D0521579

Where print meets digital and engaging content meets academic rigor

THE JUSTICE SERIES

across the CJ curriculum…

Corrections
Alarid & Reichel

Policing
Worrall & Schmalleger

Criminal Investigation
Lyman

Criminal Procedure
Worrall

Juvenile Delinquency
Bartollas & Schmalleger

CJ2013
Fagin

Criminology 2e
Schmalleger

Coming in 2014:

Criminal Law
Worrall & Moore

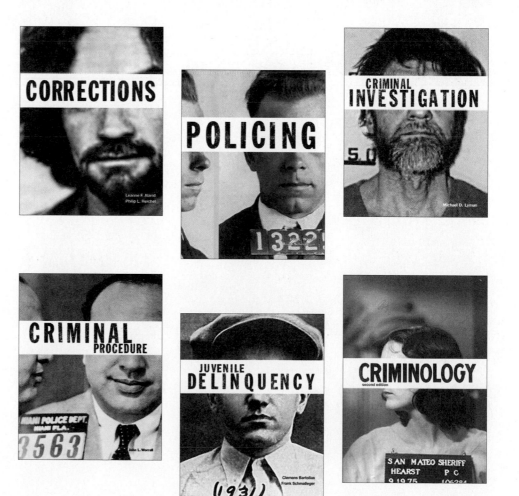

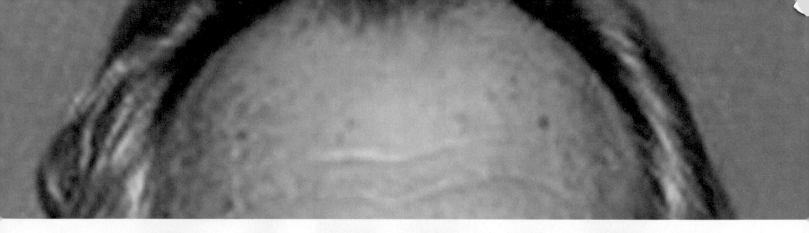

CJ 2013

James A. Fagin

Lincoln College—Normal
Normal, Illinois

PEARSON

Boston Columbus Indianapolis New York San Francisco Upper Saddle River
Amsterdam Cape Town Dubai London Madrid Milan Munich Paris Montréal Toronto
Delhi Mexico City São Paulo Sydney Hong Kong Seoul Singapore Taipei Tokyo

Editorial Director: Vernon Anthony
Acquisitions Editor: Sara Eilert
Assistant Editor: Megan Moffo
Editorial Assistant: Lynda Cramer
Director of Marketing: David Gesell
Marketing Manager: Mary Salzman
Marketing Assistant: Les Roberts
Senior Managing Editor: JoEllen Gohr
Project Manager: Rex Davidson
Senior Operations Supervisor: Pat Tonneman
Creative Director: Andrea Nix
Text Designer: Diane Ernsberger
Cover Designer: Candace Rowley
Media Director: Nichole Caldwell
Media Editor: Heather Darby
Lead Media Project Manager: Karen Bretz
Full-Service Project Management: GEX Publishing Services
Composition: GEX Publishing Services
Printer/Binder: Courier Kendallville, Inc.
Cover Printer: Lehigh-Phoenix
Text Font: Minion, 9.5/12

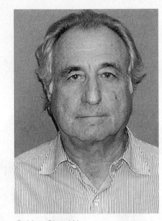

Bernard Madoff is the man behind one of the largest Ponzi schemes in history. In 2008, he was arrested by FBI agents after his sons reported him to authorities. Madoff soon plead guilty to 11 federal felonies and admitted to turning his wealth management business into a massive Ponzi scheme that defrauded thousands of investors of billions of dollars. In June of 2009, he was sentenced to 150 years in federal prison, the maximum allowed.

© Mug Shot/Alamy

10 9 8 7 6 5 4 3 2 1

ISBN 10: 0-13-296127-X
ISBN 13: 978-0-13-296127-1

This book is dedicated to my wife, Gretchen. The time necessary to produce this book was taken from her, and her understanding and support were essential in keeping me moving forward to the successful completion of this book. Also, my children, James-Jason, Elizabeth, and Emilie, constantly encouraged me and supported me in the task of preparing this book.

Brief Contents

Contents

Each chapter opener includes a quote and lists the chapter objectives to pique interest and focus students' attention on the topics to be discussed.

The book exhibits a balance between text, photos, and figures to present the information in both a text format and a visual format.

Each chapter Introduction presents a current event or story related to chapter content followed by a discussion question. This sparks interest and promotes critical thinking about chapter concepts.

Each objective has an associated icon that appears in the related chapter section and also in the end-of-chapter material. The icon is a navigational tool, making it easy to locate explanations of or find review material for a particular topic.

Important statistics pulled from the text highlight major trends and scope of issues.

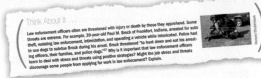

Think About It features pose questions related to chapter content, promoting critical thinking, discussion, and application.

Important quotes pulled from the text reflect the central ideas in the chapter.

in

A box at the end of each chapter directs students to chapter-specific resources and additional links to extend learning and investigation.

At the end of each chapter, a real-life case example poses analytical discussion questions related to chapter content, promoting critical thinking and application of chapter concepts.

The chapter summary displays the chapter's key information as a chart with review questions embedded throughout. This visual format is designed to be a helpful study and review tool.

Preface

Introducing the Justice Series

When best-selling authors and instructional designers come together focused on one goal—to improve student performance across the CJ curriculum—they come away with a groundbreaking new series of print and digital content: the *Justice Series*.

Several years ago, we embarked on a journey to create affordable texts that engage students without sacrificing academic rigor. We tested this new format with Fagin's *CJ2010* and Schmalleger's *Criminology* and received overwhelming support from students and instructors.

The Justice Series expands this format and philosophy to more core CJ and criminology courses, providing affordable, engaging instructor and student resources across the curriculum. As you flip through the pages, you'll notice that this book doesn't rely on distracting, overly used photos to add visual appeal. Every piece of art serves a purpose—to help students learn. Our authors and instructional designers worked tirelessly to build engaging infographics, flowcharts, pull-out statistics, and other visuals that flow with the body of the text, provide context and engagement, and promote recall and understanding.

We organized our content around key learning objectives for each chapter, and tied everything together in a new objective-driven end-of-chapter layout. The content not only is engaging to students, but also is easy to follow and focuses students on the key learning objectives.

Although brief, affordable, and visually engaging, the Justice Series is no quick, cheap way to appeal to the lowest common denominator. It's a series of texts and support tools that are instructionally sound and student-approved.

Additional Highlights to the Author's Approach

A 14-chapter format enables the instructor to cover the entire book in a standard semester and allows students to read without being pressured to cover numerous chapters in a short period of time. Also, this text is designed so that certain chapters can be omitted without disrupting the comprehensive nature and unity of the text. This design lends itself well for use in accelerated instructional formats of shorter terms where the instructor may want to omit chapters covered in other courses.

New to *CJ2013*

CJ2013 retains the outstanding format and supplemental materials associated with the Justice Series. However, there are some exciting changes in *CJ2013* compared to *CJ2012*.

- There are 14 chapters in *CJ2013* compared to 13 in *CJ2012*. The text is designed so that the chapters on criminological theory, juvenile justice, and homeland security can be included or excluded and still retain a comprehensive and unified overview of the criminal justice system.

- Enhanced material has been added to many of the chapters. This has resulted in a slightly longer text, but a text richer in detail.

- Court cases have been updated to include the latest rulings when the manuscript was submitted for publication.

- New critical thinking boxes have been added to encourage students to go beyond memorization to explore applications, conflicts, and ethical issues associated with the material.

- End-of-chapter materials have been updated and expanded and new Internet links added.

- All of the chapter openers have been updated to reflect the most current events associated with the chapter material.

- New boxes have been added to provide more detailed information about topics.

- Graphs, tables, and data have been updated.

- Many of the chapters have a new layout and new graphics to make it easier for students to comprehend the material.

- Learning outcomes have been revised and clearly presented to help students retain the major ideas of the chapter.

- A timeline has been added to some chapters to help students understand the historical development of the criminal justice system.

Groundbreaking Instructor and Student Support

Just as the format of the Justice Series breaks new ground in publishing, so does the instructor support that accompanies the series.

- **eBooks.** *CJ2013* is available in two eBook formats, *CourseSmart* and Adobe Reader. *CourseSmart* is an exciting new choice for students looking to save money. As an alternative to purchasing the printed textbook, students can purchase an electronic version of the same content. With a *CourseSmart* eTextbook, students can search the text, make notes online, print out reading assignments that incorporate lecture notes, and bookmark important passages for later review. For more information or to purchase access to the *CourseSmart* eTextbook, visit **www.coursesmart.com**.

- **TestBank** and **MyTest**. These supplements represent a new standard in testing material. Whether you use the basic *TestBank* or generate questions electronically through *MyTest*, every question is linked to the text's learning objective and page number and to level of difficulty. This allows for quick reference in the text and an easy way to check the difficulty level and variety of your questions. *MyTest* can be accessed at **www.PearsonMyTest.com**.

- **Interactive Lecture PowerPoint® Presentation** This supplement will enhance lectures like never before. Award-winning presentation designers worked with our authors to develop *PowerPoints* that truly engage students. Much like the text, the *PowerPoints* are full of instructionally sound graphics, tables, charts, and photos that do what presentation software is meant to do: support and enhance your lecture. Data and difficult concepts are presented in interactive way, helping students connect the dots and stay focused on the lecture.

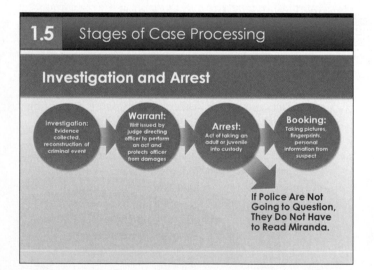

- **The Pearson Criminal Justice Online Community** Available at **www.mycriminaljusticecommunity.com**, this site is a place for educators to connect and to exchange ideas and advice on courses, content, *CJ Interactive*, and so much more.

To access these supplementary materials online, instructors need to request an instructor access code at **www.pearsonhighered.com/irc**. Within 48 hours after registering, you will receive a confirmation e-mail that includes an instructor access code. When you receive your code, go to the site and log on for full instructions on downloading materials you wish to use.

MyCJLab™ for *CJ2013*

MyCJLab is a dynamic course management and assessment program designed to support the way students learn and instructors teach. Instructors can manage their entire course online or simply allow students to study at their own pace using personalized assessment tools and preloaded interactive exercises and critical-thinking assignments. CJSearch, Pearson's new media search tool built into MyCJLab, makes it easy to integrate current events into your course. Key features of the program include:

Personalized Learning

Students are provided with a personalized study plan for each chapter in the text organized by learning objective. A pretest allows them to see what concepts they understand and what concepts they need to study further. Student responses link back to the eText and *PowerPoints* for further review. Finally, a post-test allows students to confirm their mastery of chapter concepts. Pre- and post-test results can feed to the grade book at the instructors' discretion. *"It's very impressive that both the pre- and post-tests are able to tell students exactly what areas they need to focus on."—David Pasick, Mohawk Valley Community College*

Grade Book and Performance Tracking

Grade book and performance features allow instructors to keep track of students' grades for individual learning objectives at both the class and individual level. This reporting helps instructors tailor lesson plans around concepts that need more review. *"I really like this concept. Great concept and great navigation!"*— Angela Nickoli, Ball State University

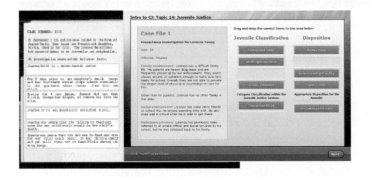

Interactive Concept Application

Interactive exercises allow students to apply chapter concepts and deepen their understanding through interactions in the criminal justice system and simulated scenarios. *"I like the reteaching aspect of the simulations. Even if the students have the knowledge to complete an activity, the information will help set up the activity and draw in the focus of the students to the task at hand."*—Jay Kramer, Central Georgia Technical College

Critical Analysis Assignments

Each chapter features assignable critical-thinking exercises that ask students to analyze crucial concepts and objectives. Students are asked to process and expand their knowledge by doing further research, going into the field, examining news or media resources, or exploring real-life issues and situations.

CJSearch: Current Event Videos, News Articles, Journal Readings, Websites

CJSearch is a database of criminal justice videos, articles, journal readings, and websites that instructors can search by topic and deliver to the class as an assignment. Each item has a critical-thinking assignment tagged to learning objectives, and the database is continuously updated and augmented, making it easy to integrate current events into the course. *"I would use*

CJSearch to prepare students in advance for class discussions of material. . . . Its utility as a teaching resource is endless."—Cornel Plebani, Husson University

Connecting Your Textbook with MyCJLab

Within the textbook, you will see icons that direct students to the following online resources:

Apply: Directs students to complete an interactive exercise.

Watch: Directs students to an online criminal justice video.

Course Resources: Directs students to relevant online tools, websites, documents, and full versions of cases discussed in the textbook.

Review: Directs students to the Study Plan where they first complete the pretest to confirm what they know and what requires further study and then complete the post-test to confirm mastery of the concepts. Key term flash cards are also available to review key terminology.

Analyze: Directs students to complete assignments as directed by their instructor.

Current Events: Directs students to explore CJSearch for current topical videos, articles, and news pieces.

MyCJLab Purchasing Options

Whether you're an expert in digital learning or new to online teaching, *MyCJLab* provides student engagement and instructor support for all levels of teaching and learning.

Printed Textbook with MyCJLab Access Code Value Packs:

- *CJ2013* print textbook with MyCJLab (without eText) for *CJ2013* Access Code Valuepack (ISBN: 0-13-340805-1)

- *CJ2013* print textbook with MyCJLab for *CJ2013* (with integrated eText) Access Code Valuepack (ISBN: 0-13-314075-X)

Students can purchase an access code separately to MyCJLab by going to **www.MyCJLab.com**.

▶ Acknowledgments

> **A book requires teamwork.**

The final product is the work of many hands, each touching the project and adding his or her contribution. Without the talents and contributions of many team members, this text would not have been possible. The production of a high-quality text with many supplements requires a sizable team of talented professionals, some of whom I have never met face-to-face but whose contributions are essential to the final product.

I regret that I cannot thank every person who contributed to the successful production of this text by name. The list would be way too extensive. I do extend my appreciation to everyone involved in this project. There are some whom I would like to single out and mention by name because of their continuous input and assistance. I cannot express enough appreciation for the tremendous job done by the production team. They took my words and added graphics and a professional layout that is first-rate.

Assistant Editor Megan Moffo's assistance has been invaluable. She worked with me from the start. I greatly appreciate the contributions of Senior Acquisitions Editor Eric Krassow, under whose leadership this project began. Acquisitions Editor Sara Eilert oversaw the completion of this project. The transition was smooth, and Sara has been very supportive. I am indebted to the professional skills and contributions of Senior Project Manager Kelly Morrison and the copy editor, Marianne Miller.

Dr. Charles A. Brawner III was an invaluable assistant and colleague in helping me complete this text. Dr. Brawner's research and input enhanced the quality of the text and instructional features. Also, I extend my thanks to Dr. Ronald D. Swan, Chief of Illinois State University Police Department (ret.) and Soviet expert, for his assistance in helping me understand the Soviet criminal justice system and for the photographs he provided.

The text was greatly improved by the input of many other dedicated publishing professionals at Pearson and the critical reviews supplied by C. Nana Derby, Virginia State University; Hilary Estes, Lakeland College; Price Foster, University of Louisville; Jon Gurney, Florida International University; David Hull, Saint Anselm College; William Kelly, Auburn University; Jack Monell, Central Piedmont Community College; Kerry Muehlenbeck, Mesa Community College; Tom Powell, Paradise Valley College; Jill Shelley, Northern Kentucky University; and Michael Witkowski, University of Detroit-Mercy.

▶ About the Author

James A. Fagin is a professor of criminal justice studies at Lincoln College–Normal (LCN), located in Normal, Illinois. In addition to being a teaching faculty member, he serves as the program director for the criminal justice science program. He founded the criminal justice studies Bachelor of Science degree at LCN.

Jim Fagin is a pioneer in criminal justice education and has been involved in innovative criminal justice education programs for nearly four decades. He developed one of the early models of statewide delivery of criminal justice undergraduate and graduate degrees. During the developing years of criminal justice education, Jim worked as a consultant and instructor for the Law Enforcement Assistance Administration (LEAA) to develop model criminal justice curriculum in research, administration, and planning to promote quality nationwide education in criminal justice. These model curriculums were developed by an elite team of practitioners and educators and were field-tested throughout the United States.

Jim wrote some of the classical literature on computer crime, police bargaining and unions, presidential candidate security, domestic disturbance resolution, and hostage negotiations. These works emerged from active involvement with federal, state, and local criminal justice agencies.

Jim was a commissioned deputy sheriff and training officer and polygraph examiner for the Wyandotte County (Kansas) Sheriff's Department and a Commissioned Reserve Police Officer in the Kansas City (Kansas) Police Department. He has worked as a consultant with federal, state, and local law enforcement agencies and correctional facilities. He served on the Kansas Victims' Rights Commission to help establish the charter victims' rights legislation for the state. He assisted in implementing the first domestic disturbance response policy for the Wichita, Kansas Police Department. He has been a criminal justice professor, graduate dean, and college president. He received his B.A. degree from the University of Nevada, Las Vegas, and his M.S. and Ph.D. from Southern Illinois University–Carbondale.

Textbooks such as this are an ongoing work in progress, and the author welcomes communication and correspondence about his work. Dr. Fagin can be contacted at Lincoln College–Normal, 715 West Raab Road, Normal, IL 61761 or at jfagin@lincolncollege.edu. Thank you for using this textbook.

Introduction to Criminal Justice

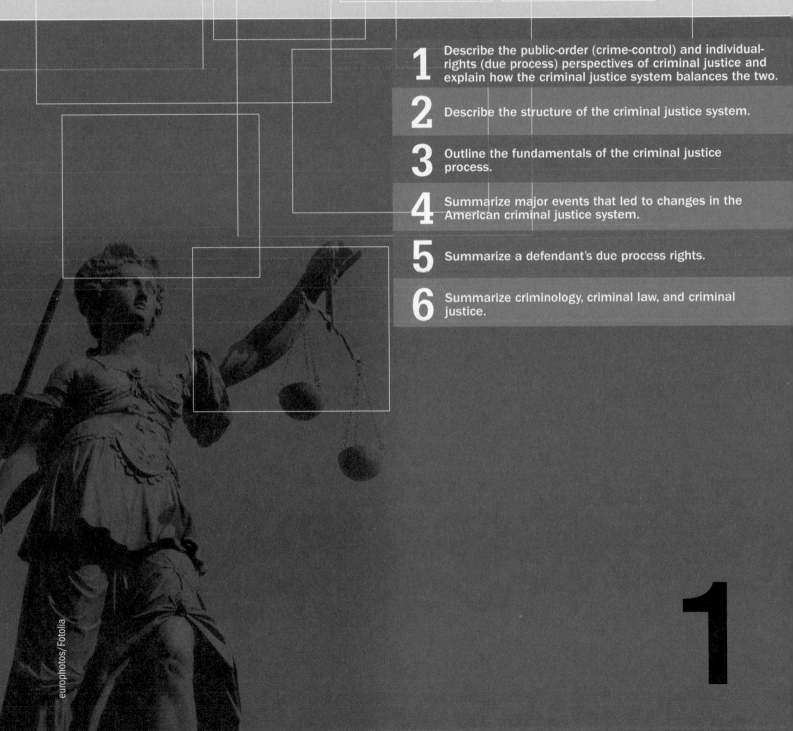

"We hold these truths to be self-evident, that all men are created equal, that they are endowed by their Creator with certain unalienable rights."

—Declaration of Independence

1 Describe the public-order (crime-control) and individual-rights (due process) perspectives of criminal justice and explain how the criminal justice system balances the two.

2 Describe the structure of the criminal justice system.

3 Outline the fundamentals of the criminal justice process.

4 Summarize major events that led to changes in the American criminal justice system.

5 Summarize a defendant's due process rights.

6 Summarize criminology, criminal law, and criminal justice.

europhotos/Fotolia

1

CONFLICT OF UNALIENABLE RIGHTS

In 2012, the Department of Health and Human Services announced a federal mandate to require all health insurance plans to offer access to free birth control. Religious groups declared that the mandate violated the First Amendment of the U.S. Constitution. The U.S. Conference of Catholic Bishops declared that the mandate would require Catholic institutions to offer services that were contrary to their core religious beliefs.[1] Cardinal Francis George declared that the issue was not whether birth control should be included in health insurance plans, but whether the government could tell a religious institution to offer a service contrary to the tradition of conscience protection traditionally protected by the First Amendment.[2] Cardinal George declared that if Catholic institutions are not exempt from the mandate, the Catholic Church will be forced to close hospitals, universities, and charities that provide essential services often to the most needy in society.

The Obama administration offered a compromise wherein the insurance companies rather than the Catholic Church as an institution would have to provide the free birth control services. Furthermore, it was noted that many Catholic institutions already offer insurance that includes birth control services. Supporters of the access to birth control mandate argue that most people favor women's access to birth control and many consider it a "woman's right" issue.[3] Cardinal George said that he could not see a compromise that would preserve the First Amendment freedoms of the Church.[4]

DISCUSS The First Amendment guarantees freedom of religion as one of the unalienable rights. How is this right interpreted and implemented in a complex, diverse society?

▶ *Balancing Public Safety and Unalienable Rights*

What does American society do when there appears to be a conflict between two or more "unalienable" rights? The criminal justice system plays an important role in resolving the issues that involve protections alleged to be provided by the U.S. Constitution. As the access to birth control health insurance mandates illustrates, there is no single viewpoint as to what constitutes an unalienable right. In some cases, there is outright conflict as the right claimed by one group is seen as a violation of the right of another group. Balancing the exercise of civil liberties against the need for law and order is a difficult and complex mission.

While the Declaration of Independence declares that people have unalienable rights and the U.S. Constitution describes those rights, from time to time, some of them may be in conflict with popular opinion, the law, or social values.

Society uses several means to balance conflicting rights and social values. In general, these means can be divided into informal and formal sanctions. **Informal sanctions** include social norms that are enforced through the social forces of the family, school, government, and religion. These social institutions teach people what is expected for normative behavior. In addition to teaching normative behavior, these primary social institutions also provide punishment when people violate **social norms**. In the informal system, parents punish children

> Balancing the exercise of civil liberties against the need for law and order is a difficult and complex mission.

Timeline of Key Events

1788	1791	1865	1868	1870
The Constitution of the newly formed U.S. government is ratified by the States.	The first ten amendments, known as the **Bill of Rights**, are added to the U.S. Constitution. These amendments are the foundation of the civil rights and due process rights of citizens.	**The Thirteenth Amendment** abolishes slavery.	**The Fourteenth Amendment** guarantees U.S. citizenship and is the basis for the due process clause of civil rights.	**The Fifteenth Amendment** prohibits the denial of voting rights based on race, color, or previous state of servitude. The Fifteenth Amendment does not extend voting rights to women, only to men.

U.S. society is not characterized by a homogeneous and stable group of people with a common belief system.

for disobedience, bosses reprimand employees, teachers discipline students, and religious groups call on offenders to repent of their sins.

The balancing of rights and public safety can also be achieved through use of **formal sanctions** (such as laws) found within the criminal justice system. Frequently, the norms and values embedded in informal systems are reflected in the formal systems of order maintenance. The more homogeneous and stable the people and their belief systems, the fewer the violations of social norms. In a homogeneous, stable society with a common belief system, there is less need for reliance on a formal **system of social control** to maintain order and regulate interactions. Social control systems operate most effectively and efficiently where there is constant and unified, overt and covert, and cultural and social support from all control agencies.[5] However, contemporary U.S. society is not characterized by a homogeneous and stable group of people with a common belief system. Rather, the United States is characterized by great diversity in race, religion, ethnicity, and values.

Limited Powers of Government

In *Two Treatises of Government* (1690), philosopher John Locke argued that all human beings are endowed with what he called "natural rights." These rights are given to people by a power higher than government, and people cannot be deprived of them. Governments exist, according to Locke, to serve individuals. People surrender certain rights with the understanding that they will receive as much, or more, in other benefits, such as safety, order, and preservation of property rights. Locke conceded that the government must have the power of physical force to protect people and their property from the physical violations of others.[6] However, this power was to be balanced against the need to preserve individual liberty. John Locke's philosophies had a great influence on Thomas Jefferson when he drafted the Declaration of Independence.[7]

When there is conflict between rights, often the U.S. Court system decides which rights are to be sanctioned. For example, the U.S. Supreme Court has recognized the right of people who have conscientious objections to killing to be exempted from combat service (the exemption does not exempt them from military service when required by law), the right to refuse childhood immunizations required by law, the right to withdraw children from public school before the age allowed by law, the right of Amish to be exempt from paying Social Security taxes, the right of Jews to be exempt from military rules that forbid nonuniform head coverings, and the right of Native Americans to use certain drugs in religious ceremonies and gather eagle feathers (which is prohibited by law for nonnative Americans). In the conflict between the Obama administration's mandate requiring access to birth control services and religious institutions' claim that the mandate violates the rights guaranteed by the First Amendment, the U.S. Supreme Court will be the final arbitrator as to which right is unalienable. Thus, the criminal justice system has assumed an important central role in public safety and **order maintenance**.

LEARNING OUTCOMES 1 Describe the public-order (crime-control) and individual-rights (due-process) perspectives of criminal justice and explain how the criminal justice system balances the two.

GLOSSARY

informal sanctions Social norms that are enforced through the social forces of the family, school, government, and religion.

social norms The expected normative behavior in a society.

formal sanctions Social norms enforced through the laws of the criminal justice system.

system of social control A social system designed to maintain order and regulate interactions.

order maintenance Activities of law enforcement that resolve conflicts and assist in the regulation of day-to-day interactions of citizens.

due process rights Rights guaranteed to persons by the Constitution and its amendments.

crime-control (public-order) model A model of the criminal justice system in which emphasis is placed on fighting crime and protecting potential victims.

due process model A model that ensures that individuals are protected from arbitrary and excessive abuse of power by the government.

1896	1920	1941	1954	1955
The U.S. Supreme Court case of **Plessy v. Ferguson** establishes the "separate but equal" doctrine of racial discrimination that permitted the legal separation of whites and blacks.	**The Nineteenth Amendment** extends voting rights to women.	**Broadcast television** begins in the United States.	**Brown v. Board of Education** declares state laws establishing separate public schools for black and white students unconstitutional. The decision overturned the *Plessy* v. *Ferguson* decision of 1896 that established the doctrine of "separate but equal" racial segregation.	**Rosa Parks** is arrested and convicted for refusing to give up her seat to a white passenger on a bus. Her arrest initiates the 381-day Montgomery bus boycott and many acts of civil disobedience.

1961	**1963**	**1964**	**1964**
Civil rights workers attempt to desegregate bus stations and waiting rooms in the South. A bus in which they are traveling is fire-bombed, and the demonstrators are beaten. NAACP leader Medgar Evers is murdered.	*Martin Luther King, Jr.* (1929-1968) delivers his "I Have a Dream" speech in the March on Washington.	*The Civil Rights Act of 1964* bans discrimination on the bases of race and gender by facilities that are open to the public, such as hotels, restaurants, theaters, retail stores, and similar establishments. Also, it extends greater protection for the right to vote. The Civil Rights Act of 1964 does not extend the ban on racial discrimination to state and local government. Thus, state and local law enforcement agencies and correctional agencies are not prohibited from racial discrimination.	*Martin Luther King, Jr.*, is the youngest person to receive the Nobel Peace Prize for his work to end racial segregation and racial discrimination through civil disobedience and other nonviolent means.

Crime Control versus Due Process

In the Declaration of Independence, Thomas Jefferson embedded Locke's arguments that government is limited in its power. This philosophy was further asserted in the Constitution and its amendments. Thus, the government has the power to act as final arbitrator of which rights are to be sanctioned, but there are checks and balances on this power. The government is charged with maintaining harmony among conflicting interests and sanctioning those who violate the rights of others. However, the government is restricted in the powers and actions it may use in its pursuit of maintaining law and order in society.

The rights guaranteed to persons by the Constitution and its amendments are called **due process rights**. There is no universal agreement as to what powers the government may exercise in the pursuit of law and order. Some would give the government more power and citizens few rights to tip the scale toward greater public order. Others would give the government less power and citizens more rights to achieve an acceptable level of crime control but maintain strict limits on government power.

There must be a balance between law and order and due process rights. Law without order is anarchy, but order without law is tyranny. In the United States, the emphasis on public order or crime control versus emphasis on due process rights resembles a pendulum that swings back and forth between the two values.

Concern for due process swung to its most liberal extent in the 1960s under Chief Justice Earl Warren and then back to the right again with the "law and order" platform on which Richard Nixon based his campaign for the presidency. Nixon's term as President (1969–1974) was characterized by a period of social unrest, violent protests and demonstrations, and high crime rates. Crime was the number one fear of citizens, and many people were receptive to the promise of crime control, public order, and swift—preferably harsh—justice for the offender. This emphasis on efficient and effective justice is known as the **crime-control (public-order) model** of criminal justice.

However, crime control cannot be achieved at the expense of constitutionally protected liberties. The emphasis on ensuring

Law without order is anarchy, but order without law is tyranny.

1968	**1968**	**1968–1982**	**1970**
Martin Luther King, Jr. is assassinated.	*The Omnibus Crime Control and Safe Streets Act* is passed. The act establishes the Law Enforcement Administration Assistance (LEAA), which provides funding, training, and professionalization of the criminal justice system. LEAA implements many of its standards through the power of the "purse strings." Agencies lose LEAA funding if they do not adopt the standards advocated by LEAA. LEAA is abolished in 1982.	*The Law Enforcement Education Program (LEEP)*, under the Law Enforcement Administration Assistance, undertakes the mission of raising the educational level of criminal justice personnel by funding grants and loans to those seeking college degrees.	On the *Kent State University (Ohio)* campus, National Guard troops open fire on unarmed students protesting U.S. involvement in the Vietnam War. Four students are killed.

Malcolm X (1925–1965), also known as Malcolm Little and El Haji Malik El-Shabazz, is assassinated by members of the Nation of Islam, an activist group that advocates black supremacy and separation of blacks and whites in the United States. Until a year before his murder, Malcolm X was a leader in the Nation of Islam, when he renounced the Nation of Islam and advocated more peaceful coexistence of the races.	A Gallup Poll reports that Americans view crime as the most serious problem in the country.	**President Lyndon Johnson** declares War on Crime.	**U.S. troops** are committed to the Vietnam War. In 1975, North Vietnam captures Saigon and Vietnam is united.

Think About It . . .

In the summer of 2011, numerous protest movements sprang up under the banner "Occupy Wall Street." The nationwide Occupy protesters demanded more from the wealthiest Americans, who the protesters called the "1%." The Occupy protestors, calling themselves the "99%," set up illegal encampments in cities across the nation. They blocked sidewalks, traffic, bridges, and public buildings as part of their protest movement. The police made thousands of arrests and used pepper spray to disperse protestors. The estimated costs to cities of police and cleanup after Occupy protests are more than $13 million.[8] Should cost be a factor in allowing people to exercise their First Amendment rights? Why or why not?

Jim West / Alamy

that individuals are protected from arbitrary and excessive abuse of power by the government is known as the **due process model** of criminal justice. Due process means that in the quest for crime control and public order, the government is bound to follow certain rules and procedures. Even if a person is guilty, if the government does not follow the rules and procedures in obtaining a conviction, the courts can refuse to prosecute the alleged offender or void a conviction obtained in violation of these rights.

One of the primary roles of the state and federal courts is to provide authoritative guidance as to the proper balance between due process and crime control that should be exercised by criminal justice personnel and agencies. Often the guidelines of the Court are the result of cases of alleged violation of constitutional and due process rights by law enforcement, the courts, or correctional personnel. For example, one of the best-known guidelines issued by the U.S. Supreme Court came from *Miranda* v. *Arizona* (1966), in which the Court mandated the specific due process rights that law enforcement must follow in arrest and interrogation of accused persons. The due process model reflects belief in the saying that it is better that a guilty person should escape the punishment of justice than an innocent person be wrongfully punished.

The twenty-sixth Amendment lowers the voting age from 21 to 18.	**The Equal Rights Amendment (ERA)** is introduced. The Amendment would ban discrimination on the basis of gender. Despite a three-year extension, the Amendment fails to obtain ratification by a sufficient number of states to become law, and the proposal dies in 1982.	**The Equal Employment Opportunity Act of 1972** extends the provisions of the Civil Rights Act of 1964. The act gives the Equal Employment Opportunity Commission the authority to file class-action lawsuits and extends the jurisdiction of the act to cover state and local governments. The effect is to require state and local law enforcement agencies and correctional agencies, which had previously been exempt from the prohibitions against discrimination based on race and gender, to abolish discriminatory hiring, employment, and promotional practices.

1972	1995	2001	2001	2010
The President's Commission on Law Enforcement and Administration of Justice concludes that most people have lost confidence in the police.	The number of serious violent crimes begins a decline that continues through the late 1990s and into the 2000s, when the numbers begin to level off.	Hijacked commercial airplanes strike the towers of the World Trade Center and the Pentagon. A third plane crashes in Pennsylvania.	**President George W. Bush** declares War on Terrorism. **The USA Patriot Act** is passed.	**The Second Amendment** is incorporated. The U.S. Supreme Court rules that the Second Amendment provides individuals the right to own firearms.

▶ The Structure of the Criminal Justice System

During the 1960s, the public lost faith in the criminal justice system. Rising crime rates, riots, demonstrations against the Vietnam War, and racial conflict resulted in many people believing that the criminal justice system was "broken" or was a "nonsystem." Concerned over the public's ebbing faith in the ability of government to maintain public safety, President Lyndon Johnson appointed a commission of experts from the criminal justice system, government, public, and academic community to examine the **criminal justice system**, describe the criminal justice process, and make recommendations to improve it. The commission was called the President's Commission on Law Enforcement and Administration of Justice. One of the main charges of the Commission was to determine whether the process of administration of justice in the United States was a system and, if so, to define the criminal justice system. The Commission issued a report in 1967 entitled *The Challenge of Crime in a Free Society*. The Commission's report concluded that there was indeed a criminal justice system and provided an outline of the agencies and processes that comprised it.

The Commission concluded that the criminal justice system was composed of (1) the agencies and people involved in the criminal justice system and (2) the processes and flow of the criminal justice system. Furthermore, the Commission concluded that the criminal justice system was a dynamic system, constantly adjusting and changing. This dynamic nature was due in large part to the interactions between agencies, the operation of checks and balances within the system, and changing environments such as new laws and U.S. Supreme Court decisions. Also, the Commission acknowledged the dual nature of the criminal justice system; that is, the criminal justice system is not a single system but is comprised of the criminal justice system of each of the 50 states and the federal criminal justice system.

Today, the criminal justice system is widely recognized as a significant component of federal, state, and local governments. The criminal justice system employs more than 2.5 million people and spends more than $228 billion per year. The per capita justice expenditures are about $755 per U.S. resident. In 2011, the expenditures by the criminal justice system were flat or slightly declining, but from 1982 to 2007, the expenditures for criminal justice increased 171%.[9]

Agencies in the Criminal Justice System

Criminal justice agencies can be divided into (1) law enforcement; (2) prosecutors and the courts; (3) the probation and parole agencies; and (4) the jails, prisons, and other correctional agencies. These agencies exist in the local, state, and federal levels of government. Each level of government has its own criminal justice agencies and process. Thus, there is not a single criminal justice system, but an interconnected system of criminal justice agencies at the local, state, and federal level. Also, there is a separate but interconnected criminal justice system for adults and juveniles at both the state and federal level of government.

Dual Criminal Justice System

The U.S. criminal justice system is distinct from criminal justice systems of other nations in which there is a centralized system of oversight and command from top to bottom. The American system can be described as a dual system, which refers to the fact that the federal government and the states each have the power to create their own semiautonomous criminal justice system. While all criminal justice systems must preserve the rights guaranteed by the U.S. Constitution, there is great diversity between states and the federal government in the details of their criminal justice systems.

Thus, while 2.5 million people are employed by the criminal justice system, each of the thousands of criminal justice agencies hires its own employees. There is no central employment agency for the criminal justice system. Each agency sets standards of employment, defines job responsibilities and duties, and pays its employees independently of central control. As a result, there

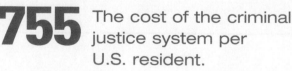

$755 The cost of the criminal justice system per U.S. resident.

is great diversity in the educational achievement, skills, knowledge, and abilities of the people who work in the criminal justice system. One law enforcement agency may require officers to have only a high school diploma, whereas another law enforcement agency may require a bachelor's degree. One state may have no requirements of legal training for its municipal judges, whereas another state may require that municipal judges meet strict standards for education and other qualifications.

Sometimes the interrelationship of local, state, and federal criminal justice agencies is described in a hierarchical relationship by comparing them to a three-layer cake—a broad layer consisting of local agencies on the bottom, a small layer of state agencies on top of that layer, and a smaller layer consisting of federal agencies on the top. However, the analogy of a three-layer cake suggests that each political entity is separate and that there is a hierarchy with local political entities at the bottom and federal government at the top. This analogy does not accurately describe the criminal justice system. Because of the semiautonomous nature of criminal justice agencies, although the agencies may interact often, the agencies are independent and there is no hierarchical authoritative relationship between them. For example, the Federal Bureau of Investigation does not have administrative powers over state law enforcement agencies and state law agencies do not have administrative powers over local law enforcement agencies. The court system does have a hierarchical relationship in that higher courts can overturn the decisions of lower courts, but separation and independence still exist between the various local, state, and federal courts.

A better analogy to describe the relationship between the local, state, and federal criminal justice agencies is the **picket fence model**. In this analogy, the three horizontal boards in the fence represent the local, state, and federal government and the vertical boards represent the various criminal justice agencies, such as law enforcement, courts, and corrections. Although separate autonomy of each agency is represented by the space between criminal justice agencies at each level of government, an interrelationship is represented by the vertical pickets.

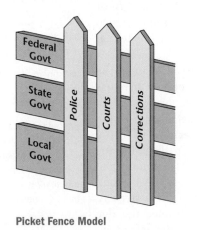

Picket Fence Model

Checks and Balances

One of the characteristics of the criminal justice system is that it reflects the mistrust of a strong centralized government by the early founders of the United States. As a result, the U.S.

One of the characteristics of the criminal justice system is that it reflects the mistrust of a strong centralized government by the early founders of the United States.

government was created with numerous checks and balances. Each person and agency in the criminal justice system has a certain amount of autonomy, but each also is controlled by interactions with other criminal justice agencies. The balance of authority exercised over other agencies and the authority of agencies to void actions of other criminal justice agencies is called the power of **checks and balances**.

The flowchart created by the President's Commission identifies five stages in the criminal justice system: (1) entry into the system, (2) prosecution and pretrial services, (3) adjudication, (4) sentencing and sanctions, and (5) corrections. The agencies that compose these stages are semiautonomous, and as discussed earlier, no one agency has the oversight powers to supervise and regulate the processing of an accused person through the criminal justice system. This separation of power acts as checks and balances to ensure fairness and to minimize the arbitrary exercise of power or abuse of power by one of the agencies.

One of the ways this power of checks and balance works is that when an accused person is transferred from one stage of the criminal justice system to another, there is the opportunity for a review of the charges against the accused. Often at these transition points, the receiving agency has the authority to refuse to continue the processing of the accused in the criminal justice system. For example, the prosecutor may alter the charges the police filed against the accused or may dismiss all charges and free the accused. The prosecutor must obtain permission of the court before the defendant can be formally tried for the alleged criminal activity. After the trial and sentencing, the defendant can appeal both the verdict and sentence. Finally, due process rights ensure that when a defendant is transferred to a correctional facility, his or her rights regarding cruel and unusual punishment and due process rights to appeal revocation of probation or parole are protected.

LEARNING OUTCOMES 2 Describe the structure of the criminal justice system.

GLOSSARY

criminal justice system The enforcement, by the police, the courts, and correctional institutions, of obedience to laws.

picket fence model The model of the criminal justice system in which the local, state, and federal criminal justice systems are depicted as horizontal levels connected vertically by the roles, functions, and activities of the agencies that comprise them.

checks and balances The authority of the legislative branch, the executive branch, and the judicial branch to provide a constitutional check on the actions of each other.

► *The Criminal Justice Process*

As mentioned, there is no single criminal justice system. Thus, a discussion of the criminal justice process cannot accurately describe the criminal justice process used by each state and the federal government. However, the criminal justice system of each state and the federal government must provide that the constitutional rights of people who have come in contact with the criminal justice system are protected. Each person must be treated with fairness and equality, and due process rights cannot be abridged. Thus, despite the differences between the criminal justice systems of the various states and the federal government, there is a commonality as governments must ensure that accused people are treated in accordance with the rights proscribed by the Constitution and that their journey through the criminal justice system is without bias and conforms to the guidelines provided by the Constitution and the U.S. Supreme Court.

In 1967, the President's Commission on Law Enforcement and Administration of Justice undertook one of the first attempts to describe the process of the American criminal justice system.[10] Prior to the Commission's study, there was little research as to the process of the criminal justice system. The Commission produced a flowchart of the criminal justice system. The flowchart was not reflective of every state's system, but it did provide a visual depiction of a generalized understanding of the process of the criminal justice system. Since the publication of the Commission's flowchart, the process described by the 1967 report has been updated by other studies and the Bureau of Justice Statistics.[11] Thus, the flowchart (Figure 1–1) has become a standard for depicting the criminal justice process.

The flowchart of the President's Commission describes the criminal justice system as a classical **input-output model**. In this model, the process describes how people are processed into the criminal justice system and then move through the system until they exit from it. (See Figure 1–2 for a description of the five stages in the criminal justice process and Figure 1–3 for the roles and functions of criminal justice personnel.)

Entry into the System

Law enforcement agencies are the primary officials responsible for detecting crime violators and bringing these individuals into the criminal justice system. Often the process of detecting crimes is a partnership between law enforcement and the public. To a large degree, law enforcement must depend on the public to report crime, to cooperate as witnesses, and to work with law enforcement in crime-prevention programs.

The arrest of a suspected criminal may be spontaneous, as when a patrolling law enforcement officer chances upon a crime in progress, or may it be the results of months, perhaps

Booking acts as the transition point to determine whether the accused will be further processed by the criminal justice system.

years, of planning that involves many different law enforcement agencies. Often arrests for major crimes, especially ongoing criminal enterprises, are characterized by extensive effort, resources, and collaboration by multiple criminal justice agencies. **Arrest** means that law enforcement can restrict the freedom of people by taking them into custody.

When a person is arrested, that individual must be transported to a facility where he or she can be booked. **Booking** is the process whereby law enforcement formally accuses a person of committing a crime. The purpose of booking is not to establish guilt, but (1) to establish the identity of the person and (2) to charge the person with a specific violation of the criminal law.

Booking acts as the transition point to determine whether the accused will be further processed by the criminal justice system.

Prosecution and Pretrial Services

In the next stage of the sequence of events in the criminal justice system, the government must decide whether the evidence presented by the police is sufficient to pursue prosecution of the alleged offender and must ensure that the due process rights of the defendant are protected. The decision to move the accused from booking to prosecution often is decided by collaboration between law enforcement officials and officials of the prosecutor's office. The government official responsible for charging and prosecuting the defendant is known by different names from state to state. Some common titles are prosecuting attorney, district attorney, and state's attorney. The prosecutor's office has complete autonomy to accept, modify, or dismiss the charges upon which the defendant was booked. If the prosecutor does not seek criminal charges against the defendant, law enforcement has no authority to bring charges against the defendant. If the prosecutor decides to bring the defendant to trial for the alleged offense(s), a number of preliminary steps must occur. The purpose of these steps is, in part, to guarantee the due process rights of the defendant.

LEARNING OUTCOMES 3 — Outline the fundamentals of the criminal justice process.

GLOSSARY

input-output model A model of how people are processed through the criminal justice system until they exit the system.

arrest To restrict the freedom of a person by taking him or her into police custody.

booking Police activity that establishes the identification of an arrested person and formally charges that person with a crime.

bail Release of the defendant prior to trial.

indictment The formal verdict of the grand jury that there is sufficient evidence to bring a person to trial.

preliminary hearing A hearing before a magistrate judge in which the prosecution presents evidence to convince the judge that there is probable cause to bring the defendant to trial.

First Appearance

If the defendant is to be prosecuted, he or she will appear before a magistrate judge. Magistrate judges are judicial officers with authority to evaluate charges filed by law enforcement against the accused and to determine whether the charges are

What is the sequence of events in the criminal justice system?

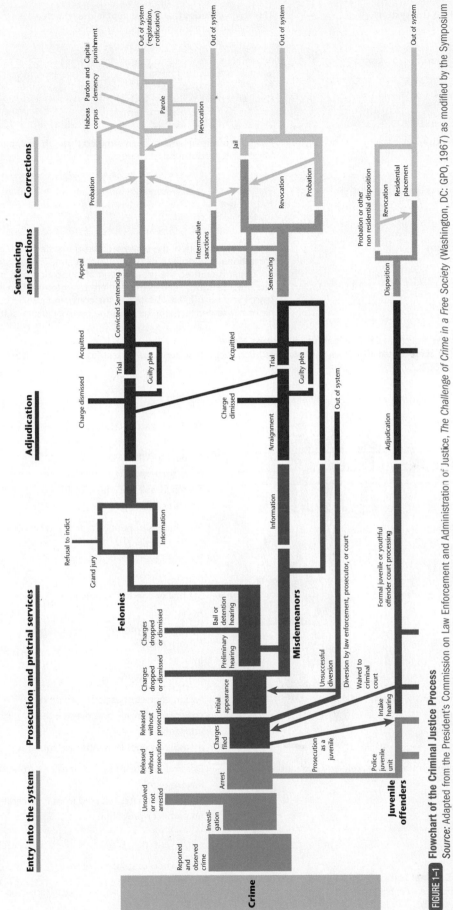

FIGURE 1-1 Flowchart of the Criminal Justice Process

Source: Adapted from the President's Commission on Law Enforcement and Administration of Justice, *The Challenge of Crime in a Free Society* (Washington, DC: GPO, 1967) as modified by the Symposium on the 30th Anniversary of the President's Commission and the Bureau of Justice Statistics.

Stage	Major Agencies and Events
Entry into the system	This stage includes the detection of crime, which can involve both the police and the public.
Prosecution and pretrial services	After the police book and charge the accused with a crime, the accused becomes the defendant. During this stage, formal charges are filed against the defendant through a process that protects the rights of the defendant and decisions are made regarding release on bail.
Adjudication	The guilt of the defendant is determined through trial, plea bargaining, or dismissal of charges.
Sentencing and sanctions	The judge sets a punishment guided by the limits established by law. The defendant and the prosecutor have the right to appeal the sentence.
Corrections	The defendant is now the convicted and is transferred to a correctional authority to carry out the sanction. The convicted no longer is granted the presumption of innocence, and many due process rights, such as those related to interrogation and search and seizure, are lost. When the convicted person completes his or her sentence, he or she exits the criminal justice system.

FIGURE 1–2 Five Stages in the Criminal Justice Process Model
Source: Adapted from Bureau of Justice Statistics, http://bjs.ojp.usdoj.gov/content/justsys.cfm (accessed February 29, 2012).

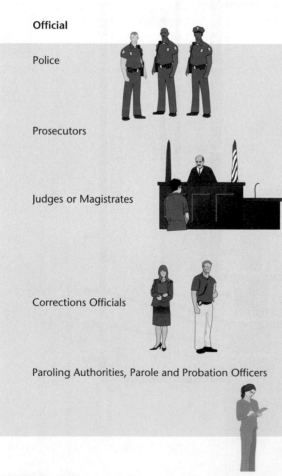

Official	Role
Police	Enforce specific laws Investigate specific crimes Search people, vicinities, buildings Arrest or detain people
Prosecutors	File charges or petitions for adjudication Seek indictments Drop chases Reduce charges
Judges or Magistrates	Set bail or conditions of release Accept pleas Determine delinquency Dismiss charges Impose sentence Revoke probation
Corrections Officials	Assign convicted persons to type of correctional facility and oversee their imprisonment Award privileges to imprisoned inmates
Paroling Authorities, Parole and Probation Officers	Determine date and conditions of parole Revoke parole Supervise inmates released from incarceration on parole or probation

FIGURE 1–3 Criminal Justice Officials and Their Role in the Criminal Justice Process
Source: Adapted from Bureau of Justice Statistics, http://bjs.ojp.usdoj.gov/content/justsys.cfm (accessed February 29, 2012).

> At the first appearance, the accused is *not* asked whether he or she pleads guilty or not guilty to the charges.

legitimate according to state statutes and federal laws. At the first appearance, the accused is advised of his or her legal rights, the magistrate must determine whether the accused has legal representation, and bail may be set. **Bail** is a promise, sometimes backed by a monetary guarantee, that the accused will return for further proceedings in the criminal justice system. The decision of bail can be revisited at several points in the criminal justice process. At the first appearance, the accused is *not* asked whether he or she pleads guilty or not guilty to the charges. The question of guilt is not raised at this time. The first appearance will be discussed in greater detail in Chapter 9, "Sentencing."

The Path to Indictment

After the first appearance, the prosecutor must obtain an indictment if he or she is to prosecute the defendant. An **indictment** is a formal, written legal document forwarded to the court, asserting probable cause that the defendant committed an offense. The indictment authorizes the court to issue an arrest warrant for the defendant and to set an arraignment hearing at which the defendant must formally respond to the charges with a plea of guilty or not guilty.

probable cause hearing
A hearing to determine whether there is a direct link between a suspect and a crime.

grand jury A panel of citizens that decides whether there is probable cause to indict a defendant on the alleged charges.

true bill A jury's decision that authorizes the prosecutor to arraign the defendant.

arraignment hearing A hearing where charges are read and the defendant is asked to enter a plea.

There are two ways the prosecutor may obtain an indictment. One way is the preliminary hearing. A **preliminary hearing** is a court hearing before a magistrate judge in which the prosecution must convince the judge that there is probable cause that (1) an offense as defined by the criminal laws of the jurisdiction has been committed within that jurisdiction and (2) the defendant accused of the offense committed the crime. The preliminary hearing is sometimes called a **probable cause hearing** because of this responsibility. Each state and the federal government have different rules regarding preliminary hearings, so the hearing differs from court to court.

Another path to obtaining an indictment is by use of a grand jury. A **grand jury** is a legal procedure that in some ways resembles a trial. Grand jury rules differ by state; in some states, the defendant's legal counsel may be present, and in others, defense counsel is barred. Similar to the preliminary hearing, the prosecutor presents evidence to the members of the grand jury to convince them that the defendant probably committed the offense. The grand jury does not determine guilt, but if the prosecutor is successful, the grand jury returns a **true bill**;

this authorizes the prosecutor to arraign the defendant. If the prosecutor is not successful, he or she cannot proceed to an arraignment.

The grand jury will be discussed in greater detail in Chapter 9, "Sentencing."

Adjudication

At the **arraignment hearing**, the charges are read and the defendant is asked whether he or she pleads guilty or not guilty. If the defendant pleads not guilty, a trial date is set. If the defendant pleads guilty (or no contest), a sentencing date is set. When a guilty plea is entered, there is no trial and the government is not required to prove guilt beyond a reasonable doubt to a jury or a judge.

Sentencing

If the defendant is found guilty, the judge will decide on a sentence guided by the limits set by law. The judge will be assisted in determining the sentence using a presentence investigation report provided by a probation officer, who will perform an extensive life history and background investigation of the convicted defendant. (The actual title of this person varies by state.) The sentence is announced at a sentencing hearing wherein both the prosecutor and the defendant's counsel can challenge the sentence and the information presented by the presentence investigation report.

The sentencing procedure for capital offenses (death penalty) is different from that of noncapital cases and will be discussed in Chapter 10, "Corrections in the Community".

After adjudication and sentencing, the defendant has the right to appeal both the criminal conviction and the sentence.

Corrections

Once the convicted defendant is sentenced, he or she is transferred to a correctional facility. For those defendants given alternative sanctions that do not require incarceration in a correctional facility, they are placed under the supervision of probation officials. (The same officers also may supervise inmates released early from correctional institutions or some form of intermediate sanction.)

Exit, Recidivism, and Multiple Dimensionality of the Criminal Justice System

There are a limited number of options as to how a person is processed into the criminal justice system, but there are numerous exit options. Some exit options occur shortly after the person enters the system; other options occur only at the end of the process model. Law enforcement officials may quickly discover that they have arrested the wrong person and release him or her before booking. Prosecuting officials may conclude that there is insufficient evidence to convict a person arrested by law enforcement and refuse to prosecute, resulting in the person exiting the system. The prosecutor may fail to win an indictment at a preliminary hearing, and the accused may exit the system. Few people who enter the system by

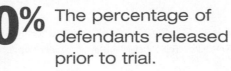

60% The percentage of defendants released prior to trial.

arrest are processed through the entire criminal justice system. Since 1990, the percentage of defendants released pretrial has remained relatively stable at about 60%.[12] (See Figure 1–4 for the latest figures on the disposition of cases.)

Furthermore, the criminal justice system is not a one-dimensional, one-way input-output model. About 43% of felony defendants who enter the criminal justice system have a least one prior felony conviction.[13] Also, many who enter the criminal justice system may be charged with a crime in multiple jurisdictions. About 18% of defendants commit new offenses while they are being processed by the criminal justice system.[14]

- -

▶ The Changing Criminal Justice System

The criminal justice system reflects the complex interaction of social values, technology, law, concepts of social justice, and economic forces. Sometimes the changes in the criminal justice system are deliberate, as when the government undertakes to change or reform the system or landmark U.S. Supreme Court decisions cause transformative change. Other forces may have unintentional influences on the criminal justice system. The invention of the revolver, the telephone, the automobile, and the television all had major impacts on the criminal justice system, resulting in transformative change.

Four meta-influences have shaped the U.S. criminal justice system since the mid-twentieth century. A **meta-influence** is a phenomenon that results in encompassing transformative changes. Meta-influences have the ability to transcend the immediate environment and objectives in which the phenomenon is situated, resulting in significant changes throughout social behavior, values, and interactions.

The four meta-influences that have resulted in transformative change of the criminal justice system:

Civil Rights Movement

Vietnam War

Rising crime rate and public's increased awareness of it

Attacks on the towers of the World Trade Center and the Pentagon by international terrrorists on September 11, 2001

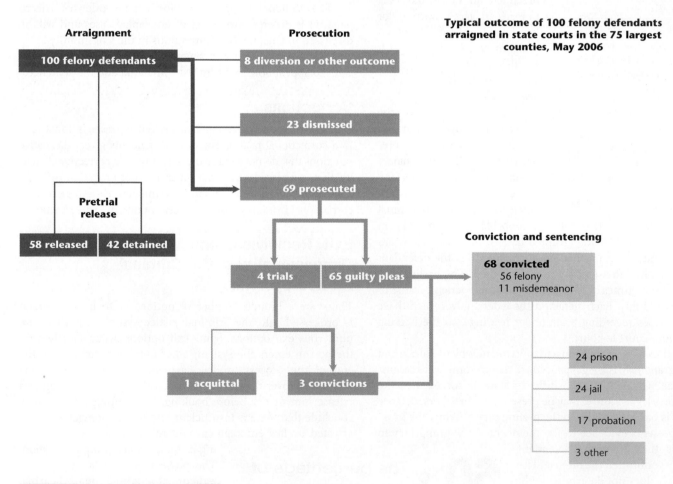

Typical outcome of 100 felony defendants arraigned in state courts in the 75 largest counties, May 2006

Arraignment
- 100 felony defendants

Prosecution
- 8 diversion or other outcome
- 23 dismissed
- 69 prosecuted

Pretrial release
- 58 released
- 42 detained

- 4 trials
- 65 guilty pleas
- 1 acquittal
- 3 convictions

Conviction and sentencing
- 68 convicted
  - 56 felony
  - 11 misdemeanor
- 24 prison
- 24 jail
- 17 probation
- 3 other

FIGURE 1–4 Typical Case Disposition in 2006
Source: Thomas H. Cohen and Tracey Kyckelhahn, "Felony Defendants in Large Urban Counties," 2006 (Washington, DC: Bureau of Justice Statistics, May 2010), p. 1.

LEARNING OUTCOMES 4 Summarize major events that led to changes in the American criminal justice system.

GLOSSARY

meta-influence A phenomenon that results in encompassing transformative changes.

slave patrols White militia who were responsible for controlling, returning, and punishing runaway slaves.

***Brown v. Board of Education Topeka* (1954)** The U.S. Supreme Court decision that resulted in the movement to integrate schools, public transportation, business, and society.

Civil Rights Act of 1964 The act declaring that it is illegal for businesses, hotels, restaurants, and public transportation to deny citizens service based on their race.

Jim Crow laws (Black Codes) Laws passed after the Civil War to overstep the basic human rights and civil liberties of African-Americans.

1972 Equal Employment Opportunity Act The act that ended discrimination in law enforcement and corrections based on race, gender, and other protected categories.

civil disobedience A nonviolent approach of protest in the civil rights movement.

Montgomery bus boycott A boycott of public transportation initiated by the arrest of Rosa Parks.

Vietnam War A war from 1955 to 1975 in Vietnam, Laos, and Cambodia.

domino theory A claim that the continued fall of governments to communist rule would threaten democracy.

The Civil Rights Movement

In a sense, the roots of parts of the U.S. criminal justice system are founded in racial discrimination. In colonial times and during the early years of the United States, slave patrols were a central component of the criminal justice system of the southern colonies and states. **Slave patrols** were composed of organizations of free white adults, sometimes called militia, who were responsible for controlling, returning, and punishing runaway slaves. In *The Police in America*, Samuel Walker describes the slave patrols as the first "modern" police organization.[15] Hence, from the founding of the United States, the criminal justice system has reflected the social values of racial discrimination.

The passage of the Thirteenth Amendment, which abolished slavery, and the Fourteenth Amendment, which prohibited the denial of due process, marked the start of a long struggle for equality within society and the criminal justice system. The U.S. Supreme Court played a central role in this struggle for equality in the ***Brown v. Board of Education of Topeka* (1954)** decision, which overturned the "separate but equal doctrine," resulting in the movement to integrate schools, public transportation, businesses, and society.[16]

The protests and demonstrations leading up to the passage of the **Civil Rights Act of 1965** were marked by extensive and widespread violence. For example, when civil rights workers attempted to desegregate bus stations and waiting rooms in the South, the bus in which they were traveling was fire-bombed and the demonstrators were beaten. NAACP leader Medgar Evers was murdered, and due to the complicity of the police in the crime, it took decades to bring his killer to justice. Civil rights protesters often feared not only the violence of the mob, but also that of local law enforcement.

> In a sense, the roots of parts of the U.S. criminal justice system are founded in racial discrimination.

The criminal justice system was at the center of this conflict as the segregation laws were enforced by law enforcement and the courts. This discrimination was reflected in so-called **Jim Crow laws** (**Black Codes**), which provided legal sanctions for customs and practices of discrimination. Also, employment in the criminal justice system was not open to minorities and females. Until the **1972 Equal Employment Opportunity Act**, law enforcement and correctional agencies could refuse employment to minorities and females with legal impunity. In *Slavery by Another Name*, Douglas A. Blackmon (2008) argues that the correctional system preserved enslavement of African-Americans until the 1940s.

The civil rights movement was divided into two distinct approaches: those who advocated violence and separation of the races and those who advocated nonviolent **civil disobedience** and integration of the races. Malcolm X was characteristic of the former; Martin Luther King, Jr., was characteristic of the latter.

King's strategy of nonviolent civil disobedience captured national attention in December 1955 with the 381-day **Montgomery bus boycott** of public transportation. This event was triggered by the arrest and conviction of Rosa Parks for violating the segregation laws because she would not give up her bus seat to a white passenger. However, King's nonviolent civil rights approach often resulted in retaliatory acts of violence, even murder, mob actions, and extensive destruction of property.

The evolution of the criminal justice system to provide fair and impartial justice for all is an underlying theme of the criminal justice system. In the twenty-first century, significant progress has been made in achieving this goal, but great challenges still face the criminal justice system. For example, Michelle Alexander, author of *The New Jim Crow: Mass Incarceration in the Age of Colorblindness*, argues that the rising incarceration rates of the late twentieth century reflect a racially based system of control to serve the perceived interests of white elites.[17]

Protests and the Vietnam War

U.S. involvement in the Vietnam War produced great acrimony in society. The conflict between antiwar protesters and the government was characterized by violent demonstrations resulting in property damage, injuries, and deaths.

The **Vietnam War** lasted from 1955 to 1975 and involved Vietnam, Laos, and Cambodia. The U.S. government considered it a war against the spread of communism based on what was called the **domino theory**. The domino theory claimed that the fall of Vietnam to communist rule would be followed by the fall of another and then another country, until democracy itself would be threatened by communist insurgency. The estimated

1–3 million The number of Vietnamese soldiers and civilians killed in the Vietnam War.

number of Vietnamese soldiers and civilians killed varies from 1 million to more than 3 million. About 58,000 U.S. service members also died in the conflict.

There was great debate as to the legitimacy of U.S. military involvement, but U.S. involvement in the war continued to escalate starting with President Kennedy and continuing under Presidents Johnson, Nixon, and Ford. In 1975, the communist government of North Vietnam militarily defended South Vietnam, officially ending the conflict.

During these approximately 15 years the United States was involved in the war, antiwar protestors staged numerous and sometimes violent demonstrations. Law enforcement officials were often in conflict with protestors, and these conflicts were lead stories for the evening news. The police were often captured on film engaged in physical conflict with the protestors. The conflicts often were such that local law enforcement was considered incapable of handling the crowd and military troops were used to respond to the demonstrations. However, military troops did not have the training in crowd control and civil demonstrators that law enforcement officers did. As a result, the presence of military troops often escalated the conflict. One example of the violent encounters between protestors and the military was the Kent State University antiwar protests in 1970. National Guard troops opened fire on unarmed student demonstrators, killing four students and injuring nine more.

The often violent encounters between law enforcement and antiwar protestors resulted in a public perception of law enforcement officials as being brutal and disrespectful of the Constitution. This rift between a large section of the public and

42% The percentage of Americans afraid to walk in their neighborhood at night in 1972.

law enforcement had a great influence on police–community relations. Also, it bred contempt for the criminal justice system because it was seen as an extension of the status quo government committed to the war effort. This perception contributed to the derogation of confidence by the public in the criminal justice system that was to become a central concern in the War on Crime.

The War on Crime

The 1960s and 1970s were periods of great social upheaval, antiwar protests, civil rights demonstrations, and rising crime rates. The combination of these events accented the public's fear of the rising crime rate. During this period, violent crime rates hit record highs and the emergence of violent juvenile crime resulted in the public's fear of criminal victimization. According to a 1965 Gallup Poll, Americans viewed crime as the most serious problem in the country.[18] In 1968, 31% of Gallup survey respondents said that they were afraid to walk in their own neighborhoods at night, and by the end of 1972, the number had risen to 42%. Many citizens thought that rather than providing a solution to the rising lawlessness, the police contributed to the problem.[19]

The criminal justice system was perceived as falling apart—failing. On July 25, 1965, President Lyndon Johnson responded by declaring a **War on Crime**. He created a series of federal presidential commissions to study crime and justice and to recommend suggested reforms to restore public confidence.

The findings of the President's Crime Commission concluded that fear of crime had eroded the basic quality of life for many Americans. It also recognized the importance of crime prevention (as opposed to crime fighting), the role of the public in public safety, and the necessity of eliminating injustices in the criminal justice system.

To further the implementation of the recommendations of the President's Crime Commission, Congress passed legislation to provide substantial resources to the various agencies of the criminal justice system. The **Omnibus Crime Control and**

War on Crime A declaration by President Lyndon Johnson in 1965 to counter crime and social disorder.

Omnibus Crime Control and Safe Streets Act of 1968 An act that provided resources to local and state government to assist in the adoption of reforms, including the Law Enforcement Assistance Administration.

Law Enforcement Assistance Administration (LEAA) A conduit for the transfer of federal funds to state and local law enforcement agencies.

Law Enforcement Educational Program (LEEP) A program created to promote education among criminal justice personnel by offering loans and grants to pursue higher education.

war on terrorism President George W. Bush's declaration regarding the response of the United States to the events of September 11, 2001.

enemy combatants The suspension of due process rights for accused terrorists under the enemy combatant executive order.

One of the goals of the National Commission on Criminal Justice Standards and Goals was to increase the professionalism and ethical behavior of criminal justice personnel, particularly law enforcement officers.

Think About It . . .

More than 40 years have passed since a comprehensive review of the criminal justice system was undertaken. U.S. Senator Jim Webb (D-VA) believes it is time to examine the criminal justice system again. In 2011, Webb introduced a bill to create the National Criminal Justice Commission, "a blue ribbon commission to look at every aspect of our criminal justice system with an eye toward reshaping the criminal justice system from top to bottom." The bill failed to pass. Is there a need for a comprehensive review of the criminal justice system to align it with the realities of the twenty-first century? Why or why not?

Senator Jim Webb

Safe Streets Act of 1968 provided resources to local and state government to assist in the adoption of reforms (for example, better training, better-qualified recruits, in-service education for police officers, funding of police–community relations programs, and other strategies to promote public safety and build up public confidence in the criminal justice system).

The Omnibus Crime Control and Safe Streets Act of 1968 created the **Law Enforcement Assistance Administration (LEAA)**. The LEAA acted as a conduit for the transfer of federal funds to state and local law enforcement agencies. However, these funds were not without "strings."

The LEAA's goal was to promote adoption of the standards and reforms outlined by the National Commission on Criminal Justice Standards and Goals. To receive the generous funds available from the federal government through LEAA, local and state agencies had to show that they had implemented or were working to implement the commission's standards and goals. Many of the advances made in law enforcement agencies were a result of the compliance with standards and goals necessary to qualify for federal funds.

One of the goals of the National Commission on Criminal Justice Standards and Goals was to increase the professionalism and ethical behavior of criminal justice personnel, particularly law enforcement officers. One of the primary strategies used to achieve this goal was to raise the educational level of criminal justice personnel. The task of the **Law Enforcement Educational Program (LEEP)** was to achieve this goal. LEEP offered loans and grants to law enforcement personnel who would pursue higher education.

The LEEP left a tremendous legacy. It not only resulted in a significant increase in the educational levels of law enforcement officers, but also helped develop criminal justice as an academic discipline. The availability of federal grants spurred many law enforcement officers to enroll in college. In turn, the growing demand for college programs stimulated many colleges and universities to develop criminal justice programs. This in turn resulted in law enforcement departments requiring higher educational levels for entry-level law enforcement positions and for promotions.

The Rise of Concern over Homeland Security

Prior to 2001, there was no Department of Homeland Security and the threat of an attack by international terrorists on U.S. soil was not a concern of the criminal justice system or the public. The biggest crisis in the twenty-first century was caused by a foreign attack on the United States. Responding to this attack by international terrorists on September 11, 2001, just as President Johnson had declared a war on crime, President George W. Bush declared a **war on terrorism**.

The impact of the war on terrorism has transformed the criminal justice system and continues to exert powerful forces for change. The 9/11 attacks resulted in creation of the Department of Homeland Security, new legislation expanding the powers of federal law enforcement agencies, and suspension of due process rights for accused terrorists labeled **enemy combatants** by the president. If labeled an enemy combatant upon the sole authority of the president, the accused loses all due process rights normally afforded to people accused of a crime. In fact, President Barrack Obama has extended the scope of the enemy combatant executive

order issued by President Bush to include the power to execute accused enemy combatants, including U.S. citizens, without trial, due process, or disclosure of the standards that are used to justify the execution.

The war on terrorism poses one of the most serious challenges to the balance between public safety and due process. The influence of the war on terrorism on the criminal justice system continues and will be discussed in greater detail in Chapter 14, "Homeland Security".

▶ Due Process Rights

The primary sources of due process rights are the state constitutions of the 50 states, the U.S. Constitution, and the Bill of Rights. However, it is the decisions of the U.S. Supreme Court that define which rights are enforced and how these rights are to be expressed in the criminal justice system. Most of these rights are contained in the first ten amendments and in the Thirteenth and Fourteenth Amendments of the U.S. Constitution.

In fact, the Fourteenth Amendment is sometimes called the **due process amendment** because its language prohibits state and local governments from depriving persons of life, liberty, or property without due process. The due process clause requires the government to recognize substantive and procedural rights of people and to apply the law equally to everyone. **Substantive due process** refers to the constitutionality of laws, and **procedural due process** refers to the process and procedure the government can use to seek a conviction for violation of a law.

Due Process Rights and the U.S. Supreme Court

The due process rights granted to the accused have varied throughout history. The protection of the due process rights guaranteed by the U.S. Constitution does not extend to state and local criminal justice systems unless the U.S. Supreme Court **incorporates** the federal rights defined by the U.S. Constitution. State constitutions may grant the accused due process rights independently from the U.S. Constitution. However, if the state constitution does not grant a right and the right has not been incorporated, the accused can only claim this right in federal court. The due process rights in the U.S. Constitution have been incorporated right by right and amendment by amendment throughout history.

Often these rights are incorporated by U.S. Supreme Court landmark decisions. A landmark decision occurs when the U.S. Supreme Court declares a significantly different interpretation of the rights guaranteed by the U.S. Constitution. Landmark decisions define rights the federal and state courts must recognize even if the law or previous court decisions do not recognize the right. For example, the First Amendment right of free speech did not apply to the states until *Gitlow* v. *New York* (1925), when the U.S. Supreme Court ruled state laws unconstitutional if they arbitrarily infringed upon free speech. The First, Fourth, and Sixth Amendments have been fully incorporated, and states must guarantee these rights to accused persons.

The Second Amendment (the right of individuals to bear arms) is the most recent amendment to be incorporated. It was incorporated in *District of Columbia* v. *Heller* (2008) and *McDonald* v. *City of Chicago, et al.* (2010).

Doug Meszler / Splash News/Newscom

What is an unalienable right? Marriage is considered by many to be an unalienable right. However, changing social values and diversity have resulted in conflict between those who believe marriage can be defined only as the union of one man to one woman and those who have a different concept of marriage. The 1996 Defense of Marriage Act (DOMA) defined marriage as between one man and one woman. In 2012, U.S. District Judge Jeffrey S. White ruled DOMA unconstitutional. Also, in the same month, the federal appeals court threw out a California voter-approved ban on same-sex marriage. Kody Brown and his four wives of the reality TV show *Sister Wives* have filed a lawsuit arguing that making polygamous unions illegal violates the due process and equal protection clauses of the Fourteenth Amendment. When there is conflict about different claims as to what is an unalienable right, how should the conflict be resolved?

In part, the incorporation of due process rights depends on the philosophy and values as reflected by the U.S. Supreme Court justices in their decisions.

Some rights guaranteed in the U.S. Constitution are not incorporated. For example, parts of the Seventh Amendment have not been incorporated. In part, the Seventh Amendment states, "In suits at common law, where the value in controversy shall exceed twenty dollars, the right of trial by jury shall be preserved. . . ." While this amendment has not been repealed, federal and state defendants are not guaranteed a right of trial by jury for all lawsuits exceeding $20.

Due Process and Liberal versus Conservative Courts

The incorporation of due process rights depends in part on the philosophy and values reflected by the U.S. Supreme Court justices in their decisions. At the beginning of the twenty-first century, the U.S. Supreme Court has often been described as a "conservative court." Unlike the U.S. Supreme Court under Chief Justice Earl Warren (1953–1969), which created many new due process rights for the accused, the U.S. Supreme Court under the leadership of Chief Justice John Roberts (2005–) has created few new due process rights and has modified or curtailed many put in place by previous Court decisions.

The decisions of the Roberts Court are described as "conservative," with more emphasis on crime control than due process. As a result, the Roberts Court has often ruled to allow law enforcement greater latitude in arrest, interrogation, and search and seizure than the U.S. Supreme Court did under Chief Justice Earl Warren.

Due Process Rights of the Accused

Due process rights protect the accused against abuse of power by police, prosecutors, courts, and corrections at the expense of swift and sure justice for the victim. By insisting that the government operate within certain limitations in securing the conviction of the accused, citizens are protected against the misuse of the power of the government that could be brought to bear in prosecuting the individual.

The central premise of due process rights is the **presumption of innocence**. Regardless of overwhelming evidence against the accused, the court proceeds on the presumption that until the guilt of the accused is proven beyond a reasonable doubt in a court of law, the defendant is treated as if he or she is not guilty of the charges in regards to the rights afforded the individual. In other words, an accused person cannot be denied constitutional rights simply because he or she is accused of a crime or because of the apparent overwhelming belief in his or her guilt prior to trial.

The First Amendment guarantees the right of freedom of speech, religion, and the press and the right of the people to assemble and to petition the government for a redress of grievances. The major due process rights granted by various other amendments as interpreted by the U.S. Supreme Court guarantee protections against unreasonable searches (Fourth Amendment), forced and self-incriminating testimony (Fifth Amendment), excessive bail and fines (Eighth Amendment), and cruel or unusual punishment (Eighth Amendment), as well as the right to a speedy public trial by jury. The way the U.S. Supreme Court guarantees these rights is to define through case law whether a law or an action violated a Constitutional right. (See Figure 1–5 for a summary of the due process rights of the accused.)

LEARNING OUTCOMES 5 Summarize a defendant's due process rights.

GLOSSARY

due process amendment The Fourteenth Amendment of the U.S. Constitution prohibiting local governments from depriving persons of life, liberty, or property without due process.

substantive due process Due process that refers to the constitutionality of laws.

procedural due process The process and procedure the government can use to prosecute an individual.

incorporate To grant rights defined by the U.S. Constitution to the citizens of a state.

presumption of innocence The most important principle of the due process model requiring all accused persons to be treated as innocent until proven guilty in a court of law.

The central premise of due process rights is the presumption of innocence.

▶ What Is Criminal Justice?

The study of criminal behavior dates to the earliest origins of civilization, but it was not until the mid-nineteenth century that a word was coined to describe this endeavor. In 1855, Italian law professor

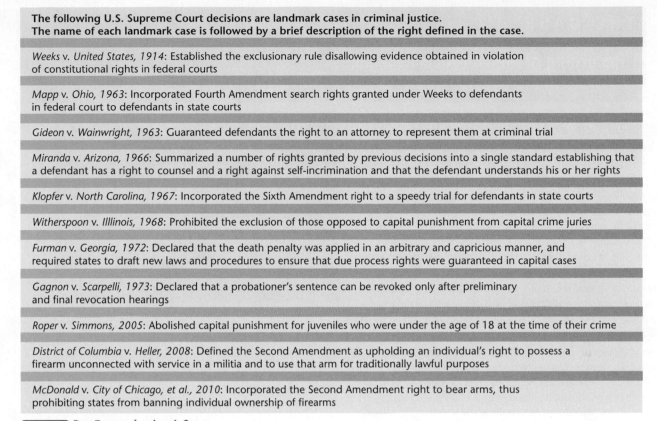

The following U.S. Supreme Court decisions are landmark cases in criminal justice. The name of each landmark case is followed by a brief description of the right defined in the case.

Weeks v. *United States, 1914*: Established the exclusionary rule disallowing evidence obtained in violation of constitutional rights in federal courts

Mapp v. *Ohio, 1963*: Incorporated Fourth Amendment search rights granted under Weeks to defendants in federal court to defendants in state courts

Gideon v. *Wainwright, 1963*: Guaranteed defendants the right to an attorney to represent them at criminal trial

Miranda v. *Arizona, 1966*: Summarized a number of rights granted by previous decisions into a single standard establishing that a defendant has a right to counsel and a right against self-incrimination and that the defendant understands his or her rights

Klopfer v. *North Carolina, 1967*: Incorporated the Sixth Amendment right to a speedy trial for defendants in state courts

Witherspoon v. *Illlinois, 1968*: Prohibited the exclusion of those opposed to capital punishment from capital crime juries

Furman v. *Georgia, 1972*: Declared that the death penalty was applied in an arbitrary and capricious manner, and required states to draft new laws and procedures to ensure that due process rights were guaranteed in capital cases

Gagnon v. *Scarpelli, 1973*: Declared that a probationer's sentence can be revoked only after preliminary and final revocation hearings

Roper v. *Simmons, 2005*: Abolished capital punishment for juveniles who were under the age of 18 at the time of their crime

District of Columbia v. *Heller, 2008*: Defined the Second Amendment as upholding an individual's right to possess a firearm unconnected with service in a militia and to use that arm for traditionally lawful purposes

McDonald v. *City of Chicago, et al., 2010*: Incorporated the Second Amendment right to bear arms, thus prohibiting states from banning individual ownership of firearms

FIGURE 1–5 Due Process Landmark Cases

Raffaele Garofalo coined the term *criminologia*, the study of crime. In 1887, French anthropologist Paul Topinard used *criminologia* to refer to any scientific concern with the phenomenon of crime.

The study of crime as an academic discipline emerged in the United States in the twentieth century and was rooted in the academic discipline of **sociology**, the study of human social behavior. American sociologist Edwin Sutherland provided a definition of criminology that is widely used. He described **criminology** as "the body of knowledge regarding crime as a social phenomenon. It includes within its scope the process of making laws, of breaking laws, and of reacting toward the breaking of laws."[20]

While criminology can include the study of the criminal justice system, criminal justice has evolved into a distinctively different discipline from criminology. Sutherland's definition of criminology emphasized that "the objective of criminology is the development of a body of general and verified principles and of other types of knowledge regarding this process of law, crime, and treatment or prevention."[21] In other words, the purpose of criminology is to develop theories that explain crime as a social phenomenon.

The discipline of criminal justice emerged in the 1960s and matured in the 1980s. Many early academic programs related to criminal justice were housed in sociology departments. Criminal justice refers to the study of the processes involved in a system of justice; the people who perform these tasks; the scope and nature of the system; and the public policy, laws, and regulations that shape the administration and outcomes of a criminal justice system. An objective of the study

of criminal justice may be to develop theories, but often criminal justice research is applied research, comparison research, descriptive research, or problem-solving research.

The study of law leading to the credentials to practice law as a licensed attorney is a distinctly different discipline from criminal justice or criminology. A career as an attorney, a prosecutor, or a judge requires completion of a graduate law degree. Lawyers tend to be professionals who work in the criminal justice system.

Today, the field of criminal justice includes many related fields in counseling, forensic science, law, medicine, psychology, science, and sociology. New fields of study such as aviation security, forensic science, homeland security, intermediate sanctions, psychological profiling, and reentry of offenders into society have created new opportunities for those who have an interest in criminal justice but do not want to enter traditional law enforcement or correctional professions. Also, as foreign language barriers become less of a challenge and travel restrictions to certain countries ease, many are finding the study of the criminal justice systems of other nations to be an exciting field. Many college-level criminal justice departments offer study-abroad programs to those who want to study another country's criminal justice system.

LEARNING OUTCOMES 6 — Summarize criminology, criminal law, and criminal justice.

GLOSSARY

sociology The study of human social behavior.

criminology The body of knowledge regarding crime as a social phenomenon.

> The discipline of criminal justice emerged in the 1960s and matured in the 1980s.

Recording of Police Officers Illegal

Nic Neish / Fotolia

On August 24, 2011, an Illinois jury returned a verdict of not guilty for Tiawanda Moore, who was charged with making an audio recording of police officers without their consent. If she had been found guilty of the felony offense, Moore could have been sentenced to 15 years in prison. Moore's crime was that she recorded her interview with two Chicago police officers. She had filed a complaint against a Chicago police officer and said she believed the two officers were trying to intimidate her into dropping the complaint and wanted evidence to prove her case.[22]

Illinois has the toughest laws in the nation prohibiting the public from recording police officers. The law specifically prohibits recording police officers while they are in uniform, in the public, and in performance of their duties.

There is debate as to the constitutionality of the prohibition against openly recording police officers who are working in public. To challenge the law, Moore has filed a lawsuit in federal court claiming that her arrest and prosecution violated her civil rights.[23] Many cities continue to enforce the law, charging people who record police officers. Other officials argue that the law is unconstitutional. The American Civil Liberties Union has filed a federal lawsuit in Chicago challenging the law as a violation of the First Amendment. One county's State's Attorney has said that he considers the law unconstitutional and refuses to prosecute people arrested for the offense.[24] State representatives have introduced legislation that would allow people to record, without his or her consent, a police officer working in public.[25] In March 2012, Stanley Sacks, a Cook County judge, dismissed charges against Christopher Drew of recording his conversations with police during his arrest, declaring the law unconstitutional.

However, the Fraternal Order of Police in Chicago has gone on record as backing the current law. They claim that the law prevents people from making baseless accusations against officers by recording them and then releasing snippets that do not reveal the full context of the incident.[26]

As a result of the mixed rulings, most believe the law will be appealed to the Illinois Supreme Court and perhaps the U.S. Supreme Court.

This case raises several interesting questions. Among them are the following:

1. Read the First Amendment and the discussion of due process in this chapter. Does the public audio recording of police officers in the course of their duties violate the due process rights of the First Amendment? Explain.

2. If new legislation is introduced, what and when should citizens be allowed to record?

3. What privacy rights do police officers have in the public performance of their duties while in uniform?

Describe the public-order (crime-control) and individual-rights (due process) perspectives of criminal justice and explain how the criminal justice system balances the two.

The need to balance each individual's due process rights with the need to protect the larger part of society poses a challenge for the criminal justice system. Balancing the exercise of civil liberties and the need for law and order is a difficult and complex task. Formal sanctions (laws) within the criminal justice system are necessary to balance individual rights and public safety. A homogeneous society has less need for reliance on a formal system of social control. However, the United States is not a homogeneous society; rather, it is a society characterized by great diversity in race, religion, ethnicity, and values.

1. Explain why public order (crime control) is necessary in our society.

2. What makes balancing public order and individual rights so complex?

3. How do the courts provide guidance in balancing crime control and due process?

informal sanctions Social norms that are enforced through the social forces of the family, school, government, and religion.

social norms The expected normative behavior in a society.

formal sanctions Social norms enforced through the laws of the criminal justice system.

system of social control A social system designed to maintain order and regulate interactions.

order maintenance Activities of law enforcement that resolve conflicts and assist in the regulation of day-to-day interactions of citizens.

due process rights Rights guaranteed to persons by the Constitution and its amendments.

crime-control (public-order) model A model of the criminal justice system in which emphasis is placed on fighting crime and protecting potential victims.

due-process model A model that ensures that individuals are protected from arbitrary and excessive abuse of power by the government.

Describe the structure of the criminal justice system.

The criminal justice system is comprised of various components. Those components include law enforcement, the courts, probation and parole, and correctional institutions. These components exist in federal, state, and local government. The distinct autonomy of each component at each level of government can be likened to a picket fence, with the local, state, and federal criminal justice systems depicted as three horizontal levels connected vertically by the roles, functions, and activities that each performs. The U.S. government has created many checks and balances to control the autonomy and to void actions of other criminal justice agencies.

1. What are the categories of agencies that comprise the criminal justice system?

2. What is meant by the term *picket fence model*?

3. How is the power of criminal justice agencies controlled?

criminal justice system The enforcement, by the police, the courts, and correctional institutions, of obedience to laws.

picket fence model The model of the criminal justice system in which the local, state, and federal criminal justice systems are depicted as three horizontal levels connected vertically by the roles, functions, and activities of the agencies that comprise them.

checks and balances The authority of agencies to void actions of other criminal justice agencies.

LEARNING OUTCOMES 3

Outline the fundamentals of the criminal justice process.

The police are responsible for investigating, arresting, and booking a defendant. If the defendant is to be prosecuted, the next step is the first appearance before a judge. A judge determines whether the charges are legitimate according to statutes, advises the person of his or her legal rights, and determines bail. A case moves from the police to the prosecutor by a preliminary hearing or a grand jury indictment. At the arraignment, the defendant is asked whether he or she pleads guilty or not guilty. Guilt or innocence is determined by the judge in a bench trial or by the jury in a jury trial. The judge determines an appropriate sentence for a convicted defendant. The sentence is announced at a sentencing hearing. The defendant has a right to appeal a verdict based on alleged judicial errors. The convicted defendant may become an inmate in a correctional facility or may be placed on probation. Under certain conditions, parole may allow for an early release from a correctional facility.

1. List the major processes a defendant faces in the criminal justice system.

2. Describe what takes place during an initial appearance.

3. How can a defendant challenge a conviction?

4. What type of punishment might a judge impose on a defendant?

arrest To restrict the freedom of a person by taking him or her into police custody.

booking Police activity that establishes the identification of an arrested person and formally charges that person with a crime.

bail Release of the defendant prior to trial.

indictment The formal verdict of the grand jury that there is sufficient evidence to bring a person to trial.

input-output model A model of how people are processed through the criminal justice system until they exit the system.

preliminary hearing A hearing before a magistrate judge in which the prosecution presents evidence to convince the judge that there is probable cause to bring the defendant to trial.

probable cause hearing A hearing to determine whether there is a direct link between a suspect and a crime.

grand jury A panel of citizens that decides whether there is probable cause to indict a defendant on the alleged charges.

true bill A jury's decision that authorizes the prosecutor to arraign the defendant.

arraignment hearing A hearing where charges are read and the defendant is asked to enter a plea.

LEARNING OUTCOMES 4

Summarize major events that led to changes in the American criminal justice system.

A number of phenomena encouraged change within the criminal justice system and led to its distinction as one of the most examined and criticized aspects of government operations. These historical events included the Civil Rights Act of 1964; the Vietnam War; President Johnson's War on Crime; and President Bush's war on terrorism following the attacks of September 11, 2001. In many respects, these four historical events were interrelated and cumulative in their effect on bringing change to the criminal justice system.

1. Name four events that stirred interest in examining the effectiveness of the criminal justice system.

2. Describe the struggle for equality within society and the criminal justice system.

3. How was the criminal justice system perceived as a failure?

4. What did the President's Crime Commission legislate to offer funding to improve the criminal justice system?

meta-influence A phenomenon that results in encompassing transformative changes.

slave patrols White militia who were responsible for controlling, returning, and punishing runaway slaves.

Brown v. Board of Education Topeka (1954) The U.S. Supreme Court decision that resulted in the movement to integrate schools, public transportation, business, and society.

Civil Rights Act of 1964 The act declaring that it is illegal for businesses, hotels, restaurants, and public transportation to deny citizens service based on their race.

Jim Crow laws (Black Codes) Laws passed after the Civil War to overstep the basic human rights and civil liberties of African-Americans.

1972 Equal Employment Opportunity Act The act that ended discrimination in law enforcement and corrections based on race, gender, and other protected categories.

civil disobedience A nonviolent approach of protest in the civil rights movement.

Montgomery bus boycott A boycott of public transportation initiated by the arrest of Rosa Parks.

Vietnam War A war from 1955 to 1975 involving Vietnam, Laos, and Cambodia.

domino theory A claim that the continued fall of governments to communist rule would threaten democracy.

War on Crime A declaration by President Lyndon Johnson in 1965 to counter crime and social disorder.

Omnibus Crime Control and Safe Streets Act of 1968 An act that provided resources to local and state government to assist in the adoption of reforms, including the Law Enforcement Assistance Administration.

Law Enforcement Assistance Administration (LEAA) A conduit for the transfer of federal funds to state and local law enforcement agencies.

Law Enforcement Educational Program (LEEP) A program created to promote education among criminal justice personnel by offering loans and grants to pursue higher education.

war on terrorism President George W. Bush's declaration regarding the response of the United States to the events of September 11, 2001.

enemy combatants The suspension of due process rights for accused terrorists under the enemy combatant executive order.

LEARNING OUTCOMES 5

Summarize a defendant's due process rights.

The Fourteenth Amendment guarantees the principle of due process to the citizens of all states. Due process means that every defendant is given procedural rights in criminal cases and receives fairness and equity while being processed through the criminal justice system. Quite often due process rights are incorporated by U.S. Supreme Court decisions. A central premise of due process is that an accused person is presumed innocent of the charges prior to trial.

1. Which amendment provides due process for anyone accused of a crime?

2. How are federal rights granted to the states?

3. What are the primary sources of due process rights?

due process amendment The Fourteenth Amendment of the U.S. Constitution prohibiting local governments from depriving persons of life, liberty, or property without due process.

substantive due process Due process that refers to the constitutionality of laws.

procedural due process The process and procedure the government can use to prosecute an individual.

incorporate To grant rights defined by the U.S. Constitution to the citizens of a state.

presumption of innocence The most important principle of the due process model requiring all accused persons to be treated as innocent until proven guilty in a court of law.

LEARNING OUTCOMES 6

Summarize criminology, criminal law, and criminal justice.

The study of criminal behavior in the United States emerged in the twentieth century. Scientific research has become a large part of the academic discipline of criminal justice today. The study of human social behavior in a society is called sociology. The scientific study of the root causes of crime in society is known as criminology. Today, the field of criminal justice includes many other related fields.

1. What are two academic disciplines that conduct research in the criminal justice field?

2. How long has crime been studied by scholars in United States?

3. What is the purpose of criminology?

sociology The study of human social behavior.

criminology The body of knowledge regarding crime as a social phenomenon.

MyCJLab

Go to Chapter 1 in *MyCJLab* to test your mastery of chapter concepts, access your Study Plan, engage in interactive exercises, complete critical-thinking and research assignments, and view related online videos.

 Review: Complete the pretest in the Study Plan to confirm what you know and what you need to study further. Then complete the post-test to confirm your mastery of the concepts. Use the key term flash cards to review key terminology.

 Apply: Complete the interactive simulation activity.

Analyze: Complete assignments as directed by your instructor.

Current Events: Explore CJSearch for current topical videos, articles, and news pieces.

Additional Links

To read or watch a video of crimes that have received national attention, visit **http://www.msnbc.msn.com/id/38739087/ns/dateline_nbc/**.

To read or download parts of the Declaration of Independence, the U.S. Constitution, and the Bill of Rights, go to **http://www.archives.gov/exhibits/charters/charters.html**.

Go to **http://www.ourdocuments.gov/doc.php?flash=true&doc=97#** to learn more about civil rights and to read the Civil Rights Act of 1964.

Go to **http://www.aclu.org** to learn about this organization's efforts to preserve and protect individual rights in legislation, courts, and communities.

Go to **http://www.criminalfindlaw.com** and learn about the stages in a typical criminal case, tips on your constitutional rights, and information about criminal records.

To read the Omnibus Crime Control and Safe Streets Act of 1968, open the PDF at **http://transition.fcc.gov/Bureaus/OSEC/library/legislative_histories/1615.pdf**.

To learn more about careers in the field of legal proceedings and projected job openings, visit the Bureau of Labor Statistics at **http://www.bls.gov/ooh/legal/home.htm**.

Crime— *The Search for Understanding*

"By age 23, almost a third of Americans have been arrested for an offense other than a minor traffic violation."

—*National Longitudinal Survey of Youth*

1 Outline the development of criminological theory.

2 Summarize major theoretical perspectives on criminal behavior.

3 Summarize modern theories of criminology.

4 Summarize factors that make it difficult for criminologists to definitively explain crime.

2

Paolese/Fotolia

For several years, social psychologist Dr. Diederik Stapel wrote dozens of academic papers discussing his research data that linked exposure to litter and graffiti to crime. The Dutch researcher published his research in prestigious professional journals. In study after study, the data from Dr. Stapel's experiments and surveys continued to support his theory that exposure to litter and graffiti makes people more likely to commit small crimes. Based on Dr. Stapel's research, others developed programs to modify the environment of children to reduce factors that were thought to promote criminal behavior. In November 2011, a report of an investigative committee at Stapel's university in the Netherlands concluded that he blatantly faked data for dozens of papers for several years.[1]

The report concluded that Dr. Stapel never collected any data from his numerous experiments and surveys, but fabricated the data to support his theories. Dr. Stapel not only faked data from his research, but also supplied false data to unaware doctoral students he supervised so that their studies would support his previous findings.[2] The scope and nature of the fraud completely discredit Dr. Stapel's theories and other research that relied on his data. While a relationship may exist between exposure to litter and graffiti and propensity to commit crime, the research fraud that Dr. Stapel committed contaminates research attempting to link the two.

Reliable data are the foundation for accurate theories concerning causes of crime. Throughout the history of criminology, popular theories of crime causation have been discarded when data revealed the principles on which the theory was formulated were not scientifically accurate. Even the theories developed by Cesare Lombroso, the "father of criminology," have been discarded as not being scientifically accurate.

> **DISCUSS** What harm can be done by accepting as accurate flawed data linking crime and certain factors?

▶ The Development of Criminological Theory

On January 8, 2011, Jared Lee Loughner, 22 years old, opened fire on a group of people at a political rally for U.S. Representative Gabrielle Giffords in Tucson, Arizona, killing 6 and injuring 13 others. Loughner had no background in political causes and no known grudge against Representative Giffords. He was a high school dropout and had been expelled from Pima Community College. He had been rejected by the military as being unfit for service. He had a history of drug and alcohol abuse but only two minor arrests. Should someone have been able to identify Loughner's potential for violence?

Why would a person deliberately murder strangers? Are there certain traits common to mass murderers? Do criminals have characteristics or behaviors that uniquely identify them? For hundreds of years, people studying crime and criminals have sought to answer those questions. Crime is pervasive throughout society. The federal government's National Longitudinal Survey of Youth found that by age 23, almost a third of Americans have been arrested for a crime other than a minor traffic violation.[3] Thus, if the factors contributing to criminal behavior were identified, it could transform society and the criminal justice system.

The study of offenders and offending is referred to as **criminology**. Criminology plays an important role in the criminal justice system the theories produced therein are often used to implement laws, prevention programs, rehabilitation programs, and sentencing strategies. From mass murderers such as James E. Holmes, Aurora, CO movie theater shooter, and Jared Lee Loughner to common thieves, researchers gather data and construct theories to explain why people commit crimes. However, no single theory explains criminal behavior. Understanding crime is best described

Jared Lee Loughner

Mug Shot / Alamy

> Criminology is the study of offenders and offending.

as a search for knowledge and variables regarding the causes of criminal behavior. Many theories claim to explain crime, but none of them are comprehensive in that they explain all criminal behavior by all people.

This chapter examines various early and modern theories proposed to explain

1692	**1768**	**1789**	**1848**	**1859**
Salem Witch Trials: Most people believe that evil spirits, the devil, and sin are causes of deviant behavior.	***Cesare Beccaria's* Of Crimes and Punishments** defines classical theory of criminology.	***Jeremy Bentham's* An Introduction to the Principles of Morals and Legislation** defines neoclassical theory of criminology.	***Karl Marx's*** **Communist Manifesto** defines class conflict as the cause of inequality and poverty.	***Charles Darwin's* Origin of Species** is published. It allows for theories that criminals are born bad.

LEARNING OUTCOMES 1 Outline the development of criminological theory.

GLOSSARY

criminology The body of knowledge regarding crime as a social phenomenon.

theory A statement regarding the relationship between two or more variables.

nonscientific theories Theories that emphasize moral weakness and evil spirits as the cause of criminality.

Classical School The school of thought that individuals have free will to choose whether to commit crimes.

biological determinism The school of thought that says that crime is caused by a biological or biochemical influence over which the offender has no control.

Diversity of Explanations of Criminal Behavior

The explanations as to the causes of criminality are numerous and diverse. Theories may even be contradictory. For example, some theories posit that crime is the result of a logical and free choice of the offender; other theories propose that criminal behavior is the result of heredity, biological traits, or other factors beyond the control of the offender.

Some theories explaining criminal behavior may appear rather bizarre, such as one theory that claims a correlation exists between unpopular names and delinquency.[4] Another theory proposes that blue lights can reduce crime and suicides in public places.[5] Some authorities in the Philippines believe that the singing of Frank Sinatra's version of "My Way" crime. These theories focus on free-will choice and biological, psychological, and sociological explanations of crime.

in karaoke bars can trigger assaults and homicides.[6] Some theories have become more accepted by the criminal justice system than others. The theories most incorporated into laws, punishment, and treatment and prevention programs are based on the premise that the causes of criminal behavior are related to social interactions and free will.

People who explore the causes of crime are interested in both the formal systems for the control of behavior, such as the legal system, and the informal systems of control, such as the family, school, social group, and religious affiliation. They are interested in observing how these systems influence behavior and what happens when there are conflicts between these various control systems. For example, the legal system prohibits people under the age of 21 from drinking alcoholic beverages. This prohibition is also supported by the informal system of institutions such as schools, religious beliefs, and family values. However, underage drinking is a common problem. What factors influence underage youths to drink in the face of formal and informal pressures not to drink? Public service campaigns, antidrinking programs, and the response of the legal system respond to the challenge of underage drinking based on the accepted beliefs of those factors that do influence youths to drink. Many antidrinking efforts seem to be based on the assumption that peer groups and peer pressure exert a strong influence on a person's decision to drink. By studying behaviors, attitudes, and social interactions, the criminologist strives to gather reliable data to construct theories that can be used to predict behavior.

A **theory** is a statement regarding the relationship between two or more variables. Theories can be based on observations (deduction) or inferences (induction). Theories are tested by

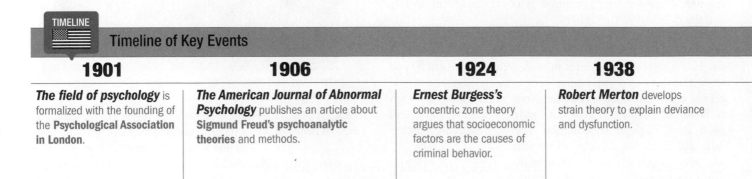

TIMELINE

Timeline of Key Events

1901	**1906**	**1924**	**1938**
The field of psychology is formalized with the founding of the **Psychological Association in London**.	***The American Journal of Abnormal Psychology*** publishes an article about **Sigmund Freud's psychoanalytic theories** and methods.	***Ernest Burgess's*** concentric zone theory argues that socioeconomic factors are the causes of criminal behavior.	***Robert Merton*** develops strain theory to explain deviance and dysfunction.

1875	1878	1892	1897	1899
Richard Dugdale's study of the Jude's family tree results in his conclusion that criminality is an inherited trait.	**Cesare Lombroso's Criminal Man** is published (published in English in 1900).	**The University of Chicago** is the first U.S. university to establish a Department of Sociology. **The Chicago School** focuses on the application of principles of the newly formed discipline of sociology to analysis of criminal behavior.	**Émile Durkheim's** Suicide introduces the importance of social integration as a causal factor in deviant behavior.	**Sigmund Freud** introduces the concept of psychoanalytic theory.

The purpose of a theory is not to predict what a specific individual will do in a specific case. Theories attempt to define general principles that will apply in a number of similar cases.

formulating a hypothesis that allows for the empirical testing of the relationship between variables. The purpose of a theory is not to predict what a specific individual will do in a specific case. Rather, theories attempt to define general principles that will apply in a number of similar cases, but not necessarily all cases. Thus, if 95 out of 100 people would act a certain way under certain conditions, the claim could confidently be made that the variables correlate significantly with the behavior, despite the fact that for five people, the variables did not cause them to commit a crime. Theories attempt to define and explain the factors that influence or determine behavior and to explain how these factors interrelate. In criminal justice research, 95% accuracy is an acceptable standard for determining reliable knowledge.

Major Theoretical Perspectives

As mentioned, there are numerous explanations for criminal behavior. These explanations are based on different standards of reliable knowledge. Some theories are merely commonly held beliefs by the public often based on prejudice, stereotyping, and limited data. Some of these theories may prescribe criminal attributes to entire groups of people. Other theories are based on a belief in supernatural forces and witchcraft.

Other beliefs may be based on authority. The belief is held because people accept the values and belief system of someone who is perceived as an authority figure. In modern society, it is not uncommon for candidates running for elective office to make assertions as to the causes of crime and disorder in society. Often these claims are not based on reliable data. For example, a common claim of conservative political candidates is that the decline of traditional social values has resulted in breeding grounds for "aberrant behavior, abandonment of traditional values of respect and honesty, and crime.[7] While beliefs based on authority may be strongly held by certain groups, the strength to which these beliefs are held does not make them accurate or reliable.

The Path from Early to Modern Theories of Crime Causation

Early **nonscientific theories** (pre-1700s) emphasized moral weakness and evil spirits as the cause of criminality. Early explanations of deviant and criminal behavior were derived

Beliefs based on authority may be strongly held, but the strength with which these beliefs are held does not make them accurate or reliable.

1938	1939	1963	1967
Frank Tannenbaum's Crime and Community emphasizes the role of stigma in delinquent behavior.	**Edwin Sutherland** introduces the theory of white-collar crime and delinquency as learned behavior.	**Howard Becker's Outsiders** is influential in promoting the importance of public reaction in the development of a delinquent identity.	**Richard Quinney's Criminal Behavior Systems** defines crime as social conflict.

1972

National Crime Victimization Survey begins gathering data on victimizations.

1975

Freda Adler introduces the liberation theory of female criminality, arguing that female criminality is caused by inequality between men and women

1997

Meda Chesney-Lind's The Female Offender: Girls, Women, and Crime hypothesizes the influence of inequality and power status between men and women as the cause of female criminality.

psychological theory The idea that criminal behavior is a result of emotions, drives, and mental defects.

Sociological School of criminology The school of thought that says that crime is caused by socioeconomic conditions and social interactions and values.

primarily from nonscientific methodologies such as superstitions, stereotypes, fear of strangers, and authority. Most of these nonscientific investigations searched for principles underlying human conduct and thought based on logic or beliefs assumed to be true but without scientific evidence to support the belief. These principles often were based on social and religious morals instead of empirical observations and facts. It was believed that deviant and criminal behaviors were caused by evil spirits, sin, agreements with evil spirits such as the devil, or magic. For example, in 1692 to 1693, more than two dozen people were sentenced to death for witchcraft in what is known as the Salem witch trials in Massachusetts Colony. It was even thought that abnormal physical appearances such as birthmarks or deformity were signs indicating that the person was marked by an evil spirit.

Modern theories of crime causation are complex because they recognize the interaction of many variables as being necessary and sufficient in explaining criminal behavior. Modern theories explaining criminal behavior are based on scientific inquiry, which involves observation and isolation of variables relating to cause and effect. Modern scientific explanations of criminality have evolved from simple theories with few variables to complex theories built on extensive data and research.

The various theories of crime causation since the 1700s can be divided into four groups based on the primary belief in the cause of criminality. These groups are called *schools*. Each

"THERE IS A FLOCK OF YELLOW BIRDS AROUND HER HEAD."

A Salem witch trial

Mary Evans Picture Library / Alamy

school of criminology has a central premise as to the cause of criminal behavior, and the various theories within that school enhance or modify the basic premise explaining criminal

Think About It . . .

In the 2012 elections, as in almost every election, many political candidates blamed moral relativism, gay rights, and the decline of traditional religious-based values for the ills that are perceived as besetting the nation. The decline of traditional values is said to contribute to rising crime rates, teen pregnancy, divorce, juvenile delinquency, and declining school performance by children. Most of these claims are generalizations without any basis in fact and often are contrary to actual facts. For example, of the 11 states with the lowest church attendance, 10 have lower homicide rates than those in states with higher church attendance.[8] Do you believe the decline in traditional values is a major cause of criminal behavior? Explain.

Bob Daemmrich / Alamy

	Classical Theories	Determinist Theories	Psychological Theories	Sociological Theories
Prime cause of crime	Free-will choice	Biological, chemical, or genetic factor	Subconscious influence	Socioeconomic factors, peer interactions, learned behavior, conflict between different group values
Degree of control by offender	Offender makes choice to commit crime	Offender often is unable to exercise control over choice to commit crime	Offender may be "driven" to commit self-destructive acts	External factors have great influence on choice to commit crime
Society's reaction	Punish offender to deter offending	Confine and isolate offender to protect society	Long-term therapeutic treatment to address underlying causes	Change in external factors will result in change in offending
Use by the criminal justice system	Extensive use in foundation of laws, early corrections theory, and popular acceptance	Influential in correctional theory in the late 1800s and early 1900s, little influence on law	Except for insanity defense, the criminal justice system has not adopted underlying principles	Most common theories underlying crime prevention, especially juvenile offending

FIGURE 2–1 Comparison of Four Schools of Criminological Theory

behavior. There are four major schools of thought regarding the causes of criminal behavior.

The earliest school of criminological thought as to the causes of criminal behavior is called the **Classical School**. It dates from the mid-1700s. It is called "classical" because it was the earliest systematic attempt to explain criminal behavior. The Classical School's primary premise is that crime is a free-will choice.

The next school of thought to emerge is called **biological determinism**. Biological determinism's primary premise is that crime is caused by a biological or biochemical influence over which the offender has little or no control. Theories based on biological determinism began to emerge in the early 1800s.

The next two schools of thought emerged about the same time at the turn of the twentieth century. They are the Psychological and Sociological Schools of criminology. The **psychological theories** are based on the primary premise that crime is caused by emotions, drives, and mental defects that are often not known to the offender. The primary premise of the **Sociological School of criminology** is that crime is caused by socioeconomic conditions and social interactions and values. These theories assume that if social and environmental conditions change, human behavior also will change. While differing in what each believes to be the primary cause of criminal behavior, all theories attempt to generalize principles that can

explain factors that influence offending, victimization, and rehabilitation. (See Figure 2–1 for a summary of the schools of criminological theory.)

▶ Classical and Neoclassical Theories

Emerging in the mid-1700s, classical and neoclassical theories of crime causation bridged the transition from early nonscientific theories to modern scientific theories of crime causation. These theories abandoned the explanations that crime was caused by sin, weak moral character, evil spirits, and magic and assumed that there was a logical explanation of human behavior.

Classical and neoclassical theorists were the first to propose that crime is a matter of free choice, criminals should have rights in the criminal justice system, and the prevention of crime should be based on altering the factors that caused crime. In classical and neoclassical theories, the explanation for crime is based on the assumption that criminal behavior is a matter of choice. The individual has free will to choose to commit or refrain from criminal behavior. The choice to commit a crime is not caused by evil spirits or magic, but is a rational choice of the offender. The individual's choice of behavior is influenced by a rational analysis of

GLOSSARY

neoclassical theories A contemporary view of Classical School theory that believes that there are mitigating circumstances for criminal acts, such as the age or mental capacity of the offender, and that punishment should fit the crime.

Cesare Beccaria The founder of Classical School theories.

pain–pleasure principle A philosophical axiom that people are rational and seek to do that which brings them pleasure and to avoid that which causes them pain.

Neoclassical School of criminology A school of thought that is similar to Classical School theories except for the belief that there are mitigating circumstances for criminal acts, such as the age or mental capacity of the offender, and that punishment should fit the crime.

felicitic calculus The balancing of pain and pleasure as a means to discourage criminal behavior.

utilitarianism A philosophy stating that a rational system of jurisprudence provides for the greatest happiness for the greatest number of people.

the gain to be achieved from committing the criminal act versus the punishment or penalty suffered for the criminal behavior if sanctioned by society. Theories that share this assumption of free will and rational choice are commonly called Classical School theories or Neoclassical School theories.

Neoclassical theories emerged after the first classical theories and were modifications of classical theories. **Neoclassical theories** of crime causation are similar to Classical School theories except for the belief that there are mitigating circumstances for criminal acts, such as the age or mental capacity of the offender, and that punishment should fit the crime. Classical theories assumed that all people, including children and adults with mental impairment, made free-will choices to commit crimes and should be held to the same standard of accountability and punishment. In other words, neoclassical theories said that the criminal behaviors of certain adults and children were not the result of free-will choices and should be treated differently by the criminal justice system.

Cesare Beccaria—Pain–Pleasure Principle

Two theorists representing the classical and neoclassical theories are **Cesare Beccaria** (1738–1794) and Jeremy Bentham (1748–1832), who are considered the founders of classical and neoclassical criminology, respectively. Their theories were a radical departure from the contemporary thought of their time, which credited spirits and demons as the cause of "bad" behavior.

While Cesare Beccaria's ideas actually preceded the development of criminology as an academic discipline, he is known as the founder of classical criminology because his theories about crime marked the beginning of a new approach to criminological thought that would eventually lead to modern theories.

Beccaria was an Italian nobleman and jurist (judge) who was dissatisfied with the justice system of his time and attempted to bring about change. During the 1700s, the Italian criminal justice system was a barbaric system that leaned toward extreme punishments and questionable justice. Laws were unwritten,

Classical and neoclassical theorists were the first to propose that crime is a matter of free choice.

arbitrary, and unfairly applied. The situation was made worse by unschooled judges whose decisions were often arbitrary and based to a large degree on the social class of the accused. The penalties handed out by the courts consisted of corporal and capital punishments that were considered a source of public entertainment. Defendants had no rights, there was no due process, and torture was regarded as an effective interrogation method.

Beccaria based his theory on what he called the **pain–pleasure principle**. Beccaria was influenced by the Age of Enlightenment. His ideas on the cause of criminal behavior were based on the philosophical axiom that people are rational. He reasoned that people seek to do that which brings them pleasure and to avoid that which causes them pain. He further assumed that members of society are responsible for their actions. There are no mitigating circumstances or excuses for one's criminal behavior. The same standard of justice and punishment should be applied to people of all ages and mental abilities. For the purpose of deterring people from committing crimes, he advocated certain, swift punishment of appropriate intensity and duration for the offense committed. According to Beccaria, the reason for the continued presence of crime in eighteenth-century Italian society was that the criminal justice system did not provide for swift, certain, and appropriate punishment.

Pain–Pleasure Principle

Beccaria opposed the death penalty. He argued that the state did not have the right to take a person's life and that the uncertainty of the punishment of death—for few judges even then were willing to send a man to the gallows for the theft of a loaf of bread—diluted the effectiveness of the threat of the death penalty.

Certain, swift punishment of appropriate intensity and duration for the offense committed would deter people from committing crimes.

Basically, Beccaria argued that even minor punishments would be more effective if they were swift and certain. If a person stole a loaf of bread and it was virtually certain that he or she would immediately receive a punishment appropriate to the crime, Beccaria argued, such punishment would be more effective than the threat of death, which was rarely carried out for minor theft. This concept—that criminal behavior is a matter of free will and choice and that certain, swift, and appropriate pain will deter people from criminal behavior—is the basic premise of the classical theory of criminology.

The English title of Beccaria's single-volume book addressing his concerns about the criminal justice system of Italy was entitled *Of Crimes and Punishments*. The book was published in Italian in 1764 and translated into English in 1768.[9] In 1771, he was appointed Counselor of State and a magistrate. Beccaria probably had no idea that his short text would become the single work responsible for a revolution in the philosophy of criminal justice. Even today, Beccaria's ideas seem quite contemporary and can be clearly identified as the foundation underlying the contemporary American criminal justice system.

Bentham and Neoclassical Theory

English philosopher and scholar Jeremy Bentham is credited with the formation of the **Neoclassical School of criminology**.[10] Neoclassical theories are similar to the Classical School in that the basic foundation is the concept that criminal behavior is a matter of free will and the choice to commit criminal behavior can be deterred by pain and punishment. The major difference between Beccaria's classical theory of criminology and Bentham's neoclassical theory is that Bentham believed that Beccaria's unwavering accountability of all offenders was too harsh.

Bentham believed in mitigating circumstances. Whereas Beccaria would hold a child of age five or six just as responsible for a violation of the law and subject to the same punishment as an adult, Bentham argued that children under the age of seven and offenders suffering from mental disease should be exempt from criminal liability. Like Beccaria, Bentham was opposed to the use of the death penalty. His most significant contribution to criminological thought was his work *An Introduction to the Principles of Morals and Legislation*, written in 1780 and published in 1789.

Like Beccaria, Bentham reasoned that people are calculating humans who logically evaluate the pleasure to be gained by the commission of an act versus the punishment to be suffered for it. When the pain of punishment outweighs the pleasure to be derived, individuals refrain from criminal behavior. Harsher prohibitions and punishments were both unnecessary and inefficient. If someone were deterred from theft by the threat of 3 strokes of the cane, then a threat of 20 strokes or of hanging made the judicial system seem ignorant and inappropriate.

Bentham's theory regarding the balancing of pain and pleasure as a means to discourage criminal behavior is known as the **felicitic calculus**—the pain versus pleasure principle. Bentham's philosophy, called **utilitarianism**, states that a rational system of jurisprudence provides for the greatest happiness for the greatest number of people. Based on the principles that people act rationally and that the punishment should fit the crime, Bentham's neoclassical philosophy became the foundation of the English jurisprudence system—and hence the American jurisprudence system.

Classical and Neoclassical Criminology and the Contemporary Criminal Justice System

When Beccaria's and Bentham's ideas about criminal behavior were published, they competed primarily with irrational arguments of demon possession, class-based justice, and harshly exaggerated punishments. Today, the ideas advocated by Beccaria and Bentham remain popular and the foundation of the American criminal justice system. The foundation of the American jurisprudence is that crime is a matter of free-will choice.

The contemporary criminal justice system is to a great deal based on the principles of classical and neoclassical criminology. Beccaria's essay clearly summarized the concept of the criminal justice system as a social contract based on logic, goal orientation, and humanistic principles. The concepts in his book, such as innocent until proven guilty, trial by a jury of one's peers, the right of appeal, the classification of crimes, equal treatment of all people before the court, prohibition against torture, and abolition of the death penalty, reflect contemporary thought.

The concept that crime is a free-will choice is central to punishment, and defendants who can prove that the crime they committed was not a result of their free will may be found not guilty or receive a reduced punishment.

Darwin
Bentham

Beccaria
Lombroso
Garofalo
Ferri

Influence of Criminological Theory

The concept that crime is a free-will choice is central to punishment.

Bentham's neoclassical philosophy became the foundation of the English jurisprudence system, and hence strongly influenced the American jurisprudence system. Bentham's principles of neoclassical theory are reflected in American jurisprudence in a separate criminal justice system for juveniles and the insanity plea that diminishes or eliminates the culpability of defendants who are insane.

Today, many opposed to what are seen as overly harsh punishments, abolishment of the death penalty, and juveniles being tried as adults often phrase their arguments in logic similar to that found in classical and neoclassical thought.

▶ Biological Theories

The Positive School

The twentieth century ushered in a new era of scientific inquiry. Many of the scientific fields that emerged at the turn of the twentieth century, such as genetic research, sociology, psychology, and psychiatry, offered innovative theories to explain human behavior. Scholars quickly adopted this new knowledge to explain criminal behavior, and often the validity of these new explanations was tested through the criminal justice system. Common to these new theories and different from

The assumption underlying the scientific method is that by repeated testing of a hypothesis, the results should be similar.

classical and neoclassical theories was the emphasis on use of the scientific method to gather reliable data about the causes of criminal behavior.

The **scientific method** is more of a philosophy than a single methodology for testing hypotheses. However, while there are differences between the academic disciplines as to the actual procedure and standards for formulating and testing hypotheses, there is general agreement that the methodology used must result in reliable data and that others must be able to replicate the methodology. The assumption underlying the scientific method is that repeated testing of a hypothesis should result in similar results. If there is different data from one procedure to another, the assumption is that the theory is faulty, errors were present in the methodology, or other unknown factors are influencing the outcome of the testing. The advantage of the scientific methodology is that by repeated testing using different methodologies with different research, the resulting data will be reliable. (See Figure 2–2 for the steps used to conduct research in criminal justice.)

Neither the classical nor the neoclassical theories were based on data produced by the scientific method. These theories were based on "logic" and "principle beliefs" that were assumed to be

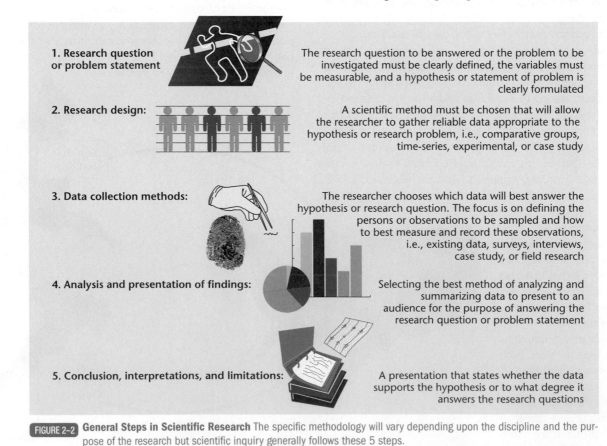

1. Research question or problem statement
The research question to be answered or the problem to be investigated must be clearly defined, the variables must be measurable, and a hypothesis or statement of problem is clearly formulated

2. Research design:
A scientific method must be chosen that will allow the researcher to gather reliable data appropriate to the hypothesis or research problem, i.e., comparative groups, time-series, experimental, or case study

3. Data collection methods:
The researcher chooses which data will best answer the hypothesis or research question. The focus is on defining the persons or observations to be sampled and how to best measure and record these observations, i.e., existing data, surveys, interviews, case study, or field research

4. Analysis and presentation of findings:
Selecting the best method of analyzing and summarizing data to present to an audience for the purpose of answering the research question or problem statement

5. Conclusion, interpretations, and limitations:
A presentation that states whether the data supports the hypothesis or to what degree it answers the research questions

FIGURE 2–2 **General Steps in Scientific Research** The specific methodology will vary depending upon the discipline and the purpose of the research but scientific inquiry generally follows these 5 steps.
Source: Adapted from Frank E. Hagan, *Essentials of Research Methods in Criminal Justice and Criminology*, 3rd ed. (Upper Saddle River, NJ: Pearson Prentice Hall, 2012).

factual and reliable but were not tested. The scientific method emphasizes that knowledge about criminal behavior should be gathered using tools such as observation, surveys, case studies, statistics, and experimentation.

The **Positive School** includes most modern theories of criminology. The positive theories can be divided into three major schools based on the emphasis of the primary cause of crime: biology, psychology, and sociology. Many of the modern positive theories of crime causation are based on the premise that, contrary to the assumption of classical theories that individuals have free will and choose to commit crime, people commit crimes because of internal or external factors that can be observed and measured. Often these factors that influence criminal behavior may be unknown to the person or may be so strong and powerful that they influence behavioral choices beyond the control of the individual. Because of this premise that these factors may compel behavior, even behavior that harms the person, scholars and scientists who advocate that one of the positive theories best explains criminal behavior are also known **determinists**. The implication is that the causes of criminal behavior are not controlled by free-will choice. Criminal behavior is influenced by factors that are beyond the control of the individual.

The Foundations of Biological Explanations

Darwin's *Origin of Species* (1859) provided an important portal for the development of new positive criminological theories. One of the dilemmas in the advancement of premodern criminological theories was the belief commonly held in Christian theologies, which influenced much of the scholarly work of the United States and Europe, that humankind was created by God in God's image and therefore is inherently good.

This foundational belief, while consistent with the free-will school of thought, posed great difficulties for any theory asserting that some people are not created good, but are bad from birth. To say that one was born "bad" seems to place the fault with God or to deny the goodness of God's creation. If people are good from birth, on the other hand, it becomes necessary to explain how someone becomes bad. The theory of evolution and adaptation of the species provided an answer to this question.

Early nineteenth century biological theories emphasized that a person's criminal nature was an inherited characteristic. That is to say, a person is a criminal because his or her parents were criminals. The original cause of the criminality was assumed to be the failure of this genealogical line to fully "evolve." The concept of Darwin's evolution of the animal species was applied to humans. According to this theory, some humans are not fully "civilized," but are defective offshoots that, while appearing similar to "fully evolved" people, are lacking in certain moral and intellectual qualities, resulting in their predisposition toward criminal behavior.

Two early studies attempting to apply a heredity model to the analysis of criminal behavior were the study by **Richard Dugdale** (1841–1883) of the Jukes family and the study of Martin Kallikak's family tree by **Henry Goddard** (1866–1957). These studies supported the conclusion that criminality is an inherited trait. However, lacking

a sophisticated development of the scientific method unbeknown to the authors of these studies, their research methodology was flawed and hence their conclusions were faulty.

Dugdale traced the family tree of Ada Jukes, showing how this one person was responsible for hundreds of criminals and imbeciles.[11] Dugdale was so impressed by the criminal lineage of **Ada Jukes** that he called her the "mother of criminals."

Goddard compared the biological offspring from Martin Kallikak's wife, "a woman of his own quality," and his illegitimate son from a servant girl. Goddard noted a significant difference in the two lineages and concluded that criminality is a degenerative trait transmitted through biology.[12]

These studies did not use the scientific method of research. The studies used observations and data, but they failed to identify and account for significant variables that might be involved in the outcomes. Thus, Goddard concluded that the illegitimate offspring of Martin Kallikak produced many more criminals than that of his wife. However, the study did not recognize the strong impact of socioeconomic variables existing at the time between Kallikak's legitimate and illegitimate offspring. Despite this and other defects in scholarship, studies such as these set the stage for developments in the Positive School of criminology. Cesare Lombroso's theory of the "criminal man" was the first important positivist theory to emerge.

Lombroso, Father of Modern Criminology

Cesare Lombroso (1835–1909) was an Italian medical doctor who took an interest in the causes of criminal behavior. He was particularly influenced by previous scholars whose writings suggested that criminality was inherited. He was influenced by Darwin's theory of adaptation

scientific method The assumption that repeated testing of a hypothesis should result in similar results.

Positive School Modern theories of crime, primarily based on sociology and psychology, that people commit crimes because of uncontrollable internal or external factors that can be observed and measured.

determinist Scholars and scientists who believe that causes of criminal behavior are not controlled by free-will choice; rather, they are influenced by factors that are beyond the control of the individual.

Richard Dugdale A psychologist who conducted an early study attempting to link heredity to criminal behavior in his study of the Jukes family.

Henry Goodard A sociologist who studied Martin Kallikak's family tree attempting to link heredity to criminality.

Ada Jukes A woman labeled by Richard Dugdale as the "mother of criminals."

Cesare Lombroso An Italian doctor who collected data to support his Darwinist-based theory that criminal behavior is a characteristic of humans who have failed to develop normally from their primitive origins.

atavism The failure of humans to fully develop into modern men and women.

criminal man Lombroso's belief that criminals were born inferior and prehuman.

Individuals commit crimes because of inherited traits or their failure to fully develop as normal humans.

and nonadaptation, and he assumed that criminals were throwbacks to an earlier stage of evolution.

For his theory explaining criminal behavior, Lombroso collected extensive data from Italian prisoners and Italian military personnel. Lombroso believed that criminal behavior was a characteristic of humans who had failed to fully develop from their primitive origins, such that criminals were closer to apes than to contemporary humans. He believed criminals could be clearly differentiated from noncriminals on the basis of distinctive physical features such as protruding jaws, sloping foreheads, left-handedness, and red hair—characteristics that made them look more like apes than humans. Lombroso concluded that criminals were cases of **atavism**—the failure of humans to fully develop into modern men and women. In other words, they were "throwbacks," "savages," or cases of "arrested development."[13]

According to Lombroso, there were two distinct species of humans: criminal and **criminal man**. Criminals were born inferior and prehuman, according to Lombroso. Thus, little could be done to prevent such people from engaging in criminal acts or to rehabilitate them. Lombroso made extensive physical measurements to define what he called the "criminal man."[14] (See Figure 2–3.) The study of the physical traits of criminals was called **atavistic stigmata**.

> Lombroso was the first person to try to unravel the mystery of criminal behavior by use of the scientific method.

Lombroso's studies led him to posit that besides "criminal man" or the "born criminal," there were other types of criminals. His research led him to the conclusion that some people did not fully fit the description of the "born criminal" because they developed criminal tendencies later in life or after traumatic brain injuries. Also, he noted that those who led a seemingly "successful" life as a career criminal did not conform to the characteristics of "criminal man." Thus, Lombroso developed other classifications of criminals, including "criminaloids" (or occasional criminals), criminals by passion, moral imbeciles, and criminal epileptics. He noted that in some of these criminals, compared to genetic factors, factors such as environment, opportunity, and poverty appeared to be more influential in determining behavior.[15]

Lombroso's basic assumption that there are two species of humans—criminal and noncriminal—has been discredited by contemporary research. Major researchers no longer believe that criminality is an inherited trait due to arrested development of one or more branches of human evolution. However, despite this rebuff of his theories of crime causation, Lombroso is known as the **father of scientific criminology**. This title is bestowed upon him because he was the first to use the scientific method in the search for an explanation of criminal behavior. He conducted meticulous observations, measurements, and data recording to develop his hypotheses. Unfortunately, he lacked knowledge of genetics, sociology, and psychology, which were not developed until the twentieth century, resulting in flawed theory development. However, his was the first attempt in the pursuit of unraveling the mystery of criminal behavior by use of the scientific method.

Lombroso's theories were further developed by Raffaele Garofalo (1851–1934) and Enrico Ferri (1856–1929). Although the theories of Garofalo and Ferri contained significant deviations from those of Lombroso, the central theme was that criminals should not be held morally responsible for crimes because they did not choose to commit the crimes. The Positive School of criminology, led by Lombroso, Garofalo, and Ferri, argued that the concept of free will is fiction. Lombroso suggested that preventive actions would have little or no impact on the prevention of criminal behavior. Ferri was more hopeful that preventive measures could overcome congenital tendencies. He favored obliging criminals to work, believing that a strong work ethic would help criminals overcome defects of character. Garofalo focused more on psychic anomalies and the reform of Italy's judicial system. For example, he argued that juries were ill-equipped to make judgments regarding the fate of criminals because criminality was more a medical condition than a moral defect.

Lombroso and the Contemporary Criminal Justice System

Despite the fact that Lombroso's theory of "criminal man" was later invalidated, it was and continues to be influential in the study of criminology and on the criminal justice system. For example, his theory influenced the way in which convicted

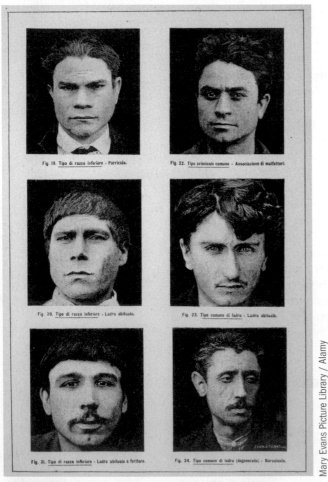

Fig. 19. Tipo di razza inferiore - Parricida.

Fig. 22. Tipo criminale comune - Associazione di malfattori.

Fig. 20. Tipo di razza inferiore - Ladro abituale.

Fig. 23. Tipo comune di ladro - Ladro abituale.

Fig. 21. Tipo di razza inferiore - Ladro abituale e feritore.

Fig. 24. Tipo comune di ladro (degenerato) - Borsaiuolo.

FIGURE 2–3 Lombroso's Image of the Model Criminal Man

people were treated in prisons in the nineteenth and early twentieth centuries. Emphasis on moral correction through religious instruction as practiced by Eastern State Penitentiary was replaced by an emphasis on identification, isolation, and extermination. Since criminals were distinct from "civilized man," prisons emphasized conditions more aligned with the imprisonment of primates than humans. One of Lombroso's beliefs was that criminal man was less sensitive to pain and unable to fully embrace cognitive learning. Therefore, prison environments emphasized obedience to strict rules, the regimentation of activities and movement, and harsh, sometimes brutal, corporal punishment.

Since this view of criminal behavior imagined that it was often impossible to reform "criminal man," the focus of corrections was to prevent the further spread of criminality rather than to rehabilitate offenders. For example, castration was a common correctional treatment based on the belief that criminality was an inherited characteristic. This belief was commonly held in American society in the early twentieth century. For example, in his opinion supporting castration as a valid treatment for criminals, U.S. Supreme Court Justice Oliver Wendell Holmes, Jr., declared, "It is better for all the world, if instead of waiting to execute degenerate offspring for crime, or to let them starve for their imbecility, society can prevent those who are manifestly unfit from continuing their kind."

This "medical model" of crime that denied that crime was a free-will choice had an enduring impact on the criminal justice system and is commonly associated today with drug-related crimes. The debate as to whether drug abuse is a free-will choice or a medical illness divides those who would criminalize and imprison drug users from those who would decriminalize and rehabilitate drug abusers.

Modern Biological Explanations

Lombroso's theories proved to be faulty explanations of criminal behavior. However, it must be remembered that Lombroso proposed his theory of criminality without benefit of the knowledge provided by modern genetic science, the mapping of the human genome, and advanced imaging and chemical analyses. As the contribution of genetics to various human conditions was recognized, several studies revisited Lombroso's basic axiom that criminality is inherited.

Modern theories reject the premise that humans are divided into criminals and noncriminals, but posit that organic factors such as genetics, biochemistry, and brain functioning may exert influences leading to criminal behavior. For example, studies of identical twins performed by Karl O. Christiansen[16] concluded that for identical twins, if one twin engaged in criminal behavior, the probability that his or her identical twin would be a criminal was statistically significantly higher. Christiansen's research suggested that biological traits were more influential than environmental factors or parenting. His research concluded that there is not nearly the link between criminality of adopted twins when one was raised by criminal nonbiological parents and the other was raised by noncriminal nonbiological parents as when one twin was criminal.

> Biological theories as the cause of criminal behavior have not been integrated into the criminal justice system.

Proponents of the biological perspective on criminal behavior argue that some people are born with a biological predisposition to be antisocial—to behave in ways that run counter to social values and norms. Unlike early biological determinists, modern biocriminologists concede that environmental factors can inhibit or stimulate hereditary predispositions for criminality. **Biocriminology** focuses on research into the roles played by genetic and neurophysiological variables in criminal behavior.

Modern biology-based theories identify a diverse number of biological, chemical, genetic, and neurological variables suspected of contributing to criminal behavior. Often these theories have emerged after scientific discoveries revealed new knowledge about how the brain works and the contribution of genetics to behavior. For example, as the role of chromosomes became clear in influencing certain human characteristics, the **XYY chromosome theory of violent behavior** emerged. The normal male has an X and Y chromosome in the cells that determine the sex of a person. It was discovered that some males have an extra Y chromosome, and studies of male prisoners convicted of violent crimes have found a high correlation between conviction for a violent crime and the presence of an extra Y chromosome.[17]

atavistic stigmata The study of the physical traits of criminals.

father of scientific criminology The title bestowed on Cesare Lombroso because he was the first to use the scientific method in the search to explain criminal behavior.

biocriminology Research into the roles played by genetic and neurophysiological variables in criminal behavior.

XYY chromosome theory of violent behavior The idea that violent behavior in males can in part be attributed to the presence of an extra Y chromosome in male offenders.

The XYY chromosome theory illustrates one of the shortcomings of many theories based on biological influences. The study of males imprisoned for violent crimes revealed a correlation between males with an extra Y chromosome. However, a correlation does not prove causation. Thus, follow-up studies revealed that the XYY chromosome pattern was also present in men who were not violent criminals.[18] This suggests that other factors that have not been identified, not the extra Y chromosome, may be the cause of the violent behavior.

Biological Theories and the Contemporary Criminal Justice System

Biological theories as the cause of criminal behavior have not been integrated into the criminal justice system. For example, defenses based on the claim that criminal behavior was inborn due to the presence of an extra Y chromosome have not been accepted by the courts. In fact, if biological theories were to be widely accepted as the cause of criminal behavior, it would require extensive reform of the criminal justice system. The criminal justice system is based on the assumption that criminal behavior is a free-will choice. If criminal behavior is not a free-will choice, it would change the concept of guilt and eliminate the bases for punishment by imprisonment. If criminality were caused by uncontrollable biological factors, it would be cruel and unusual punishment to incarcerate people for that which they had no control over and could not change and imprisonment would not change.

► Psychological Theories

Psychological Explanations

At the end of the 1800s, Sigmund Freud introduced his new **psychoanalytic theory**. In the twentieth century, the science of psychoanalysis became universally accepted as a way of understanding previously unexplainable human behavior.[19] Freud based his theory on the underlying assumption that behavior is not a choice of free will but is controlled by subconscious desires and the conflict between life and death drives. Furthermore, not all behavior is rational. Some behaviors are not only irrational, but also destructive. Yet, despite the self-destructive nature of some behaviors, Freud argued that people frequently are unable to control them.

> **psychoanalytic theory** The concept that behavior is not a matter of free will, but is controlled by subconscious desires, which includes the idea that criminal behavior is a result of unresolved internal conflict and guilt.
>
> **id** Unconscious desires and drives.
>
> **ego** The rational mind.
>
> **superego** The moral values system.
>
> **psychological profiling** Profiles based on the personality traits according to psychoanalytic theories.

At the root of Freud's theory is the concept that human thoughts and actions are controlled by the three components of the unconscious mind: the **id**, unconscious desires and conflicts; the **ego**, the rational mind; and the moral values system, or **superego**. Freud's theory of psychoanalysis was based on the theory that the motive for behaviors may not be conscious to the person. Human behavior was influenced, even controlled, by repression, transference, unconscious motives, psychosexual conflicts, and conflict between life and death drives (or *libido*). According to Freud, a person may not know his or her motives for behavior, which may only be understood through years of psychoanalytic therapy. Psychoanalytic therapy, or understanding of human behavior, was accomplished by use of dream interpretation and understanding of the subconscious drives that manifested themselves in behavior. Freud is the father of psychoanalysis, and his theories have been furthered by numerous followers, resulting in the development of different disciplines of psychoanalysis.

Freud did not focus on the study of criminal behavior. However, his theory of psychoanalysis has been applied extensively to the study of criminals. Freud's theory provides a completely different perspective on criminal behavior. To simplify a fairly complex theory, it could be said that in Freudian theory, crime is a symptom of a person's unresolved psychological conflict.[20] This conflict is caused by free-floating feelings of guilt, anxiety, repression, transference, psychosexual conflicts, and libido. In cases where the person cannot control

> Despite the self-destructive nature of some behaviors, Freud argued that people frequently are unable to control them.

these subconscious influences, he or she feels guilt and anxiety but does not know why. To alleviate the feelings of guilt, the unhealthy person commits a crime so that he or she will be caught and punished. The punishment brings temporary relief to the feelings of guilt. However, because the punishment is not really related to the source of the feelings of guilt, the guilt returns, and the person must commit another crime. This dysfunctional cycle of guilt and criminal behavior continues because, in reality, the punishment received cannot alleviate the feeling of guilt.

One of the main criticisms of theories based on psychological causes of behavior is that the underlying theory that explains the criminal behavior cannot be proven by experimentation or observation. The theory of psychoanalysis, for example, is based on axioms that no experiment or observation can disprove. Because these theories cannot be proven by use of the scientific method, some refer to them as pseudo-scientific theories and discount their reliability.

Psychological Theories and the Contemporary Criminal Justice System

Psychological theories, especially psychoanalytical theories, are not extensively used and adopted by the criminal justice system. Again, because the premise of these theories is that criminal behavior is not a free-will choice, their acceptance in the criminal justice system is limited. However, these theories have been used in the insanity plea, in criminal profiling, and in rehabilitation.

The insanity plea asserts that the defendant is not responsible for his or her behavior due to a disease or defect of the mind that rendered the defendant unable to appreciate the criminality of his or her actions. (The definition of insanity varies from state to state.) Thus, a common characteristic of a trial in which the defendant has pleaded not guilty by reason of insanity is the testimony of a number of expert witnesses composed of psychologists and psychiatrists attesting whether the defendant had such a disease. The expert witnesses cannot testify that the defendant is insane, as that is the role of the jury. However, the witnesses can testify that the defendant has a recognized medical disease that affected his or her ability to know right from wrong.

Psychology and psychiatry are the foundation of criminal profiling. Many psychoanalytic theories suggest that murder, mass and serial murder, and sexually motivated murder are rooted in psychological conflicts and subconscious drives. In some murder cases, especially mass, serial, and sexually motivated murders, where there are no physical clues to assist law enforcement in detecting the perpetrator, law enforcement may use experts to construct **psychological profiles** of the murder.

Patrick Hermans/Fotolia

In constructing theories of criminal behavior, one of the first principles is that there must be agreement as what behavior constitutes criminal or deviant behavior. The battle over gay marriage reflects the complexity and diversity of determining what is criminal behavior.

In March 2012, Maryland became the eighth state to legalize gay marriage. Maryland's law takes effect in 2013, and opponents of the law vow to overturn it before it goes into effect. Among others, the law is opposed by African-American church leaders and the Catholic Church.

It is argued that one's opinion toward gay marriage is a personal value and opinion, is a civil rights issue, or is a matter of religious freedom. Those on each side of the argument want their opinion reflected in law. About 30 states and the federal government have constitutional amendments or laws defining marriage as a union of a man and a woman. In some states, consensual sex between persons of the same sex is a criminal act.

Do you believe same-sex marriage is a right or a criminal act? If same-sex unions are not legal, are the people in these relationships criminals? If it is a right, should the rights of a minority be put to a popular vote? Why or why not? What criminological theory would best explain same-sex marriage as normal or criminal behavior?

These profiles are based on the personality traits that, according to psychoanalytic theories, are consistent with people who have the conflicts and subconscious drives that would cause them to murder.

Psychological theories of crime causation, while not embraced by the criminal justice system, are commonly used in rehabilitation. Juvenile offenders, drug offenders, and sex offenders may be treated by some form of psychoanalytic therapy. The use of group therapy sessions are one of the most common rehabilitation strategies. Rehabilitation efforts are usually undertaken by criminal justice personnel such as juvenile probation and parole officers, correctional counselors, and adult probation and parole officers rather than licensed professional psychologists and psychotherapists. The main reason is that the cost of using mental health professionals to conduct correctional rehabilitation sessions is prohibitive.

Also, most large prisons have mental health professionals on staff to respond to the needs of inmates with mental health problems.

▶ *Sociological Explanation*

Social Determinism

Theories based on the idea that forces within society—social forces and social groups and institutions—are the causes of criminal behavior reflect a philosophy called social determinism. **Social determinism** says that relations, social interactions, social expectations, and pressures exerted by peers and institutions—not free will, biology, or psychology—determine criminal behavior.

Social determinism is not restricted to theories of criminal behavior, but are often general theories seeking to explain why people behave and interact in society in general. Social determinism and the theories of criminal causation that arise from this perspective are often based in the academic discipline of sociology. The discipline of sociology emerged at the beginning of the twentieth century, and many sociology scholars chose to study deviant behavior or crime. The subfield of sociology that focuses on deviant behavior is called urban sociology or criminology.

Numerous theories are based on social determinism. Each theory emphasizes a different element within social determinism as the primary influence(s) on behavior. Two major schools of thought are those theories that focus on social structural theories and those that focus on symbolic interactionism theories. Among the more popular social structure theories are social disorganization theories, learning theories, strain theories, subcultural theories, and control theories. Symbolic interaction theories focus on the power differential between powerful institutions such as the state and less powerful groups.

social determinism The idea that social forces and social groups are the cause of criminal behavior.

anomie A feeling of "normlessness" and lack of belonging that people feel when they become socially isolated.

social disorganization theory Park and Burgess's research that criminal behavior is dependent on disruptive social forces, not on individual characteristics.

concentric zone model (Burgess model) A theory developed by Park and Burgess that social environments based on status disadvantages such as poverty; illiteracy; and lack of schooling, unemployment, and illegitimacy are powerful forces that influence human interactions.

Social Disorganization as the Cause of Crime

Early sociologists found crime and the criminal convenient and interesting subjects for study. The University of Chicago established one of the first sociology departments in the United States. Robert Ezra Park (1864–1944), one of the founders of this department, focused on explaining and understanding social disorder. Park believed that human

> # Anomie is a feeling of normlessness and lack of belonging that people feel when they become socially isolated.

behavior is influenced by the environment and that an over-crowded and disordered environment leading to social isolation contributes to deviant and criminal behavior.[21] Gathering data from the surrounding Chicago area, Park and his students engaged in a comprehensive study of the relationship between urbanization and social isolation, based on Émile Durkheim's theory of anomie. **Anomie** is a feeling of "normlessness" and lack of belonging that people feel when they become socially isolated. According to Durkheim, people with anomie lack the ties to society that would inhibit them from committing crimes against society.

The Chicago School and Social Disorganization Theory

In the early 1900s, Chicago grew rapidly as a result of industrialization and immigration. Research by Robert Park and Ernest Burgess focused on the difference in crime rates in Chicago. Crime was not randomly dispersed throughout the city, but was concentrated in certain areas. Most people identified the cause of a crime with the ethnicity of the people who lived in these high-crime areas. Park and Burgess's research demonstrated that criminal behavior was not an individual characteristic or a group-ethnic trait, but was linked to social disorganization and the environment.[22] This is called **social disorganization theory**.

The theory proposed that urban social structure exerted powerful influences on behavior independent of the ethnicity of the people living in the various territorial patterns.[23] The population within each territorial unit had a distinctive ecological niche and factors such as quality of housing, schools, medical facilities, population density, and socioeconomic level that exerted influences on the propensity for criminal behavior. This environment-based theory of urban interaction became known as the **concentric zone model (Burgess model)**. It was one of the earliest theoretical models to explain the relationship between urban social structures and crime.

Concentric Zone Theory

According to the concentric zone theory developed by Park and Burgess, social environments based on status disadvantages—such as poverty, illiteracy, lack of schooling, unemployment, and illegitimacy—are powerful forces that influence human interactions. The concentric zone theory divided Chicago into distinctive zones with common characteristics that were influential upon human interaction and behavior. According to Burgess's model (Figure 2–4), the Chicago area was divided into five zones or urban areas. Starting at the center of the city was the Loop, or central business district. As one traveled farther from the central business district, the next urban areas were the Factory Zone, Zone in Transition, Workers' Homes, Residential Zone, and Commuters. As one traveled outward

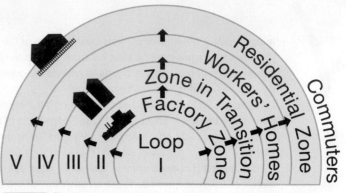

FIGURE 2–4 The Burgess concentric zone theory posited that crime was caused by the socioeconomic and physical environments of the city. Zone theory suggested that if the physical and economic environments could be improved, the crime rate would drop. According to the Burgess model, people committed crime because of external influences, not because they were "bad" or morally "defective." This perspective has been influential in modern crime-prevention programs that emphasize improving schools, housing, the environment, and employment opportunities.

from the center of the city, the urban environment improved and deviant behavior decreased.[24] Studies by Shaw and McKay showed that the highest rates of delinquency persisted in the same neighborhoods of Chicago even though the ethnic composition changed.[25] Thus, the basic cause of delinquency was not the ethnicity of the juveniles, but the social structures, institutions, and environmental variables in that zone. As one moved away from the industrial heart of the city, the rates of delinquency dropped.

Social Disorganization Theories and the Contemporary Criminal Justice System

Contemporary experiments, statistics, and observations to prove that crime is linked to socioeconomic environment and urban structure are difficult or impossible to gather. Modern transportation, new patterns of urban migration, and new forms of manufacturing and industry have made it impossible to divide modern cities into concentric circles resembling Chicago at the beginning of the twentieth century. Despite this fact, since the 1930s, social disorganization theory and especially the concentric zone theory have had a strong influence on crime-prevention efforts. Based on the assumption that social conditions such as unemployment, poor schools, and substandard housing are significant factors contributing to delinquency and crime, many government-sponsored programs have attempted to fight crime by improving employment opportunities, social services, schools, and housing. Crime prevention through environmental design (CPTED) was founded on the theory that crime prevention is related to environmental design, particularly housing design. Another crime-prevention program rooted in social disorganization theory is the broken window theory, discussed further in Chapter 5, "An Overview of Law Enforcement: History, Agencies, Personnel, and Strategies." This crime-prevention program is based on the idea that signs of neighborhood neglect, community deterioration, and tolerance of petty crime all contribute to more crime and crime-inducing environments.[26]

► Interactionism Theories

Learning Theories

Learning theory and the concept of socialization, which are shared by both sociology and psychology, were the basis for Sutherland's **differential association theory**, which proposes that criminal behavior is learned entirely through group interaction. (See Table 2–1.) This theory, proposed by Edwin Sutherland (1883–1950), argues that criminal behavior is learned in intimate peer groups that reward or reinforce antisocial or delinquent behaviors.[27] According to this theory, a life of crime is culturally transmitted through peer groups, not through heredity or urban environments.

Sutherland's explanation of deviant behavior does not refer to environmental or class factors, and it does not suggest that criminals are necessarily mentally defective, morally bankrupt, or economically deprived. Rather, Sutherland emphasizes that criminal or deviant behavior is simply learned behavior.

Because of its basis in learning theory, differential association theory can explain white-collar crime, noneconomically motivated crime, and crime by middle- and upper-class adolescents. Differential association theory emphasizes that criminal behavior is the result of learning through normal social interactions. If a "good kid" from a middle- or upper-class family has criminal friends whom he or she respects, during the normal course of social interactions with them, the "good kid" will learn criminal behavior.

Although learning theories continue to dominate criminological thought and rehabilitation programs, they have several

Criminal or deviant behavior is simply learned behavior.

Think About It . . .

Sutherland's principles of differential association were developed before the advent of broadcast television and modern music videos, violent video games, and violent-themed music. Sutherland said that learning criminal behavior must occur in face-to-face situations. Do you agree, or can learning of criminal behavior occur through exposure to violent media? Explain.

significant shortcomings. They do not adequately explain how and why a person chooses to learn criminal behavior. For example, why is it that one police officer spends a lifetime in close association with criminals without respecting their criminal values while another police officer begins to accept those values and engages in criminal behavior soon after employment?

Cultural Deviance Theories

Cultural deviance theories are based on the idea that, for the most part, the values of subcultural groups within the society are more influential upon individual behavior and interactions than are laws and norms of the larger social group. The influence of subcultural groups can be observed in such groups as military combat units, law enforcement agencies, sports teams, and extended family units. In these groups, the values embraced by the subgroup exert strong pressure on members to conform to the values, even if they are in conflict with values of the larger society. For example, law enforcement officers may band together and protect a fellow officer against a citizen's charges even if the officers must engage in illegal behavior or provide false testimony.

While the values of subcultural groups for the most part reflect the values of the larger society, there are **deviant subcultural groups** in which the group's values do not conform to social values. Organized crime families, juvenile gangs, and hate groups are examples of deviant subcultures.

Cultural deviance theories begin with the assumption that subgroups or subcultures within a society have different value systems from the larger society and that some of these values

---

TABLE 2–1 | SUTHERLAND'S PRINCIPLES OF DIFFERENTIAL ASSOCIATION

Sutherland defined the learning of criminal behavior as a nine-step process:

1. Criminal behavior is learned.

2. Criminal behavior is learned in interaction with others in a process of communication.

3. The principal part of the learning of criminal behavior occurs within intimate personal groups.

4. When criminal behavior is learned, the learning includes (a) techniques of committing the crime, which are sometimes very complicated, sometimes very simple, and (b) the specific direction of motives, drives, rationalizations, and attitudes.

5. The specific direction of motives and drives is learned from definitions of the legal codes as favorable or unfavorable.

6. A person becomes delinquent because of an excess of definitions favorable to violations of law over definitions unfavorable to violations of law.

7. Differential association may vary in frequency, duration, priority, and intensity.

8. The process of learning criminal behavior through association with criminal and anticriminal patterns involves all the mechanisms that are involved in any other learning.

9. Although criminal behavior is an expression of general needs and values, it is not explained by those general needs and values since noncriminal behavior is an expression of the same needs and values.

Source: Edwin Sutherland, *Principles of Criminology*, 4th ed. (Chicago: J. B. Lippincott, 1947), pp. 6–7.

differential association theory The concept that criminal and delinquent behaviors are learned entirely through group interactions, with peers reinforcing and rewarding those behaviors.

cultural deviance theories The idea that, for the most part, the values of subcultural groups within the society are more influential upon individual behavior and interactions than laws are.

deviant subculture group One subcultural group in which its values do not conform to social values of the larger part of society.

reaction formation A term that describes how lower-class youths reject middle-class values.

honor killings Killings for dishonoring or disrespecting cultural or religious values.

social control theory A theory that focuses on the social and cultural values that exert control over and reinforce the behavior of individuals.

neutralization theory The concept that most people commit some type of criminal act in their lives and that many people are prevented from doing so again because of a sense of guilt, but criminals neutralize feelings of guilt through rationalization, denial, or an appeal to higher loyalties.

strain theory The assumption that individuals resort to crime out of frustration from being unable to attain economic comfort or success.

are in conflict with larger social values. Cultural deviance theorists focus on differences in values and norms between mainstream society and subcultural groups.

Early cultural deviance theorists focused on studying immigrant groups that entered the United States during the first half of the twentieth century. These early immigrant groups tended to live in ethnic neighborhoods populated mostly by people of the same ethnicity. In these neighborhoods, people spoke the language of their native country, they ate foods from "the old world," they shared the same religious values, and family values reflected the norms and mores of their native country.

Albert Cohen studied the different values between the social classes. Cohen defined distinct subcultures in terms of variables such as parental aspirations, child-rearing practices, and classroom standards. Cohen used the term **reaction formation** to describe how lower-class youths reject middle-class values, which they believe they cannot achieve, and therefore create unique countercultures. For example, knowing that college education was not an achievable goal, lower-class youth would disdain the behaviors, skills, and abilities associated with aspirations of higher education. In turn, they would embrace values they identified with, such as a sense of adventure, defiance of authority, and toughness.[28]

Cultural Diversity as the Cause of Crime

Thorsten Sellin (1938) advocated that crime was not necessarily a case of bad people engaging in deliberate or negligent harm to others. Sellin argued that cultural diversity could be the cause of crime. In a homogeneous society with strong identification with the values of the group, there is little need for formal enforcement of laws, as most people will conform to the group norms and values. However, America is a diverse, complex society with many subcultural groups, often with conflicting subcultural values.

Sutherland's theory of differential association is one of the most used theories in the criminal justice system.

Sellin believed that the criminal laws of society reflect normative values of the dominant culture or ethnic group. In a society where there is a diversity of cultural or ethnic groups, the behaviors of members of the minority groups may be rejected and labeled deviant. Deviant behavior, while considered normative within the subgroup, is considered criminal by the laws of the dominant group.[29] Sellin proposed that there were two types of cultural conflict: primary conflict and secondary conflict. Primary conflict occurs when the norms of two cultures clash. Secondary conflict occurs within the evolution of a single culture, as when children reject the values and conduct norms of their parents.

Interactionism Theories and the Contemporary Criminal Justice System

Sutherland's theory of differential association is one of the most used theories in the criminal justice system. It is especially popular as a theory upon which numerous programs are based aimed at preventing juvenile delinquency or fostering juvenile delinquency rehabilitation. One reason this theory is popular is because it offers an explanation of delinquency that does not depend on correcting or improving other sociological factors that might be involved in crime causation, such as social disorganization, poor housing, substandard schools, or broken households.

The use of Sutherland's theory of differential association is especially popular in juvenile rehabilitation programs. It is one of the major strategies used by the juvenile court in rehabilitation programs.

Sutherland said that learning occurred in peer-to-peer intimate contacts. Other proponents of learning theory have developed theories that argue that learning can occur through media. According to these theories, contemporary media such as music, violent video games, and violence and sex on television and in the movies can create learning situations and influence the behavior of adolescents. Thus, those who believe learning can occur through the media have advocated for the banning of such media from juveniles. This controversy has created social, cultural, and legal conflicts.

Today's modern "global village" provides numerous examples in which cultural diversity is considered criminal. In the United States, the cultural conduct norms of subgroups may be contrary to the law. For example, parents who do not believe in childhood immunizations, compulsory schooling, or certain medical treatments to save lives and preserve the health of their children may be considered to be committing criminal behavior. Some members of religious groups find themselves in violation of the law because of their beliefs regarding polygamy. In the television reality series *Sister Wives*, one family of four "wives" strives to portray their values as "normal" and not deviant or criminal. Although polygamy is illegal in the United States, it is believed that tens of thousands of people practice it.[30]

As minority populations increase in the United States, there are likely to be more legal conflicts with the values and mores of these subcultures.

In contemporary society, a serious concern is the cultural conflict reflected in **honor killings**—killings for dishonoring or disrespecting cultural or religious values. While illegal but well documented in other counties, cases of honor killings are rare in the United States. However, they do happen. For example, in April 2011, Faleh Hassan Almaleki was convicted in Arizona for the murder of his 20-year-old daughter. Almaleki murdered his daughter because she was "too Westernized, defying Iraqi and Muslim values." As Muslim and other minority populations increase in the United States, there are likely to be more legal conflicts with the values and mores of these subcultures.

Social Control Theories

Social control theory emphasizes that social and cultural values exert control over individuals' behavior and that social institutions enforce those values. Social institutions that contribute to the formation of social values are the family, school, neighborhood, religion, and government. These institutions exert control both informally (for example, parental disapproval and social rejection) and formally (for example, school suspension and arrest). The influence of informal and formal systems of social control makes people law abiding to the extent that they identify with and conform to social expectations.[31]

Social control studies focus on the reasons people conform to norms rather than the reasons people violate norms. Social control theories attempt to answer the question of why most people do not commit crime. People of all socioeconomic backgrounds are subject to the temptation of crime and want what they do not have, yet most people do not commit crime. People also have impulses that they do not act on and desires that they do not fulfill. What, then, causes some people to turn to crime while others do not? Social control theories emphasize that both environmental variables and individual self-control are influential in preventing or suppressing criminal behavior.[32]

Neutralization Theory

Gresham Sykes and David Matza's **neutralization theory** is based on the assumption that a person cannot completely resist criminal behavior and that most people have committed some criminal or deviant act at one time or another. These theorists have argued that deviant and criminal behavior produces a sense of guilt and that the pains of conscience are sufficient to keep most people from engaging in extended and extensive criminality. Sykes and Matza say that it is necessary for criminals to learn neutralization techniques that allow them to avoid being guilt-ridden as they continue their criminality.[33]

Neutralization theory says that those who engage in a criminal lifestyle neutralize feelings of guilt through rationalization, denial, or an appeal to higher loyalties. For example, teenage shoplifters may rationalize that taking merchandise from large chain stores does not really hurt anyone. People who commit tax frauds may tell themselves that "everyone cheats on their taxes."

Strain Theory

Sociologist Robert Merton's **strain theory** is based on the assumption that people seek to fulfill the American dream of economic success.[34] His theory assumes that people are motivated to achieve the comforts and security of a middle-class lifestyle, but that some people find that they cannot achieve this goal through traditional, socially acceptable means. Those people strain to achieve the expectations and roles of the "reference group"—those who have achieved monetary success. Merton's strain theory (Figure 2–5) says that the pursuit of monetary success will exert influences on people that will affect the outcome of a situation or the way a person or group will behave. Merton said that behavior will in part depend on a person's attitude regarding the goal of economic success and his or her attitude toward the means of achieving the goal. According to Merton, a person's attitude toward the goal and the means of achieving the goal will result in four modes of adaptation: conformity, innovation, ritualism, or retreatism.[35]

Merton's strain theory posited that most people accepted the goals and the legitimate means to achieve the goals. This healthy balance was called conformity. Retreatism characterizes those who do not accept socially approved goals or the socially approved means of achieving those goals. These people are not attached to society and demonstrate retreatism, or escape from society. This behavior may be expressed in drug or alcohol abuse. Those who accept the goal but believe they do not have the means to achieve it demonstrate ritualism, or acceptance of social and role expectations but with no hope they will ever achieve the goal. Merton's strain theory defines the deviant or criminal as the person who wants to achieve monetary success but does not accept the traditional means to achieve it. They demonstrate innovation in that they find alternative means, usually illegal or socially unacceptable, to achieve the goal. Drug dealers, bank robbers, con artists, and those who engage in other criminal activities, including white-collar crime, are examples of people who want monetary success but are unwilling or unable to achieve success within the law.

Merton's strain theory has another mode of adaptation called rebellion. This mode describes those who reject traditional goals and traditional means but substitute other goals and means. This mode can describe great figures in history who effect social change and redefine the American dream.

Social Control Theories and the Contemporary Criminal Justice System

Merton believed that social conditions, especially poverty and ethnicity, are powerful factors in determining the adaptations that individuals make to socially prescribed goals and the lifestyles that develop as a result. Merton's concept of the "self-fulfilling prophesy" stated that the behavior of people who believe they could not achieve the goal and the outcome of their efforts, whether the belief was true, would be strongly affected by this belief.

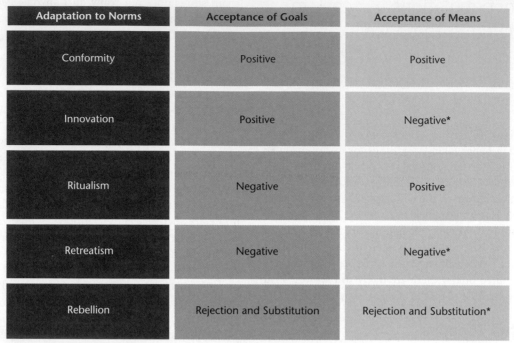

Adaptation to Norms	Acceptance of Goals	Acceptance of Means
Conformity	Positive	Positive
Innovation	Positive	Negative*
Ritualism	Negative	Positive
Retreatism	Negative	Negative*
Rebellion	Rejection and Substitution	Rejection and Substitution*

*Greater likelihood of engaging in criminal behavior

FIGURE 2–5 Merton's Strain theory is based on the assumption that economic success is the goal of all people and if that success is blocked, people become criminals or drop out.

Source: Based on Robert K Merton, *Social Theory and Social Structure* (New York: Free Press, 1957).

Thus, Merton's strain theory predicted that the greatest proportion of crime would be found in the lower classes because, Merton believed, lower-class people have the least opportunity to reach middle-class goals legitimately and believe less in their ability. Based on this premise, many crime-prevention programs have focused on improving the lot of the poor and developing programs and institutions that would instill confidence and ability in a person's belief regarding his or her potential success. Programs such as Head Start and Job Corps, which are aimed at providing economic opportunities to the poor and disadvantaged and encouraging educational achievement, are justified by the belief that economic opportunity deters crime. This theory supports prison industry programs and prison education programs that improve the self-esteem of inmates and help prepare them to support themselves through legitimate employment when released from prison.

Merton's strain theory is difficult to test by use of the scientific methodology. Also, the theory assumes a single reference group and definition of success that all in society aspire to achieve. In today's complex multicultural society, this may not be a valid assumption. The theory is based on the assumption that the motivation for criminal activity is monetary gain; thus, the theory has limited value in explaining crimes that are not motivated by economic gain.

▶ Other Theories

Criminologists continue to develop new theories of crime causation. Often these theories are based on principles proposed by earlier theories. Modern scholars review the theories of past scholars and propose new variables and perspectives to explain deviant behavior. Three examples of theories that have emerged or gained new popularity in the twentieth century include labeling theory, conflict theory, and feminist criminology.

Labeling Theory

Labeling theory focuses on explaining deviant behavior, especially juvenile delinquency, by examining society's reactions to behaviors that are defined as deviant. Advocates of labeling theory argue that everyone commits crime. It is society's reaction and the internalization of that reaction that create criminals. Juveniles who steal may be seen to have committed an error in judgment they will outgrow, or their behavior can be seen as evidence that the juvenile is morally defective and rejects social values. In turn, the attitude of those who interact with the juvenile will influence the juvenile's self-image depending on whether society's reaction is condemning or forgiving. Juveniles who internalize society's condemnation see themselves as "criminal," and this will affect their behavior and social interactions.

The single best example of belief in labeling theory is the effort of the criminal justice system to protect the identity of juveniles charged with delinquency. Laws prohibit releasing the

Programs aimed at providing economic opportunities to the poor and disadvantaged and encouraging educational achievement are justified by the belief that economic opportunity deters crime.

names of juveniles who are accused of crimes and their court proceedings. These laws are based on the premise that releasing a juvenile's name to the public may cause adverse public reaction toward the juvenile, which could have a harmful impact on his or her self-esteem and behavior.

Conflict Theories

Conflict theorists focus on how a society's system of social stratification (the division of society into social classes) and social inequality influence behavior. **Conflict theories** are based on the assumption that powerful ruling political and social elites—people, groups, and institutions—exploit the less powerful and use the criminal justice system to their own advantage to maintain their power and privilege. In this view, criminology is the study of crime in relation to society's haves and have-nots.

Theories of crime based on social inequality have their roots in the social criticisms of Karl Marx and Friedrich Engels in nineteenth-century Europe. Marxism assumes a division between the poor (workers) and the rich (property owners and capitalists) in which the rich control the various social, political, and economic institutions of society. The rich use their power and position to control the poor.[36] Present-day conflict theorists suggest that reducing social inequality is the only or best way to reduce criminal behavior.[37]

In the 1960s, Richard Quinney argued that the criminal justice system is a state-initiated and state-supported effort to rationalize mechanisms of social control, which are based on class structure. The state is organized to serve the interests of the dominant economic class. Quinney saw criminal law as an instrument the state and the ruling class use to maintain and perpetuate the social and economic order.[38] Some conflict theorists went so far as to claim that there is a deliberate conspiracy to suppress the lower classes, especially the "dangerous poor."[39]

The underlying cause of criminal behavior by females is the inequality of power between men and women.

Feminist Criminology

Feminist criminology assumes that the underlying cause of criminal behavior by females is the inequality of power between men and women. Advocates such as Freda Adler,[40] Meda Chesney-Lind,[41] Kathleen Daly,[42] and Sally Simpson[43] argue that the inequality of political, economic, and social power and wealth is the root cause of female criminal behavior.

Conflict theorists have strongly criticized mainstream criminology and the criminal justice system for ignoring class conflict and inequality as being powerful contributors to crime. For this reason, those who advocate conflict theories and class and power inequality as the causes of crime are called **radical criminologists**. They point to research data suggesting that there is no equal treatment of the poor, minorities, and females in the criminal justice system. For example, a disproportionate number of poor and minority citizens are stopped, arrested, and incarcerated compared with other groups.[44] Often there are significant differences between male and female correctional institutions in terms of quality of life, rehabilitation programs, and job training programs. Radical criminologists such as William Chambliss saw the law and the criminal justice system as a means of institutional discrimination rather than a means of providing fairness in justice.[45] While efforts have been made to address these criticisms, conflict-based theories of crime

LEARNING OUTCOMES 3 Summarize modern theories of criminology.

GLOSSARY

labeling theory The theory that explains deviant behavior, especially juvenile delinquency, by examining society's reactions to behaviors that are labeled as deviant.

conflict theories Theories that the most politically and socially powerful individuals and organizations use the legal system to exploit less powerful individuals and to retain their power and privileges.

feminist criminology The proposal that female criminal behavior is caused by the political, economic, and social inequality between men and women.

radical criminologists Those who advocate conflict theories and class and power inequality as the causes of crime.

Everyone commits crime. It is society's reaction and the internalization of that reaction that create criminals.

causation have exerted little influence on crime prevention or rehabilitation programs.

► Challenges to Explaining Crime

No single theory can explain crime. Various theories have appeared to explain crime throughout history based on the scientific knowledge and social values of the era in which they were developed. (See Table 2–2 for a summary of criminological theories.) Often advances in scientific knowledge reveal the flaws in a crime theory. Likewise, new scientific and social science theories and discoveries often result in the construction of new theories to explain crime.

It is not easy to explain crime because of its complex nature and the many variables that influence criminal behavior. Combinations of variables from several different bodies of knowledge may apply, including biology, psychology, and sociology. Also, investigation of the influence of causal variables on criminal behavior is complicated by the ethical and legal constraints concerning experimentation with humans. Experiments with humans, especially experiments in which the subjects may suffer physical or psychological harm, are strictly regulated. **Ethical standards of behavior**, which are enforced through legal sanctions, prohibit experimentation that may harm subjects and regulate the degree of deception of subjects that researchers may use in an experiment. Social researchers cannot separate identical twins at birth and assign one twin to be raised by a

criminal family and the other to be raised by a noncriminal family to observe the influence of nature versus nurture. Researchers cannot manipulate the variables of single-family homes, socioeconomic income, and peer pressure to test the various theories of crime causation. Instead, researchers must rely on secondary statistical data, correlations, and other measures without the ability to manipulate the actual variables.

Because of these limitations, often it is difficult for researchers to differentiate between causal variables and correlation. **Causal variables** directly influence the outcome of relationships. While causal variables can be identified in physical science, often it is difficult to identify causal variables in human research. It is more common in social research to establish correlations rather than causality. **Correlation** is the state of two variables being associated with each other in that when one increases, the other increases or decreases in a predictable pattern. Correlation shows relationship but does not establish causality. For example, there is a relationship between educational achievement and criminal behavior but that does not prove that there is a causal relationship between the two variables. The problem with correlations is that another variable, perhaps unbeknown to the researcher, influences the relationship.

LEARNING OUTCOMES 4

Summarize factors that make it difficult for criminologists to definitively explain crime.

GLOSSARY

ethical standards of behavior Legal sanctions that prohibit experimentation that may harm subjects and regulate the degree of deception of subjects that researchers may use in an experiment.

causal variables Variables that directly influence the outcome of relationships.

correlation The state of two variables being associated with each other in that when one increases, the other increases or decreases in a predictable pattern.

The investigation of the influence of causal variables on criminal behavior is complicated by the ethical and legal constraints concerning experimentation with humans.

TABLE 2–2 **EXPLANATIONS OF CRIMINAL BEHAVIOR**

Type of Explanation	School of Thought	Theory	Proponent	Cause of Crime	Solution to Crime	Critique
Moralism			Evil; sin, spirit possession		Elimination of offenders from society	No scientific data underlying claims of causes of criminal behavior
Free Will	Classical	Pain–pleasure principle	Cesare Beccaria	Rational free choice	Deterrence through pain of punishment over pleasure of crime	No limited liability for the young or mentally ill
	Neoclassical	Utilitarianism	Jeremy Bentham	Rational free will except for the young and the insane	Deterrence through laws fitting the punishment to the crime	Theory does not acknowledge the possible influence of biological, sociological, or psychological factors
Biological Determinism	Evolutionary	Darwinism; concept of atavism	Cesare Lombroso, Richard Dugdale (Ada Jukes)	Heredity; no free will and thus no moral accountability	Prevention is impossible; give medical treatment (and castrate or sterilize criminals)	Theory formulated prior to emergence of knowledge concerning sociological, psychological, and biological influences
		Somatotype	Willliam Sheldon	Inherited predispositions revealed through body type	Prevention through identification	Hypotheses depend on correlational statistics with little demonstration of causality
	Biocriminology	XYY chromosome; hormones; nutrition; MBD (minimal brain dysfunction)		Physiological disorders or chemically induced aggression	Medical treatment and control	Cannot isolate variables assumed to cause deviant behavior
Psychological Determinism		Psychoanalytical theory	Sigmund Freud	Psychopathology; irrational, unresolved, unconscious conflict from guilt/anxiety from childhood trauma	Counseling and rehabilitation	Understanding of behavior depends on intuitive knowledge of subconscious motives
		Criminal personality		Antisocial attitudes and lack of self-control	Early childhood intervention	Describes the thinking and behaviors but does not attribute a cause
Social Determinism	Environmentalism	Zone theory	Robert Ezra Park	Society; dysfunctional social environments	Reduce anomie through environmental design and urban renewal; reduce poverty	Most people from the same "bad" environment do not commit crimes

(continued)

TABLE 2–2   EXPLANATIONS OF CRIMINAL BEHAVIOR   (CONTINUED)

Type of Explanation	School of Thought	Theory	Proponent	Cause of Crime	Solution to Crime	Critique
	Interactionism	Differential association theory	Edwin Sutherland	Socialization in delinquent peer groups	Diversion and reeducation	More useful in explaining juvenile rather than adult behavior
		Cultural deviance	Albert Cohen	Socialization in deviant subculture or counterculture	Distinguish cultural diversity and dissent from devlance	Explains only a limited number of crimes
	Social control			Breakdown of social institutions; lack of conformity	Enforcement of social values and norms	Not possible to measure strength of "bonds"
		Containment theory	Walter Reckless	Loss of self-control and social control	Strengthening of institutions such as the family	Little consideration for biological and psychological influences
		Neutralization theory	Gresham Sykes/ David Matza	Rationalization of antisocial acts	Strengthening of social and emotional bonds to others and to society	Does not explain why some are able to justify their behavior but others are not
		Social bond theory	Travis Hirschi	Loss of sense of attachment		Explains a limited number of crimes
		Labeling theory	Howard Becker	Society's reactions to deviance		Limited applicability
	Structuralism			Social structure; structure of opportunity	Level the playing field; provide opportunity	
		Strain theory	Robert Merton	Frustration in achieving middle-class goals legitimately because of poverty or ethnicity	Eliminate frustrations and disadvantages or help people overcome them	Assumes universal aspiration for "middle-class" life
		Differential opportunity	Richard Cloward and Lloyd Ohlin	Blocked opportunities to reach goals		Assumes economic motivation for crime
		Conflict theory		Social inequality; class conflict; institutional discrimination	Social and political equality; redistribution of wealth and power in society	More a philosophy than a science
			Richard Quinney	Criminal justice system as a weapon of the ruling class; racial discrimination	Equal rights; equal protection	Assumes that class warfare is universal and irreversible
			Freda Adler	Gender inequality	Equal rights; equal protection	Major premise cannot be proven

Most modern criminologists have abandoned the belief that criminals are completely different from noncriminals. The focus of criminology is on isolating and measuring those variables that appear to have the greatest influence on human behavior in a legal and ethical manner. Thus, it is unreasonable to expect that a single theory of crime causation will emerge in the near future.

Presently, sociological explanations are most popular for use by scholars and the criminal justice system. Many of the rehabilitation, treatment, and prevention programs in the criminal justice system are based on the premises hypothesized by sociological theories. Theory must underlie the various rehabilitation, treatment, and prevention programs because without an underlying theoretical foundation, the various attempts to reduce crime and to rehabilitate offenders are nothing more than guesses.

▶ Conclusion: More Questions Than Answers

The search for the cause(s) of criminal behavior has not produced definitive answers to questions such as why people offend, how offenders are rehabilitated, or how victimization is minimized. Also, while a tremendous amount of criminal justice data has been captured since the 1970s, all this data seems to point to the fact that there are still many unanswered questions. It suggests that more data are needed.

While criminology, victimology, and criminal justice data may not be the most interesting topics to some students of criminal justice, foundational knowledge of these fields is essential to understanding what works in criminal justice and where resources should be invested to improve public safety. As previously stated, if crime-prevention programs and rehabilitation programs are not based on reliable theories, these efforts are nothing more than guesswork and success most likely will be elusive.

In 2011, the number of murders in the United States decreased by more than 5%. This was good news for the nation, but it did not describe the murder rate in New Orleans. In 2010, New Orleans' homicide rate was ten times the national average. There were 51 homicides per 100,000 residents in New Orleans in 2010, compared with fewer than 7 per 100,000 in New York and 23 per 1,000 in Oakland, California. Commenting on the high murder rate, New Orleans Mayor Mitch Landrieu said, "a student attending John McDonogh [school] was more likely to be killed than a soldier in Afghanistan."[48] New Orleans has a history of being a violent city. In 1994, a record 421 murders were recorded. The rate dropped after federal intervention, but it rose in 2000 and has increased since Hurricane Katrina.

The search for the causes of New Orleans' high murder rate are elusive. There are no large organized gangs or major drug wars in New Orleans. Most of the victims are young African-American men who had prior criminal convictions and were unemployed. Only about half of the homicide cases are cleared. Many believe that the authorities, especially the police, are more of a problem than a solution. Some of the reasons given to explain the high murder rate include a corrupt police department, lack of trust between the police and the public, budget shortfalls, and a staffing shortage.[49]

In 2011, New Orleans embarked upon a "public health" approach to bring down the high murder rates. This approach included the following[50]:

- Setting up a commission to analyze past killings and recommend prevention measures

- Working to reduce the unemployment rate among returning offenders

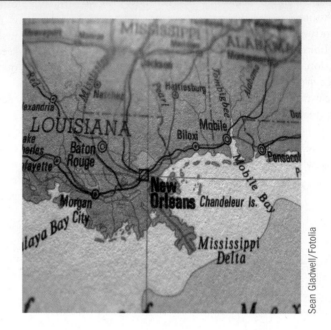

Sean Gladwell/Fotolia

- Developing counseling and intervention teams to assist in defusing conflicts in violent neighborhoods

- Seeking grants to expand community policing programs and add homicide detectives

- Using more sophisticated tools to analyze crime trends

- Encouraging citizens to supply information to police regarding crimes they witness

This case raises several interesting questions. Among them are the following:

1. Which of the various theories of crime causation or victimization best explains the high murder rate in New Orleans?

2. Why would the murder rate in New Orleans be so high compared to other cities? What is unique about New Orleans?

3. What theories of crime causation or victimization would be useful in constructing a comprehensive plan to permanently reduce the murder rate of New Orleans?

4. How could accurate crime and victimization data assist in a plan to reduce the murder rate?

5. If the murder rate goes down, how can authorities be confident that the downward trend in the homicide rate was caused by programs that were utilized and not by other factors?

6. How does the high murder rate in New Orleans affect the quality of life of citizens and the economic and business health of the city?

Outline the development of criminological theory.

The explanations as to the cause of crime vary greatly. Contemporary theories of crime causation are complex because they recognize the interaction of many variables. The cause of criminality can be divided into four different schools of thought. In the 1700s, the Classical School believed that crime was a free-will choice. By the early 1800s, biological determinism emerged as a new premise. This school of thought theorized that a biological condition influenced the offender in a way that he or she could not control. By the turn of the twentieth century, the psychological schools studied mental defects within the offender; the sociological perspective viewed the role that socialization played in criminality.

1. What is a theory?

2. List four major categories of criminological thought.

3. Define the major premise of each school of criminological thought.

criminology The body of knowledge regarding crime as a social phenomenon.

theory A statement regarding the relationship between two or more variables.

nonscientific theories Theories that emphasize moral weakness and evil spirits as the cause of criminality.

Classical School The school of thought that individuals have free will to choose whether to commit crimes.

biological determinism The school of thought that says that crime is caused by a biological or biochemical influence over which the offender has no control.

psychological theory The idea that criminal behavior is a result of emotions, drives, and mental defects.

Sociological School of criminology The theory that crime is caused by socioeconomic conditions and social interactions and values.

Summarize the major theoretical perspectives on criminal behavior.

Popular throughout the eighteenth century was the neoclassical school of thought. The neoclassical theories bridged the transition from nonscientific theories to modern scientific theory. The twentieth century ushered in scientific thought and the positivist approach. Positive theories include biology, psychology, and sociology. Scientific method emphasized that facts about criminal behavior should be gathered through observations, surveys, statistics, and experiments. In today's contemporary criminal justice system, social control theories support rehabilitation efforts through prison industry and educational programs.

1. What is a theory? Explain the role research plays in proposing theories about crime causation.

2. Describe the basic assumption of theories of criminology from a neoclassical perspective.

3. What three major schools of thought are found in positive theory?

4. What is the psychological perspective for explaining crime?

5. What is the sociological perspective for explaining crime?

6. How is social control theory used in the contemporary criminal justice system?

neoclassical theories A contemporary view of Classical School theory that believes that there are mitigating circumstances for criminal acts, such as the age or mental capacity of the offender, and that punishment should fit the crime.

Cesare Beccaria The founder of Classical School theories.

pain–pleasure principle A philosophical axiom that people are rational and seek to do that which brings them pleasure and to avoid that which causes them pain.

Neoclassical School of criminology A school of thought that is similar to Classical School theories except for the belief that there are mitigating circumstances for criminal acts, such as the age or mental capacity of the offender, and that punishment should fit the crime.

felicitic calculus The balancing of pain and pleasure as a means to discourage criminal behavior.

utilitarianism A philosophy stating that a rational system of jurisprudence provides for the greatest happiness for the greatest number of people.

scientific method The assumption that repeated testing of a hypothesis should result in similar results.

Positive School Modern theories of crime, primarily based on sociology and psychology, that people commit crimes because of uncontrollable internal or external factors that can be observed and measured.

determinist Scholars and scientists who believe that causes of criminal behavior are not controlled by free-will choice; rather, they are influenced by factors that are beyond the control of the individual.

Richard Dugdale A psychologist who conducted an early study attempting to link heredity to criminal behavior in his study of the Jukes family.

Henry Goodard A sociologist who studied Martin Kallikak's family tree attempting to link heredity to criminality.

Ada Jukes A woman labeled by Richard Dugdale as the "mother of criminals."

Cesare Lombroso An Italian doctor who collected data to support his Darwinist-based theory that criminal behavior is a characteristic of humans who have failed to develop normally from their primitive origins.

atavism The failure of humans to fully develop into modern men and women.

criminal man Lombroso's belief that criminals were born inferior and prehuman.

atavistic stigmata The study of the physical traits of criminals.

father of scientific criminology The title bestowed on Cesare Lombroso because he was the first to use the scientific method in the search to explain criminal behavior.

biocriminology Research into the roles played by genetic and neuro-physiological variables in criminal behavior.

XYY chromosome theory of violent behavior The idea that violent behavior in males can in part be attributed to the presence of an extra Y chromosome in male offenders.

psychoanalytic theory The concept that behavior is not a matter of free will, but is controlled by subconscious desires, which includes the idea that criminal behavior is a result of unresolved internal conflict and guilt.

id Unconscious desires and drives.

ego The rational mind.

superego The moral values system.

psychological profiling Profiles based on the personality traits according to psychoanalytic theories.

social determinism The idea that social forces and social groups are the cause of criminal behavior.

anomie A feeling of "normlessness" and lack of belonging that people feel when they become socially isolated.

social disorganization theory Park and Burgess's research that criminal behavior is dependent on disruptive social forces, not on individual characteristics.

concentric zone model (Burgess model) A theory developed by Park and Burgess that social environments based on status disadvantages such as poverty; illiteracy; and lack of schooling, unemployment, and illegitimacy are powerful forces that influence human interactions.

differential association theory The concept that criminal and delinquent behaviors are learned entirely through group interactions, with peers reinforcing and rewarding those behaviors.

cultural deviance theories The idea that, for the most part, the values of subcultural groups within the society are more influential upon individual behavior and interactions than laws are.

deviant subculture group One subcultural group in which its values do not conform to social values of the larger part of society.

reaction formation A term that describes how lower-class youths reject middle-class values.

honor killings Killings for dishonoring or disrespecting cultural or religious values.

social control theory A theory that focuses on the social and cultural values that exert control over and reinforce the behavior of individuals.

neutralization theory The concept that most people commit some type of criminal act in their lives and that many people are prevented from doing so again because of a sense of guilt, but criminals neutralize feelings of guilt through rationalization, denial, or an appeal to higher loyalties.

strain theory The assumption that individuals resort to crime out of frustration from being unable to attain economic comfort or success.

LEARNING OUTCOMES 3

Summarize modern theories of criminology.

Criminologists continue to develop new theories to explain crime causation. Comprising these emergent approaches to explaining crime are the labeling theory, conflict theories, feminist criminology, and radical criminologists. The work of contemporary criminologists proposes new variables and perspectives to explain crime.

1. Name four contemporary theories used by criminologists to explain crime causation.

2. Upon whom does the labeling theory primarily focus?

3. What is the feminist perspective for explaining crime?

4. What do radical criminologists believe to be the underlying cause of crime in society?

labeling theory The theory that explains deviant behavior, especially juvenile delinquency, by examining society's reactions to behaviors that are labeled as deviant.

conflict theories Theories that the most politically and socially powerful individuals and organizations use the legal system to exploit less powerful individuals and to retain their power and privileges.

feminist criminology The proposal that female criminal behavior is caused by the political, economic, and social inequality between men and women.

radical criminologists Those who advocate conflict theories and class and power inequality as the causes of crime.

LEARNING OUTCOMES 4

Summarize factors that make it difficult for criminologists to definitively explain crime.

No one theory can explain all crime causation. Rather, various theories have been developed based on the scientific knowledge and social values of a particular era. Postmodern criminologists have abandoned the belief that criminals are completely different from non-criminals. Today, sociological explanations are most popular in application by scholars within the criminal justice system.

1. Why is there no one theory to explain the cause of crime?

2. What drives criminologists to develop new theories over the course of time?

3. Which school of thought is most popular with criminologists today?

ethical standards of behavior Legal sanctions that prohibit experimentation that may harm subjects and regulate the degree of deception of subjects that researchers may use in an experiment.

causal variables Variables that directly influence the outcome of relationships.

correlation The state of two variables being associated with each other in that when one increases, the other increases or decreases in a predictable pattern.

MyCJLab

Go to Chapter 2 in *MyCJLab* to test your mastery of chapter concepts, access your Study Plan, engage in interactive exercises, complete critical-thinking and research assignments, and view related online videos.

☑ **Review:** Complete the pretest in the Study Plan to confirm what you know and what you need to study further. Then complete the post-test to confirm your mastery of the concepts. Use the key term flash cards to review key terminology.

⚙ **Apply:** Complete the interactive simulation activity.

🔍 **Analyze:** Complete assignments as directed by your instructor.

 Current Events: Explore CJSearch for current topical videos, articles, and news pieces.

Additional Links

To explore career opportunities in the field of criminology, go to
http://www.criminology.fsu.edu/p/career-opportunities-criminal-justice-jobs.php.

To read Cesare Beccaria's treaty *Of Crimes and Punishments*, go to **http://www.constitution.org/cb/crim_pun.htm**.

One of the most interesting proposals of Jeremy Bentham was the Panopticon, a unique "all-seeing" prison that provided round-the-clock observations of prisoners but prisoners could not see their observers. To obtain more information on Bentham's Panopticon, go to **http://cartome.org/panopticon1.htm**.

One of the modern treatments of Richard Dugdale's theory of inherited criminality is the play and movie *The Bad Seed* (1956), about a 12-year-old murderess and the assumption that her evil behavior was the result of genetic destiny. For more information and to see truTV's discussion, go to
http://www.trutv.com/library/crime/criminal_mind/psychology/crime_motivation/5.html.

To find extensive information about Sigmund Freud and to view his writings, go to the Sigmund Freud Archives at
http://www.freudarchives.org/.

Measuring Crime and Victimization

"Without crime statistics, it was not possible to determine the impact of money spent, resources invested, reform efforts, and new laws on the problem of crime."

—International Association of Police

1 Summarize the various methods for measuring crime and the problems related to measuring crime.

2 Summarize the various methods for gathering criminal justice data.

3 Explain the relationship between crime and social reaction to crime.

4 Summarize the Theories of Victimization.

5 Summarize the victims' rights movement.

3

The ad on Craigslist offered $300 a week, a free trailer, and unlimited fishing to "watch over a 688 acre patch of hilly farmland and feed a few cows." Three men who answered the ad were murdered, and a fourth barely escaped after being shot in the arm. The ad was a scam by Richard J. Beasley, 52, of Akron, Ohio, and Brogan Rafferty, 16, a high school student from Stow, Ohio, to lure people to their death. The "farm" was land owned by a coal company. Beasley and Rafferty apparently targeted people who would not be "missed," and after interviewing them and promising them the job, Beasley and Rafferty took them to the "farm" and murdered them.

The fourth man to answer the ad, Scott Davis, was driven to the "farm." As the three men were walking, he heard the sound of a gun being cocked; he turned, deflected the gun, ran into the woods, and hid. He was wounded in the arm but managed to escape and alert law enforcement to the crime. Beasley and Rafferty were identified and arrested. A search of the area uncovered the three other victims. Law enforcement officials speculate that other victims may be found.

The Internet has brought many advantages to people's life in modern society. However, it also has been responsible for the victimization of many. While the murder scheme of

Vicki Beaver / Alamy

DISCUSS Lifestyle victimization theories posit that those who engage in high-risk behaviors may be subject to greater rates of victimization. Are the Internet and social media high-risk behaviors?

Beasley and Rafferty may represent the extreme danger posed by the Internet, often it is the tool used by criminals to victimize unsuspecting individuals. People answering Internet ads have been robbed; assaulted; and, in some cases, murdered. Juveniles are often targeted for sexual victimization using Internet chat rooms. In cases of missing adolescent females and young women, law enforcement routinely checks their Internet activity, especially social media sites, for possible clues that they were lured into victimization via the Internet.

Parents are warned to exercise oversight of their children's use of the Internet. People who sell and trade using the Internet are warned of the potential dangers of victimization. Young women who meet men using the Internet and social media are warned to be alert to potential signs of danger.

▶ Measuring Crime and Victimization

Data about crime is important in understanding the criminal justice system, evaluating the impact of new programs, and assessing the overall level of public safety. However, counting crime can be an inexact science. Josiah Stamp, an early American critic of government statistics, said, "The government is very keen at amassing statistics. They collect them, add them, refer them to the nth power, take the cube root, to prepare wonderful diagrams. But you must never forget that every one of these figures comes in the first instance from the [village watchman], who just puts down what he damn pleases."[1]

Crime statistics and measures of the criminal justice system are subject to error, and the further one goes back in time, the more prominent the error appears. For this reason, crime data are often difficult or impossible to compare from one historical period to another due to the errors in data collection. Consider the problems in reliability suggested by the fact that the New York City coroner's office recorded

323 homicides in 1913, but the police reported only 261. Another example is the San Francisco Police Department reporting only 50 homicides but the coroner reporting 71 in 1915.[2]

This chapter discusses the various ways of measuring crime and gathering criminal justice data and victimization theories and the victims' right movement.

The Public Demand for Reliable Crime Data

The demand for accurate crime data emerged in the 1920s and 1930s. During this period, news media generated the public belief that a "crime wave" was sweeping the country. Crime was perceived as pervasive, and few public places were safe from violent crime. The news media, radio dramas, and movies reported colorful stories of organized crime figures and infamous public enemies such as John Dillinger, Charles

Crime statistics and measures of the criminal justice system are subject to error, and the further one goes back in time, the more prominent the error.

1919	1930	1933	1972	1972
Eighteenth Amendment (prohibition) is passed.	Uniform Crime Report is first published.	Twenty-first Amendment is passed, repealing the Eighteenth Amendment (prohibition).	**National Crime Victimization Survey** begins gathering data on victimizations.	Federal Bureau of Investigation publishes *Hate Crime Statistics*.

"Pretty Boy" Floyd, George "Baby Face" Nelson, and Bonnie Parker and Clyde Barrow. Bank robberies, gang shoot-outs, and gun battles with the police and the newly formed FBI were front page news nearly every day.

Passage of the Eighteenth Amendment in 1919, which prohibited the manufacture, sale, and possession of alcoholic beverages, added fuel to the fire. The **Prohibition Amendment**, or the **Volstead Act** as it was called, increased rather than decreased crimes as gangs warred for control of the lucrative illegal sale of alcoholic beverages. Crime bosses such as Al Capone often were perceived as public heroes rather than public enemies. The average citizen was left with the impression that crime was everywhere and no one could do much about it. Without a way to objectively determine accurate crime data, the public had no idea which side—the criminal justice system or the criminals—was winning. Without crime statistics, it was impossible to determine the impact of money spent, resources invested, reform efforts instituted, and new laws enacted for the problem of crime.

During this period, crime was considered mainly a "big city" problem, but many cities were experiencing rapid population growth and joining the ranks of "big cities." After World War I, more people migrated to the cities. As urban populations swelled, the public became more concerned with crime. In the 1920s, Cleveland, Ohio, and Chicago, Illinois, were among the first major cities to perform crime surveys.[3] These surveys were motivated by the desire to correct what were perceived as major deficiencies in the criminal justice system. The basic premise was that the absence of crime is the best measure of police effectiveness. If reforms to the criminal justice system were effective, it was believed that the results would be reflected in decreasing crime rates.[4]

The **International Association of Police** published the first national report of crime in the United States in 1927. Congress was convinced of the benefit of this type of data, and in 1929, the U.S. Congress authorized the Federal Bureau

There are two nationally recognized measures of crime data: (1) the Uniform Crime Report and (2) the National Crime Victimization Survey.

of Investigation (FBI) to gather nationwide crime data and publish it. The FBI published the first nationwide report of crime in 1930, entitled the Uniform Crime Report, and has published it continuously since then. For about 40 years, this was the most authoritative report of nationwide crime data.

The emphasis on collecting and disseminating more comprehensive reliable crime data did not emerge until the 1970s and was connected with government's concern that there was a crisis in public safety. As a result of this concern, greater emphasis was placed on the collection of criminal justice data from all aspects of the criminal justice system and new agencies were chartered with the purpose of collecting and disseminating data.

Today, there are two nationally recognized measures of crime data: (1) the Uniform Crime Report and (2) the National Crime Victimization Survey. (See Figure 3–1.) Other major sources of criminal justice data are the National Incident-Based Reporting System (1988), the International Crime Victims Survey (ICVS) (1989), and the National Center for Education Statistics (1994). In addition to these sources, there are numerous state surveys and surveys by private institutions such as the PEW Research Center and individual scholars.

	UCR	NCVS
Geographic coverage	National and state estimates, local agency reports	National estimates
Collective method	Reports by law enforcement to the FBI on a monthly basis	Survey of 42,093 households and 77,852 individuals age 12 or older were interviewed
Measures	8 Part I Index crimes and 19 lesser crimes reported by law enforcement	Reported and unreported crime; details about the crimes, victims, and offenders

FIGURE 3–1 Comparison of the UCR and the NCVS

There are several important differences between the crime data reported by the FBI's UCR and the Bureau of Justice Statistics National Crime Victimization Survey. These differences include who collects the data, how the data are collected, and what data are collected. The variations result in different crime statistics being reported.

Source: Bureau of Justice Statistics, http://www.bjs.gov/index.cfm?ty=pbdetail&iid=802 (accessed April 6, 2012).

LEARNING OUTCOMES 1 Summarize the various methods for measuring crime and the problems related to measuring crime.

GLOSSARY

Prohibition Amendment The Eighteenth Amendment passed in 1919 that prohibited the manufacture, sale, and possession of alcoholic beverages.

Volstead Act Another name for the Prohibition Amendment.

International Association of Police The world's oldest and largest nonprofit membership organization of police executives.

Uniform Crime Report (UCR) A database of information about reported crimes collected by the Federal Bureau of Investigation over time.

Part I offenses A Uniform Crime Report category group used to report murder, forcible rape, robbery, aggravated assault, burglary, larceny-theft, motor vehicle theft, and arson.

Violent Crime Index The rate of crimes reported in the Part I offenses.

Part II offenses A Uniform Crime Report category group used to report less serious offenses involving an arrest.

hierarchy rule An old police method of counting only the most serious crime in a single incident involving multiple crimes.

clearance rate The percentage of crimes that are solved versus crimes that are unsolved.

The Uniform Crime Report (UCR)

On June 11, 1930, Congress passed the first federal legislation mandating the collecting of crime data. The FBI was charged with the responsibility of collecting crime data from police departments and disseminating the data to the nation. The **Uniform Crime Report (UCR)** is a record of crime reported to law enforcement agencies. While law enforcement agencies and states collected crime data prior to the UCR, there was no single agency that collected the data from the various agencies and compiled it into a nationwide report. The participation of local and state agencies is voluntary because federal law does not mandate the reporting of crime data to the FBI. Today, participation by local and state agencies is near universal; however, in the early years of the UCR, that was not the case.

The UCR had its origins at a time when there were no computers, no computerized databases, and no statistical and graphics software. Crime data were collected, stored, and transmitted manually. Collecting and reporting crime data were labor-intensive processes. Most police departments kept file cabinets filled with index cards detailing each crime—one card for each crime. The cards were arranged by case number and offense and were filed under the various crime categories (murder, rape, burglary, and so forth). Anyone wanting to know the number of burglaries committed during a particular period, for example, had to go to the file cabinet, pull the cards for burglary, and count the number of cards one by one. Given these data collection methods, the FBI had to adopt rules for counting crimes that were consistent with the limitations imposed by the system.

Rules for Counting Crime

First, it was impossible to count all crimes, so only those that were considered most reflective of public safety were counted. The URC collects data on only 27 criminal violations, which are divided into two categories: serious crimes and less serious crimes. These categories were named Part I crimes and Part II crimes, respectively. Originally, there were seven Part I offenses. **Part I offenses** were considered the most serious of the violent offenses and included murder and nonnegligent manslaughter; forcible rape; robbery; aggravated assault; and the property crimes of burglary, larceny-theft, and motor vehicle theft. Arson was added to the list of Part I crimes in 1979. The rate of crimes reported in the Part I offenses is known as the **Violent Crime Index**. **Part II offenses** consist of 21 less serious offenses such as simple assault, sex offenses, and drug abuse violations. (See Table 3–1.)

Second, since crimes were listed on cards in a case where multiple crimes were committed as part of a single incident, the card would be indexed under the most serious crime. This was called the hierarchy rule. The **hierarchy rule** would count only the most serious offense when multiple offenses occurred, and it would count multiple victims of a single criminal incident as a single crime. For example, if a person were robbed, kidnapped, physically assaulted, and murdered, all of the crime data would be on a single card and it would be indexed under murder. Also, if the crime involved multiple victims (that is, a single incidence in which three people were robbed), all crime victims would be included in the single robbery report—not three separate crime reports—one for each robbery. This type of record keeping and rules for reporting statistics was essential when data was collected manually from index cards. However, the hierarchy rule resulted in underreporting of crime because less serious offenses would not be included in the crime data and multiple crime events would not be included in the count.

TABLE 3–1

FBI'S UNIFORM CRIME REPORT, PART I AND PART II OFFENSES

Part I Offenses (Crime Index)	Part II Offenses
Criminal Homicide Murder, nonnegligent manslaughter, and nonjustifiable homicide; manslaughter by negligence is a Part I crime but is not included in the Crime index	**Simple Assault** No weapon or serious injury
	Forgery and Counterfeiting
	Fraud
Forcible Rape "Carnal knowledge," includes sexual assault but not statutory offenses	**Embezzlement**
	Stolen Property Buying, selling, and receiving
Robbery "Taking" or attempting to take anything of value from a person by force, threat, or fear	**Prostitution and Commercialized Vice**
	Sex Offenses Statutory rape and offenses against morality
Aggravated Assault Attack on a person for the purpose of inflicting bodily harm, usually through use of a weapon	**Drug Abuse Violations** State or local laws against unlawful possession, sale, use, growing, or manufacturing of opium, cocaine, morphine, heroin, codeine, marijuana, and other narcotic and dangerous nonnarcotic drugs
Burglary Breaking or entering a structure to commit a felony or theft, including attempt	
	Gambling
Larceny Includes theft of property that does not involve force, violence, or fraud	**Offenses against Family and Children** Nonsupport, neglect, desertion, abuse
	Driving Under the Influence Of alcohol or drugs
Motor Vehicle Theft Does not include motorboats, construction equipment, airplanes, or farming equipment	**Liquor Laws** State or local laws
	Drunkenness
Arson Willful or malicious burning or attempt to burn any property for any reason	**Disorderly Conduct**
	Vagrancy
	All Other Violations Of state or local laws
	Suspicion Suspect released without charge
	Curfew and Loitering Laws Persons under age 18
	Runaways Persons under age 18 in protective custody

Source: Federal Bureau of Investigation, Uniform Crime Report, 2011.

The Modern UCR

The FBI claims that the modern UCR compiled with the assistance of computers and databases is the most comprehensive analysis of violent crime and public crime in the nation. The crime data is published in quarterly and annual reports. The annual report is the *Uniform Crime Report: Crime in the U.S.* (The UCR can be downloaded from http://www.fbi.gov.) In addition, the UCR Report includes arrest, clearance, and law enforcement employee data.

Clearance rate refers to the percentage of crimes that are solved versus crimes that are unsolved. *Solved* means that the police believe they know the perpetrator of the crime. *Solved* does not mean that the perpetrator has been arrested, prosecuted, convicted, or incarcerated. It merely means that the police are reasonably certain they know who committed the crime. In most cases, a crime is "cleared" by the arrest of the suspect, but police consider the crime cleared if they believe the suspect committed the crime, regardless of whether

Mark Burnett / Alamy

Think About It ...

There are 310 Indian reservations in the United States, and the violent crime rates on reservations are more than two and a half times higher than the national average. Some reservations have crime rates five to seven times the national average. Native American women are ten times more likely to be murdered compared with other Americans. They are raped or sexually assaulted at a rate four times the national average.

The FBI and the U.S. Justice Department are responsible for handling serious violent crime on Indian reservations. Data indicates that in 2011, federal prosecutors declined to file charges in 52% of cases involving the most serious crimes committed on Indian reservations. The Justice Department did not pursue rape charges on reservations 65% of the time and rejected 61% of cases involving charges of sexual abuse of children.

Why are crime rates so high and prosecution rates so low on Indian reservations? What should be done to lower the crime rates?

The FBI publishes separate reports on other crime data, including the following:

- Hate Crime Statistics
- Bank Crime Reports
- Campus Attacks: Targeted Violence Affecting Institutions of Higher Education
- Financial Crime Reports
- Financial Institution Fraud and Failure Reports
- Internet Crime Reports
- Mass Marketing Fraud Threat Assessment
- Mortgage Fraud Reports
- National Drug Threat Assessment
- National Gang Threat Assessment
- Law Enforcement Officers Killed and Assaulted

the criminal justice system takes additional action against the suspect. Reasons a case may be cleared by the suspect not being arrested or prosecuted include the suspect dies, the suspect is given immunity from arrest, or the suspect is beyond the jurisdiction of U.S. law enforcement. If a suspect is prosecuted and found not guilty and the police believe the suspect was the offender, the crime is still considered cleared.

The Crime Clock

One of the early data presentation strategies used by the FBI, which is still in use today, is the **crime clock**, which reports how often a crime occurs. The crime clock is used to emphasize that crime is occurring nearly all of the time. For example, according to the crime clock in 2010, larceny-theft occurred every 5.1 seconds, burglary was committed every 14.6 seconds, and aggravated assault took place every 40.5 seconds. Based on the crime clock, it is easy for citizens to conclude that they can hardly walk outside their homes without becoming a crime statistic. These data are distorted, however. Although it might be accurate to say that a murder occurs every 35.6 minutes, this does not mean that every 35.6 minutes a murder occurs in every community. It

Solved does not mean that the perpetrator has been arrested, prosecuted, convicted, or incarcerated.

means that every 35.6 minutes a murder occurs somewhere in the United States. Even the FBI warns that "the crime clock should not be taken to imply regularity in the commission of crime. The crime clock represents the annual ratio of crime to fixed time intervals." One use of the crime clock is to compare the intervals from year to year. If the interval is shorter, there was more crime. If the interval between crimes is longer, there was less crime.

Uses of UCR Data

Over the years, crime data collected by the FBI and published in the UCR have become useful as databases for examining crime trends. These data have numerous purposes: as a measure of crime rates, as a factor in indexes calculating the quality of life in U.S. cities, and as a factor in policy decisions. Based on UCR trend data, municipalities might decide to add more police officers to their force. Grants aimed at preventing crime and curbing drug crime use UCR data to measure effectiveness. Many agencies often anxiously await the release of new UCR data because they want to know whether recent changes such as community policing, Neighborhood Watch programs, and "get tough" sentencing policies have had an impact on the crime rate.

A Snapshot of the UCR

The UCR has reported a decrease in violent crime since 2006. In 2006, an estimated 440,000 violent offenses were committed. That figure dropped to an estimated 240,000 violent crime offenses in 2010. That is a decline of 13.2% below the 2006 level.[5] The UCR estimated that the violent crime rate was 403.6 violent crimes per 100,000 inhabitants in 2010. Preliminary data for 2011 shows a continued decline in the violent crime rate. However, while national violent crime continues to decline, some cities are experiencing an increase, especially in homicides.

2010 CRIME CLOCK STATISTICS

A Violent Crime occurred every	25.3 seconds
One Murder every	35.6 minutes
One Forcible Rape every	6.2 minutes
One Robbery every	1.4 minutes
One Aggravated Assault every	40.5 minutes
A Property Crime occurred every	3.5 seconds
One Burglary every	14.6 minutes
One Larceny-theft every	5.1 minutes
One Motor Vehicle Theft every	42.8 minutes

This representation of crime data shows the relative frequency of how often violent and property crime offenses occurred in 2010. (Note that the crime clock should not be taken to imply regularity in the commission of crime. The crime clock represents the annual ratio of crime to fixed time intervals.)
Source: http://www.fbi.gov.

According to the UCR, in 2010, aggravated assaults accounted for the highest number of violent crimes reported to law enforcement at 62.5%. Robbery comprised 29.5%, forcible rape accounted for 6.8%, and murder accounted for 1.2% of estimated violent crimes in 2010.[6] (See Table 3–2 for preliminary crime data for 2011.)

According to *Crime in the United States, 2010*, in 2010, 47.2% of violent crimes and 18.3% of property crimes were cleared. Among violent crimes, murder has the highest clearance rate at 64.8%. The clearance rate for forcible rape offenses was 40.3%, and 28.2% of robbery offenses were cleared. The clearance rate for aggravated assault offenses was 56.4%, and 19% of arson offenses were cleared.

According to *Crime in the United States, 2010*, in 2010, the clearance rates for property crimes were much lower than those for violent offenses. Only 21.1% of larceny-theft offenses were cleared, 12.4% of burglary offenses were cleared, and 11.8% of motor vehicle theft offenses were cleared.

Flaws in UCR Data

There are several major shortcomings of UCR data that encourage the collection of crime data by other means. One shortcoming is that UCR data represent only crimes that are known to the police; unreported crimes are not included. The lack of this type of information is particularly significant: People often do not report crimes because they lack confidence in the police, including the ability of the police to do something about the crime; they also fear that the police are corrupt and that harm will befall innocent people if they report a crime.

TABLE 3–2 | PRELIMINARY VIOLENT CRIME RATES FOR 2011
PERCENT CHANGE BY POPULATION GROUP, JANUARY TO JUNE 2011

Population Group	Number of Agencies	Population	Violent Crime	Murder	Forcible Rape	Robbery	Aggravated Assault	Property Crime	Burglary	Larceny-theft	Motor Vehicle Theft	Arson
Total	12,554	254,657,803	−6.4	−5.7	−5.1	−7.7	−5.9	−3.7	−2.2	−4.0	−5.0	−8.6
Cities:												
1,000,000 and over	10	25,013,346	−5.4	−7.5	+1.0	−7.8	−3.9	−4.2	−1.1	−5.8	−1.2	−6.8
500,000 to 999,999	21	14,275,754	−6.7	+1.2	+6.7	−7.7	−7.3	−3.9	−3.6	−3.6	−6.1	−8.4
250,000 to 499,999	41	14,205,510	−5.7	−1.9	+0.1	−6.6	−5.7	−0.9	−0.3	−1.1	−1.1	−5.0
100,000 to 249,999	192	28,804,343	−6.6	−4.7	−6.7	−6.3	−6.8	−5.1	−2.1	−5.7	−8.6	−13.5
50,000 to 99,999	403	28,098,401	−7.2	−21.8	−2.5	−8.9	−6.6	−3.1	−1.7	−3.5	−3.1	−10.2
25,000 to 49,999	721	24,896,068	−5.8	−18.9	−6.8	−9.5	−3.9	−4.9	−4.0	−5.1	−5.2	−9.1
10,000 to 24,999	1,607	25,413,559	−6.5	−4.9	−8.5	−7.6	−5.9	−3.6	−2.1	−4.0	−5.2	−7.5
Under 10,000	6,233	19,865,316	−6.1	+2.6	−8.7	−9.7	−5.1	−4.6	−5.7	−4.3	−4.9	−8.7
Counties:												
Metropolitan[1]	1,345	52,108,866	−7.6	0.0	−8.8	−8.6	−7.2	−3.2	−1.3	−3.2	−9.2	−5.2
Nonmetropolitan[2]	1,981	21,976,640	−6.4	−7.0	−13.7	−8.5	−5.0	−0.5	−1.7	+0.5	−3.6	−13.4

Source: FBI Uniform Crime Reports, January to June 2011, http://www.fbi.gov.

[1]Includes crimes reported to sheriffs' departments, county police departments, and state police within Metropolitan Statistical Areas.

[2]Includes crimes reported to sheriffs' departments, county police departments, and state police outside Metropolitan Statistical Areas.

The UCR data is obtained through the voluntary cooperation of local and state police agencies for data collection. In the early years, many local police departments did not report crime data because they lacked adequate record keeping or personnel to gather the facts, they feared embarrassment, or they simply did not want to report the data. To this day, there is no official sanction of local and state police for failing to report crime data to the FBI. Thus, one should do historical trend analysis of UCR data with caution. For example, data comparison of crime rates in New York in the 1930s compared with crime rates in the twenty-first century may be inaccurate due to reporting errors.

Finally, UCR data are about local and state crimes, but definitions of crimes are not the same from place to place. In one jurisdiction, a felony theft might be defined as the taking of property valued at $100, whereas in another jurisdiction, the limit for felony theft might be $1,000. One of the most troublesome problems with UCR data is the definition of *rape*. The UCR uses a definition that is not as inclusive as the one used by states that have adopted progressive sexual assault criminal codes. The UCR defines *forcible rape* as "the carnal knowledge of a female forcibly and against her will." In 2011, the UCR redefined *forcible rape* to bring it in line with the contemporary definition used by most states. Thus, there are significant differences in certain crime definitions from state to state.

> Federal crime data may be different than that published by the state.

crime clock A method used by the Federal Bureau of Investigation to report how often crimes occur.

National Crime Victimization Survey (NCVS) A survey of a representative sample of U.S. households that gathers detailed information about crimes from victims.

dark figure of crime statistics Crimes that are not reported and thus are unknown to police.

National Incident-Based Reporting System (NIBRS) An incident-based reporting system in which more comprehensive crime information is gathered.

In some cases, these differences can result in confusion because federal crime data may be different than that published by the state. Most often this difference is due to the difference in how crimes are defined rather than incompetence or the attempt to underreport crime.

National Crime Victimization Survey (NCVS)

The other major source of crime data is the National Crime Victimization Survey. The **National Crime Victimization Survey (NCVS)** is a mailed survey of a representative sample of U.S. households that gathers detailed information about crimes from victims.

The NCVS originated in 1972, when it was recognized that a significant number of crimes go unreported to the police.

> Victims do not report crime to the police because they believe the police will or can do nothing about it.

Unreported crime is called the **dark figure of crime statistics** in that it recognizes that the official data of crime reported to the police is lower than the actual crime rate. While the UCR and the NCVS report similar rates for crimes such as motor vehicle theft, they report very different crime data for other crimes, such as rape. Furthermore, it is assumed that the NCVS does not capture the true extent of the crime of rape because it also underreports this crime.

Some of the reasons crime victims do not report crime to the police are that they believe the police will or can do nothing about it, they fear retaliation and further victimization, they fear they will be arrested because of their immigration status, or they believe the police are part of the problem. In addition, victims of sexual assault may fail to report the crime because of guilt and social shame.

The NCVS collects victimization information from a representative sample of U.S. households.[7] Each household in the sample is interviewed twice a year, and a household is part of the national sample for 3.5 years. The NCVS was authorized in 1972, and the first survey was conducted in 1973. The goals of the victimization survey were as follows:

- To develop detailed information about the victims of crime
- To initiate a data collection effort detailing the consequences of crime
- To provide systematic information about the dark figures of crime by estimating the number and types of crimes not reported to police
- To provide uniform measures of selected types of crime
- To permit comparisons of crimes over time and types of areas[8]

The NCVS gathers data about crime incidents such as the relationship between the victim and the offender, any use of drugs or alcohol, bystander behavior, suspected offender gang involvement, and self-protection measures taken by the victim. The survey gathers data from crime victims; thus, it does not gather data about homicide. (See Figure 3–2 for a list of the kinds of data included in the NCVS.)

Deficiencies of the NCVS

The NCVS does provide important data not gathered by the UCR, but it also has deficiencies. The NCVS depends on self-reported data by the victim, which may be inaccurate. The survey is sent to households, so it does not reliably pinpoint the geographic location of the crimes, as do the UCR data. Also, household members who have previously withheld

1930 First Uniform Crime Report
1973 First National Crime Victimization Survey
1982 National Incident-Based Reporting System
1993 Revision of National Crime Victimization Survey

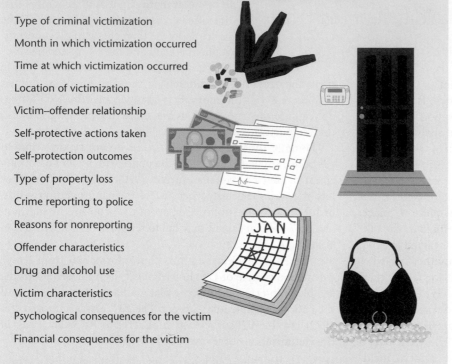

The following list shows the kinds of data included in the NCVS:

Type of criminal victimization

Month in which victimization occurred

Time at which victimization occurred

Location of victimization

Victim–offender relationship

Self-protective actions taken

Self-protection outcomes

Type of property loss

Crime reporting to police

Reasons for nonreporting

Offender characteristics

Drug and alcohol use

Victim characteristics

Psychological consequences for the victim

Financial consequences for the victim

Note: The NCVS gathers data by surveying households, so the NCVS does not report the crime of homicide since homicide victims cannot be surveyed.

FIGURE 3–2 Crime Data Included in the NCVS

information about victimization from family members are not likely to report their victimization in the NCVS.

The early surveys were called the National Crime Survey (NCS). After about two decades of data gathering, shortcomings of the NCS data were revealed. As a result of demands for better data on violence against women, the NCS was revised in 1993 to provide more information on the extent of victimization that occurred within families. Also, to increase reliability, methodological adjustments were made in the NCS to help people recall victimization more accurately. As a result of these changes, some caution should be observed when comparing trends in data prior to 1993 to trends in data after 1993. (See Figure 3–3.)

Comparisons between the UCR and the NCVS

The UCR and the NCVS were designed to serve different purposes. Thus, there are some differences between the two. The purpose of the UCR is to measure crime reported to law enforcement, whereas the NCVS attempts to gather information about crime that is not available from the UCR. For a number of

84k The number of forcible rapes reported by the UCR in 2010.

188k The number of forcible rapes reported by the NCVS in 2010.

reasons, these two measures of crime may report different data.

One purpose of the NCVS is to capture crime not reported to law enforcement. Comparisons between UCR and NCVS data have consistently confirmed the belief that there was, indeed, a vast difference between reported crime data and victimization data. For some crimes, there appears to be little difference between actual crime and reported crime. For example, both measures of crime report similar data for the crimes of homicide and auto theft. This is because the definition of homicide is similar from state to state and homicides are usually reported to law enforcement. The crime of auto theft is not underreported because most stolen vehicles are insured and insurance companies will not provide compensation to the victim unless he or she files a police report.

However, for other crimes, there is a significant gap between reported crime and actual crime. A comparison of the reported incidents of rape by the NCVS and the UCR indicates that the UCR significantly underreports sex crimes. For example, the UCR reported 84,767 forcible rapes in 2010 and the NCVS reported 188,380. The NCVS reported more than 2.2 times the number of rapes. The difference is not incompetence or inaccuracies in the data. The difference is due to the fact that many sexual assaults are not reported to the police.

The UCR reports crime against individuals, whereas the NCVS reports crimes against households. Thus, NCVS data does not have information regarding the location of the crime. The NCVS data cannot be analyzed by geographic location, but using UCR data, the crime rates of different cities or areas within a city can be examined.

Another point of difference is that the NCVS and the UCR do not have common definitions for some crimes. For a number of crimes, the UCR and NCVS have different definitions, resulting in different measures of crime. The two share a common definition for the crimes of robbery, burglary, and motor vehicle theft.

With data from two databases, researchers can compare trends in reported crime to estimated total crime. Often these data are revealing, as reported crime in the UCR might increase not because of an actual increase in the crime rate, but because of an increase in reported crime. Overall, the trend line of the two databases generally shows common characteristics. When the crime rate reported by the UCR is up, the NCVS shows a similar increase in crime reporting and vice versa.

Apparent discrepancies between statistics from the two programs can usually be accounted for by their definitional and procedural differences or the NCVS's sampling methodology of households.[9]

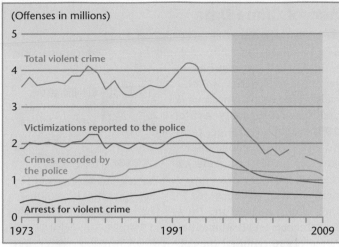

(Offenses in millions)

FIGURE 3–3 **Four Measures of Serious Violent Crime, 1973–2009**
The serious violent crimes included are rape, robbery, aggravated assault, and homicide. Although each measure is different, both the NCVS and UCR show that serious violent crime levels declined in recent years. The NCVS redesign was implemented in 1993; the area with the lighter shading is before the redesign, and the darker area is after the redesign. Also, the NCVS determined that the data for 2006 are not comparable with data from other years due to changes in survey design; therefore, the data are omitted from the chart. The data before 1993 are adjusted to make them comparable with data collected since the redesign. The NCVS is a household survey of about 134,000 people aged 12 and older in 77,200 households who are asked twice each year about their victimizations from crime.
Source: Bureau of Justice Statistics, Key Facts at a Glance, http://bjs.ojp.usdoj. gov/content/glance/cv2.cfm (accessed July 3, 2011).

Other Crime Data Sources

The National Incident-Based Reporting System (NIBRS)

The FBI recognized the shortcomings of the UCR crime data survey methods and instituted a plan to address many of the problems. In 1982, the Bureau of Justice Statistics and the FBI sponsored a study of the Uniform Crime Report Program with the objective of revising it to meet law enforcement needs of the twenty-first century.[10] The result of that study was the National Incident-Based Reporting System launched in March 1988. The **National Incident-Based Reporting System (NIBRS)** is an incident-based reporting system in which more comprehensive crime information is presented.

Taking advantage of the computer technology that is now available in crime reporting, the NIBRS is more than a simple summary of crime data. Under the NIBRS, additional data about crimes are reported, including information about the place of occurrence, the weapon used, the type and value of property damaged or stolen, personal characteristics of the offender and the victim, the nature of any relationship between the two, and the disposition of the complaint. NIBRS data provides more insight into the crime picture, and researchers will have greater success in correlating crime data with other factors suspected of contributing to the incidence of crime and effective crime prevention.

The NIBRS collects data on each single incident and arrest within 22 categories called Group A offenses. There are 11 Group B offense categories for which only arrest data are reported. The NIBRS addresses some of the shortcomings of the URC. For example, similar to the NCVS, the NIBRS uses an

> NIBRS data provides more insight into the crime picture, and researchers will have greater success in correlating crime data with other factors.

updated definition of rape that includes both male and female victims. Crimes are not reported using the hierarchy rule, so all crimes related to a single incident are reported separately. The NIBRS distinguishes between crimes that were completed and crimes that were attempted but not completed. The NIBRS collects information about crimes committed using a computer. Finally, the NIBRS reports data that can be used to establish linkage between offense, offender, victim, property, and arrestee variables that permits examination of interrelationships.[11]

The FBI has certified about half of the states to contribute NIBRS crime data to the UCR Program. The data from these states represent about 16% of the crime statistics collected by the UCR Program.[12]

▶ Other Criminal Justice Data Banks

A number of federal agencies are dedicated to data collection. The major agencies are the Bureau of Justice Statistics, the National Criminal Justice Reference Service, and the U.S. Department of Justice with its *Sourcebook of Criminal Justice Statistics*.

Bureau of Justice Statistics

The Bureau of Justice Statistics (BJS) was established by federal legislation in 1979. The BJS is a component of the Office of Justice Programs in the U.S. Department of Justice. Its mission is to collect, analyze, publish, and disseminate information on crime, criminal offenders, victims of crime, and the operation of justice systems at all levels of government.[13] The BJS publishes a number of annual and periodic reports of statistical data on law enforcement, the courts, and corrections. It is one of the primary sources of statistical data on the criminal justice system.

National Criminal Justice Reference Service

Established in 1972, the **National Criminal Justice Reference Service (NCJRS)** is a federally funded resource offering justice and drug-related information to support research, policy, and program development worldwide.[14] NCJRS data and resources can be accessed from its website at https://www.ncjrs.gov. There is no charge for the services of the NCJRS, and most of the NCJRS documents and papers can be downloaded from the website for free. NCJRS hosts one of the largest criminal and juvenile justice libraries and databases in the world, the NCJRS Abstracts Database. The collection, with holdings from the early 1970s to the present, contains more than 210,000 publications, reports, articles, and audiovisual products from the United States and other areas around the world. These resources include statistics, research findings, program descriptions, congressional hearing transcriptions, and training materials.[15]

210,000
The number of publications in the NCJRS database.

Sourcebook of Criminal Justice Statistics

Established in 1973, the *Sourcebook of Criminal Justice Statistics* brings together data from more than 200 sources about many aspects of criminal justice in the United States.[16] The *Sourcebook of Criminal Justice Statistics* is funded by the U.S. Department of Justice, Bureau of Justice Statistics. The project is located at the University of Albany School of Criminal Justice, Hindelang Criminal Justice Research Center, in Albany, New York. *The Sourcebook of Criminal Justice Statistics* includes data from a wide range of sources. As a result, data not found in more specialized databases such as the NCVS and UCR can be found in the *Sourcebook*. For example, it contains information on public opinion polls regarding attitudes about the various criminal justice agencies and personnel. Because data from the Bureau of Justice Statistics is compiled by the *Sourcebook*, it may duplicate data found in other federal databases, including the UCR and the NCVS. The web page of the *Sourcebook of Criminal Justice Statistics* is http://www.albany.edu/sourcebook.

Bureau of Justice Statistics (BJS)

The **Bureau of Justice Statistics (BJS)** is under the Office of Justice Programs, U.S. Department of Justice. The BJS was established in December 1979 under the Justice Systems Improvement Act of 1979. The mission of the BJS is "to collect, analyze, publish, and disseminate information on crime, criminal offenders, victims of crime, and the operation of justice systems at all levels of government."[17] The BJS promotes itself as "the United States' primary source for criminal justice statistics." The BJS compiles reports on many aspects of the criminal justice system, including data about federal, state, and local criminal justice authorities.

Some of the major data reports of the BJS are annual criminal victimization data, populations under correctional supervision, federal and state criminal offenders and case processing, and data regarding administration of law enforcement agencies and correctional facilities. Also, the BJS reports data on criminal justice expenditure and employment. The BJS reports special studies on various criminal justice topics such as crime on Native American reservations. The portal for accessing data disseminated by the BJS is http://www.bjs.gov.

School Crime Data

At one time, crime that occurred on K–12 campuses or college campuses was not captured because educational institutions were not required to report it to government officials. The **Crime Awareness and Campus Security Act of 1992** required college campuses to make a public disclosure of crimes occurring on their campuses whether or not these crimes were reported to the police. The **Safe and Drug-Free Schools and Communities Act of 1996** required the collection of data, frequency, seriousness, and incidences of violence in elementary and secondary schools. While this data made it possible for parents and students to obtain crime data about educational institutions, it also influenced the nation's crime data. For example, at a K–12 school in the past, when a student's lunch money was taken by force, this incident often was not reported to the police or was handled by school administration outside the criminal justice system. Now these incidents may be reported as robberies and included in the UCR. While one may think that the inclusion of these incidents will result in an increase in the crime rate, in actuality, the crime rate remains unchanged. It is just that previously unreported "school incidents" are now reported as "crimes."

LEARNING OUTCOMES 2 Summarize the various methods for gathering criminal justice data.

GLOSSARY

National Criminal Justice Reference Service (NCJRS) A federally funded resource offering justice and drug-related information to support research, policy, and other programs.

Sourcebook of Criminal Justice Statistics A publication funded by the U.S. Department of Justice, a research body that brings together data from more than 200 sources about many aspects of criminal justice in the United States.

Bureau of Justice Statistics (BJS) A primary source for criminal justice statistics that compiles reports on many aspects of the criminal justice system, including data about federal, state, and local criminal justice.

Crime Awareness and Campus Security Act of 1992 A law requiring college campuses to make a public disclosure of crimes occurring on their campuses.

Safe and Drug-Free Schools and Communities Act of 1996 A law requiring the collection of data, frequency, seriousness, and incidences of violence in elementary and secondary schools.

State Surveys and Self-Reports

State-sponsored research includes surveys of crime similar to those of the UCR, which are conducted by the individual states, and surveys of crime in public schools. Scholars, private research institutions, and government agencies conduct numerous surveys of perpetrators and offenders using self-reports. In self-reports, the data regarding offending is supplied by the people taking the survey. Often these surveys are administrated to school-age children or college students to measure drug use, driving while intoxicated offenses, underage

http://www.fbi.gov	**Uniform Crime Reports**
http://bjs.ojp.usdoj.gov/index.cfm?ty=dcdetail&iid=245	**National Crime Victimization Surveys**
http://www.bjs.gov	**Bureau of Justice Statistics**
http://www.ncjrs.gov	**National Criminal Justice Reference Service**
http://www.albany.edu/sourcebook	*Sourcebook of Criminal Justice Statistics*

drinking, and consensual crimes. The data from self-reports often indicate that UCR data regarding crimes reported to the police greatly underestimate the rate of actual offending for certain crimes, such as illegal drug use.

> Elderly individuals are the least victimized age group but have the most fear of victimization.

Crime statistics do not predict the future. Because of the delay between the gathering and reporting of crime statistics, an alarming report of rising crime rates may be inaccurate. Some data concerning the criminal justice system are gathered annually; other data are gathered periodically every several years. Crime rates might already have dropped by the time a report is issued and might continue dropping, making drastic actions and new programs unnecessary. Also, the methodology of data gathering changes and the criminal laws and social values change over time. Thus, data may be unreliable when **longitudinal comparisons** of crime data are made from one time period to another. Thus, looking at crime statistics is like looking in the rearview mirror of an automobile, which shows you where you have been but not where you are going. Crime trends may require some time before they can be established with any certainty.

▶ Caution: Crime Statistics, Public Safety, and Predicting the Future

Measures of crime data do not necessary reflect the public's fear of **victimization**. For example, victimization data indicate that elderly individuals are the least victimized age group, but surveys show that they have the most fear of victimization. Young adults are the most victimized age group, but they have the least fear of victimization. Rising crime rates can cause the public's fear of crime to rise, but lower crime rates do not necessarily result in less fear of victimization.

In one community policing program in Honolulu, Hawaii, the Honolulu Police Department (HPD) targeted a public housing project. The goal was to build better relationships with the residents and to reduce drug- and gang-related crimes. Prior to the start of the program, the HPD surveyed the attitudes of residents and found that most expressed fears of victimization, especially at night. As a result many, especially elderly residents, did not leave their residence after dark. The HPD engaged in a number of community policing programs to reduce crime and enhance public safety in the housing project. At the end of the program, the HPD surveyed the residents and took measures in the change in the crime rate. The data were unexpected in that while measures of crime showed that the crime rate had not decreased in the housing projects, the survey of residents showed that they were less fearful of victimization, were more likely to be out at night, and believed that the crime rate had decreased. The data indicated that the rise and fall of the crime rate is not directly correlated with the public's fear of crime. The public's fear of victimization depends on a number of factors, of which the crime rate is only one.

One final note regarding counting crime is the warning that crime data are only a snapshot of the past. **Crime statistics** indicate what crime has occurred, not what crime will occur.

 LEARNING OUTCOMES 3 Explain the relationship between crime and social reaction to crime.

GLOSSARY

victimization The process of being victimized or becoming a victim of crime.

crime statistics The gathering, analysis, and interpretation of crime data.

longitudinal comparisons Examinations of crime data recorded at one time period with crime data from another time period, such as year-to-year comparisons and comparisons over a number of years.

▶ The Other Side of Crime: Victimology

Understanding victimology as well as criminal behavior is an important aspect of comprehending the criminal justice system. **Victimology** is the study of victims and their patterns of victimization. From this perspective, the question is not why certain individuals (or groups) engage in criminal behavior; instead, the emphasis is on explaining why certain people (or groups) experience victimization at certain times and in certain places. Similarly, research on criminal justice has focused on how offenders are processed through the criminal justice system. Victimologists, in contrast, examine the dynamics of the administration of justice as it relates to crime victims—that is, how victims are treated by the criminal justice system and what rights they have.

The Demographics of Criminal Victimization

Like criminal offending, criminal victimization is not randomly distributed among the populace. Patterns of victimization show differences between ethnicity, income, gender, time, and age. Furthermore, for the last 30 years, victimization data show a high degree of consistency with respect to where and when victimization occurs and who is victimized. This data suggests the following observations regarding the demographics of criminal victimization:

- Individuals between the ages of 12 and 24 have the greatest chance of becoming the victims of crime, especially violent crime. (See Figure 3–4.) Generally, from the early- to mid-20s, as one gets older, the rate of victimization decreases, with those older than age 65 having the lowest rate of victimization for all crimes across gender and race. The age

> Crime data are only a snapshot of the past.

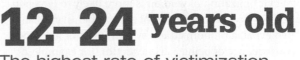
12–24 years old
The highest rate of victimization.

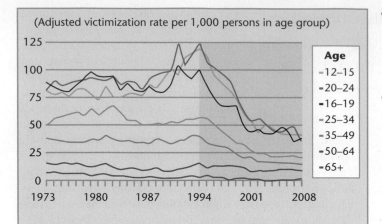

(Adjusted victimization rate per 1,000 persons in age group)

Age
- 12–15
- 20–24
- 16–19
- 25–34
- 35–49
- 50–64
- 65+

FIGURE 3–4 **Violent Crime Rates by Age of Victim, 1973–2008**
Victimization is not randomly distributed. One factor that influences the rate of victimization is the age of the victim. While the rates of victimization have changed over the years, certain relationships continue to be evident. The relationship between age of the victim and rate of victimization is one of these factors. Whether crime victimization goes up or down, the relationship between rate of victimization and age of the victim has remained constant over the past three decades. *Source:* http://bjs.ojp.usdoj.gov.

group reporting the most victimizations is 18- to 20-year-olds with a victimization rate of 33.9 per 1,000. In contract, those 65 years or older are victimized at a rate of 2.4 per 1,000.

- In 2010, for the first time since the National Crime Victimization Service began reporting differences in victimizations by sex, males and females had statistically similar rates of violent victimization. Historically, men were victimized at higher rates compared to women for every offense except sexual assault or rape and simple assault. In 2010, the rate was 15.7 per 1,000 for males and 14.2 for females. This rate reflects a trend in the convergence of male and female victimization.

- More than half of all victims of violence reported that their attacker was a nonstranger (for example, a friend or an acquaintance). However, the rate differs for males and females. Females are victimized by someone they know more than men are. Females report that in 64% of violent victimization, the offender was a friend or an acquaintance. Only 40% of men reported knowing the offender. Women are more likely to be violently victimized by family members, spouses, boyfriends, or other people they know. This relational phenomenon is known as intimate victimization. The criminal justice system has recognized this factual difference in victimization rates and has created laws, courts, and punishments to address intimate victimization. Many states have recognized the difficulties of prosecuting offenders and protecting repeat victims in intimate victimization, or, as it is commonly called, "domestic violence," and have crafted laws that allow the prosecution of offenders even when the victim does not cooperate with the prosecuting officials.

- Violent victimization of women is more likely to be repetitive and to occur over a period of time rather than as an isolated event, a random attack by a stranger, or a secondary consequence of being a crime victim (for example, a robbery victim who is assaulted by the assailant).

- Even when women are the offenders and not the victims, the data suggest that more than half of incidences in which women were arrested for killing a male intimate partner were precipitated by some sort of physical attack by their victim or claims of self-defense.[18]

- Often victimization is not reported to the police. About 80% of thefts of less than $50 were reported to the police. About 51% of violent crimes were not reported to the police. Over 58% of rapes and sexual assaults are not reported to the police by the victims. For certain victims, the rate of nonreporting can be very high. One population with a very high rate of nonreporting of sexual assaults is college females. For example, one study of 4,446 college women indicated that 95% of the women who were raped did not report it to the police and 100% of attempts of sexual coercion were not reported to the police.[19]

- The rates of victimization differ substantially by race. Compared to whites, nonwhites are victimized at rates two to three times higher. The violent victimization rate for whites is 13.6 per 1,000. The greatest rate of violent victimization (52.6 per 1,000) is among people reporting that they are two or more races. They are followed by American Indian or Alaskan natives with a victimization rate of 42.2 per 1,000. The violent victimization rate for African-Americans is 20.8 per 1,000 and 15.6 per 1,000 for Hispanics.

- One may suspect that the wealthy would suffer property crime victimization at greater rates than the poor as it seems logical that the wealthy would have more to steal. However, this is not true. Households in which property crime victimization is greatest have the least income. The overall rate for property crime victimizations per 1,000 households is 120.2. However, the rate for household incomes less than $14,999 is 170.4 and 168.7 for household incomes less than $7,500. The household crime victimization for household incomes of $75,000 or more is 119.3 per 1,000, or just slightly less than the overall average. It appears the greater the household income, the less likely the chance of property crime victimization. This pattern of greater property crime victimization among "poor neighborhoods" is one of the factors that spawned many of the theories of crime causation hypothesizing that the poor were a "criminal class" of people.

Situational Characteristics of Victimization

Just as victimization is not randomly distributed among types of people, neither is it randomly distributed in time or place. Because U.S. society is highly segregated based on people's personal characteristics, especially race and income, it is not all that surprising to find that spatial patterns of victimization are highly correlated with the demographic distribution of people. Victimization is more likely to occur in places where there is a high density of high-risk social groups. The Chicago School of

51% The percentage of violent crimes that are not reported to the police.

Criminology was one of the first to hypothesize a connection between the characteristics of the city and the crime rate.

In 2010, large urban centers reported significantly higher rates of victimization than nonmetropolitan counties. For example, the murder and nonnegligent manslaughter victimization rate was 5.0 per 100,000 for Metropolitan Statistical Areas, 3.6 per 1,000 for cities outside metropolitan areas, and 3.2 for nonmetropolitan counties. While the victimization rate is lower for all crimes in nonmetropolitan counties than in metropolitan areas, the victimization rate for some crimes is greater in cities outside the metropolitan areas and in Metropolitan Statistical Areas. For example, the rate for forcible rape is 27 per 1,000 in urban areas and 41.6 per 1,000 in cities outside metropolitan areas. Likewise, rates in cities outside Metropolitan Statistical Areas are higher for aggravated assault, burglary, and, larceny-theft.

Data indicate that the victimization rates for some crimes in rural areas and the suburbs are rising. This rising victimization rate is explained by dislocation. **Dislocation** says that as law enforcement practices and programs in larger cities make it more difficult for criminals to prey on victims, the offenders relocate to the suburbs or rural areas with fewer criminal justice resources. As a result, some small cities are now experiencing a rise in crime rates, especially violent crimes, biker gang crimes, and drug crimes.

Theoretical Explanations for Victimization

National data support the observation that crime victimization is not random. If this is the case, what factors influence who is victimized and when the victimization occurs? Scholars in the field generate both descriptive data of victimization and theories to explain this phenomenon. Just as criminologists use crime data to construct theories to explain why some people commit crimes and others do not, scholars who study victimization construct theories to explain why some people are victims and others are not.

The two most prominent explanations as to the cause of victimization are victim-precipitation theories and lifestyle theories of victimization.

Victim-Precipitation Theories

Victim-precipitation theories are based on the concept that victims themselves precipitate, contribute to, provoke, or actually cause the outcome of their victimization. These theories assume that some crimes, especially violent crimes, are interactions or transactions between victims and offenders. In this interaction, the victim often influences his or her own criminal victimization.

Victim precipitation means that the victim is not simply an object acted upon by a criminal or is selected at random. Victim precipitation is said to have three facets:

1. Victim contribution refers to a person's action or lack of action that makes his or her victimization more likely. For example, a person who goes "clubbing" and takes along a large amount of cash contributes to his or her victimization.

2. Victim proneness implies that some individuals or groups have a quality that makes them more likely to become victims of crimes. This can also refer to the fact that some

Victim-precipitation theories are based on the concept that victims themselves precipitate, contribute to, provoke, or actually cause the outcome of their victimization.

victims are "easy targets." For instance, illegal immigrants may be targeted for victimization because they cannot report victimization to the police for fear of being deported.

3. Victim provocation suggests that the victim is the primary cause of his or her victimization. Marvin Wolfgang's 1958 study of Philadelphia homicides, taken from police records for the years 1948 to 1952, brought the concept of victim provocation into the mainstream of criminological thought. Wolfgang found that in a significant proportion of criminal homicide incidents (26%), the victim had initiated the confrontation, either through verbal provocation or physical force.

Victim-precipitation theories focus on explaining violent victimization and assume an intentional interaction between offender and victim. Thus, victim-precipitation theories have limited explanation value and can be applied only to certain types of violent crime. Another critique of victim-precipitation theories is that they may be interpreted as placing the blame for the crime on the victim, not the criminal ("blaming the victim"). This critique is a concern in examining rape and sexual assaults. The theories may imply that the female victim was, to a degree, responsible for her victimization. At times, this defense is used in court when the perpetrator of the sexual assault claims that the woman's actions, the woman's dress, or other factors invited sexual intercourse.

LEARNING OUTCOMES 4 Summarize the theories of victimization.

GLOSSARY

victimology The study of victims and the patterns of how they are victimized.

dislocation Crackdowns on crime by police in larger cities that cause offenders to relocate to the suburbs or rural areas that have fewer law enforcement resources.

victim-precipitation theories Theories based on the concept that victims themselves precipitate, contribute to, provoke, or actually cause the outcome of their victimization.

Lifestyle Theories of Victimization

Lifestyle theories of victimization explain personal victimization as an outgrowth of a victim's high-risk behavior patterns and associations. These theories explain why victimization can differ in quantity but remain the same in quality. That is to say, why are the same subgroups victimized from city to city? In 1978, Michael Hindelang, Michael Gottfredson, and James Garofalo formulated a theory of personal victimization based on extensive analysis of data taken from surveys in eight cities in 1972. In examining the data, researchers found that although rates of victimization fluctuated from city to city, individual and situational factors within each locale remained much the same. For example, in all eight cities, youths were at a much greater risk of victimization than older people were and men had substantially higher rates of victimization compared to women. (Note: The gap between male and female victimization has converged since the 1972 study, and in 2010, males and females were victimized at about the same rate.)

Hindelang, Gottfredson, and Garofalo focused their attention on the situational factors surrounding victimizations and the characteristics of the people involved, both offenders and victims. They determined that for a personal victimization to occur, the following conditions must be met:

- The prime actors must have occasion to intersect in time and space.
- Some source of dispute or claim must arise between the actors in which the victim is perceived by the offender as an appropriate object of the victimization.
- The offender must be willing and able to threaten or use force (or stealth) to achieve the desired end.

The researchers believed that these factors were based largely on the victim's lifestyle. According to Hindelang, Gottfredson, and Garofalo, lifestyle "refers to the routine daily activities, both vocational activities (work, school, keeping house, etc.) and leisure activities."

According to this theory, lifestyle stands as the centerpiece of the theory of personal victimization because according to this theory, it is the patterned routines of a person's everyday activities that predict the chances of exposure to high-risk situations that can result in victimization. For example, an individual's socioeconomic status places constraints on his or her place of residence, access to postsecondary education, access to jobs, mode of transportation used, and other factors. According to this theory, a woman living in public housing and using public transportation to return home from work at night would be more likely to be victimized than a woman living

Lifestyle theories explain personal victimization as an outgrowth of a victim's high-risk behavior patterns and associations.

Lifestyle also indirectly affects a person's risk of victimization through the people with whom he or she associates regularly.

in an upper-class neighborhood who uses her automobile to return home from work in the afternoon. A woman who does not work outside the house and remains at home in her upper-class neighborhood is least likely to be victimized.

Differential Association

In addition to influencing personal victimization directly though exposure to various situational environments, lifestyle also indirectly affects a person's risk of victimization through the people with whom he or she associates regularly. **Differential association** refers to the concept that people who associate regularly with others engaged in unlawful behavior are more likely to be victimized because of their increased exposure to high-risk situations and environments.

According to this premise, perpetrators and victims share similar demographic characteristics. For example, people under the age of 24 are more likely to be victimized and are more likely to be the perpetrators of crime. Hindelang, Gottfredson, and Garofalo attributed this fact to eight propositions that explained the differential association between perpetrators and victims. (The pattern of differential association does not exist for the crime of rape and sexual assaults. Overwhelmingly, men are the perpetrators of sex crimes and women are the victims.).

Routine Activities Theory

Another theory of victimization focuses on the contexts of crime in terms of the opportunities for victimization. In 1979, Lawrence Cohen and Marcus Felson developed an approach for analyzing changes in the level of crime over time, known as the routine activities theory.[20] Like lifestyle theories, routine activities theory recognizes the importance of people's everyday actions in an explanation for criminal victimization. Routine activities theory is an analysis of changes in levels of crime over time that recognizes people's everyday actions as components of victimization.

Routine activities theory assumes that all humans are motivated by the desire to have things that give them pleasure or benefit them and to avoid those things and situations that inflict pain. Most important to the explanation for criminal victimization, according to Cohen and Felson, are the differential opportunities that exist for victimization. Differential opportunities are determined by the structure of our everyday lives: the time we leave home, the route we take to work, our mode of transportation, our favorite places for entertainment, and other routines of contemporary existence. Routine activities theory focuses on the circumstances in which crime occurs.

The routine activities approach to crime is limited to an explanation for predatory crime. Cohen and Felson define **predatory crime** as acts "involving direct physical contact between at least one offender and at least one person or object

Various victimization theories emphasize the role of environment as a factor affecting rates of victimization. In neighborhoods with capable guardians and in which high-risk environments such as bars, strip clubs, and other forms of adult entertainment are minimized or eliminated, it is hypothesized that victimization rates will be low. While victimization rates may be low in these environments, they are not eliminated. In the late 1990s, Walt Disney Company built a community called Celebration, Florida. The subdivision mirrored the Disney World theme of harmony; a pleasant environment; and, of course, no crime. However, in late 2010, within a week of each other, Celebration had a murder and a barricaded-subject situation ending in the self-inflicted death of the barricaded subject. What impact does the environment have on rates and types of victimization?

Jeff Greenberg / Alamy

which that offender attempts to take or damage."[21] Because Cohen and Felson include objects as well as people in their definition of predatory crime, their theory is not limited to interpersonal offenses such as assault, robbery, and rape. Property offenses such as burglary and larceny are considered predatory crimes as well.

Predatory victimization depends on the interaction of the following three variables in a social situation. (See Figure 3–5).

1. The presence of at least one likely offender

2. The presence of at least one suitable target

3. The absence of capable guardians (who might prevent the crime)

Unlike other explanations for criminal victimization, routine activities theory is unconcerned with the role the victim plays. In strong contrast to victim-precipitation theories, routine activities theory treats the offender as active and the victim as passive. Offenders are seen as making calculated decisions—"rational choices" to commit crime based on their perceptions of target suitability and likelihood of detection and sanction by others. Routine activities explanations for criminal victimization call attention to issues of social change that have affected guardianship, such as large-scale changes in people's routine work and leisure activities that have, in turn, affected safety and security. For example, the trend toward both parents working and houses being vacant for extended periods of time increases the likelihood of daytime residential burglary.

Rational Choice Theory of Victimization

The key assumption of routine activities theory is the idea that crime is motivated through rational choice. Rational choice theory is based on the fundamental belief that human behavior is directed toward those things that bring pleasure or benefit or that minimize painful, unpleasant experiences.

If rational choice theorists are correct, altering the balance of costs and benefits for likely offenders can reduce victimization. One way to do this is through target hardening. Target hardening is the foundation for many popular crime-reduction programs. Crime-prevention programs such as Neighborhood Watch programs, programs to increase lighting in streets and neighborhoods, and surveillance cameras are based on the assumption that these changes will cause a potential criminal to reevaluate the risk of committing a crime in these target-hardened environments. Another example of target hardening is vehicles that have integrated ignition–steering wheel locking systems, antitheft alarms, built-in global tracking devices, and satellite-activated ignition cut-off systems. These systems deter auto theft as they decrease the likelihood of the occurrence of a successful crime.

Target hardening is one of the key components of defense against terrorist attacks in the United States. Particularly attractive targets of terrorism—such as commercial aviation, nuclear reactors, federal buildings, infrastructure (for example, bridges and tunnels), and symbolic targets (for example, famous monuments and symbols of government and business)—have been examined for their vulnerability, and additional security measures have been taken to make it more difficult for someone to attack these targets.

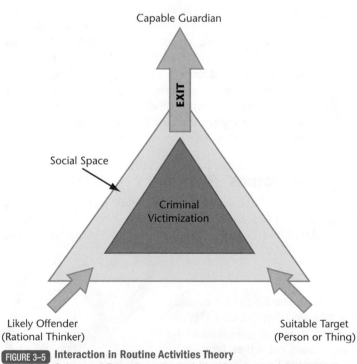

FIGURE 3–5 **Interaction in Routine Activities Theory**
Cohen and Felson's routine activities theory emphasizes that crime does not occur in a vacuum. In other words, crime requires the interaction of an offender and a victim at a particular time and place. Thus, the lifestyle choices of a victim play an important role in whether a crime occurs. Also, the presence of a capable guardian may prevent a crime from occurring. In modern society, many believe that video surveillance cameras act as a "guardian" to deter crime. As a result, video surveillance of entire metropolitan areas is common.

▶ The Victims' Rights Movement

Victimization results in financial, physical, and psychological harm to the victim. The financial costs are easiest to calculate, and often the victim will suffer longtime physical and psychological harm. Insurance may replace the property lost or destroyed in a burglary, but the feeling of vulnerability and fear may last a lifetime. Sexual assault victims may suffer the pain of the attack, the risk of sexually transmitted diseases, unwanted pregnancy, a feeling of social shame, and the dissolution of their marriage. It is impossible to calculate the costs of these harms. Victims of violent assault may suffer lifelong injuries or incapacitation due to injuries suffered in their attack. Many victims suffer post-traumatic stress disorder (PTSD), which manifests itself in numerous psychological symptoms. Families who have lost loved ones due to victimization may suffer a lifetime of grief, anger, and PTSD. (An interesting example of this is the premise that the fictional character of Batman was motivated by his desire to fight crime due to the fact that he witnessed the deaths of his father and mother during a robbery—even the entertainment media embrace the impact of victimization.)

Effects of criminal victimization often include additional suffering at the hands of unsupportive friends and family, the news media, and the criminal justice system. **Secondary victimization** refers to the victimization caused not by the criminal act, but by the inappropriate response of institutions and individuals. Victims of sexual assault may be shunned by their spouse, family, and friends and made to feel guilty and to blame themselves for the assault. Parents of missing children may be overwhelmed by demands of the news media. Even the criminal justice system can harm victims.

The **victims' rights movement** grew out of the dissatisfaction of victims with the passive role, neglect, and minimization of harm they suffered. Victims wanted the criminal justice system to provide them with certain rights, they wanted to be treated with respect and to have access to services, and they wanted the criminal justice system to acknowledge the harm they suffered as a result of victimization.

Several events were important to the emergence of the victims' rights movement. First, the 1960s brought general concern about individual rights in many arenas, including civil rights, women's rights, inmates' rights, gay rights, and students' rights. The women's rights movement was a particularly strong supporter of victims' rights because its agenda included addressing the harm caused by the way in which the criminal justice system

processed rape and domestic violence cases. Second, several government initiatives increased awareness and provided financial support for victims' assistance programs. Results from national surveys helped raise awareness of the harm caused by crime and documented the large number of victims who did not report their victimization to the police. The Law Enforcement Assistance Administration (LEAA) provided funds to assist in the professionalization of law enforcement. The LEAA also provided funds for the support of innovative programs to reduce crime and for research to evaluate the impact of these programs. Third, the number of victims' rights organizations increased dramatically, and national coordinating bodies such as the **National Organization for Victim Assistance (NOVA)** were founded. Basically, the victims' rights movement emerged from public concern about civil rights, women's rights, gay rights, students' rights, and inmates' rights and from government initiatives for increased victim awareness and financial compensation.

The accomplishments of NOVA, founded in 1976, include helping to pass the 1984 Victims of Crime Act and the 1982 Victim and Witness Protection Act, both of which provide counseling, information, referrals, and direct assistance to crime victims, as well as support and training to victim advocates. President Ronald Reagan adopted victims' rights as one of his priority domestic policy issues. In 1982, he convened the **President's Task Force on Victims of Crime**. This task force made more than 60 recommendations for new legislation to be enacted to protect the rights and interests of crime victims in the criminal justice system.

The victims' rights movement has had tremendous success. Almost all the legislative initiatives proposed by the 1982 President's Task Force have been enacted. All 50 states have passed a crime victims' bill of rights, attempting to ensure that victims are treated with dignity and compassion, are informed about the decisions made regarding their cases, and are able to participate in this decision making. Some 29 states have amended their constitutions to focus on the rights of crime victims. Several federal laws have also been passed. In 1982, the federal Victim and Witness Protection Act established policies and procedures regarding how federal officials should treat crime victims and served as a national model for state legislation.

Crime Victims' Rights Act of 2004

The 2004 federal crime victims' rights legislation was the outgrowth of an eight-year campaign led by Senators Jon Kyl (R–Ariz.) and Dianne Feinstein (D–Calif.) to provide strong

Think About It . . .

The U.S. Constitution does not provide any constitutional rights to victims. Victims' rights are defined by federal and state legislation and state constitutions. However, victims often find that when they are denied their rights, unlike accused offenders who are denied their rights, there is no accountability. The criminal justice system is weighted toward ensuring the rights of the accused, not victims. Often the rights of crime victims are unenforceable. For example, the Illinois constitution lists ten rights of crime victims. However, none of these rights can be enforced if denied or violated. Victims cannot sue the state or hold government officials accountable for failure to provide the rights outlined in the state's constitution or receive compensation if the government fails to provide them with their rights. Victims' rights activists have proposed amending the state's constitution or passing new legislation allowing victims to sue the government if rights are denied. Should victims have the right to hold the government accountable if they are denied their rights? Why or why not?

VICTIMS' RIGHTS

From 1929 to 1974, North Carolina ran an aggressive eugenics program that sterilized over 7,500 people. The program disproportionately sterilized minorities, the poor, and uneducated and mentally handicapped persons, as the purpose of the program was to reduce welfare costs and cleanse the gene pool of undesirable characteristics. In 2012, the state decided that the program violated basic human rights and that each living person sterilized in the program should receive $50,000 as compensation from the state. Nearly three dozen other states had similar eugenics programs. Is $50,000 adequate compensation? Should the compensation be limited only to living survivors? Should federal legislation provide compensation rights to all victims of state eugenics programs? Explain.

assurances to crime victims that their rights would be recognized by the criminal justice system. The federal legislation was passed by Congress in early October 2004 and signed into law by President Bush on October 30, 2004.

The new law, known as the **Crime Victims' Rights Act**, is the most successful effort of the crime victims' rights movement to date. The law amends Title 18 (Part II, Chapter 25/Section 3771) of the Federal Criminal Code. Federal law now guarantees crime victims the following rights: to be reasonably protected, notified, present, and heard at various stages in the criminal justice system; to confer with the prosecutor; to receive restitution; to expect proceedings free from unreasonable delay; and to be treated with fairness and respect.

To a large extent, the success of the Crime Victims' Rights Act of 2004 was responsible for the failure of the Victims' Rights Amendment movement. A Victims' Rights Amendment was proposed for the U.S. Constitution. However, the success of federal legislation and the adoption of victims' rights legislation by the states convinced many that a constitutional amendment was not necessary, and the Victims' Rights Amendment movement died.

Civil Remedies for Victims

Because compensation and restitution have limitations, crime victims are increasingly relying on civil litigation as another way to help them recover from the harm caused by crime. Victims have used civil remedies—civil court processes to recover from the psychological, financial, emotional, and physical harm of crime. Civil suits are particularly empowering because crime victims are directly involved. A victim decides to pursue a civil action against the offender, a third party, or both; works directly with his or her attorney to prove liability; and chooses to accept or reject a settlement offer. The goal of such civil suits is to help victims work through the trauma caused by crimes, recover expenses from crimes, and restore confidence in their ability to control their own destinies.

A good example of a civil remedy for damages is the O. J. Simpson case. Simpson was acquitted at his criminal trial in 1995 for the murders of Nicole Brown and Ronald Goldman. However, the victims' families brought a civil action against Simpson, and he was found liable for damages. The families were awarded a $33.5 million civil judgment.

Crime victims can also bring suits against third parties for contributing to their victimization. Universities, hotels, restaurants, shopping malls, and office buildings can be sued for their inability to protect victims because of negligence or security failures. These lawsuits encourage businesses and other organizations to enhance their safety and security measures and encourage others to invest in preventive actions to avoid being sued. For example, in 2012, a jury found Virginia Tech negligent for waiting to warn students about a gunman during an April 6, 2007, campus massacre that left 33 dead. The university had offered the defense that Virginia Tech had done all it could with the information available at the time to protect students. The jury disagreed and awarded $4 million to each of the two families who filed the lawsuit. The parents' attorney said that they achieved their purpose of getting at the truth about the actions of the university officials.

Despite the advantages of civil remedies, there are some disadvantages. In a civil lawsuit, the financial burden falls on the victim. The victim is responsible for obtaining and paying an attorney and all investigation costs in pursuing the civil case. Some attorneys might agree to take civil cases based on **contingency**. Contingency means that an attorney agrees to forgo payment in return for a percentage of the potential settlement. Finally, there is no guarantee of success in bringing a lawsuit against another party. The victim may lose the suit and receive no monetary compensation or remedy. Furthermore, the lawsuit may expose the victim to a countersuit in which the victim is sued.

The Killing of Trayvon Martin: Hate Crime or Self-Defense?

Why was 17-year-old Trayvon Martin killed by George Zimmerman while Zimmerman was on neighborhood watch patrol in Sanford, Florida? Was Martin killed because of racial hatred? Representative Hank Johnson (D–Ga.) issued a statement that Martin was killed because he was WWB in a GC—"walking while black in a gated community" and called for a Justice Department investigation. MSNBC commentator and activist Al Sharpton called it a "hate crime."

The case has created a national sensation. There are claims that the Sanford Police Department conducted a flawed investigation because of racial discrimination. The Sanford police chief stepped down, and the state of Florida and the U.S. Justice Department appointed special investigation teams to examine the shooting and the police investigation. The case is confusing because there are a number of unanswered questions, accusations of statements that do not appear to be backed up by observations and witnesses, and heated emotions as to whether the killing was a hate crime or self-defense.

Craig Ruttle / Alamy

One of the questions to emerge from the heated discussion is whether Martin's actions or behavior contributed to his death. Victim-precipitation theories claim that crime victims contribute to their victimization by their interactions and behavior. According to one account of the killing, Martin walked up to Zimmerman's vehicle and asked why Zimmerman was following him. Zimmerman denied following him. When Zimmerman got out of his vehicle, Martin said, "What's your problem, homie?" and then struck Zimmerman from behind. If this accurately describes the encounter, it would appear that Martin's words and actions contributed to his death. Lifestyle theories of victimization explain victimization as an outgrowth of a victim's high-risk behavior patterns. In this case, some may claim that Martin's dress, a hoodie, contributed to his victimization as the hoodie is commonly worn by gang members. Geraldo Rivera said it was the hoodie that Martin wore that contributed to his death. Representative Bobby Rush (D–Ill.) was critical of such claims, and to protest them, he wore a hoodie on the floor of the House of Representatives. Others agreed with Rush and organized protests wherein the participants wore hoodies.

Did Florida's "stand your ground" law, which allows private citizens to carry concealed firearms and use deadly force to defend themselves against attack, even against people who are unarmed, contribute to Martin's death? Critics of Martin's death claim that in most other states, Zimmerman would not have been legally justified in the use of deadly force against an unarmed juvenile assailant.

One of the criticisms of victimization theories is that they appear to "blame" the victim. That is to say, these theories would argue that Martin in some way contributed to his victimization, whether it was wearing a hoodie or walking after dark in a gated community. Many people are critical of this focus on the victim and recall similar claims leveled against female victims of sexual assault.

This case raises several interesting questions. Among them are the following:

1. Do you believe victims are in some way responsible for their victimization? Do they contribute to their victimization by their actions and words? Explain.

2. Each state has its own laws regarding carrying concealed weapons and using deadly force in self-defense, and these laws differ significantly. Some state laws are based on the assumption that the presence of a firearm contributes to victimization and do not allow citizens to carry concealed weapons. Opponents of this belief claim victimization may be deterred merely by the presence of a firearm. What is your opinion?

3. The Martin case has been called a hate crime. Hate crimes are characterized by the motives of the perpetrator, not the criminal actions committed. What are some difficulties in determining whether George Zimmerman's actions were motivated by racial hatred?

4. Did the hoodie that Martin wore contribute to his victimization? Why or why not?

Summarize the various methods for measuring crime and the problems related to measuring crime.

The demand for more accurate crime data began with the FBI's Uniform Crime Reports (UCRs) in 1930. The UCR data is gathered in two categories, known as Part I and Part II offenses. The National Crime Victimization Survey (NCVS) is another major method for gathering statistics about crime. This methodology has uncovered the fact that many crimes go unreported to the police. Because of several shortcomings with both the UCR and NCVS data collection methodology, the implementation of the National Incident-Based Reporting System now seeks to broaden the information gathered about crime and its victims.

1. Explain why the Uniform Crime Reports were developed.

2. Describe a shortcoming of how crime is measured.

3. What are dark figure of crime statistics?

4. Why is the NIBRS being implemented?

Prohibition Amendment The Eighteenth Amendment passed in 1919 that prohibited the manufacture, sale, and possession of alcoholic beverages.

Volstead Act Another name for the Prohibition Amendment.

International Association of Police The world's oldest and largest non-profit membership organization of police executives.

Uniform Crime Report (UCR) A database of information about reported crimes collected by the Federal Bureau of Investigation over time.

Part I offenses A Uniform Crime Report category group used to report murder, forcible rape, robbery, aggravated assault, burglary, larceny-theft, motor vehicle theft, and arson.

Violent Crime Index The rate of crimes reported in the Part I offenses.

Part II offenses A Uniform Crime Report category group used to report less serious offenses involving an arrest.

hierarchy rule An old police method of counting only the most serious crime in a single incident involving multiple crimes.

clearance rate The percentage of crimes that are solved versus crimes that are unsolved.

crime clock A method used by the Federal Bureau of Investigation to report how often crimes occur.

National Crime Victimization Survey (NCVS) A survey of a representative sample of U.S. households that gathers detailed information about crimes from victims.

dark figure of crime statistics Crimes that are not reported and thus are unknown to police.

National Incident-Based Reporting System (NIBRS) An incident-based reporting system in which more comprehensive crime information is gathered.

Summarize the various methods for gathering criminal justice data.

A number of federal agencies provide broad sources of data pertaining to criminal justice. Some of these sources include the National Criminal Justice Reference Service (NCJRS), the *Sourcebook of Criminal Justice Statistics*, and the Bureau of Justice Statistics (BJS). State-sponsored research includes surveys of crime similar to those of the UCR, which are conducted by the individual states. Using self-reports, scholars, private research institutions, and government agencies conduct numerous surveys of perpetrators and offenders.

1. Name three federal bodies that gather research pertaining specifically to criminal justice.

2. Why must college campuses report crime that occurs on their campuses?

3. How are incidences of violence in elementary and secondary schools gathered?

4. What is a self-report survey? What does it tell us about the actual crime picture?

National Criminal Justice Reference Service (NCJRS) A federally funded resource offering justice and drug-related information to support research, policy, and other programs.

Sourcebook of Criminal Justice Statistics A publication funded by the U.S. Department of Justice, a research body that brings together data from more than 200 sources about many aspects of criminal justice in the United States.

Bureau of Justice Statistics (BJS) A primary source for criminal justice statistics that compiles reports on many aspects of the criminal justice system, including data about federal, state, and local criminal justice.

Crime Awareness and Campus Security Act of 1992 A law requiring college campuses to make a public disclosure of crimes occurring on their campuses.

Safe and Drug-Free Schools and Communities Act of 1996 A law requiring the collection of data, frequency, seriousness, and incidences of violence in elementary and secondary schools.

LEARNING OUTCOMES 3

Explain the relationship between crime and social reaction to crime.

Measures of crime data do not accurately mirror the public's fear of victimization. Although rising crime rates might cause the public to be more fearful of crime, a decrease in crime rates does not necessarily result in less fear of victimization. Crime statistics show what crimes have occurred, not what crimes will occur in the future. Crime trends may require some time before they can be established with any certainty regarding an increase or decrease in a specific offense.

1. Does crime data correlate with the public's fear of crime? Explain.

2. Why don't crime statistics predict future crime trends?

victimization The process of being victimized or becoming a victim of crime.

crime statistics The gathering, analysis, and interpretation of crime data.

LEARNING OUTCOMES 4

Summarize the theories of victimization.

Consideration for victims is an important aspect of understanding the criminal justice system. Patterns of victimization vary based on economic and social characteristics of the victim. Victimization is also more likely to occur in areas with a high density of high-risk groups. Some theories look at the role victims play in precipitating their own victimization, while other theories view the environment as a factor affecting the rate of victimization.

1. Why should research be dedicated toward the victim?

2. Describe some of the variables that show that victimization is not randomly distributed.

3. How does rate of victimization vary by category of race?

4. Explain how a victim can precipitate his or her victimization.

5. Give an example of how lifestyle plays a role in a person being a victim of crime.

victimology The study of victims and the patterns of how they are victimized.

dislocation Crackdowns on crime by police in larger cities that cause offenders to relocate to the suburbs or rural areas that have fewer law enforcement resources.

victim-precipitation theories Theories based on the concept that victims themselves precipitate, contribute to, provoke, or actually cause the outcome of their victimization.

lifestyle theories of victimization A concept that personal victimization is an outgrowth of a victim's high-risk behavior patterns and associations.

differential association A concept that people who associate regularly with others who engage in unlawful behavior are more likely to be victimized because of their increased exposure to high-risk situations.

routine activities theory A theory that assumes that all humans are motivated by the desire to have things that give them pleasure or benefit them and to avoid those things and situations that inflict pain.

predatory crime Acts involving direct physical contact between at least one offender and at least one person or object which that offender attempts to take or damage.

LEARNING OUTCOMES 5

Summarize the victims' rights movement.

Victimization results in financial, physical, and psychological harm to the victims. The effects of criminal victimization may include additional suffering at the hands of friends, family, news media, and the criminal justice system. As a result of the harm incurred by victims, a contemporary movement has grown focusing more on victims' rights. The federal and state governments have passed new laws aimed at broadening victims' rights for protection and restitution.

1. What drove the victims' rights movement?

2. Describe the effects crime victimization may have on an individual.

3. How have victims' rights been expanded?

4. Describe federal legislation that has been passed with regard to victims' rights.

secondary victimization The victimization caused not by the criminal act, but through the inappropriate response of institutions and individuals.

victims' rights movement The dissatisfaction of victims with the neglect and minimization of harm they suffered, leading to a victims' movement for the criminal justice system to provide them with specific rights.

National Organization for Victim Assistance (NOVA) An organization that helped pass the 1984 Victims of Crime Act and the 1982 Victim and Witness Protection Act, both of which provide counseling, information, and assistance to crime victims.

President's Task Force on Victims of Crime A task force that makes recommendations for new legislation to be enacted to protect the rights and interests of crime victims in the criminal justice system.

Crime Victims' Rights Act A law enacted in 2004 that guarantees crime victims a number of rights, including the right to protection and restitution.

contingency A situation in a civil case when an attorney agrees to forgo payment in return for a percentage of the potential settlement.

MyCJLab

Go to Chapter 3 in *MyCJLab* to test your mastery of chapter concepts, access your Study Plan, engage in interactive exercises, complete critical-thinking and research assignments, and view related online videos.

 Review: Complete the pretest in the Study Plan to confirm what you know and what you need to study further. Then complete the post-test to confirm your mastery of the concepts. Use the key term flash cards to review key terminology.

 Apply: Complete the interactive simulation activity.

Analyze: Complete assignments as directed by your instructor.

Current Events: Explore CJSearch for current topical videos, articles, and news pieces.

Additional Links

Go to **http://www.fbi.gov/stats-services/victim_assistance/victim_rights** and read the eight rights that are included in Section 3771 of Title 18 of the U.S. Code pertaining to victims of federal crimes.

Go to **http://www.trynova.org/crime-victim/specializations** and learn more about the National Organization for Victim Assistance (NOVA).

Go to **http://bjs.ojp.usdoj.gov/index.cfm?ty=pbdetail&iid=2224** to read the 2010 data regarding 2010 estimates of rates and levels of criminal victimization in the United States.

See **http://www.fbi.gov/ucr/ucr.htm** to view the FBI's Uniform Crime Reports.

See **http://www.ojp.usdoj.gov** to view the BJS's *Report on Crime* and victims statistics.

Criminal Law—
Crimes and the Limits of Law

"Good people do not need laws to tell them to act responsibly, while bad people will find a way around the laws."

—Plato

1 Describe how federal, state, and local criminal laws are created and changed.

2 Describe the limits of law.

3 List the elements of a crime and their role in criminal prosecution.

4 List and describe some of the major defenses against charges of criminal conduct.

5 Explain how crimes are classified and defined according to the Model Penal Code.

4

IT'S AGAINST THE LAW

The making of laws by various governmental agencies is complex because of the diverse values within the various local, state, and federal communities of citizens. Also, some laws were enacted a long time ago and reflect historical values no longer compatible with contemporary values. In fact, some of these laws cannot be enforced because they are unconstitutional. Even though the laws are unconstitutional, some governments retain them on the books. Such laws, which are often based on religious or moral values of past times, are called Blue Laws. Blue Laws frequently prohibit selling goods on Sunday, especially alcoholic beverages, or prohibit or regulate moral behavior, especially sexual behaviors. Various reasons are given for retaining the laws, but most are based on the notion that the laws reflect community values even if these values are unenforceable and conflict with contemporary community values.

One example of a state retaining an outdated law is Kansas. In 2012, Kansas created the Office of the Repealer to recommend the elimination of out-of-date, unreasonable, and burdensome state laws that accumulate over time. In 2012, the office issued a list of 51 laws to recommend to the legislature for repeal. However, Kansas Statute 21-3505 was not on the list.[1] Kansas Statute 21-3505 is the criminal sodomy statute that prohibits same-sex couples from engaging in oral or anal sex. Sodomy laws were declared unconstitutional by the U.S. Supreme Court in *Lawrence* v. *Texas*

dendron/Fotolia

(2003), and the law is unenforceable. Despite this fact, the law was not recommended for repeal.

The decision has angered the gay community. Susan Sommer, director of a national gay rights advocacy group, said the law has a stigmatizing effect on same-sex relationships and can sometimes be wrongly cited by law enforcement officers unaware that they are no longer enforceable."[2]

DISCUSS What harm can be inflicted by states retaining unenforceable laws on the books?

▶ The Rule of Law—We the People ...

This chapter examines the role of criminal law in defining the balance between public safety and personal liberties. It reviews the making of laws and the differences between laws of the federal, state, and local government. It discusses the limits of the law, the various criminal defenses, and the elements of some of the most common crimes.

Prior to the founding of the United States, most nations were governed by monarchies, dictatorships, or religious leaders. The concept of a democratic government was an unfamiliar concept to the nations of the eighteenth century. The source of law, often the sole arbitrator of what was right and wrong, was the ruler of the state. The citizens of the state lacked input and authority to determine the laws of their nation. Laws reflected the authority of the sovereign, and often he or she was above the law. For example, in eighteenth-century England, the king or queen was the law and could not be held accountable for any law violation.

After separating from the political rule of England, the newly formed U.S. government rejected a model of government based on either the Church or the king as supreme rulers of the state. The newly formed government was based on the principle that the United States is founded on the superiority of the rule of law. The rule of law declares that the standards of behavior and privilege are established not by kings or religious leaders, but by rules and procedures that define and prohibit certain behaviors as illegal or criminal and prescribe punishments for those behaviors. All people, regardless of rank, title, position, status, or wealth, are accorded the same rights and privileges under the law. Government leaders, even the president of the United States, are subject to the rule of law. No one is above the law.

> Even though they are unconstitutional, some governments retain these laws on the books.

▶ The Making of Law

Laws represent the collective wisdom of the community as how to best promote peaceful and fair interaction among people. Why do governments—local, state, and federal—create criminal laws? The American Law Institute, a private, voluntary association of distinguished judges, lawyers, and law teachers, gives five reasons for the establishment of laws:[3]

1. To forbid and prevent conduct that unjustifiably and inexcusably inflicts or threatens substantial harm to individual or public interests

2. To subject to public control persons whose conduct indicates that they are disposed to commit crimes

3. To safeguard conduct that is without fault from condemnation as criminal

4. To give fair warning of the nature of the conduct declared to constitute an offense

5. To differentiate on reasonable grounds between serious and minor offenses

Specific laws might be passed because they prohibit actions that are thought to be harmful to society. For example, prohibitions against murder, rape, robbery, and arson are seen as serving all people in society. Such acts are prohibited because they are considered harmful in themselves, or *mala in se*. Other laws might be passed because some people believe there is a need to regulate certain actions; thus, for example, there are parking regulations, minimum drinking-age limits, and various licensing regulations. Acts that violate such regulations are *mala prohibita*—prohibited only because of the law and not because they are necessarily harmful or inherently evil.

The distinction between *mala in se* and *mala prohibita* laws is not clear-cut or based on objective criteria. Thus, much debate is generated about what laws should be passed and what purposes the laws actually serve. Some laws are based on the morals and values of a subset of the community. Laws against abortion, obscenity, same-sex marriages, and drug use often are based on moral and ethical beliefs not shared by all members of society. Some laws are passed based on public fear. For example, kidnapping was made a federal crime after the 1932 kidnapping and murder of the son of Charles Lindbergh, an aviator of international fame. Megan's Law, which requires the registration of sexual offenders, was passed after a sexual offender unknown to the community abducted and murdered a young girl.

There is often disagreement as to whether a law is passed to protect people from harm or to regulate behavior. For example, laws regarding drug use and sexual behavior are often based on the values of a subgroup within the community. Those who embrace the values advocated by the subgroup argue that the law protects people from inherently harmful consequences. Those who do not share the subgroup's values argue that the law regulates behavior that is not inherently harmful.

Federal Criminal Laws

Each level of government is responsible for crafting the laws to govern those within its jurisdiction. Federal laws apply to all people within the United States. State laws apply only to crimes committed within the state. The jurisdiction of county and local laws does not extend beyond the county or municipal boundaries. Thus, there are federal laws in addition to the 50 state law codes and the local legal codes for each of the thousands of cities and counties. The legal codes regulating behavior are complex and numerous.

There are five sources for federal criminal laws. Federal criminal laws are expressed in the following:

The U.S. Constitution
U.S. Federal Criminal Codes
Judicial decisions interpreting code
Executive orders
International treaties

The only crimes defined in the U.S. Constitution are treason and sedition. The source for most of the federal criminal laws is the U.S. Federal Criminal Codes. In a process involving Congress and the president of the United States, federal criminal laws can be created. The process is complex and reflects the necessity for compromise among the three parties: the U.S. House of Representatives, the U.S. Senate, and the president.

Federal criminal laws are written by Congress, but the courts play an important role in defining the intent of the law and its application to specific situations. Laws cannot anticipate every situation, and the passage of time may require laws to be interpreted in light of new technology. For example, the U.S. Constitution did not anticipate technologies such as the telephone and the Internet. Thus, judicial decisions often are necessary to decide how the law is to be applied in regard to new technology.

The president of the United States can issue executive orders. **Executive orders** are presidential directives regarding the execution of legislative acts that oversee the behavior of officers and agencies of the executive branch. The power to issue executive orders is not explicitly expressed in the U.S. Constitution, but the courts have held that executive orders have the full force of law. The limits of executive orders are not clearly defined, which results in congressional challenges to executive orders that are considered beyond the proper authority of the president.

Finally, federal laws can be found in international treaties. International treaties can result in agreements between nations that prohibit certain behaviors. These prohibitions have the full force of law. Criminal behaviors commonly defined in international treaties are certain laws regarding drugs; the crossing of international borders for the purpose of certain sexual crimes, such as child pornography and human sex trafficking; and actions related to terrorism, such as the regulation of biochemical substances, nuclear material, and certain explosives and firearms.

LEARNING OUTCOMES 1 Describe how federal, state, and local criminal laws are created and changed.

GLOSSARY

mala in se Acts that are crimes because they are inherently evil or harmful to society.

mala prohibita Acts that are prohibited because they are defined as crimes by law.

executive orders Presidential directives regarding the execution of legislative acts that oversee the behavior of officers and agencies of the executive branch.

common law Unwritten, simply stated laws based on traditions and common understandings in a time when most people were illiterate.

felony Serious criminal conduct punishable by incarceration for more than one year.

misdemeanor Less serious criminal conduct punishable by incarceration for less than a year.

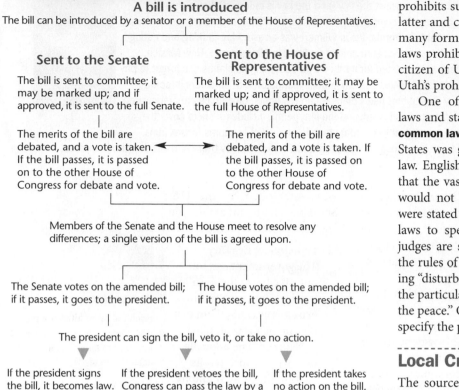

Creating a Federal Criminal Law

A bill is introduced
The bill can be introduced by a senator or a member of the House of Representatives.

Sent to the Senate

The bill is sent to committee; it may be marked up; and if approved, it is sent to the full Senate.

The merits of the bill are debated, and a vote is taken. If the bill passes, it is passed on to the other House of Congress for debate and vote.

Sent to the House of Representatives

The bill is sent to committee; it may be marked up; and if approved, it is sent to the full House of Representatives.

The merits of the bill are debated, and a vote is taken. If the bill passes, it is passed on to the other House of Congress for debate and vote.

Members of the Senate and the House meet to resolve any differences; a single version of the bill is agreed upon.

The Senate votes on the amended bill; if it passes, it goes to the president.

The House votes on the amended bill; if it passes, it goes to the president.

The president can sign the bill, veto it, or take no action.

If the president signs the bill, it becomes law.

If the president vetoes the bill, Congress can pass the law by a two-thirds vote of both Houses.

If the president takes no action on the bill, the bill may die.

State Criminal Laws

The sources of state criminal laws are the state constitution, state criminal codes, common law, judicial decisions interpreting codes and the common law, and executive orders of the state governor. Each state has the right to enact criminal laws deemed appropriate for its citizens by the state legislature with the approval of the governor. This autonomy leads to variety in state laws, but most states have similar criminal laws because (1) all state criminal laws must preserve the rights guaranteed in the U.S. Constitution, (2) many states (approximately 22) have adopted portions of their criminal codes from the Model Penal Code published by the American Law Institute in 1962, (3) state criminal laws had as their common origin early English common law, and (4) laws will serve similar public benefits in each of the states if one accepts the consensus model.

State constitutions cannot negate any right guaranteed in the U.S. Constitution, but a state's constitution can add to rights not covered by the U.S. Constitution. Most state criminal codes are passed by state governments in a manner similar to the federal criminal codes. A bill must originate in one of the state legislative bodies, be passed by both bodies, and then be endorsed by the governor of the state. Like the president, state governors have veto power and the power to create rules and regulations through executive orders.

In their particulars, state criminal codes differ significantly among states. Any person within a state is under the jurisdiction of the laws of that state, regardless of the person's state of residence

> Each state has the right to enact criminal laws deemed appropriate for its citizens.

or citizenship. Thus, a person from a state that permits carrying a concealed weapon who travels to a state that prohibits such behavior must conform to the law of the latter and cannot carry a concealed weapon there. Also, many forms of gambling are legal in Nevada, but Utah laws prohibit nearly all forms of gambling. However, a citizen of Utah who travels to Nevada is not bound by Utah's prohibitions against gambling.

One of the distinctions between federal criminal laws and state criminal laws is the area of law known as **common law**, or unwritten law. Criminal law in the United States was greatly influenced by early English common law. English criminal law was based on the assumption that the vast majority of citizens were illiterate and thus would not understand written law. Thus, written laws were stated simply, leaving judges to interpret and apply laws to specific situations. Federal courts and federal judges are specifically prohibited from operating under the rules of common law. For example, state laws regarding "disturbing the peace" may be vague and not describe the particular actions a person must engage in to "disturb the peace." On the other hand, federal criminal laws must specify the particular actions necessary for conviction.

Local Criminal Laws

The sources of local criminal laws are city or county charters, municipal or county ordinances or violations, common law, decisions of municipal judges interpreting codes and common law, and executive orders of city or county chief executive officers such as the mayor. Nearly all local criminal laws are misdemeanors or some lesser violation. Serious criminal conduct is called a **felony**, and less serious criminal conduct is called a **misdemeanor**. The difference between a felony and a misdemeanor is usually defined by the amount of time an offender spends in prison or jail as punishment for violation of a statute. Felonies commonly are state (or federal) crimes for which an offender can receive a punishment of one year or more in a state or federal prison for a federal offense. Misdemeanors are crimes for which an offender can receive a punishment of one year or less in jail or prison.

Offenses that are less serious than a misdemeanor are a relatively new classification of prohibited behaviors. Different states have various names for these offenses. They are commonly traffic laws or prohibited behaviors for which the punishment is only a fine or suspension of privilege, such as losing one's driver's license. Usually, no imprisonment is permitted for violations of these offenses.[4] Many states have redefined misdemeanor traffic offenses as noncriminal violations. The advantage is that the resources of the criminal courts are freed up for more serious cases, allowing cases to be processed more quickly through the system. Often, accused offenders have fewer rights regarding legal representation and appeals. Also, such cases may be heard by administrative officers who are not judges.

Local criminal codes are the products of city councils and county governments. Similar to the president and governors, chief executive officers of cities and counties have the power to prohibit or regulate

What should be against the law? In Manhattan, it is against the law (and the law is enforced) "for a person to open, hold open or close—or offer to open, hold open or close—any door of the vehicle" for another person unless the passenger initiates the request. In Bakersfield, California, Jason Wilmert was arrested for cooking and eating cats because it is against the law to use a pet or domesticated animal for food. In Albuquerque, New Mexico, Lauren Medina, a 23-year-old college student, was arrested for theft of a $2 pumpkin she claims she forgot to pay for after spending $75 on food at the store. In Los Angeles, the city council mandated that all actors in porno-graphic films must wear condoms during any filming that takes place within city limits. City police are empowered to perform spot checks on any set once a film permit is issued, and the film permit includes a fee to cover the cost of enforcement. Los Angeles is the first government to mandate mandatory use of condoms for sex films.

Unless there is substantial public interest, a law can be declared unconstitutional. Is there substantial public interest in these examples to justify the law? Explain.

certain behaviors through executive orders. Otherwise, there is great diversity in the ways in which municipalities and counties draft and pass local criminal codes. Local criminal codes have limited jurisdiction and are enforceable only within the city or county limits. Local criminal codes cannot deny rights guaran-teed by the state constitution or the U.S. Constitution.

Local criminal laws often address behaviors that do not rise to the level of concern by the state, and they are often a complex patchwork of conflicting laws. For example, numerous cities across the nation have adopted laws banning "saggy pants." In Lynwood, Illinois, low-hanging pants can result in fines up to $750.[5] Such fashion ordinances reflect local community values, and attempts to enact statewide bans can result in challenges to the constitutionality of the law or rejection of the bill by the larger community.

Local criminal laws may differ from city to city, resulting in confusion and uncertainty as to whether one is engaged in illegal behavior. Municipal bans on the use of cell phones while people are driving are a good example of laws that differ from city to city. For example, a survey of 270 municipalities in the Chicago area shows that more than one-quarter of them have local ordinances governing cell phone use.[6] While Illinois state laws do regulate the use of cell phones while people are driving, the cities have enacted stricter laws compared with those of the state. Some municipalities ban all use of cell phones while people are driving, and others require hands-free (for example, Bluetooth) technologies. A driver legally using a cell phone to make a call in one town may be in violation of the law after crossing the border into another town. It is unreasonable to expect drivers to know the municipal ordinances of all the cities through which they travel, but city officers write thousands of tickets to unsuspecting drivers.

▶ The Limits of the Law

The government is restricted in the making of laws. The laws made by government must conform to certain Constitutional standards. People accused of violating a law may claim that the law is unconstitutional. While there are many reasons to argue whether a law is constitutional, seven common benchmarks

Laws must be made public before they can be enforced.

were established by the U.S. Supreme Court to assess the legality of criminal laws.

1. **Principle of Legality**
   The government cannot punish citizens for specific conduct if no specific laws exist forewarning them that the conduct is prohibited or required. The **principle of legality**, which has its roots in the Roman Empire, requires that laws must be made public before they can be enforced. If there is no law prohibiting an action, the action is legal. Laws define what is illegal, not what is legal.

2. *Ex Post Facto* **Laws**
   Ex post facto ("after the fact") laws are related to the principle of legality. The **ex post facto law** declares that persons cannot be punished for actions committed before the law prohibiting the behavior was passed.[7]

   The principle of *ex post facto* law also prohibits the government from increasing the punishment for a specific crime after the crime was committed. Assume, for instance, that a person is convicted of mass murder in a state that does not have the death pen-alty. The public, upset by the brutality of the crime, might support a successful campaign to change the law and adopt a death penalty

LEARNING OUTCOMES 2 Describe the limits of law.

GLOSSARY

principle of legality The principle that citizens cannot be punished for conduct for which no law against it exists.

ex post facto laws Laws pro-viding that citizens cannot be punished for actions committed before laws against the actions were passed and that the govern-ment cannot increase the penalty for a specific crime after the crime was committed.

due process Substantive due process limits the government's power to criminalize behavior unless there is a compelling reason for the public interest to do so; procedural due process requires that the government follow standard procedures and treat all defendants equally.

rules of evidence The procedural due process laws that regulate criminal trials.

stare decisis The U.S. system of developing and applying case law on the basis of precedents estab-lished in previous cases.

void for vagueness The prin-ciple that laws not using clear and specific language to define prohibited behaviors cannot be upheld.

right to privacy The principle that laws that violate personal privacy cannot be upheld.

for mass murder. Even with the new law, however, the convicted person's sentence cannot be changed from life in prison to death.

A defendant must be tried under the rules of evidence and laws that were in effect at the time the alleged crime was committed.

3. **Due Process**

There are two types of due process rights: substantive and procedural. Substantive **due process** limits the power of government to create crimes unless there is a compelling and substantial public interest in regulating or prohibiting a certain type of conduct.

Procedural due process requires the government to follow established procedures and to treat defendants equally. Procedural laws regulate the conduct of the police, the courts, and the criminal justice system in general. The procedural due process laws that regulate the criminal trial are called rules of evidence. The **rules of evidence** define, among other things, what is fair treatment of the defendant, what order of events must be followed, and what types of evidence can be admitted at a trial, as well as the trial rights of defendants and the right to appeal.

Because of procedural due process, case law precedents play a significant role in adjudication in the U.S. system

Due process places limits on criminal law to protect the rights and freedoms of the citizens.

of justice. Attorneys can argue that the court must allow similar evidence or testimony as was admitted in the past in similar cases. This system of case law is called **stare decisis**.

To change the basis on which precedents are judged, a court must explain why it is changing its interpretation and what the new criteria for judgment are. A case in which such a change of opinion is declared by the Court is called a landmark case. When the U.S. Supreme Court decides a landmark case, the principles of the case apply to all U.S. courts. Since the 1960s, the U.S. Supreme Court has issued numerous landmark decisions affecting the criminal justice system in matters such as search and seizure, confessions, and prisoners' rights. (See the following list of Supreme Court cases.)

4. **Void for Vagueness**

The law must say what it means and mean what it says. Laws that do not provide reasonable guidelines defining the specific prohibited behaviors are **void for vagueness**. A law must clearly define what it prohibits. For instance, a New Jersey statute that made it a crime to be a member of a gang was struck down because the court declared that the word *gang* was too vague.[8]

Laws must use wording that clearly specifies what behavior or act is unlawful. Vague wording subject to different interpretations, such as *immoral, indecent, near, disrupt, too close, and interfere with*, does not provide the average person with sufficient information to determine whether his or her behavior is in violation of the law. A law that prohibits demonstrations "near" a courthouse begs the question "What is 'near'?" Is it 50 feet? 100 feet? 1,000 feet? Void for vagueness is a common claim regarding laws that people maintain violate First Amendment rights regarding speech, assembly, and protest.

5. **Right to Privacy**

Laws that violate reasonable personal privacy may be declared void. The **right to privacy** is not clearly delineated in the U.S. Constitution, but it is a constructed right that the U.S. Supreme Court has inferred from the provisions of the First, Third, Fourth, and Ninth Amendments. Some state constitutions, such as those of Alaska, Florida, and Hawaii, have explicit rights to privacy. State constitutions with strong privacy laws may prohibit

The following U.S. Supreme Court decisions are landmark cases in criminal justice. The name of each landmark case is followed by a brief description. Each case resulted in significant changes in criminal law or criminal procedure.

Case	Description
Weeks v. *United States*, 1914	Established the exclusionary rule disallowing evidence obtained in violation of constitutional rights
Mapp v. *Ohio*, 1963	Incorporated Fourth Amendment search rights to state courts
Gideon v. *Wainwright*, 1963	Guaranteed defendants the right to an attorney at trial
Miranda v. *Arizona*, 1966	Established a defendant's right to counsel and right against self-incrimination and that the defendant understands these rights
Klopfer v. *North Carolina*, 1967	Guaranteed defendants a speedy trial.
Terry v. *Ohio*, 1968	Allowed police to "pat down" a person for personal safety reasons
Witherspoon v. *Illinois*, 1968	Prohibited the exclusion of those opposed to capital punishment from capital crime juries
Furman v. *Georgia*, 1972	Declared that the death penalty was applied in an arbitrary and capricious manner
Gagnon v. *Scarpelli*, 1973	Declared that a probationer's sentence can be revoked only after preliminary and final revocation hearings
Roper v. *Simmons*, 2005	Abolished capital punishment for juveniles
District of Columbia v. *Heller*, 2008	Ruled at the federal level that the Second Amendment protected an individual's right to own a firearm
McDonald v. *City of Chicago et al.*, 2010	Incorporated the Second Amendment right to bear arms, prohibiting states from banning the possession of firearms. The case did not remove all restrictions from firearm ownership. The case recognizes that states and the federal government may make reasonable regulations regarding gun ownership for the safety of the public.

law enforcement officers from making arrests for certain actions that occur in the privacy of one's residence.

However, privacy is not an overarching right that permits otherwise harmful or prohibited behaviors merely because they are performed in one's home. For example, the U.S. Supreme Court has upheld state statutes making it a crime to possess child pornography even in the privacy of one's residence. Sexual assault, domestic violence, and child abuse are other examples of actions that are criminal even though they may be performed in the privacy of one's residence.

6. Void for Overbreadth

Laws that have been declared **void for overbreadth** are laws that go too far; that is, in an attempt to prevent a specific conduct, the law not only makes that conduct illegal, but also prohibits other behaviors that are legally protected.

A law that is void for overbreadth is not vague in what it prohibits (as in the case of a law that is void for vagueness); rather, it simply prohibits legal activities as well as illegal activities. For example, when New York City attempted to ban panhandling, the U.S. Supreme Court ruled that the law attempted to prohibit actions that were protected under the First Amendment's freedom of speech clause. New York City had to revise the statute to carefully define behaviors that were threatening to passersby rather than use its original ban on all panhandling.

void for overbreadth The principle that laws go too far in that they criminalize legally protected behavior in an attempt to make some other behavior illegal that cannot be upheld.

cruel and unusual punishment An Eighth Amendment right based on the premise of classical criminology that punishment should be appropriate to the crime.

7. Cruel and Unusual Punishment

To be valid, a law must specify the punishment to be applied for violation of the law. If that punishment is in violation of the Eighth Amendment, which prohibits **cruel and unusual punishment**, it may be declared unconstitutional. This legal philosophy appears to be based on the premise of classical criminology that punishment should be appropriate to the crime. Although the argument of cruel and unusual punishment has frequently been applied to cases involving the death sentence, the Eighth Amendment applies to the punishment for all crimes.[9]

For example, the U.S. Supreme Court has ruled that sentencing a person to prison for drug addiction is cruel and unusual because drug addiction is deemed an illness rather than a criminal behavior. However, sentencing a person for possessing or using drugs is not cruel and unusual because this addresses the behavior of the person, not his or her condition.[10]

The Supreme Court has ruled that the use of corporal punishment in prison is cruel and unusual and has prohibited such punishment. There have been many Eighth Amendment challenges to the death penalty, but the U.S. Supreme Court has consistently held that if fairly applied, the death penalty is not cruel and unusual punishment.

▶ Elements of a Crime

The actions and intent of the criminal, as well as the seriousness or harm of the crime, all carry weight in determining the punishment for a crime. Punishments specified by law are based on the principle of proportionality. Less serious harms, such as misdemeanors, carry lesser punishments than do more serious harms, which are felonies. However, there are various degrees of punishment for criminal behavior. Determining what punishment should be attached to a crime depends on a number of factors, including the conduct of the perpetrator, the intention of the perpetrator, and the harm done to the victim or society. The actions and intentions of a person who commits a crime are called the **elements of a crime**. Each crime is defined by these elements. Two important elements necessary for all crimes are *actus reus* and *mens rea*. *Actus reus* refers to the actions of the person (that is, what he or she did). *Mens rea* refers to the state of mind or criminal intent of the person. Did the person intend to harm someone, or was the harm the result of negligence or recklessness?

Think About It...

The First Amendment provides a number of civil rights, including freedom of speech. There are a number of recent examples where the courts have struck down laws as unconstitutional based on First Amendment rights.

In *Brown* v. *Entertainment Merchants Association*, No. 08-14448, the Supreme Court struck down a California law that banned the sale of violent video games to children. The law was justified as protecting children from harm. Justice Scalia rejected the argument, writing "No doubt a state possesses legitimate power to protect children from harm, but that does not include a free-floating power to restrict the ideas to which children may be exposed."

In *Snyder* v. *Phelps*, the Court affirmed that the Westboro Baptist Church's disruptive anti gay protests at fallen soldiers' funerals was protected speech despite the hurtful nature of the speech.

In 2011, Missouri Circuit Judge Jon Beetem issued a preliminary injunction blocking a Missouri law that would have prohibited teachers from having private online conversations with students through social networking sites such as Facebook. Public blacklash spurred calls for repeal of the law.

The First Amendment does not guarantee unlimited "freedom of speech," but restrictions must be carefully crafted to avoid abridging freedom of speech rights. Do you agree with the examples cited? Why or why not?

Rahul Sengupta/Fotolia

actus reus — **The actions of the person** American law is firmly rooted in the classical criminological principle that persons are punished for their actions. Thus, one of the first elements of a crime is that the law must define the actions that constitute the crime. The action must be voluntary in the sense that criminal law does not prosecute persons for accidents or unintentional actions that are not negligent or reckless. However, the law does provide that in two cases, *actus reus* can be other than direct criminal behaviors. These are failure to act and possession.

failure to act or crimes of omission The criminal intent of a crime may be failure to act when there is a legal duty to act.

In crimes of omission, hospitals, caregivers, and even bystanders can come under the requirement of a legal duty to help another. The state of Alaska requires that a motorist render assistance to stranded motorists. A number of states have passed "Good Samaritan" laws that extend legal protection to a person who helps someone in distress. Parents are considered to have a legal duty to aid and assist their children.

possession The possession of an illegal or prohibited item can constitue *actus reus.*

constructive possession: When a person knows that an item is contraband and he or she doesn't have actual possession but is in control of the item; the mailing of contraband is an example.

knowing possession: When a person has actual possession and is aware that what he or she possesses is contraband.

mere possession: When a person has actual possession but is not aware that what he or she possesses is contraband.

mens rea — **The intent of the person** The person must have criminal intent, or "a guilty mind." The action must intend harm. Harms that result from accidental actions may have civil liability but are not criminal. The only direct evidence of *mens rea* is the defendant's confession. Otherwise, in criminal law, of *mens rea* is determined primarily by circumstantial or indirect evidence. There are four types of criminal intent.

general intent: This refers to the commonsense understanding that an action may cause harm. The law infers what common sense suggests even if the defendant denies the intent. The law assumes it is logical to assume that a person who shoots and kills another but claims that he or she did not intend to shoot the person but only to "scare" the person had general intent to cause harm.

specific intent: This refers to the actions taken to knowingly commit a crime; for instance, larceny requires taking property with the intent to permanently deprive the owner of that property.

transferred intent: This covers incidences in which a person injures another but did not intend to harm that person. This includes a case in which a person is intending to hurt someone but misses and an innocent third party is injured.

constructive intent: This refers to a situation in which a person does not intend to harm anyone but should have known that his or her actions would create a risk. Shooting a gun into the air on New Year's Eve is an example of this.

The Model Penal Code distinguishes four types of intent: *purposely, knowingly, recklessly,* and *negligently*. Each has a lesser degree of criminal intent and will have a lesser punishment assigned. For instance, a person who purposely causes the death of another is guilty of murder, whereas someone who causes the death recklessly is guilty of manslaughter.

Strict Liability

Some actions are considered criminal without the necessity of *mens rea*, or criminal intent. These actions are called **strict liability crimes**. Parking violations are an example of strict liability laws. The registered owner of an illegally parked vehicle is held liable for the fine regardless of whether he or she parked the car, was operating the car, or even had knowledge of the parking violation. Strict liability crimes tend to be minor offenses such as traffic offenses or serious offenses from which society has deemed the victim deserves additional protection. In some states, sex with a minor is a strict liability crime in that the law places an affirmative burden on the defendant to affirm the legal age of the minor. In some states, even if the minor lies about his or her age, the defendant is assumed to have criminal intent. Some states have laws that require K–12 teachers and administrators to report suspected physical abuse of children. In such states, the motive or intent of the teacher for not reporting suspected abuse is not a defense for violating the law.

Incomplete Crimes, or Inchoate Offenses

One cannot be convicted of a crime for thinking about murder, rape, robbery, larceny, burglary, or any other crime. The law punishes people only for what they do, not what they think. Crimes that go beyond mere thought but do not result in completed crimes are called incomplete crimes or **inchoate offenses** and are subject to punishment. The three common inchoate offenses are described in the following paragraphs.

LEARNING OUTCOMES 3 List the elements of a crime and their role in criminal prosecution.

GLOSSARY

elements of a crime The illegal actions (*actus reus*) and criminal intentions (*mens rea*) of the actor along with the circumstances that link the two, especially causation.

actus reus An element of crime in which people are punished for their actions; thus, the law does not prosecute people for actions that are not voluntary or that are accidental and do not involve recklessness or negligence.

Solicitation

Solicitation is the urging, requesting, or commanding of another to commit a crime. The person solicited does not have to have *mens rea* or any intent whatsoever of complying with the solicitation to commit the crime. Thus, solicitation of an undercover law enforcement officer to commit a crime is punishable. Solicitation is a criminal charge against the person making the offer, command, or encouragement, not against the person to whom the offer is made. The crime of solicitation requires specific criminal intent. A person who makes a remark such as, "We should steal that car and take it for a ride," to a general group of people has not satisfied the specific intent required for solicitation. Solicitation is most removed from the actual completion of the crime and usually carries the least punishment of the inchoate offenses.

Conspiracy

Conspiracy requires no *actus reus* other than communication. A plot to commit a bank robbery is not a conspiracy if it is not shared or if no steps are taken in preparation for the planned robbery. By definition, **conspiracy** requires two or more people to plan a crime. Actions that require two people (that is, actions that cannot be committed by individuals, such as fornication, bigamy, bribery, and gambling) are not considered examples of conspiracy. Thus, if a correctional officer accepts money to help an inmate escape, the two could not be charged with conspiracy. The appropriate criminal charge would be bribery, which requires at least two people—one to make the offer and the other to accept the offer.

Conspiracy requires that two or more people take steps in preparation for the commission of a crime. Any step or steps taken may constitute conspiracy. In the case of a bank robbery that is anticipated to take months to plan and hundreds of steps to execute, the first meeting of the parties involved to discuss how to proceed constitutes a conspiracy. Furthermore, the parties to a conspiracy do not have to meet face-to-face. They may satisfy the requirements of conspiracy by any form of collaboration, including

> For most crimes that can be committed, there is a corresponding crime of attempt.

> The actions and intent of the criminal, as well as the seriousness of the crime, all carry weight in determining punishment.

verbal, written, or electronic. As another example, if two or more people plan to commit forgery and take steps to obtain a certain type of paper required to commit the crime, this is sufficient *actus reus* to constitute conspiracy. The supplier of the items needed for the commission of a crime is not guilty of conspiracy unless the supplier is aware of the illegal use planned for the materials.[11]

Attempt

What happens when things do not go as the criminal planned and he or she is not able to complete the intended criminal activity he or she started? Has a crime been committed? Yes, he or she has committed the crime of **attempt**. For most crimes that can be committed, there is a corresponding crime of attempt—that is, attempted murder, attempted kidnapping, attempted rape, attempted burglary, and so forth. Attempt is the closest act to the completion of the crime and therefore carries a greater punishment than conspiracy or solicitation does, but usually a lesser punishment than if the crime had been completed.

Renunciation of Criminal Intent

It is possible that a person might have criminal intent and might take steps toward completing a

mens rea An element of crime in which a person must have criminal intent, or a "guilty mind," for his or her actions to be criminal.

strict liability crimes Actions that are considered criminal without the need for criminal intent.

inchoate offense An action that goes beyond mere thought but does not result in a completed crime.

solicitation The requesting or commanding of another to commit a crime.

conspiracy The planning by two or more people to commit a crime.

attempt An incomplete criminal act; the closest act to the completion of a crime.

Think About It . . .

Motive, or the reason a person committed a criminal act, is an important factor in determining the seriousness of an offense or even if the actions are considered criminal. The legal term for motive is *mens rea*, which roughly translated means "guilty mind." The lack of *mens rea* or the degree of *mens rea* can be a defense to a crime, as in the crimes of necessity and homicide.

Consider the following crimes and the associated *mens rea*. In Palmdale, California, a 12-year-old girl stole more than $10,000 worth of jewelry from her home. She claimed a psychic persuaded her to steal the jewelry to lift a curse and appease evil spirits. In February 2012, singer Chris Brown was accused of taking an iPhone from fan Christal Shanae who snapped a picture of him. Angered that she had taken his picture, he grabbed her iPhone and drove off with it in his Bentley. Florida law defines his actions as "robbery by sudden snatching," a third-degree felony punishable by up to five years in prison. Self-help guru James Arthur Ray was convicted of negligent homicide in the deaths of three people in an Arizona sweat lodge ceremony. Ray was sentenced to three two-year sentences. Ray claimed that he made an error of judgment and mistakes and was sorry for the loss of life.

In determining the importance of *mens rea* in defining a crime and its punishment, what factors should legislators take into account?

crime but then change his or her mind before the crime is fully executed. Does renunciation of criminal intent absolve one of punishment? No, it does not.[12] If a person enters a bank with a mask, a gun, and a note demanding money from the teller but, noting the presence of a security officer, changes his or her mind and exits the bank without presenting the note to the bank teller, the person nevertheless has satisfied the criminal intent requirement to be charged with attempted bank robbery. (In some states, these actions may satisfy the requirements for bank robbery.) If a person intends to commit burglary but is frightened away by a noise after committing trespass, the person has satisfied the criminal intent requirement to be charged with attempted burglary. A person who demands sex under threat of force but is "talked out of it" by the victim has satisfied the criminal intent requirement to be charged with attempted rape.[13] The law does not take the view that "a stroke of luck or a retreat from criminal activity based on fear of getting caught" makes one immune from criminal prosecution. If a person is involved in a criminal conspiracy and changes his or her mind regarding becoming involved, many states have laws that require specific actions that the person must take to avoid criminal liability. Often these criteria require the person to report the criminal conspiracy to law enforcement.

▶ Criminal Defenses

The fact that a person has committed an act that, by law, may constitute a crime does not mean the person will be held criminally liable for the crime in a court of law. There are numerous **defenses** a person can offer at trial as noncriminal justification for his or her actions. Two types of defenses to criminal charges are a **perfect defense**, in which the person is excused from all criminal liability and punishment, and an **imperfect defense**, in which the person's liability or punishment is reduced. An imperfect defense may result in the defendant being found guilty of a lesser charge. Defenses are usually offered at the trial of the defendant. The most common defenses are described as follows:

- **Alibi**   The use of an alibi as a defense requires that the defendant present witnesses who will give testimony in court or other evidence establishing the fact that the defendant could not have committed the offense. The most common alibi strategy is for defendants to claim that they could not have been at the scene of the crime at the time the crime was committed and to offer witnesses who will testify to that fact. The jury is the ultimate judge of an alibi. The defendant's alibi witness may be a friend, a relative, or another person closely associated with the defendant. Thus, there may be reason to question the reliability of the alibi witness's testimony. The jury is the judge of the reliability of the testimony or evidence. The jury may choose to believe or not to believe the testimony of alibi witnesses or the evidence presented.

- **Consent or Condoning by the Victim**   The defense that the victim gave permission for the act or condoned the act is not a valid defense for some criminal actions.[14] For example, in most states, consent is not a valid defense in mercy killing or assisted suicide. Dr. Jack Kevorkian constructed a "suicide machine" to help terminally ill patients end their lives. Despite the consent—even pleas—of

the victims for his assistance in committing suicide, the Michigan court that heard the case did not recognize the defense of consent and Kevorkian was convicted. Likewise, consent is not a defense in murder–suicide pacts, and in those cases, any surviving member can be charged with murder.

Consent or condoning by the victim is a valid defense for a number of actions in which injury is a foreseeable risk and the behavior is socially and legally acceptable. Consent is a legitimate defense for certain kinds of physical violence in sporting events, even violence resulting in death. For example, if a professional boxer in a sanctioned boxing match causes the death of his or her opponent, consent is a defense against homicide. Consent is a defense for violence in some sports, such as hockey, but not in others, such as basketball, where violence is not common. Even in sports such as hockey, excessive violence, such as striking a player's head with a hockey stick, may be criminal.

- **Entrapment or Outrageous Government Conduct**   Entrapment or outrageous government conduct is related to the principle that a defendant's criminal actions must be voluntary. If agents of the government provide both the *mens rea* and the means to commit the crime, the U.S. Supreme Court has ruled that the defendant may be defended on the grounds of entrapment or outrageous government conduct. Entrapment is an **affirmative defense**, which means that the defendant must admit that he or she committed the crime as alleged. The person is not innocent, but claims that if it had not been for the actions of government

LEARNING OUTCOMES 4   List and describe some of the major defenses against charges of criminal conduct.

GLOSSARY

defenses Justifications or excuses defined by law by which a defendant may be released from prosecution or punishment for a crime.

perfect defense The defense that results in the person being excused from all criminal liability and punishment.

imperfect defense The defense that results in the defendant's liability or punishment for a crime being reduced.

affirmative defense A defense in which the defendant admits that he or she committed the *actus reas* of the crime but claims that he or she should not be found guilty of the crime because his or her actions were justified or he or she had an excuse.

diplomatic immunity The granting of immunity, or protection from any kind of criminal prosecution, to foreign diplomats.

legislative immunity The protection of senators and representatives of Congress from arrest only while the legislature is in session, except for felonies and treason.

witness immunity A situation in which a defendant admits to committing a crime but is granted immunity from prosecution in exchange for cooperating with a government investigation.

privilege A type of defense in which the defendant claims immunity from punishment for an admitted violation of the law because it was related to his or her official duties.

agents, he or she would not have committed the crime.

Entrapment is different from encouragement, in which law enforcement officers might pretend they are buyers, sellers, or coconspirators in crime. In this role, law enforcement officers may promise the suspect benefits from committing the crime or offer to supply materials or help the suspect obtain contraband, but they do not supply the motive of the offender to commit the crime. Undercover "sting operations" must be careful not to cross the line from mere encouragement to entrapment.

- **Immunity or Privilege** In the defense of immunity, the accused has special protection from the government against being prosecuted. Four forms of this defense are diplomatic immunity, legislative immunity, witness immunity, and privilege. **Diplomatic immunity** grants foreign diplomats complete immunity from any criminal prosecution, including murder and traffic violations. In return for extending immunity to foreign diplomats, U.S. diplomats in foreign countries receive the same protection. If a foreign diplomat commits a serious felony crime in the United States, the only recourse for the U.S. government is to ask for the diplomat's recall to his or her country or to request that the country voluntarily waive the diplomat's immunity.

A lesser form of immunity extended to lawmakers in the United States is **legislative immunity**. Federal and state lawmakers receive some form of immunity from arrest while the legislature is in session. The U.S. criminal justice system included legislative immunity as a defense because of the abuses of the English monocracy whereby elected representatives would be arrested on false charges to prevent them from voting on a bill. Unlike diplomatic immunity, legislative immunity only postpones the time the legislator can be arrested until after the legislative session is adjourned. Also, in some states, legislative immunity may not protect the legislator from arrest for felonies and treason.

In **witness immunity**, the defendant admits to the criminal acts as charged, but in exchange for cooperating with a government investigation or prosecution, he or she is granted immunity from further prosecution based on the offered testimony or cooperation. Witness immunity is commonly used in organized crime, drug trafficking, political corruption cases, and corporate crime cases.

The defense of **privilege** is the claim that the defendant violated the law but is immune from punishment because of his or her official office or duty. For example, the courts have recognized as a privilege the right of operators of emergency vehicles to violate traffic regulations when responding to a call. Law enforcement officers and correctional officers have the defense of privilege in certain cases involving the use of deadly force. For example, correctional officers can use deadly force to prevent an inmate from escaping from prison even if, in certain cases, there is no fear of death or great bodily harm to the officer.

> Several defenses, defined by law, can be used in court to excuse an accused offender or to lessen his or her criminal liability.

Privilege is not a valid defense when the defendant is accused of committing a crime but claims that he or she was just "following orders" from a superior government or military official. In the Watergate scandal, the accused burglars claimed privilege as a defense. Their claim was that they were following the orders of President Richard Nixon and, as president, he had the privilege of ordering them to perform actions that were illegal without the action being criminal. The court rejected the claim and convicted the defendants.

- **Involuntary Actions and Duress** Involuntary actions and duress are similar defenses. A defense of involuntary action is a claim by a person that the action or behavior was not voluntary (that is, was not committed of his or her own free will). This claim may be based on the claim that the person's behavior was accidental or was the result of actions he or she could not control and were no fault of his or her own. In February 2006, former Vice President Dick Cheney, for example, accidentally shot and seriously wounded his friend Harry Whittington in a hunting accident. Because the wounding was an accident, no criminal charges were filed. However, the defense of involuntary action cannot be used to defend against criminal liability for behaviors that occurred as a result of the initial willful behavior of the defendant. For example, a person is responsible for crimes resulting from alcohol or drug consumption if the person voluntarily consumed the alcohol or drugs.

Similar to the involuntary defense is the **defense of duress**, in which the person claims that he or she did not commit the actions of his or her own free will. However, unlike the involuntary defense, in the defense of duress, the person claims that his or her behavior was compelled by the use or threat of force by another. A simple example of this defense is when a bank teller gives the bank's money to a robber. It could be argued that the bank teller does not have the authority to give away the bank's money, but the teller has not committed a crime because the actions are not voluntary. The teller is operating under duress.

However, the defense of duress cannot be used as a defense in homicide. The law does not allow the taking of one life even to save the life of another.

- **Mistake or Ignorance of Fact or Law** Laws are published as a matter of public record, partly so that offenders cannot claim ignorance of the law as an excuse for their behavior. Most citizens know very few of the many volumes of law that govern their lives, but the law usually does not recognize ignorance of the law as a valid defense. Ignorance of the law may be considered a defense if the law in question is so unusual or obscure that the court finds that a reasonable person would not have had knowledge of it. However, simple ignorance of the law is not a defense against prosecution or punishment for crimes.

Mistake or ignorance of fact, on the other hand, may be a valid defense. If at the end of class you pick up a backpack you think is yours and walk out of the classroom, have you stolen the backpack if it does in fact belong to another student? If a person has a reasonable belief that the action he or she is doing is legal, mistake of fact may be a valid defense.

Mistake or ignorance of the law should not be confused with factual impossibility. **Factual Impossibility** is when it is not possible for the person to commit the crime intended. An example of factual impossibility would be a person who attempted to murder another person using a firearm that unbeknownst to him or her was inoperable or unloaded. Factual impossibility is not a defense. If the intent of the person was to commit a crime, the fact that the circumstances or means used could not have resulted in the commission of the crime does not negate the *mens rea*, or criminal intent, of the perpetrator.

- **Necessity**   The defense of **necessity** is sometimes known as the defense of the "lesser of two evils." Necessity is an affirmative defense in which the defendant must admit that he or she committed the act but claims that it was done because of necessity or need and not because of *mens rea*. This defense is commonly used against charges of property crime, such as trespass, theft, and burglary.[15] In the classic case in which this defense is successful, the defendant is faced with a life-threatening situation and chooses to commit an illegal act to save his or her life. For example, a cross-country skier caught in an unexpected blizzard might break into a mountain home, start a fire, and consume food found there. Under normal circumstances, these actions constitute the crime of burglary, but because of the threat of death from exposure to the elements, the court may recognize the defense of necessity as a logical defense. Necessity does not justify any and all actions. The actions must be in response to life-threatening situations. A person who has been repeatedly late for work and was told not to be late again or he or she will be fired is not justified in stealing a car because he or she missed the bus.

- **Self-Defense**   The claim of **self-defense** is a complex defense usually associated with murder and physical assault. Again, this is an affirmative defense: The defendant admits to the killing or assault but claims that he or she lacked criminal intent. The lack of criminal intent is based on the claim that the defendant was protecting himself or herself from deadly attack or serious bodily injury.[16] The courts have also recognized self-defense when applied to (1) protecting another person from deadly attack or serious bodily injury and (2) defending one's home from invasion. In most states, the act of self-defense used by the defendant must be appropriate and proportional to the force used by the attacker. Before deadly force is justified as

defense of duress A legal claim by a defendant that he or she acted involuntarily under the threat of immediate and serious harm by another.

mistake or ignorance of fact An affirmative legal defense in which the defendant made a mistake that does not meet the requirement for *mens rea*.

factual impossibility Circumstances under which it is not possible for a person to commit the crime intended.

necessity An affirmative legal defense claiming that the defendant committed an act out of need, not *mens rea*.

self-defense An affirmative legal defense in which a defendant claims that he or she acted to protect himself or herself or another person against a deadly attack or invasion of his or her home.

insanity A legal claim by a defendant that he or she was suffering from a disease or mental defect and that the defect caused the defendant not to understand the difference between right and wrong.

GARY GREEN/UPI/Newscom

George Zimmerman claimed he shot Trayvon Martin in self-defense. This defense requires Zimmerman to admit he caused the death of Martin but it claims his actions were legally justiciable and not subject to punishment.

Criminal Defenses   **83**

self-defense, the attacker must create a situation in which the defendant fears death or great bodily harm. Also, the defendant cannot have been the person who initiated the confrontation. However, state laws differ. Florida's "stand your ground" law regarding self-defense provides one of the most liberal interpretations of self-defense in the nation. As a result of the controversy surrounding this defense raised by the killing of Trayvon Martin by George Zimmerman in 2012, Florida has appointed a commission to review the law and recommend any necessary changes.

Timing is a controversial issue in capital cases involving the claim of self-defense. For example, is a routinely abused spouse or child justified in killing an attacker when not under immediate threat of deadly attack or serious bodily injury? Usually, the courts require imminent threat to justify self-defense.[17]

The laws of self-defense in protecting one's home against invasion varies significantly among states. Some states require that, when reasonable, the occupant of the house must first attempt to retreat or escape attack. Other states do not have such a requirement but follow the "castle doctrine," which means that occupants have the unqualified right to protect their home against violent trespass.[18] Most states do not permit the claim of self-defense in resisting arrest—whether lawful or unlawful—by a police officer.[19] Also, most states do not allow the use of deadly force to defend property other than one's home in cases of arson or home invasion.

- **Youth**   A 14-year-old boy steals a car, refuses to stop when pursued by the police, and ends up destroying the vehicle in a high-speed chase. Is he just a kid and therefore held to a different standard of culpability from that of an adult? Since 1899, the answer for the U.S. criminal justice system has been yes. Prior to 1899, age was a defense based on the British principle that children under 7 years of age, and possibly even under 14 years of age, could not form *mens rea*.

  In 1899, Cook County (Chicago) adopted the use of juvenile court. This separate court system operated under significantly different rules and standards of proof to adjudicate the crimes of youthful offenders under the age of 18 separately from adult offenders. The use of juvenile court quickly caught on and is now practiced in all 50 states.[20] In the last 50 years, states have restricted the use of the defense of youth. Some states, such as Pennsylvania, have removed the defense of youth for homicide, and youthful offenders may be tried in adult court. Other states have lowered the age of accountability for certain violent offenses.

- **Insanity**   The **insanity** defense has an interesting connection to Sir Robert Peel, the father of modern policing. In 1843, Daniel M'Naghten suffered the paranoid delusion that Sir Robert Peel, who was then Prime Minister of England, intended to kill him. Based on this belief, M'Naghten undertook to kill Peel first in what M'Naghten perceived as a form of self-defense. He obtained a single-shot, black power pistol and lay in wait for Peel to pass by. Fortunately for Peel but not for his secretary, Edward Drummond, M'Naghten shot, missed Peel, and struck and killed Drummond.[21]

M'Naghten was tried for murder. The state argued that because he had the "sense of mind" to acquire a pistol, operate it, and lay in wait, M'Naghten showed sufficient mental capacity to be held accountable for his crime. However, he was acquitted based on a successful insanity defense.[22] The queen was alarmed at the verdict and charged the court to change English law regarding insanity to make it more difficult for a person to be acquitted using an insanity defense. Under the new standard, a defendant could be considered insane only if he or she met two conditions: (1) He or she suffered from a disease or defect of the mind, and (2) the disease or defect caused the defendant not to know the nature and quality of the criminal act or not to know that the act was wrong. This standard for insanity became known as the M'Naghten standard—even though it was not the standard to which M'Naghten was held at his trial. This standard became the primary requirement for a successful insanity defense in Great Britain and the United States. In the latter half of the twentieth century, the standard for a successful insanity plea was modified by many states and the federal government and made less restrictive. However, after John Hinckley's assassination attempt upon President Ronald Reagan and Hinckley's verdict of not guilty by reason of insanity, the federal government and many states reverted to criteria similar to the M'Naghten standard.

Overview of Defenses

Defenses to crimes can be divided into two major categories: an alibi defense and an affirmative defense. In an alibi defense, the defendant denies that he or she committed the crime and offers proof that he or she could not have done so. Usually, this proof involves an alibi—that is, evidence that at the time of the crime, the defendant was not at or near the scene of the crime. Affirmative defenses require the defendant to admit to the *actus reus*, but the defendant claims that his or her actions lacked criminal intent. Affirmative defenses carry the risk that if the jury does not accept the defense, the defendant most likely will be convicted of the crime because he or she has already admitted to having done the actions.

Affirmative defenses can be divided into justifications, excuses, and exemptions. In each, the defendant admits to some of the elements of the crime but denies that all of the elements were present. Usually, in these defenses, the defendant admits to the *actus reus* but denies criminal intent.

In justifications, the defendant claims that he or she was entitled to perform the actions because he or she was justified by the circumstances. For example, the defendant was justified in killing the person because it was self-defense. In excuses, the defendant claims that he or she did the act because of certain circumstances, such as necessity or duress. In exemptions, the person claims that he or she was entitled by privilege or law to violate the law without immunity.

▶ Crimes by Law

Crimes are defined by laws, and the laws governing society are numerous, complex, and diverse. Federal, state, and local governments have specific, different, and overlapping criminal

The State	Persons	Habitation	Property	Public Order	Public Morals
Treason	Murder	Burglary	Theft	Disturbing the Peace	Prostitution
Sedition	Rape	Arson	Larceny	Inciting to Riot	Gambling
	Sexual Assault		Embezzlement		
	Kidnapping		Fraud		
	Robbery		Receiving Stolen Property		
	Assault		Forgery		

Classification of Laws
Laws are classified according to who is victimized.

codes. It would not be possible to address the particulars of each law in a discussion of the different crimes. Thus, law texts and criminal justice texts do not use actual federal and state laws when discussing the various crimes; instead, they use the laws and definitions of the Model Penal Code. The **Model Penal Code** is not the law of the federal government or any state government, but is a set of guidelines developed in 1962 by the American Law Institute for what are considered the best practices or legal codes. Most textbooks on criminal law discuss the laws as presented by the Model Penal Code rather than actual federal or state laws. Most law school classes are based on the laws of the Model Penal Code rather than actual state law. Since graduates of law school have not studied the actual laws of the state in which they want to practice, they must pass an examination on the laws of the state. This examination, taken after graduation from law school, is called the bar exam.

The Model Penal Code classifies crime according to the victim of the crime. Crimes are classified in the following ways:

- **Crimes against the State** Crimes against the state include treason, espionage, and sedition. Terrorism and terrorism-related crimes such as supporting terrorism are other examples of crimes against the state. The term *state* includes both the federal and state governments. In crimes against the state, there may be no individual victims. For example, Bradley Manning, a U.S. soldier, was charged in 2010 with passing classified materials to WikiLeaks. He was charged with "aiding the enemy," an offense that carries a possible death sentence. Yet, the government does not have to show that his actions resulted in actual harm to any soldier, person, or government mission.

- **Crimes against Persons** In the Model Penal Code, crimes against persons include homicide, rape, sexual assault, kidnapping, robbery, and assault and battery. These specific offenses are discussed to illustrate important points about criminal law: what elements are required for an offense, how the offense is graded, and how the offense and the punishment reflect social values.

The modern offense of burglary combines two less serious crimes—trespass and intent to commit a crime—into a serious felony crime.

Homicide The definition of **homicide**—the killing of one human being by another—takes into account the harm done to the victim and the different degrees of criminal intent in regard to the punishment for the crime. The killing of another human being can result in a punishment of a few years to death. Based on the degree of harm intended and advance planning, homicides are divided into murder and manslaughter. **Murder** is divided into first-degree murder—the premeditated and deliberate killing of another—and second-degree murder. Second-degree murder includes the killing of another without premeditation, with the intent to inflict serious bodily injury but not death, as the result of extreme recklessness and during the commission of a felony in which there was no intent to kill or injure another. **Manslaughter** is the killing of another without malice—that is, without the specific intent to kill. The Model Penal Code divides manslaughter into three categories: voluntary, involuntary, and vehicular. Examples of manslaughter include people killed in barroom fistfights where no weapons were involved; people killed through reckless actions of another, such as firing a firearm into the air in celebration

LEARNING OUTCOMES 5 Explain how crimes are classified and defined according to the Model Penal Code.

GLOSSARY

Model Penal Code Guidelines for U.S. criminal codes published in 1962 by the American Law Institute that classify and define crimes into categories.

homicide The killing of one human being by another.

murder All intentional killings and deaths that occur in the course of aggravated felonies.

manslaughter The killing of another without the specific intent to kill.

rape Sexual assault; nonconsensual sexual acts.

kidnapping The taking away of a person by force against his or her will and holding that person in false imprisonment.

robbery The taking away of property from a person by force or the immediate threat of force.

assault The act of inflicting injury on another, whereas battery is the act of unlawfully striking another.

burglary A combination of trespass and the intent to commit a crime.

arson The willful and malicious burning of a structure.

larceny The wrongful taking of another's property with the intent to permanently deprive its owner of its possession.

of an event; and motor vehicle "accidents" where the person was culpable for the death.

Rape or Sexual Assault The crime of rape, or the more contemporary term *sexual assault*, shows how criminal codes reflect changing social values. Rape is a crime wherein intent and consent determine whether the action was a crime. In most cases, consensual sex, unlike nonconsensual sex, is not a crime. The lack of consent makes **rape** a crime. Since about the 1950s, states no longer require proof of resistance. Prior to the 1950s, the laws of many states were such that lack of proof of continuous resistance, even to the point of suffering bodily injury, could be argued to be consent. The efforts of women's rights groups have resulted in changes to state laws. Starting in the 1970s, a number of reforms were instituted in state laws regarding rape. The criminal law no longer requires women to resist continuously, and lack of physical resistance or bodily injury is not considered consent. Also, many states have changed the classification of the crime from rape to sexual assault to more clearly identify the crime as an assault as opposed to a sexual act. In some criminal codes, sexual assault has been defined to include any sexual penetration with the penis or any other object and any other form of assault such as touching. States also have enacted statutes recognizing that men can be raped, by women or by men. The marital rape exception has been eliminated in many states. Under the marital rape exception, husbands could not be charged with rape of their wife under any circumstances, including situations in which the husband and wife were separated. The law was based on historical values that sexual intercourse was a right of the husband. Finally, some states have enacted rape shield laws that prohibit the defense from questioning the victim about past sexual experiences. Without rape shield laws, victims of sexual assault could be questioned regarding their entire sexual history when testifying in court.

Kidnapping **Kidnapping** is the taking away of a person by force against his or her will and holding that person in false imprisonment. In defining kidnapping, the taking of a person against his or her will is called asportation. Thus, one of the elements of kidnapping is that it must be proven that the defendant moved the victim against his or her will from one place to another. If a perpetrator does not move his or her victim, the lesser crime of false imprisonment or unlawful restraint may be applicable. Historically in England, kidnapping applied only to children unless the adult was taken out of the country.

Kidnapping did not become a serious federal crime until the kidnapping of Charles Lindbergh's 20-month-old son in 1932. In reaction to the kidnapping, Congress passed the Federal Kidnapping Act, or Lindbergh Law, that made it a federal crime to transport a kidnapped victim across state lines. Prior to *Furman* v. *Georgia* (1972), kidnapping was a capital offense in many states.

Robbery **Robbery** is the taking and carrying away of property from a person by force or threat of immediate use of force. Houses are burgled, but only people can be robbed. Robbery actually involves the elements of two crimes: theft from crimes against property and assault from crimes against persons. The commission of robbery with a weapon makes it the more serious crime of aggravated robbery. The use of a weapon in the commission of a crime can be prosecuted as a separate crime.

Assault and Battery **Assault** is defined as the act of inflicting injury on another, whereas battery is the act of unlawfully striking another. The actual state codes governing assault and battery vary significantly. Some states use the terms interchangeably or have defined the crime as *assault and battery* instead of one crime called *assault* and another crime called *battery*. Mayhem is an offense similar to battery, but the elements of mayhem require unlawfully and violently depriving the victim of full use of any part of the body, such as a hand, a foot, or an eye. If a firearm or another dangerous weapon is used in the crime, it becomes the more serious offense of aggravated assault or battery.

- **Crimes against Habitation** Burglary and arson are crimes committed against places where people live. Both offenses require specific criminal intent. Burglary requires the person to commit the crime of trespass with the specific intent to commit a crime thereafter. Arson requires the specific intent to commit a malicious burning.

  Burglary The modern offense of **burglary** combines two less serious crimes—trespass and intent to commit a crime—into a serious felony crime. The Model Penal Code and most state codes define several degrees of burglary and expand burglary to include property other than homes, such as cars, campers, airplanes, tents, and vacation cabins. Burglary does not require breaking and entering or the intent to steal.[23] A person who remains in a habitation when not authorized to do so satisfies the criminal intent of burglary. For example, someone who enters a public building during authorized hours and hides until after those hours is considered to have committed the specific intent of trespass required of burglary. Also, entering a

Think About It . . .

Consider the following two crimes: (1) A person enters a public campsite, pulls up the stakes holding down a small tent, and drags away the tent and its entire contents without authorization. (2) A person walks into a public campsite and enters a small tent. The tent "door" has no lock. Once inside, he takes items from the tent and leaves. Has the person committed the same crime in both situations? Explain.

Claude Beaubien/Fotolia

marked, restricted space may satisfy the intent of trespass even if there is no door, lock, or obstacle to open or cross.

It is common to think of burglary as a crime involving the intent to steal something. Modern burglary statutes require only that once a person commits trespass, he or she intends to commit another crime, whether it is a felony, such as theft, or a misdemeanor, such as vandalism. A person who commits only trespass with no specific intent to commit another crime has not satisfied the specific criminal intent required for the crime of burglary. Modern burglary statutes also cover a multitude of structures where people live and sleep, in addition to abandoned homes and partly constructed houses.

Arson   **Arson** is the willful and malicious burning or attempted burning of any structure, including one's own. Because of the many motivations a person might have for burning a structure and the serious harm that can come to innocent parties, nearly all malicious burnings constitute arson.[24]

Modern arson codes also include destroying a structure by the use of explosives. Arson includes the burning of homes, factories, personal property, and vehicles. If the structure is occupied, even if the arsonist is unaware of this fact, the crime is the more serious crime of aggravated arson. The crime of arson may also be considered aggravated arson if a firefighter or law enforcement officer is injured or killed while responding to the fire. Accidental burnings, or burnings without malice, are not criminal.

However, a person who burns his or her private property in a way that endangers the public may be charged with arson. For example, a person motivated to burn his or her automobile that is parked on a public street may be charged with arson even if the person owns the automobile and there is no lien or insurance claim on it.

- **Crimes against Property**   Numerous statutes define offenses against property, including theft, larceny, embezzlement, receiving stolen property, false pretenses, forgery, and uttering. Many of these offenses originated in common law and have been redefined in modern legal codes. For example, in many legal codes, forgery, the creation of a forged document, and uttering, passing a forged document, have been included in consolidated criminal codes regarding crimes against property that make it illegal to take stocks, bonds, checks, negotiable paper, services and labor, minerals, crops, utilities, and even trees. Virtually all property falls within the scope of modern larceny statutes.

  Larceny   Larceny is the most commonly committed crime in the United States. The Model Penal Code defines **larceny** as "the wrongfully taking and carrying away of another's property with the intent to permanently deprive the property's owner of its possession." The crime of larceny is a felony or a misdemeanor depending on the value of the property taken. Each state sets the criteria for the division between felony and misdemeanor, as does the federal government.

Women's Rights and the Law

There is great diversity among the values of the millions of people in the United States, so it is not surprising that great conflict is often generated over the constitutionally of laws. Abortion laws are an example of this conflict.

Prior to *Roe* v. *Wade* (1973), state laws prohibited abortions. The U.S. Supreme Court decided in *Roe* v. *Wade* and the companion case of *Doe* v. *Bolton* (1973) that the federal court had jurisdiction over this issue and could overrule state prohibitions against abortion, that abortion was a privacy right under the due process clause of the Fourteenth Amendment, and that state laws prohibiting abortions were unconstitutional. However, the Court ruled that the states had the right to regulate abortions; therefore, a balancing act existed between a woman's right of privacy and the state's right to regulate abortion. The decision divided the nation, and after four decades, this conflict still exists.

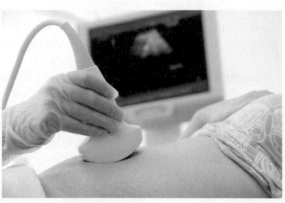

Alexander Raths/Fotolia

Pro-life groups opposed to *Roe* v. *Wade* continue to work to overturn the decision or to enact new laws that prohibit or severely restrict abortions. Recently, those opposed to *Roe* v. *Wade* in Mississippi, Oklahoma, Virginia, and Arizona introduced "personhood" bills that would have codified the fact that life begins at the moment of conception and a fertilized egg has full legal rights as a person. The Arizona bill would have established that "personhood" begins at the end of a women's menstrual cycle. This definition could call into question the legality of morning-after pills, birth control pills, and other methods of birth control. Bills have been proposed that would require women to obtain counseling and undergo ultrasound imaging prior to obtaining an abortion. On the other side of the argument, those who support *Roe* v. *Wade* continue to work to oppose new laws that would restrict abortion rights.

This case raises several interesting questions. Among them are the following:

1. When a great divide exists between the values of one group and the values of another group, how should these differences be reconciled in the law?

2. Abortion is a classic case of moral/religious beliefs versus law. To what extent should law reflect religious beliefs of certain groups?

3. Should laws reflect the majority opinion of the community, or is there an obligation to protect the values of minority communities? Explain.

4. Identify other legal issues where there are significant differences in community values.

Describe how federal, state, and local criminal laws are created and changed.

Criminal law plays a major role in defining the balance between public safety and personal liberties. Laws represent the collective understanding of a community as to how to promote peaceful and fair interaction among people. Federal criminal laws must be initiated as bills in the Senate or House of Representatives. The process for state criminal laws is similar, except the governor plays the role of the president. City councils and county governments create local criminal laws, of which most are misdemeanors or violations, in diverse ways.

1. Explain the difference between *mala in se* and *mala prohibita*.

2. Name the five sources of federal criminal law.

3. Describe the origins of common law.

4. How do sanctions differ between a felony and misdemeanor?

mala in se Acts that are crimes because they are inherently evil or harmful to society.

mala prohibita Acts that are prohibited because they are defined as crimes by law.

executive orders Presidential directives regarding the execution of legislative acts that oversee the behavior of officers and agencies of the executive branch.

common law Unwritten, simply stated laws based on traditions and common understandings in a time when most people were illiterate.

felony Serious criminal conduct punishable by incarceration for more than one year.

misdemeanor Less serious criminal conduct punishable by incarceration for less than a year.

Describe the limits of law.

Our government is restricted in making laws. Seven common benchmarks were established by the U.S. Supreme Court to define the legality of criminal laws: (1) principle of legality, (2) *ex post facto* laws, (3) due process, (4) void for vagueness, (5) right to privacy, (6) void for overbreadth, and (7) cruel and unusual punishment. The U.S. Supreme Court has held that if fairly applied, the death penalty is not cruel and unusual punishment.

1. How is government restricted in making laws?

2. Name the seven common benchmarks that define the legality of criminal laws.

3. How can punishment violate the Eighth Amendment?

principle of legality The principle that citizens cannot be punished for conduct for which no law against it exists.

ex post facto **laws** Laws providing that citizens cannot be punished for actions committed before laws against the actions were passed and that the government cannot increase the penalty for a specific crime after the crime was committed.

due process Substantive due process limits the government's power to criminalize behavior unless there is a compelling reason for the public interest to do so; procedural due process requires that the government follow standard procedures and treat all defendants equally.

rules of evidence The procedural due process laws that regulate criminal trials.

stare decisis The U.S. system of developing and applying case law on the basis of precedents established in previous cases.

void for vagueness The principle that laws not using clear and specific language to define prohibited behaviors cannot be upheld.

right to privacy The principle that laws that violate personal privacy cannot be upheld.

void for overbreadth The principle that laws go too far in that they criminalize legally protected behavior in an attempt to make some other behavior illegal that cannot be upheld.

cruel and unusual punishment An Eighth Amendment right, based on the premise of classical criminology, that punishment should be appropriate to the crime.

LEARNING OUTCOMES 3

List the elements of a crime and their role in criminal prosecution.

The elements of a crime that must be present for prosecution are *actus reus*, in which a person voluntarily committed a criminal act, and *mens rea*, in which a person committed a crime with the intent to do so. Strict liability crimes are actions that are considered criminal without the need to prove the *mens rea*. Inchoate offenses, known as incomplete crimes, are subject to punishment. The three common inchoate offenses are solicitation, conspiracy, and attempt.

1. What elements of a crime must a prosecutor prove for a conviction?

2. Which element of a crime is not necessary to show in a strict liability offense?

3. Define the term *inchoate offense*.

4. Name three types of inchoate offenses.

elements of a crime The illegal actions (*actus reus*) and criminal intentions (*mens rea*) of the actor along with the circumstances that link the two, especially causation.

actus reus An element of crime in which people are punished for their actions; thus, the law does not prosecute people for actions that are not voluntary or that are accidental and do not involve recklessness or negligence.

mens rea An element of crime in which a person must have criminal intent, or a "guilty mind," for his or her actions to be criminal.

strict liability crimes Actions that are considered criminal without the need for criminal intent.

inchoate offense An action that goes beyond mere thought but does not result in a completed crime.

solicitation The requesting or commanding of another to commit a crime.

conspiracy The planning by two or more people to commit a crime.

attempt An incomplete criminal act; the closest act to the completion of a crime.

LEARNING OUTCOMES 4

List and describe some of the major defenses against charges of criminal conduct.

A person can offer numerous criminal defenses at trial to justify his or her actions. Defenses to a criminal charge can be a perfect defense or an imperfect defense. The most common defenses against criminal charges include (1) alibi, (2) consent or condoning by the victim, (3) entrapment or outrageous government conduct, (4) immunity or privilege, (5) involuntary actions and duress, (6) mistake or ignorance of fact of law, (7) necessity, (8) self-defense, (9) youth, and (10) insanity.

1. At what stage of the criminal justice process are defenses typically offered?

2. Name types of common defenses used by a defendant.

3. What are the two major categories of defense to crimes?

4. Name three categories of affirmative defenses.

defenses Justifications or excuses defined by law by which a defendant may be released from prosecution or punishment for a crime.

perfect defense The defense that results in the person being excused from all criminal liability and punishment.

imperfect defense The defense that results in the defendant's liability or punishment for a crime being reduced.

affirmative defense A defense in which the defendant admits that he or she committed the *actus reas* of the crime but claims that he or she should not be found guilty of the crime because his or her actions were justified or he or she had an excuse.

diplomatic immunity The granting of immunity, or protection from any kind of criminal prosecution, to foreign diplomats.

legislative immunity The protection of senators and representatives of Congress from arrest only while the legislature is in session, except for felonies and treason.

witness immunity A situation in which a defendant admits to committing a crime but is granted immunity from prosecution in exchange for cooperating with a government investigation.

privilege A type of defense in which the defendant claims immunity from punishment for an admitted violation of the law because it was related to his or her official duties.

defense of duress A legal claim by a defendant that he or she acted involuntarily under the threat of immediate and serious harm by another.

mistake or ignorance of fact An affirmative legal defense in which the defendant made a mistake that does not meet the requirement for *mens rea*.

factual impossibility Circumstances under which it is not possible for a person to commit the crime intended.

necessity An affirmative legal defense claiming that the defendant committed an act out of need, not *mens rea*.

self-defense An affirmative legal defense in which a defendant claims that he or she acted to protect himself or herself or another person against a deadly attack or invasion of his or her home.

insanity A legal claim by a defendant that he or she was suffering from a disease or mental defect and that the defect caused the defendant not to understand the difference between right and wrong.

LEARNING OUTCOMES 5

Explain how crimes are classified and defined according to the Model Penal Code.

The laws governing society are numerous, complex, and diverse. The Model Penal Code is a set of guidelines that are considered the best practices for legal codes. The categories found within the Model Penal Code include (1) Crimes against the State, which includes treason, espionage, and sedition; (2) Crimes against Persons, which includes murder, rape (or sexual assault), kidnapping, robbery, and assault and battery; (3) Crimes against Habitation, which includes burglary and arson; and (4) Crimes against Property, which includes theft, larceny, embezzlement, receiving stolen property, false pretenses, forgery, and uttering.

1. What is the Model Penal Code?
2. How does the Model Penal Code classify crimes?
3. Name the various crimes against persons.
4. Name the various crimes against property.

Model Penal Code Guidelines for U.S. criminal codes published in 1962 by the American Law Institute that classify and define crimes into categories.

homicide The killing of one human being by another.

murder All intentional killings and deaths that occur in the course of aggravated felonies.

manslaughter The killing of another without the specific intent to kill.

rape Sexual assault; nonconsensual sexual acts.

kidnapping The taking away of a person by force against his or her will and holding that person in false imprisonment.

robbery The taking away of property from a person by force or the immediate threat of force.

assault The act of inflicting injury on another, whereas battery is the act of unlawfully striking another.

burglary A combination of trespass and the intent to commit a crime.

arson The willful and malicious burning of a structure.

larceny The wrongful taking of another's property with the intent to permanently deprive its owner of its possession.

MyCJLab

Go to Chapter 4 in *MyCJLab* to test your mastery of chapter concepts, access your Study Plan, engage in interactive exercises, complete critical-thinking and research assignments, and view related online videos.

 Review: Complete the pretest in the Study Plan to confirm what you know and what you need to study further. Then complete the post-test to confirm your mastery of the concepts. Use the key term flash cards to review key terminology.

 Apply: Complete the interactive simulation activity.

Analyze: Complete assignments as directed by your instructor.

Current Events: Explore CJSearch for current topical videos, articles, and news pieces.

Additional Links

Go to **http://www.ali.org** to visit the website of The American Law Institute. Its self-described mission is "producing scholarly work to clarify, modernize, and otherwise improve the law."

Go to **https://www.law.upenn.edu/fac/phrobins/intromodpencode.pdf** for more information about the Model Penal Code.

Go to **http://www.shouselaw.com/self-defense.html** for more information on California's self-defense law.

Go to **http://www.gpoaccess.gov/uscode/index.html** for further information about the U.S. Federal Code (permanent laws).

A discussion regarding the history and use of the insanity defense is available at **http://www.law.umkc.edu/faculty/projects/ftrials/hinckley/hinckleyinsanity.htm**.

An Overview of Law Enforcement—*History, Agencies, Personnel, and Strategies*

"Every society gets the kind of criminal it deserves. What is equally true is that every community gets the kind of law enforcement it insists on."

—*Robert Kennedy*

1 Outline the history and development of law enforcement.

2 Describe the roles of federal law enforcement agencies and describe some of the major federal law enforcement agencies.

3 Describe the roles and organizational structure of state law enforcement agencies.

4 Summarize the duties and administrative structure of the sheriff's office.

5 Summarize the duties and administrative structure of local law enforcement agencies.

6 Describe the hiring of, training of, and career paths for law enforcement officers.

7 Discuss the unique aspects of employment in law enforcement.

8 Describe the role and authority of special police and private protection services.

9 Describe the various styles and primary operational strategies of today's law enforcement agencies.

5

POLICE

pixarno/Fotolia

It has been less than 200 years since London's first full-time paid police officers were created by Robert Peel to patrol the streets of London. However, in the short history of the police, there have been tremendous changes in law enforcement. While the mission of law enforcement remains similar—to secure public safety, to respond to criminal activity, and to provide services to the public—the strategies utilized throughout history to achieve the mission have changed significantly.

One area that has seen significant change is the process and procedures used to hire new law enforcement officers. The process for hiring new entry-level employees is significantly different from that used by private businesses. The hiring process is long; involves multiple steps; requires extensive testing of mental, physical, and psychological traits; and is intrusive. The advent of the Internet and social media has made the process more intrusive.

Like some employers in private business, law enforcement agencies are looking at the social media postings of applications. Some departments do a search of the online postings and social media sites of applicants. Other departments request applicants to sign into social media sites to be screened as part of the interview process. A more controversial practice is for the prospective employer to ask the applicant for his or her social media password. Chief Deputy Rusty Thomas of the McLean County Sheriff's Department (Illinois) said that the department

Scott Griessel / Fotolia

is looking for "inappropriate pictures of relationships with people who are underage, or illegal behavior."[1] Chief Joseph E. Thomas, Jr., of the Southfield, Michigan, Police Department said that the department routinely checks police recruits' social pages when they apply for a job. In one case, he said, a candidate posted on his Facebook, "Just returned from the interview with the Southfield Police Department and I can't wait to get a gun and kick some ass."[2] Such statements are not conducive to a successful application for employment.

As law enforcement agencies enter the twenty-first century, there are forces acting on traditions and current practices that will force agencies to change as they strive to fulfill the mission of law enforcement.

DISCUSS Do you believe it is appropriate for law enforcement agencies to review social media postings and photographs of applicants?

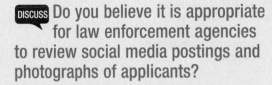

▶ Development of Policing

This chapter reviews the history and development of policing in America and discusses the personnel and agencies that comprise American policing.

Contemporary Policing

One of the most distinctive characteristics of contemporary policing in the U.S. criminal justice system is that it is a decentralized system performed by nearly 18,000 fragmented, semi-autonomous law enforcement agencies and over 1 million employees under the authority of local, state, and federal governments.[3] Each law enforcement agency has its own chief administrator, headquarters, rules and regulations, jurisdiction, and training standards.

The modern model of policing is based on Sir Robert Peel's London system, which, in 1829, was the first to establish a full-time, paid, uniformed police agency.

No single agency has oversight responsibility for all of these different police agencies. There is no central authority, person, or agency to coordinate law enforcement activities, professionalism, or administrative oversight of law enforcement agencies nationwide. There is no central authority to enforce compliance with rules, to investigate charges of abuse of power, or even to make sure the law enforcement agencies are doing a good job.

This decentralization is by design, not accident. The United States was founded on principles that reflected a distrust of a strong centralized government. The U.S. Constitution established a government divided into three branches: executive, legislative, and judicial. The purpose was to create checks and balances on government power.

LEARNING OUTCOMES 1 Outline the history and development of law enforcement.

GLOSSARY

Posse Comitatus Act of 1878 An act that limits the powers of local governments and law enforcement agencies in using federal military personnel to enforce the laws of the land.

jurisdiction The geographic limits, such as the municipality, county, or state, in which officers of the agency are empowered to perform their duties.

The British Police System

1774 The Westminster Watch Act is established to deal with the problem of public law enforcement. Using a system of night watchmen, bailiffs, and gate guards, Westminster attempts to control sex, swearing, drinking, and brawling.

1828 Sir Robert Peel is appointed Home Secretary of England. He is expected to deal with the growing problem of street crime in London.

Topham/The Image Works

The U.S. Police System

1789 The U.S. Marshals Service and the U.S. Postal Inspection Service are established.

1862 Congress creates the Office of Internal Revenue and authorizes it to investigate tax evasion.

1865 The U.S. Secret Service is founded.

1896 *Plessy v. Ferguson* This federal court case establishes the doctrine of "separate but equal" treatment of minorities, specifically African-Americans. Employment of African-American police officers, both in the South and in northern cities, is suspended.

1653 Oliver Cromwell tries a military solution to the problem of maintaining law and order in British cities. This strategy of military policing reduces personal freedoms and sharply contrasts with rising expectations of democratic values. English citizens find this solution worse than the problem.

1829 The British Parliament passes the London Metropolitan Police Act. Under Sir Robert Peel's leadership, a full-time, paid, uniformed police agency is established to promote public safety, enforce criminal codes, and bring criminals to justice.

Library of Congress

1776–1850 Gradually, various municipalities abandon the use of part-time personnel and volunteers and adopt London-style policing in an effort to promote public safety.

1850 Private security agencies such as Brinks, Pinkerton, and Wells Fargo provide investigative services and protection of private property. They fill the void created by limitations of local police to cover wide jurisdictions.

1877 Congress passes an act prohibiting the counterfeiting of any coin, or gold or silver bar.

1894 The Secret Service began informal part-time protection of President Cleveland.

Development of Policing

This philosophy was reflected in the powers invested in the authorities of the criminal justice system. To avoid a strong centralized law enforcement system that could be used as a military unit, a decentralized model was adopted. Furthermore, the U.S. model of law enforcement emphasizes that law enforcement agencies are civilian, not military, agencies. In fact, the **Posse Comitatus Act of 1878** and other laws and military regulations limit the powers of local governments and law enforcement agencies in using federal military personnel to enforce the laws of the land.

In trying to understand the country's system of policing, a good starting point is to examine the jurisdiction of the various agencies. Each law enforcement agency's powers, responsibilities, and accountability are determined by its jurisdiction. **Jurisdiction** refers to the geographic limits, such as the municipality, county, or state, in which officers of the agency are empowered to perform their duties. Jurisdiction also refers to the legitimate duties the department can perform. Some agencies have a relatively small geographic jurisdiction but a large number of legitimate duties. Other agencies have an expansive geographic jurisdiction but limited legitimate duties. For example, the geographic jurisdiction of a municipal police officer ends at the city limits, but Federal Bureau of Investigation agencies have geographic jurisdiction in all 50 states, the District of Columbia, U.S. territories, and certain federal reservations. However, the legal jurisdiction of the FBI is limited to federal laws mandated by Congress.

There are three major divisions of the political jurisdiction of law enforcement agencies: federal, state, and local. These political jurisdictions are determined by which government body (federal, state, or local) exercises authority over the agency. (Private protection services are not government agencies and are discussed later in this chapter.)

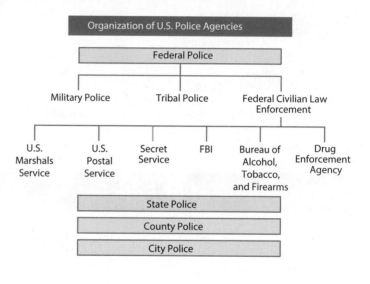

▶ *Federal Law Enforcement*

While federal, state, and local agencies might have similar responsibilities, there are distinct differences between the agencies. Federal agencies enforce only federal laws. There are different court systems for federal crimes, state crimes, and local crimes, as well as different rules of evidence in each court level. When there are overlapping responsibilities, most of the time the various agencies work cooperatively. However, there are times when agencies have conflicts.

Federal law enforcement agencies, each with a different jurisdiction and administrative leadership, have been developed to handle the enforcement of federal laws. These agencies are under the administrative control of the executive branch of the federal government (that is, the president). The president, with the approval of the Senate, appoints the chief executive officers of the various federal law enforcement agencies. Personnel within each agency are hired, trained, and supervised

1901 In response to the assassination of President William McKinley, the duties of the Secret Service are expanded to include the protection of the president.

1908 President Theodore Roosevelt creates the Bureau of Investigation, the forerunner of the FBI, to provide detective services to the executive branch of the federal government.

1913 A typical Boston police officer is recruited from the working class and makes $1,400 per year after six years of service. He works 75 hours a week with 1 day off in 15. He receives little or no training and is hired on the basis of his obedience to authority, physical strength, and size.

1934 The National Firearms Act is passed, and the Treasury Department is charged with the duty of collecting federal taxes on firearms.

1939 After World War I, Franklin D. Roosevelt charges the FBI with the responsibility for domestic intelligence matters relating to espionage and subversive activities.

Bettmann / Corbis

1972 The Civil Rights Act of 1964 is amended to prohibit discrimination by local, state, and federal criminal justice agencies.

1973 The Drug Enforcement Administration (DEA) is formed.

1995 The Office of Tribal Justice is established to coordinate Native American tribal issues for the Department of Justice.

2003 The formation of the Department of Homeland Security combines 22 existing agencies under a single command.

1905–1932 August Vollmer, Chief of Police in Berkeley, California, emphasizes education, professionalism, and administrative reform and is known as the father of modern American policing. Vollmer's contributions include scientific crime-detection practices, training for police officers, selection of police officers based on performance testing, and a vision of an expanded role of police officers in the community beyond that of "thief catchers."

1919 The emergence of the United States as the world's industrial leader after World War I brings significant changes to policing. Increased population density in New York, Boston, Philadelphia, Detroit, and Chicago, along with increased ethnic diversity, produce social disorder. Most people consider the primary threats to public order to be street violence; gangs; and vices such as gambling, drinking, and prostitution.

1952 The Office of Internal Revenue is reorganized to include the newly created Alcohol and Tobacco Tax Division.

1968 The Gun Control Act is passed, and the Alcohol, Tobacco, and Firearms Division (ATF) is created.

1970 The Organized Crime Control Act increases ATF responsibilities to include explosives.

1973 All duties related to alcohol, tobacco, firearms, and explosives are transferred from the Internal Revenue Service to the ATF.

1982 The Anti-Arson Act makes arson a federal crime and gives the ATF responsibility for investigations.

JOE MARQUETTE/ASSOCIATED PRESS

Photo Courtesy of ICE

Often federal law enforcement agencies work together due to overlapping jurisdictions, a common mission, and the unique expertise that each agency can bring to the task.

Service was added to perform investigative services and to combat counterfeiting. In 1908, after a controversial debate as to the merits of the need and appropriateness of a federal investigation agency, the Federal Bureau of Investigation was established. Over the years, other federal agencies were added, each with specialized and limited roles and responsibilities. The latest federal agency to be added was the Drug Enforcement Agency in 1973. (The Department of Homeland Security is not considered a law enforcement agency.)

Most federal agencies have jurisdiction in all 50 states, the District of Columbia, and U.S. territories. The legal jurisdiction of each agency is determined by legislation and executive orders. Federal agencies are often charged with responsibilities that are similar to those of state and local law enforcement agencies. For example, both the FBI and state and local law enforcement agencies have jurisdiction over bank robberies, kidnappings, and drug crimes. However, federal agencies can enforce only federal criminal laws. Hence, the FBI has responsibilities for kidnappings when the victim is taken across state lines or for drug crimes that violate federal drug laws, not state laws. Federal agencies can and do render assistance and service to state and local law enforcement agencies.

There are three distinctively different types of federal agencies: military police, Native American tribal police, and civilian police.

Military Police

Military police perform law enforcement duties on military bases, on certain federal lands, and in certain cases involving military personnel. Each of the four branches of military service (Army, Navy, Marines, and Air Force) has adopted its own unique strategy for providing police services, conducting criminal investigations, and maintaining order. For example, the Army utilizes military personnel to perform these activities. The Army's Military Police (MP) provides services similar to those of local police in traffic enforcement and maintenance of order. Major crimes are handled by the United States Army Criminal Investigation Division Command (USACIDC). On the other hand, the Navy has a predominately civilian employee–based agency to investigate major crimes, the Naval Criminal

by each agency. Thus, while federal agents from the different agencies may perform similar duties, each is under the unique and exclusive employment of his or her agency.

Federal Jurisdiction and Police Powers

When the United States was founded, there were only two federal law enforcement agencies: the U.S. Marshals Service and the U.S. Postal Inspection Service. In 1865, the U.S. Secret

Investigation Service (NCIS). Thus, NCIS is not a military law enforcement agency in that its personnel are civilian employees, but its jurisdiction is limited to certain violations related to criminal offenses defined by the military.

Each branch of the military service also has its own criminal justice system, including court and correctional institutions, which are separate from the civilian criminal justice system. Some of the correctional facilities are shared among the various branches of military service. Military law enforcement and military justice are based on the **Uniform Code of Military Justice (UCMJ)** rather than on state or federal criminal codes. People who want to enter military law enforcement agencies (except NCIS) must do so after enlistment in the military service. Military law enforcement is a specialty unit within the branch of the military.

Tribal Police

Native American reservations are considered sovereign territories, where local and state police have no or very limited jurisdiction. Federal police, the Bureau of Indian Affairs (BIA), and the military have limited jurisdiction on the reservations. Each Native American reservation has the legal authority to establish its own **tribal police** to provide police services. In addition to tribal police departments, police services on tribal lands are provided by the FBI and the BIA. The tribal police provide public safety services similar to those of local civilian police agencies. The FBI has responsibility for investigating felonies that occur on Native American reservations. The mission of the BIA is to enhance the quality of life; to promote economic opportunity; and to carry out the responsibility to protect and improve the trust assets of American Indians, Indian tribes, and Alaska Natives. The BIA was founded in 1824,

and prior to the emergence of the FBI, it was involved in the implementation of federal laws that have directly affected all Americans, tribal government, and quality-of-life issues. The Tribal Self-Governance Act of 1994 along with the Self-Determination and Education Assistance Act have fundamentally changed how the federal government and the tribes conduct business with each other.[4]

The jurisdiction of local and state law enforcement agencies can be complicated by the geographic location of the tribal lands, whether the offender is a registered Native American of the tribe or a non-Native American living on tribal land (for example, the non-Native American spouse of a Native American), and the crime. In general, tribal police have no or limited jurisdiction over non-Native Americans even on tribal lands. Local and state law enforcement agencies have limited jurisdiction on Native American tribal lands. The FBI's jurisdiction is limited primarily to felonies, whether the offender is a Native American or a non-Native American. Obviously, the jurisdiction of each agency is not easily defined, and at times, there may be confusion or conflict regarding jurisdiction, particularly between tribal police and the FBI.

The fact that public safety is the shared responsibility of several agencies has resulted in deficiencies in providing public safety services. Research suggests that public safety on Native American reservations has been neglected by the U.S. criminal justice system, resulting in a public safety crisis on the reservations. The rate of violent victimizations per 1,000 Native Americans aged 12 or older for 2009 was more than twice the rate for the nation as a whole (50 per 1,000 persons).[5]

The federal government has recognized this problem and has endeavored to provide better public safety services and greater coordination among agencies. These efforts have included federal grants, more personnel for reservation police departments, more crime victim services, and improvement in the judiciary. In 1995, the attorney general established the **Office of Tribal Justice** to coordinate tribal issues for the Department of Justice (DOJ). Intended to increase the responsiveness of the DOJ to Native American tribes and citizens, the purpose of the Office of Tribal Justice is to ensure better communication by serving as a permanent point of contact between the DOJ and federally recognized tribes.

Despite these efforts, crime rates on reservations continue at record high rates. In 2009, the economic stimulus package included $248 million for criminal justice infrastructure projects on Native American lands with the goal of reducing these crime rates. The main targets are domestic assaults and drug crimes. Also targeted for reduction is the unique crime of pillaging artifacts from tribal lands in the Southwest. Attorney General Eric Holder has proposed a number of changes in both federal responsibilities and the organizational structure of the DOJ to help combat the public safety crisis on Native American lands.[6]

Federal Civilian Law Enforcement Agencies

There are approximately 50 federal civilian law enforcement agencies. Some are small with limited duties, while others are major agencies with international jurisdiction. The formation of the Department of Homeland Security (DHS) on March 1, 2003, had a major influence on the organizational structure and responsibilities of federal civilian law enforcement agencies. The DHS is an executive cabinet-level agency, not a federal law enforcement agency. However, some agencies within the DHS are law enforcement agencies, as the new organization placed 22 previously independent agencies under the command and control of the DHS. In an effort to enhance national security, the goal of this reorganization was to provide unity of command for the various semiautonomous federal agencies.

The largest and most visible of the federal civilian law enforcement agencies are the U.S. Marshals Service; the U.S. Postal Inspection Service; the U.S. Secret Service; the Federal Bureau of Investigation; the Bureau of Alcohol, Tobacco, Firearms and Explosives; and the Drug Enforcement Administration.

U.S. Marshals Service The U.S. Marshals Service was one of the first federal law enforcement agencies established by the Judiciary Act of 1789. The first 13 U.S. Marshals were appointed by President George Washington. The federal Marshals Service was the first federal agency with general law enforcement powers responsible for providing security for federal courts, serving papers of the federal courts, and enforcing federal laws.

During the late 1800s, federal marshals were responsible for maintaining law and order in the western territories, but they often lacked the necessary manpower and resources to carry out such responsibilities. To supplement their manpower, federal marshals were authorized to enlist the service of civilians and the military to help them perform their duties. This power to "deputize" civilians and military troops for law enforcement purposes is known as *posse comitatus*. Lawmakers became concerned that abuses could occur if military troops were used to perform civilian law enforcement, and in 1878, Congress passed the Posse Comitatus Act, which limited the role of military troops in civilian law enforcement.

Today, the law enforcement jurisdiction of the U.S. Marshals Service still includes overseeing federal court security, serving papers of the federal courts, and performing federal law enforcement duties. However, the emergence of additional federal law enforcement agencies has impacted the law enforcement role of the U.S. Marshals Service. Agencies such as the FBI; Drug Enforcement Administration; Secret Service; and Bureau of Alcohol, Tobacco, Firearms and Explosives have assumed primary federal law enforcement responsibilities for crimes that used to be the responsibility of the U.S. Marshals Service. However, today the **U.S. Marshals Service** performs other specialized services, such as the movement and custody of federal prisoners, the capture of inmates who escape from federal penitentiaries, the management and selling of government assets, and the protection of witnesses.

The U.S. Marshals Service often works with other law enforcement agencies to assist city, county, and state police with their fugitive cases, and it is the primary U.S. agency responsible for returning fugitives from foreign countries who are wanted in the United States.

U.S. Postal Inspection Service The **U.S. Postal Inspection Service**, established the same year as the U.S. Marshals Service (1789), is a specialized law enforcement agency responsible for the security of the U.S. mail and mail carriers and for investigation of mail fraud. Its law enforcement agents are called postal inspectors and are employed by the United States Postal Service. The Postal Inspection Service has both armed and unarmed inspectors. Postal inspection agents have the power of arrest, the power of search and seizure, and the authority to carry firearms. Their geographic jurisdiction extends to wherever there is U.S. mail service; however, their primary law enforcement responsibilities are limited to crime related to protecting the integrity of mail services. The Postal Inspection Service has always had a low-key profile despite being one of the larger-staffed federal law enforcement agencies, and it has an impressive record of effectiveness. Often the positions of postal inspectors are filled from the ranks of mail carriers through competitive civil service examinations.

U.S. Secret Service Another early federal law enforcement agency was the U.S. Secret Service, founded in 1865. Initially, this agency was under the control of the Department of the Treasury, as its primary duties related to investigating the widespread counterfeiting and currency violations that followed the Civil War, when numerous legal currencies were in circulation. Counterfeiting was widespread in part because it was legal for large companies, banks, and states to print and mint legal tender, or money. Also, the technology for printing money used by the federal government was relatively primitive, and the forgery of acceptable-quality counterfeit money was not difficult.

Starting in 1894, the Secret Service provided informal part-time protection of President Cleveland. However, no agency was charged specifically with the full-time responsibility and resources for protecting the president from assassination or harm. The president, like any other citizen, went about his duties and life without the protection of federal bodyguards. Motivated by the assassination of President William McKinley

Often federal and local law enforcement agencies cooperate in criminal investigations, especially large scale drug investigations as in this major drug tunnel bust.

Photo Courtesy of ICE

at Buffalo, New York, in 1901, the duties of the Secret Service were expanded to include the full-time protection of the president.

Over time, the protective duties of the Secret Service were expanded. Today, the **U.S. Secret Service** protects not only the president, but also the president's family, the vice president and designated members of his family, former presidents and their minor children, and widows of former presidents. With the assassination of presidential candidate Robert Kennedy in 1968, Congress again expanded the protection responsibilities of the Secret Service to include major presidential and vice presidential candidates. The U.S. Secret Service also protects visiting heads of foreign governments. In addition to protecting people, the U.S. Secret Service also protects national treasures. For example, when the Magna Carta was on loan from Great Britain to the United States, it was the responsibility of the U.S. Secret Service to protect it.

The Federal Bureau of Investigation (FBI)
The Federal Bureau of Investigation was not created until the twentieth century; however, it is perhaps the most well-known of the federal police agencies. The forerunner of the FBI, the Bureau of Investigation, whose agents were unarmed, was created by executive order in 1908 by President Theodore Roosevelt. The primary purpose of the bureau was to provide detective services to the executive branch of the government. The Bureau of Investigation at first focused on finding Communist agents in the United States.

The FBI became a prominent federal police agency during the 1930s under the leadership of J. Edgar Hoover. During this time, agents of the FBI waged a "war on crime" that resulted in the FBI killing "public enemies" such as John Dillinger, "Pretty Boy" Floyd, "Baby Face" Nelson, Kate "Ma" Barker, Alvin "Creepy" Karpis, and other gangsters. Unlike the negative publicity and critical

> Most federal law enforcement agencies have jurisdiction in all 50 states, the District of Columbia, and U.S. territories and have distinct duties.

review that results today when police agents use deadly force, the social context of the time was such that the FBI's killing of gangsters was widely accepted as a great contribution to public safety.[7]

Since 1930, the responsibilities of the **Federal Bureau of Investigation (FBI)** have grown steadily. In 1939, in response to the needs caused by World War I, the FBI was charged by President Franklin D. Roosevelt with the responsibility for domestic intelligence matters relating to espionage, sabotage, and subversive activities.[8]

Through legislation such as the Mann Act in 1910, the Lindbergh Law in 1932, the Fugitive Felon Act in 1934, and the National Firearms Act in 1934, the FBI has been able to assume additional criminal responsibilities. However, the FBI is not a national police force. It does not have control or jurisdiction over state and local police agencies.

In addition to criminal investigation and domestic intelligence responsibilities, the FBI also maintains aand operates a sophisticated crime lab and makes the technical expertise of its crime lab available upon request to other police agencies free of charge.

The FBI operates the largest training academy in the United States for law enforcement agencies. The prestigious FBI training academy provides instruction in investigation, management, computer crime, homeland security, and other important subjects to local and state law enforcement personnel. As with the crime lab services provided by the FBI, no tuition is charged for those law enforcement personnel who attend the training academy.

The FBI also maintains the **National Crime Information Center (NCIC)**, the nation's largest database of computerized criminal information on wanted felons, people on parole, criminal history, and stolen items (automobiles, boats, guns, and securities). Nearly every police agency participates in the NCIC, and it has been an invaluable tool in law enforcement in this highly mobile, contemporary society. Also, the FBI is responsible for compiling the national crime data published in the Uniform Crime Report. Following the September 11, 2001, attacks, however, public and congressional scrutiny resulted in a significant reorganization of the FBI.

To combat future terrorism, FBI Director Robert Mueller asked for hundreds of new agents, better computer resources, and a redirected mission and priorities that would change the FBI's mission. The new mission resulted in the FBI shedding its traditional case-oriented focus on criminal activity.[9] Mueller saw "a Federal Bureau of Investigation whose central mission is to collect, analyze and act on information that will help prevent [terrorist] attacks." Mueller told Congress, "The FBI must become better at shaping its workforce, collaborating with its partners, applying technology to support investigations, operations and analyses, protecting our information and developing core competencies."

In this 1939 photo, FBI agents practice shooting at "public enemy" targets from a moving vehicle. Most modern police departments do not allow officers to shoot from a moving vehicle.

The new FBI priorities are as follows:

- Protect the United States from terrorist attack
- Protect the United States against foreign intelligence operations and espionage
- Protect the United States against cyber-based attacks and high-tech crimes
- Combat public corruption at all levels
- Protect civil rights
- Combat transnational and national criminal organizations and enterprises
- Combat major white-collar crime
- Combat significant violent crime
- Support federal, state, local, and international partners
- Upgrade technology to successfully perform the FBI's mission

The FBI also reorganized its Counterterrorism Division, established the Office of Intelligence, and placed more emphasis on coordinating with other agencies and using intelligence information more effectively. As a result of all these changes, the FBI is focusing its recruitment on candidates who possess skills beyond those associated with traditional criminal investigation. The critical skills the FBI is now seeking in new agents include computer science, other information technology specialties, engineering, physical sciences (physics, chemistry, and biology), foreign language proficiency (Arabic, Farsi, Pashto, Urdu, Chinese, Japanese, Korean, Russian, Spanish, and Vietnamese), foreign counterintelligence, counterterrorism, military intelligence, and fixed-wing piloting.

Bureau of Alcohol, Tobacco, Firearms and Explosives (ATF) The origins of the Bureau of Alcohol, Tobacco, Firearms and Explosives stemmed from the need of the Treasury Department to enforce tax laws on alcohol and tobacco. Responsibilities for firearms and explosives were added later. Initially, the agency's activities

The FBI training academy provides training to law enforcement officers worldwide.

were focused on tax evaders. Early in U.S. history, the taxing of alcoholic beverages became a significant source of income for the federal government, and there was a need to collect taxes from those who evaded them. In 1862, Congress created the Office of Internal Revenue within the Treasury Department and authorized the agency to investigate criminal evasion of taxes. The Office of Internal Revenue was to eventually become the ATF.

New duties were added to the Treasury Department with the passage of the National Firearms Act in 1934, as the department was charged with the duty of collecting federal taxes on certain types of firearms—machine guns. In 1937, the Marijuana Tax Act imposed a tax on cannabis, hemp, and marijuana and the Treasury Department was responsible for apprehension of those who evaded this tax. (The Marijuana Tax Act was overturned by *Leary* v. *United States* (1969) and repealed by Congress in 1979.) In 1952, the Internal Revenue division of the Treasury Department was reorganized and the Alcohol and Tobacco Tax Division was created. In 1968, the Gun Control Act was passed. In addition to regulatory responsibilities for firearms under this Act, the department also assumed responsibility for explosives. To fulfill these responsibilities, the Treasury Department created the Alcohol, Tobacco, and Firearms Division. In 1970, the Organized Crime Control Act increased the ATF's responsibilities to include explosives. In 1972, the functions, powers, and duties related to alcohol, tobacco, firearms, and explosives were transferred from the Internal Revenue Service to Alcohol, Tobacco, and Firearms (ATF). In 1982, the Anti-Arson Act made arson a federal crime and gave the ATF responsibility for investigating commercial arson nationwide.

In 2003, the Bureau of Alcohol, Tobacco, and Firearms was transferred under the Homeland Security bill to the DOJ. The law enforcement functions of the ATF under the Treasury Department were transferred to the DOJ. The tax and trade functions of the ATF remained with the Treasury Department with the new Alcohol and Tobacco Tax and Trade Bureau. The

U.S. Secret Service The federal agency that protects the president, the vice president, members of their families, major candidates for president and vice president, and visiting heads of foreign governments.

Federal Bureau of Investigation (FBI) The federal agency responsible for protecting the United States from terrorist attacks, foreign intelligence and espionage, cyber-based attacks, and high-tech crimes and for combating public corruption at all levels.

National Crime Information Center (NCIC) The nation's largest database of computerized criminal information on wanted felons; people on parole; criminal history; and stolen items such as automobiles, boats, guns, and securities.

Bureau of Alcohol, Tobacco, Firearms and Explosives (ATF) The federal agency responsible for regulating alcohol, tobacco, firearms, explosives, and arson.

Drug Enforcement Administration (DEA) The federal agency that enforces U.S. laws and regulations regarding controlled substances and that supports nonenforcement programs intended to reduce the availability of illicit controlled substances domestically and internationally.

narcoterrorism Terrorism in which drug lords in some countries operate virtually unchecked by law enforcement.

The U.S. founding fathers created a decentralized government with checks and balances. However, not all countries have adopted this model. The criminal justice system of the former Soviet Union and present-day Russian Federation illustrates a centralized criminal justice system.

According to Soviet expert Chief (retired) Ronald Swan, Ph.D., after "The Great October Socialist Revolution," Vladimir Lenin established the Cheka. The Cheka had absolute powers to protect the revolution, including summary trials and executions. Earlier in November 1917, Lenin created a people's militia, also known as the police in the People's Commissariat of Internal Affairs (NKVD). In 1954, the Militia (police) and Security Services were divided. The Ministry of Internal Affairs (MVD) was responsible for the criminal police and correctional facilities. The MVD was further subdivided into two divisions: (1) militia (police), who had primary responsibility for criminal activities, and (2) Internal Troops, an elite military force with a centralized rank structure. The Internal Troops reported directly to the Minister of Internal Affairs, maintaining their own chain of command. The Internal Troops were a powerful elite military arm under the direct control of the Communist Party.

The USSR officially ended on December 31, 1991, and in 2010, the name of the militia was changed to "Police" and placed under the MVD. The Ministry of Justice also controls the correctional system. Under the new Russian Federation, the former KGB was divided into two organizations: the Federal Security Service (FSB) and Russian Foreign Intelligence Service (SRV). The primary tasks of the FSB are domestic security, counter-intelligence, boarder security, counterterrorism, and surveillance. The primary responsibilities of the SRV are foreign intelligence and counterintelligence service.

Unlike the decentralized U.S. system, there is no local control of the police. The Russian Federation Police have military-type equipment, can be deployed as military units, and can be under military control. Also, there is no check-and-balance oversight of the various Russian Federation law enforcement agencies by local governments.

In the twenty-first century following the 9/11 attacks, there is greater emphasis on centralization of U.S. federal law enforcement agencies. Some argue that decentralization impedes effective response to international terrorism, drug trafficking, and other interstate crimes. Should there be greater centralization of command and control of U.S. law enforcement agencies? Why or why not?

agency's name was changed to the **Bureau of Alcohol, Tobacco, Firearms and Explosives (ATF)** to reflect its new mission. However, the initials ATF used to identify the agency are still in common use.

Drug Enforcement Administration (DEA) Another high-profile federal law enforcement agency is the **Drug Enforcement Administration**

The mission of the ATF is to conduct criminal investigations, regulate the firearms and explosives industries, and assist other law enforcement agencies.

(DEA). The DEA, founded in 1973, is one of the newest federal law enforcement agencies. The mission of the DEA is to enforce U.S. controlled-substances laws and regulations and to bring to criminal and civil justice systems of the United States, or any other competent jurisdiction, those organizations and principal members of organizations involved in the growing, manufacture, or distribution of controlled substances appearing in or destined for illicit traffic in the United States and to recommend and support nonenforcement programs aimed at reducing the availability of illicit controlled substances on the domestic and international market.[10]

This mission gives the DEA virtually worldwide jurisdiction, but at the same time, it makes the DEA one of the most focused of the federal law enforcement agencies. Despite its worldwide jurisdiction, unlike other federal law enforcement agencies, its mission focuses primarily on violations and education related to controlled substances.

The "war on drugs" and the new emphasis on the perceived dangers of international criminal drug trafficking and the connection between illegal drugs and terrorism have made the DEA a key law enforcement agency. There are nearly 5,000 DEA agents and a $2 billion budget. Even though many other law enforcement agencies are involved in the enforcement of drug laws,

In 2010, the DEA's Operation Tarpit in Afghanistan resulted in the seizure of $55.9 million from a clandestine heroin operation.

the DEA is the lead agency in countering the use of illicit drugs in the United States.

The worldwide jurisdiction of the DEA is attributed in part to the rise of the international drug cartels in the 1980s, particularly the Medellín cartel of Columbia. Worldwide drug cartels have created the phenomenon of **narcoterrorism**, whereby drug lords in some countries operate virtually unchecked by law enforcement. Also, the linkage of international drug trafficking as a fund-raising activity for terrorism has emphasized the role and importance of drug enforcement. For example, the DEA has ongoing missions in Mexico and Afghanistan.

Other Federal Law Enforcement Agencies

Other federal agencies with law enforcement powers include the Internal Revenue Service (IRS), the National Park Service, the National Forest Service, the U.S. Fish and Wildlife Service, the U.S. Air Marshals, and a number of small agencies with limited jurisdiction.

The Central Intelligence Agency (CIA) and the National Security Agency (NSA) are two very important federal agencies. Both of these large government agencies have responsibilities related to national security, but their focus is on threats posed by foreign governments and powers. These agencies are not federal civilian law enforcement agencies. In fact, the CIA is prohibited by law from conducting any operations on American soil other than those that are administrative. Law enforcement operations related to domestic national security are handled by the FBI.

▶ The State Police

The geographic jurisdiction of the state police is limited by state boundaries, and their legal jurisdiction is determined by legislation. State law enforcement agencies can be divided into three major types: traffic enforcement, general criminal investigations, and special investigations. Some states, such as Kentucky, have a single state police agency that is responsible for both general criminal investigations and traffic enforcement. Other states have created distinct agencies for each function. Hawaii has neither a state highway patrol nor a statewide general criminal investigation agency. The state legislature of each state has the authority and discretion to establish the state police agencies that it deems most appropriate for the needs of its state.

The Texas Rangers claim to be oldest state law enforcement agency in the United States. Stephen F. Austin is credited with the formation of the unit that was the origins of the Texas Rangers in 1823. Today, the Texas Ranger Division of the Texas Department of Public Safety is a relatively small law enforcement agency of fewer than 150 commissioned members. However, the history and reputation of the Texas Rangers as a law enforcement agency in the Old West are legendary and have been the subject of many books and movies. Texans' feelings toward the Rangers are reflected by the fact that they have the distinction of being the only law enforcement agency protected from disbandment by Texas state legislation.

Highway Patrol

State police agencies that focus on traffic enforcement are commonly called the **highway patrol**. The legal jurisdictions for these agencies are limited to enforcing the traffic laws and promoting safety on the interstate highways and primary and secondary roads of the state. Generally, state traffic enforcement officers do not provide general preventive patrol services to neighborhoods, as do municipal police, or engage in the investigation of crimes. State highway patrol officers enforce the various traffic laws of the state, render assistance to motorists, and promote highway safety. Highway patrol officers have the powers of arrest and search and seizure and are authorized to carry firearms. State highway patrol officers are commonly called "troopers." This name most likely originated from the uniform and distinctive hats worn by state highway patrol officers. During the 1970s and 1980s when CB radios were popular with truckers, when using the radios, truckers commonly referred to state troopers as "the bear."

Criminal Investigation

Some state police investigative agencies have law enforcement powers similar to municipal police detectives in that they are authorized to conduct general and specialized criminal investigations. In

One of the oldest state police agencies is the Texas Rangers.

LEARNING OUTCOMES 3 — Describe the roles and organizational structure of state law enforcement agencies.

GLOSSARY

ten-code radio communications A system of communicating events, actions, and services by use of numbered code, each beginning with the number 10 followed by another number.

highway patrol State law enforcement agencies that focus on traffic enforcement.

aijohn784/Fotolia

Contemporary law enforcement agencies are more interdependent than they have ever been. A sign of this growing interdependency is that law enforcement agencies are abandoning their **ten-code radio communications**. Since the police radio was adopted, officers and dispatchers have talked to each other using "ten codes." Events, requests for service, and cautionary advisories were spoken in "ten codes" such as "10-4," "10-6," and "10-8." Each code had a meaning, such as "acknowledge," "arrived at the scene," and "in service." Each agency had its own unique "ten codes," even agencies with a common border or agencies with overlapping geographic patrol areas such as the police department and the sheriff's department. The early adoption of these "ten codes" was based on technological limitations of police radio communications and the lack of encrypted radio frequencies that made all police radio communications available to the public.

In the aftermath of the September 11, 2001, terrorist attacks, there has been a great increase in interagency cooperation and mutual-aid agreements. This cooperation has resulted in more interagency cooperation and hence more interagency communication. Since departments have different meanings for the same radio "ten code," the probability of misunderstanding is high. Hence, law enforcement agencies are abandoning the ten-code radio communications and adopting plain language communication, meaning that a law enforcement officer uses plain English to say what he or she is doing or requesting. This change reflects how contemporary law enforcement agencies are adopting new strategies to improve services even if it means abandoning long-held traditions. What other changes would modernize or improve services provided by law enforcement agencies?

some cases, state police may also perform routine patrol and provide police services. So as not to duplicate the law enforcement services provided by municipal and county police, state police focus on the investigation of crimes more appropriate for an agency with statewide jurisdiction. For example, state investigators may assume responsibility for investigating statewide crimes, such as those involving drugs and narcotics, or crimes that occur in more than one jurisdiction, such as a mobile crime ring, organized crime, or serial murders. In counties where cities or villages do not have a local law enforcement unit and the sheriff's department cannot provide investigative services, the state police may provide investigative services to these areas in the event of a serious crime. Sometimes small towns or villages will contract with the state police to provide general police services for a fee rather than attempt to have their own police

department. In this case, state police may provide general public safety services, traffic enforcement, and investigative services.

State police can also have jurisdiction for investigation of crimes when the municipal or county police appear to be biased. In cases in which there are charges of political corruption of local officers, voter fraud, or bribery of state officials, it might make sense to give jurisdiction for these investigations to the state police.

▶ County Law Enforcement Agencies

The sheriff's office is the oldest local law enforcement agency in the United States. The sheriff was the only local law enforcement officer when the United States was founded. The office of sheriff was an Old English position appointed by the Crown and imported from England to the American colonies. When the United States won its independence, it retained the office of sheriff but transformed the position into an elective office. The sheriff is the only law enforcement chief executive who obtains his or her position by election. A candidate for sheriff must conduct a political campaign and be elected by a majority of the popular vote of county residents to obtain his or her position. In contrast, police chiefs and directors of state and federal law enforcement agencies obtain their positions through political appointment.

Originally, the term of sheriff was limited to two years, and in many cases, the sheriff could not serve two terms in a row. These limitations were due to suspicions of a strong centralized authority. The short term of office and restrictions on succeeding oneself in office proved disadvantageous and were changed. Most modern sheriffs are elected to four-year terms and may run for reelection. In many county elections, sheriffs are expected to affiliate with a political party and to raise funds to campaign for the position. Qualifications to run for sheriff are

Larry Kuivila / Fotolia

Highway patrol is limited to enforcing traffic laws and promoting safety on the interstate highways and primary and secondary roads of the state.

In November 2011, 93-year-old Myra Westray received special recognition from the Illinois Sheriff's Association as the second female sheriff in Illinois. She was appointed sheriff in 1942 to serve in place of her husband, who was called to duty in World War II. When her husband returned, voters elected him to succeed his wife. The National Sheriff's Association reports that of the approximately 3,000 sheriffs, only about 40 are women. Only within the last decade have some states seen their first female elected as sheriff. For example, in 2000, Beth Arthur was the first elected sheriff of Arlington County, Virginia. In 2004, Susan Benton was the first elected female sheriff in Florida (Highlands County). The field is a predominately male occupation, and women often encounter discrimination. Sheriff Susan Benton says that the best way for women to succeed in law enforcement is "to confront and manage discrimination." Will more women obtain top executive positions in law enforcement in the future? Why or why not?

minimal. The most common requirements are a minimum age and no felony convictions. A successful campaign, political affiliation, and public appeal are more important in obtaining the office of sheriff than are job experience, education, or law enforcement abilities. It is not uncommon for some sheriffs to have no previous background in law enforcement prior to being elected.

Because a sheriff has countywide jurisdiction, whereas local police departments have only municipal jurisdiction, the sheriff is called the **chief law enforcement officer** of the county. The chief law enforcement officer of the state is the attorney general, and the chief law enforcement officer of the United States is the U.S. attorney general.

A. T. Willett / Alamy

Referred to by the media as "the toughest sheriff in America," Joe Arpaio is sheriff of Mariocopa County (Arizona), the third-largest sheriff's office in the United States. Sheriff Arpaio has been elected sheriff a record four terms. Despite his popular appeal, he is under constant review by the Department of Justice for his alleged practices of discrimination against Hispanics.

Administrative Structure of the Sheriff's Department

The sheriff is empowered to appoint officers to help him or her carry out the duties of the office. These officers are called **deputy sheriff officers.** The sheriff's department is organized in a typical pyramid-shaped structure similar to most other law enforcement agencies. The second-in-command of the sheriff's office sometimes retains the Old English title of **undersheriff**.

Deputy sheriffs wear different uniforms from those of local police within their county to distinguish the two departments. The star-shaped badge worn by deputy sheriffs is a carryover from the Old English office of the sheriff, whereas officers in most police departments wear "shields," or oval-shaped badges.

Because the sheriff obtains his or her office by popular election, this has influenced how deputy sheriffs are selected. Historically, selecting deputy sheriffs was based on the belief that an elected sheriff should be able to appoint employees on the basis of loyalty. If a sheriff failed to win reelection, the incoming sheriff had the authority to dismiss the deputy sheriffs and award the jobs as political patronage to those who had helped him or her win office.

Until the latter half of the twentieth century, sheriffs selected their deputies based on the same criteria on which they had obtained their own office—politics. Deputy sheriffs served at the pleasure of the sheriff, and those who did not campaign or contribute to the sheriff's election effort could be fired. Deputies could be fired for supporting the sheriff's opponent or even for being perceived as a liability. Likewise, deputies could be hired as a reward for

LEARNING OUTCOMES 4 Summarize the duties and administrative structure of the sheriff's office.

GLOSSARY

chief law enforcement officer The highest-ranking law enforcement official within a system; the sheriff is the chief law enforcement officer of a county, the attorney general is the chief law enforcement officer of a state, and the U.S. attorney general is the chief law enforcement officer of the United States.

deputy sheriff officers Law enforcement officers who assist the sheriff.

undersheriff The second-in-command of the sheriff's office.

officers of the court Law enforcement officers who serve the court by serving papers, providing courtroom security, and transporting incarcerated defendants.

supporting the sheriff in his or her campaign or because they were friends or relatives.

Today, there are state-mandated minimum training requirements for law enforcement officers. As a result of court rulings prohibiting the dismissal of deputy sheriffs for failing to campaign for the sheriff (or in some cases campaigning for the sheriff's opponent), most sheriff's departments use a civil service selection process for the appointment of sworn officers. Deputy sheriffs are selected based on competitive examinations that test job knowledge, skills, and abilities and can be dismissed from their jobs only for legitimate reasons. However, some court cases still uphold the right of the sheriff to dismiss employees who campaigned for his or her opponent.

Law Enforcement Duties of the Sheriff

The sheriff's department can have three major responsibilities: performing law enforcement duties, serving as **officers of the court**, and operating the county jail. The Office of the Sheriff was the first and only local law enforcement agency in the late eighteenth and early nineteenth centuries. The sheriff and his deputies were empowered to enforce the laws of the county and state, to make arrests, to engage in preventive patrol, and to carry firearms. With the rise of municipal policing in the latter half of the twentieth century, the role of the sheriff in providing law enforcement services diminished.

Today, in practice, it is often the municipal police who assume major responsibility for law enforcement and the sheriff's department that provides police services for citizens who live in unincorporated or rural areas of the county. However, in some major metropolitan areas, very little of the county is unincorporated, and the law enforcement services of the sheriff overlap those of municipal police. In counties where the sheriff has responsibility for law enforcement and criminal investigations, some small cities or villages within the county without local policing will contract with the sheriff's office for traffic and criminal investigation services. Sheriff's offices with law enforcement units have different standards for hiring, training, and paying what are called "road" officers versus deputies who work in the jail.

The potential for conflict exists between sheriff departments and city police regarding geographic jurisdiction concerning crimes and routine patrol, as in some counties, there are overlapping jurisdictional claims. Unlike state police agencies that may offer specialized criminal investigation services to a community, the sheriff's department and the city police provide similar services, which may duplicate each other. In some large metropolitan areas, the sheriff and police have tackled this problem by forming "metro units" whereby deputy sheriff officers and municipal police officers have joint geographic authority throughout the county and share a common mission is providing law enforcement and investigative services.

▶ The City Police: "The Cops"

When most people refer to "the police," they usually mean the municipal police. In fact, many people appear not to appreciate or notice the difference between deputy sheriffs, state police, and municipal police officers. Perhaps this is partly due to the fact that municipal police officers, commonly referred to as

"the cops," far outnumber all other types of law enforcement officers combined. Local police departments account for 60% of sworn personnel.[11]

Each incorporated town or city in the United States has the power to establish its own police department and laws. Thus, there are over 12,500 local police departments.[12] Typically, the size of a municipal police department increases as the population of the city increases, and the largest police departments are found in the largest cities.

Large cities can employ thousands of police officers, but most municipal departments are much smaller. About 49% of all agencies employ fewer than ten full-time officers, and 30% of these agencies employ fewer than five officers. About 12% of these smaller agencies employ just one full-time officer or part-time equivalent.[13] Local police departments are one of the major expenses of any city. The budget for a small police department serving a population of less than 2,500 averages $263,000.[14] The typical budget for a department serving a metropolitan area of a million or more residents is $849 million.[15] The average law enforcement agency budget is $4.4 million.[16] New responsibilities related to the war on terrorism have strained the budgets of many police departments. Nationwide there is about 1 local law enforcement officer for every 400 residents.[17]

Ten Largest Local Law Enforcement Agencies by Number of Full-Time Sworn Personnel, 2008

Department	Full-Time Sworn Personnel
1. New York City (New York) Police	36,023
2. Chicago (Illinois) Police	13,354
3. Los Angeles (California) Police	9,727
4. Philadelphia (Pennsylvania) Police	6,624
5. Houston (Texas) Police	5,053
6. Washington, D.C. Metropolitan Police	3,742
7. Dallas (Texas) Police	3,389
8. Phoenix (Arizona) Police	3,388
9. Miami-Dade (Florida) Police	3,093
10. Baltimore (Maryland)	2,290

Source: Brian A. Reaves, *Census of State and Local Law Enforcement Agencies, 2008* (Washington, DC: Bureau of Justice Statistics, July 2011), p. 14.

49% The percentage of departments that employ fewer than ten full-time officers.

When most people refer to "the police," they mean the municipal police. Commonly referred to as simply "the cops," municipal police officers far outnumber all other types of law enforcement officers combined.

Often local police are involved in youth activities, drug education programs, and community activities.

Mikael Karlsson / Alamy

Jurisdiction of Local Police

The geographic jurisdiction of local law enforcement agencies is limited to the city limits. Once outside his or her municipal jurisdiction, a local police officer's powers to arrest, search, or even carry a firearm may not be recognized. Although the geographic jurisdiction of municipal police officers is more limited than that of county, state, and federal agents, their legal jurisdiction is the most comprehensive of all of the police agencies. Municipal police officers have the authority to enforce both local and state laws, and often their authority is based on common law rather than statutory law. Common law authority gives the officers broad discretion in determining what behaviors are illegal.

As cities have merged into large metropolitan areas, police departments have responded by expanding the geographical jurisdiction of municipal police officers through intercity agreements. In large metropolitan areas such as Dade County (Florida) and Las Vegas (Nevada), intercity and county agreements have established the metro police. These agreements provide for greater geographic jurisdiction to avoid the problems that would develop if the police did not have powers outside their city limits.

Roles of Local Law Enforcement

Local law enforcement agencies are responsible for a variety of services. The most commonly demanded services of local law enforcement include enforcing traffic laws, investigating accidents, patrolling and being first responders to incidents, investigating property crime, investigating violent crime, responding to requests for service and order maintenance, and investigating murders. Local law enforcement agencies also end up assuming *de facto* responsibility for many services simply because they are one of the few government agencies available 24 hours a day, 7 days a week, and they will dispatch an officer to the scene. Thus, it is common to find that some local law enforcement agencies also have responsibilities for animal control, search and rescue, emergency

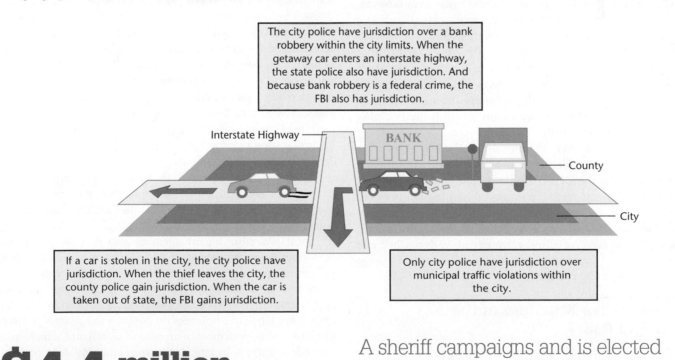

The city police have jurisdiction over a bank robbery within the city limits. When the getaway car enters an interstate highway, the state police also have jurisdiction. And because bank robbery is a federal crime, the FBI also has jurisdiction.

Interstate Highway

BANK

County

City

If a car is stolen in the city, the city police have jurisdiction. When the thief leaves the city, the county police gain jurisdiction. When the car is taken out of state, the FBI gains jurisdiction.

Only city police have jurisdiction over municipal traffic violations within the city.

$4.4 million
The nationwide average of a local police budget.

A sheriff campaigns and is elected as the chief law enforcement officer of a county and need not have any law enforcement experience.

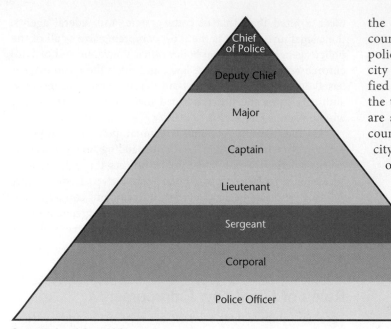

Command-and-Control Structure

The city police, or "cops," are limited by the geographic limits of the city but have the greatest legal jurisdiction of all law enforcement agencies.

medical services, civil defense, communication and technical support services, jail operations, and **order maintenance**. Order maintenance is when law enforcement officers use informal conflict resolution skills to defuse conflicts between citizens and restore order. Frequently, the police are called to a situation not because of a violation of the law or the desire to see someone arrested, but because residents need someone with authority to resolve public order conflicts or to provide certain noncrime-related services important to maintaining harmony in the community.

In an effort to save money, some smaller cities have combined the police department and the fire department. Commonly called the Department of Public Safety, the officers of these departments receive training in both law enforcement and firefighting. Officers patrol in police cars and police uniforms but carry firefighting equipment in the trunks of their vehicles. In the event of a fire, a fire engine is dispatched and officers meet the fire engine at the scene, where they change into their firefighting equipment.

Administrative Structure of the Municipal Police

Local law enforcement agencies are organized in the typical pyramid-shaped command-and-control organizational structure. The chief administrative officer of the police department is usually called the **chief of police**. The chief obtains his or her position by appointment. In smaller cities,

the chief may be directly appointed by the mayor or city council. In larger cities, the chief may be appointed by a police commission whose members are appointed by the city council. Unlike the sheriff, who is elected for a specified number of years, the chief may have no guarantee of the term of his or her appointment. For this reason, chiefs are said to "serve at the pleasure of the mayor or the city council." This political relationship between the chief and city administrators has influenced local policing throughout history. At its worst, this system becomes a political patronage system wherein the local police become an extension of the political machine of the mayor or ruling party. At various times in history, this relationship has resulted in extensive political corruption and inappropriate use of local law enforcement authority. An example of this was Tammany Hall, the Democratic Party political machine of New York City. From 1790 to the 1960s, the Tammany Hall machine utilized the police as a strategy to achieve political power and win elections.

Police departments have a system of military-style ranks in a hierarchical pyramid, with a chain of command from chief of police to patrol officer.[18] This type of organizational structure is termed a **command-and-control structure**. As mentioned, the chief executive is the chief of police. The second-in-command of the police department is usually called the **deputy chief** or assistant chief. This person is selected by the chief from among the higher-ranking police administrators. In large departments, administrators may have responsibility for the various branches of the police department. These administrators also are selected by the chief of police. Below this level of high-ranking officers is middle management, consisting of majors and captains followed by supervisors known as lieutenants. Sergeants are the first level of line or field supervisors. Below sergeants are corporals. Police departments do not use the military rank of private. Instead, departments refer to the lowest level of personnel by various names, such as "police officer," "public safety officer," or "patrol officer." These ranks may be further subdivided as "police officer 1," "police officer 2," and "police officer 3," for example.

Although also organized in terms of a command-and-control structure, many federal law enforcement agencies do not use military titles; instead, they use titles such as "field agent," "supervisor," "agent in charge," and "director."

Local law enforcement agencies also employ nonsworn personnel. **Sworn personnel** are police officers who have police powers of arrest and search and seizure and the authority to carry a firearm. **Nonsworn personnel** are employees such as secretaries, office workers, and technicians. These are civilian employees. Civilian employees do not have the powers granted to sworn police personnel of arrest and search and seizure and the right to carry a firearm. Both sworn and nonsworn personnel normally have civil service protection, which means that after completing their probationary period of employment, they cannot be dismissed from their jobs without cause and due process.[19]

► Selection of Police Officers and Career Paths

Every police department is faced with the challenge of recruiting and retaining highly qualified men and women to fill the ranks of the police department. Large cities such as New York and Chicago may have to recruit hundreds of new police officers each year. Smaller cities may recruit only one or two officers per year.

The process of becoming a police officer is unlike applying for an entry-level position in private industry. It is more intrusive and involves many steps. The hiring process takes months to complete. During this process, applicants are screened, examined, tested, observed, stressed, and evaluated in many ways. They are tested for their physical, psychological, and intellectual fitness as police officers. The objective of this extensive screening and training process is to produce police officers who can perform their duties to the high professional standards demanded by the department, the community, and the law.

There is no universal hiring process that must be used by local police agencies. Each city and county department sets its own entrance requirements, salary levels, testing procedures, and timetable. Although there are no universally required criteria and procedures, over the years—as a result of state regulations, public expectations, Supreme Court decisions, and civil and criminal liability cases—police agencies have adopted a set of hiring procedures that are fairly uniform from department to department.

Supreme Court decisions have required that hiring standards must reflect job-related requirements; cannot be arbitrary; and cannot discriminate on the basis of race, national origin, religion, or sex.[20] The major impact of these decisions has been to eliminate minimum height requirements, which were once as high as 6 feet for some police departments; to eliminate nonjob-related physical tests such as climbing 10-foot walls; and to eliminate discrimination based on race, color, and gender.

The usual process for hiring includes a written test; an oral interview; a physical examination; fitness testing; psychological testing; a background check; a drug-screening test;

GLOSSARY

order maintenance Noncrime-fighting services performed by police, such as using mediation, providing for the welfare of vulnerable people, and controlling crime.

chief of police The chief administrative officer of the police department.

command-and-control structure A hierarchical administrative structure organized by ranks with a single person responsible for all personnel in the organization.

deputy chief The second-in-command below the chief of police. In a large police department, there may be several deputy chiefs, each commanding a large unit within the police department.

sworn personnel Officers who have police powers of arrest and search and seizure and the authority to carry a firearm.

nonsworn personnel Employees such as secretaries, office workers, and technicians who do not have "police" powers and are not authorized to carry firearms.

and, in some departments, a polygraph examination.[21] Each department arranges the order of the testing according to its preference. However, most departments administer the least expensive procedures first to eliminate unqualified candidates, and only highly qualified candidates are subject to more expensive screening procedures. Most departments first require the applicant to pass a written test. The examination does not test specific knowledge of law enforcement procedures or law, as the U.S. Supreme Court has banned such tests for entry-level positions. Instead, the examination assesses general comprehension skills, basic math abilities, and reading.

A prominent change in minimum job qualifications for police officers has been an increased emphasis on recruiting from a more educated pool of applicants.[22] The requirement of a minimum of a high school education was not universal prior to the 1970s. College-educated officers were rare. Even college-educated police executives were rare, as it is estimated that less than 1% of local police chiefs had a bachelor's degree in the 1960s. Today, nearly all local police departments require a minimum of a high school diploma or general equivalency degree (GED) to apply for employment.[23]

Law Enforcement Education Program (LEEP)

A 1967 presidential commission recommended that a four-year college degree should be the minimum requirement for employment as a local police officer.[24] Although this standard has not been adopted universally, a number of police departments require some college or a four-year college degree to apply for the position of police officer. However, college education and degrees are a common requirement for promotion to higher ranks, especially higher-level administrative positions. Some federal agencies, such as the FBI, require a minimum of a four-year degree to apply for entry-level agent positions.

A major factor that promoted the emphasis on college-educated police officers was the federal **Law Enforcement Assistance Administration (LEAA) program**. From the late 1960s to the early 1980s, the federal government administered an educational loan and grant program under the LEAA, called the Law Enforcement Educational Program (LEEP), to encourage criminal justice personnel and applicants to attend college. Under LEEP, college students who indicated their desire to join a police department after graduation, as well as employed police officers, could obtain student loans to attend the college of their choice. In return for remaining in the criminal justice system after graduation from college, their educational loans were forgiven. Nearly 100,000 students took advantage of this government program.[25]

The LEEP program was discontinued in the early 1980s, but the number of college-educated police officers has continued to grow. Other factors, such as the adoption of new communication and computer technologies by the police, continue to increase the demand for college-educated police officers. For example, computer literacy is becoming a common job requirement for police officers; about 90% of police departments use field computers.[26]

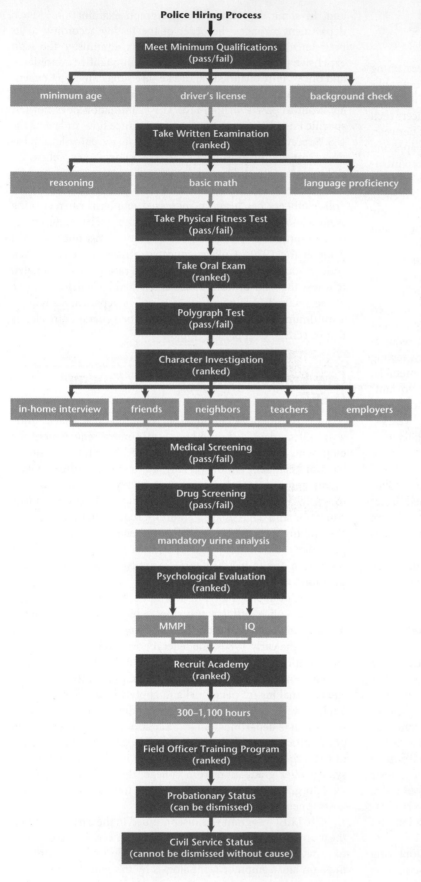

Police Hiring Process

Meet Minimum Qualifications
(pass/fail)

minimum age · driver's license · background check

Take Written Examination
(ranked)

reasoning · basic math · language proficiency

Take Physical Fitness Test
(pass/fail)

Take Oral Exam
(ranked)

Polygraph Test
(pass/fail)

Character Investigation
(ranked)

in-home interview · friends · neighbors · teachers · employers

Medical Screening
(pass/fail)

Drug Screening
(pass/fail)

mandatory urine analysis

Psychological Evaluation
(ranked)

MMPI · IQ

Recruit Academy
(ranked)

300–1,100 hours

Field Officer Training Program
(ranked)

Probationary Status
(can be dismissed)

Civil Service Status
(cannot be dismissed without cause)

Police Hiring Process
The hiring process varies from department to department, but this figure shows the typical process involved in seeking entry-level employment with most law enforcement agencies.

The Police Academy and In-Service Training

After candidates are interviewed, tested, and screened, a number of selected candidates are given notices to report to a **police academy**. The police academy is where law enforcement candidates receive specialized training in various subjects necessary to fulfill their responsibilities as law enforcement officers. Today, a new law enforcement officer will receive an average of 1,370 hours of training before he or she is allowed to exercise his or her power as a police officer.[27] In addition, many states have required every police officer to complete a minimum number of hours of training each year to retain his or her police powers. The academy emphasizes academic learning, physical fitness, and development of the recruits' aptitude for police work. In the academy, the recruit learns the specific laws of the state, county, and/or city of his or her jurisdiction.[28]

Large local law enforcement usually has its own academy. Smaller agencies may send their recruits to a common academy for most of their training and then, after they complete the academy, provide a short period of specialized training regarding local department policies and laws. In states such as California, where common learning outcomes have been established by state commissions, an alternative to the police academy is the completion of an approved curriculum at a community college. Prior to being selected as a candidate for a department, a student may complete a criminal justice curriculum at a community college, whereby upon successful graduation, he or she is certified as having completed the requirements of the training academy of the state. This option is usually used by small and medium-sized law enforcement agencies. The advantage is the financial savings to the department, as the student must pay for all costs of the program. Completion of an academy certificate curriculum at a college neither guarantees the student employment nor provides the student with police authority upon graduation.

In addition to academy training, most departments use some form of in-service training, or **field-training program**, to further evaluate the suitability of the candidate for police work after he or she graduates from the training academy.[29] During this time, the academy graduate works under the direct supervision of an experienced officer. The experienced officer evaluates the "street sense" and attitude of the new officer and assesses his or her ability to be a good cop.

The field-training program may last only several weeks, but most departments keep a newly hired officer on probation for up to a year. During this time, the department reserves the right to dismiss the officer without having to show cause. After successful completion of the academy, the in-service training, and one year of service, the employee may be granted civil service status.

Michael Matthews - Police Images / Alamy

In 2012, Detroit, Michigan, had a serious financial crisis. The crisis was due to a shrinking population, escalating costs of pensions and other legacy costs, and lower tax revenues. In January 2012, Mayor David Bing said that if immediate action was not taken, the city could run out of money within 90 days. Detroit has one of the highest crime rates of large American cities. Its murder rate has risen 14%, whereas the murder rates in other large cities has remained flat or declined. Despite these facts, Detroit chose to balance its budget by slashing the police budget. The city closed its precinct stations to the public at night. Detroit police stations will only be open to the public from 8 A.M. to 4 P.M. After hours, the public must access police services using the Internet or a telephone. The desk officers will be transferred to street duties. The city will lay off 100 police officers, bringing the number of officers to about 3,000 compared with 5,500 officers in 2001. The police perform essential public order services that no other agency is trained or authorized to perform. Has the reduction of the number of police officers and the availability of services had a significant impact on the crime rate or the public's fear of crime? Why or why not?

Civil service status, or civil service protection, means that the officer can only be dismissed under certain circumstances and that the employer must follow due process in dismissing the employee.

Career Paths

The police organizational chart differentiates the various functions that the department performs. The most common divisions are patrol, detective services, and support services. The patrol division is the largest organizational unit. Detective services include the investigation of crimes such as fraud, burglary, arson, and homicide. Larger departments allow for specialization among detectives, including juvenile officers, vice squad officers (gambling and prostitution), and other divisions based on types of crime. Support services might include human resources, research and development, special units for community crime prevention, drug education in schools, juvenile delinquency, child abuse, missing children, drunk drivers, gangs, domestic violence, repeat offenders, hate crimes, and victims' services.[30] Specialty support units include the police training academy; the air patrol unit; the bomb squad; and the reserve, or auxiliary, police (volunteers who assist in police duties).

Officers may make lateral transfers from unit to unit within the organizational structure throughout their career. **Lateral transfers** are changes in the duties the officer performs and the unit to which he or she is attached, but no changes are made in his or her rank or pay grade. Often these transfers are based on seniority or length of service rather than competitive civil service examinations and testing. For example, a patrol officer may transfer to a community policing unit or a vice detective may transfer to a burglary unit or an administrative sergeant may transfer to the training academy.

If officers do not find positive strategies to deal with job stressors, they may resort to harmful behaviors such as alcohol abuse, drug abuse, or other self-destructive behaviors.

The career path of a law enforcement officer is unlike that of a person in private business. When a private business needs a new manager or supervisor, it is likely to recruit someone from outside the company to fill the position. Promotions for the higher-level ranks within law enforcement agencies are filled from lower ranks. This policy is one of the reasons it is important to recruit highly qualified entry-level officers. It is from this initial pool of entry-level officers that the corporals, sergeants, lieutenants, captains, and majors of the department will be selected. For example, when there is an opening for lieutenant, the department will consider only qualified candidates within the department who hold the next lower rank of sergeant.

This policy of promoting from within does limit a law enforcement officer from moving from agency to agency. Most law enforcement agencies accept only entry-level employees. For example, if after ten years of experience in a medium-sized police department in one state a person had achieved the rank of sergeant and wants to move to a larger police department in another state, he or she must enter as an entry-level employee and go through the academy, probationary period, and in-service training. This policy discourages lateral transfers from department to department. A few states have established common standards and have entered into agreements whereby limited lateral transfer is possible. Most of these arrangements limit lateral transfers to the rank of sergeant.

LEARNING OUTCOMES 6 — Describe the hiring of, training of, and career paths for law enforcement officers.

GLOSSARY

Law Enforcement Assistance Administration (LEAA) program A federal grant/loan program to promote educational advancement of law enforcement officers.

police academy A facility or program for the education and training of police officers.

field-training program A probationary period during which police academy graduates train in the community under the direct supervision of experienced officers.

civil service status Protection of an employee in that his or her employment can only be terminated for cause and the employer must follow certain due process procedures in terminating the employee.

lateral transfers Transfers that involve changes in the duties the officer performs and the unit to which he or she is attached, but no changes are made in his or her rank or pay grade.

▶ Unique Aspects of Employment in Law Enforcement

Some aspects of employment as a law enforcement officer are particularly unique to the profession. These include shift work as well as stressors and danger.

Shift Work

The organizational structure of police departments is also based on geographically based units or departments. Agencies divide the geographic area for which they are responsible into small units called districts, beats, and precincts, for example. Each geographic unit is given a name or number related to its location; natural boundaries; or place in the local economy, such as business district, warehouse district, waterfront, or downtown. The size of a unit and the number of officers assigned to it are based on population density and demand for police services in the area.[31] A law enforcement officer may be rotated from geographic district to geographic district throughout his or her career. Each geographic area has its own challenges, often quite unique from those of other districts. The race and ethnicity of the population may change from geographic area to geographic area. The socioeconomic status may change. Some areas may be dominated by warehouses; others, by retail stores; and still others, by residential communities. Some patrol districts may have large areas of cemeteries, woodlands, or public lands. As an officer rotates from district to district, he or she must adapt to the challenges and demands of a new district.

The need to deliver round-the-clock service means that police departments must have multiple time-based shifts. Most small police departments have three shifts that divide the 24-hour day into three 8-hour shifts. Medium-sized and large police departments may have multiple and even overlapping shifts. Overlapping shifts provide additional coverage during times of high demand for police services. Thus, the organizational structure must provide for supervision, officers, and support for the various districts and time shifts. Officers and supervisors work various shifts. Most departments require rotating shifts wherein an officer works a certain shift for a period of time and then rotates to the next time period and then the next. In some departments, shifts may be assigned based on seniority wherein more senior members have first choice as to the shift they want to work. The length an officer works a particular shift varies from department to department. Some agencies may change an officer's shift as often as every eight weeks. Research has indicated that this rotation of work shifts can produce both physical and psychological stress for officers.

One factor that may discourage women from applying for law enforcement work is that as a new officer, women often work the night shift with split days off. For women with a family, especially young children, the night shift may be a challenge.

 LEARNING OUTCOMES 7

Discuss the unique aspects of employment in law enforcement.

GLOSSARY

internal affairs investigation unit A special unit whose mission it is to investigate the actions of officers for the purpose of recommending disciplinary actions or criminal prosecution.

suicide by police Situations created by citizens in which law enforcement officers are forced to fire on them.

move and shoot High-tech simulations that mimic real-world scenarios where officers must respond to the simulated environment to detect and respond to threats.

Stress and Danger

Law enforcement work is performed in a highly stressful environment and one in which individuals may experience great personal danger, including death. Law enforcement officers often deal with the public in times of crisis, such as motor vehicle accidents, domestic violence, riots, self-destructive behavior, and crime. During these crises, it is not unusual for people to be injured, to suffer life-threatening danger, or to be in the midst of a crisis that will have permanent and extreme consequences. Law enforcement officers must remain calm and exhibit professional behavior during times when the average citizen often cannot find the self-discipline to cope with the crisis at hand. Long-term interaction with people in crisis can impact the personality and mental health of law enforcement officers. If officers do not find positive strategies to deal with job stressors, they may result to harmful behaviors such as alcohol abuse, drug abuse, or other self-destructive behaviors.

Perhaps one of the most serious stressors that law enforcement officers must deal with is the threat of injury or death and the possibility that a law enforcement officer may have to take a life in the line of duty. Assault and death are real possibilities for law enforcement officers. According to the FBI's *Law Enforcement Officers Killed & Assaulted, 2010*, 56 law enforcement officers were feloniously killed in 2010. Fifteen of them were killed in ambush situations. An additional 72 died of accidents in the line of duty. Most of these deaths (63) were related to vehicular or motorcycle accidents. About one in ten, or 53,469, officers were assaulted in the line of duty. Over one-fourth (26.1%) of those assaulted sustained injuries.

The threat of injury or death to law enforcement officers can be the result of many different situations. Most officers (33%)

Most deaths of law enforcement officers are due to vehicular accidents.

Phase4Photography/Fotolia

56 The number of officers feloniously killed in 2010.

Marsan/Shutterstock

were assaulted responding to disturbance calls. Other situations may be when gang members and drug dealers believe that the police are rivals and open fire on them.[32] A more sinister motive is when individuals deliberately target law enforcement officers due to some grudge or to mentally unbalanced behavior. For example, in 2011, Nicholas John Smith of San Jacinto, California, was convicted of 11 felonious assaults on Detective Chuck Johnson and other officers of the Hemet-San Jacinto Valley Gang Task Force (California).[33] Smith attempted to murder officers in a string of attacks on police that included using improvised booby traps and firing a World War II–era bazooka at a police station.

Often during the interview of prospective officers, they will be asked about their feelings toward the use of deadly force. Obviously, this is a condition of employment that few employees in other occupations have to face. Estimates are that 95% of law enforcement officers will never fire their weapon in the line of duty. However, a small number will. In 2010, police killed 387 people in justified homicides, according to FBI statistics.

For those officers who do use deadly force, the impact is very different from that portrayed in the media. In the media, officers may kill numerous people and carry on as if nothing out of the ordinary happened. Some media show officers immediately returning to duty. Few show the paperwork and intensive internal investigations that follow a shooting. After every shooting, the internal affairs investigative unit of the agency conducts an intensive investigation. The **internal affairs investigation unit** is a special unit whose mission it is to investigate the actions of officers for the purpose of recommending disciplinary actions or criminal prosecution. The investigation of a shooting can take months or even years.

In real life, the use of deadly force by a law enforcement officer can take an enormous emotional toll on the officer. The emotional toll can last forever.[34] Officers who kill in the line of duty often undergo intensive interrogations and psychological examinations. In most cases, the officer is put on administrative leave. Often officers are prohibited from carrying their firearm until they are cleared by the department to do so. A killing in the line of duty is a media event, and the scrutiny the officer undergoes is very public and very intrusive. After a shooting, an officer may face professional challenges if his or her career is hindered by the incident.

One particularly disturbing aspect of killings in the line of duty is what is referred to as "suicide by police." **Suicide by police** is when citizens construct situations in which law enforcement officers are forced to fire on them. In cases of suicide by police, the victim often is suffering from some emotional, physical, or mental illness and wants to end his or her life but does not want to commit suicide. In these cases, the person

often sets up a situation whereby he or she appears to threaten others or the responding officer with deadly force. Faced with a situation in which it appears the lives of others or the officer are threatened, the officer must use deadly force to end the threat. The true intent of the perpetrator is often revealed in that his or her weapon was unloaded or was not real.[35]

In response to the threats facing law enforcement officers, many departments have adopted policies to help address the emotional and psychological needs of officers after they have been involved in shootings. Policies such as mandatory counseling force officers to obtain help rather than mask the emotions that can be the result of using deadly force. Also, there have been improvements in training programs. Firearms training for most law enforcement officers consists of firing on a range at paper targets. New programs that emphasize real-world conditions require officers to "move and shoot." **Move and shoot** are high-tech simulations that mimic real-world scenarios where officers must respond to the simulated environment to detect and respond to threats. In these simulated environments, the officer may experience the sound of gunfire, the smell of burned cordite, a change in lighting, and numerous distractors such as "innocent bystanders."[36]

▶ Special Police and Private Protection Services

In addition to local, state, and federal law enforcement agencies, there are special police and private protection services.

Special Police

Special police include airport police, park police, transit police, public school police, college and university police, public housing police, game wardens, alcoholic beverage control agency police, and special investigative units.

Special police have limited jurisdiction in geography and in police powers. They are hired, trained, and equipped separately from municipal police officers, sheriff's deputies, and state officers. The criteria for special police agents often are less than those required for general law enforcement officers. The training and the pay are less. Some special police are authorized to carry weapons and have powers of arrest and search and seizure; others do not.

Special police include agencies that have responsibility for public building, natural resources, transportation systems, criminal investigations, and special enforcement. Public building special police include agencies that have limited law enforcement responsibilities for public school districts, colleges, universities, state government buildings, medical schools/campuses, public hospital/health facilities, public housing,

LEARNING
OUTCOMES
8

Describe the role
and authority of
special police
and private
protection services.

GLOSSARY

special police Police who have
limited jurisdiction in geography
and in police powers.

proprietary services Private
protection security forces that
are owned and managed by a
company.

contract services Security
personnel who work for a third-
party company and are hired
by another company to provide
specific services at the direction
of the client.

private investigators
Investigators who are licensed
by the state and are authorized
to conduct investigations.

**American Society for Industrial
Security (ASIS)** One of the
largest professional societies
for promoting the ethics and
professionalism of private
protection services.

and other state-owned facilities. For example, many state
colleges and universities have
police departments rather
than security departments.[38]
The employees of these campus police departments have
general police powers on
the state campus, have the
right to make arrests and
conduct searches, and have
the authority to carry and
use firearms. They are law
enforcement officers, but they
provide services only for specific campuses.

Natural resource spe-
cial police have responsibility
for fish and wildlife enforcement agencies, parks and recreational areas, boating laws,
environmental laws, water
resources, forest resources, and
levee districts. Transportation
system special police are
responsible for airports, mass
transit systems, commercial
vehicles, harbor/port facilities, and bridges and tunnels.
Special police for criminal
investigations include investi-
gators to assist prosecutors, fraud investigators, fire marshals
tax/revenue enforcement, and arson investigators. (Arson investigators are usually employed by the fire department, not the
police department.) Other special enforcement agencies may be
responsible for alcohol/tobacco laws, agricultural laws, gaming
laws, and racing laws.

Although special police agencies perform essential services,
are the source of a substantial number of jobs, and contribute
significantly to the public safety of citizens, they have had
little impact or influence on the development of the criminal
justice system.[39] Special police agencies are often neglected by
the public unless there is media attention due to scandal or a
horrific crime.

Private Protection Services

The lack of competent local law enforcement during the
nineteenth century created business opportunities for private
protection services. Merchants, railroads, banks, and even the
federal government were in need of professional, competent
security and investigative services. With no public agency to
fulfill these needs, they turned to private agencies. During
the mid-1800s, private protective agencies such as Brinks,
Pinkerton, and Wells Fargo provided investigative services and
protection of private property. These private agencies filled the
void created by the widespread corruption and the geographic
jurisdiction limitations found in local law enforcement.

Today, private protection services are a multibillion-dollar
business. There are about three times as many private protection security agents as there are public law enforcement agents.
Brinks, Pinkerton, and Wells Fargo continue to be world leaders in private protection services. Merchants and citizens hire
private protection service agents today for the same reasons
they did in the past. Private protection services protect the private property of clients and investigate matters that, although
important to the client, may be of lesser importance or not
appropriate for law enforcement.

The services offered by private protection agencies vary
greatly from military-like private armies trained and equipped
with sophisticated weaponry to "rent-a-cop" unarmed security
officers who spend their days looking for shoplifters and handling unruly customers. Private security services are used by
airports, banks, corporations, hospitals, nuclear facilities, rail-
road companies, schools, and retail companies. Even wealthy
and prominent individuals may engage the services of a private
security service to provide exclusive protection.

There are basically two types of private protection services: proprietary services and contract services. **Proprietary
services** are security forces that are owned and managed by
a company. Proprietary services are usually characteristics of
large companies such as railroads, large shopping malls, and
industrial plants. The security personnel are employees of
the company. The company is responsible for the employees'
training, responsibilities, and oversight. **Contract services** are
security personnel who work for a third-party company and
are hired by another company to provide specific services at
the direction of the client. Smaller companies whose needs
for security vary and who do not have the financial resources

Largest Special Police Agencies

Agency	Full-Time Personnel	Category of Special Police
Temple University (PA)	125	University
School District of Philadelphia (Pennsylvania)	450	Public School
California Department of Parks and Recreation	654	Parks and Recreation
Port Authority of New York and New Jersey	1,667	Transportation

Source: Brian A. Reaves, "Census of State and Local Law Enforcement Agencies, 2008" (Washington, DC: Bureau of Justice Statistics, July
2011), pp. 9–12.

Experts at the 7th Annual John Jay/Guggenheim Conference on Crime in America suggested that the falling crime rates may be due to private security forces hired by business owners and technologies such as anti–car theft LoJack systems. Dr. Philip Cook, Professor of Economics and Sociology at Duke University, proposed that private action is a way "of controlling opportunity to potential criminals." Cook cited a RAND Corporation study that showed that in areas where local businesses employ private actions to reduce crime, the total violent crime rate decreased 5.9% compared with a 4.3% decrease in other areas. Not everyone agreed with Dr. Cook's analysis. Other experts attributed the drop to a lower juvenile crime rate or the effects of the economic recession. Is the use of private protection services a significant factor in the declining crime rate? Why or why not?

to maintain a company-owned security force use contract services. They negotiate with the security company to provide security services.

Private security protection personnel are not sworn law enforcement officers. They do not have the power of arrest and search and seizure. The authorization to carry firearms varies with the laws of the state. Some private protection service agents are permitted to carry firearms only while on duty. For example, the agents of armored car services who transport large amounts of cash may be allowed to carry firearms while engaged in their duties, but not concealed while off duty. When private protection agents are allowed to carry firearms, the company is responsible for training and licensing the employee. Also, the company may be liable for any abuse or misconduct by the employee.

Law enforcement officers may work as contract private protection security agents for private businesses off duty. State laws and department policies regulate the off-duty employment of these officers. The advantage of using off-duty law enforcement officers as private protection security agents is that the officer retains his or her authority as a law enforcement officer while working for the private company.

Closely related to private protection services are private investigators. Private investigators are the central figure in many media films and books. However, there is little resemblance between the work of a real-life private investigator and the one portrayed in movies and books. **Private investigators** are licensed by the state and are authorized to conduct investigations. They do not have police powers and in many states are not authorized to carry a firearm. Private investigators may be employed by companies looking into the background of suspect employees or by a private party seeking information about his or her spouse to use in a divorce settlement. Like private protection services, private investigators may be proprietary or contract agents. Large companies such as railroads, trucking and freight companies, insurance companies, and large distribution centers and warehouse companies may employee permanent, full-time employees to investigate theft, fraud, or other crimes against the company. For example, Yellow Freight has a staff of employees to investigate thefts of merchandise in transit. State Farm Insurance and most other large insurance companies have a staff of full-time employees dedicated to the investigation of fraudulent insurance claims. A person or private company that has the occasional need to obtain information may hire the services of a private investigator on a contract basis. Such services may be provided by large corporate companies or sole proprietorship agencies.

Private protection and investigative services are regulated by state law and are self-regulating. State laws (and in some cases federal law) establish the authority that private protection companies and agents may exercise. For example, state laws may establish the minimum number of hours of training before a private agent is authorized to carry a firearm or the minimum qualifications to be licensed as a private investigator. Also, private protection and investigative services are self-regulating. Given the size of the industry, a professional association exists to promote the ethics and professionalism of private protection services. One of the largest professional associations is the **American Society for Industrial Security (ASIS)**.[40] ASIS sets minimum standards and standardized testing. Also, ASIS's code of ethics provides guidelines for professional conduct by private security companies and agents.

▶ Operational Strategies

One of the more powerful influences on law enforcement operational strategies and community satisfaction with police services is how the police go about their job of providing services and what services the police think are most important to provide.[41] Police scholar James Q. Wilson proposed that rather than viewing police behavior as random and independent of community values, the style of policing—and hence the behavior of the police officer—should be viewed as closely related to the type of city government and community expectations.

An important point to emerge from Wilson's research is the premise that there is a link between police behavior and community values. The police do not act randomly, nor do they develop values in a vacuum. Police strategies reflect a department's values, which reflect community values. Wilson's study of policing strategies reported that there were three styles of policing, each shaped by and conforming to the values and politics of the community served. The three styles were watchman, legalistic, and service.[42] The **watchman style** focused on maintaining order and was associated with declining industrial, blue-collar communities. In this style, the police exercised broad discretion in the enforcement of legal codes. Often this discretion resulted in differential treatment of community groups. The **legalistic style** focused on law enforcement and professionalism and was associated with reform-minded cities with mixed socioeconomic communities. The police were expected to reflect a single standard of professionalism for the entire community. An important measure of police effectiveness was a large number of arrests and citations. The **service style** focused on protecting a homogenous community against outsiders. Due to the homogenous nature of the community, the police provided service and informal interventions for community members. This style was associated with suburban, middle-class communities.

Describe the various styles and primary operational strategies of today's law enforcement agencies.

GLOSSARY

watchman style A style of policing that focuses on maintaining order and is associated with declining industrial, blue-collar communities.

legalistic style A style of policing that focuses on law enforcement and professionalism and is associated with reform-minded cities with mixed socioeconomic communities.

service style A style of policing that focuses on protecting a homogenous suburban, middle-class community against outsiders and providing service to community residents.

team policing Teams of officers assigned to a specific geographic area with the charge to ensure public safety, maintain order, and deliver community services to the residents of that community.

community policing Decentralized policing programs that focus on crime prevention, quality of life in a community, public order, and alternatives to arrest.

broken window theory The belief that ignoring public-order violations and disruptive behavior leads to community neglect, which fosters further disorder and crime.

zero-tolerance strategy Strict enforcement of the laws, even for minor violations.

problem-oriented policing A community policing strategy that emphasizes attacking the root problem that causes crime instead of responding to the symptoms of the problem.

SARA A community policing strategy based on a highly modified version of the scientific method that attempts to identify the root cause of crime in a community.

Team Policing

During the 1960s and 1970s, the crime rate began to climb. Cities burned. Drugs, gangs, and crime became pandemic. The image of police omnipresence proved to be a myth as cities were consumed with disorder and riots that the police could neither prevent nor control. Fear of crime, increasing violence, mistrust of the police, and serious doubts about the professionalism of the police resulted in widespread dissatisfaction with police services—especially with the municipal police.[43] Thus, it is not surprising that since the 1970s, many police departments have adopted new policing strategies as a reflection of the public's dissatisfaction with traditional policing.

One of the early styles of policing with which police experimented was team policing. **Team policing** assigned teams of officers to a specific geographic area with the charge to ensure public safety, maintain order, and deliver community services to the residents of that community. In theory, a team commander, usually a lieutenant or captain, and a small team of police officers were provided with broad decentralized decision-making authority to enable them to respond to the needs of the local community. The use of team policing peaked in the early 1970s and quickly faded.[44] One of the flaws that made team policing unworkable was the premise of team policing—that the team should exercise broad decentralized decision-making authority. Team policing attempted to establish small units of police personnel who would assume responsibility for public order and crime control within a geographic area to encourage more police-community involvement. Team

> The goal of community policing was to eliminate public disenchantment with police services and criticisms of the lack of police professionalism.

policing was short-lived, but it did establish a foundation for community policing, which proved to be a more viable policing strategy.[45]

Community Policing

Community policing emerged in the 1970s in an attempt to provide a more effective style of policing.[46] The goal of community policing was to eliminate public disenchantment with police services and criticisms of the lack of police professionalism.[47] It was thought that the key to achieving this goal was more police-community interaction and community trust and confidence in the police. Community policing has endured, and a majority of contemporary police departments claim to use some of the strategies of community policing.

What Is Community Policing?

Despite its popularity and widespread use, there is no universally accepted definition of community policing. As a result, many police departments have declared that they have adopted community policing; however, each community policing program is different.[48] The common characteristics of **community policing** are these:

- Focus on decentralized strategies that promote crime prevention rather than rapid response, crime investigation, and apprehension of the criminal[49]
- Focus on promoting the quality of life of the community and public order rather than law enforcement[50]
- Use alternatives other than arrest and force to solve the problem rather than respond to the symptoms of the problem[51]

Broken Windows and Zero Tolerance

Although each police department has approached community policing differently, an underlying theme is a partnership between the police and the community and a focus on quality of life rather than crime fighting. In this partnership, the police become problem identifiers, dispute resolvers, and managers of relations rather than crime fighters, law enforcers, and the "thin blue line."[52]

One of the widely used community policing strategies developed by James Q. Wilson is the **broken window theory**.[53] The theory is based on an interesting experiment in which an automobile was parked in a neighborhood and left unattended. It was discovered that the automobile was more quickly vandalized if a window was broken than if the automobile was left undamaged. The same findings were observed when an abandoned house was substituted for an automobile. The message sent by the broken window was "Nobody cares—other acts of vandalism are okay."[54]

When applied to a neighborhood, the broken window theory means that if vacant buildings are left untended, if graffiti is tolerated, and if "minor" public order violations such as public drinking, disruptive behavior by youths, and vandalism are permitted, they will be signals that nobody cares about the community, leading to more serious disorder and crime.

One of the strategies associated with the broken window philosophy is strict enforcement for minor violations of the law, such as public drinking, after-hours use of parks, loitering, and even jaywalking. This strict enforcement strategy is called the **zero-tolerance strategy**, and the assumption behind it is that it will send the message to more serious lawbreakers that if minor offenses are noticed by the police, more serious offenses will surely bring prompt police action. According to the broken window theory, tolerance by the police and the community for people breaking "small laws" demonstrates the community's apathy and leads to more serious crime.

Police Partnership and Public Order

Studies conducted in the 1970s indicated that much police work actually involved order maintenance as opposed to crime fighting.[55] In fact, in only about 5% of all dispatched calls in most cities, the officer has a chance to intervene or make an arrest. Despite the emphasis of the police on rapid response time, these studies suggested that rapid response time was, in general, an ineffective crime-fighting strategy. The philosophy of community policing holds that order maintenance, not law enforcement, is the root of crime fighting. If a community has a high degree of public order, more serious crime is less likely to develop.[56]

Frequently, when police seek to enter into a partnership with the residents of a neighborhood to promote public order and to fight crime, both sides must learn to trust each other and to communicate. Neither the police nor the community is accustomed to working with the other. The old division between "us and them" or "police and civilians" had worked to separate the community and the police. When working in partnership with the community, the police were often surprised at community expectations. While police may tend to focus on serious crime problems such as drug trafficking, community residents often are more concerned with quality-of-life issues. Often these issues are beyond the "job of the police" in that they concern building code violations, abandoned vehicles in project housing, and use of public space.

Problem-Oriented Policing

Community policing emphasizes attacking the root problem that causes crime instead of responding to the symptoms of the problem by arresting offenders and taking victimization reports. This approach to crime fighting is sometimes called problem-solving policing or **problem-oriented policing**. Problem oriented policing emphasizes three main themes:[57]

- Increased effectiveness by attacking underlying problems that give rise to incidents that consume patrol and detective time

- Reliance on the expertise and creativity of line officers to study problems carefully and develop innovative solutions

- Closer involvement with the public to make sure the police are addressing the needs of citizens

Rather than being reactive, problem-solving policing emphasizes the role of the police as proactive—acting before crimes are committed. In traditional policing, the police are seldom, if ever, expected to take steps to find out what the cause of the crime or conflict was and what would prevent it from recurring.[58] Problem-oriented policing focuses on resolving the problems or issues that promote crime rather than arresting offenders. Problem-solving policing is based on the premise that the police cannot arrest enough offenders to create a high quality of life within the community. No matter how many criminals are arrested, they will be replaced by new criminals unless the root of the crime problem is addressed.

Scanning, Analysis, Response, and Assessment (SARA)

One commonly used technique in problem-solving policing is scanning, analysis, response, and assessment (SARA).[59] **SARA** is a community policing strategy based on a highly modified model of the scientific method that attempts to identify the root cause of crime in a community. There are four steps in the SARA strategy and a feedback loop: scanning, analysis, response, and assessment. Each of these steps is interconnected by a feedback loop.

Scanning is the process of gathering data about an incident that would allow an officer to define the problem.

Analysis is the search for information that would let an officer understand the underlying nature of the problem and its causes and consider a variety of options for its resolution.

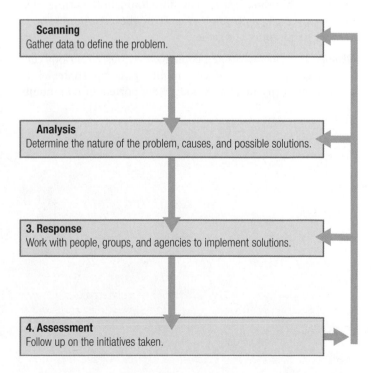

Response requires an officer to work with citizens, businesses, and public and private agencies to implement a solution that would impact the cause of the problem.

Assessment requires the officer to follow up on the initiative taken to see if it has had the desired effect.

Challenges of Community Policing

If community policing is so great, why isn't everyone doing it? Critics argue that community policing will not last because, like team policing, it requires that decision making be decentralized in the police administrative structure. Problems are solved through decisions made by the lowest-ranking people in the organization.

Decentralization of Decision Making The decentralization of decision making runs counter to the traditional paramilitary command-and-control organizational culture of the police. Some argue that "despite scholarly opinions, the street cops tend to prefer the quasi-military style."[60] This argument is based on the assumption that the traditional law enforcement strategy gives the police officer a better sense of control, structure, and direction in an otherwise chaotic environment.

Need for Retraining Community policing requires more-educated officers and officers with creative problem-solving abilities.[61] Police officers must view members of the public as a potential resource in crime fighting rather than as potential criminals. Some argue that the police officer's separation or isolation from the community makes it possible for him or her to engage in grisly interactions such as assaults, accident victims, and shootings day after day as duty demands without becoming impaired by emotional overload.[62]

Crime Displacement versus Elimination Many believe that the dislocation of crime is a major problem with community policing. Although community policing and problem-solving strategies may reduce robberies, burglaries, prostitution, and car thefts in one neighborhood, they may not eliminate the crimes, but merely drive them to another part of the community or to another community altogether.

Minority Communities Some people have expressed serious concern over the ability of community policing strategies to work in minority neighborhoods.[63] Supporters of community policing dispute this claim, and it is not clear what effect the minority race or ethnicity of an officer has on community policing efforts in minority neighborhoods.

Tyranny of Neighborhoods A final concern over community policing strategies is the "potential tyranny of neighborhoods." In an effort to promote quality of life and fight crime, neighborhoods may mistake diversity and tolerance for crime and disorder. Neighborhoods can be places of congeniality, sociability, and safety, but they can also be places of smallness, meanness, and tyranny. Like Trayvon Martin, a minority youth walking in a gated white community may find that he becomes a target of the community and the police because he is different, not because he is a criminal.

The Future of Community Policing The jury is still out on the benefits and future of community policing strategies. They are popular with the public, but police officers are not promoted to higher administrative ranks because of stellar performance in community policing. It is too early to tell if community policing strategies will be valued and universally adopted. As more police departments document their efforts at community policing strategies, data will accumulate. The data may show that community policing strategies have little impact on crime rates, but a much greater impact on the community's fear of crime.

Traditional police strategies have emphasized crime fighting and investigation and have paid little, if any, attention to citizens' fear of crime. Police have assumed that fear is caused by criminal victimization. They reasoned that if criminal victimization was reduced, fear of crime would naturally diminish. However, research has shown that the causes of fear of crime do not stem so much from criminal victimization as from other interactions and environmental cues.[64] The level of fear of crime does not necessarily diminish as the crime rate drops. Community policing may be an effective strategy for reducing citizens' fear of crime because one of its positive effects is that it promotes the belief by citizens that the community has been empowered. Citizens feel less helpless in the face of rising crime rates. Even in communities where crime rates do not decrease with the adoption of community policing strategies, the self-confidence of the community seems to improve and the fear of crime decreases.

Combating Gangs with Counterinsurgent Tactics

The deployment of American troops to fight the war on terrorism in Iraq and Afghanistan has impacted law enforcement agencies. Most of the impact has focused on the shortage of law enforcement personnel due to military reserve units being deployed and concerns regarding the possible effects of post-traumatic stress disorder on returning troops. Little has been mentioned regarding the possible positive impacts of the deployment of law enforcement personnel to war.

Massachusetts state troopers Michael Cutone and Thomas Sarrouf were deployed to Iraq with a Green Beret unit. When they returned to their civilian law enforcement position in 2009, they noticed the similarities of combating gangs in Brightwood, a low-income, largely Puerto Rican neighborhood, and combating insurgents in Avghani, Iraq. They observed that conventional policing techniques were ineffective in achieving lasting change in failing urban neighborhoods where gangs dominated the streets and ruled with fear and intimidation.[65] The two troopers drew on their military experience with counterinsurgency strategies and applied it to the Brightwood neighborhood. Their mission was "to promote a safe and secure environment and reduce gang activity and violence."[66]

Troopers Cutone and Sarrouf believed that traditional methods such as raids, stings, removal of gang leaders, and a show of force only addressed the symptoms of the problem. Their central premise was that "[t]he problem of gangs is something you have to make the community itself responsible for."[67] Applying strategies that were used in Iraq, the two men created community strategies to restore trust in the police and empower the community to overcome fear and apathy. The strategies included holding community meetings, networking, implementing new ideas offered by community residences, setting up informal intelligence networks, soliciting residents' support, and developing new methods for residents to be able to report tips anonymously.

As of 2012, the success of the program has not been validated with objective statistical data. The goal is to evaluate the impact of the program by measuring arrest rates, calls to the police, ambulances summoned for gunshot wounds, gang graffiti, litter on the streets, and other quality-of-life measurements.[68] Gang graffiti and litter were reduced in 2011, but calls for police service went up. The increase in calls for police service is seen as a positive sign that more residents are confident enough to report previously unreported crime. The geographic area of the program has been expanded to a 30-block area. Also, other cities have contacted the Massachusetts State Police seeking information about the program.

ZUMA Press, Inc. / Alamy

This case raises several interesting questions. Among them are the following:

1. Are counterinsurgency strategies used in defeating terrorist groups an effective means of combating gangs? Explain.

2. What problems might there be in using military-developed strategies to defeat a civilian problem?

3. How important an element in combating community gangs is community trust in the police?

4. How much trust in the police does the average resident in gang-dominated communities have? How do the police build up community residents' level of trust?

LEARNING OUTCOMES 1

Outline the history and development of law enforcement.

Policing in the United States is a decentralized system with approximately 18,000 law enforcement agencies. There is no central authority in our nation to coordinate law enforcement activities. This serves as checks and balances of policing powers. The Posse Comitatus Act of 1878 limits local law enforcement agencies in using federal military personnel to enforce laws. A law enforcement agency carries out legitimate duties at the federal, state, or local level.

1. Describe the concept of decentralized policing.

2. How does jurisdiction limit policing powers?

3. What are the three political jurisdictions by which government exercises law enforcement authority?

jurisdiction The geographic limits, such as the municipality, county, or state, in which officers of the agency are empowered to perform their duties.

Posse Comitatus Act of 1878 An act that limits the powers of local governments and law enforcement agencies in using federal military personnel to enforce the laws of the land.

LEARNING OUTCOMES 2

Describe the roles of federal law enforcement agencies and describe some of the major federal law enforcement agencies.

Federal law enforcement agencies are under the administrative control of the executive branch of the federal government. There are three distinctively different types of federal agencies: military police, Native American tribal police, and civilian police. All four branches of the military (Army, Navy, Marines, and Air Force) have their own strategy for providing police services. Another federal authority is found in Native American reservations, which establish their own tribal police to provide services. Finally, there are approximately 50 federal civilian law enforcement agencies. One such federal agency, the Federal Bureau of Investigation (FBI), operates the largest training academy in the United States for law enforcement agencies. In addition, the FBI maintains the National Crime Information Center (NCIC), the nation's largest database of computerized criminal information on wanted felons, criminal history, and stolen items such as automobiles and guns.

1. Which branch of the federal government oversees federal law enforcement agencies?

2. Name a federal law enforcement agency and describe its roles and duties.

3. Describe the jurisdiction of a tribal police department.

4. Discuss the new priorities of today's FBI.

5. Explain what is meant by the term *narcoterrorism*.

federal law enforcement agencies Agencies that enforce only federal laws and are under the control of the executive branch of the federal government.

military police Police who are members of the military and provide law enforcement services on military bases, on certain federal lands, and in cases involving military personnel.

Uniform Code of Military Justice (UCMJ) Legal statutes that govern the behavior of military personnel and prescribe the due process to be followed to determine guilt and punishment.

tribal police Police that provide law enforcement services on Native American reservations, where local and state police have no jurisdiction and federal police have only limited jurisdiction.

Office of Tribal Justice An office established in 1995 to coordinate tribal issues for the Department of Justice (DOJ) and to increase the responsiveness of the DOJ to Native American tribes and citizens.

U.S. Marshals Service The federal agency that provides security for federal courts; is responsible for the movement, custody, and capture of federal prisoners; and provides protection of witnesses in federal cases.

U.S. Postal Inspection Service The federal agency responsible for the security of U.S. mail and mail carriers and for investigation of mail fraud.

U.S. Secret Service The federal agency that protects the president, the vice president, members of their families, major candidates for president and vice president, and visiting heads of foreign governments.

Federal Bureau of Investigation (FBI) The federal agency responsible for protecting the United States from terrorist attacks, foreign intelligence and espionage, cyber-based attacks, and high-tech crimes and for combating public corruption at all levels.

National Crime Information Center (NCIC) The nation's largest database of computerized criminal information on wanted felons; people on parole; criminal history; and stolen items such as automobiles, boats, guns, and securities.

Bureau of Alcohol, Tobacco, Firearms and Explosives (ATF) The federal agency responsible for regulating alcohol, tobacco, firearms, explosives, and arson.

Drug Enforcement Administration (DEA) The federal agency that enforces U.S. laws and regulations regarding controlled substances and that supports nonenforcement programs intended to reduce the availability of illicit controlled substances domestically and internationally.

narcoterrorism Terrorism in which drug lords in some countries operate virtually unchecked by law enforcement.

LEARNING OUTCOMES 3

Describe the roles and organizational structure of state law enforcement agencies.

State police agencies have jurisdiction that is limited by state boundaries. State law enforcement agencies are divided into three types: traffic enforcement, general criminal investigations, and special investigations. Some state agencies, such as the highway patrol, are limited to only traffic enforcement. Other state police agencies have law enforcement to conduct general and specialized criminal investigations. Sometimes small towns and villages will contract with the state police to provide local services. State police might also have jurisdiction for investigation in cases involving charges of political corruption of local officers, voter fraud, or bribery of state officials.

1. Who has the authority to establish a state police agency?

2. Why are some agencies moving away from the use of "ten code" when talking on the radio?

3. Which agency is considered the oldest form of a state police agency?

4. Describe some of the situations wherein a state police agency could be called on to oversee a special investigation.

ten-code radio communications A system of communicating events, actions, and services by use of numbered code, each beginning with the number 10 followed by another number.

highway patrol State law enforcement agencies that focus on traffic enforcement.

LEARNING OUTCOMES 4

Summarize the duties and administrative structure of the sheriff's office.

The sheriff's office is the oldest local law enforcement agency in the United States. The sheriff is the only head law enforcement executive who obtains his or her position by election. The sheriff has jurisdiction over an entire county. Second in the command staff of a sheriff's department is the undersheriff. The sheriff's department can have three major responsibilities: performing law enforcement duties, serving as officers of the court, and operating the county jail. With the increase of municipal policing agencies in the twentieth century, the role of the sheriff in providing law enforcement services has diminished.

1. How does someone become a sheriff?

2. In what country did the office of sheriff originate?

3. Explain how the sheriff's office might overlap services provided by municipal police.

chief law enforcement officer The highest ranking law enforcement official within a system; the sheriff is the chief law enforcement officer of a county, the attorney general is the chief law enforcement officer of a state, and the U.S. attorney general is the chief law enforcement officer of the United States.

deputy sheriff officers Law enforcement officers who assist the sheriff.

undersheriff The second-in-command of the sheriff's office.

officers of the court Law enforcement officers who serve the court by serving papers, providing courtroom security, and transporting incarcerated defendants.

LEARNING OUTCOMES 5

Summarize the duties and administrative structure of local law enforcement agencies.

Municipal policing is the most visible and largest type of agency in the United States. These local law enforcement agencies are responsible for many services, including traffic enforcement, accident investigation, patrol and response to criminal activity, and order maintenance situations. To save money, some cities combine the police department and fire department into a Department of Public Safety. Police departments have a system of military-style ranks and a chain of command. Local law enforcement agencies also employ nonsworn civilian personnel such as secretaries, office workers, and technicians.

1. Which of our nation's police departments has the largest number of full-time sworn personnel?

2. What is meant by the term *order maintenance*?

3. Who is the highest administrative officer in a municipal police department?

4. Explain the hierarchical structure of a municipal police department.

order maintenance Noncrime-fighting services performed by police, such as using mediation, providing for the welfare of vulnerable people, and controlling crime.

chief of police The chief administrative officer of the police department.

command-and-control structure A hierarchical administrative structure organized by ranks with a single person responsible for all personnel in the organization.

deputy chief The second-in-command below the chief of police. In a large police department, there may be several deputy chiefs, each commanding a large unit within the police department.

sworn personnel Officers who have police powers of arrest and search and seizure and the authority to carry a firearm.

nonsworn personnel Employees such as secretaries, office workers, and technicians who do not have "police" powers and are not authorized to carry firearms.

LEARNING OUTCOMES 6

Describe the hiring of, training of, and career paths for law enforcement officers.

Police departments strive to recruit highly qualified applicants for entry-level positions. Police recruits are sent to an academy for training and then typically placed in an in-service field-training program for further evaluation of their aptitudes. Most police departments are organized by division for patrol, detective services, and support services. Specialty support units may handle a police training academy, the air patrol unit, the bomb squad, or reserve police officers. During their career, officers may make lateral twransfers from unit to unit within the organizational structure.

1. Discuss how Supreme Court rulings have impacted the police hiring process.

2. How did the LEAA program improve the level of education among our nation's police officers?

3. Describe the training process for a new police recruit.

Law Enforcement Assistance Administration (LEAA) program A federal grant/loan program to promote educational advancement of law enforcement officers.

police academy A facility or program for the education and training of police officers.

field-training program A probationary period during which police academy graduates train in the community under the direct supervision of experienced officers.

civil service status Protection of an employee in that his or her employment can only be terminated for cause and the employer must follow certain due process procedures in terminating the employee.

lateral transfers Transfers that involve changes in the duties the officer performs and the unit to which he or she is attached, but no changes are made in his or her rank or pay grade.

LEARNING OUTCOMES 7

Discuss the unique aspects of employment in law enforcement.

Law enforcement officers have a unique profession because of the facets of shift work as well as stressors and danger. Law enforcement work is a highly stressful environment and one in which individuals may experience great personal danger, including death. Long-term interaction with people in crisis can impact an officer's personality and mental health. The threat of injury or death to law enforcement officers may require an officer to use deadly force. One such situation is known as suicide by police, when someone forces a police officer to fire upon him or her. To improve good decision making in shooting scenarios, new programs that emphasize real-world conditions, called move and shoot, have been developed.

1. Name various stressors found in the nature of police work.

2. Which unit conducts internal investigations following a shooting?

3. What is meant by the term *suicide by police*?

suicide by police Situations created by citizens in which law enforcement officers are forced to fire on them.

move and shoot High-tech simulations that mimic real-world scenarios where officers must respond to the simulated environment to detect and respond to threats.

LEARNING OUTCOMES 8

Describe the role and authority of special police and private protection services.

Special police have limited jurisdictions; examples are airport police, park police, transit police, public school police, game wardens, and other special investigative units. Private protection services can be hired through contractors who offer security officers or even private investigators. The number of private protection services is three times that of public law enforcement positions. Private protection and investigative services are regulated by statc law and are self-regulating.

1. Name the types of special police jurisdictions.

2. What are the two different types of private protection services?

3. What is the purpose of ASIS?

special police Police who have limited jurisdiction in geography and in police powers.

proprietary services Private protection security forces that are owned and managed by a company.

contract services Security personnel who work for a third-party company and are hired by another company to provide specific services at the direction of a client.

private investigators Investigators who are licensed by the state and are authorized to conduct investigations.

American Society for Industrial Security (ASIS) One of the largest professional societies for promoting the ethics and professionalism of private protection services.

LEARNING OUTCOMES 9

Describe the various styles and primary operational strategies of today's law enforcement agencies.

During the 1960s and 1970s, as crime rates rose, a new strategy called team policing was adopted. Team policing was short-lived, but it served as the foundation of the concept of community policing. Community policing focuses on preventing crime, dealing with quality-of-life issues, and solving root causes of problems. Responding to the underlying symptoms of crime is sometimes called problem-oriented policing. One commonly used technique in problem-oriented policing is scanning, analysis, response, and assessment (SARA).

1. Describe the three policing styles that are shaped by different community values.

2. What is the broken windows theory?

3. Discuss the various challenges facing community policing programs.

watchman style A style of policing that focuses on maintaining order and is associated with declining industrial, blue-collar communities.

legalistic style A style of policing that focuses on law enforcement and professionalism and is associated with reform-minded cities with mixed socioeconomic communities.

service style A style of policing that focuses on protecting a homogenous suburban, middle-class community against outsiders and providing service to community residents.

team policing Teams of officers assigned to a specific geographic area with the charge to ensure public safety, maintain order, and deliver community services to the residents of that community.

community policing Decentralized policing programs that focus on crime prevention, quality of life in a community, public order, and alternatives to arrest.

broken window theory The belief that ignoring public-order violations and disruptive behavior leads to community neglect, which fosters further disorder and crime.

zero-tolerance strategy Strict enforcement of the laws, even for minor violations.

problem-oriented policing A community policing strategy that emphasizes attacking the root problem that causes crime instead of responding to the symptoms of the problem.

SARA A community policing strategy based on a highly modified version of the scientific method that attempts to identify the root cause of crime in a community.

MyCJLab

Go to Chapter 5 in *MyCJLab* to test your mastery of chapter concepts, access your Study Plan, engage in interactive exercises, complete critical-thinking and research assignments, and view related online videos.

 Review: Complete the pretest in the Study Plan to confirm what you know and what you need to study further. Then complete the post-test to confirm your mastery of the concepts. Use the key term flash cards to review key terminology.

 Apply: Complete the interactive simulation activity.

Analyze: Complete assignments as directed by your instructor.

Current Events: Explore CJSearch for current topical videos, articles, and news pieces.

Additional Links

Go to **http://www.met.police.uk/history/** to see a detailed history, including historic photographs, of the London Metropolitan police.

Go to **http://www.nyc.gov** to get the latest pictures and information about events and the operations of the New York City Police Department, the nation's largest police department.

Go to **http://www.fbijobs.gov** for the Federal Bureau of Investigation's employment information, including the physical fitness requirements and background disqualifiers.

Go to **http://www.sheriffs.org** to learn about the National Sheriffs' Association, its programs, and its publications.

Go to **http://www.asisonline.org/** to read about the efforts of the American Society for Industrial Security to increase professionalism in the private security field, as well as its certifications, seminars, and employment opportunities.

Go to **http://www.theiacp.org** and learn about the International Association of Chiefs of Police. This organization is the world's oldest and largest nonprofit membership organization of police executives, with over 20,000 members in more than 100 countries.

Oversight and Professionalism of Law Enforcement

"There is no contradiction between effective law enforcement and respect for civil and human rights. Dr. King did not stir us to move for our civil rights to have them taken away in these kinds of fashions."

—Dorothy Height

1 Explain the importance of police professionalism and integrity and the means used to promote professionalism and integrity.

2 Summarize the legal restraints placed on law enforcement and the procedures that law enforcement must follow for searches, seizures, lineups, and arrests.

3 Summarize the legal aspects of police interrogations and the Miranda decision.

4 Explain the issues of law enforcement misconduct and use of force.

5 Summarize the legal aspects of intelligence gathering and the war on terrorism.

6

Lisa F. Young / Fotolia

The U.S. Secret Service provides protective services for some of the highest-ranking officials in the U.S. government. According to Darrell Issa (R–Calif.), Chairman of the House Oversight and Government Reform Committee, it is the federal government's most elite protective unit. U.S. House Representative Elijah Cummings (D–Md.) praised the Secret Service as "an essential organization and it's an organization that is viewed like the Navy SEALs and viewed like the folks who guard the leaders of Israel. These kinds of folks are the elite." President Obama said that the Secret Service "does very hard work under very stressful circumstances." Unfortunately, the backdrop for all this praise is a sex scandal in Cartagena, Colombia, allegedly involving a number of U.S. Secret Service agents and possibly an unknown number of other personnel.

SAUL LOEB/AFP/Getty Images/Newscom

What happened in Cartagena, Colombia, definitely did not stay in Cartagena. While on assignment to protect President Obama during his trip to Cartagena, Colombia, on April 12, 2012, 11 Secret Service agents went in small groups to different nightclubs and strip joints, drank to excess, and picked up foreign national women to bring back to their hotel rooms for paid sex. A dispute over payment to one of the women resulted in the police being dispatched to the hotel, and the incident was reported to the U.S. Embassy. (Prostitution is legal in Colombia.) As a result, the actions of the agents became public knowledge. Now the Secret Service Office of Professional Responsibility, at least three Congressional committees, and the Department of Homeland Security are investigating the incident. Representative Issa said that this is the kind of incident that could compromise the security of the president. Senator Susan Collins (R–Maine) accuses the agents of engaging in "reckless, morally repugnant behavior" that could compromise the security of the president.

U.S. Secret Service Director Mark Sullivan has called the scandal an isolated incident and promised that the Secret Service's internal review will hold all involved accountable. Senator Collins said that she did not believe it was an isolated incident, as two Secret Service supervisors, each with more than 20 years of experience, were involved. She suggests that it reflects a culture of misconduct because the involvement of the supervisors "surely sends a message to the rank and file that this kind of activity is tolerated on the road." Collins is calling for an independent investigation. Senator Joe Lieberman (I–Conn.) said that records show 64 cases of alleged similar misconduct by Secret Service agents in the last five years, and he, too, believes "a culture of misconduct took root" in the agency.

The U.S. Secret Service has implemented a written code of conduct, has issued policy that agents will be held to standards of behavior appropriate to U.S. laws, and requires all agents to complete mandatory ethics training to be provided by professors of Johns Hopkins University.

> **DISCUSS** Can agencies conduct trustworthy internal investigations of alleged misconduct? Why or why not?

▶ Professionalism and Oversight

This chapter discusses the balance between crime fighting and due process rights. The U.S. Constitution guarantees certain due process rights to those accused of a crime. However, the Constitution lacks specificity regarding the interpretation and application of those rights in the twenty-first century. The process of applying and interpreting due process rights is influenced by social values, technology, scientific knowledge, and law.

Law enforcement plays an important role in determining this balance because it is the actions of law enforcement officers in activities such as stops, searches, arrests, interrogations, and use of force that define the abstract concepts of justice, fairness, and constitutional rights.

There are two opposing views of law enforcement officers. The first is that they are mere employees trained to

provide competent services as directed within the scope of their employment. The second viewpoint is that law enforcement officers are professionals and their training, knowledge, and discretion allow them to make complex decisions as to how abstract principles of law and order are to be applied in the real world on a case-by-case basis. In the first view, law enforcement officers could be considered professionals in that they render competent services, are courteous, are knowledgeable of the various laws and policies, and deal fairly with the public. However, this definition of professionalism could be applied to nearly any trade or employee. The latter viewpoint is usually applied to medical doctors, lawyers, judges, and other professionals who are required to engage in complex decision making, are

> Such activities as stops, searches, arrests, interrogations, and use of force define the abstract concepts of justice, fairness, and constitutional rights.

1914	**1918**	**1925**	**1936**	**1949**
Weeks* v. *United States establishes the exclusionary rule, which prohibits the admission in federal courts of evidence obtained in violation of Fourth Amendment rights.	***Silverthorne Lumber Co. v. United States*** establishes the "fruit of the poisoned tree doctrine," which prohibits the admission in federal courts of indirect as well as direct evidence obtained illegally.	***Carroll doctrine*** defines requirements for search of a vehicle.	***Brown* v. *Mississippi*** declares that confessions obtained by the use of force are tainted.	***Wolf* v. *Colorado*** incorporates the exclusionary rule as a state right.

self-regulating, and are dedicated to providing services to others even when self-sacrifice or danger is involved.

For the majority of the first half of the twentieth century, most people viewed law enforcement officers as employees trained to provide competent services. O. W. Wilson was one of the first people to refute this premise and argue that law enforcement officers provide services on a much higher level of professionalism. Unfortunately, his views were rejected by most of his contemporaries. The question of professionalism was raised again in 1967 when the President's Commission on Law Enforcement and Administration of Justice debated whether law enforcement officers needed college education. The answer to that question depends to a large degree on whether one considers law enforcement officers professionals or merely employees. The President's Commission recommended that law enforcement officers have a minimum of a four-year degree.

There is no universally accepted definition of professionalism in law enforcement. However, there is general agreement that professionalism includes the following factors:[1]

- An occupation that requires extensive training

- The mastery of specialized knowledge

- An occupation that requires some form of accreditation, certification, or licensing

- An internal set of standards of performance and behavior

- Aspiration to high ideals such as altruism, honor, integrity, respect, and excellence

- A code of ethics to which members are held accountable

- Self-regulation in terms of accountability to the professional standards of the occupation

Contemporary law enforcement sees itself as a professional occupation and its law enforcement officers as professionals.

Each agency has policies that define professional standards of behavior. Nationally, law enforcement acknowledges the **Law Enforcement Code of Ethics** as publicized by the International Association of Chiefs of Police as a standard of behavior to which all officers should aspire. Also, law enforcement has internal procedures and personnel for detecting, correcting, and disciplining unprofessional behavior.

Three internal strategies are used by law enforcement to achieve professionalism: (1) a rigorous procedure for selecting and training new recruits, (2) a well-developed internal standard of professional behavior, and (3) formal strategies for detection and punishment of violations of professional behavior.

Each law enforcement agency has a rigorous selection strategy to screen out applicants who do not meet the entry-level requirements. The steps in this selection process were discussed in Chapter 5. The objective is to screen out applicants who have psychological, mental, behavioral, or physical characteristics that would render them unqualified to meet the professional

LAW ENFORCEMENT CODE OF ETHICS

As a Law Enforcement Officer, my fundamental duty is to serve allkind; to safeguard lives and property; to protect the innocent against deception, the weak against oppression or intimidation, and the peaceful against violence or disorder; and to respect the Constitutional rights of all men to liberty, equality, and justice.

I will keep my private life unsullied as an example to all, maintain courageous calm in the face of danger, scorn, or ridicule; develop self-restraint; and be constantly mindful of the welfare of others. Honest in thought and deed in both my personal and official life, I will be exemplary in obeying the laws of the land and the regulations of my department. Whatever I see or hear of a confidential nature or that is confided to me in my official capacity will be kept secret unless revelation is necessary in the performance of my duty.

I will never act officiously or permit personal feelings, prejudices, animosities, or friendships to influence my decisions. With no compromise for crime and with relentless prosecution of criminals, I will enforce the law courteously and appropriately without fear or favor, malice or ill will, never employing unnecessary force or violence and never accepting gratuities.

I recognize the badge of my office as a symbol of public faith, and ethics of the police service. I will constantly strive to achieve these objectives and ideals, dedicating myself before God to my chosen profession ... law enforcement.

Source: International Association of Chiefs of Police.

standards of the department. This process screens out people who use illegal drugs; abuse alcohol; and have a record of criminal behavior, domestic violence, mental problems, and personality disorders. Furthermore, new officers undergo extensive initial training and in-service training. During this training, officers are taught the specialized knowledge required for professionalism, introduced to the required standards of behavior, and tested to ascertain that they have what it takes to be a law enforcement officer.

Next, law enforcement agencies have formalized comprehensive policies and procedures that prescribe the standards of professional conduct and the discipline for violation of these standards. These policies and procedures are frequently codified into a publication called the **standard operating procedures (SOP) manual**. The SOP manual describes the policies that regulate behavior and the performance standards. SOP policies may be general policies such as prohibiting officers from making public statements that discredit the department. Other policies may describe the specific procedures officers are expected to follow when transporting prisoners, arresting suspects, or towing a vehicle. Officers are expected to be knowledgeable of the policies and procedures in the SOP manual and to adapt their behavior to these standards.

Finally, departments have formal strategies to detect and discipline officers who violate professional standards of behavior. Violations may include gross actions such as criminal activity or corruption, abuse of power, or minor violations such as incivility to citizens. Departments detect violations through citizen complaints and investigations.

Most departments have procedures whereby citizens may lodge complaints of criminal, abusive, or unprofessional behavior. The department has a procedure for reviewing the validity of these complaints. Some common names for these oversight boards are **citizen complaint board**, citizen review board, and police review board. This review usually involves the citizen and the officer presenting testimony, evidence, or witnesses before a formal board with the power to render a judgment regarding the charges. Some boards are composed entirely of law enforcement personnel; other boards are composed of members from both law enforcement and the public. Some boards have the authority to impose discipline on officers

who have been found to violate professional standards of behavior. However, it is more common that citizen complaint boards only have the power to recommend discipline to another authority.

Finally, departments maintain standards of professional behavior by proactively investigating violations of professional behavior. In mid- to large-size departments, this investigation is done by a special unit of law enforcement officers. This unit is commonly called **Internal Affairs Unit or Office of Internal Affairs**, but it may be known by other names. The specific mission of the Internal Affairs Office is to conduct proactive investigations to detect criminal, abusive, or unprofessional behavior by law enforcement officers within the department. The Internal Affairs Office is much like a detective unit, but with a focused mission—investigating officers within the department. Usually, the Internal Affairs Unit is outside the chain of command and reports directly to the chief or another high-ranking official.

The Internal Affairs Office may conduct random or targeted investigations. In a random investigation, officers may be selected at random without any suspicion of wrongdoing. Often it is the Internal Affairs Unit that conducts random drug testing of officers. In a targeted investigation, the unit selects an officer or officers to investigate based on suspicion or probable cause that the officer or officers are involved in criminal or abusive behaviors. A common targeted investigation conducted

LEARNING OUTCOMES 1 Explain the importance of police professionalism and integrity and the means used to promote professionalism and integrity.

GLOSSARY

Law Enforcement Code of Ethics Professional standards of behavior to which law enforcement officers should aspire.

standard operating procedures (SOP) manual A manual that describes the policies that regulate behavior and the performance standards for police officers.

citizen complaint board A citizen review board that hears alleged complaints of police misconduct.

Internal Affairs Unit or Office of Internal Affairs An office that conducts investigations of criminal, abusive, or unprofessional behavior by law enforcement officers within the department.

The Internal Affairs Office is much like a detective unit, but with a very focused mission—investigating officers within the department.

1985	**2004**	**2006**	**2009**	**2010**	**2012**
Tennessee* v. *Garner prohibits law enforcement from shooting fleeing subjects unless they are a clear and present danger.	***Hiibel* v. *Sixth Judicial District Court of Nevada*** requires citizens to give their name to law enforcement.	***Hudson* v. *Michigan*** allows the exception to the exclusionary rule for entry without "knock and announce."	***Herring* v. *United States*** allows evidence obtained that involves only isolated carelessness. Introduces concept of "sliding scale."	***Berghuis* v. *Thompkins*** rules that people have a duty to assert their right to remain silent.	***United States* v. *Antoine Jones*** requires a court search warrant for use of a GPS tracking device.

by the Internal Affairs Unit is the investigation of a shooting. All shootings are investigated to determine the facts of the shooting and to determine whether the officer should be subject to discipline or criminal charges. If the shooting is controversial, the department may request that the Internal Affairs Unit of another department investigate the shooting so as to appear fair and impartial.

Officers are selected for Internal Affairs Units in several ways. A common method is rotating assignments. In a rotating assignment, officers are selected to serve for a certain period of time and then return to service within the department. This procedure is thought to keep internal affairs officers from becoming corrupt themselves. The disadvantage of this method is that since officers know they will return to the department, they may be reluctant to appear unnecessarily harsh or aggressive in investigating fellow officers for fear that those officers will resent them when they leave the Internal Affairs Unit. Most often Internal Affairs Units investigate allegations of serious wrongdoing that can result in criminal charges, dismissal, or serious disciplinary actions.

While contemporary law enforcement exercises internal oversight to ensure professionalism, it is also subject to external oversight of behavior.

▶ External Oversight of the Police

In addition to self-regulation, law enforcement is subject to external oversight. External oversight does not negate viewing law enforcement officers as professionals. External oversight, or checks and balances, is an integral characteristic of the U.S. government. The most significant sources of external oversight are laws and judicial decisions, especially U.S. Supreme Court decisions. Laws provide **direct oversight** of law enforcement because it prohibits specific behaviors and requires certain behaviors. Judicial decisions provide **indirect oversight** of law enforcement. Indirect oversight does not exercise direct control over agencies or officers, but provides a remedy, usually at a criminal trial, if the standards of the court are not observed.

The courts and law enforcement are different branches of government. Thus, the courts do not have the authority to develop and administer law enforcement policies and codes for professional behavior. However, by indirect oversight, the courts can influence the policies and behaviors of law enforcement.

The courts can indirectly influence law enforcement by determining what evidence can be presented at trials; the standards of proof needed for a conviction; and the constitutionality of law enforcement policies, practices, or behaviors. One of the ways the courts exercise indirect oversight is through procedural law.

Procedural law is a body of laws for how things should be done at each stage of the criminal justice process. These laws are developed through legislative and judicial oversight. Police practices are affected by city and county councils, state legislatures, and the federal Congress. These legislative bodies can pass laws that limit or expand police jurisdiction, create standards, and provide remedies for police practices not acceptable to the community. For example, a 1973 Washington, DC, law provided that drivers with expired license plates were to be arrested and taken to jail. The law was passed to deal with a growing crime problem because it provided officers with a tool to stop, question, and identify persons of interest with expired license plates. At the time, it was enforced primarily in selected inner-city neighborhoods. In 2011, the police department started enforcing the law citywide, resulting in the arrests of citizens unaccustomed to such policies. Public complaints resulted in the law being changed to repeal criminal penalties for driving with an expired tag, instituting fines instead.[2]

According to the separation of powers doctrine, police officers have the power to arrest people, but not the power to prosecute people for the charges on which they have been arrested. The power to file a criminal complaint against a defendant—even to decide who will be brought to court to face charges and who will not—rests with the judicial branch of government in the hands of an independent prosecutor's office and the court.

Even for serious felonies such as murder, rape, and child sex offenses, failure to provide the accused the rights guaranteed to

LEARNING OUTCOMES 2 Summarize the legal restraints placed on law enforcement and the procedures that law enforcement must follow for searches, seizures, lineups, and arrests.

GLOSSARY

direct oversight Laws and judicial decisions that prohibit specific law enforcement behavior.

indirect oversight A remedy, usually at a criminal trial, if the standards of the court are not observed by agencies or officers.

procedural law The body of laws governing how things should be done at each stage of the criminal justice process.

him or her or to follow required procedural law can result in the dismissal of charges and the person's release from the criminal justice system. The police are responsible for the detection and investigation of crimes and for the arrest of the alleged offender. However, as they perform these responsibilities, they are required to do so without violating the rights of the accused.

▶ Rules of Evidence

The police have the primary responsibility for detecting and investigating crime, gathering evidence to present in court, and arresting suspects. However, they do not have unrestricted powers in fulfilling these responsibilities and must perform these duties within prescribed limits set by legislation, judicial oversight, and the Constitution. One of the most influential criminal justice agencies regulating police behavior is the U.S. Supreme Court. The Supreme Court has the power to review cases to determine whether the constitutional rights of the accused have been preserved. It also has the power to establish the rules by which courts operate. Rules that relate to the presentation of evidence in a trial are called the rules of evidence.

Rules of evidence stipulate the requirements for introducing evidence and define the qualifications of an expert witness and the nature of the testimony he or she may give. According to the rules of evidence, for example, the prosecutor must show the defense the evidence he or she has gathered against the defendant. Rules define when evidence is relevant to the case and to particular issues in the case.

Rules of evidence affect police officers' conduct because collecting evidence is part of their job. If evidence is not collected properly, it can be declared inadmissible, in which case it cannot be used against a defendant. For example, if a defendant is on trial for illegal possession of drugs and the drugs he or she is accused of possessing are declared inadmissible as evidence, the prosecutor cannot present this evidence to the jury. Thus, the prosecutor has no case.

The Exclusionary Rule

Evidence can be declared inadmissible under the **exclusionary rule**, which prohibits the use of evidence or testimony obtained in violation of civil liberties and rights protected by the U.S. Constitution. The exclusionary rule originated with the 1914 Supreme Court case of *Weeks* v. *United States*.[3] In the *Weeks* case, the U.S. Supreme Court ruled that evidence against Weeks that had been obtained without a warrant was in violation of his protections under the Fourth Amendment.

Initially, the exclusionary rule applied only to federal courts. The rights guaranteed by the First Amendment (freedom of speech and freedom of association), the Fourth Amendment (privacy and search and seizure), the Fifth Amendment (self-incrimination and double jeopardy), and the Sixth Amendment (the right to confront witnesses) did not apply to the actions of local police or state courts. Until 1949, state courts were free to write their own rules of evidence.[4]

In 1961, the Court decided that the states had failed to act to protect the constitutional rights of the defendant.

Fruit of the Poisoned Tree Doctrine

At first, the exclusionary rule established in the *Weeks* case applied only to primary (directly obtained) evidence, not to secondary evidence. For example, if federal agents obtained the business books of a company by unconstitutional means, those books could not be used as evidence to incriminate the defendant, but a copy of the information could. Also, inadmissible evidence could lead to other evidence, which then could be introduced in court. Thus, if an unconstitutional search produced a map indicating where a defendant had buried the body of the person he or she was accused of murdering, the map could not be introduced as evidence. However, using the knowledge obtained from the map, police officers could find the body and introduce it as evidence.

Four years after the *Weeks* decision, the Supreme Court reconsidered the exclusionary rule and added another rule of evidence, known as the **fruit of the poisoned tree doctrine**. The name of the doctrine comes from the analogy that if the tree is "poisoned," the "fruit" of the tree also will be poisoned. In *Silverthorne Lumber Co.* v. *United States* (1918), the Supreme Court declared that the rules of evidence applied not only to evidence directly obtained by illegal means, but also to any other evidence obtained indirectly.[5] Under this rule, the copy of the business books and the body found through the aid of the map are not admissible as evidence.

The U.S. Supreme Court required the federal courts to follow this rule but still did not interfere in the procedures of state courts. Only 17 states chose to adopt similar rules of evidence. However, in *Wolf* v. *Colorado* (1949), the U.S. Supreme Court declared that state courts had to enact procedures to protect the rights of citizens against police abuses of search and seizure.[6] *Wolf* v. *Colorado* gave the states wide latitude in developing rules of evidence such as the exclusionary rule and the fruit of the poisoned tree doctrine to discourage such abuses. Twelve years later, in 1961, the Court decided that the states had failed to act to protect the constitutional rights of the defendant.

Application to State Courts: *Mapp* v. *Ohio*

Historically, the Supreme Court did not interfere with state courts, but with the incorporation of the exclusionary rule, this practice started to change. Without any "punishment" for gathering evidence and obtaining confessions contrary to constitutional protections, local and state law enforcement officers paid little attention to the federal constitutional rights of citizens. They knew that any evidence they obtained would be admissible at trial in state court. It was common practice for police to search without a warrant or probable cause, obtain confessions by the use of force, and in general

It was common practice for police to search without a warrant or probable cause, obtain confessions by the use of force, and in general ignore the constitutional rights of suspects.

ignore the constitutional rights of suspects. Then, in 1961, in *Mapp v. Ohio*, the U.S. Supreme Court reversed itself and required state courts to use the exclusionary rule.[7]

The facts of *Mapp v. Ohio* are that Cleveland, Ohio, police officers received a tip from an informant that a bombing suspect was at the home of Dolree Mapp and that evidence at her house would connect her to the numbers racket. When police officers went to Mapp's home and asked permission to search her house, she refused. The police officers returned and announced that they had obtained a search warrant. When she asked to see it, they showed her a piece of paper, which she grabbed and stuffed in her dress. The police officers forcibly retrieved their "search warrant," which actually was a blank piece of paper.

The police proceeded to search Mapp's house without a search warrant, probable cause, or consent. They did not find the bombing suspect or the numbers evidence, but they did find a bag of obscene books and arrested her for possession of obscene materials. Mapp was convicted in state court for possession of obscene materials. Mapp believed that her Fourth Amendment rights had been violated, but when she appealed, the Ohio Supreme Court upheld the conviction. Mapp appealed to the U.S. Supreme Court, which ruled that local police officers were accountable to the same standard as that in *Weeks v. United States*. Therefore, the evidence obtained illegally was inadmissible. Mapp's conviction was reversed.

Mapp v. Ohio was the first case in which the U.S. Supreme Court applied the exclusionary rule to state courts. All state courts were then required to adopt rules of evidence, which declared that evidence would be inadmissible in criminal court if it was gathered

> The exclusionary rule has been considered one of the most important doctrines in deterring police misconduct. It was not created by legislation and is not found in the Constitution.

rules of evidence Requirements for introducing evidence and testimony in court.

exclusionary rule A rule that prohibits the use of evidence or testimony obtained in violation of the Fourth and Fifth Amendments of the U.S. Constitution, established in *Weeks v. United States* (1914) and extended to all state courts in *Mapp v. Ohio* (1961).

fruit of the poisoned tree doctrine A rule of evidence that extends the exclusionary rule to secondary evidence obtained indirectly in an unconstitutional search, established in *Silverthorne Lumber Co. v. United States* (1918) and in *Wolf v. Colorado* (1949).

without a warrant, probable cause, or consent. The exclusionary rule has been considered one of the most important doctrines in deterring police misconduct. It was not created by legislation and is not found in the Constitution. The Supreme Court created the rule as a means to respond to violations of constitutional rights by the police.

Exceptions to the Exclusionary Rule

The 1961 landmark case *Mapp v. Ohio* is the standard for police professional conduct. Other decisions affecting the admissibility of evidence in state courts followed quickly and had sweeping effects on state criminal court procedures. However, recent decisions have modified the exclusionary rule. Recent rulings have exempted what has been called "minor police misconduct" from the provisions of the exclusionary rule calling for the complete exclusion of evidence gathered in violation of civil rights.

Hudson v. Michigan

In this case, the Court ruled in 2006 that the failure of the Detroit police to knock and announce themselves before entering the home of Booker T. Hudson was not sufficient error to justify suppressing the drugs they found under the exclusionary rule.

Herring v. United States

This case involved a more significant deviation from the exclusionary rule. Bennie Dean Herring had been arrested in 2004 based on erroneous computer records showing an outstanding warrant for his arrest. As permitted by law when making a lawful arrest, the arresting officer immediately made a search of Herring and his vehicle. The search resulted in the discovery of a pistol and methamphetamine. The pistol was illegal because Herring was a convicted felon. Within 15 minutes of the automobile stop, arrest, and search, the arresting officer was notified that the outstanding warrant was void and that the police computer was in error. Herring was convicted and appealed based on the exclusionary rule that the search was unconstitutional because without a valid warrant for arrest, there was no probable cause for the search. The facts of the case were undisputed. If the Supreme Court followed previously rulings, Herring's conviction would most likely be dismissed. However, in 2009, the Roberts Court ruled that the error by the police was minor

Mark Poprocki/Fotolia

Think About It . . .

Bloomington (Illinois) police officer Scott Sikora stopped motorist Anthony Johnson for a loud muffler. However, once stopped, Officer Sikora told Johnson that the actual purpose for the stop was because Johnson had been observed visiting a home known for drug activity. Officer Sikora told Johnson, "Our goal is not tickets. Our goal is drugs."[8] Johnson's car was searched, and officers discovered drug paraphernalia. Johnson was charged with possession of drug paraphernalia. At trial, Johnson's defense was that the police lacked legal justification to detain him or to search his vehicle. Associate Judge David Butler agreed with Johnson and ruled that the police did not have a valid reason to search a man's car during a traffic stop in which the officer made it clear that the stop was not related to a traffic offense.[9] If evidence of criminal behavior is found in a vehicle stop based on a pretense, should the evidence be banned? Why or why not?

and should be balanced against the seriousness of the crime. Writing for the majority, Justice Roberts said, "The exclusion of evidence should be a last resort and judges should use a *sliding scale* [emphasis provided] in deciding whether particular misconduct by the police warranted suppressing the evidence they had found…. To trigger the exclusionary rule police conduct must be sufficiently deliberate that exclusion can meaningfully deter it, and sufficiently culpable that such deterrence is worth the price paid by the justice system." Although the "sliding scale" is a common practice in other countries, it has been rejected in the United States since the 1914 *Weeks* decision.

▶ Search and Seizure

The rights of the accused are based on rights guaranteed by the U.S. Constitution, state constitutions, and legislation. Often the Court is called on to interpret the application of these rights to specific actions of the police. Numerous changes in law, society, and technology and science have occurred since the drafting of the Constitution. Inventions such as the telephone, the automobile, and the Internet emerged more than 100 years after the writing of the Constitution; so there is no specific reference in the Constitution as to how these modern technologies affect the constitutional rights envisioned by its authors. Thus, the Court must often interpret the intent of the Constitution as applied to modern society.

The Fourth Amendment and the Right to Privacy

The courts establish guidelines for the police through case law that provides rulings on what actions violate constitutional rights. Evidence gathered in a manner that violates the constitutional rights of the accused cannot be used in court to prove the guilt of the defendant.

The Fourth Amendment does not guarantee absolute privacy in one's person, house, papers, and effects. Actually, the "right to privacy" is not guaranteed in the Constitution, but is a right "inferred" from other rights guaranteed by the various amendments. As such, the right to privacy is not clearly defined. In some cases, the government can access what some may consider private information; in other cases, they cannot.

Medical Records

When Keith Emerich of Pennsylvania reported to his doctors, who were treating him for an irregular heartbeat, that he regularly drank more than a six-pack of beer a day, his doctors reported this information to the Pennsylvania Department of Transportation as required by a state law. The law required doctors to report any physical or mental impairments that could compromise a patient's ability to drive safely. Emerich had no traffic convictions for over 20 years, but based on the information provided by his doctors, his driver's license was suspended. Emerich objected, saying that the information he provided his medical doctor was private and confidential and should not have been reported to the Commonwealth. However, the Court, after considering the balance of medical privacy versus public safety, ruled that in this case, as in other similar cases, the concern for public safety outweighed the individual's right to privacy.

However, in 2004, when the U.S. Justice Department wanted Chicago's Northwestern Memorial Hospital to disclose records on abortions performed at the hospital, a federal appeals court rejected the demand. The Justice Department claimed that the abortion records were needed in an upcoming lawsuit to test the claims of doctors who maintained that the Partial-Birth Abortion Ban Act would prevent them from performing medically necessary procedures. The federal appeals court rejected the Justice Department's claim, saying that access to such records would violate the privacy rights of women.

Reasonable Expectation of Privacy

In some cases, the courts are required to decide what a reasonable expectation of privacy is. For example, when Lonnie Maurice Hill was arrested in 2003 for drug charges, he challenged the constitutionality of his arrest. Hill and a woman entered a convenience store's one-person unisex restroom. The store clerk called the police and reported this activity as suspicious behavior. When the police arrived, Hill and the woman refused to respond to the officer's request for them to open the bathroom door. When police opened the door, they found marijuana and cocaine inside the restroom and arrested Hill on drug-related charges. Hill appealed that he had an expectation of privacy in the restroom. At his defense, his lawyer raised the question of whether a married couple, a parent and child, or a disabled person and an assistant occupying a single-person bathroom would be considered suspicious behavior. Despite these arguments, the Eighth U.S. Circuit Court of Appeals rejected Hill's claim that his expectation of privacy in the public restroom made the drugs seized by the officer inadmissible as evidence.

Electronic Monitoring

At times, the Court must decide how new technology affects constitutionally protected rights, as in the case concerning event data recorders (EDRs). These devices are electronic monitoring systems in cars and trucks that track and record data, such as whether airbags deployed, whether passengers wore seatbelts, and what the speed of the vehicle was. EDRs are installed in 65% to 90% of 2004 and later model year vehicles.

Typically, EDRs store the last five seconds of data. However, they can easily be programmed to store months of data. The data can be retrieved—much like the black box of an airplane—in the event of a crash. Also, the data are transmitted to such services as OnStar. Many drivers are not aware that their car is recording such data. Most states have no laws requiring that drivers be advised of the presence of this device. Data from EDRs have been used by law enforcement to obtain a number of convictions for vehicular homicide because police can prove the speed of a vehicle and they know whether the vehicle was accelerating or braking at the time of an accident. Concerned that the collection of such data violates the privacy rights of drivers, North Dakota has proposed legislation that would require drivers to be informed if their vehicles have EDRs installed and would restrict access of police, insurance companies, and car manufacturers to such data. No doubt, the courts will have to decide whether such technology violates the privacy of motorists and whether evidence gathered by EDRs can be used in obtaining criminal convictions.

In 2012, the U.S. Supreme Court required law enforcement to obtain a search warrant to monitor a suspect's vehicle with a

Global Positioning System (GPS) device. Prior to *United States* v. *Antoine Jones* (No. 10-1259), law enforcement routinely used GPS devices to monitor suspects' movements without obtaining a court order. The reasoning was that the GPS device was similar to law enforcement personnel following the suspect and a court search warrant was not need to "tail a suspect."

In 2005, without a search warrant, law enforcement placed a GPS device on a Jeep Grand Cherokee used by Antoine Jones who was suspected of drug trafficking. The police tracked his movements for a month, and the evidence obtained played a key role in his conviction for conspiring to distribute cocaine. Jones appealed his conviction. The appeals court ruled that the prolonged surveillance with a GPS device amounted to a search and that a search warrant was required. The government appealed to the U.S. Supreme Court, and the Supreme Court upheld the appeal. Supreme Court Justice Scalia summarized the Court's opinion, "We hold that the government's physical intrusion on the Jeep for the purpose of obtaining information constitutes a search."

United States v. *Antoine Jones* was not decided in such a manner that it covered a broad scope of electronic tracking issues. Of future concern will be the question of using cell phones to track people. Presently, cell phone tracking is a powerful and widely used surveillance tool for federal and local law enforcement.[10] While the American Civil Liberties Union (ACLU) and other civil rights advocates raise legal and constitutional questions regarding the use of cell phone tracking without judicial search warrants, search warrants are not presently required. Cell phone tracking is used in both criminal cases and search and rescue to find missing persons. There are cases at the U.S. Court of Appeals level regarding this issue. No clear-cut judicial ruling has emerged regarding the necessity of a search warrant for cell phone tracking.[11]

search warrant Legal permission, signed by a judge, for police to conduct a search.

probable cause The likelihood that there is a direct link between a suspect and a crime.

search incident to lawful arrest The right of police to search a person who has been arrested without a warrant.

plain-view search The right of the police to gather without a warrant evidence that is clearly visible.

Carroll doctrine Terms allowing admissibility of evidence obtained by police in a warrantless search of an automobile when the police have probable cause that a crime has occurred and delaying a search could result in the loss of evidence.

pat-down doctrine The right of the police to search a person for a concealed weapon on the basis of reasonable suspicion, established in *Terry* v. *Ohio* (1968).

Search Incident to Lawful Arrest

The Fourth Amendment requires that evidence must be obtained by police with the use of a valid **search warrant** issued by a judge or by a search based on probable cause. **Probable cause** is the likelihood that there is a direct link between a suspect and a crime. Despite this seemingly limited authority to gather evidence by searches outlined in the Constitution, the courts have authorized a number of other circumstances under which the police can gather evidence without a warrant or probable cause.

The Supreme Court has granted that when police make a lawful arrest, they are entitled to make a search of the person arrested without a search warrant. This is called **search incident to lawful arrest**. The question has arisen as to how extensive a search police can make under this justification. They cannot extend their search to rooms not occupied by the person arrested and to areas beyond the person's reach because a search incident to lawful arrest is limited to the area within the immediate control of the person.[12] Otherwise, evidence obtained is not admissible in criminal court. Evidence obtained from a search incident to lawful arrest can include containers found within the reach of the arrestee, firearms within reaching distance, and evidence under the car seat or couch cushion on which the person is sitting.

In 2004, the U.S. Supreme Court expanded the authority of police to make searches incident to lawful arrest when they ruled that police do not need a warrant to search a car when the person they have arrested was recently in the car. The Supreme Court's ruling permits warrantless searches whenever the arrestee was a recent occupant and is still in the vicinity of the car. The ruling will most likely result in further appeals because it did not define "how recent is recent, or how close is close." Thus, it will be left up to future cases to determine the limits authorized by this decision.

Plain-View Searches

Evidence in the plain view of police officers is admissible in criminal court (*Harris* v. *United States*).[13] However, to be admissible, the police officer must have had the legal right to be where he or she was. For example, a police officer is invited into someone's home and that person was thoughtless enough to leave on the table a pile of marijuana that he or she was in the process of cleaning and bagging; the Supreme Court has ruled that such evidence obtained in a **plain-view search** is admissible. However, a police officer cannot move objects to get a view of the evidence.[14] For example, if the marijuana on the table had been completely covered with a cloth, the police officer could not remove the cloth (without permission, a search warrant, or probable cause) to see what was underneath it. Likewise, if a police officer were to enter a room and move electronic equipment to see the serial numbers to check against a list of stolen merchandise and find a match, such evidence would be inadmissible without permission, a search warrant, or probable cause.[15] However, the police are not required to be heedless or inattentive to their environment. In the language of the Court, "inadvertence is not necessary."[16] A police officer who sees a cloth covering something on a table and smells marijuana may have probable cause to look under the cloth.

Whether evidence from a plain-view search is admissible can depend on even minor variations. For example, if a 6-foot-tall police officer is walking by a 5-foot-high fence and sees marijuana plants growing on private property on the other side of the fence, the evidence is in plain view. If a 5'8" police officer is walking by a 6-foot-high fence and uses a ladder to look over the fence and sees marijuana plants growing on the other side, the evidence is not in plain view. Similarly, the Supreme Court has ruled that a police officer using a flashlight to look into an automobile at night does not violate the plain-view doctrine.

However, a police officer using binoculars to view evidence might violate the plain-view doctrine.

Consent to Search

If a person gives permission for a search, any evidence discovered is admissible (*Florida v. Jimeno*, 1973).[17] The person who gives permission must have the authority to do so. For example, a landlord cannot give valid permission to search an apartment currently occupied by a tenant but can give permission once the tenant vacates the apartment. A motel owner cannot give permission to search a motel room rented to a guest but can give permission to search the room after the guest checks out. A parent can give permission to search the room of a legal dependent living in the same house but cannot give permission to search the room of a boarder living in a room rented in the house. The complexity of society has resulted in numerous rulings by the courts defining who has the authority to grant permission to search.

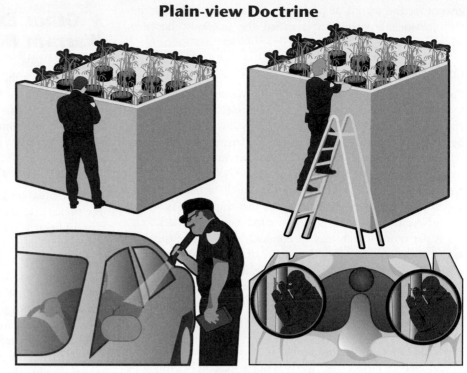

Plain-view Doctrine

left: No violation of doctrine. Evidence is admissible; **right:** Violation of doctrine. Evidence is inadmissible

Search of Automobiles

The Carroll Doctrine

As early as 1925, the Supreme Court addressed the question of the constitutionality of searches of automobiles without a search warrant. Recognizing that the mobility of automobiles adds a new dimension to searches, the Court established the Carroll doctrine, based on *Carroll* v. *United States* (1925).[18] According to the **Carroll doctrine**, evidence obtained in the search of an automobile without a warrant is admissible in criminal court if both of the following take place:

- A police officer has probable cause to believe that a crime has occurred.

- The circumstances are such that a delay in searching the automobile would result in loss of the evidence.

This rule requires that an officer must have probable cause to stop the car in the first place.[19] If an officer does not have the authority to stop the car, any evidence obtained in a search is not admissible.

Trained Dog Sniffing

In *Illinois* v. *Caballes* (2005, No. 03923), the Supreme Court extended the power of the police to search vehicles by permitting a trained dog to sniff a car for drugs without the need for any particular reason to suspect the driver of a narcotics violation. Justice Stevens, arguing for the majority opinion of the Court, said, "A dog sniff conducted during a concededly lawful traffic stop that reveals no information other than the location of a substance that no individual has any right to possess does not violate the Fourth Amendment." As long as the "search" by the dog does not unreasonably prolong the traffic stop and the

police had the legal right to stop the vehicle, the police do not need "specific and articulable facts" suggesting drug activity to justify the use of the dog.

Impounded Vehicles

Any evidence obtained during an inventory of the contents of a lawfully impounded vehicle is admissible in criminal court.[20] For example, if the police arrest a driver for driving while under the influence of alcohol and impound the vehicle, they can perform a thorough search of the vehicle, including any locked glove compartments or trunks. They also can remove any boxes, suitcases, or other items and search them. The police may even force locks for the purpose of inventorying the contents of an automobile. The philosophy is that the police assume liability for the loss of anything of value in the vehicle when they impound it and therefore are authorized to inventory the entire vehicle and its contents to establish the presence and value of any contents. Also, locked containers in a vehicle might hide things that pose a danger to police or the public, such as a bomb hidden in a suitcase in the vehicle, in which case the police have a right and duty to determine such danger.

Search of Persons

Pat-Down Search

The U.S. Supreme Court has appreciated the fact that the police operate in an environment that can be life-threatening. Thus, the police are allowed to take certain reasonable precautions in dealing with the public. In the course of taking reasonable precautions, such as frisking or patting down a detainee suspected of carrying a weapon, if the police find incriminating evidence, such evidence is admissible in criminal court. The doctrine governing the search of persons without probable cause but with reasonable suspicion is called the **pat-down doctrine,** which has its origins in *Terry* v. *Ohio*.[21]

Concealed Weapons

Police officers frequently approach or are approached by citizens to interact. At close range, a citizen's possession of a weapon could be deadly to an officer. In some contexts, the police may be able to determine by simple visual inspection whether a citizen is carrying a concealed weapon, but outer clothing often makes it impossible to tell. In such cases, officers are authorized to conduct a limited pat-down search of outer clothing when they have a reasonable concern that the citizen is armed. Probable cause is not required under these circumstances.

A pat-down search may be conducted solely to ensure the safety of the officer.[22] If in the course of a pat-down the police officer feels an object that might be a weapon, the officer legally can reach into the pocket or clothing to further explore the nature of the object. If the officer still believes the object might be a weapon, he or she may remove the object and examine it. If it is a weapon and the person is not authorized to carry it, the weapon is admissible as evidence. However, if the officer feels an object that clearly is not a weapon but might be illegal, such as a bag of narcotics, the officer may not reach into the pocket to explore the nature of the object or remove it for inspection. An object acquired in an illegal pat-down search is not admissible as evidence in a court of law unless it is immediately apparent by touching the object that it is contraband.

Stop and Identify

In 2004, the Supreme Court significantly altered the scope of warrantless searches that police may conduct, which is justified by the 1968 *Terry* v. *Ohio* case. The Supreme Court upheld the conviction of Larry D. Hiibel of Nevada for refusing to give a deputy sheriff his name.[23] Although the offense was a misdemeanor, the court's ruling upheld the concept that in a routine stop of a citizen, the police have the authority to demand that the citizen answer their questions. Previously, it was understood that the police had the power to stop citizens under the authority of *Terry* v. *Ohio* but that citizens were under no obligation to answer a police officer's questions. The Court ruled that there was no violation of the Fifth Amendment for a citizen to be required to disclose his or her name and that such information does not incriminate a citizen in violation of the Fifth Amendment. The ruling might have been influenced by the concern that if the Supreme Court did not uphold this authority, a ruling the other way would have protected terrorists and encouraged people to refuse to cooperate with police.

Drug smuggling and other drug laws have resulted in the interesting situation in which people swallow drugs wrapped a protective covering or conceal drugs in personal body cavities in an effort to prevent their detection by the police. Even if the police have probable cause to believe that someone has swallowed illegal drugs in an effort to conceal them, the Court has been fairly consistent in requiring a search warrant to retrieve drugs by medical procedures such as pumping the stomach or conducting invasive searches of the body.[24]

▶ Other Exceptions to the Warrant Requirement

Since the 1960s, the U.S. Supreme Court has restricted the situations in which the police may conduct a search without a warrant. However, the Court has continued to recognize that there are certain circumstances that may justify a warrantless search. The two most common exceptions to the requirements for a search warrant are public safety and good faith.

Public Safety Exceptions

Certain situations require immediate action by the police. If the police are chasing a person who just committed a crime using a firearm and catch the person but fail to find the firearm on him or her, the Court has ruled that the police have the right to perform a search without a warrant in places where the person may have discarded the firearm. The justification for this is the **public safety exception,** the argument that if the search is not performed immediately, the presence of the weapon in the community may pose a serious threat to public safety.[25] For example, if a person committed armed robbery and fled from the police into a mall but did not have a firearm when caught, the police would be justified in immediately searching for the weapon in the stores in the mall. There is the danger that a citizen, especially a juvenile, might find the weapon and accidentally harm someone by discharging it. The firearm, if found by police in a warrantless search, would be admissible as evidence.

Searches of Airline and Bus Passengers

Another example of the public safety exception is the acceptance of searches of airline passengers without probable cause or warrant requirement for the public good. The justification for this kind of search is that it is necessary for public safety and that passengers implicitly consent to be searched in exchange for the right to board an airplane. Law enforcement officers extended this philosophy to bus passengers. In an effort to detect drug smugglers who use public transportation to move illegal drugs from Florida to the Northeast, law enforcement officers obtained permission from bus companies to search the possessions and baggage of bus passengers. Arguing that they had the permission of the operating companies, similar to permission given by the airline industry to search air passengers, officers began routine searches of bus passengers, a practice known as "working the buses." Evidence seized in these searches could legally justify an arrest and be used as evidence in court.[26]

public safety exception The right of the police to search without probable cause when not doing so could pose a threat of harm to the public.

good faith exception An exception to the requirement that police must have a valid search warrant or probable cause when they act in good faith on the belief that the search was legal.

wiretapping A form of search and seizure of evidence involving communication by telephone.

arrest The restriction of the freedom of a person by taking him or her into police custody.

Searches of people and property at border checkpoints and entry ports do not require probable cause, reasonable suspicion, or a search warrant. Federal border officers may search people and property virtually at will.

Searches of Subway Passengers

In 2005, the police extended the public safety exception to justify random searches of subway passengers for explosives in response to perceived terrorist threats against U.S. mass transit systems following terrorist attacks on London's bus and subway system. The ACLU protested the random searches as a violation of the Fourth Amendment. The ACLU expressed concern that if random searches of subway passengers were permitted under the public safety exception, police could extend the scope of the searches to include virtually any public space. The court did not uphold the ACLU's protests.

U.S. Customs officials also have been granted greater leeway by the Supreme Court under the public safety exception to conduct warrantless searches.

Border Searches

Searches of people and property at border checkpoints and entry ports do not require probable cause, reasonable suspicion, or a search warrant. Federal border officers may search people and property virtually at will. Property may be destroyed in the search, and searches of people may be intrusive. This power is granted to border security personnel by both legislation and case law. Consent of the person to be searched is not necessary because he or she does not have the right to refuse. Evidence found of illegal activity or contraband such as drugs is admissible in criminal court.[27]

School Searches

Although not police officers, school administrators have been granted broad discretionary power to search students, students' property such as backpacks and purses, and students' school lockers. Evidence obtained in these searches can be used for both disciplinary action and criminal charges. The Court has recognized the power of school administrators to perform searches of students both on school property and "near" school property. The Court has held that students do not have an expectation of privacy concerning property in "student" lockers because the lockers are under the ownership and control of the school. However, a 2009 case concerning the strip search of a middle school student set a limit on school administrators' power to search. The Supreme Court ruled that school strip searches are not reasonable.[28]

The Good Faith Exception

Another common exception to the requirement of having a warrant or probable cause to conduct a legal search is when the police act in good faith. In most cases, the **good faith exception** applies when some type of clerical error results in the police executing what they think is a valid search warrant but in reality it is not. A common example is when the police have probable cause to obtain a valid search warrant but because of a clerical error, the address of the premises to be searched was entered incorrectly in the search warrant document. Acting in good faith that they have a valid warrant, the police search the location described in the search warrant. What happens if in the course of this mistaken search the police find evidence of criminal activity such as illegal drugs? Because the search was not authorized by the warrant and the police had no probable cause to perform the search of the "innocent" party, is the evidence discovered at the wrong premises admissible in criminal court? Initially, the Court did not support the good faith exception, taking the position that good faith by the police does not override the violation of the valid search warrant requirement.[29] However, the Court later reversed itself and allowed evidence obtained in good faith but without a valid search warrant to be admitted in evidence.[30] This principle may be expressed as the exclusionary rule applying only in cases in which police misconduct is involved.

Issues of Privacy

Wiretapping

Another area affected by the Fourth Amendment in which the Supreme Court has changed its position on the admissibility of evidence is the issue of obtaining evidence by **wiretapping**, a form of search and seizure of evidence involving telephone communications. At the time the U.S. Constitution was drafted and the rights of citizens were enumerated in the Bill of Rights, there obviously was no mention of the right of privacy of one's telephone communications or messages sent by computer or e-mail. A hundred years after the drafting of the Constitution, the telephone was invented and law enforcement officers began listening in on private telephone conversations between bootleggers. Using the information obtained by listening to these conversations, the police were able to make arrests and win convictions. In one case, the bootleggers appealed their conviction, and in 1928, the Supreme Court heard its first case in the area of electronic communications (*Olmstead* v. *United States*, 1928).[31]

Initially, the Court ruled that the telephone lines and public telephone booths were not an extension of the defendant's home and were therefore not protected by the constitutional guarantee of privacy. Thirty-nine years later, the ruling in *Olmstead* was reversed, and it was declared that electronic communication was indeed private communication and protected as a constitutional right (*Katz* v. *United States*, 1967).[32] Violating this privacy without consent, probable cause, or a warrant constitutes illegal search and seizure.

Electronic Communications

The issue of privacy in relation to electronic communications has gone beyond court-mandated rules of evidence, requiring new legislation. Major pieces of legislation addressing privacy of electronic communications are the Electronic Communications Privacy Act of 1986, the Communications Assistance for Law Enforcement Act of 1994, the Telecommunications Act of 1996, and the USA PATRIOT Act. These laws provide specific details governing the collection of evidence by wiretaps and other means and the definition of what electronically transmitted information is protected by the expectation of privacy.

Except in cases of suspected terrorism, law enforcement officers generally must satisfy stringent requirements before they can obtain information transmitted electronically or stored in computer databanks, such as stored e-mails. If law enforcement officers fail to follow the provision of the law, besides the evidence not being admissible in court, for some violations, the officer may be subject to fines or incarceration.

Homeland Security

The USA PATRIOT Act, presidential executive orders, and other legislation have significantly altered the limits of the power of law enforcement to perform searches. In cases of homeland security, searches can be performed without a warrant, whereas in a criminal case, the search is unconstitutional. The impact of new legislation on the power of law enforcement agencies is discussed in Chapter 14.

Incarceration

Once incarcerated in a correctional institution, the inmate loses all expectation of privacy and can be searched, including invasive searches, without a warrant or probable cause. Visitors to correctional institutions are considered to have consented to search by their presence in the institution. The Court has distinguished between inmates and people who police hold temporarily in "holding cells." People who have been arrested are subject to search.

Arrest

The court has the authority to issue arrest warrants. To obtain an arrest warrant from a court, the police must present probable cause evidence that a crime has been committed by the person identified in the warrant. Arrest warrants can also be obtained as the result of a grand jury issuing a "true bill."

Limitations on police powers of arrest stem from abuses by the English government during the colonial period in the American colonies and in England. As a result of historical suspicion against the government's power to incarcerate citizens on questionable charges or without due process, the powers of the police to make an arrest are limited. Law enforcement officers can initiate an **arrest** only under the following conditions:

1. With an arrest warrant issued by the court
2. When they observe a violation of the law
3. Under exigent circumstances—that is, circumstances in which unless immediate action is taken by the police, the evidence may be destroyed or the suspect may escape
4. When they have probable cause to believe that someone has committed a crime

In many states, the police are limited to arresting a person justified by probable cause that he or she has committed a crime only when the crime is a felony.

▶ Interrogations and Confessions

The Fifth and Sixth Amendments govern the admissibility of testimony obtained through interrogations and confessions. The confession is an effective method of convincing a jury that the defendant has committed the crime of which he or she has been accused. In fact, nearly a quarter of all convictions overturned in recent years based on DNA and other evidence have involved false confessions.[33] For example, in the infamous 1989 Central Park jogger case, five young defendants provided elaborate and detailed confessions as to how they committed the crime and were found guilty by a jury. As unexplainable as it seems, the confessions were false. After these men had served 13 years for a crime they did not commit but to which they confessed, the real offender, Matias Reyes, confessed to the crime. His confession was confirmed by DNA and other evidence and the five defendants were released.

Waiver of Rights

In some cases, the accused provides a confession to the police. However, confessions must be obtained within court-imposed criteria. Even if the police are successful in obtaining a confession, it may be inadmissible in court if it was not obtained properly. To be admissible, a confession must be given knowingly and voluntarily, it cannot be obtained as a result of threat or pain, and the suspect must be informed of his or her rights.

Use of Physical Punishment and Pain

Law enforcement practices traditionally have not been conducive to protecting citizens' Fifth Amendment rights. The U.S. Supreme Court has addressed the admissibility of confessions obtained by the use of force in several landmark cases:

- *Brown* v. *Mississippi* (1936): The court ruled that confessions obtained by force were tainted.
- *Ashcraft* v. *Tennessee* (1944): The court ruled that confessions obtained by the use of around-the-clock interrogation were not voluntary and were therefore inadmissible.

- The confession must be given knowingly and not as a consequence of lies or deception.
- The suspect must be informed of his or her rights.
- The confession must be voluntary.
- Confessions may not be obtained through threats, such as threatening to turn an illegal foreign alien over to immigration authorities for deportation, threatening to report an abusive mother to child protective services so that her children are taken away from her, or threatening to report suspects to a welfare agency for the purpose of having their welfare benefits suspended.
- Confessions may not be obtained through use of pain or through constructive force, such as beating up one suspect in front of another and telling the second suspect that he or she is next if a confession is not forthcoming.

Standards for an Admissible Confession

Despite these rulings, the use of force or torture to obtain a confession continues to be a concern. In 2001, for example, former Chicago police commander Jon Burge was sentenced to four and one-half years for his role in detectives' torture of suspects to obtain confessions.[34] In 2011, Juan Rivera was tried for a third time for the 1992 rape and murder of 11-year-old Holly Staker. The former trials required jurors to weigh the confession of Rivera against DNA evidence suggesting that he did not commit the murder. The confession was revised several times to eliminate inconsistencies and add vital elements to the crime that were missing from earlier confessions. Defense attorneys suggested that when combined with the circumstances under which the confession was obtained, the confession was improperly obtained and false.[35] The outcome of the trial is interesting in that while the jury convicted Rivera for a third time for the murder, appeals judges reversed Rivera's conviction, calling the believability of the confession into question.[36]

The Right to an Attorney

Because of concern that the rights of a suspect protect him or her from **self-incrimination**, the court has required that the suspect is entitled to have an attorney present when he or she is interrogated by the police, as well as in court.

Right to an Attorney in Court

The right to have the benefit of an attorney when accused of criminal charges was established in the landmark case of *Gideon* v. *Wainwright* (1963).[37] The details of the case are striking because they illustrate the influence a single case concerning a relatively obscure defendant can have on the entire criminal justice system.

Gideon was convicted of burglary and sentenced to an extended prison term under the habitual offender act. He did not have the funds to hire an attorney to represent him in court, and the state refused to grant him one free of charge. Left to defend himself, Gideon apparently did not do very well against the trained and experienced state prosecutors, and he was convicted of the crime. While in prison, Gideon sent a handwritten letter to the Supreme Court in which he protested the unfairness of his conviction. He argued that it was unfair for him to have to defend himself, without the benefit of counsel, in a court of law against the resources of the state.

After due consideration, the Court agreed with Gideon's position and issued an opinion that he was entitled to a new trial and that at this trial he was entitled to be represented by an attorney. If he could not afford an attorney, the state would have to provide one free of charge. Gideon was found not guilty in his retrial. Gideon's case established the practice of **indigent defense**. If a person cannot afford an attorney, the duty of the state is to provide legal counsel.

Extensions of the Right to an Attorney

Once this right was established, it was extended beyond the criminal trial. In *Argersinger* v. *Hamlin* (1972), the right to an attorney was extended to include anyone facing a potential sentence of imprisonment, not just a felony. It was extended to juveniles accused of crimes in *In re Gault* (1967).[38] In *Escobedo* v. *Illinois* (1964), the right to an attorney was extended to include the right to have an attorney present during police interrogation.[39]

Limitation on the Right to an Attorney

The Court has made several changes regarding the right to an attorney when suspects are questioned. In *Michigan* v. *Jackson* (1986), once a person requests an attorney, the police must cease their questioning. In *Maryland* v. *Shatzer* (2010), the Court ruled that if the suspect requests an attorney and refuses to answer questions, police may reinitiate questioning without counsel 14 days after release from custody.

> **indigent defense** The right to have an attorney provided free of charge by the state if a defendant cannot afford one, established in *Gideon* v. *Wainwright* (1963).
>
> **Miranda rights** Rights that provide protection from self-incrimination and confer the right to an attorney, of which citizens must be informed before police arrest and interrogation, established in *Miranda* v. *Arizona* (1966).
>
> **police lineup** An opportunity for victims to identify a criminal from among a number of suspects.

Delayed Court Appearance

A 1968 law known as the McNabb-Mallory rule placed a six-hour time limit between the interrogation of a suspect and his or her first court appearance. The purpose of the law was to limit abuses made possible by extended detention and interrogations without the benefit of legal rights. The Supreme Court acknowledged that confessions obtained after lengthy detention and interrogation called into question the credibility of those confessions.

Limits on Deception

Court rulings have not clearly prohibited police from obtaining a confession by lying to the suspect.[40] For example, confessions have been admitted even when obtained by police falsely telling one suspect that his partner in crime had confessed and named him as the "trigger man." Also, confessions have been obtained by placing a police officer dressed in prisoner clothing in the same cell as the suspect. Confessions have been prohibited when obtained through the use of other types of deception. In *Leyra* v. *Denno* in 1954, the police used a psychiatrist to obtain a confession from the suspect, who thought he was receiving treatment for a medical

The McNabb-Mallory rule placed a six-hour time limit between the interrogation of a suspect and his or her first court appearance.

condition. The psychiatrist persuaded the suspect that he would feel better if he confessed to his crime. The court ruled that such deception was beyond the acceptable limits of professional police conduct and that the confession was inadmissible.[41]

Miranda Rights

In the famous case of *Miranda* v. *Arizona* (1966), the court issued an opinion in which it summarized all of the rights of a citizen during police arrest and interrogation.[42] Initially, the court was very strict in requiring that these rights, known as the **Miranda rights**, were spoken word for word to all suspects during arrests and interrogations. Gradually, however, the Miranda protections have been weakened by exceptions. Courts have decided that it is not necessary to advise people of all Miranda rights and that they do not have to be advised of their rights at the beginning of questioning. Controversies surrounding Miranda have included concerns of law enforcement that the requirement to advise people of their rights impedes efficient police work.

Interrogating outside Miranda

This is an interrogation tactic used by law enforcement. In this practice, the officer first questions the suspect without advising the suspect of his or her rights. If a confession is obtained, the suspect is advised of his or her rights and a second interrogation is performed. The assumption is that it is easier to obtain a confession without advising the suspect of his or her Miranda rights. The first confession is discarded, and the second confession, the one in which the suspect was advised of his or her rights, is used in court. The Court ruled that this tactic was a police strategy "adapted to undermine the Miranda warnings."

Exceptions to Miranda

However, not all confessions require that the suspect be advised of his or her Miranda rights. Confessions given freely prior to an opportunity for police to advise a suspect of his or her rights are admissible, and confessions given to third parties are admissible. An example of the former is a spontaneous confession given by a suspect immediately after the arrival of the police, such as the case in which a husband who murdered his wife exclaimed, "I murdered her!" to the police when they arrived. Another example involved a Southern California couple bragging on the Dr. Phil show about how they took part in a large-scale shoplifting scheme; police used that information in their investigation. The information was not obtained through interrogation by the police. Therefore, the information could be used even though the couple was not advised of their Miranda rights.

In *Berghuis* v. *Thompkins* (2010), the U.S. Supreme Court issued a significant reversal of the rights granted by Miranda. The Court required that the suspect must clearly tell police that he or she does not want to talk. Previously under Miranda, the police had the burden of showing that a Miranda warning had been given and that the accused

DNA evidence has exposed a number of cases in which a witness mistakenly identified a person as the offender, only to be exonerated at a later time by DNA evidence.

understood it. The Court's decision ruled that a written waiver is not necessary and that if a Miranda warning is given, an uncoerced statement by the accused "establishes an implied waiver of the right to remain silent."

Right to Remain Silent

Miranda rights are based on the rights against self-incrimination guaranteed in the Fifth Amendment. Thus, defendants have the well-known "right to remain silent," or "Fifth Amendment" right, during interrogations and their trials. Defendants cannot be compelled to provide testimony that may incriminate them. Furthermore, the law provides that the prosecution cannot say or imply to the jury that a defendant's silence or refusal to testify at his or her trial implies guilt.

Police Lineups

The Fifth Amendment also protects the rights of suspects in participating in a **police lineup**. In a police lineup, a victim or witness is given an opportunity to identify a suspected perpetrator from among a number of suspects. What are a suspect's rights in a lineup?

Rulings have suggested that suspects' guarantees against self-incrimination apply in police lineups, but not to the degree they apply in police interrogations. Law enforcement officers need to perform certain investigative tasks essential to gathering information about a crime. So long as the police act in a professional and fair manner, they have greater latitude than in interrogations.[43] For example, police officers can drive a witness by a suspect to see if the witness can identify the person as someone who

Landmark cases have addressed the following questions:

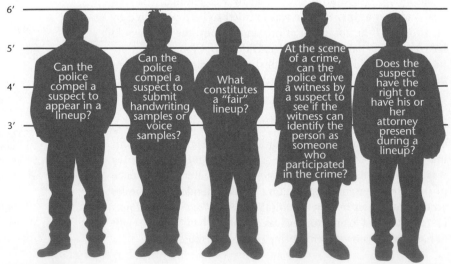

Can the police compel a suspect to appear in a lineup?

Can the police compel a suspect to submit handwriting samples or voice samples?

What constitutes a "fair" lineup?

At the scene of a crime, can the police drive a witness by a suspect to see if the witness can identify the person as someone who participated in the crime?

Does the suspect have the right to have his or her attorney present during a lineup?

participated in the crime, and this can be done without informing the suspect or obtaining the suspect's consent. Suspects can be required to participate in a lineup without their consent and can be required to give a handwriting or voice sample.[44]

Lineups must be fair, however, and must meet the following requirements:

- Suspects have the right to have an attorney present.

- A lineup must include suspects who are similar and match the description given by the witness.

- A lineup must include actual suspects and not police personnel masquerading as suspects.[45]

- A lineup must include people who are known to the police not to be capable of being the offender. The inclusion of these people acts as a check on the witnesses' credibility.

One of the abuses of lineup standards that gained nationwide publicity was the Duke lacrosse rape case. In the case, lacrosse players from Duke University were accused of sexually assaulting a female dancer at a party. Using a photo lineup, the prosecuting attorney had the victim select those men who had assaulted her. However, the prosecutor included only pictures of Duke lacrosse players who were at the party. Thus, no matter whom the victim selected, he was a possible offender.

DNA evidence has exposed a number of cases in which a witness mistakenly identified a person as the offender, only to be exonerated at a later time by DNA evidence. Although eyewitness identification is persuasive in convincing jurors of the guilt of the defendant, some research questions the accuracy of lineup identification.

Juveniles

The standards for the interrogation of juveniles differ from those for adults. Juvenile rights are discussed further in Chapter 13. Basically, juveniles are not considered capable of waiving their right to remain silent. The consent of a guardian or the juvenile's attorney is normally necessary prior to police interrogation.

▶ Law Enforcement Misconduct

Numerous issues are related to law enforcement misconduct, ranging from criminal behavior to incompetence. Some of the more serious concerns are (1) use of force, (2) corruption and criminal behavior, (3) racial profiling, (4) high-speed vehicular pursuits, and (5) entrapment.

Use of Force

Public safety is at the crux of the issue regarding the use of force. There are two considerations in the use of force: (1) use of deadly force and (2) use of less than deadly force. **Deadly force** is the use of force, most commonly a firearm, that is likely to cause death or serious injury. Thus, a situation in which a person is shot but does not die is still considered a deadly force incident because the force used could have caused death. Prior to 1985, one common situation in which law enforcement used deadly force was shooting fleeing suspects who refused to stop as commanded.

Prior to 1985, many police departments had SOP detailing the circumstances under which an officer was justified in firing warning shots or using deadly force. It was common policy for departments to allow officers to use deadly force against fleeing people who were only "suspected" of committing crimes, and some jurisdictions did not differentiate between misdemeanors or felonies when using deadly force against a fleeing suspect. This practice was known as the fleeing suspect doctrine or **fleeing-felon doctrine**. The police justified this practice on the basis of public safety. They argued that a suspect allowed to escape could be a potential danger to the community. If the person was suspected of having committed murder, they reasoned, a failure to apprehend might create an undue risk for the public—a justification for use of deadly force.

Prohibition against Deadly Force

In *Tennessee* v. *Garner* (1985), the Supreme Court disagreed with that reasoning.[46] Attorneys representing Garner, who had been slain by a police officer who was pursuing Garner when he refused to stop, made the argument that the officer's use of deadly force was a form of search and seizure for which the officer lacked probable cause or a warrant. The Court accepted the validity of the argument and ruled that the search and seizure by deadly force against a fleeing suspect was a violation of the person's constitutional rights. The ruling in *Tennessee* v. *Garner* immediately superseded the rules of all police departments and the laws of the states that had permitted the practice. All law enforcement officers (local, state, and federal) were immediately prohibited from using deadly force as a means to stop a fleeing suspect. If the ruling was ignored, the officer and department could be held liable in a lawsuit for violation of the person's constitutional rights.

This ruling caused great confusion as law enforcement officials and state legislators tried to determine the limits of the prohibition.[47] For example, if a person committed murder in the presence of a police officer and then threw down his or her weapon and fled from the scene and there was no other way to stop the person from escaping, could the officer use deadly force? The argument for the use of deadly force is based on the potential threat that an escaped murderer poses to a community. The argument against the use of deadly force is based on the fact that after the person threw down his or her weapon, that person was no longer an immediate threat to the officer or the public, such that the use of deadly force was an unreasonable violation of his or her constitutional rights. If deadly force were used and the person died, he or she would have been deprived of the right to a trial by jury for the alleged criminal conduct.

Clear and Present Danger

Although there are legitimate arguments to support the prohibition and sanction of the use of deadly force in this case, the present legal position is that when there is a **clear and present danger** to the public posed by the escape of the person, deadly force may be justifiable.[48] In the lack of a clear and present danger, the use of deadly force to apprehend a fleeing suspect or criminal is a violation of the person's constitutional rights.

Continuum of Force

In 2008, an estimated 17% of U.S. residents aged 16 or older had face-to-face contact with police.[50] The most common reason for

In March 2012, Oscar Carrillo called Pasadena 9-1-1 and reported that two young African-American men had put a gun in his face and had stolen his backpack. When officers arrived at the scene and found Kendrec McDale, a 19-year-old African-American man, two blocks from the scene, they attempted to stop him, but he ran. Carrillo had reported that the robbers were armed; so when McDale reached for his waistband when he was about 10 feet from the officers, they thought he was reaching for a gun and fired approximately eight times, killing McDale. McDale's 17-year-old partner was arrested but was unarmed. Police searched for days in an unsuccessful attempt to find the firearms the two men had allegedly used. When police reinterviewed Carrillo, he confessed that he had lied to the 9-1-1 dispatcher about the men having weapons, in the hope the police would respond faster.

The shooting occurred less than a month after the shooting of Trayvon Martin in Florida. Previously in 2009, Pasadena police officers shot Leroy Barnes, Jr., an African-American man, during a traffic stop, resulting in recommendations for major change by the Office of Independent Review. Joe Brown, president of the Pasadena chapter of the NAACP, said that the perception of the Pasadena police officers is that "they [African-American men] are all gangbangers, or they are all packing. It does increase the instances of shoot-to-kill with law enforcement." Pasadena police have asked the County of Los Angeles Office of Independent Review to investigate McDale's shooting. They also charged Oscar Carrillo with suspicion of involuntary manslaughter because he lied to the police about the suspect being armed.[49] They claim that this lie contributed to the officer's decision to shoot.

To what degree, if any, is Oscar Carrillo responsible for the police officers shooting McDale? Is the decision to charge Carrillo an attempt by the Pasadena police to relieve the officers from being blamed for the shooting? Explain.

contact with police was being a driver in a traffic stop. In 2010, nationwide, law enforcement made an estimated 12,120,947 arrests, or about 4,258 arrests per 100,000 residents.[51] Of this large number of contacts and arrests, the good news is that in about 9 out of 10 incidents, citizens who had contact with police believed the police acted properly. The bad news is that about 10% did not think the police acted properly.[52] A common complaint is that police use excessive force. When officers use force, injury rates to citizens range from 17% to 64%, depending on the agency.[53]

Officers are authorized to use force in a number of situations. The use of force, including deadly force, is authorized to remove the threat of death or serious bodily injury to the officer or the public, to apprehend a person who is a clear and present danger, and to effect an arrest. Most state statutes permit officers to use force to defeat attempts to resist arrest even if it is a misdemeanor arrest. However, in all of these situations, officers are expected to use only the minimum force necessary to achieve their lawful objective.

The public and the courts presume that law enforcement agencies have policies and training that set standards for the use of force in various situations.[54] Most agencies have a use of force continuum policy. **Use of force continuum** requires officers to use appropriate force depending on the circumstances. The force used must match the threat and resistance encountered.[55]

9 out of 10

citizens said that police acted properly during contact they had with the police.

The least force is verbal commands. If a person does not respond to verbal commands or offers resistance, an officer may use soft empty-hand tactics (that is, pushing). The next level of force is the use of chemical agents and hard empty-hand tactics. If there is the threat of great bodily injury, the use of force may escalate to conducted energy devices, or Tasers. **Conducted energy devices (CEDs)** deliver powerful electric shocks, causing incapacitation. Taser is the most common brand used by law enforcement agencies. The final levels of use of force are impact devices such as batons and deadly force.

CEDs are used in more than 15,000 law enforcement and military agencies.[56] More than 200 persons have died after being shocked by Tasers.[57] This number represents less than 0.3% of people who were shocked by CEDs.[58] Despite this low number of deaths, both Amnesty International and the ACLU have questioned whether Tasers can be used safely.[59] While use of CEDs is not risk-free, no clear medical evidence shows a high

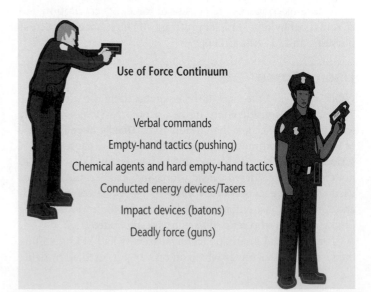

Use of Force Continuum

Verbal commands

Empty-hand tactics (pushing)

Chemical agents and hard empty-hand tactics

Conducted energy devices/Tasers

Impact devices (batons)

Deadly force (guns)

risk of serious injury or death from their direct effects. A preliminary review of deaths following CED exposure found that many were associated with continuous or repeated shocks.[60]

Serious injury or death may be related to three issues: (1) insufficient training, (2) use on vulnerable populations, and (3) failure of the device to subdue the victim with one shock. In most agencies, officers receive four to six hours of training in the use of CEDs.[61] Officers may need additional training or annual training to ensure that they understand the risks associated with CED use. A second possible contributor is the use of CEDs on vulnerable populations. The use on vulnerable people and circumstances that pose potential heightened risk to the subject may be a factor in serious injuries. Vulnerable populations include pregnant women, the elderly, and juveniles. Potentially higher-risk circumstances include drivers of moving vehicles, handcuffed suspects, people in elevated areas, and people near flammable substances.[62] Finally, in one study, about 9% of the time, a Taser did not work properly or did not have the desired effect of subduing the subject.[63] In such incidences, officers may have administered repeated shocks that resulted in serious injury.

One issue raised by the use of less lethal force such as CEDs is that some officers may move too quickly from verbal commands to the use of CEDs. The ease and effectiveness of CEDs may entice some officers to become too reliant on them as a way to control subjects rather than use conflict resolution skills. This tendency to forgo conflict resolution skills in favor of CEDs is referred to as the **lazy cop syndrome**.[64]

High-Speed Vehicular Pursuits

Such pursuits of fleeing people have posed a difficult question as to the right of police to engage in them. A number of high-speed pursuits have resulted in death or bodily harm to the person being pursued and to innocent parties. Lawsuits have been filed asking the courts to prohibit or at least restrict high-speed vehicle pursuits by the police, but in general, the courts have upheld the right of the police to pursue a fleeing person even when there is no reasonable suspicion or probable cause that the person has committed a crime other than a traffic violation. However, police departments have adopted rules and guidelines aimed at reducing deaths and injuries caused by such pursuits by regulating when officers can engage in them and when they should be discontinued.

Misconduct and Law Enforcement

Ever since Sir Robert Peel founded the first full-time professional police department, one of the major issues has been to ensure that those entrusted with a position of power and authority do not abuse that trust. Peel is credited with developing a set of guidelines to reflect the ethical behavior expected of London bobbies. (See Peel's Principles of Conduct, which follow.) If law enforcement officers were to follow these principles, undoubtedly there would be significantly less police misconduct. Obviously, this has not been the case.

Misconduct has been a constant problem for U.S. law enforcement throughout its history. The scope and nature of law enforcement misconduct has been documented numerous times by commissions, legislative investigation, and criminal prosecutions. The scope of law enforcement misconduct includes the largest police departments [the New York City Police Department (NYPD) and the Los Angeles Police Department (LAPD), for example] as well as small rural departments. For example, the Knapp Commission in 1970 and the Mollen Commission in 1993 documented extensive, serious citywide corruption within the NYPD. The investigation and prosecutions of the LAPD Rampart Division resulted in more than 100 falsely obtained convictions, 20 officers suspected, and 7 convicted of crimes.

Law enforcement misconduct can range from minor transgressions such as accepting gratuities and free meals contrary to department policies to more serious offenses of accepting

SIR ROBERT PEEL'S PRINCIPLES OF CONDUCT

1. The basic mission for which the police exist is to prevent crime and disorder.

2. The ability of the police to perform their duties is dependent upon the public approval of police actions.

3. Police must secure the willing co-operation of the public in voluntary observation of the law to be able to secure and maintain the respect of the public.

4. The degree of co-operation of the public that can be secured diminishes proportionately to the necessity of the use of physical force.

5. Police seek and preserve public favour not by catering to public opinion, but by constantly demonstrating absolute impartial service to the law.

6. Police use physical force to the extent necessary to secure observance of the law or to restore order only when the exercise of persuasion, advice, and warning is found to be insufficient.

7. Police, at all times, should maintain a relationship with the public that gives reality to the historic tradition that the police are the public and the public are the police; the police being only members of the public who are paid to give full-time attention to duties which are incumbent upon every citizen in the interests of community welfare and existence.

8. Police should always direct their action strictly towards their functions, and never appear to usurp the powers of the judiciary.

9. The test of police efficiency is the absence of crime and disorder, not the visible evidence of police action in dealing with it.

Think About It . . .

Historically, law enforcement has been characterized by incompetency, misconduct, and corruption. While advances have been made, these issues continue to be a concern. For example, when Mafia figure James "Whitey" Bulger was arrested in 2011, many feared he would reveal the names of politicians and law enforcement officials who had helped him elude capture. Bulger claimed that during his criminal career, which included 19 murders, he made payoffs to Boston police officers as well as FBI agents. A 2011 Justice Department investigation of the New Orleans Police Department concluded that "[t]he department is severely dysfunctional on every level: one that regularly uses excessive force on civilians, frequently fails to investigate serious crimes and has a deeply inadequate, in many cases nonexistent, system of accountability." The trial of Captain Jon Burge of the Chicago Police Department revealed systemic police torture and violation of civil rights. Rural departments are not exempt. In southern Illinois, Gallatin County Sheriff Raymond Martin was sentenced to life in prison for 15 felony drug counts and a foiled plot to have potential witnesses killed. Some police misconduct may be motivated by racial discrimination, as in the Dallas (Texas) Police Department, in which officers were citing immigrants for being "non-English-speaking drivers" when there was no such law. What can be done to help reduce the culture of misconduct within law enforcement?

ZUMA Press/Newscom

bribes, committing crimes, and even carrying out criminal enterprises that include homicide and drug trafficking under the color of one's law enforcement position. The Knapp Commission divided misconduct into two categories: grass eaters and meat eaters. **Grass eaters** are police officers who engage in minor illegitimate activities, much of which is accepted as "acceptable behavior" by fellow officers. **Meat eaters** are officers who engage in serious criminal conduct, corruption, and illicit money-making opportunities. Meat eaters solicit bribes and use threat to achieve gain, whereas grass eaters are passive, accepting what comes their way.

Contemporary departments continue to battle law enforcement misconduct. In 2012, officers of the New Orleans Police Department were convicted of homicide. In 2011, officers of Chicago's elite Special Operations Section were convicted of theft, bribery, drug trafficking, and civil rights violations. Law enforcement misconduct is not confined to local law enforcement because officers of federal agencies, including the Federal Bureau of Investigation (FBI), have been convicted of serious felony misconduct.

Racial Profiling

The history of law enforcement in the United States has its roots in racial discrimination. The Southern states established a system of militias and Black Codes to protect the white slave owners from rebellious and runaway slaves. From *Plessy* v. *Ferguson* (1896) to the 1972 Equal Employment Opportunity amendment of the Civil Rights Act of 1964, minorities were virtually excluded from law enforcement. During the 1960s, law enforcement was used to defend the status quo against protestors and activists seeking racial equality. Thus, it is no surprise that tensions and distrust exist between law enforcement and minorities.

In contemporary times, minorities—both juveniles and adults—have disproportionally more negative contact with the criminal justice system. Minority communities often perceive law enforcement officers as prejudiced and believe that they target minorities for arrest and are more likely to use deadly force on minorities. Numerous examples substantiate these perceptions. For example, in a period of eight months, Miami police officers shot and killed seven African-American men.[65] Michael Daragjati, a New York City police officer, was under FBI surveillance for other crimes when FBI agents intercepted text messages and calls by officer Daragjati. In those communications, he bragged about falsifying a police report to charge an African-American man with resisting arrest when the man complained about the officer's behavior and asked for his name and badge number.[66]

Racial profiling is not limited to African-Americans. Hispanics and Muslims have also been the targets of racial profiling. Hispanic/Latino racial profiling appears to be related to the immigration problem. Some states have enacted legislation that provides law enforcement with broad powers to stop and question Hispanics/Latinos such that the U.S. Department of Justice (DOJ) has intervened. The DOJ has filed numerous lawsuits against states—and in some cases specific law enforcement agencies—to remedy what it claims is unconstitutional discrimination against Hispanics/Latinos. Prominent among these DOJ interventions have been the lawsuits filed against the state of Arizona and Sheriff Joe Arpaio of the Maricopa County Sheriff's Department.

> **LEARNING OUTCOMES 4** Explain the issues of law enforcement misconduct and use of force.
>
> **GLOSSARY**
>
> **deadly force** The power of police to incapacitate or kill in the line of duty.
>
> **fleeing-felon doctrine** The police practice of using deadly force against a fleeing suspect, made illegal in *Tennessee* v. *Garner* (1985), except when there is clear and present danger to the public.
>
> **clear and present danger** A condition related to public safety that may justify police use of deadly force against a fleeing suspect.
>
> **use of force continuum** A policy that requires officers to use appropriate force depending on the circumstances they confront.
>
> **conducted energy devices** Devices that deliver powerful electric shocks, causing incapacitation.

An egregious example of racial profiling by law enforcement was the East Haven, Connecticut, Police Department scandal documented in 2012 by the DOJ and the FBI. Police officers were accused of tyrannizing Hispanics/Latinos, particularly immigrants. They would stop and detain people without justification; assault handcuffed victims; and engage in biased policing, unconstitutional searches and seizures, and the use of excessive force at will.[67] In January 2012, FBI agents arrested four New Haven officers on numerous charges related to civil rights violations. Janice K. Fedarcyk, assistant director in charge of the FBI office in New York, called the officers "a cancerous cadre that routinely deprived East Haven residents of their civil rights."[68] According to prosecutors, the misconduct reached to the highest ranks of the department and the police union. Upon the arrest of the New Haven officers, East Haven Mayor Joseph Maturo, Jr., voiced his public support of the chief and the officers. The chief was an unindicted co-conspirator. When the mayor was asked by the news media what he was doing for the Hispanic/Latino community in light of the indictments and misconduct directed against them, he responded on camera, "I might have tacos when I go home. I'm not sure yet."[69]

Racial profiling and law enforcement misconduct against Muslims appeared after the September 11, 2001, terrorist attacks. Racial profiling against Muslims is unique in that many people, including public officials, have endorsed racial profiling in incidences such as airport screening and homeland security. For example, the NYPD Intelligence Division has extensively targeted its intelligence-gathering efforts on young college-age Muslim men. This community is targeted for secret observations and intelligence gathering without evidence of wrongdoing or threat to homeland security. While there may be issues of violations of constitutional rights regarding the New York Police Department's actions, public polls show that the citizens of New York support the department's actions.

Entrapment

Law enforcement often uses tactics in which they pose as providers or buyers of illegal substances or goods. These operations are commonly called **stings** when law enforcement poses as buyers of illegal substances or goods and **reverse stings** when they pose as providers of illegal substances, goods, or services. For example, in a sting, law enforcement officers may pose as people interested in buying illegal drugs. In a reverse sting, law enforcement officers may pose as people selling illegal drugs. In addition to sellers and buyers of illegal goods or services, law enforcement may simply create conditions conducive to criminal activity. For example, in the television series *Bait Car*, law enforcement officers leave a parked car (with the keys in it) in an area known for criminal activity, sometimes with the door open or the engine running. The assumption is that a person interested in stealing an automobile will see this car as an easy target and take it. Since law enforcement is providing only the means to steal the vehicle and not the motivation, the use of a bait car is not considered entrapment.

The U.S. Supreme Court has required that a criminal conviction cannot be contingent on **entrapment**. Entrapment is when law enforcement provides both the motivation and means for committing a crime (*Jacobsen* v. *United States*, 1992).[72] The law requires that the *mens rea*, or criminal intent, must

Think About It . . .

African-American and Hispanic/Latino lawmakers of New York are working to pass legislation to curb racial profiling spawned by the NYPD's policy of "stop, question, and frisk." The aggressive policy resulted in a record 684,330 stops in 2011. African-American and Hispanic/Latino lawmakers say the stop-and-frisk policy results in racial stereotyping and out-of-control stop-and-frisk practices against minorities.[70] Lawmakers point to the fact that 87% of those stopped were African-American or Hispanic/Latino, and of those thousands of stops, only about 10% led to arrests and 1% to the recovery of a weapon, according to the Center for Constitutional Rights. Police Commissioner Raymond Kelly defended the policy. He says that stop-and-frisk has recovered 8,000 weapons, 800 of them handguns, and that in the last decade, the number of murders has dropped by 51%.[71]

michaeljung/Fotolia

Minority lawmakers have introduced bills that would make it illegal for the NYPD to set a quota for the number of stops officers must make, to prohibit racial profiling, to make it mandatory for officers to inform people they stop that they can refuse to be searched, and to require officers to give those people they stop a business card with a phone number in case they want to file a complaint.

Minority lawmakers accuse white lawmakers of creating a racial divide. Minority lawmakers claim that white lawmakers and citizens do not support reform because they cannot identity with the abuse caused by the policy. For example, opinion polls indicate that 59% of white voters approve of the stop-and-frisk policy whereas only 27% of African-American voters do. African-American and Hispanic/Latino lawmakers say that they can relate to the abuse because they have personally experienced it. Furthermore, David Paterson, the first African-American governor of New York, said, "It's a feeling of being degraded. I think that's what people who it hasn't happened to don't understand."

Is there a racial divide between whites and minorities as to what constitutes good policing? Why or why not? If so, what should be done about it?

lazy cop syndrome A term used to refer to officers who eschew the use of conflict resolution skills in favor of Tasers to control subjects.

grass eaters Police officers who engage in minor illegitimate activities that are considered "acceptable behavior" by fellow officers.

meat eaters Officers who engage in serious criminal conduct, corruption, and illicit money-making opportunities.

stings Tactics in which law enforcement officers pose as buyers of illegal substances or goods.

reverse stings Tactics involving law enforcement officers who pose as providers of illegal substances, goods, or services.

entrapment The illegal arrest of a person based on criminal behavior for which the police provided both the motivation and the means, tested in *Jacobsen* v. *United States* (1992).

sovereign immunity Immunity from civil lawsuits granted to federal and state governments.

actual damages Losses or harm that can be documented and on which a monetary value can be placed.

punitive damages Claims for a monetary award to punish the defendant for his or her misconduct.

consent decree A court order that establishes a monitoring team over a law enforcement agency.

originate with the offender. Law enforcement can provide the opportunity or means to commit the crime, but criminal intent must originate with the perpetrator.

Entrapment can occur when law enforcement engages in a reverse sting to sell cocaine but offers to sell the drug for a price much lower than the market value. For example, if law enforcement offers to sell cocaine with a street value of $10,000 for $100, this is considered entrapment. It is entrapment because a person who had no criminal intent to buy cocaine may be motivated to buy it solely because of the potential for profit if he or she resells it. For these reasons, when law enforcement engages in sting operations, it is important that they have accurate knowledge of the street value of the goods or services involved.

In overzealous enforcement efforts, law enforcement may cross the line and commit entrapment. A number of contemporary cases have involved undercover operations in which people infiltrated terrorist groups posing as a fellow terrorist. Once in the group, the undercover agent provides the bomb or explosive device to be used in an attack. Often the defense argues that the undercover agent provided both the motivation and the means and that his or her clients were entrapped by outrageous government conduct. The defense claims that had it not been for the government's actions, his or her defendants would not have committed the crime.

Remedies for Law Enforcement Misconduct

In a National Institute of Justice survey of subjects who were shocked with Tasers, almost all of them said that officers used excessive force and that they were not resisting arrest. However, when officers and the police reports were reviewed, a different version of events emerged.[73] Some subjects had failed to mention that they were armed or were fleeing or that they threatened the officer. Citizens file tens of thousands complaints of

33–45
The number of citizen complaints per department of excessive force used each year.

use of excessive force each year. Nationwide there are about 33 to 45 complaints per department.[74]

There are several remedies in response to allegations of police misconduct. Generally, allegations of police misconduct are lodged with the law enforcement agency, and the department does an internal investigation. For more serious allegations, a criminal investigation is conducted by the prosecutor, the DOJ, or a special state or federal commission. For the likelihood of allegations of misconduct to result in administrative discipline or punishment other than criminal charges, complaints are investigated internally by the agency or a citizens' complaint review board. In such an investigation, a citizen files a complaint with the department, usually the Internal Investigation Unit. The complaint is investigated, and a hearing is held. At the hearing, the citizen and officer present evidence and witnesses, and the board makes a decision regarding the validity of the charges. Of the thousands of complaints filed against law enforcement officers, only about 8% are sustained by citizen review boards or department investigation.[75] In smaller departments without citizen complaint boards, complaints are usually handled by a high-ranking administrative officer. In some small municipal police departments and sheriffs' offices, the chief or sheriff may make the final determination as to the disposition of the complaint.

More serious allegations of wrongdoing are usually handled by the prosecutor's office or a special commission empowered to investigate and criminally charge officers. Such investigations usually involve allegations of serious criminal behavior. In cases of egregious criminal behavior or widespread misconduct throughout a department, the DOJ has the authority to investigate local, state, and federal agencies and file criminal charges if appropriate. When the DOJ pursues allegations of wrongdoing, the FBI does the actual investigative work to document the misconduct. At the completion of its investigation, the DOJ can file federal criminal charges against officers when it believes there is sufficient evidence to obtain a conviction. If convicted, officers are subject to the same criminal penalties as nonsworn citizens.

Also, citizens can chose to bring civil law suits against officers and departments who are accused of wrongdoing. Civil lawsuits are complicated by the fact that the federal government and states have what is called sovereign immunity. **Sovereign immunity** grants federal and state governments immunity from civil lawsuits unless the government waives its immunity.[76] Because local governments do not have sovereign immunity, civil lawsuits can be brought against municipal police officers and departments.[77] However, officers of local departments have limited immunity when they are exercising actions under court orders, such as the case of serving a search warrant.[78] Civil lawsuits against local police officers generally name as parties to the suit the officer(s) accused of misconduct and the department. In some cases, the officer's supervisor may be named as a party to the lawsuit.

The purpose of a civil lawsuit is to punish the officers and the department for misconduct by claiming monetary awards for damages. There are two types of damages. **Actual damages** are losses or harm that can be documented and on which a monetary value can be placed. **Punitive damages** are claims for a monetary award to punish the defendant for his or her misconduct. One of the purposes of punitive damages is to discourage similar misconduct in the future. Punitive damages can be for millions of dollars.

Citizens who bring lawsuits against officers who are accused of misconduct must bear the entire costs of litigation. Some attorneys will take a case on contingency, meaning that in lieu of payment from the client, the attorney will take a share of the award if he or she wins the case. However, there are no guarantees in a lawsuit. The lawsuit may be rejected for technical reasons, the jury may decide against the citizen, or the jury may award only a small monetary amount for the misconduct.

The "nuclear" option in remedies for misconduct is the **consent decree**. A consent decree is a court order that establishes a monitoring team over a law enforcement agency. Consent decrees are considered the "nuclear option" because they transfer oversight of the law enforcement agency to a court-appointed monitor. This is considered a very serious action and is used only in the most extreme cases.

The consent decree can remove all final decision-making authority from department officials; require mandated training; require departments to develop new policies; or require substantial improvements in various aspects of the officers' work, knowledge, training, or testing. Consent decrees are sought by the DOJ in federal court when corruption and misconduct are so pervasive and systemic that the department is considered incapable of correcting the misconduct on its own. A number of police departments in major cities have fallen under consent decrees, including the LAPD, Oakland Police Department (California), Prince George County Police Department (Maryland), Detroit Police Department (Michigan), Cincinnati Police Department (Ohio), Pittsburgh Police Department (Pennsylvania), and dozens of other departments.

▶ Intelligence Gathering

During the 1950s, 1960s, and early 1970s, many police departments, especially large departments, engaged in active intelligence gathering. Intelligence gathering occurs when the police gather information about people who are not currently under suspicion or investigation for a specific crime. The following were primary targets for police intelligence units during these decades:

- Suspected members of the Communist Party, defined as a danger to the United States

- People engaged in or suspected of engaging in protests against U.S. involvement in the Vietnam War

- People engaged in civil rights protests

At the time, it was thought that these activities posed a significant risk to the United States and that people engaged in these activities were likely to use violence or to overthrow the country.

The federal law enforcement agency most actively engaged in the gathering of intelligence information was the FBI under the directorship of J. Edgar Hoover. Hoover conducted intensive intelligence operations to discover "communist agents" in the United States. He believed that there was a real threat of violence from communist agents, as their intent was to contribute to the overthrow of the U.S. government.

In general, the justification for intelligence gathering is that if a crime occurs, to quickly identify suspects and make arrests, law enforcement will already have sufficient information about people who may have committed the crime, thereby protecting the public from subversives and terrorists. However, in the 1960s and 1970s, abuses by federal and local law enforcement led to public concern, legislative initiatives prohibiting intelligence-gathering activities, and Supreme Court cases condemning the targeting of citizens for intelligence operations who were not under suspicion of committing a crime. The full extent of FBI abuses finally became known through the Freedom of Information Act, and law enforcement intelligence activities came to be seen as an unjustifiable intrusion on the constitutionally protected privacy of citizens.

However, attitudes toward law enforcement intelligence changed again dramatically on September 11, 2001. The terrorist attacks on the World Trade Center in New York City and the Pentagon in Washington, DC, changed the balance between privacy and security, with far-reaching consequences.[79] New legislation has enhanced the intelligence-gathering capability of the FBI.

▶ Intelligence Gathering and the War on Terrorism

The USA PATRIOT Act has greatly enhanced the intelligence-gathering authority of the FBI and federal law enforcement agencies; its goal is to prevent another attack similar to the one on September 11, 2001. Also, local and state law enforcement agencies have renewed the resources devoted to intelligence gathering. The NYPD has the most sophisticated intelligence-gathering unit of local agencies. Most of the focus has been on enhancing the powers of federal agencies.

Critics accuse the Justice Department of denying due process to many people accused or suspected of terrorism because of the desire to obtain intelligence information. For example, a report by the Human Rights Watch accuses the federal government of indiscriminate and arbitrary arrests of men from predominately Muslim countries without sufficient probable cause or even reasonable suspicion.[80]

Also, the Human Rights Watch and the ACLU have accused the Justice Department of abusing the material witness law to detain terror suspects. The **material witness law**, enacted in 1984, allows federal authorities to hold a person indefinitely without charging him or her with a crime if they suspect the person has information about a crime and might flee or be unwilling to cooperate with law enforcement officials.[81] The Human Rights Watch and the ACLU charge that the Justice Department has used the material witness law to detain 70 people, about one-third of them U.S. citizens, on suspicion of terrorism, although questionable evidence exists for these detentions. The Justice

Department has apologized to at least 13 people for wrongly detaining them under the material witness law.[82] One of the more publicized abuses of the material witness law was the detention of Portland, Oregon, lawyer Brandon Mayfield, whom the FBI wrongly accused of being connected to the Madrid train bombings of 2004.

Interrogations and the War on Terrorism

Recent issues have arisen regarding the civilian trials of people originally detained as enemy combatants. The government was more interested in gathering intelligence by interrogating these enemy combatants in an effort to prevent future terrorist attacks and to gather information that would allow the United States to capture or kill leaders of terrorist organizations. In this effort to gather intelligence, enemy combatants were not treated as prisoners of war or as accused criminals. They were denied due process rights, were not charged with a crime, and did not have access to an attorney or the courts. Enemy combatants were interrogated using **enhanced interrogations methods**. Enhanced interrogation methods allow for the use of pain, threats, and waterboarding. **Waterboarding** involves pouring large volumes of water over a bound person to simulate the sensation of drowning. There are allegations that some interrogations involved even more aggressive techniques, including electric shock. Initially, the objective was to extract information from a person with little regard to criminal charges and trial.

After more than a decade now, the government is turning its attention to the prosecution of these enemy combatants. Frequently, confessions were obtained during their enhanced interrogation. Now a common situation arises when accused terrorists being tried in U.S. courts claim that their confessions were obtained through torture when they were captured or transported outside the United States for interrogation. Under the rules of evidence for civilian trials, such confessions and the evidence obtained from enhanced interrogations are not admissible. For example, Ahmed Omar Abu Ali was tried in a Virginia federal court in 2005 on charges that he was a member of al-Qaeda and was plotting to assassinate President Bush. Abu Ali's lawyers wanted their client's confession ruled inadmissible because Abu Ali claimed that the confession was obtained through torture. He claimed that he was arrested in Medina, Saudi Arabia, in June 2003 and gave a false confession to stop the torture. Also, he later gave a confession to the FBI, but that confession was ruled invalid because the FBI disregarded Abu Ali's request for an attorney. Therefore, when he was tried in a U.S. federal court, the prosecution relied on the confession he gave in Medina. The judge ruled that there was insufficient evidence to establish that the confession was obtained through torture and allowed it as evidence. There will likely be further allegations comparable to this incident as more people are tried for terrorism under similar circumstances. Courts will have to give consideration to what evidence is necessary to establish that a confession was obtained through torture and whether such a confession is admissible.

LEARNING OUTCOMES 5 Summarize the legal aspects of intelligence gathering and the war on terrorism.

GLOSSARY

material witness law A law that allows for the detention of a person who has not committed a crime but is suspected of having information about a crime and might flee or refuse to cooperate with law enforcement officials.

enhanced interrogations Interrogation methods that allow for the use of pain, threats, and waterboarding to extract information from a subject.

waterboarding An interrogation technique in which a large volume of water is poured over a bound person to simulate the sensation of drowning.

NYPD's Demographics Unit

The NYPD has one of the most sophisticated and controversial police intelligence units in the United States. Since the September 11, 2001, attacks on the towers of the World Trade Center, the NYPD has engaged in extensive secretive investigations of mosques and Muslims, especially young college Muslims. The unit known as the Demographics Unit utilizes undercover officers known as "rakers" to visit Islamic bookstores, cafés, businesses, clubs, Internet sites, and mosques. The rakers monitor community bulletin boards, photograph and video-record people, and engage in "conversations" to gather information. Mayor Michael Bloomberg describes what the unit does as "looking around just to kind of get familiar with what's going on."[83]

The Demographics Unit targets people considered "ancestries of interest." Ancestries of interest are mostly people from Muslim

Jolanta Mayeroeg/Fotolia

countries.[84] According to Police Commissioner Raymond W. Kelly the NYPD Intelligence Division has been essential to thwarting 14 terrorists plots since 9/11.[85] Public polls show that most New Yorkers strongly support the NYPD's counterterrorism efforts and do not believe police unfairly target Muslims. Mayor Bloomberg said the intelligence-gathering performed by the unit was "legal, appropriate, and constitutional."

However, there is considerable controversy regarding Mayor Bloomberg's assessment. For example, the intelligence unit partnered with the Central Intelligence Agency (CIA) to conduct covert surveillance. One of the targets was Muslim Student Associations (MSAs) at numerous colleges, including Yale, Columbia, Syracuse, Rutgers, New York University, and Brooklyn College, as well as public state universities. The Demographics Unit undertook the task of photographing every mosque in Newark. Using intelligence and census data and other databases, the Unit built databases showing where Muslims live, where they buy groceries, what Internet cafés they use, and where they watch sports. The Unit used undercover officers to infiltrate groups and gather personal data.

It appears that this intrusive surveillance and data mining was done without any evidence of wrongdoing, reasonable suspicion, or evidence of criminal activity. Also, the investigation focused almost exclusively on Shiite Muslims. The intelligence unit operates in secrecy with little outside oversight.[86] College administrators and New Jersey and Pennsylvania officials have expressed surprise to learn that the NYPD was conducting such investigations. People who have read the report claim that it contains numerous errors in identifying Muslim-owned businesses. Attorney General Eric Holder has testified before Congress, saying that the DOJ is beginning a review to decide whether to investigate possible civil rights violations by the NYPD.

This case raises several interesting questions. Among them are the following:

1. What are the legal and constitutional limits of gathering information on people not suspected of criminal activity?

2. If intelligence data result in greater protection against terrorist attacks, should civil rights be ignored? Explain.

3. What limits should be placed on police intelligence units to gather information outside their jurisdiction, such as other states and countries?

4. Should citizens be concerned that the police gather information about them and photograph them if they are not doing anything wrong? Why or why not?

Explain the importance of police professionalism and integrity and the means used to promote professionalism and integrity.

Police professionalism is an important hallmark to ensure competent services, while balancing crime fighting and due process rights. Three strategies are used to maintain integrity within a police department: (1) a rigorous selection process in hiring new officers, (2) formalized policies and procedures, and (3) a procedure for investigating allegations of misbehavior should a citizen complaint be alleged. Through the process of an internal investigation, disciplinary action may result against an officer who violated a professional standard.

1. What challenges do law enforcement agencies face in balancing crime fighting and due process rights?

2. Discuss the principles of the Law Enforcement Code of Ethics.

3. Describe what is contained in an SOP manual.

4. What process could a citizen utilize to make a complaint about police misconduct?

Law Enforcement Code of Ethics Professional standards of behavior to which law enforcement officers should aspire.

standard operating procedures (SOP) manual A manual that describes the policies that regulate behavior and the performance standards for police officers.

citizen complaint board A citizen review board that hears alleged complaints of police misconduct.

Internal Affairs Unit or Office of Internal Affairs An office that conducts investigations of criminal, abusive, or unprofessional behavior by law enforcement officers within the department.

Summarize the legal restraints placed on law enforcement and the procedures that law enforcement must follow for searches, seizures, lineups, and arrests.

The police do not have unrestricted powers in performing their duties. An external oversight of police powers is the courts, especially the U.S. Supreme Court. Courts can prohibit and require certain behaviors of police in their gathering and presentation of evidence for a trial. The rules of evidence require that police officers must collect evidence properly; otherwise, it can be declared inadmissible in court. Hence, improperly obtained evidence can be declared inadmissible under the exclusionary rule. There are exceptions to the exclusionary rule that allow police to conduct search and seizures without a warrant in certain situations of public safety. Courts have also recognized that police operate in a dangerous environment; thus, they are allowed to take precautions (conducting pat-downs, for example) to protect themselves.

1. Explain the difference between direct and indirect oversight of law enforcement behaviors.

2. What is meant by the term *exclusionary rule*? How does it affect police procedure?

3. Describe various exceptions to the exclusionary rule.

4. What is a plain-view search?

5. Why can a police officer conduct a pat-down without probable cause that a crime has occurred?

direct oversight Laws and judicial decisions that prohibit specific law enforcement behavior.

indirect oversight A remedy, usually at criminal trial, if the standards of the court are not observed by agencies or officers.

procedural law The body of laws governing how things should be done at each stage of the criminal justice process.

rules of evidence Requirements for introducing evidence and testimony in court.

exclusionary rule A rule that prohibits the use of evidence or testimony obtained in violation of the Fourth and Fifth Amendments of the U.S. Constitution, established in *Weeks* v. *United States* (1914) and extended to all state courts in *Mapp* v. *Ohio* (1961).

fruit of the poisoned tree doctrine A rule of evidence that extends the exclusionary rule to secondary evidence obtained indirectly in an unconstitutional search, established in *Silverthorne Lumber Co.* v. *United States* (1918) and in *Wolf* v. *Colorado* (1949).

search warrant Legal permission, signed by a judge, for police to conduct a search.

probable cause The likelihood that there is a direct link between a suspect and a crime.

search incident to lawful arrest The right of police to search a person who has been arrested without a warrant.

plain-view search The right of the police to gather without a warrant evidence that is clearly visible.

Carroll doctrine Terms allowing admissibility of evidence obtained by police in a warrantless search of an automobile when the police have probable cause that a crime has occurred and delaying a search could result in the loss of evidence.

pat-down doctrine The right of the police to search a person for a concealed weapon on the basis of reasonable suspicion, established in *Terry* v. *Ohio* (1968).

public safety exception The right of the police to search without probable cause when not doing so could pose a threat of harm to the public.

good faith exception An exception to the requirement that police must have a valid search warrant or probable cause when they act in good faith on the belief that the search was legal.

wiretapping A form of search and seizure of evidence involving communication by telephone.

arrest The restriction of the freedom of a person by taking him or her into police custody.

LEARNING OUTCOMES 3

Summarize the legal aspects of police interrogations and the Miranda decision.

To be admissible in court, a suspect's confession must be obtained properly. Moreover, a confession must be given knowingly and voluntarily. When suspects are held in custody and subject to interrogation, they must be advised of their Miranda rights before questioning begins. The Fifth and Sixth Amendments provide due process rights to protect a suspect from self-incrimination. If a person cannot afford an attorney, the duty of the state is to provide legal counsel through the practice of indigent defense.

1. What must be demonstrated during a confession for it to be admissible in court?

2. Explain how Miranda rights affect a police interrogation.

3. Describe a suspect's rights during a police lineup.

self-incrimination Statements made by a person that might lead to criminal prosecution.

indigent defense The right to have an attorney provided free of charge by the state if a defendant cannot afford one, established in *Gideon* v. *Wainwright* (1963).

Miranda rights Rights that provide protection from self-incrimination and confer the right to an attorney, of which citizens must be informed before police arrest and interrogation, established in *Miranda* v. *Arizona* (1966).

police lineup An opportunity for victims to identify a criminal from among a number of suspects.

LEARNING OUTCOMES 4

Explain the issues of law enforcement misconduct and use of force.

Public safety is at the core of any controversy surrounding the use of force by police officers. A threat of death or serious bodily injury must be present to justify the use of force, including deadly force in the apprehension or arrest of a suspect. An officer should use the appropriate level of force that matches the threat or resistance encountered. Another area of concern in police practices is police misconduct. Law enforcement misconduct can range from minor offenses such as accepting gratuities to more serious violations such as accepting bribes. Several remedies may be used in response to these allegations. Allegations of police misconduct can be lodged with the law enforcement agency for an internal investigation; more serious allegations may be investigated by a special prosecutor to determine whether criminal charges are warranted.

1. Discuss the fleeing-felon doctrine.

2. What is meant by the term *continuum of force*?

3. How does a CED work when it is deployed?

4. Explain the difference between a grass eater and a meat eater.

5. Provide an example of racial profiling.

deadly force The power of police to incapacitate or kill in the line of duty.

fleeing-felon doctrine The police practice of using deadly force against a fleeing suspect, made illegal in *Tennessee* v. *Garner* (1985), except when there is clear and present danger to the public.

clear and present danger A condition related to public safety that may justify police use of deadly force against a fleeing suspect.

use of force continuum A policy that requires officers to use appropriate force depending on the circumstances they confront.

conducted energy devices Devices that deliver powerful electric shocks, causing incapacitation.

lazy cop syndrome A term used to refer to officers who eschew the use of conflict resolution skills in favor of Tasers to control subjects.

grass eaters Police officers who engage in minor illegitimate activities that are considered "acceptable behavior" by fellow officers.

meat eaters Officers who engage in serious criminal conduct, corruption, and illicit money-making opportunities.

stings Tactics in which law enforcement officers pose as buyers of illegal substances or goods.

reverse stings Tactics involving law enforcement officers who pose as providers of illegal substances, goods, or services.

entrapment The illegal arrest of a person based on criminal behavior for which the police provided both the motivation and the means, tested in *Jacobsen* v. *United States* (1992).

sovereign immunity Immunity from civil lawsuits granted to federal and state governments.

actual damages Losses or harm that can be documented and on which a monetary value can be placed.

punitive damages Claims for a monetary award to punish the defendant for his or her misconduct.

consent decree A court order that establishes a monitoring team over a law enforcement agency.

LEARNING OUTCOMES 5

Summarize the legal aspects of intelligence gathering and the war on terrorism.

Since the attacks of September 11, 2001, new legislation has enhanced the intelligence-gathering capacity of the FBI. Critics argue that the Justice Department is denying due process to many people accused or suspected of terrorist activities. At the heart of this controversy is the material witness law. This law allows federal authorities to hold a person indefinitely without charging him or her with a crime. These so-called enemy combatants have been subjected to interrogations involving waterboarding and other torture to gather intelligence or obtain confessions.

1. How have interrogations of suspected terrorist circumvented due process rights?

2. What does the term *enhanced interrogation* mean?

3. Describe the practice of waterboarding.

material witness law A law that allows for the detention of a person who has not committed a crime but is suspected of having information about a crime and might flee or refuse to cooperate with law enforcement officials.

enhanced interrogations Interrogation methods that allow for the use of pain, threats, and waterboarding to extract information from a subject.

waterboarding An interrogation technique in which a large volume of water is poured over a bound person to simulate the sensation of drowning.

MyCJLab

Go to Chapter 6 in *MyCJLab* to test your mastery of chapter concepts, access your Study Plan, engage in interactive exercises, complete critical-thinking and research assignments, and view related online videos.

☑ **Review:** Complete the pretest in the Study Plan to confirm what you know and what you need to study further. Then complete the post-test to confirm your mastery of the concepts. Use the key term flash cards to review key terminology.

⚙ **Apply:** Complete the interactive simulation activity.

🔍 **Analyze:** Complete assignments as directed by your instructor.

 Current Events: Explore CJSearch for current topical videos, articles, and news pieces.

Additional Links

Go to **http://www.law.cornell.edu/wex/exclusionary_rule/** to learn how the exclusionary rule prevents the government from using most evidence gathered in violation of the U.S. Constitution. This site provides links to other related Supreme Court decisions.

Go to **http://www.mirandarights.org** for further explanation of a suspect's Miranda rights.

Go to **http://www.youtube.com/watch?v=dcSi_NB7a_w** to watch a one-minute video of a Taser deployment.

Go to **http://www.law.cornell.edu/supct/html/historics/USSC_CR_0392_0001_ZS.html** to read the Supreme Court decision of *Terry* v. *Ohio*, which provided the foundation for police pat-downs.

Go to **http://www.nij.gov/topics/law-enforcement/officer-safety/use-of-force/continuum.htm** to learn more in-depth details about the use of force continuum.

Go to **http://www.nytimes.com/2011/03/03/us/politics/03witness.html/** to read how the Supreme Court appears to back the material witness law.

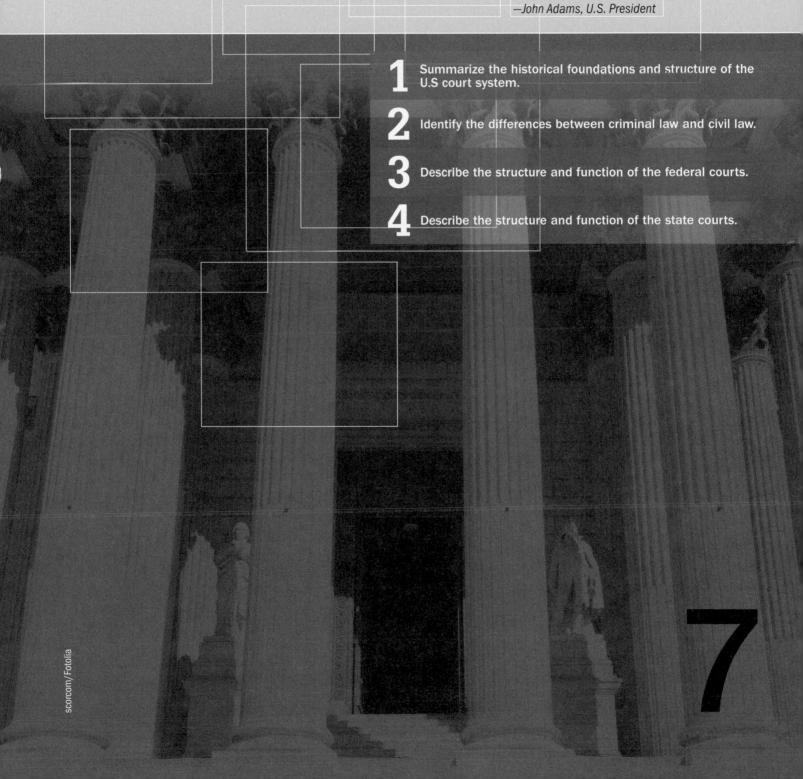

The Court System

"The way to secure liberty is to place it in the people's hands, that is, to give them the power at all times to defend it in the legislature and in the courts of justice."

—John Adams, U.S. President

1 Summarize the historical foundations and structure of the U.S court system.

2 Identify the differences between criminal law and civil law.

3 Describe the structure and function of the federal courts.

4 Describe the structure and function of the state courts.

scorcom/Fotolia

7

The U.S. Constitution provides for three branches of government. At the head of the judiciary branch is the Supreme Court. The Supreme Court has broad powers as the final authority to arbitrate controversies between individuals, states, and foreign powers.[1] Each term about 10,000 petitions are filed with the Court. Of these cases, the Court issues formal written opinions in only about 100 cases.[2]

The Court has guided the course of judicial history in decisions as such *Bush* v. *Gore; Citizens United* v. *Federal Elections Commission;* and various cases concerning Obamacare, same-sex unions, and state immigration laws. Historically, the public has had high confidence in the Supreme Court. However, according to a 2011 Gallup Poll, this confidence is eroding. Since 2001, public approval of the Supreme Court has dropped from a high of 62% in 2001 to a historical low of 46% in 2011.

The public is concerned about the Court's isolation, secrecy, and lack of impartiality.[3] Presidential candidate Newt Gingrich spoke critically of federal judges, saying "judges who have ruled in favor of gay marriage or against prayer in school are 'activists' who should be thrown out." He said that judges should be compelled to explain their decisions before Congress, and if they refuse to appear, they should be arrested.[4] Referring to Supreme Court justices as "unelected" officials, President Obama has voiced concern that the Court would overturn health care legislation approved by the elected Congress. In 2012, the Senate Judiciary Committee approved a bipartisan bill that would require the Court to permit television coverage of most of its arguments. The Court's response was to remind the Committee that the prerogative of the Court is to make the rules governing its operations.[5]

A tradition of the Court is that white quills are placed on counsel tables each day the Court sits.[6] In this modern age, quill pens have faded from use and serve only as a symbolic tradition. Many cases are awaiting review by the Supreme Court, and it is important that the public be confident in the wisdom and fairness of the Court's decisions. If the Court does not adopt contemporary practices and public confidence continues to erode, the Court could become like the quill pens—outdated.

DISCUSS Should the Supreme Court permit televised coverage of its cases? Why or why not?

▶ *Foundation and Structure of the Judicial System*

This chapter examines the organization of the federal and state U.S. court system and the role of the criminal courts within the criminal justice system. Most people's knowledge of the courts comes from the entertainment media. Movies and television shows compress criminal trials into short timelines and give the illusion that the path through the courts is simple, direct, and quick. Often there is little distinction between the various courts and the full range of functions of the courts. This illusion is far from the truth.

Over the centuries, society's ways of dealing with harms against others have changed. At one time, people believed that if another person harmed their reputation, they could challenge the offending party to a duel to the death, as when Vice President Aaron Burr killed Secretary of Treasury Alexander Hamilton in a duel in 1804. In the western frontier of the late nineteenth century, disputes sometimes were settled by gunfights. Today, however, people are prohibited from seeking private revenge and personal justice through the use of violence. The government requires that all wrongs—whether accidental, negligent, or criminal—be handled by the criminal justice or civil justice system.

The concept of a "court" vested with the power to arbitrate disputes can be traced back to the earliest times. One of the earliest references to court refers to the power of kings, rulers, and nobility to resolve disputes. Disputes were brought before the king or ruler, and the parties to the dispute argued their case. The opinion of the monarch frequently was unchallengeable and based primarily on his or her personal power, values, and interpretation of the dispute. As society became more sophisticated, it became necessary to develop a system of **jurisprudence**—a philosophy of law—to settle disputes. In such a system, a body of written law regulates interactions. These laws or codes provide people with guidelines that regulate behavior.

The jurisprudence system of the United States was influenced primarily by the Justinian Code, the Napoleonic Code, and the common law of Great Britain. The Justinian Code, developed under the Roman emperor Justinian I, was influential in shaping the

> The government requires that all wrongs—whether accidental, negligent, or criminal—be handled by the criminal justice or civil justice system.

civil law of Europe and that of the Spanish colonies in Mexico and Latin America. The Napoleonic Code, designed by Napoleon Bonaparte to unify the laws of his empire, became the basis of the legal system of the state of Louisiana, a French colony. English common law was the main foundation on which the American jurisprudence system was built.

Dual Court System

In the **dual court system**, the court systems of the various states are sovereign governmental jurisdictions, each equal in importance and with separate political jurisdictions. The term *dual* means that there are two systems of courts. The federal courts are distinct from the state courts but do have limited jurisdiction over the state courts. Thus, within both the federal and state systems, there are many further distinctions and divisions of the jurisdiction of the courts. The jurisdiction of the federal courts is defined in **Article 3, Section 2** of the U.S. Constitution:

> The judicial power shall extend to all cases, in law and equity, arising under this Constitution, the laws of the United States, and treaties made or which shall be made, under their authority; to all cases affecting ambassadors, other public ministers and consuls; to all cases of admiralty and maritime jurisdiction; to controversies in which the United States shall be a part; to controversies between two or more states; between citizens of the same state claiming lands under grants of different states; and between a state or the citizens thereof, and foreign states, citizens, or subjects.

The **Eleventh Amendment**, ratified in 1795, restricts the jurisdiction of the federal courts by declaring that a private citizen from one state cannot sue the government of another state in federal court. The **Tenth Amendment** provides that powers not specifically delegated to the federal government are reserved to the states. Under this authority, each state has the responsibility and power to establish its own court system. Modern American jurisprudence, both federal and state, includes codes of civil, criminal, and public law as well as codes of civil and criminal procedures.

Unlike the thousands of police departments that operate independently of each other, the courts are organized in a hierarchy of authority whereby the decisions of each lower court can be reviewed and reversed by a higher court. (See Figure 7–1.) Also, unlike the police, wherein federal agencies have no authority over state and local agencies, federal courts do

GLOSSARY

jurisprudence A philosophy or body of written law used to settle disputes.

dual court system The political division of jurisdiction into two separate systems of courts: federal and state; in this system, federal courts have limited jurisdiction over state courts.

Article 3, Section 2 The part of the U.S. Constitution that defines the jurisdiction of the federal courts.

Eleventh Amendment A provision that prohibits a citizen from one state from suing the government of another state in federal court.

Tenth Amendment A provision that states that powers not specifically delegated to the federal government are reserved for the states.

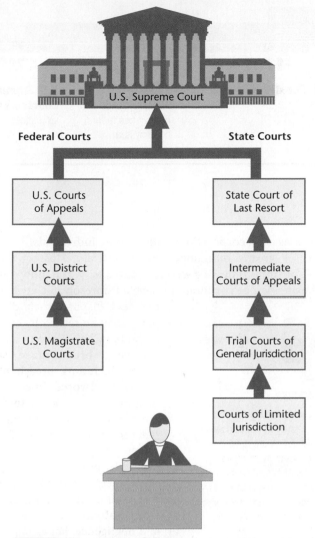

FIGURE 7–1 Hierarchy in the Judiciary
The state and federal courts are arranged in a hierarchy from lowest to highest. State courts may differ from what is shown in the figure because each state court system is unique. When a defendant has exhausted all appeals in the state court system, he or she may appeal to the U.S. Supreme Court.

have authority over state courts.[7] Each state has a final court of appeals, but it is possible to appeal a state decision to the U.S. Supreme Court, which may or may not choose to hear the case. Decisions of lower federal courts also can be appealed to the federal court of appeals and ultimately to the U.S. Supreme Court. When the U.S. Supreme Court makes a ruling regarding the constitutionality of a law, due process right, or rule of evidence, that decision is binding on all federal and state courts.[8]

▶ Civil versus Criminal Law

Individuals are responsible for seeking redress in a civil court when they are harmed by a violation of a civil law. **Civil law** is referred to as private law because it addresses the definition, regulation, and enforcement of rights in cases in which both the person who has the right and the person who has the obligation are private individuals. Civil law is also called "business law" because many of the lawsuits involve

TIMELINE
Timeline of Key Events

1787	1789	1789	1791	1794
U.S. Constitution is ratified.	**Federal Judiciary Act** establishes federal court system.	**U.S. Supreme Court** consists of six justices.	**Tenth Amendment** is adopted, which grants powers not enumerated in the U.S. Constitution to the states.	**Eleventh Amendment** is adopted, which restricts jurisdiction of the federal courts.

businesses and corporations rather than individuals. Civil law cases greatly outnumber criminal trials. Most of the court's business is dealing with civil lawsuits. When individuals, businesses, or corporations have an unresolvable civil or business dispute, such disputes may be settled by civil lawsuits. Civil lawsuits can involve a broad range of issues, including breach of contract, divorce, medical malpractice, and torts. **Torts** are claims of personal injury that are not criminal. Tort injuries may include injuries caused by purposeful actions or by negligence. Common tort claims include injuries from automobile accidents and negligence. For example, if a person slips and falls on business premises due to negligence of the business owner, he or she can file a tort claim for injuries suffered in the fall. The action upon which a tort claim is based does not have to be criminal or illegal. There is some overlap whereby an injury can be both a criminal action and a tort. For example, if someone is physically assaulted by another person and suffers bodily harm, the assault may be a criminal action and the injured party may file a tort suit for medical, physical, and emotional harm suffered as a result of the assault.

The state and federal courts are divided into civil courts and criminal courts. However, judges and attorneys may handle both civil and criminal cases. A private attorney may handle divorces, torts, homicides, robberies, and burglaries. Likewise, judges may hear both civil and criminal cases.

There are significant differences between the civil justice system and the criminal justice system. A significant difference is the burden of proof. The burden of proof in a civil court is a **preponderance of the evidence**, whereas the burden of proof in a criminal court is **beyond a reasonable doubt**.[9] Preponderance of the evidence means that a simple majority of the jury votes. In a 12-person jury, a vote of 7 to 5 decides the case. Beyond a reasonable doubt requires a unanimous vote of the jury. All members must vote guilty for a conviction. The difference in the burden of proof can have a profound impact on the outcome of a case. For example, in the O. J. Simpson case, Simpson was on trial in criminal court for the alleged murder of his ex-wife, Nicole Brown Simpson, and Ron Goldman. The government was unsuccessful in proving the criminal charges against the defendant, and he was found not guilty of the criminal charges. However, the family of Ron Goldman filed a civil lawsuit against O. J. Simpson, alleging injury. The civil lawsuit did not require a unanimous jury vote, and they were able to obtain a judgment for monetary damages in civil court.[10]

LEARNING OUTCOMES 2 Identify the differences between criminal law and civil law.

GLOSSARY

civil law Also called private law, the body of law concerned with the definition, regulation, and enforcement of rights in noncriminal cases in which both the person who has the right and the person who has the obligation are private individuals.

tort A private wrong that causes physical harm to another.

preponderance of the evidence A majority vote of the jury—the standard required for a judgment in a civil case.

beyond a reasonable doubt A unanimous verdict—the standard required for a verdict in a criminal case.

TIMELINE
Timeline of Key Events

1867	1869	1919	1937	1967
U.S. Supreme Court consists of eight justices.	**U.S. Supreme Court** consists of nine justices.	**Congress** adds the Sixteenth Amendment making personal income tax constitutional.	**President Franklin D. Roosevelt** attempts to increase the number of U.S. Supreme Court justices to 15, but Congress does not approve the change.	**Thurgood Marshall** is first African-American appointed to the U.S. Supreme Court.

1803	1804	1807	1863	1866
Marbury v. Madison establishes power of judicial review for the courts.	U.S. Vice President Aaron Burr kills **Secretary of Treasury Alexander Hamilton** in a duel.	**U.S. Supreme Court** consists of seven justices.	**U.S. Supreme Court** consists of ten justices.	**U.S. Supreme Court** consists of nine justices.

	Civil Law	versus	**Criminal Law**
Scope of the law	• Private law • Contract law • Negotiable instruments • Redress for harm or injuries, including libel, slander, and fraud • **Torts**—which are private wrongs that cause physical harm to others • Civil lawsuits alleging violation of constitutional rights		• Violation of criminal law
Burden of proof	• Preponderance of the evidence		• Belief beyond a reasonable doubt
Who brings the case to court	• Private parties • The **plaintiff**, the person who is suing • The defendant, the person who is being sued *Each side is responsible for its own expenses and witnesses.*		• The government is responsible for bringing a case to court. The government bears all responsibility for trial expenses related to prosecution; the prosecutor is the government agent responsible for litigation; the defendant is the person accused of a crime. • If the defendant cannot afford an attorney, the government will provide one at no cost to the defendant.
Punishment	• Monetary damages • Enforcement of terms of a contract		• Fines, imprisonment, restriction of liberty, or death
Naming the case	• Last name of the parties involved, plaintiff listed first (e.g., *Hazelwood* v. *Cranberry*) • A government agency or corporation may be part of a suit.		• The government agency prosecuting the case, followed by the last name of the defendant (e.g., *State of Nevada* v. *Hazelwood*)
Similarities	*Judges, courtroom, jury, due process rights, and rules of evidence*		
Overlap	Some actions can be both a private civil case and a criminal case.		

1981	1993	2000	2009
Sandra Day O'Connor is first female appointed to the U.S. Supreme Court.	**Ruth Bader Ginsburg** is first Jewish female appointed to the U.S. Supreme Court.	**Bush v. Gore** decides the 2000 presidential election winner.	**Sonia Sotomayor**, first Latina, is appointed to the U.S. Supreme Court.

Civil versus Criminal Law   **153**

Private Parties Must Initiate Civil Cases

Redress for civil wrongs, contract violations, and torts must be initiated by the individual and fall within the jurisdiction of the civil court. The party initiating the civil suit is known as the **plaintiff**, and the party being sued is known as the **defendant**. Each party is responsible for the financial expenses related to the lawsuit. In some cases, the courts may require the losing party to reimburse the legal expenses of the other party. In a criminal case, the defendant is found guilty or not guilty. In a civil case, the outcome of the trial is a **judgment**. A judgment is a ruling by the court regarding the liability for injury or the claim alleged by the plaintiff. In a civil lawsuit, the court may assign a degree of blame to each party. In criminal cases, the defendant can appeal a guilty verdict only on the grounds that a significant judicial error could have affected the verdict or on constitutional grounds. A civil judgment may be appealed on other grounds, including a challenge as to the damages awarded by the jury.

The criminal justice system is responsible for detecting, prosecuting, and punishing people who violate criminal laws that have been created by political bodies such as the city, county, state, or federal government. After a criminal law is passed, the responsibility of the police is to detect violators of the law. The court is responsible for determining whether a person violated the law. Finally, the responsibility of corrections is to punish offenders for violation of the law. In civil cases, each party must perform the roles of "police" and "prosecutor." As to "punishment" in civil cases, it is limited to monetary damages and remedies.

> **plaintiff** The party who files a civil lawsuit against the party who is alleged to have done harm.
>
> **defendant** The party whom a lawsuit is brought against.
>
> **judgment** A ruling by the court regarding the liability for injury or the claim alleged by the plaintiff.

► The Federal Court System

The authority for establishing a federal court system is in Article 3 of the U.S. Constitution. Congress created the lesser courts referred to in Article 3 on September 24, 1789. Congress passed the **Federal Judiciary Act** that established 13 courts, one for each of the original states. Initially, the federal courts had few cases because there were few federal laws. Given the light caseload, judges were required to travel from city to city and hold court in each city rather than have judges assigned to a single city. This practice was known as "riding the circuit," and the geographic divisions of the federal court system are still referred to as **circuits**. The Supreme Court originally consisted of six justices, but today there are nine justices—one chief justice and eight associate justices—on the Supreme Court. The number of justices is not determined by the U.S. Constitution.[11]

Overview of the Federal Court System

Marbury v. Madison

For the first three years of its existence, the authority of the U.S. Supreme Court was limited. The landmark decision that established the modern power and role of the Supreme Court, and by inclusion its lesser courts, was ***Marbury v. Madison*** (1803).

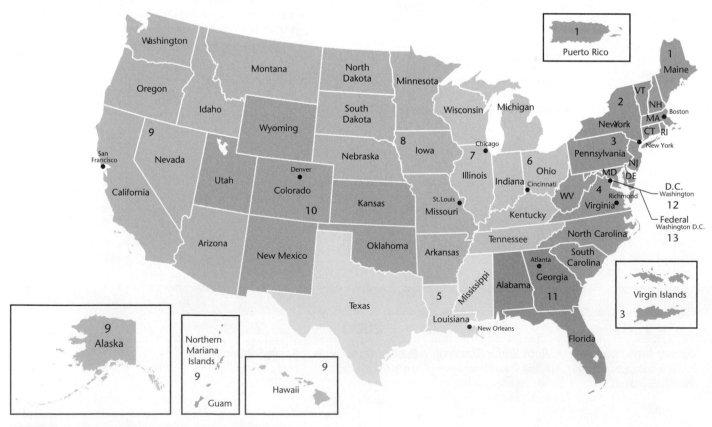

FIGURE 7–2 The Federal Judicial Circuits and Appeals Courts

In *Marbury* v. *Madison,* under the leadership of Chief Justice John Marshall, the Supreme Court claimed the power to review acts of Congress and the executive office (president) and pronounce whether congressional and presidential acts were constitutional.[12] This claim gave the Supreme Court the power to nullify acts of Congress and the president. It also asserted that the Court has the power to review congressional or presidential acts without having to wait for a case to be brought before the Supreme Court. This power to declare congressional and presidential acts unconstitutional—the power of **judicial review**—is the most important power of the Supreme Court. The Supreme Court sees its primary mission as the guardian of the Constitution and accomplishes that goal by exercising its power of judicial review.[13]

Structure of the Federal Court System

The federal court system has undergone significant revisions during its history. Today, the federal judiciary has a unified four-tier structure system. The 94 judicial districts are organized into 12 regional circuits, each of which has a U.S. court of appeals in addition to a Thirteenth Circuit for Washington, DC. A court of appeals hears appeals from the district courts located within its circuit, as well as appeals from decisions of federal administrative agencies. Federal judicial circuits include more than a single state. The largest judicial circuit is the Ninth Judicial Circuit, which includes seven western states, Alaska, Hawaii, Guam, and the Northern Mariana Islands.[14] (See Figure 7–2.)

In addition, there are specialty federal courts that do not handle criminal trials or traditional civil cases. These include U.S. Bankruptcy Courts, U.S. Court of Appeals for the Armed Forces, U.S. Court of Federal Claims, U.S. Court of International Trade, U.S. Tax Court, and U.S. Court of Appeals for Veterans Claims.

The federal court system is responsible for the enforcement of all federal codes in all 50 states, U.S. territories, and the District of Columbia. This includes responsibility for civil, criminal, and administrative trials.[15] The federal court system is also responsible for trials involving local codes and ordinances in the territories of Guam, the Virgin Islands, and the Northern Mariana Islands. If a person violates a federal law, he or she can be tried at any federal district court within the circuit. Thus, a person accused of terrorism in Oklahoma can be tried in Oklahoma, Arizona, Colorado, Kansas, New Mexico, Utah, or Wyoming.

The federal court system is responsible for both civil and criminal cases, but there are many more federal district court civil trials than there are criminal trials. Criminal trials, especially trials for violent crimes, are only a small part of the workload of the federal court.

Four-Tier Structure

As shown in Figure 7–3, the federal court is divided into four tiers of responsibility: the U.S. magistrate courts, the trial courts, the appeals courts, and the U.S. Supreme Court. **U.S. magistrate courts** are federal lower courts whose powers are limited to trying lesser misdemeanors, setting bail, and assisting district courts with various legal matters. In 2011, there were 574 authorized positions for U.S. magistrate judges.[16] **U.S. district courts** are the federal system's trial courts of original jurisdiction, meaning that these are the first courts to hear charges against defendants and to render verdicts regarding the charges. In 2011, there were 677 authorized positions for U.S. district judges. Cases were filed against 102,931 defendants. There were 8,453 criminal trials completed.[17]

The U.S. court of appeals handles appeals from U.S. district courts, and the U.S. Supreme Court has both original and appellate jurisdiction.

U.S. Courts of Appeal

Appeals are guaranteed by congressional act. Rather than have the Supreme Court handle all appeals, the federal judiciary uses **U.S. courts of appeal** to hear appeals from U.S. district courts. In 2011, there were 179 authorized positions for U.S. Appeals judges.[18] The right of appeal applies to both civil and criminal cases, but the focus of this discussion is on criminal appeals.

Criminal appeals to the U.S. court of appeals must be based on the claim that the defendant was denied a fair trial or that the law the defendant was convicted of violating was

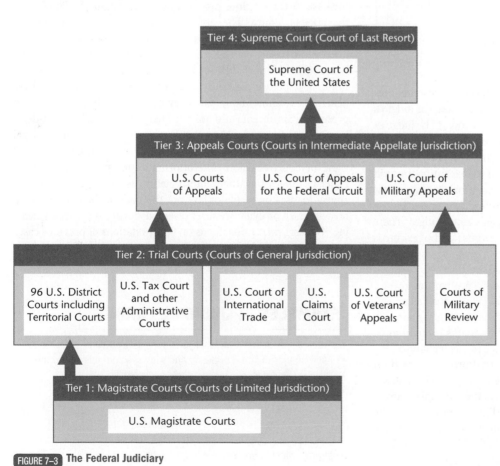

FIGURE 7–3 The Federal Judiciary

Authorized judgeships in 2011:

574 U.S. magistrate judges

677 U.S. district judges

179 U.S. Appeals judges

9 U.S. Supreme Court justices

U.S. District Courts

- Trial courts of original jurisdictions—they decide whether the defendant is guilty and, if so, the punishment

- Special courts
  Hear civil and criminal cases—the majority of the cases are civil; 95 district courts in the United States

U.S. Magistrate Courts

- Organized by the Federal Magistrates Act of 1968
- Prisoner litigation, such as habeas corpus, and civil rights appeals
- Bail review
- Detention hearings
- Arraignments
- Preliminary examinations
- Initial appearance hearings
- Issues search warrants and arrest warrants
- Assists district courts
- Tries Class A misdemeanors and petty offenses

The public may be outraged when a conviction is reversed on appeal. However, to convict a defendant in a court of law, rules must be followed and the rights of the defendant must be protected.

In the U.S. appeals courts, a panel of three federal judges hears appeals from the U.S. district courts. Appeals are based on the defendant's claim that he or she did not receive a fair trial. This claim is based on the claim that a substantial judicial error occurred that could have significantly affected the verdict. Also, the appeal can be based on the claim that the law the defendant was convicted of violating was unconstitutional.

One must remember that there is a difference between judicial error and not guilty. The defendant may indeed have committed a criminal act and is, without question, guilty in the eyes of the public. There may be video or eyewitnesses who document the defendant's commission of the crime, and the public may be outraged when a conviction is reversed on appeal. However, to convict the defendant in a court of law, rules must be followed and the rights of the defendant must be protected.

U.S. courts of appeal are required to hear the cases brought to them on appeal from the federal trial courts within their circuit. The U.S. court of appeals does not conduct a jury trial. Rather, a panel of federal appeals judges, usually three, reviews the case. A review does not mean the defendant appears before the appeals court. The appeals court may decide to review only the written briefs submitted by the attorneys and to make a decision based on the information contained in the briefs. If the appeals court decides to hear oral arguments, the attorneys come before the court and present their reasoning. These hearings are short. Each side may be given only 30 minutes to present its arguments and answer questions posed by the judges.

Often there are legitimate differences of opinion among legal professionals regarding an interpretation of a law, constitutional right, or court decision. The attorneys attempt to persuade the panel of judges that their interpretation is the correct one. The appeal focuses on a rule of law, not the guilt of the defendant; so no witnesses or evidence are presented during the appeals hearing. The arguments may focus on interpretations of previous cases and explain how this present case is similar to or different from previous cases. If a U.S. court of appeals decides that a substantial

unconstitutional. Defendants cannot appeal on the grounds they are innocent. The question of guilt is a question of **original jurisdiction** and is addressed in the U.S. district court: The judge or the jury heard the facts of the case and rendered a decision regarding the criminality of the defendant's behavior. Thus, the U.S. appeals court will not conduct another trial to determine the guilt of the defendant. The appeals court conducts hearings that review the questions of judicial error or constitutionality raised by the defendant. The case is heard by three appeals court judges. There are no witnesses or evidence because the purpose of the hearing is to make a judicial decision, not a decision of guilt.

A fair trial does not mean the defendant's trial was without error, but it does mean no substantial judicial error could have affected the outcome of the court's decision. During the defendant's trial in district court, the responsibility of the defendant's attorney is to object to any procedure or court ruling that is thought to be unfair or unconstitutional. The district judge makes a ruling on the objection raised by the attorney, and the trial proceeds based on the judge's ruling. The objection of the defense counsel is entered into the transcript of the trial. After the trial, if the defense counsel believes that the ruling of the district judge was not correct, the judge's ruling can be appealed. If at the time of the trial the defense attorney fails to object to an unfair practice, the absence of such an objection can be considered a reason to deny the appeal.

EXAMPLES OF JUDICIAL ERRORS

- Admitting evidence that has been improperly obtained
- Allowing prosecutorial evidence and witnesses not relevant to the trial
- Disallowing defense evidence and witnesses
- Improper trial conduct
- Misbehavior by the jury
- Instructions by the judge prohibiting the jury from considering a lesser offense
- Improper instructions by the judge to the jury

94 judicial districts

12 regional circuits

2 appellate courts in Washington, DC

judicial error has been made, the court determines the appropriate action to be taken to correct the error. The appeals court does not declare the defendant not guilty and does not "throw out" the lower court's conviction. The decision of the appeals court may mean that the defendant receives another trial in which the judicial error is corrected, or the sentence of the defendant may be modified. If the appeals court orders a new trial and the prosecutor determines that a conviction may not be possible given the instructions to correct the judicial error, the prosecutor may drop the case and not file charges against the defendant for another trial.

The 94 judicial districts are organized into 12 regional circuits, each of which has a U.S. court of appeals. Also, there is one U.S. court of appeals for the Federal Circuit.[19] Each of the federal judicial circuits has one location that is the principal seat of federal courts of appeal, and two courts of appeal are located in Washington, DC. (One of the Washington, DC courts of appeal handles civil cases related to patents, copyrights, tax disputes, and claims against the federal government.) Appeals court circuits were first established in the original 13 colonies and spread westward as the United States expanded. This geographic origin of the various federal appeals circuits resulted in a disproportionate division of circuit courts east and west of the Mississippi River. There are only four U.S. circuit courts of appeal west of the Mississippi River.

As a result of the shift of the population centers from the East Coast to the West Coast, western U.S. circuit courts of appeal have more cases to review and greater diversity in the values and cultures of the people within a circuit. The Ninth U.S. Circuit Court of Appeals, for instance, includes seven western states, Alaska, Hawaii, and the U.S. territories of Guam and the Northern Mariana Islands. When there is widespread diversity, judges of the U.S. courts of appeal do not always have the same interpretation of the Constitution, the law, or criminal procedures. Nevertheless, the federal court system requires that decisions of the U.S. Circuit Court of Appeals are binding on all U.S. district courts within that circuit. For example, an opinion regarding the constitutionality of a search without a warrant in the Ninth U.S. Circuit Court of Appeals would be binding on all U.S. district courts in the Ninth Circuit, but not binding on the district courts in the other circuits. Although not binding, decisions from other jurisdictions can be cited as guidelines. When appellate courts issue conflicting rulings, the U.S. Supreme Court has the authority to provide a single binding ruling for all courts.

The U.S. Supreme Court

The **U.S. Supreme Court** is the highest court in the American judicial system. This means there is no higher authority to which a defendant can appeal a decision of the Supreme Court. A decision by the Supreme Court is final and cannot be overruled by Congress. The only way to affect Supreme Court decisions is for Congress to pass a statute or constitutional amendment altering the wording of a law the Supreme Court

LEARNING OUTCOMES 3 Describe the structure and function of the federal courts.

GLOSSARY

Federal Judiciary Act The congressional act of 1789 that created the lower federal courts.

circuits Geographic divisions of the federal court system.

Marbury v. Madison The 1803 case that established the court's power of judicial review.

judicial review The power of the courts to declare congressional and presidential acts unconstitutional.

U.S. magistrate courts Federal lower courts whose powers are limited to trying lesser misdemeanors, setting bail, and assisting district courts with various legal matters.

U.S. district courts The federal system's trial courts of original jurisdiction.

Think About It . . .

President Obama made a significant impact on diversity in the federal judiciary. Nearly three of every four people nominated by Obama and confirmed as federal judges have been women or minorities. This is more than twice the number of minorities and women nominated by President Bush and 20% more than President Clinton nominated. Obama's successful nominations include the first female Latina on the Supreme Court, the first time three females have served on the Supreme Court, and the first openly gay man to a federal judgeship. About 21% of Obama's confirmed nominees were African-American, 11% were Hispanic, 7% were Asian-American, and 47% were women.[21]

Nan Aron of the Liberal Alliance for Justice claims, "The more diverse the courts, the more confidence people have in our judicial system. Having a diverse judiciary also enriches the decision-making process."[22] However, this claim can be controversial. One of the criticisms of Justice Sonia Sotomayor during her nomination hearings concerned statements she had made about the ability of minorities to bring a new perspective to judicial decision-making. Her critics argued that judicial decision should be fair and impartial and should not take into account gender or race.

Do you agree with Aron's statement that the more diverse the courts, the more confidence people have in the judicial system? Explain. Is it important to have diversity in the judicial system? Why or why not? What are some obstacles to achieving greater diversity in the judicial system?

Library of Congress

Justice Thurgood Marshall, First African-American Appointed to the U.S. Supreme Court, 1967

For more than 140 years, no females or minorities were among the nation's federal judges. Landmarks for females and minorities in the federal judiciary include the following:

- Starting in 1934 minorities and females were added to the ranks of federal judges.
- 1950 Burnita Shelton Matthews is the first female U.S. district court judge.
- 1961 Reynaldo G. Garza is the first Hispanic federal judge.
- 1967 Thurgood Marshall is the first African-American Supreme Court justice.
- 1971 Herbert Choy is the first Asian-American U.S. Circuit Court of Appeals judge.
- 1981 Sandra Day O'Connor is the first woman Supreme Court justice.
- 1993 Ruth Bader Ginsburg is the second female Supreme Court justice and the first Jewish female justice.
- 1994 Deborah A. Batts is the first openly homosexual federal judge.
- 2009 Sonia Sotomayor is the first Latina Supreme Court justice.
- 2010 Elena Kagan's appointment was the first time there were three women justices on the U.S. Supreme Court.
- 2011 Bernice Donald is the first African-American woman on the Sixth U.S. Circuit Court of Appeals.

has declared unconstitutional. For example, when the Supreme Court ruled that congressional legislation to create the assessment of personal income tax was unconstitutional (because the legislation violated Article 1, Section 9 of the Constitution), the law could not be enforced. The only way to institute personal income tax was to change the Constitution. Thus, in 1919, Congress passed the Sixteenth Amendment authorizing the federal government to lay and collect taxes on personal incomes.

In addition to its role in the criminal justice system, the Supreme Court exercises other important judicial powers. The Supreme Court is the legal mediator for lawsuits between states and between the United States and foreign countries. The Supreme Court also is the final authority for legal opinions binding on the federal government.[20] For instance, when controversy arose over the legality of ballots cast in Florida in the 2000 presidential election, the Supreme Court provided the final judgment regarding the vote count.

Reviewing Cases and Landmark Cases

Unlike the U.S. circuit courts of appeal, the U.S. Supreme Court does not have to hear a criminal case on appeal. The Supreme Court chooses cases that the justices believe address important constitutional issues. According to Justice Samuel A. Alito, Jr., the task of the Supreme Court in regard to judicial review is "to establish legal principles that will apply to countless cases." Technically, the Court must review cases when:

1. A federal court has held an act of Congress to be unconstitutional.
2. A U.S. court of appeals has found a state statute to be unconstitutional.
3. A state's highest court of appeals has ruled a federal law to be unconstitutional.
4. An individual's challenge to a state statute on federal constitutional grounds is upheld by a state's highest court of appeals.

In all other cases, the Court can decline to review a case. If a majority of justices do not want to review a case, this is the same as affirming the lower court's decision. If the Court decides not to review a case, there is no further appeal to the Court's decision.

In its role of judicial review of a case, the Supreme Court does not conduct jury trials and does not determine whether the defendant is guilty. The purpose of the Supreme Court's review is to look at cases that have important procedural and constitutional questions and determine whether a significant judicial error was made by the lower court and, if so, determine the appropriate remedy.

The Supreme Court has the power to review civil lawsuits, criminal cases, and juvenile hearings. The Court is very

HOW CASES GET TO THE U.S. SUPREME COURT

The defendant is found guilty in the court of original jurisdiction (i.e., a U.S. magistrate court or U.S. district court). ▶

The defendant appeals, claiming that a judicial error occurred during the trial that substantially affected the outcome of the trial (i.e., a guilty verdict or the law that the defendant was convicted of breaking is unconstitutional). ▶

A panel of judges, usually three, reviews the case. The appeals court can review the case by:

1. A review of the appeal and case documents.
2. A review of the written briefs of the two sides.
3. A hearing in which the two sides submit written briefs and the court hears oral arguments. ▶

Finding ▶

TIM SLOAN/AFP/Getty Images/Newscom

The U.S. Secret Service provides protective services for many government officials. One notable exception is protective services for the nine members of the U.S. Supreme Court. These nine men and women comprise the leadership of the judiciary, the third branch of government. The cases they decide can change society and the criminal justice system in profound ways. In controversial cases, the vote of a single Supreme Court justice can alter the course of history. Despite this influence, Supreme Court justices receive relatively few protective services.

When in Washington, DC, the justices are protected mainly by the court's own small force. When the justices leave Washington, the U.S. Marshals Service and local police provide protective services. When they are overseas, justices may have no protective services at all. They rely primarily on their low-key profile and anonymity to thwart attacks.[23] As a result, justices are relatively free to travel and engage in social events with minimum security concerns or encumbrances. Justices enjoy an unparalleled degree of personal freedom compared to other high-ranking officials.

Justices attribute their low profile in part to the fact that Supreme Court hearings are not televised. As a result, even in the most controversial cases, only a few hundred observers can crowd into the courtroom to witness the proceedings. As a result, most people do not recognize Supreme Court justices.

There have been no assassination attempts or serious attacks upon any Supreme Court justice. Justices have been the target of common crimes, but most likely the criminals did not recognize their victims as Supreme Court justices.[24] Based on these facts, there are no calls for greater protective services for justices or by the justices.

As Supreme Court justices become more visible through media interviews and public appearances, should the Secret Service provide protective services for Supreme Court justices? Could televising the Supreme Court hearings result in a greater security threat to the justices? Explain. Why do justices have such anonymity compared to other government officials?

selective in deciding what cases to review and will not hear a case until all other appeals have been exhausted. For a state case, that means the case must have been reviewed by the state's highest court before the Supreme Court will consider it for review. Furthermore, the case must involve a substantial federal or constitutional question.

The process by which the Supreme Court chooses which cases to review begins with a clerk for a Supreme Court justice— an attorney who performs legal research for the justice. Clerks review the numerous cases that petitioners have forwarded to the Supreme Court, select those that may merit consideration, and forward them to the Supreme Court judges. Each judge reviews the cases and decides whether a case has the potential to raise a significant federal or constitutional question. If four or more members of the Supreme Court believe that a case meets this criterion, it is selected for review. For cases selected for review, the Court issues a writ of *certiorari*. This authority to select cases for review is known as **certiorari power**. A **writ of**

certiorari is an order to the lower court, state or federal, to forward the record of the case to the Supreme Court.

When the Supreme Court selects a case for review, this does not mean the defendant is not guilty, is freed, or is immediately entitled to a new trial. The Court has several options in reviewing a case. The Court can do one of the following:

1. Examine the trial record and facts of the case and determine that no further review is necessary.

2. Ask the attorneys representing the appellant to submit a written statement, called a **brief**, stating the substantial federal or constitutional issue they think needs to be decided. (The attorney from the other side submits a rebuttal brief, and the Court decides on the basis of information in the briefs.)

3. Decide that the case deserves a hearing.

A substantial judicial error affecting the outcome of the verdict was committed.	The case is returned to the lower court with orders to fix the error. The lower court may: 1. Retry the defendant. 2. Correct the sentence. 3. If the error cannot be corrected and still leaves sufficient evidence to convict, the prosecutors may decide to drop the case.	▶ New trial ▶ New sentence ▶ Charges dismissed
The law is unconstitutional.		
No judicial error		
There was judicial error, but it did not substantially influence a verdict of guilty.	The verdict is voided.	
The law is constitutional.	The verdict of the court of original jurisdiction is upheld.	▶ The defendant can appeal to the U.S. Supreme Court.

U.S. courts of appeal The third tier of the federal court system where decisions of lower courts can be appealed for review of significant judicial error that may have affected the verdict.

original jurisdiction The first court to hear and render a verdict regarding charges against a defendant.

U.S. Supreme Court The highest court in the U.S. judiciary system whose rulings on the constitutionality of laws, due process rights, and rules of evidence are binding on all federal and state courts.

certiorari power The authority of the Supreme Court, based on agreement by four of its members that a case might raise significant constitutional or federal issues, to select a case for review.

writ of certiorari An order to a lower court to forward the record of a case to the U.S. Supreme Court for review.

brief A written statement submitted by an appellant's attorneys that states the substantial constitutional or federal issue they believe the court should address.

per curiam opinion A case that is disposed of by the U.S. Supreme Court without a full written opinion.

affirm the case A finding by the Supreme Court that there was no substantial judicial or constitutional error and that the original opinion of the lower court stands.

reversing the case A finding by the Supreme Court that a judicial error or an unconstitutional issue was central to the lower court's decision and voided the lower court's ruling.

remanded After the U.S. Supreme Court's reversal of a decision of a lower court, the return of the case to the court of original jurisdiction with instructions to correct the judicial error.

stare decisis The legal principle of determining points in litigation according to precedent.

landmark case A U.S. Supreme Court case that marks a significant change in the interpretation of the Constitution.

If the Court decides the case requires a hearing, two sides are invited to present oral arguments before the full Supreme Court in Washington, DC. Few cases are decided by oral hearings. The purpose of the hearing is to allow the parties to present arguments in support of their brief that the case involves a substantial federal or constitutional issue. The parties to the case may be given only one hour to argue their case. In addition to the arguments being presented, unlike criminal trials, the Supreme Court justices will ask questions of the attorneys.

After reviewing a case, the Court declares its decision and can issue a written opinion explaining the reasons for its decision. A case that is disposed of by the Court without a full written opinion is said to be a **per curiam opinion**. The Court can **affirm the case** or reverse the lower court's decision. In affirming a case, the Supreme Court finds that there was no substantial judicial or constitutional error and that the original opinion of the lower court stands. In a criminal case, this means that whatever sentence was imposed on the defendant may be carried out or continued. An opinion by the Supreme Court voids rulings or decisions by any lower court, including state courts.

Remedies for Judicial Error

Reversing the case means that the Court found that a judicial error or an unconstitutional issue was central to the lower court's decision. Most cases are not reversed. The Court has reversed about 25% of all of the cases decided on merit.[25] In a criminal case, reversal does not mean that the defendant is freed, is not guilty, or receives a reduced sentence. It means that the

Supreme Court found the conviction of the defendant to be flawed and that the conviction is "vacated." After the case is reversed, it is remanded. **Remanded** means that the case is returned to the court of original jurisdiction—the court that first convicted the defendant—with the instructions to correct the judicial error, called a "remedy."

If the judicial error involved the introduction of inadmissible evidence, such as an unconstitutional confession or search and seizure or inappropriate testimony, the remedy requires a new trial in which the inadmissible evidence cannot be used. If a conviction cannot be obtained without this evidence, the prosecution may decide not to ask for a new trial. In that case, the charges are dismissed and the defendant is set free. If the prosecution decides to retry the case, the defendant may or may not be convicted at the new trial. The decision to retry the case does not violate the Constitutional protection against double jeopardy or a person being tried twice for the same offense.

Not all judicial errors require a new trial. Judicial errors also can involve an incorrect sentence being assessed against a defendant, and the court of original jurisdiction may be instructed to recalculate the sentence. A common criminal appeal for a reduction of sentence is the appeal for a reduction of a death sentence to the lesser sentence of life in prison.

When a long-incarcerated individual appeals on a writ of *habeas corpus*, the appeal to the Supreme Court can take decades. Although long delays are unusual, in some cases, defendants have served the length of their sentence by the time the Supreme Court hears their case. Delays often are due to the large caseload of the Supreme Court and its limited ability to review and decide on appeals. Some critics of the judicial system have argued that such a delay in justice is the same as justice denied. There appears to be no immediate solution to this problem because new issues involving substantial questions of constitutional rights, due process, human rights, and civil liberties come before each session of the U.S. Supreme Court.

In deciding a case, the U.S. Supreme Court follows the principle of **stare decisis**. *Stare decisis* is the legal principle of determining points in litigation according to precedent. Case law requires equal justice, meaning that as one case was decided, so must other cases be decided that are the same. However, the U.S. Supreme Court can change the legal principles or foundations upon which legislation and constitutional rights are interpreted. This does not happen often. When it does, the case is called a **landmark case**. In a landmark case, the Supreme Court issues a new interpretation of a legal principle or constitutional right that differs from previous cases. A landmark case is important because once the U.S. Supreme Court makes a ruling, the lower courts must fall in line with that ruling. Landmark cases can change the practices of law enforcement or corrections throughout the nation. Some famous landmark cases are *Brown* v. *Topeka Board of Education*, in which the Court reversed *Plessy* v. *Ferguson*, striking down the "separate but equal" practice in racial discrimination, and *Mapp* v. *Ohio*, in which the Court incorporated the requirements of the Fourth Amendment requiring states to adopt the exclusionary rule. Landmark cases end diversity in practices among state courts and rulings among the various circuit courts of appeal. U.S. Supreme Court rulings on constitutionality also are applicable to state and juvenile courts. Landmark cases are important in defining the constitutional rights of the defendant.

▶ Structure and Function of the State Courts

State courts are authorized and organized autonomously by each state. If there is a legal dispute between states, the federal courts have jurisdiction. The purpose of state courts is to try defendants charged with violations of state laws or the state constitution. A state also contains smaller political jurisdictions, such as cities and counties, and each of these has its own legal codes. Therefore, states must establish court systems that provide for a defendant to be tried for allegedly violating a city or county ordinance. Like the federal court system, the state court system has a number of specialized courts dealing with noncriminal cases. As in the federal courts, civil lawsuits compose the majority of the state court's trials.[26]

State court systems uniquely reflect the history of each state. For example, Pennsylvania's judiciary system began as a disparate collection of courts, some inherited from the reign of the Duke of York and some established by William Penn. They were mostly local, mostly part-time, and mostly under control of the governor. All of the state courts were run by nonlawyers, and final appeals had to be taken to England. The Judiciary Act of 1722 was the colony's first judicial bill. It established the Pennsylvania Supreme Court and the Court of Common Pleas.[27] The court system changed again with the Pennsylvania Constitution of 1776 and the Constitution of the United States. After that, the most sweeping changes in Pennsylvania's judiciary came in 1968. The Constitution of 1968 created the Unified Judicial System, consisting of the supreme court, superior courts, and commonwealth courts; common pleas courts; the Philadelphia municipal court; the Pittsburgh magistrate court; the Philadelphia traffic court; and district justice courts. Pennsylvania's judicial system is illustrated in Figure 7–4.[28]

The history of each state court reflects the unique historical development of the state. However, many of the state courts have similar structures because they evolved from British common law courts. The original courts of Louisiana and Illinois had a different structure and process from that of the other state courts because they were French territories and their early courts adopted the continental law tradition of the French courts.

Like Pennsylvania, the original 13 colonies made significant changes to their court system when the colonies became part of the United States. Territories were under the authority of the federal judicial system. As territories were designated as states and admitted into the Union, each new state developed its own court system. Thus, the states consisting of the original 13 colonies have the oldest state court systems; Alaska and Hawaii have the newest. Over time, the philosophy, mission, and values of the citizens of the states change and many states have found it necessary to redesign their state court system. For example, Illinois has revised its court system four times.[29]

Most states have chosen judicial models that resemble the four-tier federal court system. Some states have a three-tier

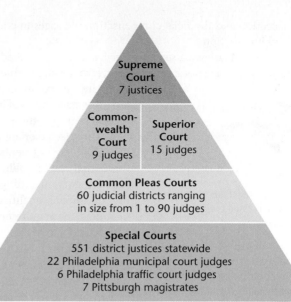

FIGURE 7–4 Each state court system is unique, but most, like the four-tier structure of the Commonwealth of Pennsylvania court system, are similar to the federal court system. Each state establishes its own unique court structure, but basically they are similar to the same organizational structure used by the U.S. Supreme Court.

system, and some have a four-tier system. For those states with a four-tier system, the tiers consist of the following:

1. Courts of limited jurisdiction
2. Courts of general jurisdiction
3. Courts of intermediate appellate jurisdiction
4. Courts of last resort

For those states with a three-tier system, the courts of limited jurisdiction and courts of general jurisdiction are usually combined into a single tier. Each state has unique names for the various courts within its system. Each state has granted different jurisdiction to the various courts within its system based on geography, subject matter, and hierarchy. Each state has a hierarchy of appeals from the lowest court to the court of last resort.

Courts of Limited Jurisdiction

State courts with **original jurisdiction**—the power to determine whether the defendant is guilty—are divided into courts of limited jurisdiction and general trial courts. Some of the names for **courts of limited jurisdiction** are justice of the peace courts, municipal courts, justice courts, and magistrate's courts. These courts handle traffic violations and criminal violations, misdemeanors, and local ordinances and laws within the geographic jurisdiction of the local government.[30] In addition to these criminal matters, courts of limited jurisdiction may also handle a number of civil matters, such as "small claims" lawsuits, landlord/tenant disputes, permits, and dispute resolution. Other functions of courts of limited jurisdiction may include accepting passport applications and performing marriages. Also, these courts of limited jurisdiction perform functions such as issuing search and arrest warrants, setting bail, and arraigning defendants. Usually, the local government is responsible for the selection and financial compensation of judges in courts of limited jurisdiction.

In states that have a separate tier for courts of limited jurisdiction, judges may not have to be lawyers. In fact, in some cases, there are no requirements for judges of state courts of limited jurisdiction. In these states, judges are elected or appointed by local governments and there may be absolutely no requirements regarding legal or educational qualifications, including the requirement for a high school diploma.[31]

Describe the structure and function of the state courts.

GLOSSARY

original jurisdiction The power to determine whether the defendant is guilty.

courts of limited jurisdiction State courts of original jurisdiction that handle traffic violations and criminal violations, small claims, misdemeanors, and violations of local ordinances and laws within the geographic jurisdiction of the town or village.

courts of record Courts in which trial proceedings are transcribed.

trial *de novo* A new trial granted by an appellate court.

general trial courts State courts of original jurisdiction that hear all kinds of criminal cases.

appellate courts State courts that have the authority to review the proceedings and verdicts of general trial courts for judicial errors and other significant issues.

court of last resort A state court of final appeals that reviews lower court decisions and whose decisions can be appealed to the U.S. Supreme Court.

Courts of limited jurisdiction frequently are not **courts of record**. A court of record is when a word-for-word transcript is made of the proceedings of the court and the ruling of the judge. In courts of limited jurisdiction that are not courts of record, there is no record or transcript of the trial proceedings except for the judges' personal notes and the verdict. There is no record of the witnesses, the testimony, or the evidence presented. In courts of limited jurisdiction, defendants often represent themselves and there may be no state or local government prosecutor. For example, in traffic courts, the law enforcement officer may "prosecute" the case and the person ticketed may act as his or her own defense counsel. In courts of limited jurisdiction, defendants may not be entitled to state-appointed attorneys.

A conviction in a court of limited jurisdiction may be appealed to a court of general jurisdiction. Even traffic criminal law convictions can be appealed to a court of general jurisdiction. However, because there is no record of what happened in the court of limited jurisdiction, if the case is appealed, a new trial is necessary. This is called **trial *de novo***. Thus, unlike appeals from courts of general jurisdiction to state appellate courts in which the appellate court examines only the legal issues regarding judicial error or constitutionality, in a trial *de novo*, the court of general jurisdiction conducts a new trial to determine the guilt of the defendant, not just a review of disputed judicial errors. A new trial is required because there is no written record of the lower court's proceedings to determine whether a judicial error occurred.

Traditionally, justice of the peace courts are associated with rural geographic jurisdictions, whereas municipal courts are associated with urban geographic jurisdictions. Another court of limited jurisdiction is the county court, where counties can try defendants for violations of county laws. Some cities have municipal courts, which have jurisdiction for traffic violations and criminal law offenses within the geographic jurisdiction of the city. Usually, only larger municipalities have city courts due to the cost of financing them.

Courts of General Jurisdiction

The general trial courts of the state judicial system are the workhorses of the criminal justice system. State **general trial courts** handle all kinds of criminal cases—from traffic violations to murder. General trial courts are courts of record. A full transcription (that is, a word-for-word recording of the proceeding) is made for every trial in a general trial court. Nearly all appeals for criminal cases originate from state general trial courts. General trial courts are called circuit courts, superior courts, district courts, courts of common pleas, and courts of first instance. In addition to criminal trials, state courts of general jurisdiction handle civil cases and many other legal responsibilities.

Modern state court systems require that judges and lawyers must meet minimum qualifications for courts of general jurisdiction and higher. These qualifications may be established by the state's constitution or by the state's agency or commission charged with regulating and disciplining judicial officers. State prosecutors (known by different names in each state) are responsible for the presentation of cases in courts of general jurisdiction. While defendants may invoke the right to represent themselves, this is rare. Most defendants are represented by an attorney. If the punishment for the offense can result in a sentence of six months or more and the defendant cannot afford an attorney, the state has the constitutional duty to provide one for the defendant at no cost to him or her.

Appellate Courts

Most states have intermediate appellate courts that act in a similar capacity as the U.S. court of appeals. Some common names for these are court of criminal appeals, court of appeals, appellate court, court of special appeals, appellate division of superior court, superior court, and commonwealth court. These **appellate courts** do not have original jurisdiction and review cases for judicial error and other significant issues concerning due process, civil rights, and federal and state constitutional questions. Similar to federal appellate courts, these courts do not conduct trials where each side presents evidence and witnesses. The purpose of the appellate courts is not to determine whether the court of general jurisdiction convicted an innocent person, but whether a significant judicial error occurred during the trial that may have affected the outcome of the case.

The procedure of the state appellate courts is similar to that of the federal appellate courts in that a panel of judges, usually three, reviews the alleged judicial errors or constitutional issues.

The power of the state appellate courts is similar to that of the federal appellate courts in that if they determine a judicial error occurred, they can remand the case back to the court of original jurisdiction to correct the error. Such an action does not free the defendant or mean that the defendant is not guilty. The court of original jurisdiction must correct the error. This correction may require a new trial in which evidence that was previously allowed is excluded or evidence is allowed that was previously excluded. If the prosecutor decides that he or she cannot obtain a conviction under the conditions imposed by the appellate court's ruling, he or she may decide not to prosecute the case again. This action results in the defendant being released from incarceration.

In many states, the defendant has an automatic right to appeal his or her conviction to a state appellate court. In such states, this right to appeal is usually limited to a specific period of time following the conviction. The time limit for declaring that a case will be appealed may be as short as 30 days.[32]

Courts of Last Resort

Each state has a court of final appeals. Some of the names given to these courts of last resort are supreme court, supreme judicial court, court of appeals, and high court. Most states have a single court of last resort. Oklahoma[33] and Texas[34] have two separate courts of last resort. (In Oklahoma, the Court of Civil Appeals handles civil cases and the Court of Criminal Appeals is the highest court with appellate jurisdiction in criminal cases. In Texas, the Supreme Court is the highest court of appellate jurisdiction for civil and juvenile cases and the Court of Criminal Appeals has final appellate jurisdiction in criminal cases.) Each state determines the number of judges that sit on the court of last resort, typically five to nine justices. Justices may be selected by election, appointment, or some combination of election and appointment. The terms of justices for these courts are usually determined by the state's constitution. Unlike federal justices on the U.S. Supreme Court, state justices are not appointed for terms of "good behavior" (that is, life terms), but usually have definite terms of service. The length of service may be as long as ten years in some states.

The state **courts of last resort** have appellant jurisdiction and original jurisdiction similar to that of the U.S. Supreme Court. State courts of last resort select the criminal cases they review. The primary purpose of the court's review is to review a selected number of cases that may have a significant state or federal question. These courts do not conduct trials to determine guilt, but focus on a review for judicial error or constitutional issues. The procedures for review by state courts of last resort are similar to those of the U.S. Supreme Court. That is, after reviewing the case, the state's court of last resort can decide to affirm the case or reverse and remand the case back to the court of original jurisdiction for correction.

The state court of last resort is the final legal authority within the state. However, after a criminal defendant has exhausted all appeals in the state court system, he or she can appeal the case to the U.S. Supreme Court. State criminal cases can be appealed to the U.S. Supreme Court only after all appeals in the state court system have been exhausted. If a case is appealed to the U.S. Supreme Court, the U.S. Supreme Court has the authority to remand the case back to the state court of original jurisdiction for correction of a judicial error or constitutional issue. The interesting aspect of a ruling by the U.S. Supreme Court regarding a state case is that a ruling by the U.S. Supreme Court is binding on all state courts, not just the state from which the case originated.

New York Justice Courts: Too Small to Fail

In England, the Act of 1327 established unpaid "conservators of the peace" to exercise summary justice or common law justice to provide for local justice. In 1391, the name of these conservators was changed to "justice of the peace." It is this fourteenth-century model upon which the town and village courts of New York are based.

There are nearly 1,300 town and village courts (collectively known as the justice courts). Judges in these courts are known as "justices," and they handle close to 2 million cases a year. Justice courts handle small claims cases, landlord/tenant claims, prosecution of misdemeanors, violations committed within the town's or village's geographic boundaries, arraignments and preliminary hearings, and traffic law misdemeanors and traffic infractions.[35]

An in-depth investigation of New York's Justice Courts by the *New York Times* in 2006 revealed a broken system of justice presided over by poorly paid, incompetent small-town justices who often had no knowledge of the law or disregarded the law and preferred "common sense" over constitutional rights.

Justice courts are part of the New York judicial system, but justices are paid by the towns and villages; thus, the state court system has limited administrative and financial control of justice courts. Justices in the smaller towns and villages are often poorly educated. Elected justices are not required to be lawyers, and about 75% of them are not lawyers. Of those who are not lawyers, about a third have no formal education beyond high school and about 40 did not complete high school.[36] Most are retirees, farmers, mechanics, or former police officers. At least 30 justices are in their eighties. In 2006, newly elected justices received only six days of state-administered classes.[37]

The investigation by the *New York Times* documented numerous abuses and incompetence by the justices. Justices often openly expressed distain for constitutional rights and racial and gender equality.[38] One justice denied a restraining order for a woman, saying that "women needed a good pondering. " Another judge ordered defendants to perform community service work to pay for their court-appointed lawyers. When informed that this was unconstitutional, he replied, "The only unconstitutional part is for these freeloaders to expect a free ride."[39] Justices jailed defendants for months without bail hearings, fined defendants more than the law allowed, gave preferential treatment to family and friends, and intimidated people into pleading guilty or dropping charges. Justices make up about 66% of all New York judges, but they constitute 76% of the judges who have been removed from office by the Commission on Judicial Conduct.[40]

scorcom/Fotolia

This case raises several interesting questions. Among them are the following:

1. The assumption behind justice courts is that local judges know their community and provide appropriate ruling. Can a judge be "too familiar" with defendants so that judicial decisions reflect bias? Explain.

2. Defendants in New York Justice Courts have complained of racial and sexual bigotry "so explicit it seems to come from some other place and time."[41] How does this behavior influence the public's opinion of the larger criminal justice system?

3. New York is one of about 30 states that still relies on non-lawyers as judges for lower-level courts. Should the federal government require states to abandon this practice and require that all local judges be lawyers? Explain.

Summarize the historical foundations and structure of the U.S court system.

Our nation's court system is described as a dual system, with both distinct federal and state courts. Unlike police departments that operate independently of each other, the courts are organized in a hierarchy whereby decisions of a lower court can be reviewed and reversed by a higher court. The Tenth Amendment of the Constitution gives each state the authority to establish its own court system. Each state has a final court of appeals, but it is possible to appeal a state decision to the U.S. Supreme Court.

1. Why is the United States referred to as a dual court system?

2. How does the Tenth Amendment affect state courts?

3. Which court ultimately has the highest appellate authority?

jurisprudence A philosophy or body of written law used to settle disputes.

dual court system The political division of jurisdiction into two separate systems of courts: federal and state; in this system, federal courts have limited jurisdiction over state courts.

Article 3, Section 2 The part of the U.S. Constitution that defines the jurisdiction of the federal courts.

Eleventh Amendment A provision that prohibits a citizen from one state from suing the government of another state in federal court.

Tenth Amendment A provision that states that powers not specifically delegated to the federal government are reserved for the states.

Identify the differences between criminal law and civil law.

Civil law is referred to as private law because it addresses rights in cases between private parties. Civil lawsuits can include breach of contract, divorce, and medical malpractice. Criminal law addresses the prosecution and punishment of people who violate city, county, state, or federal laws. A significant difference between civil and criminal law is the burden of proof. The burden of proof in a civil court is only preponderance of the evidence, whereas the burden of proof in a criminal court is beyond a reasonable doubt.

1. Give an example of one type of civil lawsuit.

2. How does the burden of proof differ between a civil and criminal case?

civil law Also called private law, the body of law concerned with the definition, regulation, and enforcement of rights in noncriminal cases in which both the person who has the right and the person who has the obligation are private individuals.

tort A private wrong that causes physical harm to another.

preponderance of the evidence A majority vote of the jury—the standard required for a judgment in a civil case.

beyond a reasonable doubt A unanimous verdict—the standard required for a verdict in a criminal case.

plaintiff The party who files a civil lawsuit against the party who is alleged to have done harm.

defendant The party who sued in a lawsuit.

judgment A ruling by the court regarding the liability for injury or the claim alleged by the plaintiff.

Describe the structure and function of the federal courts.

The federal court system is responsible for the enforcement of all federal codes in all 50 states, U.S. territories, and the District of Columbia. The federal court is divided into four tiers of responsibility with the U.S. magistrate courts, the trial courts, the appeals courts, and the U.S. Supreme Court. The U.S. Supreme Court is the highest appellate court in the American judicial system. The U.S. Supreme Court can change the legal principles upon which legislation and constitution are interpreted through a landmark case.

1. Which court has the highest appellate authority in the United States?

2. How many federal judicial circuits are there?

3. How many U.S. district courts are there?

4. What is meant by the term *judicial review*?

5. How many justices comprise the U.S. Supreme Court bench?

Federal Judiciary Act The congressional act of 1789 that created the lower federal courts.

circuits Geographic divisions of the federal court system.

Marbury* v. *Madison The 1803 case that established the court's power of judicial review.

judicial review The power of the courts to declare congressional and presidential acts unconstitutional.

U.S. magistrate courts Federal lower courts whose powers are limited to trying lesser misdemeanors, setting bail, and assisting district courts with various legal matters.

U.S. district courts The federal system's trial courts of original jurisdiction.

U.S. courts of appeal The third tier of the federal court system where decisions of lower courts can be appealed for review of significant judicial error that may have affected the verdict.

original jurisdiction The first court to hear and render a verdict regarding charges against a defendant.

U.S. Supreme Court The highest court in the U.S. judiciary system whose rulings on the constitutionality of laws, due process rights, and rules of evidence are binding on all federal and state courts.

certiorari power The authority of the Supreme Court, based on agreement by four of its members that a case might raise significant constitutional or federal issues, to select a case for review.

writ of certiorari An order to a lower court to forward the record of a case to the U.S. Supreme Court for review.

brief A written statement submitted by an appellant's attorneys that states the substantial constitutional or federal issue they believe the court should address.

affirm the case A finding by the Supreme Court that there was no substantial judicial or constitutional error and that the original opinion of the lower court stands.

per curiam opinion A case that is disposed of by the U.S. Supreme Court without a full written opinion.

reversing the case A finding by the Supreme Court that a judicial error or an unconstitutional issue was central to the lower court's decision and voided the lower court's ruling.

remanded After the U.S. Supreme Court's reversal of a decision of a lower court, the return of the case to the court of original jurisdiction with instructions to correct the judicial error.

stare decisis The legal principle of determining points in litigation according to precedent.

landmark case A U.S. Supreme Court case that marks a significant change in the interpretation of the Constitution.

Describe the structure and function of the state courts.

Most states have a judicial model that resembles the four-tier federal court system. States with a four-tier system consist of (1) courts of limited jurisdiction, (2) courts of general jurisdiction, (3) courts of intermediate appellate jurisdiction, and (4) courts of last resort. Once a criminal defendant has exhausted all appeals in the state court system, he or she can appeal the case to the U.S. Supreme Court. The Supreme Court has the power to grant a trail *de novo*, which provides a new trial for the defendant.

1. What is a court of original jurisdiction?

2. Which tier in the state structure is considered the workhorse of the criminal justice system?

3. Why are trial courts subject to transcribing records?

4. To where can a defendant appeal after a verdict in a state court of last resort?

original jurisdiction The power to determine whether the defendant is guilty.

courts of limited jurisdiction State courts of original jurisdiction that handle traffic violations and criminal violations, small claims, misdemeanors, and violations of local ordinances and laws within the geographic jurisdiction of the town or village.

courts of record Courts in which trial proceedings are transcribed.

trial de novo A new trial granted by an appellate court.

general trial courts State courts of original jurisdiction that hear all kinds of criminal cases.

appellate courts State courts that have the authority to review the proceedings and verdicts of general trial courts for judicial errors and other significant issues.

court of last resort A state court of final appeals that reviews lower court decisions and whose decisions can be appealed to the U.S. Supreme Court.

MyCJLab

Go to Chapter 7 in *MyCJLab* to test your mastery of chapter concepts, access your Study Plan, engage in interactive exercises, complete critical-thinking and research assignments, and view related online videos.

 Review: Complete the pretest in the Study Plan to confirm what you know and what you need to study further. Then complete the post-test to confirm your mastery of the concepts. Use the key term flash cards to review key terminology.

Apply: Complete the interactive simulation activity.

Analyze: Complete assignments as directed by your instructor.

Current Events: Explore CJSearch for current topical videos, articles, and news pieces.

Additional Links

Go to **http://www.cnn.com/JUSTICE/index.html** to watch the latest news and video about crime, the law, and the courts.

Go to **http://www.uscourts.gov** to learn about federal rules and statistics. The site also has useful links to educational resources and employment opportunities.

Go to **http://www.supremecourtus.gov** for more information on the U.S. Supreme Court.

Go to **http://www.findlaw.com** to look up landmark U.S. Supreme Court cases.

Go to **http://www.youtube.com/watch?v=Wq9MV8wdJHw** to watch live testimony in an actual murder trial.

Go to **http://www.uscourts.gov/FederalCourts/UnderstandingtheFederalCourts/DistrictCourts.aspx** and learn more details about the operations of the U.S. district courts.

Courtroom Participants and the Trial

"I'm no idealist to believe firmly in the integrity of our courts and in the jury system—that is no ideal to me, it is a living, working reality. Gentlemen, a court is no better than each man of you sitting before me on this jury. A court is only as sound as its jury, and a jury is only as sound as the men who make it up."

—Harper Lee, American writer

1 Describe the jurisdiction of the courts.

2 Describe pretrial proceedings and the process of developing charges for the arraignment hearing.

3 Summarize the purpose of bail and the various forms of bail.

4 Summarize the process of plea bargaining.

5 Explain the right to a speedy trial.

6 Describe the participants and the process of the criminal trial.

8

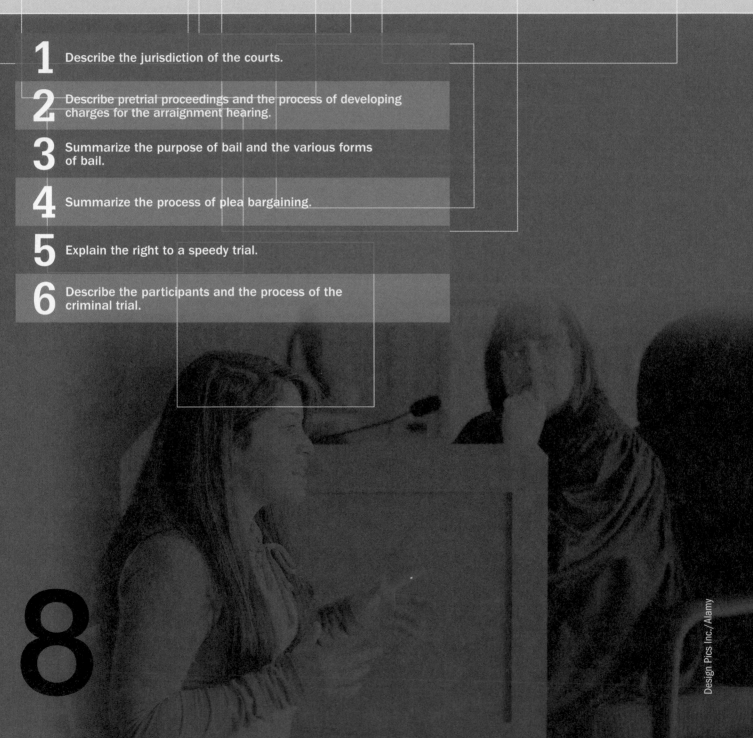

Design Pics Inc./Alamy

AN IMPERFECT SYSTEM OF JUSTICE

Prosecutors have been called the most powerful officials in the criminal justice system."[1] The prosecutor is the final authority as to who will be charged with a crime, what charges will be filed, and whether the accused will be offered a plea bargain. When prosecutors abuse their power, innocent people often suffer severe consequences.

The Brady rule, established in *Brady v. Maryland* (1963), requires prosecutors to disclose evidence favorable to the defendant. In *Smith v. Cain*, No. 10-8145 (2012), the Supreme Court overturned the conviction of Juan Smith for killing five people in 1995. The Court ruled that the New Orleans District Attorney's Office failed to disclose reports of interviews with eyewitnesses that could have impacted the jury's decision. Prior to the *Smith* decision, four death sentences and eight other noncapital cases tried by the New Orleans District Attorney's Office were overturned for violations of the Brady rule.

Other high-profile violations of the Brady rule include the corruption trial of the late Senator Ted Stevens (R–Alaska) and the 2006 Duke lacrosse sex scandal. In 2012, a judicial investigation into the Stevens case concluded that prosecutors engaged in "systematic concealment of significant evidence from Steven's [sic] attorneys. In the 2006 Duke lacrosse sex scandal, four players from the men's lacrosse team were accused of sexual assault of a dancer at a team party. A year after charging the four defendants,

Chris Hill/Shutterstock

North Carolina district attorney Mike Nifong was dismissed from the case, lost his law license, and was convicted of criminal charges of willfully making false statements to the court regarding the evidence against the defendant and withholding evidence from the defense attorneys.

Defendants have limited options in regard to punishing prosecutors who withhold evidence. In *Connick v. Thompson* (2011), the U.S. Supreme Court ruled that prosecutors are protected from civil liability. The Court argued that professional discipline, including sanctions, suspension, and disbarment, was the appropriate remedy for prosecutorial misconduct, not civil remedies.

DISCUSS **In the absence of civil remedies, what options would help prevent gross violations of the Brady rule and other miscarriages of justice?**

▶ *The Adjudication Process*

This chapter discusses what normally happens in the criminal trial and describes the roles of the criminal trial participants. A criminal trial is a complex event involving many participants. Many of these participants do their work behind the scenes. Most trials attract little media attention, but sensational trials can command nationwide media coverage. The public's perception of a criminal trial is strongly influenced by the media because few people outside the criminal justice system have reliable knowledge of the adjudication process. Many people, however, have watched criminal trials portrayed by the media. Some media presentations of trials are essentially complete fiction. The guilty party rarely, if ever, bursts forth from the public seating and confesses to the crime in the middle of the trial. Despite the importance and complexity of trials, most trials last only a couple of days. There are public broadcasts of actual criminal trials that provide an accurate view, but few viewers have the interest and patience to watch a criminal trial from start to finish because it can be boring.

The legal philosophy of the American criminal justice system is that the trial is a combative encounter between the state and the defendant. Unlike the Continental system, trials are not a "search for truth." A not guilty verdict does not mean the defendant is innocent in the sense that he or she did not do the alleged crime. Trials seek to establish the guilt of the defendant and, if guilty, to determine appropriate punitive sanctions. Trials are complex because many criminal justice agencies and personnel—police, prosecutors, judges, jurors, victims, offenders, and many more—must interact in the pursuit of justice. Often the parties in a trial are in conflict with each other, so there is no guarantee the process will go smoothly. Police officers seek to have the most serious charges possible filed against defendants, whereas prosecutors seek charges for which they can get a guilty plea or verdict. Prosecutors seek to convict defendants, whereas defendants hope for a verdict of not guilty. Victim and defendant may offer different accounts of events.

This chapter provides a description of the adjudication phase—in other words, the criminal trial. It examines the people involved in this process, the decisions that must be made to bring a defendant to trial, and the opposing ideologies that play out in the adjudication process. These opposing ideologies are the pursuit of punishment for the guilty and the desire to provide the accused with constitutional rights to protect him or her from abuse by the criminal justice system.

▶ *Jurisdiction*

Civilian criminal trials occur in federal court when the offense is a violation of federal law and in state or local courts when the offense is a violation of state or local law. When the offense is a federal felony, the trial occurs in a district court with **jurisdiction** over the offense. Usually, jurisdiction means that some part of the crime was committed within the geographic jurisdiction of the district court. If the offense is a misdemeanor, the trial occurs in a federal magistrate court. Defendants accused of violating state statutes are tried in a state court of limited jurisdiction for misdemeanor crimes and in a state court of general jurisdiction for felony crimes.

Trials in Courts of Limited Jurisdiction

Trials in **courts of limited jurisdiction** usually concern misdemeanor crimes, violations of criminal traffic laws, and lesser offenses. These include cases such as simple assault, disorderly conduct, trespass, and larceny. In a typical case, the defendant is arrested by a local police officer and appears before the court for a trial within a few weeks. Often the defendant is not guaranteed the right to an attorney because the punishment does not exceed the threshold at which the government must provide defendants with an attorney if they cannot afford legal counsel. Most trials consist of the police officer telling the judge what law the defendant is alleged to have violated and the evidence supporting his or her assertion, followed by the defendant's rebuttal. For the most part, these trials are fairly simple affairs. Few witnesses are called to testify, and only a minimum of evidence is introduced. The entire trial may last only minutes.

Many courts of limited jurisdiction are not courts of record, so no transcript is made of the proceedings. Scheduling of trials is simple in that many defendants are given the same trial date and time. The court starts the day with the first case and proceeds through the others as time permits. These are not jury trials, and the judge renders an immediate decision following the conclusion of the arguments. The defendant has the right to appeal the decision to a court of general trial jurisdiction.

Each local or municipal court has its own distinctive procedures depending on factors such as the legal training of the judge, the judicial resources of the municipality or county, and the number of cases the court hears. In rural areas, the court may be held only once a week, whereas in large urban cities, the municipal court may hear cases daily. Because of the diverse and variable nature of trials in courts of limited jurisdiction, the focus of this chapter is on trials in state courts of general jurisdiction and federal district courts.

Trials in Courts of General Jurisdiction and Federal District Courts

Most felony criminal trials occur in state **courts of general jurisdiction** or U.S. district courts. Because there are more felony crimes committed in violation of state laws than federal

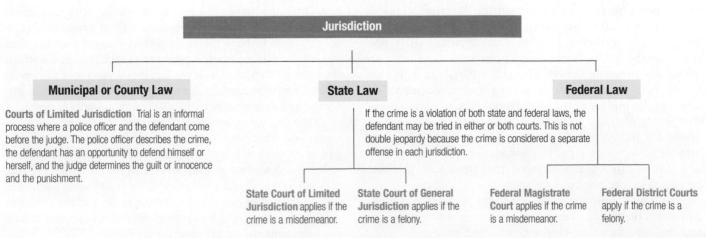

Following the arrest and booking

Arraignment

The defendant must be arraigned before the court, federal or state, that will exercise jurisdiction over the case. Usually, federal agents take the accused to a U.S. magistrate court for arraignment, whereas local and state law enforcement officers take the accused before the appropriate state court. Because both courts may have jurisdiction in the case, a defendant in some cases may be charged with both federal and state crimes and will be arraigned before each court.

Jurisdiction

Municipal or County Law

Courts of Limited Jurisdiction Trial is an informal process where a police officer and the defendant come before the judge. The police officer describes the crime, the defendant has an opportunity to defend himself or herself, and the judge determines the guilt or innocence and the punishment.

State Law

If the crime is a violation of both state and federal laws, the defendant may be tried in either or both courts. This is not double jeopardy because the crime is considered a separate offense in each jurisdiction.

State Court of Limited Jurisdiction applies if the crime is a misdemeanor.

State Court of General Jurisdiction applies if the crime is a felony.

Federal Law

Federal Magistrate Court applies if the crime is a misdemeanor.

Federal District Courts apply if the crime is a felony.

laws, the number of state felony criminal trials is much higher than the number of federal felony trials. Trial procedures for state and federal courts of general jurisdiction are similar. This chapter discusses the general procedures that apply to state and federal courts and highlights any differences between the two.

One of the first decisions that must be made when a person is arrested for a felony crime is which court has jurisdiction. The general guidelines for determining jurisdiction have to do with which laws were violated and the geographic location of the crime. If the crime was a violation of both federal and state laws, the defendant may be tried in either or both courts. Violations of federal and state laws are considered different offenses, and trying the person in both federal and state court does not constitute **double jeopardy**. Double jeopardy, which is the act of trying a person twice for the same offense, is prohibited by the Fifth Amendment of the Constitution.

As a practical matter, however, most defendants are not tried in both federal and state courts. Usually, the federal or state prosecutor with the strongest case takes the lead in bringing the case to trial. For example, Timothy McVeigh, who killed 168 people when he blew up the Alfred P. Murrah Federal Building in Oklahoma City in 1995, violated federal and state laws. He was tried in federal court and sentenced to death. The Oklahoma court did not bring charges against McVeigh. When a defendant can be charged in both federal and state court, the arresting agency often is a factor in determining who files charges.

Federal courts claim jurisdiction for crimes committed in the United States; its territories; maritime jurisdictional limits; federal, Native American, and military reservations; and U.S. registered ships at sea. For a state court to have jurisdiction of a case, all or part of the crime must have been committed within the state. If part of the crime is committed in a state, the state may claim jurisdiction over other parts of the crime, even crimes committed in another state. It is not considered double jeopardy to try a defendant in two or more states for what would appear to a layperson to be the same crime. States are sovereign political entities; thus, violation of the laws of several states is not considered the "same crime," and each state retains jurisdiction.

For example, if a person is abducted in one state and transported across the state line, where he or she is murdered, both states can claim jurisdiction over the crime. Both states can try the defendant for kidnapping and murder even though the kidnapping happened in one state and the murder in another. If two (or more) states claim jurisdiction over a crime, the state officials must negotiate to determine who will prosecute the defendant first. The states also must negotiate whether the defendant will be tried in both states if he or she is convicted by the first state. If the defendant is convicted and is to be tried in the second state, the states must negotiate whether the trial will occur before or after the convicted defendant has served his or her sentence for the crime. If the crime is first-degree murder and one state has the death penalty but the other state does not, the decision concerning in which state to try the defendant becomes even more important.

The ability to try a defendant in both state and federal court can act as checks and balances in the criminal justice system. If state courts fail to provide equal and fair justice for victims, the federal courts may file charges against the defendant even if the defendant was acquitted in state court. This strategy was used in the 1960s when southern state courts did not convict defendants for racially motivated crimes due to prejudices shared by the jurors. It can also be used in high-profile cases in which there is concern regarding the outcome of the state court's verdict. For example, the Los Angeles Police Department officers who beat Rodney King were tried in both state court and federal court. In their first trial in state court, the officers were acquitted. After their acquittal, the federal government filed charges of violation of civil rights and convicted the officers in federal court.

▶ Charges and Proceedings before Trial

The Constitution requires that citizens must be informed of the charges against them before they are tried in a court of law. The first step toward bringing a person to trial is arresting and booking the person, which formally charges him or her with having committed a crime. From that point, the process of bringing a person to trial involves the joint activity of the police and the prosecutor. There are many steps between booking and arraignment. One of the first is to determine whether the defendant will be arraigned before a state court or in the U.S. magistrate court. The defendant must be arraigned before the court, federal or state, that will exercise jurisdiction over the case. Usually, federal agents take the accused to a U.S. magistrate court for arraignment, whereas local and state law enforcement officers take the accused before the appropriate state court. Because both courts may have jurisdiction in the case, a defendant who is first arraigned before one court may later be arraigned before another.

LEARNING OUTCOMES 2 — Describe pretrial proceedings and the process of developing charges for the arraignment hearing.

GLOSSARY

due process Court rules that define the standards for a "fair" trial.

prosecutorial discretion The power of a prosecutor to decide whether to charge a defendant and what the charge(s) will be, as well as to gather the evidence necessary to prosecute the defendant in a court of law.

grand jury An alternative method, which is confidential, to determine whether there is sufficient evidence to charge the defendant with a crime.

arraignment A criminal proceeding where the defendant is formally charged with a crime and is asked to enter a plea.

competent to stand trial The defendant's ability to comprehend the charges against him or her and to assist counsel in his or her defense.

Determining the Charges: The Police and the Prosecutor

When the accused is first arrested, the law enforcement officer files a report charging the person with a crime. After the person is booked, a magistrate reviews the charges filed against the accused and determines that the police

Pretrial Proceedings

When the police arrest a suspect, the prosecutor has a very short time to decide if the charges are appropriate and if the evidence, even though incomplete at this stage, is sufficient to bring the case to trial. In some cases, the police and the prosecutor may have worked together to investigate and compile the necessary evidence prior to the arrest of the suspect.

Due Process The government must present evidence to an impartial judicial body that a crime has been committed and that there is reasonable belief that the person accused committed the crime.

Prosecutorial Discretion The prosecuting attorney decides if he or she wants to proceed with the case or drop it. The prosecutor may decide to:
- Drop the charges.
- Add additional charges.
- Reduce the charges.

Initial Appearance

Initial Appearance After the paperwork is forwarded to the prosecuting attorney, the accused is brought before a magistrate judge for a first appearance. The magistrate judge reviews the charges, advises the defendant of his or her rights, and sets bail. If charges filed could result in a prison sentence of six months or more, the judge will determine whether the person has funds for a lawyer and, if not, will arrange for a lawyer to represent him or her at no charge.

Preliminary Hearing

Preliminary Hearing This is sometimes referred to as the "probable cause" hearing. The judge will take an active role in questioning the prosecution and defendant. It is the prosecution's responsibility to convince the judge that there is probable cause to believe that (1) a crime has been committed and (2) the defendant committed the crime. Defense counsel can challenge the evidence. The judge determines whether the case should be dismissed or whether the defendant should be arraigned.

Grand Jury

Grand Jury Some states and the federal government make use of grand juries to determine if a case should go forward. The grand jury is made up of a panel of citizens selected to hear evidence against an accused person. Much like a jury, there is a presiding judge and the prosecution presents evidence and witnesses to convince the jury that a crime has been committed. The major difference is that the defendant and his or her attorney are not present. If the grand jury determines that there is probable cause, an indictment is written. This is called a true bill.

Arraignment

The defendant is formally charged with the crime or crimes he or she is alleged to have committed and is asked to enter a plea. If the defendant pleads not guilty, a trial date is set. If the defendant pleads guilty, there is no trial and a sentencing hearing is set.

Pretrial Motions

motion for discovery a pretrial motion filed by the defense counsel requesting that the prosecutor turn over all relevant evidence, including the list of witnesses, that the prosecution might use at the trial

motion for suppression a pretrial motion made by the defense to exclude certain evidence from being introduced in the trial

motion for change of venue a pretrial request, made either by the prosecutor or the defense, to move the trial to another courtroom in the same jurisdiction

motion for continuance a pretrial request made either by the prosecutor or the defense to delay the start of the trial

motion for dismissal a pretrial defense motion requesting that the charges against the defendant be dismissed

motion for a bill of particulars a pretrial motion that allows the defense to receive more details as to exactly what items the prosecution considers illegal if a defendant is charged with possession of burglary tools, illegal weapons, drug paraphernalia, or illegal gambling paraphernalia

motion for severance of charges or defendants a pretrial request that the defendant be tried for each multiple charge separately or that multiple defendants charged with the same crime be tried separately

---

have filed constitutional charges against the person and have provided the person with his or her constitutionally protected rights. While the police and the prosecutor then work together to bring the case to trial and to secure a conviction without violating due process, the prosecutor has the final authority in determining the charges and prosecuting the defendant.

Due Process

The framers of the U. S. Constitution included the provision that due process must be used in bringing a person to trial for a criminal offense. Recall that **due process** has been interpreted to mean that the government must present evidence to an impartial judicial body that a crime has been committed and that there is reasonable belief the person accused committed the crime. The prosecutor, not the arresting officer, is responsible for presenting this evidence.

Prosecutorial Discretion

After reviewing the police reports and in some cases talking to the arresting officers, the prosecuting attorney must decide if he or she wants to proceed with the case or drop it. The fact that the police have arrested and booked a suspect is no guarantee that the prosecutor will see the same merit in the case the police did. The prosecutor may decide that the police do not have sufficient evidence to prove the charges beyond a reasonable doubt and may refuse to move the case forward. Figure 8–1 summarizes the disposition of federal suspects arrested in 2008. About 16% of cases presented to federal prosecutors are not accepted for further action.

It is also very common for the prosecutor to modify the charges alleged by the police before moving the case forward. The prosecutor has the following options:

- Dropping some or all of the charges
- Adding additional charges
- Reducing the charges

The police may have arrested a person for first-degree murder, but the prosecutor may believe that the evidence warrants only charges of second-degree murder. This power of prosecuting attorneys is called **prosecutorial discretion**. The prosecutor also exercises power in the preliminary hearing and with regard to information, indictment, and arraignment.

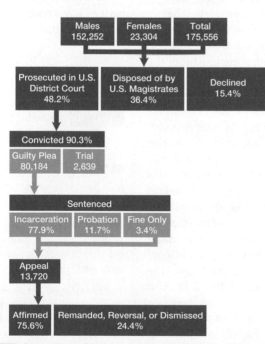

FIGURE 8–1 **Disposition of Federal Suspects Arrested in 2008 October 1, 2007–September 30, 2008**
Federal prosecutors refused to advance about 15% of suspects to trial. Less than 4% of suspects were convicted by trial.
Source: Bureau of Justice Statistics, Federal Justice Statistics 2008 (2011), http://bjs.ojp.usdoj.gov/index.cfm?ty=pbdetail&iid=1745.

Relationship between Prosecutor and Law Enforcement

Law enforcement and the prosecution are each autonomous criminal justice agencies, but without cooperation between them, it is difficult to achieve a successful prosecution. When the police arrest a suspect, the prosecutor has a very short time to decide whether the charges are appropriate and whether the evidence, even though incomplete at this stage, is sufficient to bring the case to trial. The relationship between the prosecutor and law enforcement is an important factor in this decision. Serious felony crime is most likely handled by veteran detectives who have an ongoing relationship with the prosecutor. The prosecutor depends on the detectives' professionalism and competence in making the decision to take the case.

In some major cases, the police and the prosecutor work together prior to the arrest of the suspect. In important cases, taking months or years to investigate and compile the necessary evidence, the prosecutor may be an active partner with the police. Some prosecutors even have their own investigative staff that can gather additional evidence to help support the charges. In major felony cases in which the prosecutor and law enforcement officers work together, the prosecutor may use the **grand jury** to obtain an arrest warrant rather than have the police arrest the suspect on probable cause. The grand jury process allows the prosecutor to obtain multiple arrest warrants without disclosing this fact to the public or the defendants.

Arraignment

Checks and balances against police and prosecutorial power are provided by the initial screening of the first appearance and preliminary hearing. In addition, the prosecutor must present evidence to the court at the **arraignment** that the defendant should be tried for the offense. The arraignment is the final stage before the trial, and the charges filed at this time are the charges on which the defendant will be tried. The arraignment is the first time in the pretrial process that the defendant is asked to formally declare a plea of guilty or not guilty. At the arraignment hearing, the prosecutor has the dilemma of how much evidence he or she should present to convince the court. The prosecutor needs to present enough evidence to convince the court that the defendant should be held over for trial. However, the more evidence the prosecutor presents, the more information the defense has to prepare for the trial. Thus, the prosecutor wants to present enough evidence to secure a trial date but not so much that the defense will be able to determine the entire prosecution strategy.

Competency to Stand Trial

Prior to the trial, the responsibility of the court is to determine that the defendant is **competent to stand trial**. Competent to stand trial means that the defendant can comprehend the charges against him or her and is able to assist counsel in his or her defense. While all defendants must be competent to stand trial, for most cases, this issue is not raised because there is no reason to suspect that the defendant is not competent to do so.

Competency to stand trial usually is determined by the ruling of a federal magistrate court judge or similar-level state judge. Health is one of the most common reasons a pretrial

Alternatives to Traditional Bail

Bail

▼

Bail As part of the initial appearance, the magistrate decides whether the defendant should be released on bail or held in a correctional facility until trial. For minor charges, the amount of bail may be set by a schedule of established fees. The amount of bail is typically based on the fines levied if the person is found guilty. Bail can be denied for reasons of community safety or the belief that the defendant is a flight risk.

Bail Bonds Agent is an agent of a private commercial business that contracts with the court to guarantee the defendant's return to court. The accused pays a fee to the bonds agent that is usually ten percent of the bond.

Alternatives to Traditional Bail

Release on Recognizance (ROR) The accused's release is based on the promise that he or she will return for trial.	**Conditional Release** The accused is released with conditions such as drug or alcohol treatment programs.	**Unsecured Bond** The defendant signs a promissory note to pay the court if he or she does not return.	**Signature Bond** is used for minor offenses such as traffic violations. The accused is released immediately after signing a promise to appear in court.

defendant may not be competent to stand trial. A defendant who has a serious disease and is undergoing treatment can experience serious side effects that affect his or her judgment. A defendant who is wounded by the police may not be competent to stand trial because of the need for medical treatment. A defendant with a medical condition affecting intellectual capacity may be considered incapable of understanding the charges against him or her. Declaring a pretrial defendant not competent to stand trial is a temporary ruling. When the defendant becomes competent to stand trial, the court will order that the trial proceedings resume or begin.

In some cases, the defendant may never be deemed competent to stand trial. The unconscious defendant may never regain consciousness, or the defendant's incompetence may be related to a permanent condition or mental illness. In these cases, the charges against the defendant are indefinitely suspended.

If a defendant is not competent to stand trial, that does not mean the defendant is insane. The claim that a defendant is not guilty by reason of insanity is an affirmative defense that must be made prior to the trial. After the insanity defense is declared, the court orders a series of psychiatric examinations to assess the defendant's mental state. The results of examinations are admissible as evidence during the defendant's trial. A finding of not guilty by reason of insanity is not determined by the medical professionals who examine the defendant, however, but by the jury.

▶ *Bail*

One of the hallmarks of the American criminal justice system is the assumption that defendants will be treated as if they are innocent until they are proven guilty. Essential to the fulfillment of that principle is the premise that a defendant will not be incarcerated prior to conviction unless it is absolutely necessary for public safety. The mechanism to provide for the pretrial release of the defendant is bail.

Bail has its roots in English history and has been used since before the Norman conquest in 1066. In an era before prisons were used to detain people prior to trial, the English magistrate would place prisoners with private parties who would guarantee that they would be delivered to the court when it was time for trial. To ensure that these custodians would perform their duties properly, they were required to sign a bond, known as a private surety, promising that if they failed to produce the prisoners on the trial date, they would forfeit a specified sum of money or property. The new American government adopted a variation of this pretrial procedure. Rather than entrust the accused to a private custodian, the Eighth Amendment of the Constitution recognized the concept of bail and specified that excessive bail should not be required of the accused. In the U.S. criminal justice system, **bail** is a system of pretrial release of the accused in a criminal proceeding based on a guarantee by the accused—or a bail bonds agent—that the accused will appear in court as required. The traditional method of guaranteeing the appearance of the defendant is to require a cash bond or some property of value.[2]

The Eighth Amendment does not specifically state that a defendant is guaranteed bail. It states only that excessive bail should not be required. The U.S. Supreme Court has interpreted the wording of the Eighth Amendment to mean that the defendant does indeed have a right to bail.[3] Initially, the

LEARNING OUTCOMES 3 Summarize the purpose of bail and the various forms of bail.

GLOSSARY

bail Temporary release of the defendant prior to trial.

excessive bail Bail that is prohibited by the Eighth Amendment, but there is no uniform standard as to what "excessive" is.

bail bonds agent An agent of a private commercial business that has contracted with the court to act as a guarantor of a defendant's return to court.

constitutional guarantee of bail was not a state requirement, but applied only to the federal courts.[4] However, the question of whether a state defendant has a guarantee of bail has never been a significant constitutional issue because state constitutions and judiciary practices have provided defendants with this right. Both federal and state courts have recognized that the right to bail is not an unrestricted right.

The controversy over bail has centered on the following factors:

1. What is excessive bail?
2. When can bail be denied?
3. Does the bail system discriminate against the poor?

Excessive Bail

The Supreme Court has declared that **excessive bail** must be based on standards relevant to guaranteeing that the defendant will not take advantage of his or her freedom and flee prior to the trial.[5] Thus, no standard limits of excessive bail apply to all cases. The court has the power to consider each case individually based on the totality of the circumstances. The court can consider factors such as the seriousness of the crime, the defendant's prior criminal record, the strength of the state's case, and the defendant's financial status. In some cases, the court set bail at millions of dollars, which was not considered excessive.

Bail is considered at various stages in the criminal justice system and is a revocable court decision. For example, in the Florida case of George Zimmerman, who was accused of killing Trayvon Martin, the Florida court initially granted Zimmerman bail based on his statement of financial assets. However, when it came to light that Zimmerman had significantly understated these assets, the court revoked his bail and remanded him back to custody. Also, the court can initially refuse to grant a defendant bail and agree at a later time to grant bail.

Denial of Bail

Bail is not an absolute guarantee, and defendants, under some circumstances, can be denied bail (*United States* v. *Salerno*).[6] Initially, the Supreme Court narrowly defined the purpose of bail as ensuring that the defendant would appear for trial. However, both the federal judiciary and the state judiciaries recognized cases in which the defendant's pretrial release could pose a potential danger to society and bail should be denied. Starting in the 1970s,

state judiciaries enacted danger laws that allowed the court to deny bail for certain offenses in which public safety could be a concern. The most common use of this denial of bail was for allegations of murder, organized crime and gang crime, and drug trafficking. The 1984 federal Bail Reform Act provided the same authority to federal judges.[7] This act allowed the court to assume that the defendant may pose a danger to others or to the community. Once the court makes this determination, it is the burden of the defendant to demonstrate that he or she is not a flight risk and is not a danger to people or the community.[8] If the defendant cannot meet this standard of proof, he or she is denied bail.

For most misdemeanor offenses, bail is set based on a fixed fee schedule; that is, for most common offenses, a predetermined bail is set by the judge in advance, committed to written record, and used by booking to know what bail to set without a judge's specific instructions for the defendant. Bail is an integral part of the initial appearance hearing. It is the first consideration of bail for the defendant.

For more serious felony cases, bail is usually determined at a bail hearing in which the prosecutor and the defense argue before the judge the merits of pretrial release. In the federal judiciary, bail hearings are held before magistrate judges. In most state courts, bail hearings are handled by courts of limited jurisdiction. Bail hearings are not decided by a jury, and following short oral arguments, the judge has wide discretionary powers as to granting bail and setting the amount. As mentioned, the judge's decision as to the granting of bail and the amount of the bail can be revisited. For example, if a defendant is granted bail on the condition that he or she cannot have any contact with the victim and the defendant violates that condition, the judge can revoke bail and incarcerate the defendant.

Discrimination against the Poor

If bail requires the posting of a cash bond, it seems obvious that low-income defendants are not going to have access to the right of bail because of their lack of available money. Without the ability to post a cash bond, the poor are likely to remain incarcerated until the trial. Given the fact that even simple felony cases may take months before they come to trial, the poor may spend more time in jail awaiting trial than the length of sentence they receive at the end of the trial. (When this happens, defendants are credited with time already served and are released.) Accused people who are not incarcerated have greater opportunities to assist in their defense. Thus, if

> Without the ability to post a cash bond, the poor are likely to remain incarcerated until the trial.

bail discriminates against the poor, the poor may not receive the same quality of justice as the rich. Recognizing that a cash bail system may discriminate against the poor, the judiciary has established alternatives.

The Bail Bonds Agent

A **bail bonds agent** is an agent of a private commercial business that has contracted with the court to act as a guarantor of the defendant's return to court. A bail bonds agent is not a state or federal employee, but rather a private party operating a for-profit business. Other than the Philippines, the United States is the only country to use a commercial for-profit business independent of the judicial system to secure bail for a defendant. In fact, in England and Canada, it is a crime for another person to agree to pay a defendant's bond for profit. Even in the United States, four states (Illinois, Kentucky, Oregon, and Wisconsin) have abolished commercial bail bonds. In these states, bail is a responsibility of the courts.

A bail bonds agent acts as an intermediary and posts the bond for the accused. For a fee paid by the defendant, the bail bonds agent guarantees to the court that the defendant will show up for all scheduled court appearances, This fee is usually 10% of the bond, but it may be higher because there is no set limit on the bail bond company's fee. At a 10% fee, a person whose bail is set at $1,000 would have to pay the bail bond company $100 for its services. A person whose bond is set at $50,000, a more realistic figure for a serious felony crime, would have to pay $5,000. The fee the defendant pays to the bail bonds agent is nonrefundable. Bail bond companies can refuse to underwrite the bail of a defendant if they do not believe the defendant is a good risk. The defendant is responsible for securing a bail bonds agent to post bail. For this reason, it is not uncommon for many bail bond businesses to set up shop as close to the courthouse as possible to increase their chance that defendants will use them.

Bond Jumpers and Bounty Hunters

A person who fails to appear for a court appearance is said to have "**jumped bond**." When a person jumps bond, the court will allow the bail bonds agent a certain amount of time to return the defendant to the custody of the court before revoking the posted bond. Bail bond businesses are not criminal justice agencies, but when they post bail for a defendant, they are considered agents of the court. This power allows the bail bonds agent to require the defendant to sign a legally binding contract, waiving the right of extradition. This means the agent can track down and bring back the bond jumper.

As an agent of the court, the bail bonds agent, who is not a law enforcement officer, does not have to observe the restrictions placed on the police in seeking the return of the person who fails to appear for his or her court appearance. Essentially, the bonds agent may use any means necessary to return the person to the jurisdiction of the court. The bonds agent may be authorized to carry firearms depending on the laws of the state, can use the threat of force to compel the defendant to return, and can even kidnap the defendant and forcibly return him or her to the court against his or her will. The bonds agent does not need an arrest warrant to enter a private residence where the defendant has sought refuge and can trespass anywhere the defendant is hiding. The bonds agent is allowed to pay a third party to search for and return a bond jumper. There are no minimum requirements or mandated training for people who track down and return defendants. Commonly called "bounty hunters," bonds agents have greater powers than police officers in the pursuit of bond jumpers.

Alternatives to Cash Bond

Despite the widespread use of the bail bond system, there are criticisms of it and of the conduct of bail bonds agents in returning bond jumpers. One of the primary criticisms is that even with fees at 10% of the total bond, the bail bond system still discriminates against the poor, and a disproportionate number of the poor who are accused of crimes and have bail set are persons of color. Charges of institutionalized racial discrimination have led both federal and state courts to implement a number of alternatives to the cash bond system.

Release on recognizance (ROR) means to secure the pretrial release of the accused based merely on the defendant's unsecured promise that he or she will return for trial. The success of the program has caused many states to adopt the use of ROR. The provision is most appropriate for nonviolent offenses when the defendant has ties to the community and is not a flight risk.

Unsecured bond and signature bond are pretrial release systems that allow the defendant to be released on his or her promise to return for trial. An **unsecured bond** releases the defendant from incarceration after he or she signs a promissory note to pay the court a predetermined amount similar to a cash bail bond if he or she does not fulfill this promise.

A **signature bond** is commonly used for minor offenses such as traffic law violations. It is similar to ROR but much simpler. There are no prequalifications for a signature bond, and no one makes an assessment of the defendant's flight risk or danger to the community. A signature bond allows the police officers, acting as agents of the court, to release the accused immediately after he or she is charged with the offense if he or she signs a promise to appear in court. When a law enforcement officer asks a motorist to sign a traffic citation, the motorist's signature is not a confession of guilt, but a promise to appear in court. If the motorist does not sign the citation, he or she forfeits the right to a signature bond and the law enforcement officer has the authority

jumped bond Failed to appear for a court appearance.

release on recognizance (ROR) To secure the pretrial release of the accused based merely on the defendant's unsecured promise to appear at trial.

unsecured bond Bond that releases the defendant based on his or her signing a promissory note agreeing to pay the court an amount similar to a cash bail bond if he or she fails to fulfill the promise to appear at trial.

signature bond Bond that releases the defendant based on his or her signature on a promise to appear in court, usually for minor offenses such as traffic violations.

conditional release A bail alternative in which the defendant is released from custody if he or she agrees to court-ordered terms and restrictions.

50% The percentage of people arrested who are released within 24 hours.

to take the motorist into custody. After booking, the motorist will be required to post bond to be released from custody.

Conditional release and third-party custody are interesting alternatives to cash bail. Conditional release and a closely related type of bail, called supervision release, require the defendant to agree to a number of court-ordered terms and restrictions. Common terms of conditional release include participation in drug or alcohol treatment programs, attendance at anger management classes, compliance with a restraining order, and regular employment. Supervision release has the additional stipulation that the defendant, similar to someone on parole or probation, must report to an officer of the court at regular intervals. Third-party custody allows the court to release a pretrial defendant to the custody of an individual or agency that promises to be responsible for the defendant's behavior and to guarantee his or her participation in the legal process. The two most common conditions are placing a defendant with his or her family or with attorneys who assume responsibility for their clients. Youthful offenders are most likely to be placed with their families. An adult member of the family assumes responsibility for a defendant's day-to-day behavior and appearances at scheduled court appointments.

Pros and Cons of Bail

Whereas 50% of individuals who are arrested are released from jail within 24 hours, approximately 28% are not released until one week after their arrest and 10% remain incarcerated after one month of their arrest. For those who will not be prosecuted (recall that about 25% of those arrested will not be prosecuted), 1 to 30 days or more in prison can be a significant burden. For those who have been wrongly arrested, spending from 1 to 30 days in jail while waiting for dismissal of the charges can seem unfair and unnecessarily punitive. Thus, there are important reasons for an effective bail system and alternatives to traditional cash bails.

▶ Plea Bargaining

Another pretrial activity is **plea bargaining**, and 97% of federal cases and 94% of state cases are disposed of by this method without ever going to trial.[9] Justice Anthony Kennedy said of the plea bargaining process, "Plea bargaining is not some adjunct to the criminal justice system; it is the criminal justice system."[10]

Both the police and the victim often object to the practice of plea bargaining, but the prosecutor must make the best use of the resources of his or her office. The police and the victim object to plea bargaining on the grounds that the offender typically is not punished to the fullest extent of the law. After working to gather the necessary evidence and witnesses to help convict the defendant, law enforcement officers would like to see the defendant prosecuted on the most serious charges. Victims often want the same thing, but often for revenge or retribution or satisfaction that justice has been provided. Yet, prosecutors often decide to offer defendants the opportunity to plead guilty to lesser charges.

Time and Cost

One reason for a plea deal is that preparation for trial is a time-consuming and costly endeavor. The prosecutor's office has the responsibility for trial preparation and bears the majority of the costs associated with gathering evidence, interviewing witnesses, and handling other preparations. Most prosecutors have only a limited staff and budget and cannot take every case to trial. Furthermore, the court has only so much time to hear cases. Thus, the prosecutor's office must select which defendants to take to trial and to which defendants to offer plea bargains. Many offenses are settled by plea bargains, whereas a small percentage of defendants are convicted by trial. With few exceptions, plea bargaining is an integral part of the path in a criminal trial because it keeps the costs of justice affordable.

Community Interest

In deciding whether to offer or accept a plea to a lesser charge, the prosecutor must make an important professional decision as to how to best serve community interests with the limited departmental resources. A plea bargain guarantees a guilty verdict. The prosecutor wins a conviction in approximately 80% of the cases that are taken to trial, but without plea bargaining, the prosecutor would not be able to devote the personnel and resources necessary to prepare for trial in these cases. Thus, plea bargaining helps free up time for more difficult cases. Also, without plea bargaining, the prosecutor risks a substantial investment in time and resources, only

According to Justice Anthony Kennedy, "[p]lea bargaining is not some adjunct to the criminal justice system; it is the criminal justice system."

to have the defendant found not guilty, avoiding all punishment. A guilty plea obtained by a plea bargain ensures that the defendant will have a criminal record and will receive some punishment or treatment.

The irony is that career criminals seem to benefit more from this practice than do minor criminals or the innocent. Obviously, the innocent can only be harmed by the practice of plea bargaining. For fear of being wrongfully convicted and executed, a defendant accused of a serious crime (capital murder, for instance) who is not guilty may be tempted to accept or offer a plea bargain for a lesser crime that does not carry the threat of the death penalty. Plea bargaining most benefits major criminals, such as the burglar who has committed 300 burglaries, the serial rapist who has committed numerous sexual assaults, and the drug dealer who has constantly engaged in drug trafficking.

Clearing Cases

The prosecutor might not have sufficient evidence to convict a career burglar for all of the burglaries he or she committed and might not even know about all of them. One of the reasons the prosecutor may offer a plea bargain to a career criminal is for the purpose of **clearing cases**. If the prosecutor agrees to charge the defendant with only a single burglary in return for a confession to 300 burglaries, what does the prosecutor gain? First, the prosecutor and the police are able to "clear" the 299 burglaries, even though the defendant is not prosecuted for them. By accepting this offer, the police and the prosecutor can report a higher clearance rate to the public. Second, the prosecutor knows that even if a defendant is convicted of multiple offenses, he or she may end up serving the prison sentences concurrently instead of consecutively. Thus, the extra time and effort required to obtain the multiple convictions may make little difference in the actual outcome.

Questionable Confidence in the Case

Finally, the prosecutor might not be completely confident of the evidence or witnesses. Perhaps the prosecutor believes that at the last moment a victim may refuse to testify. Witnesses to crimes committed by gang members or organized crime figures may become concerned about their safety or the safety of their families, for instance, and may refuse to testify or may give weak and inconclusive evidence. A young witness, especially a child, may pose special difficulties for the prosecutor. In other instances, the prosecutor might believe that the reputation of the arresting police officer or reliability of evidence gathered by the police will not stand up to cross-examination. Any of these reasons may make the prosecutor reluctant to take the case to trial.

Initiation of Plea Bargaining

Plea bargaining can be initiated by the prosecuting or defending attorney at many different points in the criminal justice process up until the jury renders a verdict. Plea bargaining can center on the charges or the sentence. At arrest, the police and prosecutor typically charge the defendant with as many crimes

as possible, beginning with the most serious one. In return for dropping the more serious charges, the defendant offers his or her guilty plea. Plea bargaining can involve the police, prosecutor, judge, and defense counsel, but seldom involves the victim. In some cases, the victim is not even informed of the decision to accept a plea bargain. The defendant may provide the police with information regarding other criminals or crimes in return for his or her help in convincing the prosecutor to accept the defendant's plea bargain. The defendant may not have been the principal offender and may offer to testify against other defendants in exchange for a plea bargain. Plea bargains for testimony against fellow partners in crime is risky, however, because the information often is unconvincing to a jury.

Sentence Bargaining

In **sentence bargaining**, the defendant seeks leniency. Sentences can range from probation to life imprisonment. The defendant may offer to plead guilty to the charges in return for the prosecutor's recommendation to the judge for a minimum sentence. A sentence of probation, even a long period of probation, is preferable to hard time in prison. Some defendants want to negotiate about where they will serve their time, what type of facility it is, or what its security level is. Because they control the charges to be filed against the defendant, prosecutors can bargain for reduction of the charges directly. However, the judge has control over the sentence; so sentence bargaining frequently involves pretrial negotiation between the prosecutor, defense counsel, and judge. Although the prosecutor and the defense may propose plea bargains, the judge must approve of any negotiated guilty plea to ensure that the rights of the defendant are protected. Thus, it is contrary to the ethics of the court for judges to initiate plea bargains or to encourage a defendant to agree to a plea bargain. The standards of the American Bar Association recommend that the "trial judge should not participate in plea discussions."[11] The Federal Rules of Criminal Procedure also state that the court should not participate in negotiating guilty pleas.[12] Some states have similar prohibitions.

Effective Counsel in Plea-Bargaining Law

In *Gideon* v. *Wainwright* (1963), the U.S. Supreme Court ruled that defendants have the right to counsel at critical points in the criminal justice process. The Court did not include pretrial negotiations as a critical point at which defendants had the guarantee of counsel. In 2012, the Court revised the right to effective counsel in **Missouri v. Frye**, No. 10-444, and **Lafler v. Cooper**, No. 10-209, and extended the constitutional rights of criminal defendants to effective counsel during plea negotiations.

In the majority opinion, Justice Anthony Kennedy wrote, "The right to adequate assistance of counsel cannot be defined or enforced without taking account of the central role plea bargaining takes in securing convictions and determining sentences." These rulings will have a significant impact on the criminal justice system because they open the door for defendants who believe their lawyers failed to secure them the best possible plea bargain, failed to inform them of a plea bargain offer, or failed to provide effective counsel in advising them

Think About It . . .

The requirement of a unanimous verdict in a civil criminal trial is not a constitutional requirement or a universal practice. For example, the U.S. Uniform Code of Military Justice does not require a unanimous verdict for criminal military trials. If a jury cannot reach a unanimous verdict, the judge declares a mistrial due to a hung jury and the government has the option of retrying the case. When the 2010 trial of former Illinois governor Rod Blagojevich ended in a hung jury, the government retried the case and obtained guilty verdicts on 17 counts of corruption. The 2012 trial of former presidential candidate John Edwards also ended in a hung jury, but the government decided not to retry the case.

Trials are expensive, and high-profile trials can cost millions of dollars to prosecute. To avoid hung juries, should less than a unanimous verdict be required for a guilty verdict? Why or why not?

whether to take a plea bargain or appeal a conviction to the Supreme Court.

The cases are controversial in they appear to guarantee the defendant not a fair trial, but the most favorable outcome possible.[13] This concern is highlighted by the tendency for longer mandatory sentencing. Many states have adopted harsh penalties that make plea bargains appear "attractive" as the defendant may be looking at a 2-year prison term offered by a plea bargain or a 50-year prison term if found guilty at trial.[14] The phenomenon is referred to as **trial penalty**. Trial penalty refers to the fact that the sentences for people who go to trial have grown harsher relative to sentences for those who agree to a plea.[15] In some jurisdictions, the gap has widened so much that it has become coercive and is used to punish defendants for exercising their right to trial, some legal experts say.[16] Given this concern, the constitutional right to effective counsel during pretrial negotiations is critical to ensuring justice and due process.

> The sentences for people who go to trial have grown harsher relative to sentences for those who agree to a plea.

▶ The Right to a Speedy Trial

After arraignment—assuming that the defendant is competent to stand trial, no alternative diversion is offered, and no plea bargain is struck—the case proceeds forward in the criminal justice process. It becomes one of the few arrests that actually results in a criminal trial. For a case to come to trial, it must be placed on the **court docket**, or calendar. Attorneys, defendants, and courtroom personnel must know when the case is scheduled for trial and how long the trial is expected to last because the demand for judges and courtrooms exceeds the limited resources of the criminal justice system.

Defendants released on bail, especially when guilty, may want to postpone their day in court as long as possible. However, the actual time a defendant must wait for his or her day in court is not left to the defendant or the government. The Sixth Amendment of the Constitution guarantees that defendants will receive a speedy trial, but the Constitution does not define what constitutes "speedy." The right to a speedy trial is not the same as the statute of limitations. The **statute of limitations** is the length of time between the discovery of the crime and the arrest of the defendant. Various crimes have different acceptable lengths of time between the crime and the arrest. Usually, less serious crimes have a shorter period for prosecuting the defendant, and more serious crimes have longer periods. Customarily, there is no statute of limitations for the crime of murder.

The Sixth Amendment Right to a Speedy Trial

Like other amendments in the Bill of Rights, the Sixth Amendment right to a speedy trial originally extended only to federal crimes in federal courts. Not until 1967 did the Supreme Court incorporate the Sixth Amendment (that is, made the Sixth Amendment applicable to state courts as well). Before then, states did not have to provide a speedy trial unless guaranteed by the state constitution.[17] The definition of speedy trial differed substantially among states. Some states required that the trial take place in less than two months, and others allowed a case to come to trial years after the defendant was arrested. Initially, the Supreme Court did not provide specific guidelines to help determine what constitutes a speedy trial. The Court took the view that a speedy trial is a relative matter and may vary in length of time from arrest to trial because of the circumstances of the case.[18]

Klopfer v. North Carolina

The judicial interpretation of the right to a speedy trial changed dramatically in the late 1960s and early 1970s, beginning with the 1967 case of **Klopfer v. North Carolina**[19]. Peter Klopfer, a professor at Duke University, was arrested for trespassing while engaged in a sit-in at a segregated motel and restaurant. Klopfer initially was tried for trespassing, which resulted in a hung jury. In such cases, the state has the right to retry the defendant. The prosecutor decided not to bring the case to trial, but at the same time refused to dismiss the charges

 LEARNING OUTCOMES 5 — Explain the right to a speedy trial.

GLOSSARY

court docket The schedule of cases and hearings.

statute of limitations The length of time between the discovery of the crime and the arrest of the defendant.

Klopfer v. North Carolina The case that requires states to grant defendants a speedy trial.

Barker v. Wingo The case in which the court ruled that the defendant's failure to request a speedy trial does not negate the defendant's right to a speedy trial.

Speedy Trial Act of 1974 The act that requires a specific deadline between arrest and trial in federal courts.

In 2011, the New Jersey Supreme Court adopted new rules regarding eyewitness testimony. The New Jersey Court required judges to hold a hearing to consider a broad range of issues related to the reliability of eyewitness identification and to give detailed explanations to jurors on influences that could heighten the risk of misidentification.[21]

In *Perry* v. *New Hampshire* (2012), the defendant appealed his conviction in which disputed eyewitness identification played a significant role in his conviction to the U.S. Supreme Court. The appeal requested that the U.S. Supreme Court require similar standards to those in New Jersey for all eyewitness evidence. The appeal cited 2,000 studies demonstrating that eyewitness misidentification is the single greatest cause of wrongful convictions.

The Supreme Court declined to require special instructions for eyewitness evidence based on the reason that "the jury, not the judge, traditionally determines the reliability of evidence."[22] Do you agree with the U.S. Supreme Court's decision that the jury is competent enough to judge the reliability of eyewitness testimony without special instructions? Explain.

Junial Enterprises/Fotolia

2,000 The number of studies demonstrating that eyewitness misidentification is the single greatest cause of wrongful convictions.

against Klopfer. The laws of North Carolina allowed the prosecutor to postpone a trial indefinitely, even over the defendant's demand for a speedy trial. At the time, North Carolina did not guarantee defendants the right to a speedy trial.

Thus, Klopfer was left in a state of legal limbo. At any time, the prosecutor could decide to reactivate the criminal charges against the defendant, and the defendant had no recourse for lack of a speedy trial. The prosecutor used this uncertainty as a strategy to detour Klopfer from further participation in civil rights protests under the threat that further participation would result in a new trial for the old trespassing charges. Klopfer's case was appealed to the U.S. Supreme Court on the grounds that North Carolina denied him his constitutional rights. On appeal, the Supreme Court agreed and declared the North Carolina law unconstitutional. The right to a speedy trial was incorporated in or extended to state courts, and spurred by the *Klopfer* case, many states adopted speedy trial legislation. The Sixth Amendment right applies even if a defendant, for whatever reason, does not object to a delay. In 1972, in **Barker v. Wingo**, the Supreme Court issued a ruling that a defendant's failure to demand a speedy trial does not amount to a waiver of the Sixth Amendment right.[20]

Although guaranteeing the right to a speedy trial, the Sixth Amendment does not specify the remedy if this right is denied. If a defendant is denied a speedy trial, what should the court do? After the *Klopfer* v. *North Carolina* ruling that extended this right to state courts, the Supreme Court found it necessary to review cases in which some state defendants failed to receive a speedy trial. In 1973, the Supreme Court decided that the remedy applied when a defendant does not receive a speedy trial is permanent dismissal of the charges against the defendant; subsequently, the prosecutor will not be allowed to bring these charges against the defendant. However, the Court also ruled

that delays caused by the defendant's actions, such as requests for postponement and claims related to competency to stand trial, cannot be considered denial of the right to a speedy trial.

The Speedy Trial Act of 1974

These Supreme Court rulings caused both federal and state courts to change the way they did business. Previously, prosecutors could select some cases for prosecution and leave others to a later time without any concern for the delay in bringing a case to trial. After the Supreme Court's ruling, prosecutors had to be mindful of bringing all cases to trial in a timely manner or risk losing the ability to prosecute. The Speedy Trial Act of 1974 turned this concern into a crisis. The **Speedy Trial Act of 1974** required a specific deadline between arrest and trial in federal courts. Fully implemented in 1980, the act required that, except in a few well-defined situations and barring delays created by the defendant, the defendant would be brought to trial within 100 days of his or her arrest or the charges could be dismissed and could not be reinstated. When a federal defendant is charged with a crime, the clock starts and the prosecutor has 30 days to seek an indictment or formally charge the defendant with a violation of the law. If the defendant is indicted, the prosecutor has 70 days after the indictment or information to start the trial.[23] The clock is stopped for delays attributable to the defendant, such as postponements or escape to avoid prosecution. The clock may not stop when the delay is attributable to the prosecutor, however, even if the delays are beyond the prosecutor's control.

▶ Rules of Evidence

The rules of evidence govern the process of the criminal trial. Each court is governed by certain rules of evidence. **Rules of evidence**

LEARNING OUTCOMES 6 Describe the participants and the process of the criminal trial.

GLOSSARY

rules of evidence Administrative court rules governing the admissibility of evidence in a trial.

contempt of court A charge against any violator of the judge's courtroom rules, authorizing the judge to impose a fine or term of imprisonment.

gag order A judge's order to participants and observers at a trial that the evidence and proceedings of the court may not be published, broadcast, or discussed publicly.

The Judge

Witnesses

Witnesses There are two types of witnesses: lay and expert. Lay witnesses can testify to what they saw, heard, felt, smelled, or otherwise directly experienced. Lay witnesses cannot provide testimony as to the motivation of the defendant. Expert witnesses can testify as to conclusions or hypothetical questions based on scientific certainty, the cause of death, or the identity of an unknown substance that was tested.

The Judge is a central figure in the trial and is a neutral party. His or her role is similar to that of a referee at a sports game. The judge determines what evidence can be presented at the trial, which witnesses can testify and about what, and when there will be courtroom breaks. The judge has authority over courtroom personnel, attorneys, the jury, members of the media, and the public in the courtroom.

The Jury

The Clerk of Court

The Court Reporter

The Jury decides if the evidence and witnesses prove beyond a reasonable doubt the guilt of the defendant. This is an awesome responsibility, and it is given to 12 laypersons. The jury hears evidence from the prosecution and the defense and decides which is more credible. If the defendant pleads not guilty by reason of insanity, the jury decides whether the defendant was insane.

The Clerk of Court works directly with the trial judge and is responsible for court records and paperwork both before and after the trial. Usually, each judge has his or her own clerk of court. The clerk of court issues summonses and subpoenas for witnesses, receives pleas and motions and forwards them to the judge for consideration, and prepares all case files that a judge will need for the day. During the trial, the clerk of court records and marks physical evidence introduced in the trial and swears in the witnesses.

The Court Reporter, also called the court recorder, transcribes every word spoken by the judge, attorneys, and witnesses during the trial. He or she is responsible for making a permanent written record of the court's proceedings.

The Bailiff

The Bailiff is usually a county deputy sheriff or a U.S. Deputy Marshal. The county sheriff is responsible for providing bailiffs for court security for state courts, and a U.S. Marshal is responsible for providing court security for federal courts. The bailiff is an armed law enforcement officer who has the power of arrest and the power to use deadly force if necessary. For most bailiffs, courtroom security consists of escorting the jury in and out of the courtroom and maintaining order in the court at the direction of the judge.

The Defense

The Prosecutor

The Prosecutor is not an employee of the court, but does represent the government. The prosecutor brings charges against the defendant, gathers evidence necessary to prosecute the defendant, and presents evidence at trial. The prosecutor's primary goal is not to convict the defendant but to see that the person who committed the crime is brought to justice and to demonstrate to the court that the evidence supports a conviction beyond a reasonable doubt.

The Defendant is the person accused of committing a crime in a criminal case. The defendant may choose to assist in his or her defense or may choose to remain passive and let the defense attorney handle the case.

The Defense Attorney In any criminal trial in which the maximum punishment exceeds six months in prison, the defendant is entitled to a jury trial and the right to be represented by an attorney. There are two types of defense attorneys: public defenders and private defense attorneys. The defendant may hire any defense attorney registered to practice law before the court and as many private defense attorneys as he or she can afford. If the defendant cannot afford to hire a private defense attorney, the court will appoint and pay for an attorney to represent the defendant. In rare cases, the defendant may choose not to have a defense attorney but to represent himself or herself.

are procedural laws or administrative rules that influence law enforcement and court practices. Rules of evidence define how the trial will be conducted, how evidence will be introduced, how the parties to the trial will act, and what the order of the proceedings will be. Deviation from rules of evidence constitutes a judicial error, which leads to appeals. If a rule of evidence is violated, the prosecution or the defense can appeal the case. If an appeals court finds that the violation is a serious breach of the rules and could have influenced the outcome of the trial, the defendant has not received a fair trial.

Each state court and the federal courts have different rules of evidence. To represent clients in a particular court, attorneys are

Many people are involved in making a criminal trial possible. Those present at the trial can be divided into the four groups shown below.

1. Government employees responsible for the business of the court

2. The defendant and his or her legal counsel

3. The jury

4. Witnesses (including the victim). Note that the only role the victim has in the trial is that of a witness.

required to demonstrate that they have competent knowledge of the rules of evidence for the court hearing the case. To represent a client in a court of appeals or the state or federal Supreme Court, attorneys may need to pass an examination on the rules of evidence.

Usually, attorneys qualify for practice in state trial courts of limited and general jurisdiction by virtue of their good standing in the state bar association. However, the federal trial courts have different rules of evidence, requiring that the lawyer demonstrate competency in these rules before he or she can present a case in federal court.

The rules of evidence regulate nearly every aspect of the trial. Rules of evidence can be mundane, such as the rule that only the original of a document can be introduced as evidence. In addition, rules of evidence determine what evidence is relevant, what evidence is permissible, what evidence cannot be introduced, what evidence an expert witness may present to the jury, what questions can be asked of witnesses, and what is required before an item of physical evidence can be introduced at the trial.

If during the trial the prosecutor or defense counsel believes that a rule of evidence has been violated, he or she has a duty to raise objections to the judge. To do this, the attorney says, "I object on the grounds that…." For example, if the prosecution

> **bench trial** A trial in which the judge rather than a jury makes the determination of guilt.
>
> **bailiffs** The people who provide courtroom security. Deputy sheriffs provide security for state courts, and Deputy U.S. Marshals provide security for federal courts.
>
> **indigent defense** A defense counsel provided for a defendant who cannot afford a private attorney.
>
> **Taylor v. Louisiana** The case that ruled that the exclusion of women from jury duty created an imbalance in the jury pool.

asks a witness a question that the defense believes the witness is not competent to answer, the defense attorney objects on the grounds that the question calls for the witness to make a conclusion that he or she is not competent to make. Objections include questions that are not relevant to the present case or that call for the witness to comment about the mental state of the defendant (for example, whether the defendant was angry). If the judge agrees, he or she declares that the objection is sustained and the witness is instructed not to answer the question or the evidence will not be presented to the jury. If the judge does not agree, he or she overrules the objection. After the trial, the case can be appealed if the prosecution or defense believes the judge made a judicial error.

▶ Duties and Rights of Participants

Power of the Judge

The power of the judge lies in his or her absolute and immediate ability to fine or imprison people for contempt of court. If the judge believes an attorney, either defense or prosecution, or any other participant in the trial or audience has violated a professional standard of conduct during the trial, he or she can impose a fine or term of imprisonment for **contempt of court**. For attorneys, unprofessional conduct includes being late for court, continuing to argue with the judge when told to stop, or being guilty of more serious violations with regard to witness and evidence integrity. It is difficult to appeal a contempt of court decree. Contempt of court is not a crime; thus, the person does not have the same rights as a defendant accused of a crime. Contempt of

Think About It …

Judges, prosecutors, and defense attorneys practice what is known as "public law," and they comprise a minority of lawyers. The path to becoming a lawyer is similar for both public and private attorneys. Attorneys must successfully complete two to three years of postgraduate law school. After law school, to become a licensed attorney, graduates must pass the state bar examination in the state in which they want to practice. Some states require hours of public service before the law school graduate can be admitted to the State Bar Association, a requirement to practice law.[25] Admission is very competitive and based in part on one's undergraduate grade point average and score on the Law School Admission Test (LSAT).

George Wada/Fotolia

There are many civil service positions for attorneys, but those who want to become prosecutors or judges frequently must obtain their office by political election. Defense attorneys are either public defenders employed by the government or private defense attorneys. Those who practice public law, including judges, often make less money than those who go into private practice. Public defenders make the least, with a national average of $40,976 to $78,987. Would you consider public law as a career? Why or why not?

court can bring substantial penalties. For example, witnesses who will not testify may be held in prison for up to two years.[24]

The public, the jury, and the members of the media may be fined or imprisoned for contempt of court. If people in the courtroom are unruly, the judge can impose a fine or hold them in jail for contempt of court. The power of the judge even extends to appropriate dress of people in the courtroom. Jury members can be fined or imprisoned for violating the orders of the judge not to discuss the case. The media most often run afoul of the judge's authority by violating a **gag order**—an order that the evidence, the witnesses, or proceedings of the court may not be published or discussed publicly. If disclosure of evidence or testimony may jeopardize the defendant's chance at receiving a fair trial, the judge has the authority to order all parties to refrain from discussing or publishing this information. Members of the media who violate this order can be held in contempt of court.

Bench Trial

The judge's role can be complicated in a **bench trial** when the judge, not a jury, determines whether the defendant is guilty. In a bench trial, the judge must act as impartial mediator during the trial and, at the conclusion of the trial, must make a determination of guilt. Some states prohibit bench trials in cases involving serious felonies.

Courtroom Security

Courtroom security is provided by sheriff's deputies in state courts and by deputy U.S. Marshals in federal courts. When acting in the role of courtroom security, both are called **bailiffs**. The parties before the court are often emotionally charged, and judges and court personnel often express concerns that security may not be adequate to ensure their safety. Although security checkpoints and metal detectors enhance the security of the court, there is still the ever-present threat to court personnel. Several high-profile security incidents in 2005 emphasized the serious security threats that bailiffs face. One, in Atlanta, Georgia, on March 11, 2005, Brian Nichols, aged 34, on trial for rape and kidnapping, grabbed a gun from a sheriff's deputy during the trial and began shooting in the courtroom. He killed Superior Court Judge Rowland Barnes and his court reporter.

4 million

The number of indigent defenses a year at a cost of $1 million.

While escaping from the courthouse, Nichols killed another deputy who had confronted him, as well as a federal customs agent. The incident sparked concern for improved court security and more security personnel.

The Defendant

The defendant does not have to testify during the trial, and the prosecutor cannot indicate that the defendant's choice not to testify might show that he or she is guilty. The defendant may actively assist his or her attorney or may remain passive during the trial. In some cases, the defendant may be his or her own attorney. If the court deems the defendant competent, even if the defendant has no formal legal training or license, in some cases, he or she may represent himself or herself. In some states, even if a defendant represents himself or herself, an attorney is appointed to assist the defendant in his or her defense. The courts discourage defendants from representing themselves.

Indigent Defendants

A defendant who cannot afford a private attorney is known as an indigent defendant. When a defendant is charged with a crime, a judge inquires as to the defendant's ability to afford an attorney. Defendants indicating that they cannot afford an attorney are required to complete a financial statement and submit it to the court. The court examines the defendant's finances and decides if the defendant is eligible for an indigent defense. About half of all criminal defendants accused of a felony crime cannot afford an attorney, and for larger counties, this number increases to 80%.[26] **Indigent defense** services represent a substantial expense in the criminal justice system. For example, the largest 100 counties handle over 4 million indigent defenses a year at a cost of over $1 billion.[27]

Jury Service

Jurors are citizens required by law to perform jury duty. The court wants jurors who are fair, competent, and able to serve. Major challenges for the court include selecting a fair and competent jury and deciding whether excuses given by citizens who do not want to serve on the jury are legitimate.

Junial Enterprises/Fotolia

Jury of One's Peers

The Constitution requires that defendants be tried by a jury of their peers. The Supreme Court has not interpreted this literally, however. A white middle-class man does not get a trial by a jury of white middle-class men. Rather, the jury pool is selected from a broad base of citizens who are representatives of the community, not the specific characteristics of the defendant. Many jurisdictions have used voter registration lists as the pool from which to select jurors. Studies have clearly demonstrated, however, that this pool of candidates is biased because voter registration lists underrepresent minorities and people with lower income.[28] The current practice in many courts is to select jurors from more representative sources, such as licensed drivers, people with state identification cards, and even people with published telephone numbers.

Exemptions from Jury Duty

Citizens are paid for jury duty by the government, but the rate of pay is very low, ranging from only a few dollars to $40 per day. Most jurors serve for short periods but may be asked to serve longer; for some jurors, even a few days impose a severe hardship. Also, some citizens may not be competent to serve as jurors. For these and other reasons, the court may excuse citizens from jury duty. Each jurisdiction determines the rules for excusing citizens from jury service, but the rules must not discriminate against a person because of race, gender, or other characteristics that are in violation of the law. For example, until 1975, many states automatically excluded women, especially women with children at home, from jury duty. In **Taylor v. Louisiana** (1975), the Supreme Court decided that the exclusion of women from jury duty created an imbalance in the jury pool and was not justified.[29] Legitimate reasons for being excused from jury duty include illness, conviction of a felony crime, personal interest in the case, and an inability to understand English. Members of certain professional groups, such as physicians, may be excluded from jury duty based on the reasoning that jury service would be detrimental to community safety. Other members of professional groups, such as attorneys, police officers, and legislators, may be excluded from jury duty based on the reasoning that they may not be able to be neutral and make decisions based only on the evidence presented in court. However, in many states, these criminal justice personnel are not excused from jury duty and the court depends on the *voir dire* process to eliminate potential jurors who may be biased. Most jurisdictions require jury service only once a year.

> Legitimate reasons for being excused from jury duty include illness, conviction of a felony crime, personal interest in the case, and an inability to understand English.

Jury Requirements

Although essential to ensuring a fair and public trial by one's peers, jury duty is disdained by some people. Thus, the court must ensure that despite any reluctance by citizens to respond to a summons for jury duty, those who are called do serve. As a result, there are penalties, including fines and jail time, for those who unlawfully avoid jury duty and for anyone, such as employers, who interfere with, intimidate, or threaten citizens to prevent them from fulfilling their civic duties.

The Constitution does not require a jury of 12 people. This number is a tradition but not a legal requirement, and obtaining 12 people to serve on a jury can be a challenge. All states require 12 jurors for capital cases, and all but six states require 12 jurors for felony trials. Fourteen states allow misdemeanor trials with only six jurors. Other states allow criminal trials with a jury of seven or eight.[30]

▶ Conclusion—Justice Is the Goal

Police charges against a defendant are merely suggestions to the prosecutor. The prosecutor's charges at arraignment are but a hope. The decision of guilt is decided at a trial. Despite a constitutional guarantee of a trial by jury, over 90% of those charged with felony crimes choose to forgo this procedure and plead guilty. A great number of professionals come together to make a trial possible. In the American judicial system, the trial is a conflict between the prosecutor and the defense. At the trial, the playing field is not level, but is tipped in favor of the defendant by design. The U.S. judicial system recognizes the incredible power of the state compared to the limited resources of the accused; therefore, it provides a number of opportunities to balance the power between the state and the defendant. Thus, even if the defendant is convicted, he or she has the right to appeal, a right denied to prosecutors if they lose the case. The procedure and rules of the trial are well defined, but the strategy and risk that go into the decision making and presentation of evidence are left to the professional judgment of the participants in the trial. Despite the differences among the various courts, all work toward a common objective—justice.

Plea Bargaining

In the landmark case of *Gideon* v. *Wainwright* (1963), the U.S. Supreme Court guaranteed defendants the right to counsel during critical points in the criminal justice process. In 1963, plea bargaining was not considered a critical point at which the defense was entitled to effective counsel. Plea bargains were often verbal agreements made in informal settings.

Two 2012 cases have changed the landscape of plea bargaining and the criminal justice system: *Missouri* v. *Frye*, No. 10-444, and *Lafler* v. *Cooper*, No. 10-209. The decisions affirm a defendant's right under the Sixth Amendment to have the assistance of an effective lawyer during pretrial negotiations. These decisions acknowledge the fact that in the modern criminal justice system, 97% of federal cases and 94% of state cases are disposed of by a plea bargain. Justice Anthony Kennedy said in the majority opinion, "Criminal justice today is for the most part a system of pleas, not a system of trials."

As a result of these decisions, a defendant may be entitled to a court remedy if his or her attorney fails to provide effective counsel during the pretrial process. In the *Frye* case, Galin Frye's attorney failed to tell his client of a plea bargain offer, resulting in Frye receiving a sentence of three years compared to the plea bargain offer of a 90-day sentence. In the *Cooper* case, Anthony Cooper rejected a plea bargain based on bad legal advice from his attorney.

The cases have created more confusion than clarity as to the rights of the defendant. The Court's decision does not provide clear-cut guidelines as to what is "effective counsel," and the remedy is not clearly defined. Justice Kennedy suggested that the proper remedy is to require that the plea deal be reoffered.

This case raises several interesting questions. Among them are the following:

1. How should the courts handle the flood of postconviction appeals from defendants who will claim that they did not receive effective counsel during their pretrial bargaining?

2. If a defendant admits his or her guilt in exchange for a lesser sentence, has the defendant received a fair trial regardless of whether he or she could have received a lesser sentence through a plea bargain? Explain.

Design Pics Inc./Alamy

Describe the jurisdiction of the courts.

The authority of a court within a specific geographic jurisdiction to conduct a trial is called jurisdiction. Cases involving violations of federal law are heard in district court. Misdemeanor violations of state laws are heard in courts of limited jurisdiction, whereas felonies trials are held in state courts of general jurisdiction. The Fifth Amendment prohibits trying a person twice for the same offense unless that offense violated both federal and state law. Being able to try a defendant in both state and federal courts can serve as checks and balances in the criminal justice system. Should a state court fail to provide equal and fair justice for a victim of a civil rights violation, the federal court may file charges against the defendant even if the defendant was acquitted at the state court level.

1. Which court has jurisdiction to conduct trials for violating federal statutes?

2. What is meant by the term *double jeopardy*?

3. Explain why criminal trials are so complex.

4. Is it considered double jeopardy to try a defendant in two or more states for the same crime? Why or why not?

jurisdiction The authority of the court to try a case. Usually, jurisdiction is established when some part of the crime was committed within the geographic jurisdiction of the district court.

courts of limited jurisdiction Courts that handle misdemeanor crimes, violations of criminal traffic laws, and lesser offenses.

courts of general jurisdiction Courts that handle felony crimes.

double jeopardy The act of trying a person twice for the same offense.

Describe pretrial proceedings and the process of developing charges for the arraignment hearing.

Law enforcement and the prosecution are autonomous criminal justice agencies, but in most cases, they work together to determine the charges to be brought against the defendant. In some cases, the prosecutor may use the grand jury to obtain an arrest warrant rather than have the police arrest the suspect on probable cause. The Constitution requires that before trial, a defendant must be informed of the charges brought against him or her. The defendant is arraigned in a federal or state court that will have jurisdiction over the case. Prior to trial, a judge establishes the defendant's competency to stand trial.

1. Explain what proceedings take place at an arraignment.

2. What options does a prosecutor have in modifying charges alleged by the police?

3. What happens if a defendant is deemed incompetent to stand trial?

due process Court rules that define the standards for a "fair" trial.

prosecutorial discretion The power of a prosecutor to decide whether to charge a defendant and what the charge(s) will be, as well as to gather the evidence necessary to prosecute the defendant in a court of law.

grand jury An alternative method, which is confidential, to determine whether there is sufficient evidence to charge the defendant with a crime.

arraignment A criminal proceeding where the defendant is formally charged with a crime and is asked to enter a plea.

competent to stand trial The defendant's ability to comprehend the charges against him or her and to assist counsel in his or her defense.

Summarize the purpose of bail and the various forms of bail.

The Eighth Amendment of the Constitution recognizes the concept of bail and the fact that bail should not be excessive. Both state and federal courts have recognized that the right to bail is not guaranteed, and under some circumstances, it can be denied. Knowing that a cash bail system might discriminate against the poor, the judiciary has established alternatives to cash bonds. These alternatives involve a release on recognizance (ROR), a signature bond, and a conditional release. A conditional release calls for a supervised release, wherein the defendant agrees to court-ordered terms and restrictions.

1. What are the historical roots of the bail system?

2. Describe three controversial factors with regard to bail.

3. How does a bail bonds agent work?

4. Who issues a signature bond? What offenses might include this type of bond?

5. What percentage of people are released within 24 hours of arrest?

bail Temporary release of the defendant prior to trial.

excessive bail Bail that is prohibited by the Eighth Amendment, but there is no uniform standard as to what "excessive" is.

bail bonds agent An agent of a private commercial business that has contracted with the court to act as a guarantor of a defendant's return to court.

jumped bond Failed to appear for a court appearance.

release on recognizance (ROR) To secure the pretrial release of the accused based merely on the defendant's unsecured promise to appear at trial.

unsecured bond Bond that releases the defendant based on his or her signing a promissory note agreeing to pay the court an amount similar to a cash bail bond if he or she fails to fulfill the promise to appear at trial.

signature bond Bond that releases the defendant based on his or her signature on a promise to appear in court, usually for minor offenses such as traffic violations.

conditional release A bail alternative in which the defendant is released from custody if he or she agrees to court-ordered terms and restrictions.

Summarize the process of plea bargaining.

The prosecutor's office has the responsibility for trial preparation and bears the costs associated with gathering evidence, interviewing witnesses, and overseeing other pretrial arrangements. Plea bargaining plays an essential role in saving the courts time and money. Plea bargaining can focus on a reduction in the charges or the defendant's length of sentence. As a result of the plea bargaining process, a prosecutor may allow a defendant to plead guilty to lesser charges to avoid a trial. Sentencing for defendants who go to trial is more severe than sentences given to those who accept a plea offer.

1. Explain why plea bargaining is so crucial to the criminal justice system.

2. Cite reasons a prosecutor might offer a plea bargain to a career criminal.

3. Who is responsible for approving a plea agreement?

plea bargaining A pretrial activity that involves the negotiation between defendant and prosecutor for a plea of guilty for which in return the defendant will receive some benefit, such as reduction of charges or dismissal of some charges.

clearing cases In reference to the status of a criminal offense, knowing the perpetrator of the crime, as asserted by the police or prosecutor.

sentence bargaining Negotiating with the prosecutor for a reduction in length of sentence, reduction from capital murder to imprisonment, probation rather than incarceration, or institution where the sentence is to be served in return for a guilty plea.

Missouri* v. *Frye* and *Lafler* v. *Cooper The two cases that extended the constitutional rights of criminal defendants to effective counsel during plea negotiations.

trial penalty The fact that the sentences for people who go to trial have grown harsher relative to sentences for those who agree to a plea.

Explain the right to a speedy trial.

For a case to go to trial, it must be placed on a court docket, or calendar. Courtroom participants need to know when a case is scheduled to be heard because the demand for judges and courtrooms exceeds available resources. The Sixth Amendment provides that a defendant will receive a speedy trial, but the Constitution does not define what time frame constitutes a speedy trial. The Supreme Court has ruled that delays caused by the defendant, such as requests for postponement and claims related to competency to stand trial, cannot be considered denial of a speedy trial.

1. How does the right to a speedy trial differ from the statute of limitations?

2. How many days does a federal prosecutor have after indictment to start the trial?

3. What could be the outcome if a prosecutor failed to meet the speedy trial requirement?

court docket The schedule of cases and hearings.

statute of limitations The length of time between the discovery of the crime and the arrest of the defendant.

Klopfer* v. *North Carolina The act that requires states to grant defendants a speedy trial.

Barker* v. *Wingo The case in which the court ruled that the defendant's failure to request a speedy trial does not negate the defendant's right to a speedy trial.

Speedy Trial Act of 1974 The act that requires a specific deadline between arrest and trial in federal courts.

LEARNING OUTCOMES 6

Describe the participants and the process of the criminal trial.

Rules of evidence direct the process of the criminal trial. This affects how the trial will be conducted and how evidence will be introduced. If a rule of evidence is violated, the prosecutor or the defense attorney can appeal the case. If the judge believes that the prosecutor or the defense attorney has violated a professional standard of conduct during trial, the judge can impose a fine or term of imprisonment for contempt of court. In a bench trial, the judge determines the verdict. Bailiffs provide courtroom security for trials. A jury trial uses citizens who determine the guilt of the defendant, not the judge. The constitution does not require the jury to number 12 people.

1. How do the rules of evidence affect the admissibility of evidence at trial?

2. What happens when a judge imposes a gag order?

3. What is an indigent defense?

4. How are potential jurors identified for service in a jury pool?

rules of evidence Administrative court rules governing the admissibility of evidence in a trial.

contempt of court A charge against any violator of the judge's courtroom rules, authorizing the judge to impose a fine or term of imprisonment.

gag order A judge's order to participants and observers at a trial that the evidence and proceedings of the court may not be published, broadcast, or discussed publicly.

bench trial A trial in which the judge rather than a jury makes the determination of guilt.

bailiffs The people who provide courtroom security. Deputy sheriffs provide security for state courts, and Deputy U.S. Marshals provide security for federal courts.

indigent defense A defense counsel provided for a defendant who cannot afford a private attorney.

Taylor v. Louisiana The case that ruled that the exclusion of women from jury duty created an imbalance in the jury pool.

MyCJLab

Go to Chapter 8 in *MyCJLab* to test your mastery of chapter concepts, access your Study Plan, engage in interactive exercises, complete critical-thinking and research assignments, and view related online videos.

Review: Complete the pretest in the Study Plan to confirm what you know and what you need to study further. Then complete the post-test to confirm your mastery of the concepts. Use the key term flash cards to review key terminology.

Apply: Complete the interactive simulation activity.

Analyze: Complete assignments as directed by your instructor.

Current Events: Explore CJSearch for current topical videos, articles, and news pieces.

Additional Links

Go to http://www.uscourts.gov to learn more about the federal courts, rules and policies, and jury service.

Go to http://www.usmarshals.gov/judicial/index.html and learn about courtroom security provided by U.S. Marshals and careers with this agency.

Go to http://www.lsac.org/JD/LSAT/about-the-LSAT.asp for information about the law school admission's test (LSAT exam).

Go to http://www.americanbar.org/groups/legal_education/resources/aba_approved_law_schools/in_alphabetical_order.html for a complete list of approved law schools and direct links to them.

Go to http://www.pbs.org/newshour/news/supreme-court/index.html to watch videos and read articles pertaining to Supreme Court decisions.

Go to http://www.nytimes.com/2012/03/22/us/supreme-court-says-defendants-have-right-to-good-lawyers.html?pagewanted=all and read how the U.S. Supreme Court expanded the rights of the accused during the plea bargaining process.

Sentencing

"Capital punishment kills immediately, whereas lifetime imprisonment does so slowly. Which executioner is more humane? The one who kills you in a few minutes, or the one who wrests your life from you in the course of many years?"

—Anton Chekhov, Writer

1 Describe the purpose of sentencing.

2 Explain how the criminal justice system sentences the offender who claims to be mentally ill.

3 Identify the factors that can influence whether the defendant receives a fair sentence, including the role and process of the presentence investigation and sentencing hearing.

4 Describe the various sentencing models and explain their influence on the sentence.

5 Summarize the challenges to the death penalty sentence, and explain how U.S. Supreme Court rulings have affected the death penalty sentence.

9

Dr. Conrad Murray, 58, the physician convicted of involuntary manslaughter in the 2009 death of Michael Jackson, was sentenced to four years in prison. However, because California prisons are overcrowded, Dr. Murray is likely to be released much sooner than that. In addition to prison time, he also will be obligated to pay restitution to Jackson's estate and family and will lose his medical license.

Keith Randulich, 18, stabbed his four-year-old half-sister 30 times in the throat with a 5-inch knife. He said that he loved his sister and he hated to kill her but it was the only way to save her. He believed she had been molested by a relative, and because he could not afford to buy a gun to kill the molester, he killed her to save her. Investigators were not able to find any evidence of abuse. Randulich was found to

have personality disorders but was deemed psychologically fit for trial. He pleaded guilty and was sentenced to 40 years without any credit for good behavior for early release. He will be 58 years old when he is released.

Dr. Conrad Murray

PAUL BUCK / POOL/EPA/Newscom

In May 2012, 11 people were charged with felonies and 2 with misdemeanors in the hazing death of Florida A&M band member Robert Champion. The felony charges can result in a six-year prison term. Police continue to gather evidence on others who may have been involved in the hazing death but have not been charged. The Champion case is one of the largest criminal cases ever built on a hazing death. The Champion family had hoped for the state to bring murder or manslaughter charges against those responsible because it carried a more severe sentence.[1]

DISCUSS **What is the purpose of criminal sanctions? Is it to punish the offender, to rehabilitate the offender, or to obtain revenge for the victim and the victim's family?**

▶ *Purpose of Criminal Sanctions*

This chapter discusses the purposes and types of sentences, sentencing models, and the death penalty. Imposing a sentence is a complex interaction of people and philosophies. This chapter discusses the various reasons given to justify criminal sanctions, the process by which judges determine appropriate sentences, and the growing public concern regarding the insanity defense and the death penalty.

Each country determines its own criminal sanctions, and the range of sentences is diverse. Nations practicing Sharia law have sentences of corporal punishment that include whippings, caning, and amputations. The United States has abolished corporal punishments as a criminal sentence. Most European countries have eliminated the death penalty. In the United States, the death penalty is retained by 33 states, the federal government, and the military.

What is the purpose of criminal sanctions? Is it to punish the offender, to obtain revenge, to provide an example to deter others, to rehabilitate the offender, or to protect society from further harm? In the United States, there is no one answer to that question. The courts, both state and federal, have adopted diverse sentencing options. Sentencing options have

frequently been adopted based on fear, loss of confidence in the criminal justice system, or belief that offenders cannot be rehabilitated. Evidence-based research offers little insight into the relationship between the sentence imposed and the effect on the offender and public safety.

While sentencing models are diverse and each state and the federal government have autonomy in sentencing, the U.S. Supreme Court has oversight responsibility to determine that sentences do not violate constitutional rights under the Eighth Amendment, which provides that punishments should not be cruel and unusual. The Court has required major reforms in capital cases. At one time, the Court halted all death sentences until states could demonstrate that the death penalty was not applied capriciously and arbitrarily. The Court has also issued rulings regarding the process that states must use in carrying out the death penalty. For example, the Court has issued opinions on the methods used to execute the prisoner. For example, in *Presley* v. *Georgia* (2010), the Court ruled that "judicial proceedings conducted for the purpose of deciding whether a defendant shall be put to death must be conducted with dignity and respect."

> Convictions and sentencing must be fair and respectful of constitutional rights. When sentences are considered unfair, often there is public outcry for justice.

GLOSSARY

corporal punishment The administration of bodily pain as punishment for a crime.

deterrence The philosophy and practices that emphasize making criminal behavior less appealing.

Convictions and sentencing must be fair and respectful of constitutional rights. When sentences are considered unfair, often there is public outcry for justice. Some examples include the movement to change the 100:1 sentencing disparity for crack versus powder cocaine, the movement to abolish the death penalty, and the demand for options for individuals to appeal their conviction based on a claim of factual innocence.

With over 1 million sentences handed down by judges each year, there is a great variety in the sentencing of defendants. Some sentences can be quite unusual. For example, an Olathe, Kansas, high school student convicted of battery for vomiting on his Spanish teacher was sentenced to spend four months cleaning up after people who threw up in police cars.[2] However, it proved impractical to implement the sentence due to the logistics of coordinating the student's time and the need for cleanup. Also, a North Dakota man was sentenced to two days in jail for failing to license his cat.[3] In another case, Family Court Judge Marilyn O'Connor of Rochester, New York, sentenced a dysfunctional, drug-addicted couple not to procreate again until their children were being raised by a natural parent or were no longer being cared for at the expense of the public.[4] Sentences can be influenced by a number of factors. For instance, convicted rapist Stephen Terry Bolden was sentenced for multiple crimes, including first-degree rape, by Arizona Circuit Judge George Greene to 99 years plus two consecutive life sentences. When Bolden told Judge Greene that he (Greene) was "real rude during the sentencing hearing," Greene added an additional five days in prison to the sentence.[5]

Some cases attract national attention, such as the sentence given to Joseph Pannell. In 2008, 58-year-old Joseph Pannell pleaded guilty to the 1969 shooting of a Chicago police officer, Terrence Knox. Knox was not killed, but his right arm was permanently damaged by the shooting. After the shooting, while he was released on bail, Pannell fled to Canada, where he married a Canadian and worked as a library research assistant. He was arrested in 2004 but was not extradited to the United States until 2008. He was charged with aggravated battery, attempted murder, and bail jumping, for which he could have been sentenced to up to 23 years in prison. According to the Bureau of Justice Statistics, the average sentence for a violent felony offense is 92 months in prison. Pannell received a sentence of 30 days in jail, two years' probation, and a $250,000 fine to be paid to a foundation that helps the families of injured Chicago police officers.[6] Such a sentence is rare, especially one involving a large donation to a foundation. Mr. Pannell said of the sentence,

"We must seek to move away from adversarial confrontation and towards peaceful reconciliation and conflict resolution."[7]

How do judges determine the appropriate punishment for a crime? Judges are guided by the law because it must provide the type and range of punishments that may be imposed after conviction. However, these laws are passed by legislators based on public sentiment as to the purpose and effect of various punishments. Also, judges are guided by sentencing guidelines and case precedents. Sentences must be fair and cannot discriminate on factors such as race, gender, or religion. Minority offenders, for example, cannot be sentenced to longer terms of imprisonment than white offenders for similar offenses.

The history of punishment in the United States is rooted in economic sanctions, corporal punishment, and death. However, the concept of serving time in prison or jail as punishment for a crime is a fairly new philosophy of the criminal justice system. Historically, punishments in England and the American colonies consisted primarily of fines, restitution, ordeals, corporal punishment, and torture. Criminals who could not afford to pay the fines or restitution imposed on them could be sold into economic servitude, a form of slavery, to pay the fines. **Corporal punishment** included whipping, branding, dunking, confinement to the stocks or pillories, and other pain-inflicting rituals.

Five contemporary philosophies regarding the purpose of punishment are as follows. (See Table 9–1 for a summary of the philosophies.)

1. Deterrence
2. Incapacitation
3. Retribution
4. Rehabilitation
5. Restorative justice

These are simple categories for classifying punishment, but often the law and circumstances are not so simple. Criminal sanctions may have more than one purpose and may have unstated or contradictory purposes.

Deterrence

Deterrence is based on the principle that punishment should prevent the criminal from reoffending. The problem is to identify what punishment or threat of punishment effectively prevents people from committing crimes or criminals from reoffending. Punishments based on deterrence include economic sanctions, corporal punishment, and threat of bodily harm, all of which are based on the premise that people seek pleasure and avoid pain. For example, as a means to stop Hartford, Connecticut, high school students from cursing, a joint effort by school and police officials gives citations to students who swear while defying teachers and administrators. Students who swear are fined $103. If the

1 million The number of sentences handled by judges each year.

TABLE 9–1

PHILOSOPHIES OF PUNISHMENT

Types of Punishment	Purpose of Punishment	Examples	Pros and Cons
Deterrence			
General Deterrence	Prevent nonoffenders from committing crimes	Expose nonoffenders to punishment received by offenders	Little cost, simple to administer Assumes free-will model of criminal behavior
Specific Deterrence	Prevent offenders from reoffending	Infliction of pain and punishment to make crime less attractive than the rewards	Little cost, simple to administer Assumes free-will model of criminal behavior
Incapacitation	Prevent offender from the opportunity to reoffend	Banishment, transportation, warehousing, "lock and feed" Confiscation of cars of DUI and profits of criminals	Effective if the offender is removed from the community Long-term incarceration is expensive; provides no provisions for reentry or rehabilitation
Retribution	To "repay" the offender with like punishment; to satisfy the desire of the victim for revenge	Infliction of injuries similar to what the victim received Physical punishments during incarceration Death penalty for murder	Provides emotional satisfaction to victims and survivors Little or no emphasis on rehabilitation; courts have prohibited inflicting intentional pain on prisoners; death penalty is very expensive
Rehabilitation	"Cure" the offender	Medical model; drug treatment, counseling, education, job skills training	Emphasizes reentry and rehabilitation Offender seems to receive benefits, but victim is ignored
Restorative Justice	"Heal" the community and conflict resolution	"Truth commissions," "healing ceremonies," restoration mediation, and victim-offender mediation	Goal is to promote public safety and restore offenders to community Often involves difficult and long-term process Better results in small, close-knit community

student cannot pay the fine, the student's parents are required to pay it. The theory underlying the use of fines is that the painful experience of the fines will discourage students from continuing to swear. In this case, the practice seems to support the theory: Although there are critics of the actions of the police and school officials, officials report that the incidents of swearing have dropped to "almost nothing."[8]

Corporal Punishment

Some people profess that corporal punishment is an effective deterrent to misconduct in raising properly behaved children and ensuring proper conduct in schools. As a result of this deeply rooted belief, attempts to pass laws prohibiting the use of corporal punishment against children and students by parents and teachers have been unpopular and have been met with limited success.[9]

Because corporal punishment has been considered an effective strategy in shaping children's behavior, there is little surprise that many consider it effective in influencing adult behavior. Corporal punishment was commonplace in America sentencing and corrections until the mid-1900s. Although corporal punishment has been abandoned as an official punishment in the United States, many foreign countries continue to use some form of corporal punishment as official sentences. In 2000, Nigeria introduced Islamic law, which sanctions the use of corporal punishment. Despite this fact, Nigeria received international criticism in January 2001 for flogging a 17-year-old Muslim girl 100 times for having premarital sexual relations and later, in August, for sentencing a 20-year-old woman to 100 lashes with a cane for having an extramarital affair.[10] Also in 2001, in just four days, Iran sentenced 20 people to be lashed. Their crime was drinking alcohol, an offense against Islamic law. Each offender received 80 lashes.[11]

Some people still advocate that the return of corporal punishment would benefit crime control. For example, in 2005, Las Vegas Mayor Oscar Goodman suggested that whippings or canings should be brought back for children who got into trouble. Goodman said, "I also believe in a little bit of corporal punishment going back to the days of yore. I'm dead serious. Some of these [children] don't learn. You have got to teach them a lesson. They would get a trial first."[12] Despite such vocal advocates for the return of corporal punishment (or the adoption of the practice of caning, a common practice for a number of other nations), to the American criminal justice system, there appears to be little support for this movement.

From January 1 through April 1, 2012, Chicago recorded 120 homicides and 490 nonfatal shootings. This was a 60% increase from the same period in 2011. In one weekend in April 2012 alone, 49 people were shot—10 of them fatally. While homicides increased, other major crime rates decreased as much as 15%. Criminologist James Alan Fox blamed the warm weather. The police union blamed the reduction in street officers. Police superintendent Garry McCarthy blamed retaliatory gang shootings. No one blamed sentencing. Do you believe harsh sentencing deters crime? If not, what is the purpose of incarceration?

kilukilu / Fotolia

Specific and General Deterrence

Specific deterrence is when an individual who has committed a crime is deterred from committing that crime in the future by the nature of the punishment. Punishment with the power of specific deterrence would cause offenders not to drink alcohol again, for example, or not to harass women again because of the unpleasant experience they suffered for their last offense.

General deterrence is the ability to prevent nonoffenders from committing crimes. General deterrence is based on the logic that people who witness the pain suffered by those who commit crimes will want to avoid that pain and hence will refrain from criminal activity. Based on this belief, corporal punishment was often carried out in public so that people could witness the event. For example, in the Iranian floggings for drinking alcohol, over 1,000 people gathered in Vali-e-Asr Square in Tehran to watch the lashings. In England and the United States, hangings were once public events and parents brought their children to witness what happened when someone broke the law. Some advocates of general deterrence today propose that the death penalty would be a greater deterrent to crime if executions were broadcast live on television.

Sterilization and Deterrence

The dark side of deterrence is the historical belief, first made popular by Cesare Lombroso, that crime is hereditary and that criminals should be sterilized to prevent future crime. Sterilization of criminals was practiced in the United States during the early twentieth century. In the United States today, a chemical version of castration is legal, but the few cases in which it was used have drawn criticism and protest. Supreme Court Justice Oliver Wendell Holmes argued for sterilization as an effective means to prevent crime. One criminologist has even argued that the drop in crime in the 1980s and 1990s was a result of the increase in abortion in the general population. Other countries have used sterilization to reduce the births of "socially undesirable" people. Between 1935 and 1975, Sweden sterilized more than 63,000 citizens to improve the country's genetic stock. It is alleged that between 1944 and 1963, approximately 4,500 Swedish citizens were lobotomized, often against their will, as a form of treatment for homosexuality.[13] Until 1996, Japanese law allowed the forced sterilization of people with a broad range of mental or physical handicaps, hereditary diseases, and leprosy. Japanese Health Ministry statistics indicate that nearly 850,000 people were sterilized between 1949 and 1996.[14] The law was changed in 1996 as a result of a change in public sentiment.

Incapacitation

Another view of punishment is that if criminals cannot be deterred from committing further crimes, they should be prevented from having the opportunity to commit other crimes, a condition referred to as **incapacitation**. The theory of incapacitation assumes that offenders cannot be rehabilitated and it will never be safe to release them back into society. The death penalty is an extreme form of incapacitation in that those offenders executed are guaranteed not to be capable of reoffending. In the absence of the death penalty, incarceration in a correctional institution is the alternative to incapacitating the offender.

Two of the oldest forms of incapacitation are banishment and transportation. Banishment as a criminal sanction may have begun in prehistoric times. **Banishment** removed offenders from society, often under the stipulation that if they returned, they would be put to death. This removal could be for a period of time or forever. In societies in which the protection and support of the group were essential to survival, banishment was considered a punishment nearly equal to death. **Transportation** removed offenders from society by literally moving them to another place. England made extensive use of transportation as a criminal sanction. Until the American Revolutionary War, prisoners were transported to the American colonies. After the American Revolution, English convicts were transported to Australia until the mid-nineteenth century.[15]

Modern society has made transportation of offenders to penal colonies impractical. However, some states still practice limited forms of banishment or legal exile whereby offenders

specific deterrence A concept based on the premise that a person is best deterred from committing future crimes by the specific nature of the punishment.

general deterrence The concept based on the logic that people who witness the pain suffered by those who commit crimes will want to avoid that pain and will refrain from criminal activity.

incapacitation Deterrence based on the premise that the only way to prevent criminals from reoffending is to remove them from society.

banishment The removal of an offender from the community.

transportation The eighteenth-century practice by Great Britain of sending offenders to the American colonies and later to Australia.

Until the 1800s, it was commonplace for executions, mostly hangings, to be a public event. The last public execution in the United States was in 1936 in Owensboro, Kentucky. An estimated 20,000 people attended the event. The adoption of the gas chamber, the electric chair, and lethal injection was the downfall of the public execution because these could not be conducted outdoors with large audiences. Today, the technology exists to allow in-prison executions to be recorded and broadcast to the public. Videos of executions carried out in other countries are readily available on the Internet. Do you favor public broadcasting of executions? Why or why not?

akg-images/Newscom

Execution of Rainey Bethea, the last public execution in the United States, 1936

are prohibited from residing within the state. Kentucky, New York, and Oklahoma have banished offenders from their state as a condition of the offenders' sentence. Also, in a sense, the federal government uses a form of transportation with regard to enemy combatants imprisoned at Guantanamo Bay, Cuba. The federal government has removed enemy combatant prisoners from captivity at Guantanamo Bay and has paid other countries to take them.

Modern means of incapacitation include confiscating the cars of accused drunk drivers and the property and valuables of drug dealers and members of organized crime. The argument of those in favor of the law is that without a car, it would be impossible to drive while intoxicated and without wealth, it would be impossible to engage in illegal businesses such as drug dealing.

The most common form of incapacitation, however, is imprisonment. The public belief underlying this practice is that, behind bars, a criminal is effectively prevented from having the opportunity to commit more crimes. This belief underlies proposals for long prison sentences, especially for repeat offenders. Such a philosophy is sometimes referred to as "warehousing" or "lock and feed." These terms emphasize that the primary purpose of sentencing is to separate the offender from the public for as long as possible. Those who view imprisonment as incapacitation do not place value on prison programs such as education, drug treatment,

retribution Deterrence based on the premise that criminals should be punished because they deserve it.

rehabilitation Deterrence based on the premise that criminals can be "cured" of their problems and criminality and can be returned to society.

medical model The rehabilitation model that views criminality as a disease to be cured.

restorative justice A model of deterrence that uses restitution programs, community work programs, victim-offender mediation, and other strategies not only to rehabilitate the offender, but also to address the damage done to the community and the victim.

and rehabilitation. They have essentially given up on the ability of these programs to change the offender.

Those opposed to incapacitation as the primary purpose of sentencing point out that although incarceration may appear to protect the public from the offender, it does not. Nearly all prisoners are released back into society. When they reenter society, if underlying behavioral and psychological problems have not been addressed through rehabilitation and treatment, offenders will reenter society as even more of a danger than when they were incarcerated. Also, while incarceration may protect the general public from victimization, fellow inmates and correctional officers are at risk.

Retribution

Retribution, or just-desserts, is the argument that criminals should be punished because they deserve it. Retribution is associated with "get tough" sentencing and the philosophy of an eye for an eye, which advocates that those who do wrong should pay for their crimes in equal measure. Traditionally, retribution was the victim's revenge. The victim was entitled to inflict punishment or to see that punishment was inflicted on the offender. Many who favor the death penalty argue that it is the most appropriate punishment for convicted murderers. Many family members attend the execution of the offender who murdered their spouse or relative with the belief that "they will feel better" when they see the offender die for the murder he or she committed.

Retribution relates to people's emotional response to a crime. For example, Kim Davis, 34, stole a car in Independence, Missouri. When he discovered that a six-year-old child had been left in the vehicle, he tried to shove the boy outside. The boy became tangled in the seat belt, but Davis refused to stop. Horrified motorists who witnessed the awful scene pursued him for five miles before he was stopped. The boy did not survive the ordeal. Davis was charged with second-degree murder, robbery, child abuse, and kidnapping. A witness to the crime suggested that Davis should be "dragged

> Many family members attend the execution of the offender who murdered their spouse or relative with the belief that "they will feel better" when they see the offender die for the murder he or she committed.

himself, just like he dragged that kid."[16] In retribution, the criminal suffers—perhaps in a like manner—for the crime.

Those who believe that the purpose of sentencing is retribution are often disappointed that the offender does not suffer enough as a result of the sentence imposed. For example, the parents of Robert Champion, who died due to hazing at Florida A&M, were disappointed when the state charged the offenders with the lesser crime of hazing resulting in death. They wanted the offenders to be sentenced to a longer period of imprisonment.[17]

Historically, surviving relatives were allowed to carry out the punishment against the offender. In fact, in some Middle Eastern countries today, the law still allows relatives, even juveniles, to carry out the punishment against the offender, even if it is execution. However, the U.S. criminal justice system does not allow this, nor is the offender brutalized by corporal punishment. Torture and the infliction of pain with the intent to "pay back" the offender or to make him or her suffer in like manner are prohibited. Today, retribution emphasizes long prison terms for offenders. The belief in retribution is reflected in the statement of Malissa Wilkins. Wilkins's two young children were killed when Jennifer Porter, a former elementary school dance teacher, hit the children with her car and killed them. Porter fled the accident. After Porter's arrest and conviction, Florida Circuit Judge Emmett Battles could have sentenced Porter to 15 years in prison. However, the judge took into account Porter's clean past record and other factors and sentenced her to three years of probation and 500 hours of community service. At the sentencing, Wilkins sobbed and urged the judge to sentence Porter to prison. Wilkins said, "I want her to be punished. I want her to go to prison. I want her to see what it's like to lose someone." Wilkins's sentiments reflect the underlying philosophy of retribution.

During the nineteenth and twentieth centuries, many prison officials and the public favored the idea that the purpose of punishment was retribution. As a result, prison conditions often were deliberately harsh and cruel and physical punishment was administered liberally to inmates while incarcerated. Many early prisons were built with physical facilities to accommodate the punishment of inmates, such as whipping posts and special cells designed to induce pain and suffering. The public expected that prisoners would be punished while incarcerated.

Rehabilitation

Rehabilitation and restoration are more contemporary philosophies defining the purpose of criminal sanctions. **Rehabilitation** calls for criminal sanctions to "cure" the offender of criminality. The rehabilitation model often is referred to as the **medical model** in that it views criminality as a disease to be cured. Some believe that rehabilitation of offenders is impossible and offenders cannot be cured. Those who believe in the rehabilitation model tend to reject the theory that crime is a free-will choice as advocated by classical and neoclassical criminological theories. Advocates of rehabilitation favor approaches involving psychology, medical

> "I want her to be punished. I want her to go to prison. I want her to see what it's like to lose someone."

treatment, drug treatment, self-esteem counseling, education, and programs aimed at developing ethical values and work skills. The foundation of most rehabilitation models is that the offender has a "defect" of which he or she may not be aware or able to control that needs to be "fixed." Most rehabilitation efforts focus on juvenile delinquents and youthful offenders. It is thought to be easier to "cure" a 13-year-old shoplifter than a 43-year-old child molester. The juvenile justice system is based on the principle that its primary purpose is to rehabilitate the offender.

The criminal justice system and the public may accept that the purpose of criminal sanctions is to rehabilitate children and first-time youthful offenders, but they often reject this premise for repeat and career offenders. Thus, the public may be willing to give the 18-year-old marijuana user the chance to turn around his or her life, but they would just as soon see the 45-year-old sexual offender receive a life sentence than give the system a chance to rehabilitate him or her. When 68-year-old former Penn State football coach Jerry Sandusky was found guilty of child molestation and it was evident that he would spend the rest of his life in prison, the hundreds of spectators outside the courthouse erupted in cheers. There was no regret among the members of the crowd about the long sentence.

Restorative Justice

Restorative justice focuses on rehabilitating the victims rather than the offenders. Rehabilitation often is criticized for forgetting the victim. The focus in rehabilitation is on the offender and what needs to be done to make him or her a productive, normal member of society. Restorative justice does not forget the victim, but sees the relationship between offender, victim, and society in a different light. The restorative justice model goes beyond rehabilitation of the offender. The restorative justice model is a holistic model that contends that there is a bond between offender, victim, and society. Crime has a harmful effect on the victim and society, and justice requires that as much of this harm as possible be removed. Restorative justice programs use restitution, community work programs, victim–offender mediation, and other strategies to rehabilitate the offender and to address the damage done to the community and the victim. South Africa used this model to help heal the division between African-Americans and whites after the overthrow of white rule of the country. South Africa's Truth and Reconciliation Commission allows those who committed hate crimes against minorities during apartheid and confessed and repented of their crimes to escape criminal sanctions. The purpose was to "heal" the country rather than leave a great

The rehabilitation model often is referred to as the medical model in that it views criminality as a disease to be cured.

racial divide that would eventually tear the country apart or lead to civil war.

One of the characteristics of restorative justice is the concept that the offender should be made to provide some contribution to the community and to the victim to heal the harm he or she caused. In the American criminal justice system, this concept is translated into practice by sentencing the offender to additional penalties other than or in addition to incarceration. The most common penalties related to restorative justice include sentences requiring restitution to the victim and community service. This sanction is most often used in property offenses and least used in drug and weapon offenses. Restorative justice is not central to the modern criminal justice system. Community service is included as a penalty in only about 5% of all offenses. Community service is based on the philosophy that the offender should provide services that help the community as a way to make up for the harm he or she did.

► The Special Case of Offenders with Mental Illness

The offender who commits bizarre and shocking crimes poses a special challenge to the criminal justice system. Guilt is based on the assumption that the defendant is **legally sane**. This means that the defendant can distinguish between right and wrong and committed his or her offenses of his or her own free will. Some offenders commit offenses that call this assumption into question. For example, in 1967 to 1968, serial killer David Berkowitz, known as the "Son of Sam" or the ".44 caliber killer," killed six people in New York. He claimed that a demon that possessed his neighbor's dog commanded him to kill. Berkowitz was found guilty and sentenced to 365 years in prison.

In 2001, Andrea Yates drowned her five children in her Houston area home. She said that she did so because the devil made her do it. Initially, she was found guilty and sentenced to 40 years in prison. On appeal, she was found not guilty by reason of insanity and was remanded to a mental health institution.

On July 28, 2009, San Antonio police responded to a crime scene to find that a 3½-week-old boy had been beheaded and his brain and three of his toes eaten. The police describe other injuries as too horrific to report to the public. At the scene, his hysterical mother, Otty Sanchez, had a self-inflicted wound to her chest and her throat partially slashed. She screamed to police, "I killed my baby! I killed my baby! The devil made me do it."[19] At her trial, three psychologists testified that she was schizophrenic and did not know right from wrong. The prosecutors did not contest the findings. The judge took five minutes to review the plea and decide that Sanchez was not guilty by reason of insanity.

As mentioned in the chapter opener, Keith Randulich, 18, stabbed his stepsister 30 times in the throat. He said he was saving her from physical abuse by a relative because he could not afford a gun to kill the relative. He was sentenced to 40 years in prison.

Why do some people "escape" punishment by use of the not guilty by reason of insanity plea while others who commit

> Crime has a harmful effect on the victim and society, and justice requires that as much of this harm as possible be removed.

horrific crimes are held responsible? The criminal justice system is based on the fundamental principle that an offender must have committed the criminal act of his or her own free will. The insanity defense is based on the legal principle that defendants lack the necessary *mens rea* to be held criminally liable for their actions. In other words, they did not commit the crime of their own free will. Criminal law provides a similar defense for young children and for people with diminished intellectual capacity or mental retardation. Because the insanity defense is based on the claim of mental illness, people often mistake insanity as a mental health term. However, insanity is a legal term, not a mental health term.[20] Only a jury, not mental health professionals, can pronounce a defendant insane.

Defining Insanity

Federal and state courts have different standards for defining insanity, but all federal courts use the same standard. The federal standards for the insanity plea were changed following the assassination attempt on President Reagan. When John Hinckley attempted to assassinate President Ronald Reagan, Hinckley was acquitted in federal court based on a plea of not guilty by reason of insanity. The federal test of insanity in the early 1980s was whether defendants lacked the capacity to appreciate the wrongfulness of their conduct or to conform their conduct to the requirements of the law. This definition did not require that the defendant did not know right from wrong. Because of the public outrage over the laxity of the federal insanity standard, however, this standard was made more conservative, making it more difficult to prove claims of insanity.[21] The U.S. Congress passed the Insanity Defense Reform Act of 1984, under which the federal courts adopted a new standard of insanity. A defendant must prove insanity at the time of the crime by clear and convincing evidence. Mental disease or defect is no longer considered sufficient to avoid criminal responsibility. The reason a person who meets the criteria for insanity is not guilty is that "psychiatric evidence which negates *mens rea* … negates an element of the offense rather than constituting a justification or excuse."[22] Thus, the insanity plea is not like a plea

LEARNING OUTCOMES 2 Explain how the criminal justice system sentences the offender who claims to be mentally ill.

GLOSSARY

legally sane An assumption that a defendant knows right from wrong and that his or her behavior was willful.

not guilty by reason of insanity A verdict by which the jury finds that a defendant committed the crime but was insane.

civil commitment examination A determination of whether the defendant should be released or confined to an institution for people with mental illness.

guilty but mentally ill A new type of verdict in which the jury finds a defendant mentally ill but sufficiently aware to be morally responsible for his or her criminal acts.

of self-defense that offers a justification for the defendant's actions, but completely exempts the defendant's actions from criminal liability.

All defendants are considered sane. Thus, the insanity defense is an affirmative defense, meaning that the defendant must declare the defense in advance of the trial. The defendant admits to the acts of the crime but claims that he or she lacked *mens rea*. When the defendant pleads not guilty by reason of insanity, the court arranges for the defendant to be examined by mental health professionals prior to the trial. The court, the defendant, and the prosecutor have input as to who is selected to examine the defendant. At the trial, these mental health professionals are called as expert witnesses to give their opinion as to the defendant's state of mind at the time of the crime. The defense must prove that the defendant could not understand that his or her actions were criminal due to mental illness. The prosecution must present evidence that the defendant was capable of forming the necessary *mens rea* to be held accountable for his or her criminal actions. It is not unusual at a trial to have mental health professionals give very different assessments of the defendant's mental health. The jury must digest the evidence and decide whether the defendant's mental health meets the legal standard of insanity. If the jury finds the defendant sane, he or she is convicted of the criminal charges. A verdict of **not guilty by reason of insanity** means the defendant will not be criminally sanctioned for his or her acts. In order words, the defendant is not guilty.

The Insanity Defense Reform Act of 1984

The Insanity Defense Reform Act of 1984 requires that in federal courts, the defendant found not guilty by reason of insanity must undergo a **civil commitment examination** within 40 days of the verdict. The civil commitment process determines whether the defendant should be released or confined to an institution for people with mental illness. The purpose is to determine whether defendants are a danger to themselves or the public. If found to be a danger to the public or themselves, defendants may be involuntarily confined to a civil mental health institution until the medical staff determines that they are no longer a danger. In addition, defendants may be forced to undergo medical and drug treatment and may be denied their liberty for the rest of their lives. Because a successful insanity defense may lead to a sentence that differs little from life imprisonment, the insanity defense is seldom used for misdemeanors or lesser felonies. It is used almost exclusively in first-degree homicide cases.

State Courts and the Insanity Plea

State courts have adopted diverse standards for a successful insanity defense. Some still use the awareness-of-right-and-wrong test, others have adopted the Model Penal Code substantial capacity test, and a few have adopted standards combining elements of both. A number of states have adopted a new verdict: **guilty but mentally ill**. In 1975, Michigan was the first state to adopt this verdict. The verdict provides the jury the option of finding that the defendant, indeed, has mental illness, is perhaps suffering from a serious mental illness, but was "sufficiently in possession of his faculties to be morally blameworthy for his acts."[24]

In states that have adopted it, the guilty but mentally ill verdict is an alternative to the not guilty by reason of insanity verdict. Thus, the jury has the option of finding defendants mentally ill but morally responsible for their acts or finding them insane and lacking the *mens rea* to be held criminally liable. In the latter case, the defendant is involuntarily confined to a civil mental health facility, but if found guilty but mentally ill, the defendant is sentenced to incarceration in a state prison following psychiatric treatment. During confinement at a mental institution, if doctors determine that the defendant is no longer suffering from mental illness, he or she is not released, but is transferred to the state prison to serve his or her sentence. The time the offender spent in the mental institution counts toward the sentence to be served. Once returned to the regular prison population, offenders may still be considered mentally ill to some degree, but their medical and psychiatric problems do not excuse them from incarceration for their crimes.

Public Fear of the Insanity Plea

The public fear that the successful use of the insanity defense poses a grave danger because it allows defendants to escape incarceration does not appear to be justified. A very small number of defendants choose to plead not guilty by reason of insanity.[25] Offenders found to be not guilty by reason of insanity rarely obtain their freedom following the verdict.[26] Media coverage has sensationalized unusual cases, such as that of Lorena Bobbitt, who successfully pleaded temporary insanity to a charge of cutting off her husband's penis and was freed within two months of the verdict, and John Hinckley, who escaped possible lifetime incarceration by use of the insanity plea. However, these cases are not typical of defendants found guilty by reason of insanity.

Another limiting factor of the insanity plea is that it is not often used by defendants. Technically, the defendant could enter a plea of not guilty by reason of insanity for any crime from shoplifting to murder. However, it is rare for the plea to be used for any crime other than first-degree murder. If the defendant is found to be not guilty by reason of insanity, the follow-up is that the defendant will be involuntarily committed to a mental health institution for an indefinite period of time. The defendant will remain in the mental health institution until medical doctors pronounce him or her not to be a risk to self or community. The defendant could be held in the mental health facility for life.

What happens in sentencing when a defendant is not successful in his or her insanity plea? The judge may require that after conviction, the offender undergo another mental competency examination. If the offender is found mentally unfit for incarceration in the state or federal prison, he or she is placed in a maximum-security mental health facility that can provide appropriate psychiatric treatment. Some states have special correctional facilities for such patients. Medical authorities determine if or when the offender can be returned to the prison population. The time spent in the medical institution counts toward the sentence to be served.

▶ A Fair Sentence

The public and the ethics of the criminal justice system demand a sentence that is fair and unbiased. The following six major factors may have a significant impact on the fairness of a sentence. See Table 9–2 for a brief explanation of these factors.

A fair and impartial judge is the cornerstone of justice. One of the important considerations in securing fair and impartial judges is the selection process.

Laws

Laws are enacted by legislation and must specify the punishment for an offense. If the law is unjust or discriminatory, it fails to provide justice. Laws that are inequitable and discriminate by race, gender, religion, or other constitutionally protected groups are most often targeted for change. Over time, many laws have been considered racially inequitable. Perhaps the most egregious were the Jim Crow laws, which provided for inequality in treatment of African-Americans and access to the criminal justice system. Although legislation has been passed in an attempt to eliminate such laws, there are still debates as to the equality of contemporary laws and punishments. One of the most controversial laws directly related to a fair sentence was the 100:1 ratio in sentencing for crack cocaine versus powder cocaine. The sentence for 50 grams of crack cocaine was a minimum of ten years. The amount required to trigger a ten-year sentence for powder cocaine was 5000 grams. The difference in sentencing is significant in that 80% of criminals sentenced for crack-related offenses are

1. The law
2. The judge
3. The prosecutor
4. The defense attorney
5. The jury
6. The presentence investigator

A fair sentence depends upon six major factors

TABLE 9–2 | FACTORS THAT CAN PREVENT A FAIR SENTENCE

Courtroom Participant	Possible Misconduct	Negative Impact on the Criminal Justice System
Legislation	Unfair, unconstitutional, or discriminatory legislation	Loss of respect for the law, civil and violent protest against the law
Judge	Selection of incompetent or biased judges, criminal misconduct regarding judicial decisions, abuse of powers, biased decisions	Wrongful convictions, verdicts based on bribery and influence, distrust of the courts
Prosecutor	Prosecutorial misconduct	Wrongful prosecution of defendants, guilty defendants escape justice, public sees the criminal justice system as biased and unfair
Defense Attorney	Overburdened public defenders unable to provide adequate representation	Innocent defendants failing to receive a fair trial, wrongful convictions resulting from inadequate representation, delays in trials resulting in innocent defendants spending unnecessary pretrial time in jail
Jury	Biased	Unfair decisions based on emotion or prejudice rather than facts
Presentence Investigator	Inaccurate presentence investigation report	Sentencing recommendations based on inaccurate information resulting in recommendations for sentence lengths that are excessive or insufficient
		Because the presentence investigation is based on the assumption that the defendant is guilty, the protests of a wrongfully convicted defendant will be held against the defendant and the defendant will be seen as being uncooperative and unwilling to take responsibility for his or her actions.

African-American. Attorney General Eric Holder called the disparity egregious.[27] The Fair Sentencing Act of 2010 narrowed the sentence disparity to 18:1, but some still think the sentence disparity is not justified.

Judges

A fair and impartial judge is the cornerstone of justice. One important consideration in securing fair and impartial judges is the selection process. Federal judges are nominated by the president and approved by the Senate. Once confirmed by the Senate, federal judges can be removed only by **impeachment**, a process that has rarely been used or successful. The founding fathers selected this method with the hopes that it would shield federal judges from political influences in their judicial duties and decisions.

Concerns about the Election of State Judges

However, the states took a different approach to selecting judges. Most of the states adopted a selection process that depends in one way or another on popular elections. According to the National Center for State Courts, 87% of all state court judges face elections. The use of popular elections to select judges is unique to the United States because only two other nations use popular elections in the selection of judges (Switzerland and Japan). Furthermore, in those two countries, the use of popular elections applies only in certain cases and is not generally used.

The concern is that election pressures can influence a judge's judicial decisions. For example, one study found that all judges increase their sentences as reelection nears.[28] Perhaps of greater concern is the fear that election campaign donations will prejudice judges. The cost of judicial campaigns has greatly increased, and some judicial campaigns spend millions of dollars in a bid to get elected. There are two concerns. First, the cost of a judicial election is so great that highly qualified candidates may be eliminated by candidates who have fewer qualifications but more money. Second, large donors may "buy" special consideration. One West Virginia case concerning the possible judicial bias that could occur as a result of large campaign contributors is *Caperton* v. *A. T. Massey Coal Co.* (2009). Caperton, the owner of a small coal company, successfully argued in court that the much larger A. T. Massey Coal Company forced him into bankruptcy because of unfair business practices, resulting in Caperton receiving a $50 million jury award. Massey appealed the $50 million award. In the West Virginia judicial elections, Massey had contributed $3 million to the campaign of Brent Benjamin for state Supreme Court justice. The newly elected Judge Benjamin was party to the panel of five appellate judges hearing the appeal, and he refused to recuse himself. The vote was 3 to 2, with Benjamin casting the deciding vote. Caperton unsuccessfully appealed to the U.S. Supreme Court that Benjamin was biased by the large campaign donation from Massey.

Despite calls for reform, the U.S. Supreme Court has refused to intervene in the selection process for judges used by states. In 2008, a case before the U.S. Supreme Court challenged the method used by New York State to choose its trial judges. The case claimed that its system of choosing candidates for judges by convention rather than primary elections was a patronage-tainted system that favors party cronies and minimizes voters' input because they have no voice in the selection of the candidates on the ballot. The U.S. Supreme Court ruled that states are free to use the method of their choice to select judges, even if that system has obvious flaws.

Prosecutors

A fair and unbiased prosecutor is an essential element of a fair trial and sentence. Prosecutors are supposed to use the immense powers of the government to discover who committed a crime, gather evidence to prosecute the defendant, and present the best possible case against the defendant. It is unethical for the prosecutor to demonstrate bias in selecting which crimes to prosecute or to charge defendants without regard for the evidence regarding their possible innocence. The criminal justice system is not perfect, and there are incidences wherein prosecutors have not acted professionally and within ethical standards. One notorious example was the unethical behavior of former Durham, North Carolina, prosecutor Michael B. Nifong in 2007. As prosecutor, Nifong charged students of the Duke University lacrosse team with sexual assault and other crimes even though evidence he possessed demonstrated that the defendants were not guilty. Besides Nifong's behavior being considered unethical, he was found to have committed criminal actions, resulting in a one-day jail sentence as well as disbarment.

Defense Attorneys

The quality of the accused's defense attorney can have an influence on the fairness of the verdict and sentence. The extensive use of public defenders in the criminal justice system to represent the indigent raises concerns that those who cannot afford a private attorney may receive less competent representation, resulting in conviction and longer sentences. The public defender system is in crisis in many states. The extent of this crisis is illustrated by the fact that some public defenders have begun rejecting new cases, arguing that it would be unethical to overburden themselves to the point that they are unable to provide each defendant with adequate representation.

(Think About It ...

In 2012, the New Orleans Police Department initiated a policy of putting signs on houses indicating that the owners were being *investigated* for drug offenses. When challenged by the American Civil Liberties Union (ACLU), the police department discontinued the policy.[29] This is just one example of the numerous additional sanctions for convicted and accused offenders. Sex offenders and child abuse offenders can be made to publish information on offender registers. Convicted felons lose their voting rights, the right to own firearms, and to work in certain occupations. Are these sanctions justified? Why or why not?)

Juries

The criminal justice system attempts to provide juries that are unbiased. In a high-profile case, the *voir dire* **process** can be lengthy and expensive. However, there are possible faults with the jury process wherein jury members may be biased, resulting in both wrongful convictions and guilty defendants being freed. During the 1960s, there were a number of high-profile civil rights cases where juries failed to convict people accused of civil rights violations because of their personal racial prejudices. Other examples of juror misconduct include jurors who engage in wrongful actions such as conducting their own investigations, discussing the case with other people, or disregarding the judge's instructions. One example of blatant misconduct occurred in the trial of former Orange County Sheriff Michael S. Carona on federal corruption charges. Radio "shock jocks" John Kobylt and Ken Chiampou of KFI-AM in Los Angeles urged citizens who were prospective jurors to lie to the court during *voir dire* with the purpose of getting on the jury and voting guilty based on pretrial public information suggesting that the former sheriff was guilty.[30]

▶ Presentence Investigation Report

The presentence investigation reports play a very important role in arriving at a fair sentence for a convicted defendant. A **presentence investigation** involves gathering information about the convicted offender to help determine the best sentence. Following conviction, by either plea or trial, the defendant is returned to jail and the judge begins the process of determining the appropriate sentence. Federal and state judges of general trial jurisdiction are assisted in this process by a staff of people who conduct a presentence investigation.

Unlike the impression of trials and sentencing given on television and in movies, in which arrest, trial, and sentencing follow in rapid succession, the process from arrest to sentencing is rather lengthy. One-half of all people arrested for a felony are sentenced in 184 days. Generally, the more serious the crime, the longer the time from arrest to sentencing.[31] For example, the median time from arrest to sentencing for larceny is only 99 days, but the median time from arrest to sentencing for murder is 412 days.

The Offender's Background and Attitude

The **presentence investigator** is a person who works for the court and has the responsibility of investigating the background of the convicted offender and the circumstances surrounding the offense. Federal courts use federal probation and parole personnel to serve as presentence investigators. Each state court has its own method for staffing presentence investigators. Some states use state probation and parole officers, whereas in other states, presentence investigators are employees of the court. The presentence investigator has the responsibility of investigating the life the offender led, any previous crimes and punishments received, the offender's attitude toward his or her crime, and the impact of the crime on the community and victims. The presentence investigation is based on the assumption that the defendant is guilty. Therefore, protests by a wrongfully convicted defendant that he or she is not guilty will be held against the defendant and the defendant will be seen as being uncooperative and unwilling to take responsibility for his or her actions.

After conviction, a defendant is expected to cooperate with presentence investigators and does not have the right to remain silent. All previous crimes committed by the offender may be considered in the sentencing process. The defendant's employment history, family relationships, and reputation in the community may all be considered. Other factors that influence the recommendation include prior convictions and the seriousness of the current offense, including the extent of harm to others as a result of the crime.

The offender may be required to complete interviews and life history forms as part of the presentence investigation. Defendants who refuse to provide information may be classified as uncooperative, which can be a factor in sentencing. Convicted defendants who do not accept responsibility for their guilt or do not express remorse for their crime may receive a more severe sentence.

The Presentencing Recommendation

The **presentence investigation report** contains a recommendation for specific criminal sanctions, including a recommendation for prison time, probation, fines, community service, or other sanctions. If an offender is assessed a fine and is unable to pay it, he or she cannot be imprisoned in lieu of the fine. Thus, the presentence investigator will review the convicted offender's financial resources to determine what he or she can pay in fines or restitution. When the report is completed, the presentence investigator will forward it to the judge for review. The judge will forward a copy of the report to the prosecutor and the defense attorney. The investigator's role is important. In over 90% of cases, the judge accepts the recommended sanctions outlined in the presentence

GLOSSARY

impeachment A process for removing judges or elected officials from office.

voir dire **process** The questioning of potential jurors to determine whether they have biases that would disqualify them from jury service.

presentence investigation An in-depth interview and investigation into the background of a convicted defendant and the impact of his or her crime on victims and the community.

presentence investigator A person who works for the court and has the responsibility of investigating the background of the convicted offender and the circumstances surrounding the offense.

presentence investigation report A report that contains a recommendation for specific criminal sanctions, including a recommendation for prison time, probation, fines, community service, or other sanctions.

sentencing hearing A hearing at which the prosecution and the defense have the opportunity to challenge the recommended criminal sanctions.

victim impact statements Testimony by victims at a convicted offender's sentencing hearing.

investigation report. Both the prosecution and defense will have an opportunity to rebut the presentence investigation recommendation.

Sentencing Hearing and Victim Impact Statements

The judge sets a date for a **sentencing hearing**, at which the prosecution and the defense have the opportunity to critique the recommended criminal sanctions. The presentence investigator may be called to testify as to how he or she compiled the data for the report and what influenced him or her in making a specific recommendation for criminal sanctions.

The judge also may allow **victim impact statements** at the presentence hearing, in which victims of the crime have a chance to influence sentencing. Victim impact statements are controversial. Technically, defendants are punished for what they did, regardless of who the victims were. Sentencing is not supposed to be based on whether the victim was a homeless person or a beloved member of the community. Because of the emotional nature of the victims' testimony, some civil rights advocates consider victim impact statements prejudicial and biased.[32] Defenders of victim impact statements argue that the harm and suffering caused to others is an appropriate factor in determining the offender's sentence. Both the defense and the prosecutor can appeal the sentence.

▶ Sentencing Models

Juries (except in bench trials) determine the guilt of defendants, but judges are responsible for determining the sentence that defendants receive. In sentencing, judges evaluate the circumstances of the cases of everyone who pleads guilty or is convicted of an offense. A judge must also evaluate the possible sentences allowed by law and then select the sentence that best fits the case. All criminal laws passed by the state legislature or the U.S. Congress must specify the punishment or range of punishments a judge can impose if a defendant is found guilty of violating a law. The only constitutional guideline for sentencing is the Eighth Amendment prohibition against cruel and unusual punishment. The U.S. Supreme Court has allowed a broad interpretation of this amendment; thus, few punishments have been found to be cruel and unusual.

Sentencing Models

The traditional criminal sanctions that a judge may impose are fines, imprisonment, community service, restitution, probation, or some combination of these. (Parole is early release from imprisonment after an offender has served some of his or her sentence; it is not a sentence given by a judge.) Federal judges in U.S. District Courts, military judges, and state judges in courts of general trial jurisdiction in states with the death penalty also may sentence a defendant to death. Judges are guided by the law as to the minimum and maximum sentence a convicted defendant can receive. However, especially for state judges, the difference between the minimum and maximum punishment varies greatly. Thus, each sentence requires the judge to give careful consideration to the individual circumstances of the case. Seldom is sentencing an automatic or routine function in which the outcome is always predictable. (See Table 9–3 for an overview of the various sentencing models.)

At one time, state and federal judges had great discretion in sentencing an offender because most states and the federal courts used the indeterminate model of sentencing. The **indeterminate sentencing** model gives the judge the most power and flexibility in setting the sentence of the offender. In the late nineteenth century, as incarceration became a common punishment for serious crimes, the predominant correctional philosophy was that offenders should demonstrate that they had changed their criminal attitudes and lifestyles as a condition of release. Thus, judges were given wide latitude in the sentences they could impose for crimes. Because no one could predict when offenders would demonstrate that they were rehabilitated, offenders were given sentences of indeterminate length. For example, an offender might

LEARNING OUTCOMES 4 — Describe the various sentencing models and explain their influence on the sentence.

GLOSSARY

indeterminate sentencing A model of sentencing in which judges have nearly complete discretion in sentencing an offender.

structured sentencing A sentencing model (including determinate sentencing, sentencing guidelines, and presumptive sentencing) that defines punishments rather than allowing indeterminate sentencing.

determinate sentencing A model of sentencing in which the offender is sentenced to a fixed term of incarceration.

mandatory sentencing The strict application of full sentences in the determinate sentencing model.

habitual offender laws Tough sentencing laws that punish repeat offenders more harshly.

three-strikes law The law that applies mandatory sentencing to give repeat offenders longer prison terms.

sentencing guidelines A sentencing model in which crimes are classified according to their seriousness and a range of time to be served is mandatory for crimes within each category.

TABLE 9-3 | SENTENCING MODELS

Sentencing Model	How Sentencing Works	Advantages/Disadvantages
Indeterminate Sentencing	Legislation provides a very broad range for crimes (for example, 1 to 20 years), and the judge decides the sentence based on individual circumstances.	Allows for discretion to adjust the length of the sentence to fit the individual circumstances. Can result in intentional or unintentional discrimination. Sentences may vary from judge to judge so much as to appear to be unfair.
Structured Sentencing Determinate	Legislation mandates a range of incarceration, usually in months, for crimes, and the judge decides a sentence within these ranges (for example, 18 to 24 months). The sentence is reduced for factors such as being a first offense, being a youthful offender, and cooperating with the police but is increased for aggravating factors.	Strives to ensure that all offenders receive an equal sentence for the same crime. Still allows the judge leeway for individual circumstances. Often the range of the sentence is not based on any research regarding the effectiveness and appropriateness of the sentence range.
Structured Sentencing Mandatory	Legislation provides a fixed sentence for offenders found guilty. The judge has no discretion in sentencing. Usually used for certain crimes such as those involving firearms and drugs.	Guarantees that defendants will not receive a light sentence at the judge's discretion. Provides no discretion for individual circumstances. Offenders who may have benefited from diversion, counseling, or probation will be sentenced to imprisonment.
Structured Sentencing Mandatory—Habitual Offender	Similar to mandatory sentencing in that legislation specifies a period of incarceration on a finding of guilt with no discretion given to the judge to alter the sentence. However, it is applied only to repeat offenders.	Provides the public with a sense of public safety that dangerous offenders will receive long prison sentences. Can be triggered by minor offenses, and when applied to youthful offenders, can result in long sentences, which can be very expensive with little impact on rehabilitation or release of the offender.
Structured Sentencing Presumptive	1984 federal legislation and sentencing guidelines issued by the U.S. Sentencing Commission provided specific guidelines based on the "primary" offense, which then increased or decreased by the presence of mitigating or aggravating factors.	Its goal is to provide fair and unbiased sentences. The judge has little discretion based on individual circumstances. U.S. Supreme Court rulings declared the use of the federal sentencing guidelines unconstitutional. Sentencing guidelines are only constitutional when considered advisory for the judge.

All criminal laws passed by the state legislature or the U.S. Congress must specify the punishment or range of punishments a judge can impose if a defendant is found guilty of violating a law.

receive a sentence of a minimum of 1 year and a maximum of 20 years in prison. The exact number of years to be served would be determined by the prisoner's behavior and progress toward rehabilitation.

Indeterminate sentencing came under criticism in the late twentieth century. In addition to giving the judge wide latitude in sentencing, indeterminate sentencing also gave extensive power to prison authorities. In reality, it was prison authorities, not the judge, who determined the term of the sentence to be served. Prison officials could arbitrarily exercise this power with little or no oversight. To cure the ills of indeterminate sentencing, state and federal legislation adopted **structured sentencing** models, including the following:

1. Determinate sentencing
2. Mandatory sentencing and habitual offender laws
3. Sentencing guidelines
4. Presumptive sentencing

Determinate versus Indeterminate Sentencing

In **determinate sentencing**, the offender is sentenced to a fixed term of incarceration. This term may be reduced by parole or good behavior, but other than that, the inmate knows when he or she is scheduled for release from prison. Determinate sentences are also known as flat sentences or fixed sentences. Determinate sentencing was a sentencing reform that emerged in the 1970s to provide more equity and proportionality in sentencing. Proponents claimed that it would eliminate racial discrimination.[33]

Determinate sentencing reform did not become popular, however. Only Arizona adopted a determinate sentencing model. A few other states (California, Illinois, Indiana, and Maine) adopted sentencing models based on determinate sentencing but still provided for discretion in sentencing.[34]

> The Innocence Project has identified 292 wrongful convictions through postconviction DNA exoneration since 1989. However, North Carolina is the only state that has an agency to review inmates' appeals of their sentence based on a claim of factual innocence. Established in 2006, the North Carolina Innocence Inquiry Commission has had nearly 1,000 petitions. In only one case has an inmate been exonerated. Should the sentencing process be changed so that all states and the federal courts are required to have a means for a convicted person to appeal based on a claim of factual innocence? Explain.

Mandatory Sentencing and Habitual Offender Laws

A controversial sentencing model is **mandatory sentencing**— the strict application of full sentences adopted because of public perception that offenders were "getting off too light." Concerned that judges were too lenient in sentencing, many states adopted legislation mandating that offenders convicted of crimes serve the sentence for that crime as specified by law. Thus, sentencing was not left to the discretion of the judge. Mandatory sentences have been applied mostly to crimes involving drugs or the use of firearms. For crimes with mandatory sentences, if the defendant is convicted, the sentence for the crime is specified by the law and the judge has no authority to change the sentence based on mitigating circumstances. For example, if the law states that the prison term for committing a crime with a firearm is two years, the judge must sentence the defendant to two years. Critics of mandatory sentencing argue that unique circumstances in a case may make mandatory sentences inappropriate. Judges are critical of mandatory sentences because they greatly reduce the authority of the judges in determining the sentence.

One area in which mandatory sentences have been applied is for crimes of domestic violence. Concerned that the criminal justice system was ignoring domestic violence or not taking domestic violence cases seriously, several states adopted mandatory sentencing for conviction of domestic violence. Sometimes these sentences are for short periods, such as

83% The amount of increase in the number of felons serving life sentences since 1992.

48 hours, or involve only probation. Nevertheless, the convicted offender finds that he or she can no longer escape punishment for domestic violence.[35]

Mandatory sentencing also has been applied to repeat offenders through **habitual offender laws**. California has received much press concerning its **three-strikes law**, in which repeat offenders receive longer mandatory sentences. Proponents argue that "getting tough on crime" reduces crime by taking repeat offenders off the streets. Opponents argue that the three-strikes law creates situations in which offenders are receiving disproportionately long prison terms for minor crimes such as possession of drugs.

Habitual offender sentencing has been responsible for much of the increase in prison populations. As a result of the "get tough" sentencing policies, especially the three-strikes policy, the number of convicted felons serving some kind of life sentence has increased 83% since 1992.[36] For example, California's use of habitual offender laws has resulted in a crisis in prison overpopulation to the point that the U.S. Supreme Court has ordered the state to reduce its prison population.

Supporters of these new sentencing policies defend long sentences by citing the significant decline in crime since their

Federal Sentencing Classifications—Section 3559, Title 18

Felony
Class A Maximum sentence of life imprisonment or, if authorized, death
Class B Maximum sentence of 25 years to life imprisonment; death penalty is not permitted
Class C Maximum sentence of 25 years of imprisonment but no less than 10 years
Class D Maximum sentence of 10 years of imprisonment but no less than 5 years
Class E Maximum sentence of 5 years of imprisonment but more than 1 year
Misdemeanor
Class A Maximum sentence of 1 year of imprisonment but no less than 1 month
Class B Maximum sentence of 6 months of imprisonment but no less than 30 days
Class C Maximum sentence of 30 days of imprisonment but no less than 5 days

Federal crimes are classified into levels of seriousness; then a sentence range is set for violations.
The sentence of the judge must fall within the range specified by the sentence guidelines.

$1,000,000

The cost to keep the average inmate locked up for life.

adoption, but opponents criticize the long sentences, pointing out that it will cost about $1 million to keep an inmate locked up for life. With over 125,000 inmates sentenced to life terms, the costs, which fall primarily on state taxpayers, of getting tough on criminals are extremely high. As a result of these costs and claims that factors other than long prison terms may account for the significant drop in crime, many states are reconsidering mandatory sentencing and three-strikes laws.[37] The American Bar Association (ABA) has recommended an end to mandatory minimum sentences and overly harsh prison terms for nonviolent offenders.[38]

A 2004 report by the ABA said that long prison terms should be reserved for criminals who pose the greatest danger to society and who commit the most serious crimes. Ennis Archer, ABA president in 2004, critiques overly harsh and mandatory sentences, saying, "For more than 20 years, we have gotten tougher on crime. Now we need to get smarter."[39] Even Supreme Court Justice Anthony M. Kennedy has criticized overly harsh prison terms for nonviolent drug offenders, saying, "Our resources are misspent, our punishments too severe, our sentences too long."[40]

Sentencing Guidelines

Sentencing guidelines have been adopted by most states and the federal courts. In **sentencing guidelines**, crimes are classified according to seriousness, and a range of time is mandated for crimes within each category. Each state has its own classification for the seriousness of a crime and the corresponding length of sentence that can be imposed for that crime. Federal crimes are defined by Section 3559, U.S. Code, Title 18 into felonies and misdemeanors and are representative of the scheme used by most states in setting sentencing guidelines. The federal court distinguishes five classifications for felony crimes and three classifications for misdemeanors.

Presumptive Sentencing

Presumptive sentencing is a structured sentencing model that attempts to balance indeterminate sentencing with determinate sentencing. Presumptive sentencing gives discretionary powers to the judge within certain limits. The best-known presumptive sentencing model is used by the federal court according to the Sentencing Reform Act of 1984. This act set minimum and maximum terms of imprisonment for the various federal offenses. It then provided an adjustment for the offender's criminal history and for aggravating or mitigating circumstances. **Aggravating factors** are actions that may increase the seriousness of the crime and thus the length of the punishment. Aggravating factors may include using a firearm, discharging a firearm, or injuring a victim. **Mitigating factors** are actions that show

the offender's remorse or responsibility. Mitigating factors may include actions such as cooperation with the police, the return of stolen money or merchandise, or the youthful age of the offender. After conviction, the judge must sentence the offender using the *Federal Sentencing Guidelines Manual*.[41] Based on the offense and the offender's history, a base sentence is determined in months (for example, 135 to 180 months). The offender's sentence can be increased by adding months for aggravating factors such as the use of a firearm, failure to cooperate with arresting authorities, lack of remorse, and failure to recover stolen property. The offender's sentence also can be shortened by months for mitigating factors such as cooperating with arresting authorities, making restitution, and providing information to authorities leading to the arrest of others involved in the crime. The judge literally calculates a sentence using the base sentence in months listed in the *Federal Sentencing Guidelines Manual* and adding and subtracting months to this base sentence based on aggravating and mitigating factors. If the judge departs significantly from the federal sentencing guidelines, he or she must provide written reasons for this deviation at the sentencing hearing. The prosecution or defense can appeal the sentence.

> **presumptive sentencing** A structured sentencing model that attempts to balance sentencing guidelines with mandatory sentencing and at the same time provide discretion to the judge.
>
> **aggravating factors** Actions that may increase the seriousness of a crime.
>
> **mitigating factors** Actions that show the offender's remorse or responsibility.
>
> **truth in sentencing** Legislation that requires the court to disclose the actual prison time the offender is likely to serve.

Federal judges protested the imposition of the federal sentencing guidelines, arguing that they violated the separation of powers clause. The argument was that the legislative branch of the government did not have the authority to dictate sentencing guidelines to the judicial branch of the government. Ironically, the U.S. Supreme Court was the final arbiter of the dispute.[42]

Restrictions on Plea Bargaining

The Sentencing Reform Act of 1984 restricted but did not abolish plea bargaining. First, sentence-reduction plea bargaining cannot permit the offender to receive less than the minimum mandatory sentence for the offense.[43] Second, if plea bargaining results in reduced charges, the court record and plea bargaining agreement must fully disclose the details of the actual crime. Thus, if the crime of sexual assault is reduced to burglary, the court record will still contain the details of the crime of sexual assault.

Each state has its own classification for the seriousness of a crime and the corresponding length of sentence that can be imposed for that crime.

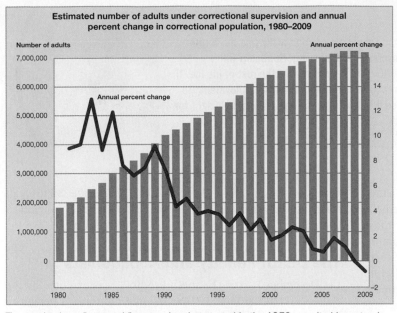

Estimated number of adults under correctional supervision and annual percent change in correctional population, 1980–2009

Number of adults — Annual percent change

The emphasis on "get tough" sentencing that started in the 1970s resulted in a steady increase of adults under correctional supervision. The actual number of adults under correctional supervision increased from 1980 to 2005 and then started to level off. However, around 1990, the annual percentage began to decrease.
Source: Lauren Glaze, *Correctional Populations in the United States, 2009* (Bureau of Justice Statistics, Washington, DC, 2010).

This record is public information. Thus, offenders cannot hide their crimes from the public and the media by plea-bargaining to a lesser included crime.

Abolishment of Parole

One consideration in the use of presumptive sentencing is that it abolishes parole, or early release from prison. This is a stumbling block for states that want to adopt a presumptive sentencing model similar to the federal court model. Parole provides for the possibility that an offender sentenced to serve nine years in prison may serve only one-third of that time. Many states depend on parole to move offenders through the correctional system because there are not enough prison beds to accommodate the number of sentenced offenders. Thus, before these states could adopt a presumptive sentencing model, they would have to build more prisons. The federal correctional system has the ability to move inmates throughout the United States, which allows the federal government to manage prison overcrowding by moving prisoners to less crowded facilities. State corrections systems do not have this option.

Unconstitutionality

Presumptive sentencing, specifically the federal sentencing guidelines, was struck down as unconstitutional by the U.S. Supreme Court in January 2005. The Court first ruled in June 2004 that Washington State's sentencing law, which was modeled on the federal sentencing guidelines, was unconstitutional because it violated the right to a trial by jury. The reasoning was that under the state's sentencing guidelines, similar to the federal guidelines, in determining the sentence

of the offender, judges could take into account actions and circumstances related to the case that were not introduced during the trial. The review of state sentencing guidelines was sparked by the review of the financial fraud case of Jamie Olis, who was sentenced to 24 years in prison. In the Washington State sentencing guidelines, many aggravating and mitigating factors allowed a judge to increase or decrease the length of a prison term, one of which was financial losses caused by fraud. The U.S. Supreme Court ruled that any factor that increases a criminal's sentence, except prior convictions, must be proven to a jury beyond a reasonable doubt before it can be considered as a factor to increase sentence length.

The Washington State decision affected other states with similar sentencing guidelines. In January 2005, the U.S. Supreme Court ruled that the same reasoning made federal sentencing guidelines invalid (*United States* v. *Booker*, No. 04 104, and *United States* v. *Fanfan*, No. 04-105). The Court ruled that the federal sentencing guidelines violated defendants' right to trial by jury by giving the judges the power to make factual findings that increased sentences beyond the maximum that the jury's finding alone would support. For example, in 2002, Mohamad Hammoud was convicted of smuggling cigarettes to raise money for the Lebanese terrorist group Hezbollah. He faced a 57-month sentence for that crime, but because of the terrorism connection and other findings by the judge, he was sentenced to 155 years.[44] The Court ruled that such increases are not constitutional.

The U.S. Supreme Court ruled that federal sentencing guidelines are "merely advisory." Justice Breyer, writing for the majority decision, said, "Judges must consult the guidelines and take them into account in imposing sentences. But at the end of the day the guidelines will be advisory only, with sentences to be reviewed on appeal for reasonableness."[45]

As a result of the Court's rulings in the Washington State case, in *United States* v. *Booker* and in *United States* v. *Fanfan*, state and federal courts must review those cases in which defendants were sentenced under state or federal sentencing guidelines. Also, the Supreme Court's ruling has renewed the struggle between Congress and the judiciary for control over setting criminal punishment.[46] In June 2005, then-Attorney General Albert Gonzales cited the "drift toward lesser sentences" in federal criminal cases and urged Congress to enact a new sentencing system that would incorporate mandatory minimum sentencing rules. However, the U.S. Supreme Court continued to affirm that to be constitutional, sentencing guidelines published by the U.S. Sentencing Commission must be advisory, not mandatory.

Truth in Sentencing

Because they cannot eliminate parole, some states have taken another approach, called truth in sentencing. **Truth in sentencing** legislation requires the court to disclose the actual prison time the offender is likely to serve. Some states

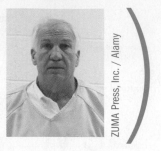
(Arizona, California, and Illinois) have gone one step further and adopted what is known as the 85 percent requirement rule, which states that for some offenses, the offender must serve at least 85% of his or her sentence before becoming eligible for release. Thus, an offender sentenced to 10 years in prison would have to serve 8.5 years before being eligible for early release. Because offenders in many states routinely serve only one-third to one-half of their sentences, the 85 percent requirement significantly increases the actual time in prison.

▶ Sentencing and the Death Penalty

Capital punishment—the death penalty—can be traced back to the earliest records of human history. In English common law, the roots of the American system of justice, even minor thefts could be punished by death, and the prisoner could be tortured in the process. The American colonists did not shun the use of the death penalty. The criminal codes of 1642 and 1650 of the New Haven Colony mandated the use of the death penalty not only for crimes of murder and treason, but also for crimes such as denying the true God and His attributes, bestiality, theft, horse theft, and children above the age of 16 striking their natural father or mother.[47]

Many Western countries, including England, France, Germany, and Italy, have banned the death penalty. Some nations have retained the death penalty in forms that are alien to U.S. values, such as execution by Sharia law, law based on Islamic religious values. For example, in March 2000, Judge Allah Bakhsh Ranja of Pakistan sentenced to death a man convicted of strangling and dismembering 100 children. The judge ordered Javed Iqbal, aged 42, to be executed in a Lahore park in front of his victims' parents. He told the prisoner, "You will be strangled in front of the parents whose children you killed. Your body will then be cut into a hundred pieces and put in acid, the same way you killed the children."[48]

In the United States, lethal injection is the primary method of execution for states. Some states have alternative methods. In states with alternative methods, the inmate may be allowed to choose his or her method of execution. (See Figure 9–1.)

The federal government uses lethal injection for offenses prosecuted under 28 Code of Federal Regulations, Part 26. Federal cases prosecuted under the Violent Crime Control Act of 1994 (18 United States Code 3596) call for the method used in the state in which the conviction took place.[49]

The Death Penalty and Abolitionists

On December 1, 2005, Kenneth Lee Boyd was executed by the state of North Carolina. He was the one-thousandth person to be executed by the United States since 1976, when the Supreme Court upheld states' rights to order the death penalty. As of June 2012, there have been 1,299 executions. The number of executions per year has declined from a high of 98 in 1999 to 43 in 2011. Also, polls show that public support of the death penalty is dropping. In 2009, approximately 60% of Americans supported use of the death penalty, but that number is down from a high of 80% in 1994.[50] A 2010 poll by the Death Penalty Information Center found that only 33% of respondents would choose the death penalty for murder if other alternatives were available. Most (39%) would choose a sentence of life without parole and restitution.[51]

Some people are opposed to the death penalty in specific cases for specific reasons, such as their belief that the person is innocent, the person did not receive a fair trial, or there is reasonable doubt that justifies an alternative other than death. However, some people oppose the death penalty under all circumstances and for all reasons. They do not believe that the government has the right to execute citizens. Those universally opposed to the use of capital punishment are called **abolitionists**.

The debate between abolitionists and those who favor capital punishment is very old. One of the earliest debates about the death penalty was recorded by Greek philosopher Plato regarding Socrates, who was convicted by the Athenians of corrupting the morals of the youth and was sentenced to death. A friend tried to convince Socrates that he should escape because he was wrongfully convicted and told him that other cities would welcome him as a citizen, recognizing that the

LEARNING OUTCOMES 5 Summarize the challenges to the death penalty sentence, and explain how U.S. Supreme Court rulings have affected the death penalty sentence.

GLOSSARY

capital punishment The sentence of death.

abolitionists People opposed to the death penalty.

bifurcated trial A two-part trial structure in which the jury first determines guilt or innocence and then considers new evidence relating to the appropriate punishment.

157 Electrocution

3 Hanging

11 Gas chamber

3 Firing squad

1,125 Lethal injection

FIGURE 9-1 **Executions since 1976 by Method Used**
Source: Death Penalty Information Center, "Facts about the Death Penalty," http://www.deathpenaltyinfo.org (accessed June 21, 2012).

sentence was unjust. Socrates refused, however, arguing, "But whether in battle or in a court of law, or in any other place, he must do what his city and his country order him; or he must change their view of what is just…. He who has experience of the manner in which we order justice and administer the State, and still remains, has entered into an implied contract that he will do as we command him."[52] This argument—that there is an implicit contract between the individual and the state—is the crux of one of the most controversial debates in sentencing—the role of capital punishment.

Supporters of capital punishment claim the death penalty is an effective deterrent to crime, or the death penalty is justified by the philosophy of an "eye for an eye." That is to say, since the person murdered another, the death penalty is the appropriate punishment. Both arguments are based on the assumption that the state has the legal and moral authority to execute citizens.

The question of whether the death penalty deters crime is disputed by research data. Cesare Beccaria, the father of classical criminology, argued that the death penalty was not an effective deterrent. He argued that compared to death, life in prison was a greater punishment and was more dreaded by the offender. Some research studies claim that 3 to 18 murders

are prevented for every inmate put to death. Other research studies claim that there is an inverse relationship between the use of the death penalty and the crime rate—crime goes down as the use of the death penalty goes up. For example, in 2010, the southern states had the highest murder rate but accounted for over 80% of executions. The northeastern states accounted for less than 1% of all executions but tied with the western states for the lowest murder rate.[53] Criminal justice practitioners and academic scholars do not support the effectiveness of the death penalty in reducing crime. A 2009 poll of police chiefs found that they ranked the death penalty last among ways to reduce violent crime.[54] In a survey of criminology experts, 88% rejected the notion that the death penalty acts as a deterrent to murder.[55]

Most experts believe that the research is inconclusive and unreliable. Many factors influence the crime rate, and the number of people executed is so small compared to the number of offenses that experts do not think that the deterrent effect of the death penalty can be accurately gauged. When there have been only 22 to 70 executions per year since 1992 and these executions occur years (even decades) after the crime was committed, researchers argue that correlations and data regarding the impact of the death penalty are unreliable.

Abolitionists claim that capital punishment is ineffective in preventing crime, is unfairly administered, and is sometimes administered in error, but the central premise of their arguments is that government does not have the right to take a person's life.[56] For example, the Southern Center for Human Rights argues against the death penalty, quoting freed slave Frederick Douglass, who became a champion of civil rights: "Life is the great primary and most precious and comprehensive of all human rights … whether it be coupled with virtue, honor, and happiness, or with sin, disgrace, and misery, the continued possession of it is rightfully not a matter of volition; … [it is not] to be deliberately or voluntarily destroyed, either by individuals separately, or combined in what is called Government."[57] Both abolitionists and proponents of the death penalty also argue for their views on the basis of religious values.

Until 1968, abolitionists could be excluded from capital murder juries simply because they opposed the death penalty. Abolitionists opposed being barred from capital murder juries and appealed to the U.S. Supreme Court. In *Witherspoon* v. *Illinois* (1968),[58] the U.S. Supreme Court declared unconstitutional the common practice of prosecutors excluding abolitionists from capital murder juries. After the *Witherspoon* decision,

Presselect / Alamy

the composition of juries in capital murder cases changed in that people opposed in principle to the death penalty could not be excluded from the jury.

It is difficult for prosecutors to obtain a death penalty conviction at trial. A 2008 study by the Urban Institute found that in cases in which prosecutors sought the death penalty, in only about one-third of the cases did the jury return a death verdict, and most of those death sentences were overturned on appeal. Obviously, the inclusion of abolitionists on capital murder cases makes it harder, or even impossible, for prosecutors to obtain a unanimous verdict for the death penalty.

The Death Penalty and Civil Rights

In the United States, the death penalty sentence can be imposed by the state, federal courts, military courts, and military tribunals. The use of the death penalty by federal courts, military courts, and military tribunals is governed by federal laws, executive orders, and the U.S. Supreme Court. Each state has the option of adopting the death penalty as a legal punishment for crime. In 2012, 33 states permit the death penalty. States that use the death penalty as a sanction must preserve the civil rights of the condemned prisoner as defined by the state and federal constitutions. Appealing to the U.S. Supreme Court has been a common strategy of abolitionists. Most appeals are based primarily on the Eighth Amendment, prohibiting cruel and unusual punishment, and the Fourteenth Amendment, providing for equality in justice.

The Issue of Cruel and Unusual Punishment

An early appeal to the U.S. Supreme Court based on the Eighth Amendment was *Wilkerson* v. *Utah* (1878).[59] Wilkerson appealed to the U.S. Supreme Court that his sentence of death by firing squad was cruel and unusual, but the Court upheld the constitutionality of the sentence.

The first execution by electrocution took place at Auburn Prison (New York) on August 6, 1890. William Kemmler was sentenced to be executed for murder by use of the newly invented electric chair. Kemmler appealed to the Court that electrocution was cruel and unusual punishment. The Court disagreed, however, and execution by electrocution was added as another method of carrying out the death sentence.[60] In 1947, the Court was asked to take up another gruesome debate concerning electrocution: What if the person survives the first attempt at electrocution? Willie Francis, a 15-year-old African-American, was convicted of killing Andrew Thomas by shooting him five times. The apparent motive was robbery; Francis took the victim's watch and $4. When the

state of Louisiana attempted to execute Francis, the electric chair failed to provide a fatal surge of electricity and Francis survived. He appealed a second attempt as cruel and unusual punishment, but the Court disagreed and he was electrocuted in the second attempt.[61]

The most recent U.S. Supreme Court Eighth Amendment challenge to the death penalty involved two Kentucky inmates under sentence of death who appealed their sentence on the grounds that the three-cocktail drug mixture used in lethal injection could result in unnecessary suffering and pain.[62] The challenge brought to a halt executions in most states because lethal injection and the drug mixture used by Kentucky was the most common method of execution. In April 2008, the U.S. Supreme Court denied the inmates' appeal and ruled that the method of execution was not a violation of the Eighth Amendment.

Other Civil Rights Issues

The U.S. Supreme Court has also addressed other civil rights issues and the death penalty. For example, the Supreme Court has ruled that people cannot be excluded from capital murder case juries because of their race. This situation most often arose when the defendant was African-American and the prosecutor excluded African-Americans from the jury by use of peremptory challenges. The Court ruled that exclusion of African-Americans from the jury when the defendant was African-American was racial discrimination. In 2002, the Supreme Court ruled that only juries, not judges, could decide sentences in capital cases. This ruling overturned state sentencing policies wherein the jury decided the guilt of the defendant but the judge decided whether the defendant would receive life in prison or the death penalty. The Court ruled that only the jury had the right to decide if the defendant should be eligible to be executed. Also, in 2002, the Supreme Court barred the execution of people with mental retardation, and in 2005, it barred the execution of juveniles.

Challenges to the Death Penalty

Furman v. Georgia

In 1972, the U.S. Supreme Court effectively banned the use of the death penalty. In *Furman* v. *Georgia*,[63] the Court issued its most significant ruling regarding the death penalty. Rather than focus on the physical and emotional pain of the prisoner as the grounds for capital punishment to be considered cruel and unusual, Furman's defense argued that the death penalty,

TIMELINE — Timeline of Key Events			
1878	**1890**	**1947**	**2008**
Wilkerson appeals firing squad as cruel and unusual punishment.	Kemmler appeals electrocution as cruel and unusual punishment.	Francis appeals second attempt at electrocution as cruel and unusual punishment.	Two Kentucky inmates appeal lethal injection as cruel and unusual punishment.

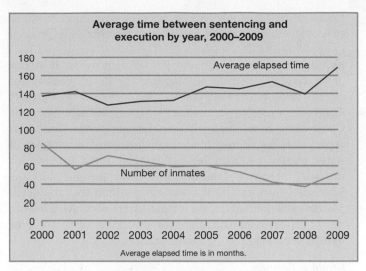

Average Time between Sentencing and Execution by Year

Source: Tracy L. Snell, *Capital Punishment*, 2007—Statistical Tables (Bureau of Justice Statistics, Washington, DC, 2010).

as applied, was arbitrary and capricious. This argument presented evidence that a person convicted of a capital offense may or may not be executed because the law and the state courts did not systematically apply the death penalty. Who was executed and who was not appeared to be determined randomly. The only common element in executions was not the crime, but the socioeconomic and racial characteristics of the offenders—poor and African-American. (See Figure 9–2.)

The Supreme Court agreed, and all death penalty sentences were suspended until the state could prove that the death penalty was applied fairly. The death penalty was reinstated four years later in *Gregg* v. *Georgia*. (See Figure 9–3 for the number of executions from 1976 to 2012.) Despite this renewal of the death penalty after the Court's approval of the laws and practices of each state, challenges to the fairness of the application of the death penalty continue. Cases continue to be appealed to the Court on the grounds that the death penalty is racially biased.

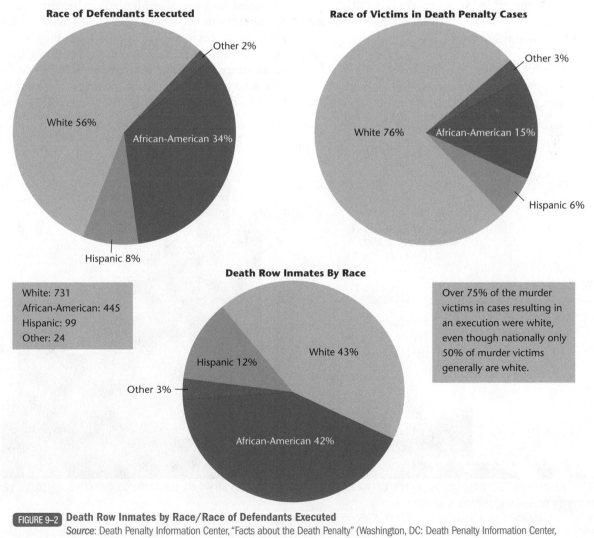

FIGURE 9–2 Death Row Inmates by Race/Race of Defendants Executed
Source: Death Penalty Information Center, "Facts about the Death Penalty" (Washington, DC: Death Penalty Information Center, 2012), pp. 1–2.

There are two important points to note about the *Furman v. Georgia* decision. First, it did not declare that the death penalty was unconstitutional, only that the manner in which it was applied was unconstitutional. Second, all states were required to submit proof to the U.S. Supreme Court that their use of the death sentence was fair, equitable, and proportional to the crime. In effect, this ruling voided all existing death penalties and death penalty laws. Every prisoner in every state under the sentence of death was given a reprieve. However, rather than require new trials for all prisoners sentenced to death, the Court required only that the death sentence be reexamined. As a result of this ruling, each state that wanted to keep the death penalty as a sanction had to submit legislation to the Court for approval prior to resuming the use of the death penalty. Some states chose to abolish the death penalty rather than review and submit new legislation to the Court for approval.

In addition to claims of racial bias, defendants who are executed have lower educational achievement than the national average. The median education of prisoners who were under sentence of death was eleventh grade. In 2004, over 52% of prisoners sentenced to death did not graduate from high school or have a graduate equivalency degree (GED). Lack of formal education is not a valid appeal of the death penalty. However, an intellectual disability is. In *Atkins* v. *Virginia* (2002), the U.S. Supreme Court ruled it was unconstitutional to execute defendants with "mental retardation."

Criteria for the Death Penalty

Some states attempted to satisfy the criteria by adopting mandatory death penalties for first-degree murder. The Court refused to allow this strategy, however, and required states to be more specific in defining the criteria to be used in applying the death penalty.[64] The Court further defined its criteria for proportionate punishment when it struck down Georgia's statute authorizing the death penalty for rape.[65] The Court ruled that the death penalty was grossly disproportionate to the crime. In 2008, the U.S. Supreme Court again considered whether the sentence of death was appropriate for crimes other than homicide. A number of states wanted to enact legislation that would provide for the death penalty for the rape of a child. In June 2008, the Supreme Court upheld its previous position that the death penalty was limited to the crime of murder. As a result, nearly all death penalties are for the crime of first-degree murder with aggravating circumstances.

Gregg v. Georgia

In 1976, the U.S. Supreme Court issued another landmark decision in *Gregg* v. *Georgia*,[66] which required a **bifurcated trial** structure. This required that trials for capital offenses had to be conducted in two separate parts. In the first part of the trial, the jury determines the guilt of the defendant. In the second part of the trial, after the defendant has been convicted, additional evidence can be introduced relevant to the punishment appropriate for the crime. Prior to 2002, although it was common to allow the jury to exclude the death penalty as an appropriate sanction for the crime, in some states, the judge determined whether the defendant was sentenced to the death penalty.[67] In *Ring* v. *Arizona* (2002), the Supreme Court ruled that a jury, not a judge,

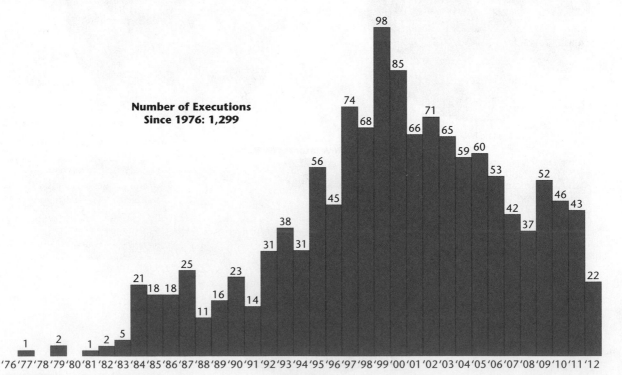

Number of Executions Since 1976: 1,299

FIGURE 9–3 **Executions, 1976 to June 2012**
Executions have declined from a high of 98 per year in 1999 to about one-half that number in 2011. The decline reflects waning public confidence in the fairness of the death penalty and the concern regarding the hundreds of wrongfully convicted defendants who have been exonerated, many of them on death row. Do you think death sentences are fair and equitable?
Source: Death Penalty Information Center, "Facts about the Death Penalty" (Washington, DC: Death Penalty Information Center, 2012), p. 1.

An apology for the wrongful execution of a prisoner is insufficient and does not restore the injustice done or heal the harm to innocent people.

130 The number of death row inmates who have been exonerated nationwide.

must make a finding of "aggravating factors" when those factors underlie a judge's choice to impose the death penalty rather than a lesser punishment.[68]

Reconsideration of the Death Penalty

Many states have reconsidered the use of the death penalty. Some states have abandoned the death penalty, and others have suspended its use until critical questions and protocols can be resolved. For example, when more death row inmates were exonerated than executed in 2003, then-Governor George Ryan of Illinois commuted the sentence of all inmates on death row to life in prison and called for an investigation into the use of the death penalty.[69] Illinois abolished the death penalty in 2011. The ABA called for a national moratorium on capital punishment, and 16 other states decided to examine their death penalty laws in 2000.[70] After years of debate, Florida ended the use of the electric chair in 2001.[71] In response to much criticism, Texas joined 15 other states and the federal government in passing a ban on executing murderers with mental retardation.[72] In December 2001, the Kansas Supreme Court ruled that the way the state's death penalty was handed down was unfair and must be changed, saying, "The provisions of the death penalty violated the federal constitutional provisions against cruel and unusual punishment and the guarantee of due process." This opinion voided the use of the death penalty until the state could rewrite the sentencing language.[73]

In 2007, New Jersey adopted legislation that abolished the death penalty. In 2008, the state Supreme Court of Nebraska ruled that the electric chair is cruel and unusual punishment. This ruling effectively abolished the death penalty in Nebraska because it was the only state that still relied solely on electrocution. Although the death penalty remains in Nebraska, there is no means to carry out the sentence. Unless the state adopts new legislation authorizing the use of lethal injection, there will be no executions in Nebraska. In 2012, the Arkansas Supreme Court struck down the state's lethal injection protocol, leaving the state without a lawful way to carry out executions.

The Innocent Convicted

Perhaps the most significant argument behind the reexamination of the death penalty is the alarming number of people who have been wrongfully convicted and sentenced to death.

The death penalty is final and cannot be reversed or corrected. An apology by the criminal justice system for the wrongful execution of a prisoner is insufficient and does not restore the injustice done or heal the harm to innocent people. For example, 60 years after Lena Baker, the only woman ever

put to death in Georgia's electric chair, was executed, the state of Georgia announced that it would posthumously pardon her. Baker, a 40-year-old African-American woman, was put to death in 1945 for killing her employer, a white man named E. B. Knight. At her trial, she contended that he held her as a kind of sex slave and she shot him in self-defense as he was attacking her with a crowbar. An all-male, all-white jury convicted her of capital murder in a one-day trial, and she was executed in Georgia's electric chair less than a year later.[74] However, the Georgia Board of Pardons and Parole made it clear that the board did not find that Baker was not guilty of the crime, but it did find that the decision to deny her clemency in 1945 "was a grievous error, as this case called out for mercy."[75] Unfortunately, the admission of this "grievous error" does little for Lena Baker. One study suggests that as many as 23 innocent defendants were executed between 1900 and 1988.[76] However, state officials do not acknowledge that any innocent defendant has ever been executed.

The criminal justice system is approaching a near crisis of credibility regarding the wrongful convictions of people accused of crime. Partly as a result of DNA evidence, many convicted prisoners are being freed from prison and death row. The impact of DNA evidence combined with recent revelations of official misconduct and corruption by police and prosecutors and allegations of racial discrimination has led many people to question the continued use of the death penalty as a fair and just punishment.

Official Misconduct and Error

A study considering 125 cases published in the *North Carolina Law Review* found that the leading causes of wrongful convictions for murder were false confessions and perjury by codefendants, informants, police officers, or forensic scientists.[77] The three groups of people most likely to provide false confessions are those with mental retardation, those with mental illness, and juveniles.

Some defendants have been convicted because of flawed forensic evidence. For example, Malcolm Rent Johnson was convicted of rape and murder in 1982. Johnson claimed he was innocent, but forensic evidence disputed his protests of innocence. Johnson was executed on January 6, 2000. An investigation a year later into the accuracy of the forensic chemist's testimony, which was instrumental in convicting Johnson, strongly suggests that she gave false testimony about the evidence. Also, the evidence suggests that there may be at least two other cases in which the results stated in the lab report and confirmed by the state's forensic chemist contradict independent expert reexamination of the actual physical evidence.[78]

Some prisoners appear to have been wrongfully convicted because they were framed by police and/or prosecutors.

For example, Ronald Jones, who said police had beaten a confession out of him, was exonerated of charges of rape and murder.[79] In another case, after Rolando Cruz was convicted of murder and sentenced to death, a reexamination of his case resulted in his release. In addition, charges of conspiracy to obstruct justice and to commit official misconduct were filed against the police and district attorney lawyers who prosecuted Cruz.[80] In another case, the investigation into the abuse of power of Los Angeles Police Department officers in the Rampart division uncovered evidence that police framed numerous innocent citizens and obtained convictions on the basis of false evidence given by police officers.[81] While there are numerous other examples, one final example is that of Walter McMillian. McMillian was released in 1993 after six years on death row based on findings that the sheriff framed him for the murder.[82]

Ineffective Counsel

Some prisoners have ended up on death row because of inadequate legal representation at trial. For example, Gary Wayne Drinkard was convicted and spent five years on Alabama's death row. Drinkard was released after it was determined that his defense failed to introduce critical evidence and witnesses who would have proven his innocence. As an example of the need for death penalty reform, Southern Center for Human Rights director Stephen B. Bright presented Gary Drinkard as a witness at hearings on the Innocence Protection Act of 2001. Bright told the committee, "We have been very fortunate that the innocence of some of those condemned to die in our courts has been discovered by sheer happenstance and good luck.... The major reason that innocent people are being sentenced to death is because the representation provided to the poor in capital cases is often a scandal." The committee heard testimony that defendants were given lawyers fresh from law school or lawyers who had never before tried a death penalty case.[83]

In another case in December 2001, a judge overturned the murder conviction of a man imprisoned for 27 years for murder. The judge ruled that the trial "was plagued by multiple problems which, cumulatively, present the inescapable conclusion that he was denied a fair trial." Even the widow of the murdered victim concurred, saying, "There's so much evidence

> African-Americans and Hispanics are treated more harshly than whites are at every level of the criminal justice system, from investigation to sentencing.

that it wasn't him, and it doesn't look like there was any that says it was him."[84] Other prisoners who were wrongfully convicted have been released after 13 years,[85] 17 years,[86] and 24 years[87] of wrongful incarceration.

Racial Bias

A report by the Leadership Conference on Civil Rights, a coalition of 180 civil rights groups, released in May 2000 concluded that African-Americans and Hispanics are treated more harshly than whites are at every level of the criminal justice system, from investigation to sentencing.[88] A racially biased criminal justice system is deep-rooted in American history. In Virginia during the 1830s, there were only 5 capital crimes for whites but at least 70 for African-Americans.[89] Furthermore, there was a difference in severity of sentencing in which African-Americans could receive the death penalty for any offense for which a white would receive three or more years of imprisonment.[90] In 1967, the President's Commission on Law Enforcement and Administration of Justice concluded, "The death penalty is most frequently imposed and carried out on the poor, the Negro, and the members of unpopular groups."[91] A 1973 study of offenders convicted of rape and sentenced to death shows that 13% of African-Americans convicted of rape were sentenced to death, but only 2% of whites convicted of rape were sentenced to death.[92] African-Americans convicted of raping white women were more likely to be sentenced to death than were African-Americans convicted of raping African-American women or white men convicted of raping either white or African-American women.

Furman v. *Georgia* (1972) explicitly recognized the application of the death penalty as potentially arbitrary and capricious and sought to put an end to sentencing abuses once and for all. The effectiveness of ending racial discrimination in the use of the death penalty is debatable, however. A 1996 Kentucky study of death sentences between 1976 and 1991 found that African-Americans still had a higher probability of being sentenced to death than did homicide offenders of other races.[93]

The racial bias of the death penalty continues to be controversial. In December 2001, a federal judge overturned the death sentence of Mumia Abu-Jamal. Abu-Jamal had been convicted for the first-degree murder of a Philadelphia police

(Think About It ...

In *Abbott* v. *U.S.*, Kevin Abbott challenged a federal law that allows tougher sentences for using a firearm while selling drugs or committing violent acts. The law requires a mandatory five-year sentence for having a gun, seven years if the firearm is brandished, and ten years if it is discharged. Abbott was sentenced to a 15-year mandatory sentence for being a felon in possession of a firearm, plus an additional five years. Abbott argued that the law intended offenders to serve a minimum of five years, not an additional five years. The Court disagreed. Do tough gun laws deter criminals from using firearms? Why or why not?

michaklootwijk/Fotolia

officer, Daniel Faulkner, in 1981. Abu-Jamal claimed that he was a political prisoner and a victim of racial discrimination.[94] In another case, a federal judge asked prosecutors to explain why they were seeking the death penalty against three alleged Latino drug gang members but not against mob boss Joseph Merlino and three other codefendants. Lawyers for the defense argued, "No distinction other than the race of the defendants … satisfactorily (or rationally) explains the filing of a death notice in the case at hand … and the decision not to return it in the Merlino matter."[95] Despite the decades of statistical data indicating that the death penalty is not color-blind, the U.S. Supreme Court has refused to admit statistical evidence of racial discrimination as a justification for reversing death sanctions against African-Americans. In *McCleskey* v. *Kemp* (1987), the Court said that statistical data alone do not provide the level of proof necessary to claim that a specific death penalty violates the Eighth or Fourteenth Amendment.[96] A convicted person can obtain relief from the death penalty under the claim of racial discrimination only in both of the following circumstances:

- The decision makers in the case acted with discriminatory intent.

- The legislature enacted or maintained the death penalty statute because of an anticipated racially discriminatory effect.[97]

The report of the Leadership Conference on Civil Rights does not blame overt racial bias for the disparities in the criminal justice system. The report, written by lawyers, says that "a self-fulfilling set of assumptions about the criminality of Blacks and Hispanics influences the decisions of police, prosecutors and judges in a way that accounts for the gap."[98] The report argues that these assumptions about the criminality of African-Americans and Hispanics are far-reaching and are a primary cause for police abuses such as preparing false arrest reports, lying under oath, and planting evidence against minorities.[99]

What is the evidence for racial discrimination in American criminal justice? Should this be accepted as a self-fulfilling prophecy? Would statistics about racial discrimination in sentencing influence a jury to give a lighter sentence? Would a defense attorney use this argument to appeal a death sentence or to try to win a stay of execution?

DNA Evidence

The advent of DNA testing in the late 1980s has had a tremendous impact on the criminal justice system. By 1997, the FBI crime lab's DNA Analysis Unit had exonerated about 3,000 suspects. Nearly one in four of the suspects were exonerated but had already been charged with a crime before lab results were returned.[100] There are continuous reports of inmates freed from wrongful incarceration as a result of DNA evidence demonstrating that they could not have been the offenders.[101]

Collection of people's DNA continues to expand to create vast DNA databases. In April 2009, the FBI and 15 states collected DNA samples from people awaiting trial and from detained immigrants. In 2009, the FBI DNA database had 6.7 million profiles. The FBI projects that by 2014, it will add 1.2 million DNA profiles per year. In 35 states, minors are required to provide DNA samples upon conviction. Sixteen states take DNA from people who have been convicted of misdemeanor crimes.

Difficulties in Introducing DNA after Conviction

The reliability of DNA evidence and the release of wrongfully convicted prisoners, often after serving years on death row, prove the fallibility of the criminal justice system. Often the inmates who were released had to fight to get the courts to reconsider their cases. Courts have adopted rules limiting the amount of time that may pass before new evidence will be considered[102] or have refused to allow DNA testing of prisoners who have already been executed.[103] In many cases, the criminal justice system has refused to reopen cases for which DNA testing could provide new evidence.[104]

A comprehensive study of 328 criminal cases over the last 15 years in which the convicted person was exonerated suggests that there are thousands of innocent people in prison today.[105] The study identified 199 murder exonerations, 73 of them in capital cases. Yet, only two states, Illinois and New York, give inmates the right to use the latest DNA testing. Appeals procedures make it difficult to introduce DNA evidence after a conviction. Except in North Carolina, convicted defendants are not entitled to appeal the court's decision of guilt based on a claim of innocence. Most courts allow appeals based only on trial errors that could have had a

16 The number of states that collect DNA samples from people convicted of misdemeanors.

ZUMA Press/Newscom

(Think About It …

In 2010, Oklahoma passed a state constitutional amendment that forbids state judges from considering international or Islamic law in deciding cases. While there are many similarities between U.S. and Sharia law, there are striking differences and some incompatibility with a democratic state.

The amendment was declared unconstitutional on the grounds that it discriminated against a religious group because the amendment specifically mentioned Islamic law. However, it was suggested that states could ban the use of any law or standard other than that of the United States.

Should courts be banned from deciding cases using international law? Why or why not?

significant effect on the verdict or on new evidence that was not available at the time of the trial. Appeals based on DNA evidence commonly claim the latter.

However, new evidence alone is not sufficient for a successful appeal. For a case appealed based on new evidence, the court requires the defendant to demonstrate that there is a reasonable possibility that the new evidence would prove his or her innocence. If the court determines that the evidence presented at the original trial provides substantial proof of the inmate's guilt, the court will reject appeals for DNA testing. Thus, if there is physical evidence such as fingerprints, bloody clothing, the murder weapon, and reliable eyewitness testimony, the court will deny an inmate's appeal for DNA testing. The U.S. Supreme Court has upheld the denial of requests for DNA testing. In *District Attorney's Office for the Third Judicial District* v. *Osborne* (2009), the Court ruled that prisoners do not have a constitutional right to DNA testing after their conviction.

In some cases involving prisoners who have demonstrated through post-trial DNA testing that the trial evidence does not support their guilt, prosecutors still have refused to accept that the convicted defendant may be innocent.[106] The law does not protect the right of convicted inmates to appeal based on DNA evidence, and some states routinely destroy rape kits and other evidence that could be used to establish prisoners' innocence.[107] A study by Brandon L. Garrett at the University of Virginia School of Law found that prosecutors opposed DNA testing in about 20% of cases. However, in about 43% of DNA testing cases, the DNA test identified the perpetrator.[108]

Cost of the Death Penalty

The economic recession and the serious financial impact falling revenues have had on state budgets have caused serious reconsideration of the economic wisdom of the death penalty. According to the Death Penalty Information Center in Maryland, an average death penalty case results in a death sentence cost of approximately $3 million.[109] The cost of each execution for the state of Florida is $24 million. In North Carolina, it costs $2.16 million more per trial for capital cases compared to life imprisonment cases. In Texas, a death penalty case costs an average of $2.3 million, about three times the cost of imprisoning someone in a single cell at the highest security level for 40 years.[110] The cost of death sentences adds a tremendous strain to state budgets. It is estimated that since 1978, the cost of the death penalty in California has added $4 billion to the budget.[111] Given the economic burden on strained state budgets, many states have asked whether the costs associated with the death penalty are worth it.

▶ Conclusion: The Debate Continues

What is the purpose of sentencing? Is it to punish the offender, to rehabilitate the offender, or to protect the community? The National Institute of Justice sponsored research that examined the crime-control effects of sentences over a 20-year period based on 962 felony offenders sentenced in 1976 or 1977 in Essex County, New Jersey.[112] The purpose of this longitudinal study was to examine the effects of the different sanctions on the offenders' subsequent criminal careers. The study concluded that the main sentencing choices available to the judges had little effect on crime-control aims.[113]

The overall conclusion of the study was that empirical data suggested that sentences made little difference in crime-control perspective.[114] Such data do not provide a happy ending to the discussion on sentencing. Innovative sentencing strategies are constantly being tried. Laws defining the punishment for crimes and sentencing guidelines are being revised. People are examining the effect of sentencing and the fallibility of the criminal justice system and are making new recommendations to improve it.

Sentencing is an important crossroad in the criminal justice system. It is harmful to convict the innocent and to impose sentences that do not deter criminality. Also harmful are the many possibilities for error in the use of the death penalty. Sentencing and sentencing reform will continue to be subjects of study and debate.

- Except for the effect of incapacitation, whether the offender was sentenced to confinement made no difference in the rate of reoffending.
- Where the offender was confined made little difference—except for the unfavorable effect of placement in a youth facility.
- The length of the maximum sentence made no difference.
- The length of time actually confined made a slight difference.
- When jail was imposed along with probation made no difference.
- Fines or restitution made no difference.

Analysis of 962 felony sentences and the impact on recidivism
Source: National Institute of Justice, *Effects of Judges' Sentencing Decisions on Criminal Careers* (Washington, DC: U.S. Department of Justice, November 1999).

Race and the Death Penalty

In *McCleskey* v. *Kemp* (1987), the U.S. Supreme Court ruled that statistical evidence of a significant racial disparity in death sentences in Georgia was not sufficient reason to overturn a Georgia man's death verdict. The decision has been called the "Dred Scott decision of our time" for its indifference to racial equality.

Statistics suggest otherwise. For example, 42% of death row inmates are African-American and 34% of defendants executed were African-American. Studies indicate that in Louisiana, the death sentence is 97% more likely for those whose victim was white. In California, those who killed whites were three times more likely to get the death penalty. In North Carolina, people who murdered white victims were 3.5 times more likely to be sentenced to death. A Michigan State University study of 173 capital trials found that prosecutors used peremptory challenges to remove African-Americans from the juries at a rate more than twice that of whites.[115]

North Carolina has repudiated *McCleskey*, and its Racial Justice Act allows future defendants and current death row inmates to present evidence, including statistical patterns, suggesting that race played a major role in their being sentenced to death.[116] The law allows defendants on death row to present evidence that (1) a death sentence was more likely to be sought or imposed on defendants of one race, (2) a death sentence was more likely when the victim was a certain race, or (3) racial bias influenced jury selection. The defendant does not have to deny factual guilt.

Nearly all of the inmates on North Carolina's death row have filed claims under the Racial Justice Act.

This case raises several interesting questions. Among them are the following:

1. Are statistical data sufficient to establish racial bias in the death penalty? Why or why not?

2. Opponents of North Carolina's Racial Justice Act claim that the true purpose of the law is to end the death penalty by making it too complicated and too expensive. Do you agree with this argument? Why or why not?

3. Is there is a conspiracy of prosecutors, mostly white, plotting to obtain capital convictions for African-Americans defendants? Explain.

Mikael Karlsson / Alamy

Describe the purpose of sentencing.

Historically, punishments in England and the American colonies consisted of fines, restitution, ordeals, and corporal punishment. Corporal punishment included whipping, branding, and confinement to the stocks or pillories. In modern-day society, punishment is not to be cruel and unusual; hence, judges are guided by the law as to the type and range of punishments that may be imposed. Sentences must be fair and cannot discriminate on factors such as race, sex, or religion. There are five contemporary philosophies concerning the purpose of punishment: deterrence, incapacitation, retribution, rehabilitation, and restorative justice.

1. How many sentences are handed down annually by judges across the United States?

2. Describe what comprises corporal punishment.

3. What type of punishment should the Eighth Amendment prevent?

4. Which sentencing philosophy removes the offender permanently from society?

5. Which sentencing philosophy focuses the most on victims' rights?

corporal punishment The administration of bodily pain as punishment for a crime.

deterrence The philosophy and practices that emphasize making criminal behavior less appealing.

specific deterrence A concept based on the premise that a person is best deterred from committing future crimes by the specific nature of the punishment.

general deterrence The concept based on the logic that people who witness the pain suffered by those who commit crimes will want to avoid that pain and will refrain from criminal activity.

incapacitation Deterrence based on the premise that the only way to prevent criminals from reoffending is to remove them from society.

banishment The removal of an offender from the community.

transportation The eighteenth-century practice by Great Britain of sending offenders to the American colonies and later to Australia.

retribution Deterrence based on the premise that criminals should be punished because they deserve it.

rehabilitation Deterrence based on the premise that criminals can be "cured" of their problems and criminality and can be returned to society.

medical model The rehabilitation model that views criminality as a disease to be cured.

restorative justice A model of deterrence that uses restitution programs, community work programs, victim-offender mediation, and other strategies not only to rehabilitate the offender, but also to address the damage done to the community and the victim.

Explain how the criminal justice system sentences the offender who claims to be mentally ill.

Guilt in the criminal justice system is based on the assumption that the defendant can distinguish between right and wrong. However, a defendant might plead not guilty by reason of insanity. If a defendant is found not guilty by reason of insanity, he or she will not be criminally sanctioned, but placed in a mental institution. Should a jury find the defendant sane, he or she is convicted of a criminal charge. If an offender is found mentally unfit for incarceration in the state or federal prison system, he or she will be placed in a mental health facility to undergo psychiatric treatment.

1. What is a civil commitment examination?

2. Describe limiting factors of the insanity plea.

3. What happens in sentencing when a defendant is not successful in his or her insanity defense?

legally sane An assumption that a defendant knows right from wrong and that his or her behavior was willful.

not guilty by reason of insanity A verdict by which the jury finds that a defendant committed the crime but was insane.

civil commitment examination A determination of whether the defendant should be released or confined to an institution for people with mental illness.

guilty but mentally ill A new type of verdict in which the jury finds a defendant mentally ill but sufficiently aware to be morally responsible for his or her criminal acts.

LEARNING OUTCOMES 3 Identify the factors that can influence whether the defendant receives a fair sentence, including the role and process of the presentence investigation and sentencing hearing.

The presentence investigation report is important in providing a fair sentence. A presentence investigation gathers information about the convicted offender to help the judge determine the appropriate sentence. This report includes the defendant's employment history, family relationships, and reputation in the community. The judge also might consider a victim impact statement, during which the victim of the crime has an opportunity to speak and influence sentencing.

1. How are state-level judges selected? How could that create biases?

2. What happens during the *voir dire* process?

3. Who prepares the presentence investigation report?

4. At what stage of a trial could a victim impact statement be given?

impeachment A process for removing judges or elected officials from office.

***voir dire* process** The questioning of potential jurors to determine whether they have biases that would disqualify them from jury service.

presentence investigation An in-depth interview and investigation into the background of a convicted defendant and the impact of his or her crime on victims and the community.

presentence investigator A person who works for the court and has the responsibility of investigating the background of the convicted offender and the circumstances surrounding the offense.

presentence investigation report A report that contains a recommendation for specific criminal sanctions, including a recommendation for prison time, probation, fines, community service, or other sanctions.

sentencing hearing A hearing at which the prosecution and the defense have the opportunity to challenge the recommended criminal sanctions.

victim impact statements Testimony by victims at a convicted offender's sentencing hearing.

LEARNING OUTCOMES 4 Describe the various sentencing models and explain their influence on the sentence.

At sentencing, a judge might impose fines, imprisonment, community service, restitution, or probation when delivering a sentence. There are two types of sentencing models: indeterminate and determinate. The indeterminate sentencing model gives the judge broad discretion in determining a range of sentences. The determinate sentencing model limits the judge's flexibility, as the offender is given a fixed term of incarceration. Habitual offenders might be sentenced under a three-strikes law, in which repeat offenders receive longer mandatory sentences.

1. Which sentencing model allows a judge the greatest discretion?

2. How does presumptive sentencing balance indeterminate sentencing with determinate sentencing?

3. Whom are habitual offender laws designed to punish?

4. Explain the difference between aggravating and mitigating circumstances.

indeterminate sentencing A model of sentencing in which judges have nearly complete discretion in sentencing an offender.

structured sentencing A sentencing model (including determinate sentencing, sentencing guidelines, and presumptive sentencing) that defines punishments rather than allowing indeterminate sentencing.

determinate sentencing A model of sentencing in which the offender is sentenced to a fixed term of incarceration.

mandatory sentencing The strict application of full sentences in the determinate sentencing model.

habitual offender laws Tough sentencing laws that punish repeat offenders more harshly.

three-strikes law The law that applies mandatory sentencing to give repeat offenders longer prison terms.

sentencing guidelines A sentencing model in which crimes are classified according to their seriousness, and a range of time to be served is mandatory for crimes within each category.

presumptive sentencing A structured sentencing model that attempts to balance sentencing guidelines with mandatory sentencing and at the same time provide discretion to the judge.

aggravating factors Actions that may increase the seriousness of a crime.

mitigating factors Actions that show the offender's remorse or responsibility.

truth in sentencing Legislation that requires the court to disclose the actual prison time the offender is likely to serve.

LEARNING OUTCOMES 5

Summarize the challenges to the death penalty sentence and explain how U.S. Supreme Court rulings have affected the death penalty sentence.

The use of the death penalty by federal courts, military courts, and military tribunals is overseen by federal laws, executive orders, and the U.S. Supreme Court. The U.S. Supreme Court hears many challenges to the death penalty based on the position that it violates the Eighth Amendment as cruel and unusual punishment. In addition, the U.S. Supreme Court must address civil rights issues that arise in death penalty cases. Today, many states have reconsidered their use of the death penalty; some have even abolished its use.

1. How do abolitionists view the death penalty?
2. What effect did the *Furman* v. *Georgia* decision have on the death penalty?
3. What is a bifurcated trial structure?

capital punishment The sentence of death.

abolitionists People opposed to the death penalty.

bifurcated trial A two-part trial structure in which the jury first determines guilt or innocence and then considers new evidence relating to the appropriate punishment.

MyCJLab

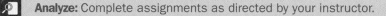

Go to Chapter 9 in MyCJLab to test your mastery of chapter concepts, access your Study Plan, engage in interactive exercises, complete critical-thinking and research assignments, and view related online videos.

☑ **Review:** Complete the pretest in the Study Plan to confirm what you know and what you need to study further. Then complete the post-test to confirm your mastery of the concepts. Use the key term flash cards to review key terminology.

⚙ **Apply:** Complete the interactive simulation activity.

🔎 **Analyze:** Complete assignments as directed by your instructor.

▭ **Current Events:** Explore CJSearch for current topical videos, articles, and news pieces.

Additional Links

Go to **http://www.cnn.com/2012/06/12/justice/pennsylvania-sandusky-trial/index.html** and read testimony from the Jerry Sandusky sex abuse trial and conviction.

Go to **http://www.youtube.com/watch?v=AJFtAjzIjGg** and watch a short documentary film about a North Carolina death row lethal injection.

Go to **http://www.sentencingproject.org** and learn how The Sentencing Project works for a fair and effective U.S. criminal justice system by promoting reforms in sentencing policy, addressing unjust racial disparities and practices, and advocating for alternatives to incarceration.

Go to **http://www.ussc.gov/index.cfm** and learn about the U.S. Sentencing Commission and its efforts to establish sentencing policies; to advise and assist Congress; and to collect, analyze, and conduct research regarding sentencing.

Go to **http://www.innocenceproject.org** to learn about this national litigation and public policy organization that is dedicated to exonerating wrongfully convicted people through DNA testing as well as reforming the criminal justice system to prevent future injustice.

Go to **http://www.curenational.org**, the website of Citizens United for Rehabilitation of Errants (CURE). CURE is a nonprofit national organization dedicated to reducing crime through rehabilitation programs and reforms of the criminal justice system.

Go to **http://www.deathpenalty.org** to read viewpoints by an organization that argues against the death penalty; then go to **http://www.prodeathpenalty.com** and read an opposing viewpoint by an organization that argues for the death penalty.

Jails and Prisons

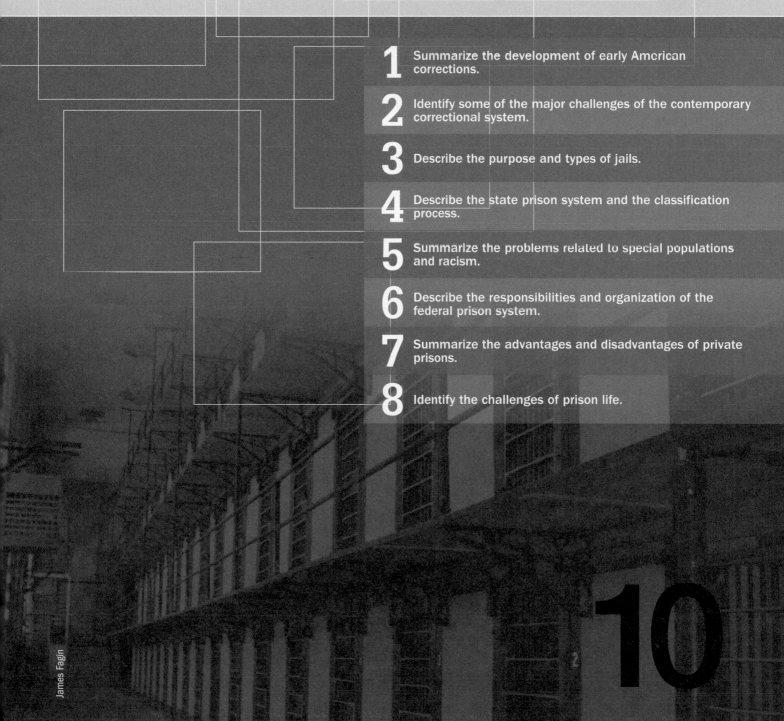

"One of the many lessons that one learns in prison is, that things are what they are and will be what they will be."

—*Oscar Wilde*

1 Summarize the development of early American corrections.

2 Identify some of the major challenges of the contemporary correctional system.

3 Describe the purpose and types of jails.

4 Describe the state prison system and the classification process.

5 Summarize the problems related to special populations and racism.

6 Describe the responsibilities and organization of the federal prison system.

7 Summarize the advantages and disadvantages of private prisons.

8 Identify the challenges of prison life.

10

James Fagin

Today, more jails and prisons are becoming institutions for holding the mentally ill. For example, Cook County Jail is the largest de facto mental institution in Illinois. It has almost four times the number of inmates that suffer from some form of serious mental illness than the state's mental health center.[1]

People with serious mental illness are more likely to engage in conduct that leads to arrests. They are less likely to be able to post bond; so even for minor offenses, they are more likely to remain in jail. While incarcerated, their inappropriate and noncompliant behavior is often mistaken by staff as deliberate refusal to obey commands and rules.

Inmates with mental illness are more likely to fight with other inmates, as they are often confused, feel threatened, or are paranoid. Also, they are more likely to be assaulted, abused, or robbed by other inmates who take advantage of their disability. Inmates with mental illness can cost three to ten times more to house than other inmates.[2] In addition, they can require significantly more time of the jail and prison staff than other inmates.

Jails and prisons were not designed for treating people with mental illness. Staff members do not receive the training that enables them to recognize behaviors related to mental illness compared to disobedience to authority. The projections are that this trend will continue and, other than overcrowding, inmates with mental illness may become one of the most serious problems in corrections.

Some argue that the significant increase of incarcerated people with mental illness is due in large part to unintended consequences of "get tough sentencing" policies.

DISCUSS **What is the appropriate policy for dealing with people with mental illness who are incarcerated?**

▶ *Development of American Jails and Prisons*

This chapter reviews the history and role of jails and prisons in the United States. It discusses the diversity of people confined in jails, state prisons, and federal facilities. It examines the classification system and the challenges associated with special prison populations. It closes by discussing important issues associated with institutional incarceration such as prison life, the financial crisis, and the use of private prisons.

The first institutions for **incarceration** of prisoners in Colonial America and the United States were local jails, which served primarily for detention prior to trial or execution rather than for punishment or rehabilitation of the criminal.[3] In 1681, for example, the community of West Jersey required that condemned people be kept in safe confinement until the next General Assembly after the governor had reviewed their cases.[4] Prisoners were confined until their punishments could be determined. Prisoners incarcerated in local jails were expected to work for their daily keep or to pay for it. They were not housed at the expense of the community.[5] In Colonial America, jails were, for the most part, operated by private parties, and after the Revolutionary War, they were operated by the sheriff. Early jails were more like secure houses than the fortified structures of today. Apparently, early jails were not all that secure, however, because prisoners often escaped from them. The colony of New Jersey reported 1,830 escapes between 1751 and 1777, an average rate of 67 per year.[6]

Inmates with mental illness may become one of the most serious problems in corrections.

16 The number of prisoners who were housed in one 12-foot by 12-foot cell in a 1767 Boston jail.

Early Jail Conditions

Conditions in early jails were deplorable, and descriptions of them are difficult to imagine. As jails were increasingly used not only to confine criminals, but also to incarcerate those with mental illness and the poor, overcrowding became a serious problem. One 1767 description of an early jail in Charlestown (Boston) reported that 16 debtors were housed in a single 12-foot by 12-foot room. The cell was so crowded that one of the prisoners died of suffocation but could not be removed until all of the other prisoners were made to lie down so that the dead prisoner could be retrieved.[7]

In early jails, the prisoners were responsible for providing their basic necessities of life with their own funds or with the help of outside benefactors. The state had no obligation to provide food or medical treatment for indigents. The more wealthy prisoners could buy additional cell space, food, and privileges, and liquor was commonly made available to those who could afford it.[8] Prisoners who could not afford to pay for their accommodations were required to toil on public works projects in exchange for their keep. Those who could not work were allowed to beg passersby for food or money. Records indicate that some prisoners who were unable to provide their daily needs were allowed to die of starvation.[9]

LEARNING OUTCOMES 1 Summarize the development of early American corrections.

GLOSSARY

incarceration The bodily confinement of a person in a jail or prison.

penitentiary A correctional institution based on the concept that inmates could change their criminality through reflection and penitence.

silent system The correctional practice of prohibiting inmates from talking to other inmates.

inside cell block Prison construction in which individual cells are stacked back-to-back in tiers in the center of a secure building.

congregate work system The practice of moving inmates from sleeping cells to other areas of the prison for work, meals, and recreation.

solitary confinement The practice of confining an inmate such that there is no contact with other people.

convict lease system The practice of some southern penal systems leasing prisoners to private contractors as laborers.

chain gang In the southern penal system, a group of convicts chained together during outside labor.

prison farm system In the southern penal systems, the use of inmate labor to maintain large, profit-making prison farms or plantations.

The portrait of American local jails at the birth of the nation is unpleasant to say the least. The jails were filled with all sorts of people—criminals as well as victims of misfortune. Men, women, and children were confined in the same cell, and no attempt was made to protect women and children from aggressive male prisoners. Sick prisoners were not separated from the healthy, so contagious diseases quickly and easily spread in the crowded, unsanitary conditions. Jails were not heated, did not have plumbing, and did not provide adequate per person sleeping and living space. A primary factor in keeping the local jail population down was the death of many prisoners.[10] In 1777, English reformer John Howard traveled extensively in Europe, visiting jails and prisons. As a result, he wrote *State of Prisons*, a critical review of the brutality and inhumane conditions of Europe's penal systems. Howard's book was very influential and contributed to efforts at prison reform on both sides of the Atlantic.

Reform at Last: The Walnut Street Jail

In America, the prison reform movement had its origins with a group of Quakers called the Philadelphia Society to Alleviate the Miseries of Public Prisons.[11] In 1787, Benjamin Rush argued for prison reform at a meeting of the Society for Promoting Political Inquiries at the home of Benjamin Franklin. The Philadelphia Society to Alleviate the Miseries of Public Prisons was formed as a result, and this group lobbied the Pennsylvania legislature for humane treatment of prisoners. The group was successful, and in 1790, the Pennsylvania legislature passed a law calling for the renovation of the Walnut Street Jail in Philadelphia.[12] In addition to a humane physical facility and adequate food and water supplied at public expense, the reform effort was successful in abolishing the practice of placing men, women, and children in the same cell and allowing prisoners to buy better treatment; prohibiting the consumption of alcohol by the prisoners; and separating the debtors and those with mental illness

In early jails, the prisoners were responsible for providing their basic necessities of life with their own funds or with the help of outside benefactors.

from the criminal population.[13] Children, many confined only because they were orphans, were removed from the jail and housed in a separate building.[14]

Prisoners in the Walnut Street Jail were required to work, but they were paid for their labor and could earn early release for good behavior. The new jail was a great improvement over previous conditions of imprisonment, and people came from other states and countries to investigate the possibility of adopting the Walnut Street Jail model.[15] However, the Walnut Street Jail ultimately failed because of overcrowding, which destroyed its ability to accomplish its mission. As a result of receiving state funding for renovation, the Walnut Street Jail became a temporary state prison, allowing prisoners from other cities in Pennsylvania to be housed there. The jail quickly filled beyond capacity.[16] Conditions deteriorated, and the cost of operating the jail became prohibitive. The goal of making prisons places for rehabilitation was crushed.

Bigger Is Better: Eastern State Penitentiary

By 1820, the hopes that the Walnut Street Jail would be the model for prison reform were dashed, and overcrowding of the prison required that a new institution be built. Pennsylvania's Eastern State Penitentiary, built in 1829, was an enormous investment of state resources and was based on a new philosophy of rehabilitation. Built at a cost of $500,000 to house 250 prisoners, it was the most expensive public building in the New World and the first in the country to have flush toilets and hot-air heating.[17]

Penitence

Eastern State Penitentiary was not designed as a jail or a prison but as a penitentiary. In a **penitentiary**, it was expected that inmates would reflect on their lives of crime and change their ways. To encourage this transformation, Eastern State Penitentiary had an individual cell for each prisoner. Prisoners were required to become proficient at a skill that would support them after their release, such as woodworking or leatherworking. When not working or exercising, prisoners were expected to read the Bible, the only literature allowed in their cells. Prisoners were kept in isolation from one another to avoid corrupting influences, and a "silent system" was enforced. The **silent system** required that prisoners communicate only with guards or prison officials; communication with other prisoners was forbidden. The goal of incarceration was to evoke penitence in the prisoner, with the idea that guilt and remorse or repentance would lead to rehabilitation, and prisoners could be released to lead normal, productive lives. This philosophy was compatible with the classical criminology theories

Built in 1829, Eastern State Penitentiary was the first public building to have flush toilets and hot-air heating.

James Fagin

James Fagin

and religious values of the period, emphasizing that crime was a rational choice made by the offender.

Self-Contained Cells

Eastern State Penitentiary was a maximum-security, walled, self-contained institution. It had seven wings, like the spokes of a wheel that extended from a hublike center. Inmate cells were located on either side of the wings with outside windows. In the middle of the wing was a central passageway for use by guards and prison officials. Following the model of solitary confinement, the cells were designed so that inmates could not see any part of the prison other than the wall that was directly in front of the cell. Cells were 12 feet long by 7.5 feet wide and had a window. Some inmates had a small outside exercise yard but seldom had a chance to leave their cell. The institution's design called for all activities—working, exercising, eating, and sleeping—to be performed within the individual prisoner's cell.

As with the Walnut Street Jail, many people came to view Eastern State Penitentiary to see if it could be a solution to their penal problems. The single-cell model reduced problems with inmate discipline. Inmates rarely had the chance to violate rules because they seldom left their cells or interacted with other inmates. As a result, corporal punishment was practically eliminated. Inmates were motivated to be productive and abide by the rules in exchange for the chance of early release and financial reward for their work.

The Auburn System

During the early history of American prisons, the Pennsylvania model of individual cells competed for popularity against the Auburn, New York, prison model of the congregate work system as new prisons were constructed. The single-cell plan was expensive, and as prison populations increased, many states found that the cost of single-cell construction was prohibitive and turned to New York's Auburn system as the model for constructing new prisons. Built in 1816, Auburn Prison was a

walled, maximum-security prison with multiple-level inmate cells located in the center of a secure building. The cells in Auburn were smaller (7 feet long, 4 feet wide, and 7 feet high), with back-to-back cells stacked five tiers high. This arrangement made it possible to house many more prisoners in much less space with less expense. Unlike the design of Eastern State Penitentiary, Auburn's design housed inmates in the center of the building without an outside window or exercise area. The cells were poorly lit and lacked access to fresh air. Also, the cells in the Auburn model did not have flush toilets or central heating. The cells stacked one on top of another created a unique prison architecture, called an **inside cell block**. This architectural model for housing prison inmates became a distinctive feature of the American penal system.

Work and Punishment

Auburn's cells were too small to be the inmate's "home," as in the Eastern State Penitentiary. Auburn's cells were only for sleeping; during the day, inmates were moved to other areas for work, dining, and recreation. This pattern is known as the **congregate work system**. Because inmates were moved from place to place

The goal of incarceration was to evoke penitence in the prisoner, with the idea that guilt and remorse or repentance would lead to rehabilitation, and prisoners could be released to lead normal, productive lives.

within the prison, Auburn required a different type of administration and correctional security. To minimize the opportunity for plotting escapes or uprisings, inmates were not permitted to talk to one another. However, unlike the Eastern State Penitentiary, the silent system was more difficult to enforce because inmates worked and ate together and met as they moved from place to place in the prison. To enforce silence, Auburn adopted a system of corporal punishment for violations of the rule. Flogging was administered as punishment, not for the crime, but for violation of prison rules. The floggings were designed to be painful but not to maim the inmate or require medical attention.[19]

Prisoners being moved from one location to another were required to march in a lockstep formation—marching in unison with one hand on the shoulder of the man ahead and all heads turned in the direction of the guard. When the inmates arrived at their destination, they continued to mark time until commanded to stop. Also, all prisoners had a similar short haircut and were required to wear distinctive striped clothing to clearly identify their status as prison inmates. Thus, the prisoners' schedule, movements, and appearance were strictly regulated.[20]

Solitary Confinement

In 1821, the New York legislature passed a law requiring that the "worst inmates" held at Auburn be placed in **solitary confinement**.[21] These inmates were cut off from all contact with other people, including visitors, and were confined to their cells with only a Bible to read. Unlike inmates at Eastern State Penitentiary, however, Auburn inmates in solitary confinement had no work to do, no exercise yard, and a very small cell. Lacking knowledge of the harmful effects of long-term solitary confinement (the sciences of sociology and psychology did not emerge until the 1900s), the legislature had created a prison environment antithetical to rehabilitation. Inmates in solitary confinement had mental breakdowns and committed suicide. The alarming debility and death rates forced the state to abandon this practice.[22]

> # Inmates in solitary confinement had mental breakdowns and committed suicide.

Economic Self-Sufficiency

Because inmates worked together in the Auburn system, the prison could combine their labor in larger and more profitable industries and construction projects. The sale of prison-made goods was so successful that the prison was virtually economically self-sufficient and required few resources from the state budget.[23] However, the Eastern State Penitentiary model required more and more state resources to operate as the prison population rose. Only 13 years after Auburn opened, the warden announced that he no longer needed state funds to run the prison.[24] The Auburn system became the prototype of the American prison. The economic advantages appealed to other states, and between 1825 and 1969, 29 state prisons were built using the Auburn model.

Pennsylvania System versus Auburn System

	Auburn System	Pennsylvania System
Correctional Philosophy	Purpose of incarceration is punishment	Create environment to promote penitence and reform of inmate
Housing	Interior cell block—small cells stacked five tiers high—no plumbing or central heat	Single cell with plumbing, central heat, and work area and some with outside exercise area
Inmate Movement	Inmates move, using lockstep formation, to separate facilities for dining, work, and recreation	Inmates remain in their cells—no inmate movement
Use of Corporal Punishment	Frequent use of corporal punishment to enforce prison rules	Infrequent use of corporal punishment as inmates have little opportunity to violate prison rules
Solitary Confinement	Used for punishment of the "worst inmates"	The norm—all inmates are in solitary confinement all the time
Silent System	Prisoners are prohibited from talking to other inmates, but the rule is difficult to enforce due to numerous opportunities for inmate interaction	Prisoners are prohibited from talking to other inmates, and there is little opportunity for inmates to violate the rule because they are in solitary confinement
Prison Industry	Congregate work system in which prisoners combine their labors to produce products for prison industry to sell to the public	Individual craft work with inmates retaining any income from their products
Funding of Prison	Auburn prison is self-sufficient and does not require state funding due to profits from prison industry	Pennsylvania system is state-funded. As inmate population increases, so does the operating budget of the prison

Angola State Prison is one of the largest prison farms in the United States.
Source: http://angoloamuseum.org/?q=History

AP Photo/Judi Bottoni

LEARNING OUTCOMES 2 Identify some of the major challenges of the contemporary correctional system.

GLOSSARY

Lombroso-based correctional philosophies Philosophies that divided people into two distinct types: criminal and noncriminal. Criminals were biologically determined and therefore not amenable to rehabilitation or reform.

prison industry The sale of convict-made products and services.

civil death The legal philosophy that barred a prison inmate from bringing a lawsuit in a civil court related to his or her treatment while incarcerated or related to conditions of incarceration.

Warren Court The U.S. Supreme Court years (1953–1969) during which Chief Justice Earl Warren issued many landmark decisions greatly expanding the constitutional rights of inmates and defendants.

Many of these institutions, such as New York's Sing Sing, are still in use today.[25]

Southern Penal Systems

Convict Lease System

Many northern states used the Auburn system as a prison model. Southern states, however, developed their own unique prison system, based on different historical circumstances. The South retained an agrarian economy rather than an industry-based factory economy. Southern prisons practiced the **convict lease system** to supply farms with labor once provided by slaves. Rather than build large maximum-security prisons to produce prison labor–made goods, southern states leased prisoners to private contractors. Inmate labor was used for agricultural work, some factory work, and construction work. The private contractor assumed all responsibility for the care and support of inmates and paid the state a fee for the inmates' labor. This prisoner lease system permitted southern states to deal with great increases in the prison population following the Civil War without requiring the states to finance the construction of prisons. For some states, a significant amount of their income was derived from the sale of convict labor.[26]

Chain Gangs

Following the Civil War, approximately 90% of those incarcerated in the South were free blacks. Work and living conditions for inmates were wretched, and convicts worked 12 to 15 hours a day. States did not set minimum standards for living conditions and did not inspect the sites where inmates were housed. Inmates who performed agricultural work often were housed in temporary, portable cages near the worksite. Thus, prisoners were no better off than slaves, and discipline was brutal.[27] To prevent escapes when the prisoners worked in open areas, they were shackled together in what came to be known as the **chain gang**. The prisoner death rate in this system used in the South was over twice as high as in northern prisons.[28]

Prison Farms

The prisoner lease system was used until the 1930s, when it was replaced by the **prison farm system**, or plantation system. Rather than lease prison labor to private contractors, the state used inmate labor to maintain large prison farm complexes. These prison farms were expected to be self-sufficient and profit-making. Some states expanded the concept and used prison labor to operate other profit-making industries. To reduce the costs of operating prison farms and prison industries, states often used inmates as guards and supervisors of other inmates.

Changing social consciousness in the southern states eventually ended for-profit prisons and use of inmate "trusties" to maintain security. Arkansas, however, continued to use the prison farm system, with its many abuses, until the 1960s.[29] A series of U.S. Supreme Court cases then ruled the penal practices in Arkansas unconstitutional.[30] The Court also decided that whipping for disciplinary purposes and the use of electric shock were cruel and unusual punishments. In its decision, the Court declared, "For the ordinary convict a sentence to the Arkansas Penitentiary today amounts to a banishment from civilized society to a dark and evil world completely alien to the free world culture."[31] Texas also practiced the plantation farm system and came under public criticism and the scrutiny of the Court. As in the case of Arkansas, a series of U.S. Supreme Court rulings forced Texas to reform its prison system.

▶ The Contemporary Correctional System

Highest Incarceration Rate in the World

At the turn of the nineteenth century, American prisons were considered to be at the cutting edge of correctional philosophy. American prisons attracted visitors from other states and foreign countries to study the innovations. Many of these visitors returned home, encouraging the adoption of these new correctional philosophies and architecture. However, by the beginning of the twenty-first century, American prisons had become known worldwide not for their innovations, but for their high incarceration rate of inmates. With less than 5% of the world's population and a quarter of the world's prisoners, the United States has the highest incarceration rate of any country in the world. This record includes not only the number of persons incarcerated, but also the length of incarceration and the crimes for which offenders are incarcerated.[32] The Bureau of Justice Statistics (BJS) indicates that about 2.3 million people were incarcerated in jails and prisons in 2010. According to the Pew Center on the States, the United States is the first nation ever to reach a 1:100 ratio for incarceration, with an incarceration rate of 1,000 people for every 100,000 in the population, whereas England's rate is 151 and Germany's is 88. Japan incarcerates only 63 people per 100,000 of the population. The United States has more inmates than the leading 35 European countries combined. The U.S. incarceration rate is six times the median of 125 for all nations.

Country	Comparison to U.S. Inmates Incarcerated
U.S.	Base
Israel	4 times more
Canada	6 times more
China	6 times more
Germany	8 times more
Japan	13 times more

Nonviolent Offenders

Less than half of those incarcerated are behind bars for violent offenses. The United States incarcerates people for nonviolent crimes such as writing bad checks and using and possessing drugs, which rarely produce prison sentences in other countries.[33] For example, about 20% of inmates are incarcerated for drug offenses. In fact, one of the factors driving the increase in prison population is the "war on drugs," which has resulted in over a 300% increase of drug offenders sentenced to prisons since 1985. Furthermore, compared to other countries, the United States incarcerates people longer. For example, the average sentence for burglary in the United States is 16 months compared to 7 months in England and 5 months in Canada.[34]

Causes of High Incarceration Rates

How did the United States come to have the highest incarceration rate in the world? The U.S. response to the rising concern for public safety during the 1970s and 1980s was a "lock and feed" philosophy of incarceration that emphasized incapacitation rather than rehabilitation. The reliance on incarceration as a major response to crime resulted in legislative changes in sentencing, such as emphasizing mandatory sentencing, long prison terms, reduced discretion of judges to adjust sentences downward for individual circumstances, and enhanced sentences for repeat offenders (sometimes life sentences). As these sentencing changes were engaged, the correctional population rapidly grew from a rate of about 130 per 100,000 (a number similar to the

25% The percentage of the world's prisoners that are incarcerated in jails and prisons in the United States.

1 in 32 The number of adults in the U.S. on probation, on parole, in jail, or in prison.

world's median today) in 1980 to 1 in 100 in 2009. According to the BJS, at year-end 2010, about 7 million people in the United States were under supervision of adult correctional authority, 3% of all U.S. adult residents, or 1 in every 32 adults.

The fact that the United States incarcerates offenders at a much greater rate than any other country is in and of itself not necessarily an indictment that the American criminal justice system is seriously flawed. If the United States has more crime and more criminals than other countries and incarceration provides the greatest enhancement of public safety, then the use of incarceration may be justified. The opposing sides argue strongly that their worldview reflects the reality of the use of incarceration. Proponents of the use of incarceration, such as Tom Riley, spokesperson for the Office of National Drug Policy Initiatives, argue that the record use of incarceration has lowered the crime rate and enhanced public safety. Riley defends the use of incarceration, saying, "It's true, we have way too many people in prison. But it's not because the laws are unjust, but because there are too many people who are causing havoc and misery in the community."[35] On the other hand, James Q. Whitman, a specialist in comparative law at Yale, claims that the American criminal justice system is "viewed with horror" by the rest of the world.[36] The Pew Center on the States argues that the United States incarcerates too many nonviolent offenders and too many people for minor crimes and violations of probation or parole.

Statistics support both sides of the argument. For example, as the use of incarceration rose in the 1980s, the crime rate did indeed drop. However, when one examines specific states, the results are not consistent with the overall drop in crime and rise in the use of incarceration. Florida has almost doubled its prison population over the past 15 years, but has experienced a smaller drop in crime than that of New York, which has reduced its number of inmates to below that of 15 years ago.[37] Also, comparison with foreign countries does not support the argument that there is a connection between the decline in crime and the increase in incarceration. For example, Canada has a prison population about one-seventh of that of the United States, and both crime and incarceration rates have declined at about the same rate as that of the United States.[38]

The Rising Cost of Incarceration

States often spent no money to house state prisoners in early prisons. In fact, some states expected that prisons would produce a profit for the state. Today's prisons are significantly different from the model of self-sufficient, no-cost-to-the-state prisons of the nineteenth century. Today, incarceration is a significant cost to local, state, and federal governments. Three changes had a significant influence on the rising cost of incarceration. Figure 10–1 highlights those factors that have contributed to the rising cost of imprisonment.

Education and Rehabilitation Programs

The first change was the abandonment of **Lombroso-based correctional philosophies** that criminality is an inherited trait. This philosophy assumes that criminals are biologically distinct from and inferior to noncriminals. Furthermore, Lombroso's philosophy assumes that because criminality is a biological trait and the biological nature of the criminal cannot be changed, there is little or no need for rehabilitation programs—only incarceration and isolation from the community are necessary.

Lombroso's theory was very influential on correctional practices in the late 1800s and early 1900s. Lombroso's theory replaced the nonscientific and classical theory that criminals were sinners or weak-willed people who chose of their own free will to commit crime. Because criminals were thought to be biologically predisposed to crime and did not choose it of their own free will, rehabilitation was not a reasonable goal of the criminal justice system. Earnest Hooton (1887–1954), typical of those who believed in the inherited nature of the criminal man theory, argued that prisoners should be placed on self-contained, self-governing reservations completely isolated from society. Hooton favored the permanent incarceration of what he called "hopeless constitutional inferiors who on no account should be allowed to breed."[39]

This was the pervasive philosophy of correctional institutions in the United States throughout the early 1900s. Prisons were places of confinement with few or no rehabilitation programs, few comforts, strict discipline, and severe physical punishment for violation of the rules. Without the financial burden of education and rehabilitation programs, the cost of incarceration was appreciably less expensive than that of modern prisons. As the philosophy of the criminal man was replaced by correctional philosophies founded on sociological theories, educational and rehabilitation programs were

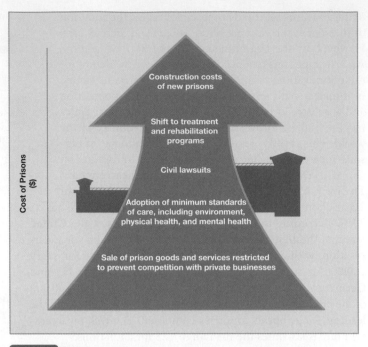

FIGURE 10–1 **Factors Contributing to the Rising Cost of Imprisonment**
Early prisons were expected to generate revenue to cover the costs of incarceration. Today, many factors have made this expectation an impossibility.

introduced as a primary mission of prisons, which greatly added to their cost.

Restrictions on Prison-Made Goods and Services

Next, the cost of incarceration was significantly impacted by legislation passed during the Great Depression (c. 1929–1940). During the Great Depression, the federal government and many states passed laws prohibiting the sale of convict-made products and services, which competed with local businesses on the open market. Prior to these restrictions, **prison industry** provided significant income for prison operations. The operating capital that prisons had been able to generate through prison industry–made goods and services dried up. Prison-industry goods and services were limited to supplying products to the government, a much smaller market with limited needs for goods and services.[40] During this era, state prisons became the exclusive manufacturers of license plates for some state governments.

Recognition of Constitutional Rights of Prisoners

Finally, the abandonment of the philosophy of **civil death** for incarcerated inmates resulted in significant increases in the cost of incarceration. Civil death is rooted in the law of

Think About It . . .

Starting with the Warren Court (1953–1969), in case-by-case decisions, the U.S. Supreme Court abandoned the hands-off, or civil death, doctrine that deprived convicted felons of nearly all civil rights, including the right to file civil lawsuits for alleged violations of constitutional rights. Under this doctrine, felony inmates were considered "slaves of the state." Today, the Supreme Court has affirmed many civil rights of inmates, including the right to sue. Inmates have won lawsuits over issues such as vegetarian meals, dreadlocks, cell size, and religious worship. How does the right to file civil lawsuits affect prison administration and the cost of incarceration?

Adam Booth/Fotolia

If prison administrators and states refuse to make the necessary changes to meet the minimum conditions of imprisonment, the court can take administrative control of the prison and force implementation of the necessary changes.

medieval Europe and the concept of outlawry. The laws of medieval Europe provided that any person who committed a felony was outside the protection of the law. That is, he could receive no benefit of the court for any reason or appeal any cause to the court. He was an "outlaw"—outside the law. Such a person was at the mercy of others because he had no redress for any harm done to him and could not appeal to the law for protection.

This concept was adapted by the United States in regard to incarcerated felony inmates. The established law of the land in the United States up until the 1960s was that incarcerated inmates had no right to bring to the courts any civil suit for any reason related to their imprisonment.[41] It was not until the **Warren Court** (1953–1969) that the U.S. Supreme Court ruled that constitutional protections extended to prisoners and prisoners were given the right to file civil lawsuits concerning the conditions of their incarceration. The earlier decision of *Cooper* v. *Aaron* (1958) ruled that states were bound by Court decisions and could not ignore them. Thus, when the Warren Court voided the doctrine of "civil death," lawsuits challenging conditions of imprisonment and denial of civil rights flooded the courts. As prison administrators and states were held accountable for providing minimum standards of living, food, and protection of civil rights, the cost of incarceration increased. Also, prisons violating minimum standards of incarceration and civil rights were subject to punitive damages and court takeover. If prior administrators and states refused to make the necessary changes to meet the minimum conditions of imprisonment, the court could take administrative control of the prison and force implementation of the necessary changes.

Number of Prisons

The end result of these and other influences is that contemporary prisons are expensive. One of the obvious reasons for the rising cost of corrections is that the record incarceration rate has resulted in a record number of prisons. The cost of prisons is

1,000 The number of prisons in the United States today.

expensive in that as the incarceration rate rises to record levels, the number of prisons required to house the inmates increases. In 1923, there were 61 prisons in the United States. It was not uncommon for a state to have a single prison to house all of its inmates. The number of prisons grew to 592 in 1974 and has expanded to over 1,000 today. Prison construction is one of the most expensive construction projects because of the security and sophisticated technology required. In addition to the costs of construction, there is also the cost of staffing. As a result, it is estimated that the cost of housing an inmate ranges from $20,000 to nearly $100,000 per year depending on the security level of the prison and the type of institution. The most expensive prisons to operate are maximum-security prisons and prisons for geriatric inmates.

Cost of Corrections

Prison costs are one of the fastest-rising costs to state governments. State spending on corrections has increased 127% in the last 20 years. Five states (Connecticut, Delaware, Michigan, Oregon, and Vermont) now spend more on corrections than on higher education. One out of nine state employees works in corrections. At a cost of about $29,000 per inmate, states are spending an average of 7% of their budget on corrections. Prisons cost state governments about $50 billion a year and the federal government $5 billion more. The cost of imprisonment is forcing states to examine alternatives because state deficits are at record highs. Some states are forced to slash prison budgets, lay off staff, and release prisoners early because there are insufficient funds to continue to pay for the high cost of incarceration. For example, California has been ordered by the U.S. Supreme Court to release 40,000 inmates or build adequate facilities to house them. In 2012, Pat Quinn, the governor of Illinois, sought to balance the state budget by closing prisons. The challenge is to reduce the costs of corrections without sacrificing public safety. This crisis is forcing some states to turn to community corrections programs instead of institutional incarceration.

- -

▶ Jails

The major institutions of modern civilian institutional corrections are jails, state prisons, and federal penitentiaries. In addition to these civilian facilities, special categories of inmates are held

(Think About It . . .

In 2009, every California state prison had an arts coordinator who oversaw an active program in theater, painting, and dance. Today, the programs have been cut due to the state's financial crisis. The prison arts program started in 1979 and was praised for its many benefits, including a way to channel aggression, break down racial barriers, teach social skills, and prepare inmates for the outside world. How does the removal of such programs affect prison life and rehabilitation opportunities?

JEAN PIERI KRT/Newscom

by Native American Nations, Immigration and Customs Enforcement (ICE), military prisons, and U.S. territories and commonwealths. These institutions differ significantly from civilian correctional institutions and contain only a small percentage of the corrections population. These institutions hold special populations. For example, the largest population of inmates is held by ICE. Its facilities have about 30,000 inmates who are being held pending deportations.

Short-Term Facilities

Jails are unique short-term facilities that, compared to any other type of correctional institution, are used for more purposes. Jails hold defendants awaiting trial, defendants convicted of misdemeanor crimes, state and federal prisoners, people with mental illness who are waiting to be moved to appropriate health facilities, and adults and juveniles of both genders. Jails hold local, state, federal, and military prisoners; convicted prisoners; absconders; pretrial and post-trial defendants; and even witnesses to crime. The majority of inmates in local jails have not been convicted of a crime. They are waiting to be charged, tried, or transported to another institution. Jails hold everyone, including those accused of murder as well as traffic misdemeanors.

In addition to the fact that they are multipurpose, jails are unique as a gateway into the criminal justice system and corrections in particular. When a person is detained or arrested for any crime, misdemeanor, or felony, he or she first is confined in a jail. (Jails should not be confused with police holding cells. Upon initial arrest and booking, a person may be confined in a police holding cell. Police holding cells are not jails.) Only convicted offenders can be confined in state and federal prisons. Thus, all prisoners and most defendants enter the criminal justice system through jails. There are three types of jails: Native American country jails, federal civilian jails, and local civilian jails.

Native American Country Jails

Native American country jails incarcerate only Native Americans living in Native American country who have been sentenced by a Native American court for an offense

All prisoners and most defendants enter the criminal justice system through jails.

committed there. Although Native tribes are regarded with a certain degree of autonomy by the federal government, they are restricted as to the crimes and punishments over which they have control. Basically, serious crimes (felonies) are the authority of the Federal Bureau of Investigation, and offenders are tried in federal courts and serve time in federal civilian institutions. Thus, although the number of inmates in Native American country jails is small, about 2,220 in 2010, 13 times that many Native American inmates (22,098) are confined in state and federal facilities.

The maximum sentence for people confined in Native American country jails is one year. Therefore, most inmates are confined for misdemeanors. Native American country jails are not part of the United States civilian correctional system, are not under local or state authority, and operate independently of the Federal Bureau of Prisons. About one-third of the Native American country jails are located in Arizona. These jails suffer from many of the same problems as their civilian counterparts, with overcrowding being the primary problem. According to the BJS, in 2010, 16 of 75 **Native American country jails** had inmate populations beyond their maximum rated capacity. Another 21% had inmate populations between 75% and 100% of their maximum rated capacity.[42] The second challenge of Native American country jails is providing treatment and counseling programs to effectively address the many behavioral and addiction problems of inmates given the cultural context in which they live.

Federal Jails

Federal jails are similar to local jails in that they house inmates incarcerated for misdemeanor offenses (sentences no more than one year). However, there are more differences than similarities between the two. Federal jails do not house the diverse population of prisoners that is characteristic of local jails. The primary purpose of federal jails is to hold federal jail inmates convicted of misdemeanor crimes and federal jail inmates awaiting adjudication or transfer. Often federal inmates awaiting trial (including felony trials) are incarcerated in local jails for a fee. Also, federal jail inmates may be transferred to 1 of the 11 federal jails if the jail population becomes too large or if an inmate is a disciplinary problem. Local civilian jails do not have these options.

City and County Jails

Local civilian jails face some of the most difficult challenges of the various correctional institutions. About 750,000 inmates reside in over 3,300 local or county jails. The size of the inmate populations of these jails varies significantly. About 47% of these jails have a capacity of fewer than 50 inmates. Less than 3% of the jails have a capacity of more than 1,000 inmates.[43] A few jails have very large populations. Four of the largest jails are Rikers Island, the Los Angeles County Jail, the Maricopa

County (Arizona) Jail, and Cook County Jail (Chicago). Rikers Island, the city jail for New York City, is one of the largest jails in the United States both in size and population. Rikers Island is a 415-acre complex of ten detention facilities located on an island in the river. It has an $860 million budget and is staffed by 7,000 officers and 1,500 civilians. In 2010, Rikers Island had 95,383 admissions with an average population of 13,049. Cook County Jail has nearly 10,000 inmates. The Los Angeles County Jail and the Maricopa County Jail house over 7,000 inmates each.

Varying Jail Conditions

Local governments must support and staff their jails. Thus, jail facilities vary with the economic prosperity of the city or county. In cities and counties with expanding jail prisoner populations, it can be difficult for the city or county to provide quality care and facilities for inmates. For example, Maricopa County Jail uses the controversial practice of housing inmates in tents due to a lack of physical facilities.

Thus, prison life in jails can range from good to bad. When cities and counties are economically challenged and do not have the resources to finance jail operations, conditions in jails can result in lawsuits by inmates and takeover by the courts. For example, in July 2004, Fulton County Jail (Georgia) was sued by inmates, it was censured by the Southern Center for Human Rights, and the Court threatened to appoint a receiver to oversee the jail. The jail opened in the mid-1980s. While it was under construction, it was determined to be too small and the number of bunks was doubled, even though the number of showers, toilets, and other utilities remained the same.[44] After it opened, a third bunk was added to many cells to accommodate the increasing population. When that was insufficient, some inmates slept on mattresses in the common area. Court papers described the jail as having "windowless, steamy rooms, where the air-conditioning is broken; 59 inmates in one cellblock sharing two showers with backed-up sewage; inmates without clean underwear and uniforms due to broken laundry service; faulty record keeping that left inmates locked up although they had served their time; attacks; beatings; escapes. Blocks designed to have 14 guards have only 2."[45]

Jail Operation

All states except Connecticut, Delaware, Hawaii, Rhode Island, and Vermont operate local jails, but these five states do have a combined jail–prison system operated by the state. Initially, local jails were operated by the county sheriff, and there was only one jail per county. In many states, this is still true. About 78% of sheriffs' offices operate a jail.[46] Jail operation is still a major responsibility of sheriffs' offices. Fully one-third of all sworn personnel in sheriffs' offices work in jail-related positions, and 56% of civilian personnel work in jail-related positions.[47] Jails not operated by a sheriff's office are managed by a county department of corrections employing only civilian personnel. Sheriffs' departments and **county departments of corrections** otherwise perform the same jail functions.

Jails house a variety of inmates; thus, jail staff and facilities must have the ability to serve all of them. (See Figure 10–2.) Local jails house adults and juveniles of both genders, people convicted of offenses, and people being detained for other reasons.

Characteristic	2008	2009	2010
Sex			
Male	87.3%	87.8%	87.7%
Female	12.7	12.2	12.3
Adults	99.0%	99.1%	99%
Male	86.4	86.9	86.7
Female	12.6	12.1	12.3
Juveniles[a]	1.0%	0.9%	1.0%
Held as adults[b]	0.8	0.8	0.8
Held as juveniles	0.2	0.2	0.3
Race/Hispanic origin[c]			
White[d]	42.5%	42.5%	44.3%
Black/African American[d]	39.2	39.2	37.8
Hispanic/Latino	16.4	16.2	15.8
Other[d,e]	1.8	1.9	1.3
Two or more races[d]	0.2	0.2	0.6
Conviction status[b]			
Convicted	37.1%	37.8%	38.9%
Male	32.3	33.0	—
Female	4.8	4.8	—
Unconvicted	62.9	62.2	61.1
Male	55.2	54.8	—
Female	7.8	7.4	—

Note: Detail may not sum to total due to rounding.
[a]Persons under age 18 at midyear.
[b]Includes juveniles who were tried or awaiting trial as adults.
[c]Estimates based on reported data and adjusted for nonresponse.
[d]Excludes persons of Hispanic or Latino origin.
[e]Includes American Indians, Alaska Natives, Asians, Native Hawaiians, and other Pacific Islanders.

FIGURE 10–2 Jail Population by Characteristics, 2008–2010
Percent of Inmates in Local Jails by Characteristics, Midyear 2010
Source: Lauren E. Glaze, *Correctional Populations in the United States, 2010* (Washington, DC: Bureau of Justice Statistics, December 2011), p. 8.

Functions of Locally Operated Jails

The following list of functions performed by local jails make it difficult to operate them and manage the inmates. Inmates range from people waiting to post bail to murderers. Many inmates are in jail for only a brief time. For example, the average stay for detainees at Rikers Island was 50.6 days and 36.1 days for sentenced inmates. Some detainees may be held for only hours until they post bond or are transferred to another institution.

- Receive individuals pending arraignment and hold them until trial, conviction, or sentencing
- Readmit probation, parole, and bail-bond violators and absconders
- Temporarily detain juveniles pending transfer to juvenile authorities
- Hold people with mental illness pending their movement to appropriate health facilities
- Hold individuals for the military, for protective custody, for contempt, and for the courts as witnesses
- Release convicted inmates to the community upon completion of sentence
- Transfer inmates to federal, state, and other authorities
- House inmates for federal, state, or other authorities because of crowding of the facilities

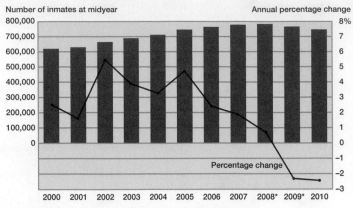

FIGURE 10–3 Number of People Held in Jail, 2000–2010

From 1980 to 2006, the population of jails rose, as indicated by the red bars and the number of inmates on the left side of the graph. However, since 2005, the percentage of increase of new admissions has rapidly and significantly declined, as indicated by the black line and the annual percentage change on the right side of the graph.

- Relinquish custody of temporary detainees to juvenile and medical authorities

- Operate community-based programs with day reporting, home detention, electronic monitoring, and other types of supervision

- Hold inmates sentenced to short terms (generally a maximum of one year but most sentences are much shorter)

Jail Population

The jail population has doubled since 1983. Since 2009, the rate of increase of the jail population has declined. Figure 10–3 illustrates this increase and decline in jail population. According to the BJS, in 2008, 785,556 inmates were held in the nation's local jails, an increase of about 5,300 inmates from 2007. In 2008, nine out of ten jail inmates were adult males. African-Americans were three times more likely than Hispanics and five times more likely than whites to be in jail. Nearly half of jail inmates have not been convicted of an offense. Thus, the majority of jail inmates have not been convicted of a crime. They are being held for pretrial detention or awaiting transfer to another facility.

During the 1980s and 1990s, the jail population rose rapidly in part because of the rise in state prison populations. Because jails are the gateways for felony inmates, as their numbers rise, there is a corresponding increase in the number of inmates. The reason is that before a person can be convicted of a felony drug offense, he or she is first incarcerated in jail for pretrial detention.

To keep pace with the influx of new jail inmates, counties were forced to construct new jail facilities at the rate of about 500 new beds each week.[48] Some counties experienced such a rate of growth in the jail population that there was not

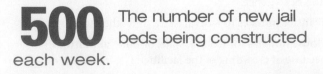

500 The number of new jail beds being constructed each week.

enough new bed space, and prisoners were housed in corridors, outdoor tents, and trailers. Overcrowding and the use of makeshift facilities can present serious problems for local jails. For example, in May 2009, the director of Arizona state prisons suspended the use of unshaded outdoor holding cells after an inmate died when left in an unshaded enclosure for nearly four hours in 100 degree temperatures.[49] Despite the new building efforts, local jails operate at about 95% capacity and many operate beyond capacity.

Municipal Jails

Historically, local jails also included local prison facilities maintained by municipal police departments. In some counties, the sheriff maintained the county jail and the police department maintained a separate municipal jail. These counties had both a municipal court and a county court, with each court housing its prisoners in the appropriate facility. Most municipalities have abandoned the use of the municipal or police jail. Recent state and federal regulations and standards regarding the housing of inmates have made it difficult for cities and towns to support local jails. These regulations have mandated physical facilities, staffing requirements and qualifications, medical facilities, and other requirements that have made it too expensive for municipalizes to operate a separate jail. Also, the liability due to civil lawsuits since the lifting of the hands-off doctrine exposes the city to huge financial penalties.

Municipal jails should not be confused with **police holding cells**, booking cells, or lockup facilities. Nearly all police departments have secure detention facilities that may look like jail cells. The primary purpose of these holding cells is to temporarily house arrestees until they can be booked and moved to another facility or pay their bail or until detectives can determine whether they are to be charged with a crime. These are not correctional institutions, and prisoners are not sent to these facilities to serve time as their punishment for a crime. Prisoners typically are confined in holding cells no longer than 48 hours.

▶ State Prisons

Unlike jails, **state prisons** are correctional institutions containing only convicted offenders, usually felony inmates sentenced to prison as punishment for a crime. State prisons do not house pre- and post-trial detainees. Furthermore, the population of a state prison tends to be limited to inmates with similar characteristics. For example, there are separate prisons for female and male offenders, for youthful offenders (usually 18- to 26-years-olds), and for more serious violent offenders. Also, juvenile offenders are housed in separate facilities. Each state operates its own correctional system, and these systems differ significantly from state to state. States also vary in the number of inmates that are housed in the correctional system. Inmates in state prisons usually have been sentenced to prison term of a year or more. Thus, different services, procedures, and policies are needed for prisoners than those provided in local jails. Inmates in state prisons require educational, counseling, vocational, and recreational programs usually not required of local jails.

93% The percentage of state prison inmates who are male.

As previously discussed, until about 2009, the number of inmates in state prisons continued to climb to record incarceration rates. Since 2009, the overall population of state prisoners has slightly declined (less than 1%). Overall, state prisons are between 1% below capacity and 15% above capacity.[50] According to the BJS, overall the state prison population has increased from 1,104,424 in 2000 to 1,216,771 in 2010.[51] According to data from *The Sentencing Project* and the BJS, most state prisoners are male (93%) minorities (60%) convicted of a violent crime (53%) or drug offense.[52] (See Table 10–1 for comparisons of inmates held in 2000 compared to 2010.)

However, the growth or decline in state prison populations varies significantly by state. (See Figure 10–4.) Some states are experiencing double-digit growth, whereas other states are experiencing a decline in state prisoner population. Figure 10–4 presents an interesting and complex picture of the status of the states' prison population. After years of record prison population growth, some states have "hit the wall" in that they can no longer afford the large prison populations that have accumulated over the past years. California is a good example. Figure 10–4 indicates that from 2000 to 2009, the California prison population increased about 1%. However, this data does not reflect the fact that the California prison population decreased nearly 4% from 2009 to 2010 and is expected to decrease even more in future surveys. California is under court order to reduce its prison population by 30,000 to 40,000 inmates by 2014. As a result, future statistics will show an even greater decrease in California's prison population.

The example of California is reflected in other states. New York, Texas, Kentucky, Vermont, and Rhode Island all show a reversal of the trend for 2009 to 2010. Rhode Island, for example, had about a 1% increase in its prison population for 2000 to 2009, but showed a dramatic drop of over 8% in prison population from 2009 to 2010.[53] It is expected that those states that have in the past incarcerated record numbers of inmates due to "get tough" sentencing laws will find it necessary to reduce the number of newly sentenced inmates. Those already sentenced to long mandatory prison terms will continue to take up prison beds, so there will be less room for newly sentenced inmates. States will have to build more prisons or find alternative punishments for newly sentenced defendants.

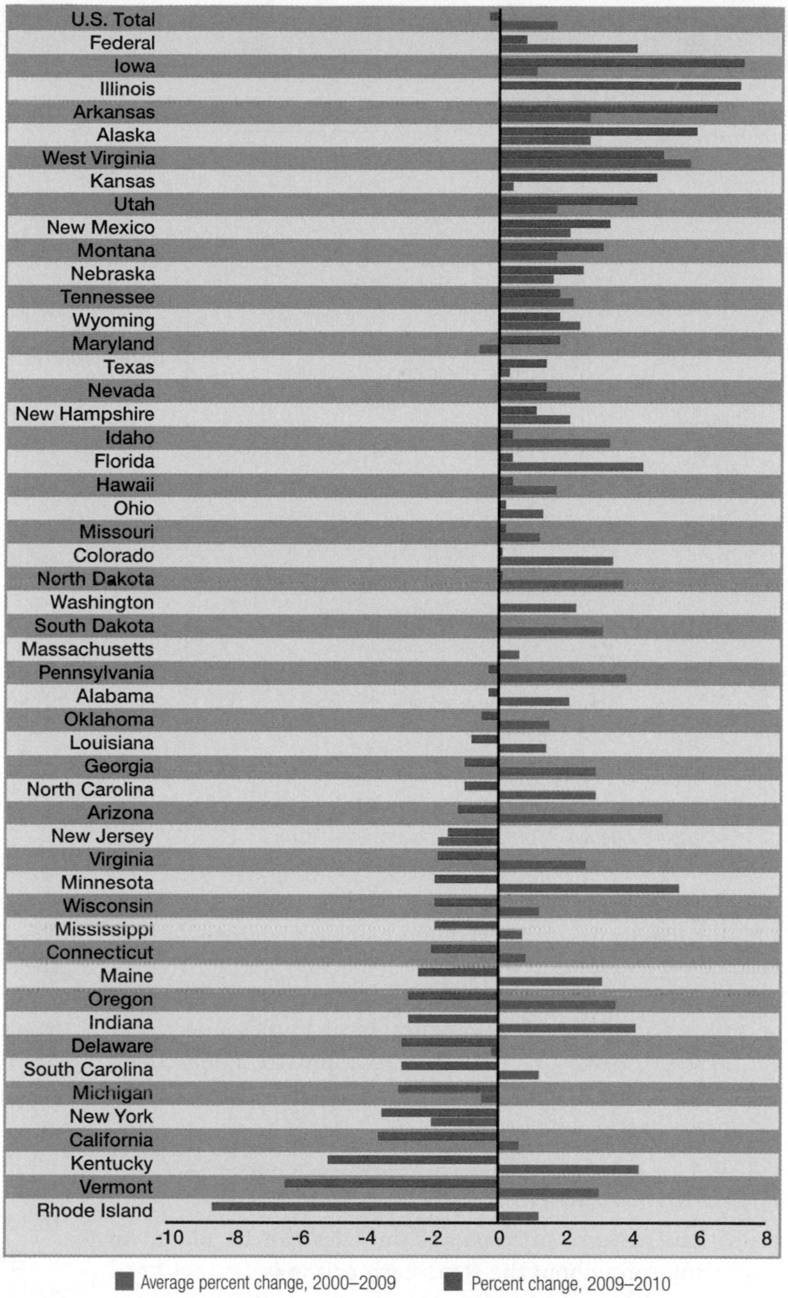

In the early nineteenth century, most states built one large prison to house all state inmates. It was thought that this economy of scale would provide the best solution to the problem of housing prisoners. Little effort was given to separating prisoners on the basis of age, type of offense, length of term, or criminal history. From the beginning, however, early state prisons, unlike early jails, separated prisoners by sex, maintaining separate facilities for female prisoners. Until the late twentieth century, women comprised a very small percentage of felony offenders. Thus, while early prisons for male offenders were built to house thousands of inmates, institutions for female prisoners usually were one-tenth the size. Furthermore, prison architecture reflected the assumption that male prisoners were more aggressive and dangerous

■ Average percent change, 2000–2009   ■ Percent change, 2009–2010

FIGURE 10–4 Change in Imprisonment Rates, 2009–2010
In 2010, the total prison population dropped after nearly 40 years of record-high increases. Future data will be examined to determine whether this is the start of a period of decline or only a temporary reduction. Prison count dropped in half the states, but the federal prison population has continued to grow due to tougher federal drug sentencing laws.
Source: Paul Guerino, Paige M. Harrison, and William J. Sabol, *Prisoners in 2010* (Washington, DC: Bureau of Justice Statistics, December 2011), p. 3.

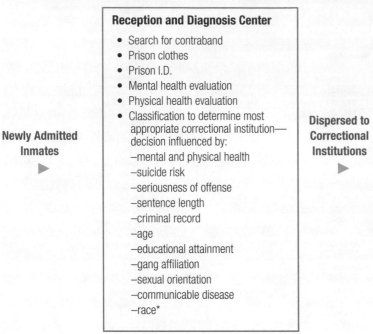

Reception and Diagnosis Center

- Search for contraband
- Prison clothes
- Prison I.D.
- Mental health evaluation
- Physical health evaluation
- Classification to determine most appropriate correctional institution—decision influenced by:
  - mental and physical health
  - suicide risk
  - seriousness of offense
  - sentence length
  - criminal record
  - age
  - educational attainment
  - gang affiliation
  - sexual orientation
  - communicable disease
  - race*

Newly Admitted Inmates ▶

Dispersed to Correctional Institutions ▶

Race alone cannot be a criterion for classification. Usually, race is relevant because it is often associated with gang membership.

Maximum Security Minimum emphasis on programs and rehabilitation and maximum emphasis on security. Inmates may work unsupervised outside of confinement on prison farms, for example, or in community-based educational or vocational programs.

Medium Security Strong security measures but a variety of education, counseling, and rehabilitation programs. Cell-type and dormitory housing.

Minimum Security Fencing or no perimeter security. Inmates may work unsupervised outside of confinement on prison farms, for example, or in community-based educational or vocational programs.

Mental Health Institutions Medical hospitals for mentally ill inmates. Strong physical security measures but the institution resembles a hospital more than a walled prison. May be combined with a medical facility.

Medical Facility A medical hospital for inmates. Medium and maximum security institutions may have a small medical facility within the walls of the prison. Large medical facilities usually treat chronically and terminally ill prisoners. May be combined with a mental health facility.

Private Prison Some prisoners are selected to be sent to private prisons, which usually accept minimum- and medium-security inmates. May be located out of state. Primary purpose is to reduce overcrowding of state prisons.

Transfer to Another Jurisdiction In rare cases, state prisons may "trade" inmates. Exceptional high security–risk inmates (for example, state witnesses for organized crime inmates) may be transferred to another jurisdiction. In turn, the state agrees to accept a similar inmate from the other jurisdiction.

and that female prisoners were more docile and less violent.[54] Based on this assumption, correctional institutions for women often lacked the fortresslike architecture and brutal discipline of prisons for men. Today, states have numerous prisons within their jurisdiction and distribute inmates among them according to a system of prisoner classification. For example, California has 33 state prisons.

Prisoner Classification

States have diverse prisons, and inmates can be placed in any prison throughout the state. Each prison is distinguished by its security level and the programs available to inmates. Before incarceration in a state prison, an inmate undergoes an extensive examination and assessment to determine his or her assignment to a particular facility. Because inmates remain in state custody for a relatively long time, the system attempts to determine their needs and any characteristics that might influence placement. The correctional system also evaluates the security risks, staffing impacts, and institutional needs when deciding where inmates go. Jails use a modified form of classification. However, because of the inmates' short-term incarceration, the lack of counseling and treatment programs, and the diversity of the inmate population, classification often sorts prisoners by just a few

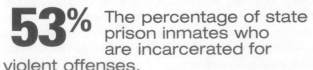

53% The percentage of state prison inmates who are incarcerated for violent offenses.

characteristics, such as gender, juvenile or adult, security risks, and special populations. Jails often have people awaiting trial on serious felony charges in the same environment as inmates serving time for misdemeanors.

This process of **prisoner classification**, performed in a specially designated facility, is commonly known as reception and diagnosis. At the state's reception and diagnosis facility, the classification process includes identification of the inmate, examination of the inmate's criminal record, evaluation of the inmate's mental capacity and psychological stability, and assessment of other factors that may influence his or her assignment (for example, gang membership, age, and educational achievement).

Prison Consultants and Prison Classification

The incarceration of prominent political figures (mayors, senators, and governors, for instance), celebrities, and wealthy people has given rise to the increased use of private prison consultants to help these people secure as favorable a classification as possible. **Prison consultants** are private for-profit advisers who are familiar with the prison culture and classification process. Sometimes prison consultants have obtained their expertise by serving time. High-profile, wealthy offenders often hire prison consultants to lobby for good prison placement, to mitigate sentence length, and to offer crash courses in prison culture. All of the following used the services of a prison consultant prior to their incarceration: Rob Blagojevich, former governor of Illinois; Martha Stewart; football star Michael Vick; former Pennsylvania state senator Vincent Fumo; and Bernie Madoff.

Prison officials deny that prison consultants are effective in receiving preferential treatment for their clients. They claim that all inmates are treated equally. However, prison consultants often advise their clients on the classification process, such as how to negotiate for assignment to the best prison and how to present themselves during the classification process so that they receive the lowest possible risk evaluation. In addition to helping with the classification process, prison consultants offer advice on how to behave in prison to minimize risk. Tim Miller of the San Diego–based Dr. Prison consultant service says, "It's like going to a foreign country that you've never been to before with different language, people's mannerisms."[55] These inmates were once wealthy (and still may be) and powerful. They are used to privilege; freedom of choice; and comfortable, even luxurious, lifestyles. They are ill-prepared to enter the prison culture. Larry Levine of the Los Angeles–based Wall Street Prison Consultants offers his clients a primer called "Fed Time 101" to help them prepare for incarceration. The federal prison system also provides inmates with information prior to incarceration, advising them how to best adjust to their new environment.

Induction into the Prison

At the classification facility, the inmate is inducted into the state's prison system. Prisoners exchange their clothing for prison clothing, undergo extensive and intrusive searches for weapons or contraband, are photographed and fingerprinted, and are assigned a prisoner identification (ID) number. This ID number becomes the unique identifying number for the inmate, similar to a person's Social Security number. (In fact, when prisoners die in prison and are buried in prison cemeteries because no one claims the body, the headstone is inscribed with the inmate's prison ID number.) This process is similar to the booking process that occurs when a person is first arrested for a crime, but it must be repeated because the inmate reporting for prison may not be the person who was convicted of the crime. Such a case was discovered in October 2000 when a federal prisoner walked away from a minimum-custody federal correctional facility. When police found and returned the escapee, prison officials found that he was an impostor.[56] The convicted offender had arranged for another person to report to prison and serve time in his place. Officials had failed to detect this switch before the impostor had served 18 months of the other man's sentence.[57]

Inmate Placement

One of the important decisions made in the classification process is of the many prisons in which the inmate may be permanently assigned, which one best matches the needs of the inmate and the state. **Initial placement** includes decisions such as to which correctional facility the inmate should be assigned, the inmate's security risk level, and the living environment of the inmate. The inmate's length of sentence, seriousness of the offense, and past criminal record are important factors in deciding in which facility the inmate will be placed initially. Inmates with long prison sentences, serious offenses, and past criminal histories will be assigned to high-security facilities. Nonviolent offenders with shorter sentences and youthful offenders with no serious criminal record may be assigned to minimum- or medium-security institutions. Inmates with mental illness may be assigned to medical facilities, where they will receive treatment in a secure environment.

Living Environment

The living environment refers to whether the inmate will be housed in a single cell, a multiple-inmate cell, or dormitory-style housing. This can be a life-and-death decision because improper assignment may result in injury or death to an inmate. For example, injury or death may result if prison authorities assign a white inmate who belonged to a white supremacist group to share a cell with a minority inmate who belonged to a minority-based gang. Also, assigning inmates belonging to rival gangs may have deadly consequences. A mistake in classification may have serious, even deadly, consequences. For example, a wrongful death lawsuit was filed against Illinois correctional officials for assigning first-time inmate Joshua Daczewitz as a cell mate to Corey Fox, a murderer and mentally ill inmate who had previously threatened to kill any cell mate assigned to him. After correctional officials placed Daczewitz as Corey Fox's cell mate, Fox strangled Daczewitz.[58]

Change in Classification

A prisoner's classification may be changed based on behavior, a change in status, or other considerations. For instance, a prisoner assigned to maximum security may be reassigned to medium security based on good behavior and time served. A prisoner assigned to minimum security who tries to escape, on the other hand, may be reassigned to a higher-security prison. A primary reason for classifying and assigning prisoners to various security levels is to enhance the safety of the prison environment for both the inmates and the staff. Thus, any change in an inmate's behavior suggesting that he or she would be an escape risk or a danger to staff, other

State prisons are correctional institutions containing only convicted offenders, usually felony inmates sentenced to prison as punishment for a crime.

inmates, or himself or herself can trigger a change in the inmate's classification. A change in classification is accompanied by a change in housing or even transfer to another prison. In theory, as an inmate approaches the end of his or her sentence, he or she is transferred to less-restrictive housing. Ideally, when the inmate is within months of release, he or she can be transferred to a community-based facility to promote his or her successful transition from prison to society.

> Before incarceration in a state prison, an inmate undergoes an extensive examination and assessment to determine his or her assignment to a particular facility.

protecting other inmates and staff from infectious diseases.

Age

Young prisoners, usually under 26 years of age, may need to be separated from older, more hardened offenders. Elderly prisoners, an increasing challenge to correctional institutions, also may need to be protected from the general prison population. The "graying of inmates" is becoming more of a problem for prisons because of longer prison sentences and demographic factors such as aging baby boomers in the prison population.

Gang Affiliation

Gang affiliation also is an important consideration in determining where to house a prisoner and can be a real dilemma. Gang members placed together may pose a security risk because they will conspire together. However, an inmate placed in a housing unit with rival gang members may be assaulted. In some cases, groups of gang rivals forced to live together may engage in gang warfare.

Women

Until the nineteenth century, it was believed that female offenders were "fallen" women and could not be rehabilitated.[59] In the nineteenth century, there were not many female offenders and those few were housed in a section of the men's prison and supervised by male correctional officers. Elizabeth Gurney Fry is credited with establishing the early theoretical and practical bases for women's corrections at Newgate Prison in London in the early nineteenth century. In America, between 1844 and 1848, Eliza W. B. Farnham instituted many of Fry's principles at the women's section of Sing Sing prison in New York. However, public outrage over "soft" treatment of the female offenders resulted in Farnham's dismissal. The first institution expressly for women was the Indiana Reformatory Institution for Women and Girls, built in 1873.

Recent years have seen an increase in the number of females arrested and incarcerated, but a wide gap still exists between male and female prisoners. Today, about one-tenth the number of female offenders as male offenders are incarcerated. In 2010, a total of 1,446,000 males were incarcerated, whereas only 104,600 female offenders were incarcerated. The rate of incarceration of females for violent crimes has increased more than the rate for male offenders. About 36% of female offenders are serving time for a violent offense compared to about 55% of male offenders.[60] Over half of female offenders are incarcerated for property crime (29.6%) or drug offenses (25.7%). Compared to men (3.3%), more women are incarcerated for larceny (8.8%) and crimes of fraud (10% for females and 1.9% for males).

There are different arguments as to why the rate of offending and incarcerate for females is increasing. One viewpoint is

▶ Special Prison Populations

Some prisoners may not be suited to transfer to the **general prison population**. Because of age, mental illness, depression, other health status, or other characteristic, an inmate may need to be kept out of the general population. Inmates with characteristics that may result in significant risks to themselves, other inmates, or staff are referred to as **special prison populations**.

Mental Stability

During the classification process, the inmate is administered psychological tests to determine his or her mental stability. Incarceration can trigger intense depression; as a result, some prisoners are high suicide risks. Prison officials attempt to identify such prisoners, provide assistance, and place them under constant observation in what is known as suicide watch. Some inmates require psychiatric treatment or medications and would be a danger to others or themselves if placed in the general population. During classification, these inmates are identified and often transferred to appropriate mental health care facilities.

Lifestyle

During the classification process, prison officials also try to determine whether the inmate's lifestyle or special needs should influence placement. Specific assignments may be based on the inmate's age, sexual orientation, gang affiliation, or physical health. Inmates with significant health problems, such as AIDS or tuberculosis, require extensive care in prison. Prison officials are responsible for providing appropriate health care and

LEARNING OUTCOMES 5 Summarize the problems related to special populations and racism.

GLOSSARY

general prison population The nonrestricted population of prison inmates who have access to prison services, inmate interactions, programs, and recreation.

special prison populations Inmates with characteristics that may result in significant risks to themselves, other inmates, or staff.

prison economy The exchange of goods, services, and contraband by prisoners in place of money.

disproportionate confinement The nonrandom distribution of people by race in correctional institutions. If the prison population reflected the same demographics as the general population, confinement would not reflect racial bias.

1873
The date the first state prison exclusively for women is built.

Andrew Aitchison/ Alamy

that female offending reflects a different power status between males and females. According to this theory, female offending is caused by male domination, which is why women commit property, drug, and sex crimes. These crimes are committed because they are sources of income for males. Other viewpoints hypothesize that female offending and incarceration has increased due to changing socioeconomic norms and values. Since World War II, women have entered the workplace, have become financially independent, and have more role models and opportunities than ever before. With this changing landscape, some women have turned to criminal activities. Other theories blame the media. The argument is that the violence depicted in the media that causes juvenile male criminal behavior also causes female criminality.

Another argument as to why the rate of female offending and incarceration is increasing links the increase to drug use and drug laws. Some argue that the shift to tougher mandatory sentencing for drug offenses is a major reason for this dramatic rise in women's incarceration rates. In many states, the rate of incarceration of female offenders for drug offenses has nearly doubled since 1990.[61] The history of the rise in female incarceration and "get tough" drug laws coincide. For example, in 1999, female offenders accounted for over 15% of defendants charged with a drug offense in U.S. district courts.[62] The number of boys charged with drug offenses in juvenile court from 1989 to 1998 dropped by 2%, but the number of girls charged with drug crimes rose by 2%.[63] Female offenders comprise 16% of the drug cases in juvenile court. In state prisons, 65% to 73% of female offenders admitted to regular drug use before incarceration.[64] Furthermore, it is estimated that many female offenders serving time for property and sex crimes were motivated to commit these crimes by the need to obtain money for drugs.

Equality of Male versus Female Prisons

Female offenders are usually housed in separate facilities from male offenders. Under the law, male and female correctional facilities should provide the same services. However, because of the much smaller number of female prisoners, female correctional institutions often lack the range of services and programs provided at male correctional facilities.

The increasing number of female offenders has created major problems for the correctional system. Female institutions are

Female offenders are more likely to suffer from HIV infection and mental illness than are male inmates.

80% The percentage of female inmates who have dependent children.

becoming overcrowded, and female offenders have less access to vocational, educational, medical, and rehabilitation programs. For example, the percentage of female offenders receiving drug treatment while in prison is declining significantly, despite the high rate of drug use among female offenders. Today, only 15% of state prison inmates and 10% of federal prison inmates obtain drug treatment while in prison, whereas in 1991, 29% of state and 19% of federal female offenders reported participation in these programs.[65]

Female prisons often lack the opportunities for vocational training and educational programs compared to male prisoners. In a male prison with thousands of inmates, it is possible to provide a variety of vocational and educational programs. It is not uncommon for male prisons to offer hands-on vocational training and internship programs as well as educational programs that include postgraduate degrees. The smaller number of women in prison makes such a variety of programs financially impracticable. Vocational training in women's prisons is often limited to cooking, sewing, and cosmetology. (It is interesting to note that in many states, cosmetology is a licensed profession and a felony conviction can bar a person from obtaining the required state license.) While lawsuits have been filed to seek equality in male and female prisons, the economic distress that most states are facing makes investment in female correctional facilities financially impossible.

Another interesting challenge for the women's prisons is staffing. There is a shortage of women interested in employment as a correctional officer in female (and male) prisons. As a result, women prisons are forced to use large numbers of men as correctional officers. The use of male correctional officers in women's prisons is often cited as a potential problem for women's privacy and sexual abuse.

Health Issues for Women

Although female offenders suffer many of the same physical and mental health problems in prison as do male prisoners, statistics indicate that female offenders are more likely to suffer from HIV infection and mental illness than are male inmates. At year-end 2002, about 2.9% of female inmates in state prisons were infected with HIV, compared to about 1.9% of male inmates. About 24% of female inmates in state and federal prisons reported suffering from mental illnesses, compared to 16% of male inmates.[66]

Victimization

Some see female offenders as victims of men.[67] This is the view of feminist criminological theories, which argue that female offenders are victimized by a social and criminal justice system that is biased toward male dominance. Evidence of female offenders as victims of men is seen in the high rate of sexual and physical abuse reported by female offenders. About 57% of state female inmates and 40% of federal female inmates report that they were sexually or physically abused before admission, whereas only 16% of state male inmates and 7% of federal male inmates report that they were abused, and the proportions are similar for jail inmates.[68] Abuse of female offenders continues after incarceration because frequent scandals involve correctional officers demanding sex from female inmates. Many former female inmates allege that during their incarceration, sex with male correctional officers in exchange for favors was commonplace. "Sexual favors are part of a hidden **prison economy**, in exchange for avoiding retribution, getting drugs, or obtaining extra privileges, such as staying up after hours."[69]

Dependent Children and Broken Families

More than 1.5 million children in the United States have parents in prison. [71] The burden of incarceration falls heavier on female offenders than on male offenders. Families are more likely to be broken by a woman's confinement in the criminal justice system than by a man's.[72] On average, about 80% of female inmates have dependent children.[73]

In the classification process, an important factor is the placement of inmates within a reasonable distance of family members for the purpose of visitation. If a federal inmate from Florida is placed in a federal prison in California, it will be a hardship for family members to visit the inmate. Likewise, if a state prisoner from southern California is placed in a state prison in northern California, it will be a hardship for family members to visit. The burden placed on family members to visit may be considered in classification, especially for women.

Although most mothers plan to return to their families after being released, they are often poorly prepared for this task. Female offenders have fewer visits with family during their incarceration than do male offenders. One reason is that as a result of few female prisons, female offenders often are incarcerated farther from home than are male offenders. Another reason is that when male offenders are incarcerated, custody of children typically remains with the mother, whereas when females are imprisoned, grandparents frequently become the caregivers of the children. Most data suggest that incarcerated women do not see their children at all.[74] Some innovative programs try to keep female offenders united with their families. A promising program that is effective, inexpensive, and easy to administer is Girl Scouts Beyond Bars, which provides regular mother–daughter contact through Girl Scout programs conducted in prisons.[75]

Upon their return to the community, female offenders are likely to face significant problems, including parental poverty, unemployment, substance abuse, low self-esteem, and ill health. Often the problems of the parent result in child abuse and neglect. Children of incarcerated parents are five times more likely to offend than are children whose parents have not been incarcerated. This starts a vicious cycle of crime that is difficult to break.

Institutional Racism and Incarceration

An indicator of the criminal justice system's discrimination against minorities is the ratio of minorities to whites in prison. Many other indicators may not clearly show that minorities are treated differently by the system, but incarceration rates demonstrate that there is a **disproportionate confinement** rate for minorities. If recent incarceration rates remain unchanged, an estimated 1 of every 20 people (5.1%) will serve time in a prison during his or her lifetime.[76] However, the likelihood of going to state or federal prison is disproportionate when one examines the likelihood of going to prison by race. When the numbers are adjusted for percentage of the general population, the differences by race are enormous. A white male has a 1 in 23 chance of serving time in prison; a Hispanic male has a 1 in 6 chance; an African-American male has a greater than 1 in 4 chance.[77]

Some argue that the criminal justice system does not incarcerate innocent people; thus, all the African-American men in prison have committed a crime and deserve to be incarcerated. Others argue that the criminal justice system discriminates against minorities from the beginning, especially African-American men, because they are more likely to be stopped, arrested, charged, convicted, and sentenced to prison than are white men. For example, a Center for Constitutional Rights study found that 87% of the 575,000 people stopped by the police in New York City in 2009 were African-American or Latino.[78]

> Upon their return to the community, female offenders are likely to face significant problems, including parental poverty, unemployment, substance abuse, low self-esteem, and ill health.

TABLE 10–1

INMATES HELD IN CUSTODY IN STATE OR FEDERAL PRISONS OR IN LOCAL JAILS, DECEMBER 31, 2000, AND 2009–2010

Inmates in custody	Number of inmates			Average annual change, 2000–2009	Percent change, 2009–2010
	2000	2009	2010		
Total	1,937,482	2,291,912	2,266,832	1.9%	−1.1%
Federal prisoners[a]	140,064	205,087	206,968	4.2%	0.9%
Prisons	133,921	196,318	198,339	4.2	1.0
Federal facilities	124,540	171,000	173,138	3.5	1.3
Privately operated facilities	9,381	25,318	25,201	11.0	−0.5
Community Corrections Centers[b]	6,143	8,769	8,629	4.0	−1.6
State prisoners[c]	1,176,269	1,319,391	1,311,136	1.3%	−0.6%
State facilities	1,104,424	1,224,145	1,216,771	1.1	−0.6
Privately operated facilities	71,845	95,246	94,365	3.1	−0.9
Local jails[c]	621,149	767,434	748,728	2.3%	−2.4%
Incarceration rate[d]	684	743	731	0.9%	−1.7%
Adult incarceration rate[e]	926	981	962	0.6	−1.9

Note: Data may not be comparable to previously published BJS reports because of updates and changes in reference dates. Total includes all inmates held in state or federal prison facilities or local jails. It does not include inmates held in U.S. territories, military facilities, U.S. Immigration and Customs Enforcement (ICE) facilities, jails in Indian country, and juvenile facilities.

[a]After 2001, responsibility for sentenced prisoners from the District of Columbia was transferred to the Federal Bureau of Prisons.

[b]Nonsecure, privately operated community corrections centers.

[c]Counts for inmates held in local jails are for June 30 of each year.

[d]The total number in custody as of December 31 per 100,000 U.S. residents. Resident population estimates were as of January 1 of the following year.

[e]The total number in custody as of December 31 per 100,000 U.S. adult residents. Adult resident population estimates were as of January 1 of the following year.

Source: Lauren E. Glaze, "Correctional population in the United States, 2010." (Washington, DC: Office of Justice Programs, 2011), p. 7

Deprivation of the Right to Vote

One of the effects of the 28.5% likelihood of incarceration for African-American men is their disenfranchisement from the political system. The District of Columbia and 46 states deprive felons of the right to vote while they are in prison. In addition, 32 states bar offenders from voting while they are on probation, and 29 states bar felons from voting while they are on parole. In 14 of these states, felons are barred from voting for life.[79] It is estimated that 13% of the nation's African-American male population cannot vote because they have been convicted of a felony.[80] In states such as Alabama and Florida, which have a higher percentage of African-American male inmates, it is estimated that one in three African-American men is denied voting rights because of felony convictions.[81]

1895
The year the first federal prison for men is built in Leavenworth, Kansas.

▶ Federal Prisons

For over 100 years after the founding of the United States, there were no federal prisons. Federal prisoners were housed in state prisons for a fee. It was not until 1895 that the first federal prison for men was constructed at Leavenworth, Kansas. Using the labor of military prisoners at the nearby U.S. Disciplinary Barracks at Fort Leavenworth, the first federal prison was built in the architectural style of the times. Leavenworth Prison

(Think About It …

Michelle Alexander, author of *The New Jim Crow: Mass Incarceration in the Age of Colorblindness*, criticizes "mass incarceration" as a racially based system of control that exists to serve the perceived interests of white elites. She claims that the move away from "get tough" sentencing policies reflects the desire of the white middle class to avoid raising taxes, not a newfound interest in social justice. She calls for the dismantling of mass incarceration while acknowledging the economic engine generated by imprisonment. Do you agree with her claim? Why or why not?

Dan Bannister/Shutterstock

was a walled, maximum-security prison based on the Auburn concept of inside cell blocks and congregate work. As in state prisons and local jails, the number of federal female offenders was only about one-tenth that of male offenders; so the building of federal prisons for females lagged behind prisons for males. The first federal prison for women was Alderson Federal Prison Camp in West Virginia, which opened in November 1928. It was a minimum-security prison with no wall or barbed wire security perimeter. Both prisons are in operation today.

Like state prisons, oversight of federal prisons is balanced between the legislative, executive, and judicial branches of the federal government. The U.S. Congress funds federal prisons, which are under the executive control of the Office of the President. The U.S. Supreme Court has the power of judicial review and can declare that prison conditions are unconstitutional or that inmate rights have been violated.

The Federal Bureau of Prisons (BOP)

Prohibition created many new federal offenses for trafficking in illegal alcoholic beverages, spurring the growth of federal prisons. In 1930, the federal government unified its prisons under the administrative control of the newly formed **Federal Bureau of Prisons (BOP)**. After repeal of prohibition, the number of federal prisoners continued to increase as a result of federal drug prosecutions, firearms violations, and, recently, mandatory sentencing.

As the federal prison population exploded, overcrowding became a serious problem, so it was necessary to construct new federal prisons. Because of the nationwide jurisdiction of the federal prison system, new prisons could be built anywhere in the United States. Federal inmates could be housed in any federal prison in the country and could be transferred between the prisons at will. This authority to transfer federal inmates anywhere in the United States has been a great advantage of the federal prison system. The ability to transfer inmates from one prison to another, often separated by hundreds or thousands of miles, allows the BOP to move troublemakers and instigators from prison to prison. It also allows inmates in overpopulated prisons to be transferred to less populated prisons. Because the BOP was 40% over capacity in 2004, this ability to transfer inmates to relieve overcrowding is important.

Alcatraz

In 1934, the newly formed BOP built one of the most infamous prisons in U.S. history—the United States Penitentiary at Alcatraz, California, in San Francisco Bay. The most violent and highest security-risk inmates were then transferred from the various federal prisons to Alcatraz, a maximum-security prison without any rehabilitation, educational, or treatment programs. Its primary goal was the incarceration of high-risk inmates, and it gave little, if any, attention to rehabilitation goals, vocational programs, or educational programs. Alcatraz, which at one time housed Al Capone, prided itself on being escape-proof. In 1946,

1934
The year Alcatraz prison is built in San Francisco Bay by the newly formed Federal Bureau of Prisons.

Alcatraz erupted in violence as two **correctional officers** and three inmates were killed during an escape attempt. Public perception of federal prisons was shaped by this event and by movies about notorious Alcatraz inmates. The prison was closed permanently in 1963 and today remains a popular tourist destination.

Federal Correctional Facilities

Today, the BOP operates over 100 federal correctional facilities throughout the United States. The BOP's central office in Washington, DC, has six regional offices to oversee the operation of federal prison facilities. Federal prisons range from the **administrative-maximum prison** (ADX) in Florence, Colorado, to minimum-security federal prison camps. The federal government even operates "coed" minimum-security correctional facilities, the largest of which is in Lexington, Kentucky. Some federal prison facilities serve primarily as medical centers for federal prisoners; others, as detention centers and prison camps.

As in state prisons, the chief executive officer at a federal prison facility is the warden, who has various associate and assistant wardens to help run the administrative units and correctional officers; they are responsible for custody, movement, and control of inmates. In addition, the prison has numerous civilian employees, as a large federal prison is much like a city. Federal prisons are self-contained and provide infrastructure services such as power, water, sewage, and housing. Also, it must provide human services such as food, medical, recreational, and communication services. Federal prisons also provide counseling services and rehabilitation programs. Employees of the BOP are federal employees who generally receive better pay and benefits than do state prison or local jail employees. Generally, the hiring standards are higher for BOP positions. Also, BOP employees may transfer from one federal facility to another; so opportunities for advancement are greater

Alcatraz Prison was built on an island in San Francisco (CA) bay to enhance security.

Dorling Kindsersley

than in state prisons or local jails. As in state prisons, staffing in federal prisons is divided between employees who perform primarily security duties and those who provide administrative and treatment services.[82]

Federal Military Prisons

In addition to federal civilian prisons, there are federal military prisons. Members of the armed services who are convicted of offenses under the Uniform Code of Military Justice and sentenced to imprisonment are incarcerated in military, not civilian, facilities. Each branch of the service (Army, Navy, Marines, and Air Force) operates confinement facilities. Military correctional facilities are known as military prisons, disciplinary barracks, brigs, detention facilities, or confinement facilities. Military facilities that function similar to civilian jails are known as guardhouses, stockades, or brigs.

Military prisons are not under the authority of the BOP. Military prisons are administered by the military and staffed by military personnel and house only military personnel who have been convicted of offenses or are being held for trial. Civilians may be employed for noncustodial staff positions such as secretaries, teachers, and other support positions.

One of the oldest military prisons is the U.S. Disciplinary Barracks (USDB) located in Fort Leavenworth, Kansas. The USDB, known as "the Castle," is the U.S. military's only maximum-security facility. Only enlisted prisoners with sentences over five years, commissioned officers, and prisoners convicted of offenses related to national security are confined to the USDB. The Castle was built by prison labor starting in 1875. Prisoners of the USDB also were used to build the United States Penitentiary, Leavenworth from 1895 to 1903. This penitentiary was one of the first maximum-security federal prisons. The USDB was built using the architectural model of Eastern State Penitentiary and the administrative and housing model of the Auburn system.

Other military prisons are located throughout the United States and the world. Overseas military prisons are necessary due to the large number of military personnel stationed outside the continental United States. In addition, the military has confinement facilities, or brigs, aboard a number of U.S. naval ships.

The appearance and operation of modern military facilities closely resembles that of civilian prisons. One of the most visible differences is that correctional personnel are uniformed military personnel and inmates wear military-style uniforms. Since military prisons employ primarily members of the armed services, if someone wanted to work in a military prison as a warden, an administrator, or another professional, he or she would have to join a branch of the military. Military personnel who work in military prisons receive specialized training from the military.

Military detainment facilities for enemy combatants are distinctly different from military prisons. Perhaps the most well-known facilities for enemy combatants are the Guantánamo Bay detainment facility located at Guantánamo Bay Naval

The U.S. Disciplinary Barracks at Fort Leavenworth, Kansas—the first and largest military prison.

Base in Cuba and Abu Ghraib Prison in Iraq. Military detainment facilities for enemy combatants are operated under different rules and assumptions, and those confined have significantly fewer civil rights compared to other military or civilian inmates.

Privatization

A trend in corrections has been the **privatization** of jails and prisons. In 2010, states and the federal system reported that about 120,000 inmates were held in privately operated facilities. In 2010, there were 25,201 federal inmates held in private prisons and 94,365 state inmates held in private prisons. This number is down slightly from 2009.[83] Texas and Oklahoma reported the largest populations in private facilities.

> **LEARNING OUTCOMES 7** Summarize the advantages and disadvantages of private prisons.
>
> **GLOSSARY**
>
> **privatization** The trend to house inmates in privately administered prisons.
>
> **private prisons** Prisons that house local, state, or federal inmates for a fee.
>
> **state liability** A state's liability for violations of an inmate's constitutional rights.

Cost-Reduction Benefits

The primary reason given for housing prisoners in private facilities is to reduce costs. The cost of new prison facilities is extremely expensive. Private prisons allow local jails and state and federal prisons to house prisoners in private facilities and pay a per diem rate per prisoner rather than build new prisons to accommodate the increasing demand for bed space.

As the nation's financial crisis continues to erode the fiscal health of the states, many states are turning to private prisons to squeeze every last dollar out of the budget. Financially challenged states such as Arizona, Florida, and Ohio are turning to private prisons to save state dollars. The primary force behind this movement is the belief that private prisons save the states money, but a study by the Arizona Department of Corrections challenges this assumption.

A 2011 study by the Arizona Department of Corrections suggests that the cost difference between housing inmates in

119,564 The number of prisoners held in private prisons in 2010.

TABLE 10–2 | FEDERAL PRISON SECURITY CLASSIFICATION

Security Designation	Security Level	Characteristics
FPC—Federal Prison Camps	Minimum Security or Federal Prison Camps	Relatively low staff-to-inmate ratio, dormitory housing, limited or no perimeter fencing or guard towers. Work- and program-oriented; frequently adjacent to larger institutions, where inmates help serve the labor needs of the larger institution. Inmates may be allowed limited unsupervised travel and community access.
FCI—Federal Correctional Institutions	Low Security	Double-fenced perimeters. Mostly dormitory or cubicle housing, strong work and program components (education programs or vocational training). Higher staff-to-inmate ratio than FPCs. Inmates may be allowed community access for work and education programs.
FCI and USP—United States Penitentiaries	Medium Security	Medium-security institutions include both FCI and USP institutions. Strengthened perimeters (double fences and electronic detection systems), higher staff-to-inmate ratio than in FCI. In low-security institutions, internal movement of prisoners is more restricted, mostly cell-type housing. May include wide variety of work and treatment programs. Very restricted community access.
USP—United States Penitentiaries	High Security	Highly secured perimeters (high walls extending underground, reinforced fences, armed guard towers), multiple- and single-occupant cell housing, highest staff-to-inmate ratio, close control of inmate movement. Inmates not permitted to have access to work or education programs in the community.
FCC—Correctional Complexes	Different security level institutions located in close proximity	Mission and security levels differ by institution. Interaction of the institutions (for example, FPC may provide services or products, such as agricultural products, to USP).
Administrative—MCC, MDC, FDC, FMC, FTC, MCFP, and ADX	Multiple security levels depending on the mission of the institution. Missions include detention of pretrial offenders; medical treatment of inmates; and housing of extremely dangerous, violent, or escape-prone inmates.	Characteristics of facility vary greatly depending on the mission. Medical facilities may have only minimum-security architecture. ADX administrative-maximum (supermax) are the most secure federal prisons and have extensive security features.
Satellite Campus and Satellite Low-Security facilities	Small minimum- or low-security camps or satellite facilities adjacent to the main institution	Located adjacent to the main facility to provide inmate labor and off-site work programs.

private prisons versus state prisons may be as little as 3 cents per day. Furthermore, when other factors are taken into account, private prisons may actually cost more per inmate compared to state prisons.

A factor often not included in comparing the costs of private versus state prisons is that the contracts of private prisons limit the type of inmates they will accept. Private prisons are typically medium-security prisons, and their contract excludes maximum-security inmates, inmates with limited physical capacity, inmates with severe physical disabilities, inmates with chronic illness, or inmates with high-cost medical needs or high-need mental health conditions. Basically, the private prisons take those inmates who are the least expensive to house, leaving the state with the high-cost inmates. As a result, the Arizona study concludes that when these factors are taken into account, a comparison of the costs of imprisonment may show that there is little difference between the costs of private prisons and state prisons and that state prisons may actually be less expensive.

There are few other studies with which to compare the findings of the Arizona study. Advocates for private prisons argue that even if these data are accurate, private prisons save

the state millions of dollars in upfront construction costs and provide the ability to handle temporary increases in the prison population without the state having to commit to permanent personnel and facility costs.

Some states are questioning the cost savings of private prisons. For example, in February 2012, the Florida Senate rejected a bill to privatize 27 prisons. Those in favor of privatizing the prisons argued that it would save the state $16.5 million a year. Opponents questioned that estimate, worried about job losses among correctional officers, and said that the shift could jeopardize public safety.[84]

Private prisons look similar to government prisons. The difference is that private prisons are for-profit businesses that take prisoners from the local, state, and federal government and house them for a fee. Charges for housing an inmate in a private facility vary, ranging from $25 to $100 a day per inmate. Thus, a private prison may house prisoners from several counties and states. Also, there may be prisoners from local as well as state and federal prisons. Some prisoners are sent long distances to be housed in private prisons. For example, Hawaii sends prisoners to private prisons in Texas. These transfers can separate inmates from their family, their friends, support services, and even their lawyers.

In building and operating a private prison, the prison must pay for all expenses from its revenue and still be able to show a profit. Thus, controlling the cost of building and operating a private prison is important to the corporation that wants to make a profit from its venture. Private prisons keep costs down in several ways. Companies often receive tax breaks for building private prisons and grants for training employees. Often private prisons are built in rural areas where land and construction costs are low and wages are below the national average.[85]

Criticisms of Privatization

Critics of the privatization of corrections argue that given the emphasis on containing costs, private companies provide less training and lower salaries to prison personnel and have higher inmate-to-correctional officer ratios than do government prisons.[86] Critics also express concern that for-profit prisons do not provide the same quality of care and supervision or the same educational, recreational, and rehabilitative services that public prisons do.

Opponents argue that beyond the question of cost comparisons, there are inherent flaws in the use of private prisons, including state liability and alleged substandard staff and lack of treatment programs, rehabilitation programs, job training, and educational programs.

Proponents of private prisons focus almost entirely on cost savings. Often local, state, and federal prisons are under great pressures, including lawsuits, to reduce prison overcrowding. Unable to afford the high cost of constructing new prisons, governments turn to the use of private prisons.

Detriments to the Surrounding Community

Although private prisons help relieve the burden on overcrowded state and federal prisons, they often are criticized as being detrimental to low-income communities, where most private prisons are located. Private companies market their services to the state on promises of providing jobs in low-income communities and providing inmate labor for community projects.[87] With some exceptions, however, pay and benefits, as well as prison conditions, often are below state standards.[88]

State Liability

Another concern of critics is the issue of **state liability** for violation of inmates' constitutional rights and the abuse of inmates while housed in a private prison. Because it placed the inmate in the prison, the state retains liability but little control. Employees of private prisons are not government employees, and they and the companies that operate the prisons do not have immunity from certain lawsuits by inmates that government prisons enjoy.[89] Nevertheless, thousands of lawsuits are filed against state as

Private prisons look similar to government prisons. The difference is that private prisons are for-profit businesses that take prisoners from the local, state, and federal government and house them for a fee.

well as private prisons for violations of inmates' rights and substandard prison conditions.[90] For example, in April 2009, a Texas jury awarded $42.5 million to the family of an inmate who was beaten to death in 2001 at a private Texas prison facility in Willacy County. The award against the GEO Group, Inc., formerly named Wackenhut, is among the largest punitive damages ever ordered against a private prison company.[91]

Escaped Prisoners

Some question the ability of private prisons to prevent escapes due to cost-cutting measures. For example, the 2010 escape of three inmates from a private prison in Kingman, Arizona, and their murderous assault upon the community suggests to some that private prisons fail to provide adequate public safety regardless of the costs.

A unique problem for private prisons is the jurisdiction of law enforcement over escaped prisoners. Not all states have enacted legislation that recognizes the potential status of inmates in private prisons as escapees. Thus, a prisoner who escapes from a private prison may not have broken a state law! Also, an assault by an inmate on a correctional officer at a private facility is an assault on a private citizen (a tort), whereas an assault on a state or federal correctional officer is defined as a more serious crime.

▶ Prison Life

Life in prison poses special problems for inmates, correctional authorities, and the community. When the government incarcerates someone, it becomes legally responsible for the health and well-being of that person. Although the mission of correctional institutions is to protect the community by keeping prisoners securely incarcerated, there are other threats to the community. In securing inmates and protecting the community from harm, correctional institutions must do so without violating the constitutional rights of inmates. Some of the major challenges for correctional authorities are reducing/eliminating sexual violence in prison; reducing the risks caused by prison gangs; providing for the health, both physical and mental, and well-being of inmates; and reducing overall violence.

Sexual Violence in Prisons

Sexual violence in prison has become a national concern. Anecdotal stories, incomplete statistics, and testimonies before legislative bodies and public forums suggest that nonconsensual sexual violence is a serious problem. Inmate lawsuits claim that prison officials turn a blind eye to sexual violence in prison.[92] Some inmates who claim that they were raped in prison state that they were considered the "property"

Inmate lawsuits claim that prison officials turn a blind eye to sexual violence in prison.

of prison gangs and would be bartered for money or favors.[93] Human Rights Watch issued a report concluding that "rape, by prisoners' accounts, was no aberrational occurrence; instead it was a deeply-rooted, systemic problem. It was also a problem that prison authorities were doing little to address."[94] Spurred by public demands for more accurate information on sexual violence in prisons, President George W. Bush signed into law the **Prison Rape Elimination Act of 2003** (P.L. 108-79). The legislation requires the BJS to develop new national data collections on the incidence and prevalence of sexual violence in correctional facilities.

2004 Data on Sexual Violence

In 2004, the BJS issued its first report. It surveyed 2,700 correctional facilities and found that 8,210 allegations of sexual violence had been reported and that correctional authorities substantiated nearly 2,100 incidents of sexual violence.[95] The most serious forms of sexual violence reported were inmate-on-inmate nonconsensual sexual acts and staff sexual misconduct. Nearly 42% of the reported allegations of sexual violence involved staff sexual misconduct, 37% involved inmate-on-inmate nonconsensual sexual acts, 11% pertained to staff sexual harassment, and 10% applied to inmate-on-inmate abusive sexual contact. Juvenile facilities reported the highest rates of alleged sexual violence. The survey data indicated that most allegations of sexual violence could not be substantiated due to a lack of evidence. Males comprised 90% of victims and perpetrators of nonconsensual sexual acts in prison and jail.

Sanctions for Sexual Violence

The 2004 survey further reported that jail and prison authorities had several sanctions for inmates who were found to have committed sexual violence. The most common sanctions included moving the perpetrator to solitary confinement, changing the inmate to a higher custody level, transferring the inmate to another facility, losing good-time credit, losing privileges, and confining the inmate to his or her cell or quarters. Staff members found to have committed sexual violence were discharged, disciplined, or referred for prosecution. Juvenile systems reported the largest numbers of staff referred for prosecution (41%).

The 2007 report of the Rape Elimination Act still notes that preventing and responding to sexual victimization of inmates does not appear to be a priority of prison administration. U.S. District Judge Reggie B. Walton, Commission Chairman of the report, recommends a zero-tolerance policy on prison sexual victimization. Other suggestions to combat the sexual victimization of inmates include conducting background checks on staff and training staff to help victims of sexual assault secure emergency medical and mental health treatment.[96]

2012 Data on Sexual Violence

Since the inception of the Prison Rape Elimination Act, the BJS continues to issue annual reports of sexual victimization in jails and prisons. The 2012 survey changed the survey methodology to elicit fuller reporting of victimization by surveying only former inmates. Thus, the results of the 2012 survey cannot be reliably compared to previous years' surveys because of the difference in the participants. Also, the new methodology required former inmates to complete the

9.6% The percentage of former state prisoners who reported one or more incidents of sexual victimization.

survey by interacting with a computer-administered questionnaire using a touch screen and provided synchronized audio instructions via headphones.[97]

The 2012 survey reported the following findings:[98]

- An estimated 9.6% of former state prisoners reported one or more incidents of sexual victimization.

- About 5.4% of former state prisoners reported an incident involving another inmate, and 5.3% reported an incident involving facility staff.

- An estimated 1.2% of former prisoners reported that they unwillingly had sex or sexual contact with facility staff, and 4.6% reported that they "willingly" had sex or sexual contact with staff.

- More than three-quarters of all reported staff sexual misconduct involved a male inmate with female staff.

- Among former state prisoners, the rate of inmate-on-inmate sexual victimization was at least three times higher for females (13.7%) than for males (4.2%).

- Among heterosexual males, an estimated 3.5% reported being sexually victimized by another inmate. In comparison, among males who were bisexual, 34% reported being sexually victimized by another inmate. Among males who were homosexual or gay, 39% reported being victimized by another inmate.

- Following their release from prison, 72% of victims of inmate-on-inmate sexual victimization indicated that they felt shame or humiliation. Seventy-nine percent of unwilling victims of staff sexual misconduct said that they felt shame or humiliation.

Prison Gangs

Gang activity, a major factor in many prisons, has implications for in-prison and postprison behavior.[99] The first prison gangs appeared in 1950. Prior to that time, strict control of prisoner movement, limited contact with the outside world, absence of work-release programs, and a harsh disciplinary code prevented the formation of gangs. Today, prison gangs, known as special threat or **security-risk groups**, are a serious problem. For example, Rikers Island in New York has identified 44 security-risk groups that operate within the prison.[100] Among the more common gangs operating in prison are the Aryan Brotherhood, the Black Guerilla Family, the Bloods, the Crips, La Nuestra Familia, the Latin Kings, the Mexican Mafia, Mexikanemi, Ñeta, and the Texas Syndicate. Most prison gangs are organized along lines of racial and ethnic identity.

Prison gangs pose special security risks and create a higher risk of violence because of the following:

- Gang codes of conduct discourage obedience to prison rules.

- Gangs frequently are involved in trafficking of prison contraband and protection.

GLOSSARY

Prison Rape Elimination Act of 2003 An act that required the Bureau of Justice Statistics to survey jails and prisons to determine the prevalence of sexual violence within correctional facilities.

security-risk groups Groups in prisons that raise special threats, such as prison gangs.

contraband Smuggled goods, such as drugs, cigarettes, money, and pornography.

Section 1983 lawsuits Civil lawsuits filed in federal court alleging that the government has violated a constitutional right of the inmate.

HIV/AIDS A disease that damages the body's immune system. Acquired immunodeficiency syndrome (AIDS) is caused by the human immunodeficiency virus (HIV). A person can be HIV-positive and not have AIDS.

tuberculosis (TB) A contagious infectious disease caused by a bacterial infection that primarily affects the lungs.

deinstitutionalization The movement of mentally ill offenders from long-term hospitalization to community-based care.

total institutions Prisons that meet all of the inmate's basic needs, discourage individuality, punish dissent, and segregate those who do not follow the rules.

prisonization Socialization into a distinct prison subculture with its own values, mores, norms, and sanctions.

prison code The informal rules and expected behavior established by inmates. Often the prison code is contrary to the official rules and policies of the prison. Violation of the prison code can be punished by use of violence or even death.

Gang codes require absolute loyalty to the gang. Often to show one's commitment to the gang, new members must pass initiation tests, rituals that require the new member to make a "hit" on a rival gang member or correctional staff member. The hit usually requires only that the gang member attack the person and draw blood.[101]

Trafficking in Contraband

Gang membership extends outside the prison. Prison gangs use this characteristic to have fellow gang members smuggle contraband inside the prison during visits, through staff members who have been bribed, or during work detail or other forms of release when the prisoner is outside the prison walls. Prison gangs then use trafficking in **contraband**—such as drugs, cigarettes, money, and pornography—to buy favors, recruit members, pay prison debts, and make a profit. Prisoners who compete with the prison gang business, who inform prison officials about gang activities, or who are unable to pay for gang contraband may become targets of gang violence.

Inmate Protection

Many inmates join a gang for protection, so an unintended consequence of longer prison terms has been an increase in gang affiliation. Because prisoners must stay in prison longer, they feel a greater need to be affiliated with a prison gang to provide them with protection from other gangs, from other inmates, and from correctional staff members. Gang affiliation guarantees retaliation for any harm caused to a member by others. In extreme cases, such retaliation can lead to a vicious cycle of gang wars, as each gang continues to retaliate for the last attack. Because fear of gang retaliation

As more prisoners are incarcerated and with longer sentences, the cost of prisoners' health care increases dramatically.

may be stronger than fear of official prison sanctions, whenever prison rules and gang codes conflict, gang members obey their gang code.

Physical Health in Prisons

Daniel Tote, aged 47, missed his release date from prison. In fact, he remained in prison ten months beyond the expiration of his sentence. Tote was not released because he was in a persistent vegetative state as a result of head trauma he had suffered in an attack while in prison. When his sentence expired, there was no place to send him. Nursing homes would not take him because, as a prisoner, he was not eligible for Medicaid. He had no insurance and no family to care for him. Thus, he remained in the prison infirmary despite the fact he was a free man. Eventually, the state found a nursing home in which to place him, at a cost to the state of about $40,000 a year.[102] Daniel Tote is an extreme example of a serious problem in the criminal justice system: The physical and mental health of offenders, both incarcerated and released, has become a costly and sometimes deadly public health problem with no end in sight.

Prisoners have significant physical and mental health problems. The health of an average 50-year-old prisoner approximates that of an average 60-year-old person in the free community.[103] In a survey by the Office of Justice Programs, about 40% of state inmates and 48% of federal inmates aged 45 or older said that they had had a medical problem since being sent to prison.[104] While they are in prison, their health care is the responsibility of the state. When they are released from prison, as most are, these problems do not go away when they reenter the community. Often the released inmate enters the community with significant physical and mental health problems that can have a serious—even deadly—impact on the public.

Long-Term Health Care

The trend toward incarceration of offenders has created an unintended consequence: the creation of long-term health care obligations. As more prisoners are incarcerated with longer sentences, the cost of prisoners' health care increases dramatically.[105] The impact of this problem can be seen in the fact that the most common **Section 1983 lawsuits** against jails and prisons involved claims of substandard medical treatment.[106] The leading causes of death in state prisons are heart disease and cancer, which account for half the deaths there. Most of these

$65,000 The average cost per year
to provide round-the-clock health care to an elderly, ill inmate.

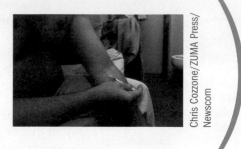

One of the challenges to prison security is preventing the smuggling of drugs into prisons. Drug smugglers use complex and high-tech methods to get Suboxone, a drug of choice, into prisons. Suboxone is prescribed to treat addiction to heroin and other drugs, but it also can be used to achieve a state of euphoria. Suboxone can be hidden under postage stamps, crayon scribblings, stickers, and glitter glue and can be hidden in seams of clothing. Prisons have adopted policies to eliminate the smuggling of Suboxone, including opening all inmates' mail. What, if any, are the limits on prisoners' rights in securing prisons?

Chris Cozzone/ZUMA Press/Newscom

inmates were aged 45 or older, and most of the deaths in prison (68%) for medical reasons were from preexisting conditions prior to admission. Many prison facilities now contain geriatric wings to house the high number of elderly inmates. These facilities provide long-term care units staffed by nurses instead of correctional officers. Older, ill inmates receive round-the-clock care that costs the state about $65,000 per year.[107]

The Burden of Health Care Costs

For some states, the cost of health care, especially for the chronically or terminally ill inmate, is so burdensome on the state that state legislators and parole boards have provided for early release of these prisoners to reduce the cost to the state. Other states, such as California, Illinois, and Texas, are turning to cost-cutting strategies such as telemedicine and the use of inmates to provide assistance to other inmates who are chronically or terminally ill. Telemedicine provides video consultations, avoiding the cost of transporting the prisoner outside the prison to medical facilities and making it easier and cheaper to secure the services of medical doctors and specialists.

The standard of health care provided by cash-starved California fell below acceptable standards of care, and a court-appointed receiver was charged with improving the health care system of California state prisons. The court mandated that the state significantly reduce its prison population or build more facilities. California appealed the decision to the U.S. Supreme Court, and in 2011, the Court affirmed the lower court's order. California was ordered to reduce its prison population to a maximum of 110,000 by 2013 or build more facilities. Given California's financial crisis and limited budget, the state will be unable to build additional facilities; so it appears that the state will have to offer early release to 30,000 to 40,000 inmates.

Studies indicate that, statistically, the risk of recidivism drops significantly with age. However, prisons, especially federal prisons and prisons in states that have abolished parole, often cannot release these inmates. In other cases, elderly offenders cannot be released because they are serving mandatory terms or because there are no community-care facilities to release them to, as in the case of Daniel Tote. As a result, the care of geriatric inmates has become an expensive burden on the criminal justice system. In a system that is constantly competing for public funding of other needs—for example, drug-treatment programs, juvenile

rehabilitation programs, community policing, and even public schools and highways—it is difficult to justify spending $65,000 a year on care for each elderly prisoner.

Prisoners cannot be released just because they are old and it is expensive to take care of them. Despite the fact that the offender is elderly, he or she still may be a serious threat to community safety. About 45% of inmates aged 50 and older had only recently been arrested. Older felons tend to be locked up for more serious crimes, such as rape, murder, and child molestation.[108] Pedophiles and sex offenders often continue their sexual violence throughout their life. For example, in the Penn State scandal, Jerry Sandusky was 68 years old when he was convicted of sexually assaulting his victims. Obviously, these offenders need to be incarcerated for the protection of the public and cannot be released from prison simply because of their age and health care costs.

Drug-Treatment Programs

Drug-treatment programs for addicted inmates are another significant challenge for prison officials. Over 50% of prisoners can be classified as drug dependent. An estimated 21% of state and 55% of federal inmates were incarcerated in 2004 for drug law violations. About 17% of state prisoners reported that they committed their crimes to obtain money for drugs. Given these high numbers of drug-dependent prisoners, it is important that prisons offer drug-treatment programs to inmates. However, only about 39% of drug users were able to participate in a prison drug abuse program in 2004.

Drug monitoring programs that screen arrestees for the presence of drugs when arrested continue to indicate that most arrestees test positive for drug use at the time of arrest. From this data, it can be inferred that those convicted of offenses and incarcerated have a drug addiction problem. Contemporary practice has been to try to divert offenders with serious and obvious drug addiction problems to drug court and to drug-treatment programs rather than prison. However, this is complicated by mandatory sentencing laws for certain drug offenders. Drug users who are convicted for selling drugs, often as a means to obtain income for their habit, may be sentenced for drug trafficking, which carries a mandatory prison sentence. Thus, the challenge of obtaining in-prison drug treatment for offenders is still a serious problem.

> Prisoners cannot be released just because they are old and it is expensive to take care of them. Despite the fact that the offender is elderly, he or she still may be a serious threat to community safety.

30,000 to 40,000

The number of inmates California corrections has been ordered to release by 2013.

Feeding Inmates

Providing for the health and well-being of inmates can be as simple as feeding them. Complaints about food have been one of the reasons inmates give for protesting and rioting. Perhaps one of the most extreme examples of failing to feed inmates properly was the case of the Morgan County jail in Alabama in 2009. Morgan County provided the sheriff with a budget for feeding inmates. Historically, because the pay for sheriffs was low, they were allowed to keep any unused funds that were to be used for the feeding of inmates. Under this system, the wives of many sheriffs provided meals for the inmates to secure a little more income. Morgan County continued the use of this scheme to supplement the sheriff's salary. However, Sheriff Greg Bartlett appeared to go to the extreme. The state food allowance was $1.75 per prisoner per day; yet, on this meager allowance, Sheriff Bartlett was able to pocket $212,000 over three years in unused food money.[109] Shocked at the failure to provide a minimum standard of care for inmates, U.S. District Judge U. W. Clemon issued an arrest warrant for Sheriff Bartlett for contempt for failing to feed inmates adequately and incarcerated him in his own jail.

HIV/AIDS and STDs

Sexually transmitted diseases (STDs), including **HIV/AIDS** and other communicable diseases, pose serious challenges to administrators of both adult and juvenile justice systems.[110] In 2002, the overall rate of confirmed AIDS cases among the nation's prison population was 3.5 times that of the U.S. general population. Official statistics indicate that about 2% of state prison inmates and 1 percent of federal prison inmates are known to be infected with HIV.[111] However, the rate of HIV/AIDS infection is not uniform throughout the criminal justice system. New York, for example, has an HIV-positive prison population of nearly 8%, but California has a rate of less than 1%.[112] The percentage of HIV-positive inmates has declined since 1998.[113] The problem affects both male and female inmates, but a greater percentage of women (2.9%) than men (1.9%) are HIV-positive, as reported in 2002.[114]

HIV/AIDS

Acquired immunodeficiency syndrome (AIDS) is caused by the human immunodeficiency virus (HIV). The disease damages the body's immune system. A person can be HIV-positive and not have AIDS.

AIDS-related deaths in prison have dropped dramatically, from over 1,000 in 1995 to 176 in 2005.[115] The drop in the death rate is attributed primarily to advances in medical treatments that are available for HIV-positive patients and better identification and management of HIV-infected inmates by prison administrators.

Testing for and Treating HIV/AIDS

Prisons are a critical setting for detecting and treating STDs. The testing of inmates for HIV/AIDS varies from state to state. About 19 states test all inmates at admission, whereas other states test inmates only upon request or those who belong to a specific high-risk group. Most HIV-positive inmates were positive when admitted. Inmates contract HIV/AIDS from high-risk behavior, such as intravenous drug use or unprotected sex with partners who are infected. Many female inmates contract HIV/AIDS from prostitution. As most inmates will be released back into the community, the identification of those with HIV/AIDS is important because they constitute a significant percentage of the total number of Americans with HIV/AIDS.[116] Unfortunately, only 10% of state and federal prisons and 5% of city and county jails offer comprehensive HIV-prevention programs for inmates.[117]

Risks to Others in the Prison

Inmates who are HIV-positive pose special problems for correctional employees. Those inmates cannot be completely isolated from the general prison population. In fact, federal laws regarding inmates' rights of privacy often prohibit prison administrators from making it generally known which inmates are HIV-positive. Thus, prison staff and other inmates may not know which inmates are affected. This lack of knowledge creates concern among the prison staff because they do not know if they are at risk of HIV infection when they handle inmates. Lacking this knowledge, the prison staff must treat all inmates as if they are potential infection risks. HIV-infected inmates may deliberately attempt to infect prison officials by biting them or using other means.

Risks to the Community upon Inmates' Release

When inmates who are HIV-positive are released back into the community, they may create a public health hazard if they don't receive proper care or education. While in prison, inmates receive free medication and treatment, but after release, they may be responsible for their own medical expenses, including treatment. Released inmates may pose a serious health hazard if they engage in unprotected sex or share needles from intravenous drug use. Female offenders pose a community health risk because many return to prostitution to obtain the cash they need.

Tuberculosis and Other Communicable Diseases

Prisons and jails also present optimal conditions for the spread of diseases such as hepatitis C, staph infections, swine flu (H1N1 flu), and **tuberculosis (TB)**.[118] TB can be more difficult to control than HIV because it is more easily spread by contact

Providing for the health and well-being of inmates can be as simple as feeding them. Complaints about food have been one of the reasons inmates give for protesting and rioting.

with active cases. TB-infected inmates released back into the community have the potential to spread the disease further because it can remain infectious for a long time. One study reported that in 31 state prison systems, 14% of inmates had positive tuberculin skin test results at intake.[119]

Inmates who receive only partial treatment for TB increase the threat of epidemic in the general population. Incomplete treatment raises the risk that the disease will become resistant to medications used to treat it and will not respond to subsequent treatment. Drug-resistant forms of TB can be transmitted to others, with the result being a widespread public health disaster. Treatment of TB is complicated. A primary TB control measure is complete isolation of infectious cases to stop the disease from spreading to other inmates. This type of isolation requires negative-pressure isolation rooms with ventilation that does not flow into the general ventilation system. Another complication of TB is that inmates may be coinfected with TB and HIV. Because TB can be spread through the ventilation system, prison administrators must take precautions to keep general prison populations from being exposed to the germs. Failure to do so may result in a lawsuit.

Mental Health in Prisons

Mental illness is pervasive in jails and prisons. According to the BJS, in 2005, 64% of local jail inmates, 56% of state prisoners, and 45% of federal inmates had a mental health problem.[120] A comprehensive Justice Department study of the rapidly growing number of incarcerated, emotionally disturbed people concluded that jails and prisons have become the nation's new mental health care facilities.[121] According to the report, "Jails have become the poor person's mental hospitals."[122]

Deinstitutionalization

In the 1960s, legislation was passed that made it difficult to commit mentally ill people who had not committed a crime to civil mental health facilities against their will. As a result, public mental hospitals were forced to release people committed against their will unless the state could prove that they were a danger to themselves or the public. The intention of the legislation was that mentally ill people would receive community-based care instead of long-term hospitalization that differed little from incarceration. It was thought that with proper medication, community-based care would be a more humane alternative to long-term hospitalization. [123] Despite the good intentions of legislators, **deinstitutionalization** did not work as planned. There were too few community-based facilities, those with mental illness did not take their medications, and jails and prisons became the dumping ground for such individuals.[124] People with mental illness end up in jails and prisons for bizarre public behavior; petty crimes such as loitering, public intoxication, and panhandling; and serious violent crimes such as murder, sexual assault, and property crime. About half of inmates with mental illness are in prison for a violent offense.[125]

> Jails and prisons have become the nation's new mental health care facilities.

Behavioral Problems

Mentally ill inmates frequently are unable to abide by prison rules and discipline. This is partly because of their mental illness and partly because of the overcrowded conditions and stresses of the correctional institution. Also, because they are unable to have "normal" interpersonal relations—a difficult challenge even for the mentally stable in prison—they are more likely to engage in fights and other violent behaviors. Unable to conform to the rules or to restrain their violent behavior, the mentally ill spend many hours in solitary confinement or segregated housing. Unfortunately, this punishment greatly increases the likelihood of depression and heightened anxiety in the mentally ill inmate.[126] The experience of being incarcerated typically exacerbates inmates' mental illness.[127] As a result, incarcerated, emotionally disturbed inmates in state prisons spend an average of 15 months longer behind bars compared to other prisoners. In many cases, the difference is attributed to their delusions, hallucinations, or paranoia, which makes them more likely to get into fights and receive disciplinary reports.[128]

Prisons as Contributing Factors of Mental Illness

Prison environments contribute to mental health problems. Prisons are **total institutions**, a term sociologist Erving Goffman coined in his study of prisons and mental hospitals.[129] In prison, the inmate has little responsibility, does not have to make decisions, does not have to engage in problem solving, and does not have to plan for tomorrow. The institution meets all of the inmate's basic needs. The institution dictates the inmate's schedule. Institutional rules are made without any input from the inmate. The environment is rigid, and inmates are expected to conform to the values and expectations of the institution. Individuality is discouraged, dissent is punished, and failure to follow the rules can result in segregation from the prison population. As a consequence, the prison environment:

- Does not promote effective treatment of mentally ill offenders—even people without mental health problems become depressed and mentally ill when exposed to this environment.

- Encourages the development of **prisonization**—socialization into a distinct prison subculture with its own values, mores, norms, and sanctions.

Prisonization results in a subculture for inmates in which the rules of conduct are distinctly different from the official rules of the institution and from society in general. Prisoners learn to adapt to this prison code and conduct their life in prison by it. However, the prisoner with mental illness, who has difficulty adapting to society in general, often is unable to relate to fellow prisoners and conform to the **prison code** while at the same time maintaining the appearance of obedience to the institutional rules and norms. Often the result of this failure to adapt to the prison code is dangerous ostracism by both inmates and administrators.

Think About It . . .

A 2011 report by the Chicago-based John Howard Association, a prison watchdog group, reported that the total number of grievances filed by female inmates at the Illinois female maximum-security prison doubled compared to 2010. One of the factors cited was inappropriate behavior by male correctional officers working in the women's living quarters where showers and bathrooms are visible to the officers.[132] Male correctional officers work in the living quarters because the state cannot find enough women interested in jobs as correctional officers. This is a nationwide trend. Why is there a shortage of female correctional officers?

Problems for the Community

All prisoners are affected by prisonization, which is why most prisoners demonstrate maladaptive behaviors when they are returned to the community. Accustomed to being told what to do, when to do it, and how to do it, released inmates often demonstrate few of the job skills employers want. Prisoners who have been incarcerated for long terms may have lost the ability to plan for the future, take responsibility for their actions, and exhibit proactive behaviors. They have become passive, dependent, and fixated on the rules.

When released back into the community, the offender with mental illness is seldom cured as a result of the treatment received while incarcerated. Even if treatment and medication in prison had made a significant impact on his or her behavior, it is doubtful that a released offender with mental illness will continue treatment or medication. For example, a survey by the BJS reported that although an estimated 13% of probationers were required to seek mental health treatment as a condition of their sentence, fewer than half fulfilled this requirement.[130]

Neither police nor correctional institutions have been able to make a significant impact on the problem of the offender with mental illness. Providing medications in prison is a temporary approach to a more serious community problem. In addition to the public-order crimes they commit, offenders with mental illness commit serious offenses. For example, about 13% of inmates with mental illness in prisons were convicted of murder, and about 12% were convicted of sexual assault. Andrea Yates, for example, was mentally ill when she murdered her five young children by drowning them one by one in the bathtub of her home. Mental health professionals posit that a significant percentage of youths involved in the juvenile justice system have unmet needs for mental health and substance abuse services.[131]

Prison Violence

Prisons are violent environments. Prison violence includes inmate-on-inmate violence and excessive use of force by staff. Experiments simulating prisoner-staff environments have demonstrated that the prison environment and the guard-inmate

All prisoners are affected by prisonization, which is why most prisoners demonstrate maladaptive behaviors when they are returned to the community.

relationship have great potential to trigger violence by staff against inmates. Many times, staff violence appears to be related to hiring practices in which staff members are not qualified or they have backgrounds that should have disqualified them from employment. For example, in 2008, investigations revealed that more than a dozen correctional officers at the Prince George's County Jail had criminal backgrounds, including charges of theft, assault, domestic violence, DUI, and sexual assault.[133]

Prison violence is also associated with practices by prison officials that permit the use of inmates to supervise other inmates. In some cases, such as the Texas prison system in the 1960s, the use of inmates to supervise other inmates was the formal policy. As a result of lawsuits, this practice has disappeared because the formal policy of the prison has been replaced by a clandestine informal policy. For example, investigations by the Civil Rights Division of the U.S. Department of Justice and the Office of the United States Attorney into the conditions at Cook County Jail in 2008 alleged systematic and widespread use of violence against inmates by staff and poor supervision of inmates, resulting in unchecked inmate-on-inmate violence. A 2009 wrongful death lawsuit against correctional officials at Rikers Island accused the jail of "letting inmates run Rikers Island jail." The lawsuit claimed that prison officials did not just turn a blind eye to violence, "[t]hey authorized and directed it."[134]

▶ Conclusion: Prisons—The Human Cage

Jails and prisons are designed to hold humans in a secure environment to prevent their escape. Frequently, the concern of the public is not the conditions of the jails or prisons, but the perceived risk of escape and fear of harm from prisoners who have escaped. Most citizens strongly object to a jail or prison being built in their neighborhood.[135] Some citizens appear to have little sympathy for incarcerated inmates. For example, in response to a report on four suicides in a municipal jail, one editorial dismissed concerns about the deaths, arguing, "These suspects had been arrested for murder, kidnapping, burglary, drug dealing, assault and drunken driving. I do not consider these deaths as tragic losses. Rather, these four saved the overburdened taxpayers a great deal of money by taking their fates into their own hands." [136]

Jails and prisons represent a substantial financial burden and directly compete with other needed services. Often people see every dollar that goes into jails and prisons as one less dollar that could go to other services, such as schools, hospitals, medical care, public safety, and transportation. For example, when a Pennsylvania jail warden turned in a request for $500,000 for new computers for an educational program for Pittsburgh jail inmates, the county refused to process the invoice.[137] The computers were to be purchased from profits from the jail's commissary, where inmates buy candy, snacks, and toiletries, but the county government argued that the money should be returned to the taxpayers. As one official expressed, "We have taxpayers who can't even afford (computers). Before we give that type of convenience to prisoners, we should balance the budget. It's not our responsibility to educate and entertain the inmates."[138]

Recidivism rates show that jails and prisons have not proven to be very effective. They have not protected the public from criminal activity in the long run. They have not deterred people from committing crimes through the threat or pain of incarceration, nor have they rehabilitated inmates, whether through penitence, educational training, or harsh discipline. Some have argued that prisons are nothing more than warehouses in which inmates are placed because society cannot think of a more effective solution to an age-old problem. The public has become frustrated with the cost and lack of effectiveness of locking criminals in cages and waiting.

Solitary Confinement

Today, the use of solitary confinement is increasing with the growing use of supermax or segregation units whose purpose, according to claims, is to isolate the "worst-of-the-worst" from the general prison population. Inmates housed in supermax prisons are isolated 24 hours a day. They do not leave their cells except when shackled. They get one hour a day for solitary exercise. There are no recreation programs, rehabilitation programs, vocational training programs, or counseling programs for these prisoners. Visitation is extremely limited, and inmates are allowed to have very few items in their 80-square-foot cell.

Today, 44 states use solitary confinement. There is no limit as to how long an inmate can be housed in solitary confinement. The average stay is 2.7 years, but in some cases, inmates have been kept in isolation for more than a decade. Mentally ill inmates are not supposed to be housed in long-term solitary confinement, but they frequently are. For example, 173 of the 505 inmates housed in long-term solitary confinement at Red Onion State Prison (Virginia) were considered mentally ill.[139]

There are several challenges to the widespread use of solitary confinement. Solitary confinement is the most expensive form of incarceration in terms of the physical facilities and staffing. Studies have shown that many inmates are inappropriately classified and should be in housing for people with mental illness or do not need to be housed in supermax units. States could save millions of dollars by reducing the use of solitary confinement. Inmates held in isolation for long periods of time suffer from higher suicide rates, increased depression, decreased brain function. and hallucinations. Many inmates held in solitary confinement are released back into society with no transition or preparation.

The American Civil Liberties Union, the American Bar Association, the United Nations, and the American Correctional Association call for a ban on the use of solitary confinement or a maximum limit of one year.

This case raises several interesting questions. Among them are the following:

1. Should there be strict limits on who is housed in solitary confinement and how long the confinement should be? Explain.

2. Is it cruel and unusual punishment to use solitary confinement when the adverse mental and physical outcomes are well documented? Explain.

3. What is the potential harm to the community when inmates are released directly from solitary confinement into society without the benefit of a transition program, reentry program, or counseling?

James Fagin

LEARNING OUTCOMES 1

Summarize the development of early American corrections.

Conditions in early colonial American jails were shocking. Local jails had no obligation to provide food or medical treatment for prisoners. The first state prison, Eastern State Penitentiary, was built in Pennsylvania in 1829. This single-cell plan utilizing the solitary confinement system became too expensive as prison populations increased over time. Eventually, New York's Auburn system served as the model for new prisons, with its use of inside cell block construction. Southern states developed a unique prison system, providing farm laborers through the convict lease system. The prisoner lease system was replaced by the prison farm system, which utilized inmate labor to maintain large prison farms.

1. Describe the conditions of an early colonial jail.

2. What was the goal of the silent system?

3. Why did New York's Auburn system prevail as the model for constructing new prisons?

4. How did southern prisons profit from the convict lease system?

incarceration The bodily confinement of a person in a jail or prison.

penitentiary A correctional institution based on the concept that inmates could change their criminality through reflection and penitence.

silent system The correctional practice of prohibiting inmates from talking to other inmates.

inside cell block Prison construction in which individual cells are stacked back-to-back in tiers in the center of a secure building.

congregate work system The practice of moving inmates from sleeping cells to other areas of the prison for work, meals, and recreation.

solitary confinement The practice of confining an inmate such that there is no contact with other people.

convict lease system The practice of some southern penal systems leasing prisoners to private contractors as laborers.

chain gang In the southern penal system, a group of convicts chained together during outside labor.

prison farm system In the southern penal systems, the use of inmate labor to maintain large, profit-making prison farms or plantations.

LEARNING OUTCOMES 2

Identify some of the major challenges of the contemporary correctional system.

The United States has the highest incarceration rate of any country in the world. During the 1970s and 1980s, a "lock and feed" philosophy of incarceration fueled significant prison population growth. Today, prison costs are one of the fastest-rising expenses in state governments. Given rising inmate costs, some states are turning to community corrections programs as an alternative to institutional incarceration.

1. How did the United States come to have the highest incarceration rate in the world?

2. What factors have influenced the significant rise in the cost of incarceration?

3. How did the Warren Court view prisoners' rights and their conditions of incarceration?

Lombroso-based correctional philosophies Philosophies that divided people into two distinct types: criminal and noncriminal. Criminals were biologically determined and therefore not amenable to rehabilitation or reform.

prison industry The sale of convict-made products and services.

civil death The legal philosophy that barred a prison inmate from bringing a lawsuit in a civil court related to his or her treatment while incarcerated or related to conditions of incarceration.

Warren Court The U.S. Supreme Court years (1953–1969) during which Chief Justice Earl Warren issued many landmark decisions greatly expanding the constitutional rights of inmates and defendants.

LEARNING OUTCOMES 3

Describe the purpose and types of jails.

Jails hold local, state, and federal pre- and post-trial defendants. The majority of inmates in local jails have not been convicted of a crime. They are waiting to be charged, tried, or transported to prison. Since 1983, the nation's jail population has doubled. Because jails house a diversity of inmates, jail staff and facilities must be able to serve a variety of inmates' needs. Typically, the sheriff maintains the county jail, while local police maintain a separate municipal jail.

1. Name the three categories of jails.

2. What is the difference between a federal jail and local jail?

3. Who is in charge of maintaining a county jail?

jails Short-term multipurpose holding facilities that serve as the gateway into the criminal justice system.

Native American country jails Short-term incarceration facilities on Native American land under the sovereign control of the Native American tribe.

county department of corrections An independent county department that supervises a county jail when the sheriff does not.

municipal jails City incarceration facilities separate from the county jail for holding detainees and inmates sentenced for violation of city codes.

police holding cells Also called booking cells and lockup facilities, secure detention facilities for the purpose of temporarily housing arrestees until they can be booked, can be moved to another facility, can pay their bail, or are released.

LEARNING OUTCOMES 4

Describe the state prison system and the classification process.

State prisons are correctional institutions housing only convicted felons. Before incarceration in prison, an inmate undergoes an examination and assessment to determine his or her assignment to a specific facility. The inmate's length of sentence, seriousness of offense, and past criminal record are weighed in determining in which facility the inmate will be placed initially. A prisoner's classification may be changed based on good behavior, resulting in the prisoner being reassigned to a lower-level security facility.

1. Describe the differences between a state prison and a jail.

2. What happens during prisoner classification?

3. What factors influence prisoner classification?

state prisons Correctional facilities for prisoners convicted of state crimes.

prisoner classification The reception and diagnosis of an inmate to decide the appropriate security level in which to place him or her and the services of placement.

prison consultants Private people who give convicted defendants advice and counsel on how best to present themselves during classification and how to behave in prison.

initial placement The assignment by the classification process as to the first institution placement and security level of a convicted defendant.

LEARNING OUTCOMES 5

Summarize the problems related to special populations and racism.

Prisoners who are not suited to be housed in the general prison population are referred to as special populations. An inmate's unsuitability for general population might be based on age, mental illness, depression, or other health conditions. Gang affiliation also is an important consideration in determining where to house a prisoner, as gang members placed together pose a security risk. Another area of concern is the rising rate of female offenders being incarcerated. Finally, incarceration rates clearly demonstrate that there is a disproportionate confinement rate of minorities that needs to be examined as an area of discrimination.

1. What factors might place a prisoner in a special prison population?

2. Describe concerns with the placement of inmates with a gang affiliation.

3. Upon her return to the community, what challenges might a former female inmate face?

general prison population The nonrestricted population of prison inmates who have access to prison services, inmate interactions, programs, and recreations.

special prison populations Inmates with characteristics that may result in significant risks to themselves, other inmates, or staff.

prison economy The exchange of goods, services, and contraband by prisoners in place of money.

disproportionate confinement The nonrandom distribution of people by race in correctional institutions. If the prison population reflected the same demographics as the general population, confinement would not reflect racial bias.

LEARNING OUTCOMES 6

Describe the responsibilities and organization of the federal prison system.

The first federal prison, at Leavenworth, Kansas, was constructed in 1895 to house male convicts. Today, over 100 federal correctional facilities throughout the United States are operated by the Federal Bureau of Prisons (BOP). Federal prison security levels range from minimum-security federal prison camps to administrative-maximum. In addition, members of the armed services who are convicted under the Uniform Code of Military Justice are sent to federal military prisons. The appearance and operation of military facilities closely resembles that of civilian prisons.

1. What is the highest level of security in the federal prison system?

2. How did the federal government combine the administrative control of its prisons in 1930?

3. Describe the characteristics of a minimum-security or federal prison camp.

Federal Bureau of Prisons (BOP) The agency responsible for the administrative oversight of federal prisons and jails.

correctional officers Uniformed jail or prison employees whose primary job is the security and movement of inmates.

administrative-maximum prison The highest security level of prison operated by the U.S. Bureau of Prisons. Supermax prisons are considered escape-proof regardless of the resources of the inmate.

LEARNING OUTCOMES 7

Summarize the advantages and disadvantages of private prisons.

Private prisons are very similar to government prisons. However, private prisons are for-profit businesses that receive prisoners from the local, state, and federal government and house them for a fee. The main reason for housing prisoners in private facilities is to reduce the government's costs of incarceration. Critics of for-profit prisons claim that these services do not provide the same quality of care and supervision or the same educational, recreational, and rehabilitative services as do public-run prisons.

1. What is an advantage to using a private prison?
2. What are some of the criticisms of a privately run prison?
3. Describe some of the services a private prison might not provide at the same level as a public prison.

privatization The trend to house inmates in privately administered prisons.

private prisons Prisons that house local, state, or federal inmates for a fee.

state liability A state's liability for violations of an inmate's constitutional rights.

LEARNING OUTCOMES 8

Identify the challenges of prison life.

Securing inmates and protecting the community from harm, correctional institutions must do so without violating the constitutional rights of inmates. Some of the major challenges for correctional authorities include reducing sexual violence, reducing the security risks associated with prison gangs, and providing for both physical and mental health. Prison environments are total institutions, where inmates have little responsibility, do not have to make decisions, and do not have to engage in problem solving. Consequently, the prison environment creates a subculture for inmates in which the rules of conduct are discernibly different from the rules of conduct for society in general. As a result of this environment, recidivism rates for those released from jail or prison have been high.

1. How do prison gangs pose a threat to prison security?
2. What is the most common reason for Section 1983 lawsuits against jails?
3. What type of infectious diseases might be present in a prison?
4. Describe factors that contribute to mental illness in a prison.

Prison Rape Elimination Act of 2003 An act that required the Bureau of Justice Statistics to survey jails and prisons to determine the prevalence of sexual violence in correctional facilities.

security-risk groups Groups in prisons that raise special threats, such as prison gangs.

contraband Smuggled goods, such as drugs, cigarettes, money, and pornography.

Section 1983 lawsuits Civil lawsuits filed in federal court alleging that the government has violated a constitutional right of the inmate.

HIV/AIDS A disease that damages the body's immune system. Acquired immunodeficiency syndrome (AIDS) is caused by the human immunodeficiency virus (HIV). A person can be HIV-positive and not have AIDS.

tuberculosis (TB) A contagious infectious disease caused by a bacterial infection that primarily affects the lungs.

deinstitutionalization The movement of mentally ill offenders from long-term hospitalization to community-based care.

total institutions Prisons that meet all of the inmate's basic needs, discourage individuality, punish dissent, and segregate those who do not follow the rules.

prisonization Socialization into a distinct prison subculture with its own values, mores, norms, and sanctions.

prison code The informal rules and expected behavior established by inmates. Often the prison code is contrary to the official rules and policies of the prison. Violation of the prison code can be punished by use of violence or even death.

MyCJLab

Go to Chapter 10 in *MyCJLab* to test your mastery of chapter concepts, access your Study Plan, engage in interactive exercises, complete critical-thinking and research assignments, and view related online videos.

 Review: Complete the pretest in the Study Plan to confirm what you know and what you need to study further. Then complete the post-test to confirm your mastery of the concepts. Use the key term flash cards to review key terminology.

 Apply: Complete the interactive simulation activity.

Analyze: Complete assignments as directed by your instructor.

Current Events: Explore CJSearch for current topical videos, articles, and news pieces.

Additional Links

Go to **http://www.bop.gov** and visit the Bureau of Prisons to learn more about the federal prison system.

Go to **http://www.easternstate.org** to see photos and learn about the grand architecture and strict discipline that was part of the nation's first prison.

Go to **http://www.aclu.org/prisoners-rights/private-prisons** to see a video of a prisoner being beaten in a private correctional facility and learn more about the criticism of privately administrated prisons.

Go to **http://www.schr.org/incarceration** to see the call by the Southern Center for Human Rights for humane treatment of prisoners and recommended videos to watch about jail and prison conditions.

Go to **http://www.youtube.com/watch?v=khaCA4EowEQ** and watch a MSNBC video of life in San Quentin State Prison.

Probation and Parole

"I never went to school, so I never growed [sic] up to read and write too good, so I have stayed in jail and I have stayed stupid, and I have stayed a child while I have watched your world grow up, and then I look at the things that you do and I don't understand. ..."

—*Charles Manson*

1 Explain why the criminal justice system provides for early release of inmates and the differences between diversion, probation, and parole and between mandatory release, good-time release, and pardon or commutation of sentence.

2 Identify the origins of, reasons for, processes of, and pros and cons of probation.

3 Identify the origins of, reasons for, processes of, and pros and cons of parole.

4 Summarize how people on probation and parole are supervised.

11

ZUMA Wire Service/Alamy

Oscar Lopez Rivera is a 70-year-old convicted terrorist serving time in federal prison. He was the leader of the Puerto Rican freedom movement known as FALN (Spanish initials for Armed Forces of National Liberation). FALN was responsible for over 100 bombings in New York, Chicago, and other cities, several of which resulted in deaths. He denied responsibility for any of the bombings, but in 1981, he was convicted in U.S. federal court of seditious conspiracy to overthrow U.S. control of Puerto Rico and other charges. He was sentenced to 70 years in prison.

In 2011, he petitioned for parole. The U.S. Parole Commission received more than 4,000 letters supporting his release; letters came from members of the Puerto Rican community, prominent community leaders, and four Puerto Rican members of Congress. The Parole Commission denied his request for parole.

His supporters call Oscar Lopez Rivera "the longest held political prisoner" in the United States. In 1999, President Clinton offered clemency to other members of FALN, but Rivera refused the offer. In 2006, the United Nations called

for the release of Rivera, calling him a "political prisoner." Rivera's sentence is 20 times longer than the typical sentence, and he has spent 22 of his 31 years in solitary confinement. He claims that his sentence and conditions of confinement are due to his political views advocating a Puerto Rico free from the United States.

The 12 FALN members who accepted President Clinton's offer of clemency have posed no risk to the community after their release. Supporters of Rivera's release claim that he too would be no risk to the community after having served more than 31 years in prison. Rivera's younger brother Jose Lopez is a prominent citizen in the Chicago Puerto Rican community. Jose claims that his brother's imprisonment has taken a great toll on his family and advocates his release. Also, support for Rivera's release runs high in the Chicago Puerto Rican community.

During his 31 years in prison, Rivera has not expressed remorse for his crimes, continues to identify himself as a political prisoner, and continues to endorse the idea of a Puerto Rico independent of the United States.

DISCUSS What are the reasons for releasing an inmate on parole?

▶ States Turn to Diversion, Probation, and Parole

This chapter discusses the history of early release from prison, the arguments for and against early release, and the various types of early release that can be granted to an inmate. (See Table 11–1.) Prisons are expensive, and many states are forced to evaluate whether they can afford to continue locking up criminals for long periods of time. Since the 1970s, the number of state prisoners has increased 500%, making prisons the fastest-growing item in state budgets. Many states are finding that prison spending competes with other needs. Taxpayers are reluctant to keep spending money on corrections if that means less money to spend on schools. As a result, many states are seeking ways to reduce prison costs. States have closed prisons and cut prison budgets, but that has not been enough. Studies suggest that although imprisonment is necessary for some offenders to ensure public safety, not all offenders need to or should be incarcerated. About half of all convicted offenders are nonviolent, nonsexual offenders. Studies suggest that long-term incarceration may not be the best use of public resources for them. Thus, states are turning to greater use of probation and parole as a means to curtail corrections costs.

Some offenders do not serve any prison time, whereas others are sentenced to prison but released before the end of their term of punishment. Still other offenders may not serve time in prison because they are diverted from the criminal justice system or because their sentences are suspended. Thus, before discussing probation and parole in greater detail, it is important to define and distinguish what is meant by diversion, probation, and parole.

Diversion and Probation

In **diversion**, the defendant is offered an alternative to a criminal trial, possible conviction, and prison sentence, such as drug court, boot camp, or a treatment program. When a defendant is convicted in a criminal court and sentenced to prison but the prison term is suspended, the defendant does not have to serve time in prison and is said to be on **suspended sentence**, or probation. Probation, a sentencing option of the trial judge, diverts the offender after being convicted but prior to serving prison time.

Parole

In **parole**, the offender has been sentenced to prison, serves a portion of his or her time, and is released before the maximum term of the sentence. The decision to parole a prisoner is made by a parole board. Prisoners released under probation or parole are subject to continued supervision in the community and can be returned to prison if they violate the terms of their release. Other means by which a prisoner can be released from prison other than probation and parole include mandatory release, good-time release, pardon, and commutation of sentence (a form of pardon).

Mandatory Release

When prisoners serve the entire length of their maximum sentence, it is required by law that they be released. This is called **mandatory release**. An inmate cannot be held in

TABLE 11–1 | COMPARISON OF EARLY-RELEASE OPTIONS

	Governing Authority	Impact on Sentence	Supervision	Comment
Diversion	Judge/Court System	Defendant can avoid criminal trial and imprisonment	Depending on placement (for example, drug program, deferred guilty agreement), conditional release with stipulated behavioral/treatment requirements	Can be returned to prison if conditions of diversion are not met
Probation	Judge	Sentence of convicted defendant is suspended	Probation officer (same as parole officer)	Can be returned to prison if conditions of probation are not met
Parole	Parole Board	Provides early release from incarceration	Parole officer (same as probation officer)	Can be returned to prison if conditions of parole are not met
Good-Time Release	State/Federal Laws	Shortens the length of the inmate's sentence based on good behavior while incarcerated—similar to parole	Parole officer	Can be returned to prison if conditions of parole are not met
Mandatory Release	State/Federal Laws	Inmate serves the complete sentence	Inmate is released into the community without conditions or supervision	Inmate can be returned to prison only for a new crime
Pardon	Governor/U.S. President	Can shorten sentence imposed by the court or change a death penalty sentence to life in prison	If released into the community, inmate is released without conditions or supervision	Inmate can be returned to prison only for a new crime

LEARNING OUTCOMES 1 Explain why the criminal justice system provides for early release of inmates and the differences between diversion, probation, and parole and between mandatory release, good-time release, and pardon or commutation of sentence.

GLOSSARY

diversion An alternative to criminal trial and a prison sentence, such as drug court, boot camp, or a treatment program, offered to a defendant.

suspended sentence Another term for *probation*, a sentence based on the fact that convicted offenders must serve their full sentence if they violate their terms of release.

parole The release of an inmate before his or her maximum sentence has been served.

mandatory release The release of prisoners required by law after they have served the entire length of their maximum sentence.

prison beyond the length of his or her sentence. Even if the prisoner is not rehabilitated or prepared for reentry into society, he or she must be released after serving his or her time. These prisoners are released without any supervision, without any restrictions on their behavior, and frequently without any support or rehabilitation plan. Mandatory release requires that prison officials release a prisoner who has served the maximum sentence regardless of the danger the prisoner may pose to the community. Some states have tried to protect the community from offenders who have been identified as sexual predators by prohibiting such mandatory releases until they are no longer a danger to the community upon release. Hence, one of the arguments for early release through probation or parole is that such release, unlike mandatory release, lets probationers and

parolees reenter the community with supervision; provides behavioral restrictions; and offers social, mental health, and drug counseling services to released inmates.

Good-Time Credit

Another form of mandatory release is when prisoners have served less than their full sentence but have earned good-time credit that entitles them to early release. **Good-time credit** toward early release is a strategy that encourages prisoners to obey institutional rules, refrain from violence and drug use, and participate in rehabilitation and vocational programs. In place of punishment for disobedience, good-time release gives inmates an incentive to comply with prison authority and rules. When the inmate is processed into the system, a percentage of the inmate's sentence is converted into good-time behavior. For many states, this is 15% or more of the time to be served. For example, an inmate with a ten-year sentence could receive a credit of 15% of the sentence, or 1.5 years, as good-time behavior. Good-time computation in the federal system is less generous than in state prison systems. The Comprehensive

Prison authorities use the deduction of good-time days to regulate nearly every aspect of an inmate's behavior. Loss of good time can be used as a punishment for both minor and major offenses.

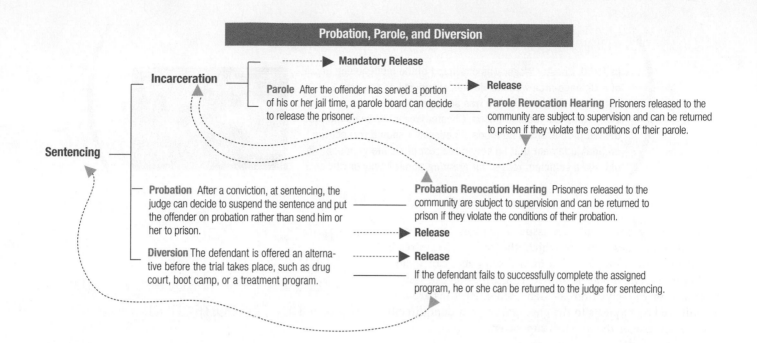

Probation, Parole, and Diversion

Sentencing

Incarceration

- - - ► **Mandatory Release**

Parole After the offender has served a portion of his or her jail time, a parole board can decide to release the prisoner. - - - ► **Release**

Parole Revocation Hearing Prisoners released to the community are subject to supervision and can be returned to prison if they violate the conditions of their parole.

Probation After a conviction, at sentencing, the judge can decide to suspend the sentence and put the offender on probation rather than send him or her to prison.

Probation Revocation Hearing Prisoners released to the community are subject to supervision and can be returned to prison if they violate the conditions of their probation.

- - - ► **Release**

Diversion The defendant is offered an alternative before the trial takes place, such as drug court, boot camp, or a treatment program.

- - - ► **Release**

If the defendant fails to successfully complete the assigned program, he or she can be returned to the judge for sentencing.

Crime Control Act of 1984, which includes the Sentencing Reform Act of 1984, reformed the federal good-time provisions such that federal prisoners earn a maximum of 54 days annually after completing the first year of a sentence.

Prison authorities use the deduction of good-time days to regulate nearly every aspect of an inmate's behavior. Loss of good time can be used as a punishment for both minor and major offenses. An inmate can lose days for not lining up when told to do so, for reporting late to work, for being in a restricted area, for being insubordinate, for engaging in arguments, for attacking other inmates or correctional officers, or for possessing contraband. However, prison authorities cannot add to prison time beyond the court-ordered sentence without a conviction for a new crime. With more serious violations, such as attempted escape or felony crime, the inmate is returned to court for trial and, if convicted, is sentenced to additional time.

Good-Time Credit

Sentenced by the judge to two years for burglary, how long will the inmate serve?

When an inmate is processed into the system, a percentage of his or her sentence is converted into good-time credit. The percentage varies by state; here we assume a 20% credit.

24 months x 20% = 4.8 months

-4.8

19.2 months

If there are no infractions to deduct from the inmate's good-time credit, his or her mandatory parole date is in 19.2 months.

Good-time credit will be reduced for violations of the rules.

The inmate's sentence cannot be extended beyond the maximum sentence.

The primary purpose of good-time credit is to motivate inmates to obey prison rules.

Good-time credit does not apply equally to all sentences. States have set good-time limits for certain crimes. Some crimes, such as heinous murder, may not be subject to any good-time credit. Other crimes, such as nonviolent drug offenses, may be subject to more liberal good-time credit provided the prisoner participates in rehabilitation programs. Thus, the good-time credit must be calculated by the prison administration for each inmate entering the institution.

Executive Pardons

Prisoners may be released early or may be exempted from serving any of their sentence through parole or commutation. Pardon and commutation are forms of executive forgiveness, not forms of probation or parole. Pardons are sometimes referred to as clemency. Pardon and commutation of sentence can be performed only by the governor of the state for state prisoners and by the president of the United States for federal and military prisoners. Pardons and commutations of sentence are acts of mercy and do not indicate that an inmate is not guilty or was wrongfully sentenced.

There are no limitations on the number of pardons governors and presidents may grant, and there are no guidelines or laws regulating whom they may pardon and under what conditions. No one has the authority to revoke a pardon or to overrule the governor or president. They may seek advice in issuing a pardon, but the absolute authority to issue pardons rests entirely with the executive authority. Also, there is no time limit for issuing a pardon.

good-time credit A strategy of crediting inmates with extra days served toward early release in an effort to encourage them to obey rules and participate in programs.

executive pardon An act by a governor or the president that forgives a prisoner and rescinds his or her sentence.

commutation of sentence A reduction in the severity or length of an inmate's sentence issued by a state governor or the president of the United States.

Think About It . . .

In 1960, Chester Weger was convicted of the bludgeoning death of a Chicago-area woman. He was suspected as the assailant in two other deaths. He was sentenced to life in prison. In 2011, after 51 years in prison, Chester Weger, 72 years old, was denied parole. The parole board believed it should respect the original judgment that he spend the rest of his life in prison.[4] Is old age a sufficient reason for granting parole? Why or why not?

A governor or president can issue a pardon for a crime committed decades ago for which the person has already served the entire length of his or her sentence, can issue a pardon while an inmate is still serving time, or can issue a pardon prior to conviction and sentencing. Pardons are usually initiated by requests to the governor or president directly from the inmate or the inmate's supporters.

Commutation of Sentence

Closely related to **executive pardon** is executive commutation of a prisoner's sentence. In **commutation of sentence**, the governor or president reduces the severity of an inmate's sentence. The most common use of executive commutation is to reduce a prisoner's sentence from death to life in prison and from life without parole to life with parole.

Also, commutation of sentence can be used to reduce a convicted offender's sentence without acknowledging that he or she was wrongfully convicted. For example, in August 2009, Virginia governor Tim Kaine commuted the sentence of three sailors who were convicted in a 1997 murder and rape case that had become a national cause célèbre as an example of wrongful convictions based on coerced confessions.[1] Governor Kaine reduced their life sentences to time served, which resulted in their release. In issuing the commutation rather than a full pardon the governor said, "The petitioners have not conclusively established their innocence, and therefore an absolute pardon is not appropriate. However, I conclude that the petitioners have raised substantial doubts about their convictions and the propriety of their continued detention."[2]

Perhaps one of the most well-known commutations was that of former Illinois governor George Ryan. Governor Ryan was indicted on federal criminal corruption charges and ultimately incarcerated. However, in 2003, two days before he left office, Governor Ryan commuted the sentences of 167 inmates on death row and pardoned 4 others. Governor Ryan said that he was motivated by concern that the inmates had been unfairly sentenced to death, so he commuted the sentences of every Illinois inmate on death row to life in prison even though the inmates had not filed a clemency petition to the governor's office. Critics were concerned about the questionable circumstances surrounding the clemency decision of the governor given the fact that he was under federal indictment and his actions in providing clemency to so many inmates who had not requested it were highly unorthodox. Critics challenged the governor's actions in court. However, the Illinois Supreme Court upheld his right to commute the

By releasing prisoners, chief executives can intervene to correct or erase perceived abuses or errors in sentencing or corrections.

sentences of prisoners, saying, "The governor may grant reprieves, pardons, and commutations on his own terms, and the decisions are unreviewable."[3]

The powers of pardon and commutation give the executive branch checks and balances on the powers of the courts and legislature. By releasing prisoners, chief executives can intervene to correct or erase perceived abuses or errors in sentencing or corrections. However, there are no checks and balances on the executive power to issue pardons, creating a potential for abuse. For example, critics accused President Clinton of granting presidential pardons in his final days of office to those who had made large political contributions.

▶ Probation

Probation is a relatively new experiment in American corrections. The roots of probation can be traced to the efforts of John Augustus (1785–1859), a wealthy Boston shoemaker who devoted himself to bringing reform to the eighteenth-century criminal justice system. He intervened in Boston's municipal court to divert a number of defendants who were sentenced to serve time in the Boston House of Corrections. Augustus was not an officer of the court, and he was not connected to the criminal justice system. As a private citizen, he used his personal finances to guarantee bail for defendants selected for diversion from jail. He was critical of the conditions of the jails and prisons of his time and believed that, for many offenders, prison would lead to further harm, not rehabilitation.

In 1841, Augustus initiated what came to be known as **probation**. He was in Boston's municipal court when a defendant was convicted of being a common drunk. Augustus asked the judge not to sentence the man to jail, but to release him to his custody instead. Augustus assumed responsibility for the man's behavior and provided for his rehabilitation. After three weeks, he brought the man back to court for evaluation. Augustus reported that "the judge expressed himself much pleased with the account we gave of the man, and instead of the usual penalty

LEARNING OUTCOMES 2 Identify the origins of, reasons for, processes of, and pros and cons of probation.

GLOSSARY

probation The conditional release of a convicted offender prior to his or her serving any prison time.

probation officer A state or federal professional employee who reports to the courts and supervises defendants released on probation.

technical violation Grounds for imprisonment of a probationer or parolee based on his or her violation of a condition of release.

of imprisonment in the House of Corrections—he fined him one cent and costs, amounting in all to $3.76, which was immediately paid." From that time on, John Augustus monitored court trials and rescued more than 2,000 defendants from incarceration.[5]

Other volunteers continued Augustus's work after his death until Massachusetts passed the first probation statute in 1878. By 1900, four other states had passed similar legislation. By 1920, every state permitted juvenile probation and 33 states had adopted a system of adult probation. Today, more people are on probation and parole than are sentenced to prison.

In 2010, 4,055,500 adults under federal, state, or local jurisdiction were on probation and about 840,700 were on parole.[6]

Probation Services

Local Courts

When determining whether to grant probation, local and county court judges typically have little information on which to base their decision. Because most criminals in these courts of limited jurisdiction are convicted of misdemeanors or violations, there is less risk to the community in the event the judge grants probation. Thus, most local and county courts do not have access to probation services that will provide them with presentence investigation reports. Also, because of the short sentences provided for the offenses (maximum of one year) that are handled by these courts, probation plans requiring the probationer to participate in long-term treatment, education, rehabilitation, drug counseling, or anger management are not practical.

Judges in state courts of general trial jurisdiction and federal courts have more access to probation personnel to provide presentence investigations. Also, because of the length of sentences for felons tried in these courts, probation plans can specify that the probationer participate in a long-term program. Federal probation services are provided to the courts by the U.S. Probation and Pretrial Services System. As the name suggests, this office provides assistance to the courts in presentence investigation and in probation services.

State Probation Offices

State probation offices are organized in different ways under different authorities. Five common organizational structures for state probation are

1. Within the state executive branch (governor)
2. Within local (county or municipal) executive departments
3. Under the state judiciary (courts)
4. Under local courts
5. Under various combinations of the previous four

4 million The number of adults on probation in the United States in 2010.

However, probation is not under the authority of law enforcement, the prosecutor, or corrections. In many states, like the federal government, probation and parole services are provided by the same agency. In these agencies, officers may handle probation, parole, and pretrial services.

Probation Officers

The status of **probation officers** as law enforcement officers varies state by state. Federal probation officers may be authorized to carry concealed weapons on and off duty. Some states grant probation officers the right to carry concealed weapons; some do not. Likewise, states grant juvenile probation officers different privileges with regard to carrying firearms. Probation officers (both adult and juvenile) do not have the same arrest powers as police officers do. The arrest powers of probation officers tend to be limited to probationers. However, with regard to the powers of arrest and search and seizure of probationers, probation officers have more extensive authority because they do not need search warrants to search a probationer, his or her residence, or his or her automobile. Furthermore, probation officers do not have to advise probationers of their Miranda rights when questioning them and probationers do not have the right to remain silent when questioned by probation officers.

Decision to Grant Probation

Probation is a sentencing option of judges. Probation, which is also called suspended sentence, for juveniles and adults can be used as a sentence for both minor and serious crimes. In fact, about half of those individuals on probation committed misdemeanors; the other half committed felonies. (See Table 11–2 for other characteristics of adults on probation and parole.) An important factor in determining whether the defendant receives a suspended sentence is information about potential risks to the community if the offender is released. Judges must decide if the criminal's release poses a serious threat to the community. In states without mandatory sentencing and sentencing guidelines, judges have great discretion in the use of probation and can suspend the sentences of those convicted of murder as well as traffic offenses. However, the federal courts and some state courts have limited judges' discretion in the use of suspended sentences through legislation requiring minimum sentences, mandatory sentencing, and structured sentencing. In these jurisdictions, judges may be prohibited from using probation for certain crimes.

When sentencing offenders to probation or suspended sentences, judges assume the following:

- A sentence of prison time is an inappropriate punishment.
- The public will not be at serious risk if the offender is released into the community.

TABLE 11–2

COMPARISON CHARACTERISTICS OF ADULTS ON PROBATION/ PAROLE, 2010

	Probation	Parole
Gender		
Male	76%	88%
Female	24%	12%
Race		
White	55%	42%
African-American	30%	39%
Hispanic or Latino	13%	18%
American Indian/Alaska Native/ Pacific Islander, two or more races	2%	2%
Type of Offense		
Felony	50%	95%
Misdemeanor	47%	5%
Other	2%	–
Most Serious Offense		
Drug	26%	35%
Property	28%	24%
Violent	19%	27%
Public Order	18%	–
Other	11%	12%
Weapon	–	3%

Source: Lauren E. Glaze and Thomas P. Bonczar, *Probation and Parole in the United States, 2010* (Washington, DC: Bureau of Justice Statistics 2011), pp. 33, 43.

- The offender will not benefit from any prison-based rehabilitation/vocational program.
- The offender will be self-supporting if released into the community.
- The offender should not be confined due to serious mental illness (terms of probation can include mental health care).
- The offender will not commit other crimes.

The judge relies to a great extent on the presentence investigation report to make a judgment about the appropriateness of probation. The decision to grant probation as a sentence depends on the quality of information the judge has about the defendant and his or her past record, social and family interaction, psychological profile, and employment status.

The U.S. Probation and Pretrial Services System provides federal judges with presentence reports to help them decide if probation is appropriate. State judges rely on state probation and parole services to provide presentence investigations. After conviction, the presentence investigation officer performs an intensive investigation of the convicted defendant's lifestyle, criminal activities, financial assets, psychological profile, and role in the community. This information and a sentencing recommendation are compiled into a report that is submitted to the court.

Presentence investigation reports contain information about the following:

- A narrative of the circumstances of the offense
- The defendant's entire criminal history
- A description of the defendant's lifestyle, including employment and financial responsibility, support to family, and contribution to the community
- Available sentencing options for the crime(s)
- Factors that would support a decision for probation (for example, potential for rehabilitation, lack of risk to the community, restitution to the victim, and costs to the criminal justice system)

The sentencing recommendation and the data in the presentence investigation report can be challenged by both the prosecutor and the defense counsel.

Active Supervision and Treatment

Probation is usually combined with the requirement for supervision and treatment. About 73% of probationers are under active supervision, which requires them to report regularly to a probation authority in person, by mail, or by telephone.[7] Probationers may be required to report to their probation officers on a daily, weekly, or monthly basis, depending on a number of factors. In this meeting, the probation officer monitors and verifies the probationer's compliance with his or her terms of probation. During these visits, the probationer may be required to submit to drug testing to see if he or she is using illegal drugs. In addition to supervision, probationers may be required to seek professional treatment or counseling. In fact, one of the advantages of probation is that it allows the court to mandate treatment programs. Often probationers must pay for treatment programs on their own. In 2010, about 26% of probationers were drug offenders.[8] For these offenders, the conditions of their release usually require that they complete drug-treatment programs and submit to regular drug testing. Probationers must submit to drug tests whenever probation officers so order. Frequent mandatory drug testing has proven to be an effective strategy in drug rehabilitation.

Pros and Cons of Probation

Fear versus Cost

The concerns associated with probation are fear of further criminal activity by the offender and lack of punishment for the crime committed. (See Figure 11–1.) However, at a cost of about $1,000 per person per year, probation is much cheaper than prison.[9] If the probationer commits new crimes, however, the cost of the property loss or damage and the intangible costs of victims' pain and suffering present a different picture. On the other hand, probation promotes rehabilitation through employment, opportunities for normal social relationships, and access

$1,000
The yearly per person cost for probation.

Probation promotes rehabilitation through employment, opportunities for normal social relationships, and access to community services and resources.

to community services and resources. Probationers are usually required to be employed or to attend school or vocational training. Employment enables offenders to support themselves and their families if they are married and to pay taxes. Therefore, the probationer is not a burden to the taxpayer.

Attachment to the Community

Probationers live in a "normal" environment. By remaining in the community, the probationer avoids the detrimental effects of the prison environment and retains relationships with family and other support groups and services. As you will recall from Chapter 2, "Crime: The Search for Understanding," a number of criminological theories of crime causation suggest that positive attachments to the community are a powerful factor in preventing criminal behavior.

Conditions of probation provide for supervision of the probationer's behavior and lifestyle. Standard conditions require that the probationer maintain employment, have a place to live, refrain from drug and alcohol use, and avoid socializing with known criminals. The probationer is monitored to ensure that he or she abides by these conditions. Additional conditions may include successful completion of a drug or alcohol rehabilitation program. While on probation, the probationer is supervised and must comply with all of the terms and conditions of probation. Proponents of probation argue that long-term oversight of offenders at low cost to the community is much preferred to unsupervised release of prisoners.

Decision to Revoke Probation and Due Process Rights

The decision to grant offenders probation is revocable because it is granted under the stipulation that offenders meet all of the conditions of their release. Probation status can be revoked at any time if offenders fail to conform to their conditions of probation. Common reasons for the revocation of probation include testing positive for drugs, possessing weapons, committing a new crime, losing a job, or failing to complete a treatment program. Offenders whose probation status is revoked are returned to prison to serve their entire sentence.

Prior to the Warren Court, in *Escoe* v. *Zerbst*, the Court ruled that probation was considered an "act of grace" and the Court did not recognize that the probationer has any due process rights following revocation of probation. In 1967, however, the Court reversed that opinion in *Mempa* v. *Rhay* and ruled that probationers are entitled to due process hearings to establish that they violated their conditions of probation.[10] In 1973 in the case of *Gagnon* v. *Scarpelli*, the Court ruled that probationers also are entitled to certain due process rights before their probation is revoked.[11]

Compared to those of a trial, different rules of evidence apply to the probation revocation hearing. For example, probation officers have the right of search and seizure of the probationer and his or her residence without obtaining a search warrant, getting consent, or having probable cause.[12] Probation officers do not have to advise probationers of their rights against self-incrimination, and probationers have only limited protection against self-incrimination.[13] Probation officers also can enter and search the probationer's vehicle at any time without permission. Probationers do have the right to counsel at their revocation hearing, and if they cannot afford counsel, they are entitled to a defense counsel paid for by the government.[14] Finally, the burden of proof differs for revocation of probation. Whereas in a criminal case the standard of proof is beyond a reasonable doubt, in a probation revocation hearing, the standard is less stringent. If the evidence suggests that it is more likely than not the probationer violated his or her conditions of probation, he or she can be returned to prison.

Technical Violations

The probationer can be returned to prison for violating a condition of probation. This is called a **technical violation**. In 2010, about 6% of probationers were returned to prison for this violation.[15] (About 16% of parolees return to prison for technical violations.[16]) Drug and alcohol use is the most frequent reason. Imprisonment for committing a new crime is not punishment for the new crime, but for the crime committed previously for which the individual received probation. If an offender commits a new crime, he or she is arrested and tried. If the probationer is found guilty, the sentence for the new crime is added to the sentence he or she must serve for the previous crime. However, even if the probationer is not convicted in court of committing the new crime or if charges are reduced through plea bargaining or are dismissed, the court still may revoke probation.

Probationers cannot be returned to prison for technical violations such as failure to pay a fine or restitution if it can be proven that the probationer was not responsible for this failure. For example, probationers might lose their job through no fault of their own, incur medical bills that prevent them from making payment, or experience some other financial crisis not under their control.

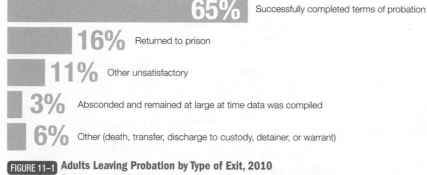

65% Successfully completed terms of probation

16% Returned to prison

11% Other unsatisfactory

3% Absconded and remained at large at time data was compiled

6% Other (death, transfer, discharge to custody, detainer, or warrant)

FIGURE 11-1 **Adults Leaving Probation by Type of Exit, 2010**
Source: Lauren E. Glaze and Thomas P. Bonczar, *Probation and Parole in the United States, 2010* (Washington, DC: Bureau of Justice Statistics), p. 6.

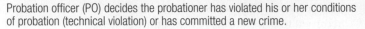
Probation officer (PO) decides the probationer has violated his or her conditions of probation (technical violation) or has committed a new crime.

The PO may arrest the probationer,

or the PO will direct the police to make the arrest.

The PO writes a report detailing the alleged violation or new crime and forwards it to the court, and a hearing is held to determine if probable cause exists to revoke probation.

Yes, probable cause exists

No probable cause exists, return to the community

A **probation revocation hearing** is held. The hearing official renders a decision based on the following:
Is the alleged violation sufficient to revoke probation?
Is the evidence sufficient and trustworthy?

Revoked If probation is revoked, the probationer is returned to court for resentencing.

Not Revoked If probation is not revoked, the probationer is returned to the community.

These probationers cannot be returned to prison because they lack the money to fulfill their conditions of probation. However, personal bankruptcy ultimately does not excuse the probationer from paying court-ordered fines or restitution.[17]

▶ Parole

People often minimize the distinction between probation and parole, but the two are very different practices and have distinct characteristics. Whereas the origins of probation can be directly traced to the early practices of John Augustus, the origins of parole are more diverse. The concept of parole encompasses the practice of conditionally releasing prisoners to the community and the supervision of the released prisoner, or the parolee, in the community. The parolee's early release from prison is conditional, based on compliance with the conditions of release and absence of criminal activity.

Parole d'Honneur

The historical roots of parole can be traced to practices of the French, English, and Irish. The term *parole* comes from the French phrase ***parole d'honneur***—the practice of releasing a prisoner for good behavior based on his word of honor that he would obey the law upon release.[18]

The Mark System

Alexander Maconochie often is credited with developing the **mark system**, a forerunner of the parole system. Maconochie developed this early type of parole system between 1840 and 1844 while he was administrator of Norfolk Island, a prison colony off the coast of Australia. He pioneered the innovative penal strategy of releasing prisoners early on the basis of points, or marks, for good behavior and work performed in prison. The system operated according to a prison token economy in which the prisoners earned marks for good behavior. Upon imprisonment, each prisoner was assessed a debt in marks to be paid. Additional marks could be assessed against the prisoner for misbehavior or violation of prison rules. At the same time, the prisoner could earn good-credit marks for working, participating in educational programs, and behaving well. Prisoners who earned enough marks to offset the debt of their crime—and any additional debts they incurred while in prison— could "buy" their freedom with these marks. If prisoners had more than enough marks to buy their freedom, the extra marks could be redeemed for cash upon their release.

Maconochie's mark system was based on the premise that prisoners must demonstrate rehabilitation to earn their release from prison. This same basic assumption underlies the modern use of parole. Parole is based on the idea that prisoners should be released not because they have served a fixed amount of time, but because they have changed their ways. However, unlike modern-day parole, the **ticket of leave** that Maconochie's prisoners purchased with their marks granted them an unconditional release from prison. Released prisoners were neither supervised in the community nor subject to any terms of conditional release. Today, on the contrary, parole is always conditional. Parolees can be returned to jail or prison for rule violations or other offenses.

GLOSSARY

parole d'honneur The practice of releasing a prisoner for good behavior based on his word of honor that he would obey the law upon release.

mark system An early form of parole invented by Alexander Maconochie in which prisoners demonstrated their rehabilitation by earning points for good behavior.

ticket of leave In the mark system, the unconditional release from prison purchased with marks earned for good behavior.

Irish system An early form of parole invented by Sir Walter Crofton based on the mark system in which prisoners were released conditionally on good behavior and were supervised in the community.

indeterminate sentence A sentence in which the defendant is sentenced to a prison term with a minimum and maximum number of years to serve.

parole board Individuals appointed to a body that meets in prisons to make decisions about granting parole release to inmates.

independent model The system in which decision making about parole is under the authority of an autonomous parole board.

consolidated model The system in which decision making about parole is a function of a state department of corrections.

U.S. Parole Commission (USPC) The agency responsible for parole decisions of federal and Washington, DC, inmates.

parole hearing A meeting with an inmate, his or her attorney, and others in which the parole board decides whether to grant, deny, or revoke parole.

> Parole is based on the idea that prisoners should be released not because they have served a fixed amount of time, but because they have changed their ways.

The Irish System

Sir Walter Crofton pioneered the practice of conditional release for inmates prior to completing their sentences based on good behavior. In 1854, Crofton was chairman of the board of directors of Irish prisons. He adopted Maconochie's mark system and ticket of leave to solve the problem of prison overcrowding. However, Crofton's **Irish system** provided a continuum of conditions of supervision based on the prisoner's behavior. Initially, prisoners were placed in solitary confinement but could work their way to more freedom. In the final stages of the Irish system, prisoners were assigned to work programs outside the prison and could earn a ticket of leave entitling them to early release under supervision. If they disobeyed the terms of their release or committed a new crime, they could be summarily tried and, if convicted, have their ticket of leave revoked. Crofton's Irish system is the model on which the American parole system is based.

Pros and Cons of Parole

Youthful Offenders

Good-time laws were passed as early as 1817 in New York, and they allowed the early release of prisoners with sentences of five years or less.[19] However, parole did not emerge as common practice until the end of the 1800s. Even the term *parole* was not used in the United States until 1846.[20] The development of parole came with the use of indeterminate sentencing and efforts to address the correctional needs of youthful offenders. In 1869, Michigan adopted the first indeterminate sentencing law.[21] An **indeterminate sentence** bases release on behavior that demonstrates signs of rehabilitation rather than on a fixed prison term. In indeterminate sentencing, the defendant is given a prison term with a minimum and maximum number of years to serve. Indeterminate prison terms can be from one year to life in prison, a wide range between the minimum and maximum sentence.

The indeterminate sentence was used extensively at the Elmira Reformatory for youthful offenders in New York. Prior to the twentieth century and the adoption of the juvenile court system, youthful offenders were not entitled to special treatment in the criminal justice system. Warden Zebulon Brockway instituted the practice of early release at Elmira Reformatory in 1876 as a means to promote rehabilitation, not punishment, of youthful offenders. Brockway's use of early conditional release combined with mandatory community supervision was the first significant use of parole in America.[22] As in the origins of probation, the first parole officers were volunteers.[23]

Promoting of Rehabilitation

Although it promoted the rehabilitation of offenders in the community, parole did not become an overnight success. By 1900, 20 states had adopted parole statutes, but it was not until after World War II that every state had a parole system. The first federal parole statute was adopted in 1867, providing for the reduction of sentences of federal prisoners for good conduct. However, the federal parole system was not created until 1910. Even during Maconochie's time, the public was opposed to the concept of early release, as indicated by the fact that Maconochie was removed as prison administrator because of opposition to his mark system.

Public Opposition

In the United States, public opposition to parole is still widespread. This disdain for parole is reflected in the abandonment of the practice by the federal court system and many states. Twenty states have restructured or eliminated state parole boards, substituting various forms of mandatory and supervised release for parole. The public seems to want criminals who have been sentenced to prison "to get the amount of time they deserve."[24] This belief is based in part on the public's fear that prisoners released early will return to a life of crime. For example, in 1994, when Virginia eliminated parole, Governor George Allen predicted that it would prevent 120,000 felonies over ten years. Allen said, "Virginia is a safer place because we abolished parole."[25] One reason the public fears the release of parolees into the community is that parolees (and probationers) do commit a significant number of crimes after being released from prison.

Rates of Reoffending

In 2010, 22% of parolees—about 1 in 5—did not successfully complete parole and were returned to prison. Another 6% absconded.[26] Of the 22% returned to prison, 6% were returned because they committed a new crime.[27] Reliable contemporary data are not available as to the total number of crimes committed by people on probation and parole. Older data (Table 11–3) suggest that probation and parole violators committed a substantial number of crimes. These data suggest that in 1991, people on probation and parole were responsible for over 13,000 murders and nearly 13,000 rapes and that over 50% of the victims were under the age of 12. They committed nearly 40,000 robberies, 19,000 assaults, and 40,000 burglaries. Those opposed to early release, especially parole, say that if these offenders had remained in prison, it could be argued that these crimes would not have occurred. They argue that the cost of the crimes committed by the probation and parole violator often is not taken into account when the cost effectiveness of probation and parole is calculated.

States That Have Abolished Discretionary Release

This fear is not entirely groundless, especially for prisoners released on parole. In 2010, only 52% of adults successfully completed the conditions of parole, compared to 65% of adults who successfully completed probation.[28] Thirty-three percent

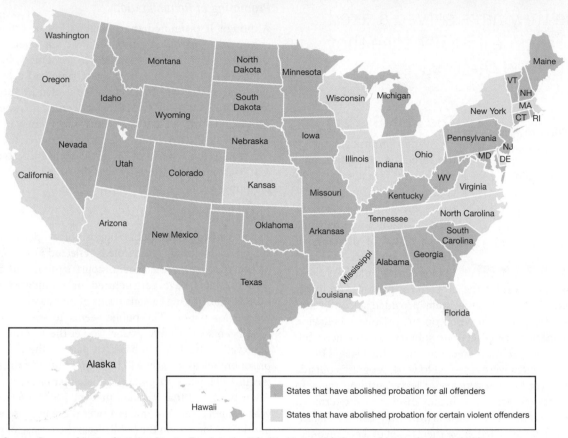

States That Have Abolished Discretionary Release

States that have abolished probation for all offenders

States that have abolished probation for certain violent offenders

Source: Bureau of Justice Statistics, *Reentry Trends in the U.S.* (Washington, DC: Bureau of Justice Statistics, 2009).

of adults on parole were returned to incarceration, compared to 17% of adults on probation. Nine percent of adults on parole simply vanished. They ran away and could not be located by the criminal justice system, compared to 3% of people on probation who absconded.[29] The failure rate for adults on parole is high, despite the fact that 82% of them are under active supervision, which requires them to report regularly to a parole authority, compared to 73% of adults on probation.[30]

The public disdain for early release, especially parole, is illustrated by the fact that discretionary early release of prisoners on parole has dropped significantly since 1980. In 2010, the most prisoners (51%) were released on parole through mandatory release. (See Figure 11–2.) Mandatory release requires the early release of the inmate due to reasons such as good-time credit.

Public distrust of parole reflects concerns that parolees pose a danger to public safety. In 2010, 9% of people released on parole committed new offenses. That is, over 75,000 inmates released on parole into the community committed a crime. It could be argued that if these people had not been released, there would have been 75,000 fewer victimizations. This distrust is reinforced by recidivism studies, which indicate that the long-term success

TABLE 11–3	CRIMES COMMITTED DURING PROBATION AND PAROLE

Probation Violators	Parole Violators
6,400 murders	6,800 murders
7,400 rapes or sexual assaults (33% of the victims were under the age of 12; 63% under 18)	5,550 rapes or sexual assaults (21% of the victims were under the age of 12; 47% under 18)
17,000 robberies	22,500 robberies
10,400 assaults	8,800 assaults
16,600 burglaries	23,000 burglaries
3,100 motor vehicle thefts	4,800 motor vehicle thefts

Crimes committed by 162,000 state probation violators while under supervision in the community an average of 17 months and 156,000 state parole violators during 13 months in the community.

Source: Bureau of Justice Statistics, *Probation and Parole Violators in State Prison, 1991* (Washington, DC: U.S. Department of Justice), p. 10.

52% The percentage of adults who successfully complete the conditions of parole.

65% The percentage of adults who successfully completed probation.

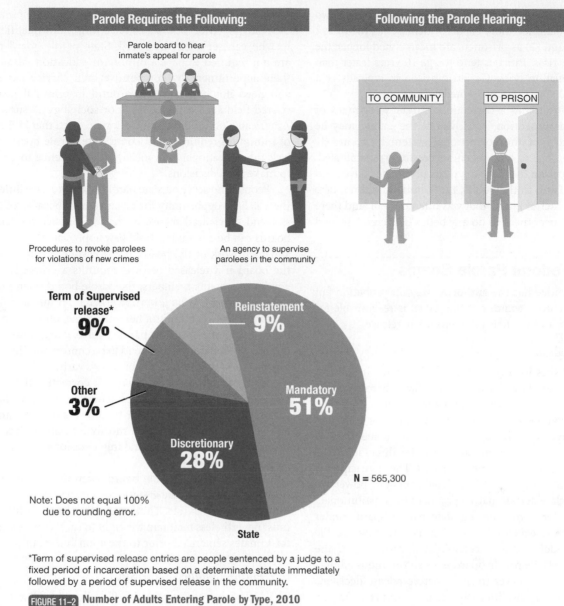

Parole Requires the Following:

Parole board to hear
inmate's appeal for parole

Procedures to revoke parolees
for violations of new crimes

An agency to supervise
parolees in the community

Following the Parole Hearing:

TO COMMUNITY

TO PRISON

Term of Supervised
release*
9%

Reinstatement
9%

Other
3%

Mandatory
51%

Discretionary
28%

N = 565,300

Note: Does not equal 100%
due to rounding error.

State

*Term of supervised release entries are people sentenced by a judge to a
fixed period of incarceration based on a determinate statute immediately
followed by a period of supervised release in the community.

FIGURE 11–2 **Number of Adults Entering Parole by Type, 2010**
Source: Lauren E. Glaze and Thomas P. Bonczar, *Probation and Parole in the United States, 2010* (Washington, DC:
Bureau of Justice Statistics, 2011), pp. 7–8.

rate for nonviolent inmates released from state prisons is dismal. (See Table 11–4.) For three years after being released in 1994, the Bureau of Justice Statistics tracked offenders from 15 states with large prison populations. After three years, 67.5% of released inmates had been rearrested, 46.8% had been reconvicted, and 25.4% had been returned to prison with new sentences. Although nonviolent offenders are more likely to succeed in reentry compared to violent offenders, the success rate for nonviolent offenders as measured by rearrest suggests that offenders are not able to reenter the community successfully.

Cost

Public disdain for early release has a cost. The number of adults incarcerated in jails and prisons continues to increase; so as fewer inmates are released on parole, the demand for bed space in jails and prison increases. Since abolishing parole, Virginia's inmate population has risen 25% and the state has had to build new prisons to accommodate over 3,000 prisoners at a cost of over half a billion dollars.[31] In many states, the prison population continues to increase due to "get tough" sentencing laws that keep inmates in prison longer, a decrease in discretionary early release, and the rising number of people incarcerated for nonviolent drug

TABLE 11–4	**RECIDIVISM RATES OF OFFENDERS RELEASED IN 1994**

Cumulative percentage of released nonviolent offenders who were:

Time after release	Rearrested	Reconvicted	Returned to prison
6 months	29.9%	10.6%	5.0%
1 year	44.1%	21.5%	10.4%
2 years	59.2%	36.4%	18.8%
3 years	67.5%	46.8%	25.4%

Source: Patrick A. Langan and David J. Levin, *Recidivism of Prisoners Released in 1994* (Washington, DC: Bureau of Justice Statistics), p. 3.

offenses. These factors increase the costs of corrections in two ways: (1) the demand for more capacity increases as the prison population rises and (2) as prisoners are incarcerated longer, the cost per prisoner rises. Inmates tend to age 10 years faster than the general population does. Geriatric prisoners typically cost $60,000 to $70,000 per year due to medical care costs.

Parole is advocated as a correctional strategy for many of the same reasons probation is. However, the public may be wary of the ability of the correctional system to accurately predict which prisoners have been successfully rehabilitated. Before going to prison, nearly two-thirds of inmates have been on probation.[32] Thus, to the public, those inmates did not take advantage of the "act of grace" that was offered them, and there is no reason to expect them to do any better if offered a second chance through parole.

State and Federal Parole Boards

The sentencing judge has the authority to grant probation but not parole. The **parole board**, not the judge, is responsible for deciding whether an inmate is to receive early release.

State Parole Boards

Each state establishes its own parole board, and no agency has oversight of all the state parole boards. State parole boards are established by state legislation and administered under the authority of the state's executive branch (the governor). The legislature retains oversight through its powers of lawmaking and budget approval. The governor appoints the director of the parole board and often the members as well. The state supreme courts and the U.S. Supreme Court have oversight powers in that they can declare certain parole practices unconstitutional.

Two models for administering state parole boards under the authority of the executive branch of government are the independent model and the consolidated model.[33] In the **independent model**, the parole board is an autonomous administrative unit with the power to make parole release decisions and to supervise all conditionally released inmates. In the **consolidated model**, the parole board is under the authority of the state Department of Corrections as a specialty unit within the department that makes decisions about conditional early releases.

State parole boards usually have fewer than a dozen members who may be full-time or part-time appointees. Final decision-making authority for selecting prisoners to release on parole lies with the parole board. Most parole board members obtain their position through an appointment by the state governor. Few states have minimum qualifications as to who can serve on the board. State parole board members are not required to have a minimum education, do not obtain their appointment by competitive civil service examination, and need not have any background in criminal justice or a related field such as psychology or sociology. A survey by the American Correctional Association revealed that in the absence of minimum requirements, some state parole board members lack the educational and vocational experience to equip them to make such decisions.[34]

People who serve on state parole boards receive little pay, and there is little opportunity for advancement because of the small size and specialized nature of the job. Service on state parole boards can be a thankless task. Few appreciate the responsibility and hard work of the board, but everyone is quick to criticize the board if a released parolee commits a crime. Because the governor appoints members, the parole board often reflects the political agenda of the governor. Also, if an inmate released by the parole board commits a heinous crime, often the public will blame the governor for the parole board's decision to release the inmate. Thus, parole boards tend to be conservative in their judgment as to whether to release prisoners early.

State parole board members are correctional officers, law enforcement officers, or judges. They do not have the power to carry concealed firearms, or the powers of arrest and search and seizure. Their duties are mostly administrative, with the primary responsibility of making decisions about the early release of prisoners.

All states have a parole board, even those that have abolished the practice, because states cannot retroactively revoke an inmate's right to parole. Thus, states that have abolished parole must nevertheless maintain the right to early conditional release for inmates sentenced prior to the abolishment of parole.

U.S. Parole Commission (USPC)

The U.S. Congress created the U.S. Board of Parole in 1930, creating the first federal parole board. In 1976, the Parole Commission and Reorganization Act retitled the agency the **U.S. Parole Commission (USPC)**. The commission consists of a chairperson and commissioners appointed by the president; regional offices are staffed by hearing examiners, case analysts, and clerical staff. Despite the increasing numbers of federal inmates, the USPC is in the process of closing down its operations. The Comprehensive Crime Control Act

Think About It . . .

It was Bill Wallshleger's sixth parole hearing. Convicted of violent sexual assaults, the former police officer had undergone treatment for a diagnosed psychosexual disorder, earned four degrees, and had a spotless disciplinary record. He was denied parole because one of his victims chose to testify at his parole hearing about the brutality of the assault and the impact in had on her life.

The Maryland parole board reports that of the 10,000 parole hearings annually, fewer than three rape victims a year typically come to speak. Should victims be encouraged to testify at parole hearings? Explain.

Picsfive/Shutterstock

of 1984 abolished eligibility for parole for federal offenders who committed crimes on or after November 1, 1987. Thus, only federal prisoners who committed crimes prior to that date are eligible for parole. The act provided for the abolition of the Parole Commission on November 1, 1992. However, judicial challenges to the elimination of or reduction in parole eligibility for those sentenced prior to November 1, 1987, resulted in the Judicial Improvements Act of 1990 that extended the life of the Parole Commission until November 1, 1997. The Parole Commission Phaseout Act of 1996 again extended the life of the Parole Commission. This act authorized the continuation of the Parole Commission until November 1, 2002. The National Capital Revitalization and Self-Government Improvement Act of 1997 gave the Parole Commission significant additional responsibilities, including responsibility for parole within the District of Columbia. More responsibilities have been added by other legislation, such as making decisions about prison terms in foreign transfer treaty cases for offenses committed on or after November 1, 1987, and having jurisdiction over all state defendants who are accepted into the U.S. Marshals Witness Security Program. The 21st Century Department of Justice Appropriations Authorization Act of 2002 again extended the life of the Parole Commission until November 1, 2005.

Today, the USPC continues to operate, but as a much smaller federal agency. While it still has jurisdiction over some federal prisoners (those sentenced prior to 1987), the majority of cases it oversees are Washington, DC, criminals. The USPC is a semiautonomous agency within the Department of Justice that handles all matters of parole for eligible federal and District of Columbia (D.C.) prisoners. According to information on its website, the USPC makes parole release decisions; authorizes method of release and the conditions under which release occurs; issues warrants for violation of supervision; determines probable cause for revocation process; prescribes, modifies, and monitors compliance with the terms and conditions governing offenders' behavior while on parole or mandatory or supervised release;

> State parole boards have tremendous discretion in deciding to which inmates to grant early conditional release, and inmates have little power to appeal those decisions.

revokes parole, mandatory, or supervised release of offenders; releases from supervision those offenders who no longer pose a risk to public safety; and issues rules, regulations, and guidelines pertaining to the national parole policy.

The Parole Hearing

Parole boards make decisions through parole hearings. State parole boards have tremendous discretion in deciding to which inmates to grant early conditional release, and inmates have little power to appeal those decisions. Parole hearings are not like trials, and each state and the federal Parole Commission have different procedures for conducting parole hearings.[35] Generally, parole hearings are brief, are private rather than public, and are held in the prison where the prisoner is housed. **Parole hearings** are convened by the parole board or by a hearing examiner who acts as the authorized representative of the parole board. The examiner presides over the hearing and makes a recommendation, which is forwarded to the parole board for formal action.

When an inmate is processed into prison, his or her file is forwarded to the parole board to determine a first hearing date. The parole board reviews the circumstances of the crime and the information about the offender and sets a date. For most offenders, the first parole hearing is set after they have served one-third of their prison time. The parole board may recommend what it expects inmates to do during this time to increase their chances of parole. Usually, recommendations relate to participation in educational or treatment programs, vocational training sufficient to allow inmates to support themselves if released, and obedience to prison rules.

The powers of the parole board to grant early release and the public's expectation that the prisoner will serve his or her sentence have created considerable public debate. In states using indeterminate sentencing, the sentence handed down by the judge may be different from the time actually served.

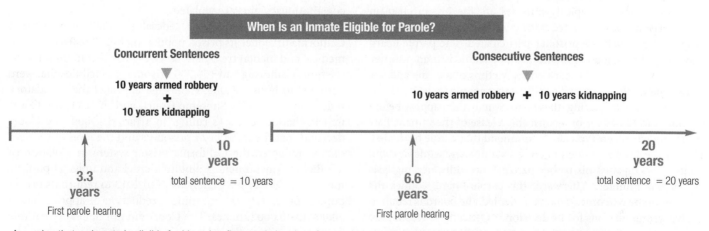

| When Is an Inmate Eligible for Parole? |

Concurrent Sentences

▼ 10 years armed robbery + 10 years kidnapping

3.3 years — First parole hearing

10 years — total sentence = 10 years

Consecutive Sentences

▼ 10 years armed robbery + 10 years kidnapping

6.6 years — First parole hearing

20 years — total sentence = 20 years

Assuming that an inmate is eligible for his or her first parole hearing after serving one-third of the total sentence, he or she will be eligible for the first parole hearing much sooner under concurrent sentencing.

As the states face financial crises, they are turning to probation and parole as revenue generators. States are assessing "legal financial obligations" fees, or "LFOs," for probation and parole services. LFOs fund state budgets. They move the burden of financing state operations from taxpayers to a mostly indigent population of convicted offenders. LFOs can be thousands of dollars. Offenders unable to pay LFOs can be imprisoned. Do LFOs for probation and parole services create an undue hardship on convicted offenders? Explain.

Natalia Merzlyakova/Fotolia

The judge may sentence a defendant who has committed multiple crimes to two sentences of ten years for each crime, to be served consecutively. In this case, the inmate is effectively sentenced to 20 years in prison.

However, in some states, the parole board has the power to decide if the first parole hearing will be based on the totality of the sentence or just the longest sentence. In consecutive sentencing, the inmate must serve one sentence and then the other. In concurrent sentencing, the inmate serves time for all crimes sentenced at the same time. In effect, in concurrent sentencing, the inmate's eligibility for his or her first parole hearing is dependent upon the longest sentence, not the totality of all the sentences. The difference between these two interpretations has a great impact on calculating when an inmate is eligible for a first parole hearing. Often the public is critical of parole boards that disregard the judge's instructions and permit concurrent sentences. This lack of truth in sentencing has led many states to adopt new sentencing guidelines that reduce or eliminate parole.

The parole hearing is conducted in a meeting room in the prison, not in a courtroom. The board reviews the history of the case and all available information about the prisoner; then the inmate is brought into the room to state his or her case for parole. All inmates are required to submit a parole plan, which contains detailed plans for employment, education, and living arrangements if released. These parole plans also contain statements explaining why inmates think they are ready for parole, what they have done to prepare for release, what they have done to rehabilitate themselves while in prison, and why they are sorry for the crimes they committed.

In some states, inmates can call witnesses to support their petition, but they do not have the power to subpoena or order a witness to testify. Typical witnesses are the prison chaplain or the prison staff associated with educational or rehabilitation programs in which the prisoner participated. The parole board may deny this request. Inmates are not entitled to an attorney at the parole hearing. In many states, victims of a crime and law enforcement officers must be notified that an inmate is scheduled to receive a parole hearing; these parties may then appear before the board to testify for or against the release of the inmate. Law enforcement officers typically recommend that parole be denied. The prisoner is not entitled to cross-examine any witnesses who testify for or against his or her parole. The entire hearing lasts only a few minutes. Afterward, the parole board notifies the prisoner of the outcome. If parole is denied, the board is required to give written reasons for its decision.[36] Often these reasons are vague, such as encouraging the inmate to continue to participate in educational or rehabilitation programs. If the parole board denies early release, it will set a date for the inmate's next parole hearing. There is no appeal of the board's decision.

Standards for Granting Parole

There is no standard judicially mandated burden of proof for the parole board to adhere to in deciding whether to grant early release. Ultimately, the decision reflects the best guess of the parole board members. Thus, the parole board's task is difficult because predicting which prisoners are ready and able to reintegrate into the community is virtually impossible. Board members often rely on feelings, common sense, and a sense of what the community would think. Some states and the USPC have developed decision-making aids to help them decide whether to grant parole. The probability or risk that a parolee will reoffend or be a danger to the community can be ranked on a scale from 1 to 10. However, in those states that use such an instrument, the parole boards are not bound by these devices and have the authority to deny parole even if the prisoner's score indicates a low risk. The American Law Institute has suggested a model protocol for parole boards based on identifying who should not be paroled rather than who should.

Prison Overcrowding and Parole

One of the most difficult decisions parole boards have to make is whom to release when the prison system is ordered to reduce its population due to overcrowding. If the conditions of imprisonment caused by overcrowding violate the Eighth Amendment against cruel and unusual punishment, the state or federal court may order a mandatory reduction in the number of inmates. Overcrowding in itself is not a violation of the Eighth Amendment, but when the overcrowding causes a significant deterioration in the standard of care, prisoners' constitutional rights are violated.

In 2009, for example, a federal judicial panel ordered California to reduce its prison population to 110,000 to improve medical and mental treatment services provided to inmates. At the time, California had 150,000 prisoners in facilities that were designed to house 80,000. California appealed the mandatory reduction to the U.S. Supreme Court, and in 2011, the Court upheld the lower court's ruling. In a rare decision, the Court declared that the number of prisoners and the level of services offered rendered the California prison system in violation of the Eighth Amendment prohibiting cruel and unusual punishment. The Court gave California until 2013 to reduce its prison population to 110,000, meaning a reduction of approximately 30,000 to 40,000 inmates. The Court did not mandate that this number of inmates be released, only that the state's prisons be reduced by this number. California has several options, most of

32.5% The percentage of parolees who are successful in maintaining their freedom three years after release.

them involving some form of early release. It can give inmates additional good-time credit, reduce the number of prisoners sent back to prison for technical parole violations, house inmates in private prisons, and increase the number of inmates eligible for various early-release programs such as house arrest.

California is not the only state that has found itself under court order to reduce or limit its prison population. Many states have found themselves in a similar situation. In these cases, the parole board must meet and decide which inmates can be released immediately, even ahead of their scheduled release date, to make room for new inmates.

At these "midnight parole hearings," the parole board must meet quickly and release inmates even before they have a parole plan in place. For example, in the late 1990s, Hawaii was under a court order to limit the state prison population to a capped number. To comply with the court order, if the evening prisoner count exceeded the cap, the parole board had to meet during the night to release prisoners before the official morning count. Such parole practices are not sound correctional policy but are political and legal necessities.

Prison overcrowding also has encouraged states to give inmates liberal good-time credit to speed releases. At the height of overcrowding in the Florida state prison system, some inmates were serving only a small percentage of their original sentence.[37] In 1990, states such as Arkansas, California, Indiana, and Louisiana were granting inmates more than 30 days' good-time credit per month.[38] The parole board's task of deciding whom to release early is complicated by mandatory sentencing laws. These laws prohibit early release for drug offenders, for example. Thus, instead of releasing nonviolent drug offenders, parole boards are forced to give early release to violent offenders who are not serving mandatory sentences.

Conditions of Parole

Parolees are subject to conditions of release similar to those for probationers. The conditions of release relate to security (whether the parolee will abide by the conditions of release) and to plans for treatment and rehabilitation. Each state has different standard conditions of release, but most are similar to those of the USPC. Federal parolees are required to abide by 14 **standard conditions of release**.[39] These standards require the parolee to report to his or her parole adviser within three days of release, restrict where the parolee can live and work, require him or her to abide by all laws, and report contact with the police to his or her parole officer. The conditions prohibit consumption of alcoholic beverages to excess, the use of illegal drugs, association with criminals, and possession of firearms. Parolees are required to cooperate with their probation officer and to submit to drug tests whenever ordered.

In addition to these standard conditions of release, parolees may, and often do, receive other conditions that are applicable to their crime and circumstances. For example, sex offenders may be prohibited from living or being near schools, playgrounds, or other areas where children are present. Those convicted of domestic violence may be prohibited from having contact with their victims. Prisoners with a history of drug or alcohol abuse may be required to attend treatment programs.

Revocation of Parole

Violations of Parole and New Crimes

Similar to probation, parole is revocable. Parole can be revoked for violation of a condition of release, for a technical violation, or for commission of a new crime. Revocation of parole is common because less than 33% of parolees are successful in maintaining their freedom three years after being released.[40] Compared to probationers, parolees are more likely to be returned to prison for the commission of a new crime.[41] Prisoners released on parole (and probation) are prohibited from possessing firearms, yet 21% reported possessing one while under supervision. According to the Department of Justice, of those arrested for committing a new offense, almost three out of every four reported having been armed when they committed their offense.

The U.S. Supreme Court has decided that parolees are entitled to certain due process rights, although these rights are substantially less than those of defendants in a trial. Most rights of parolees were established in the 1972 case of *Morrissey* v. *Brewer*, which gave parolees some protection against arbitrary and capricious revocation of parole. **Morrissey v. Brewer** secured the right to notice and a revocation hearing.[42]

The supervising parole officer initiates proceedings for parole revocation by filing notice of a technical violation or a charge that the parolee has committed a new crime. As noted earlier, the parole officer can file notice of revocation of parole even if charges against the parolee are dropped. A standard of proof that is not sufficient for conviction in court may nevertheless be sufficient to revoke parole.

Revocation Hearings

Revocation hearings most often are held in a prison facility and are conducted by the parole board or hearing officers representing the parole board. The parolee has the right to present evidence on his or her behalf and to cross-examine witnesses, but may not have the right to representation by an attorney. The U.S. Supreme Court has ruled that states do not have to provide parolees with appointed legal counsel if they cannot afford one. Normally, it is the inmate's responsibility, not the state's, to arrange for legal representation at revocation hearings.

Parole violators returned to prison are still entitled to additional parole hearings and may be released on parole at a later date. According to the USPC, only 16% to 36% of rereleased parolees successfully complete parole on their second attempt. For most state and federal parolees, at least a portion of their "street time" will be credited toward their original sentences. Usually, the parole time preceding the violation, noncompliance, or commission of a new crime is counted toward completion of the original sentence. For example, an offender with five years left on his or her original sentence who successfully completes three years of parole must serve only two years upon his or her return to prison to complete the sentence.

U.S. PAROLE COMMISSION STANDARD CONDITIONS OF RELEASE FOR U.S. CODE OFFENDERS

1. You shall go directly to the district shown on this CERTIFICATE OF RELEASE (unless released to the custody of other authorities). Within three days after your arrival, you shall report to your parole advisor if you have one, and the United States Probation Officer whose name appears on this Certificate. If in any emergency you are unable to contact your parole advisor, or your Probation Officer or the United States Probation Office, you shall communicate with the United States Parole Commission, Department of Justice, Chevy Chase, Maryland 20815.

2. If you are released to the custody of other authorities, and after your release from physical custody of such authorities, you are unable to report to the United States Probation Officer to whom you are assigned within three days, you shall report instead to the nearest United States Probation Officer.

3. You shall not leave the limits fixed by this CERTIFICATE OF RELEASE without written permission from your Probation Officer.

4. You shall notify your Probation Officer within 2 days of any change in your place of residence.

5. You shall make a complete and truthful written report (on a form provided for that purpose) to your Probation Officer between the first and third day of each month, and on the final day of parole. You shall also report to your Probation Officer at other times as your Probation Officer directs, providing complete and truthful information.

6. You shall not violate any law. Nor shall you associate with persons engaged in criminal activity. If you are arrested or questioned by a law-enforcement officer, you shall within 2 days report such contact to your Probation Officer or the United States Probation Office.

7. You shall not enter into any agreement to act as an "informer" or special agent for any law-enforcement agency.

8. You shall work regularly unless excused by your Probation Officer, and support your legal dependents, if any, to the best of your ability. You shall report within 2 days to your Probation Officer any changes in employment.

9. You shall not drink alcoholic beverages to excess. You shall not purchase, possess, use or administer marijuana or narcotic or other habit-forming or dangerous drugs, unless prescribed or advised by a physician. You shall not frequent places where such drugs are illegally sold, dispensed, used or given away.

10. You shall not associate with persons who have a criminal record unless you have permission of your Probation Officer.

11. You shall not possess a firearm/ammunition or other dangerous weapons.

12. You shall permit confiscation by your Probation Officer of any materials which your Probation Officer believes may constitute contraband in your possession and which your Probation Officer observes in plain view in your residence, place of business or occupation, vehicle(s) or on your person.

13. You shall make a diligent effort to satisfy any fine, restitution order, court costs or assessment, and/or court ordered child support or alimony payment that has been, or may be, imposed, and shall provide such financial information as may be requested, by your Probation Officer, relevant to the payment of the obligation. If unable to pay the obligation in one sum, you will cooperate with your Probation Officer in establishing an installment payment schedule.

14. You shall submit to a drug test whenever ordered by your Probation Officer.

Source: United States Parole Commission.

► *Supervision of Probation and Parole*

Social Work and Rehabilitation Skills

The actual supervision of defendants released on probation and inmates released on parole is the work of state and federal **probation officers and parole officers**. As noted earlier, in many states and in the federal system, the same officers supervise both probation and parole and perform pretrial investigation reports for the court. Probation and parole officers perform essentially three roles: law enforcement officer, social worker, and community resource broker.

Probation and parole officers enforce **compliance with the terms of release** and oversee the client's lifestyle for potential signs of danger to the community. As such, federal probation and parole officers are considered law enforcement officers, with the power to carry concealed weapons and with the limited powers of arrest and search and seizure. The status of state probation and parole officers as law enforcement officers varies by state. All states grant probation and parole officers the powers of arrest and search and seizure as those powers relate to the probationers and parolees under their supervision. They do not have general powers of arrest and search and seizure over other people. States differ as to whether probation and parole officers are granted the right to carry concealed firearms or other weapons.

In addition to their role as law enforcement officers, probation and parole officers also perform roles as social workers and community resource brokers. Probation and parole officers are expected to perform rehabilitation work. The mission of probation and parole is to successfully integrate the client back into the community. Success means keeping the client out of prison.

The responsibilities of the probation and parole officer strongly emphasize social work and rehabilitation skills as opposed to investigative and police skills. As social worker, the probation and parole officer works with his or her clients to achieve rehabilitation and develop skills, values, and abilities that will provide for successful reentry. Often officers are responsible for therapeutic individual counseling and group counseling to help clients address problems such as drug abuse, life skills, and social responsibility.

As a **community resource broker**, the probation and parole officer helps his or her clients secure the services and necessities that are required for successful reentry. For example, probation and parole officers often assist clients in finding employment, housing, medical care, and low-cost counseling programs. (Often participation in a counseling program such as for drug and alcohol abuse or anger management is a condition of probation or parole.)

One indicator of the preference for this skill mix is the fact that a federal probation and pretrial services officer must have a bachelor's degree and postgraduate experience in fields such as probation, pretrial services, parole, corrections, criminal investigations, and substance abuse or addiction counseling and treatment. Basic experience as a police officer, a correctional officer, or a security officer does not meet this requirement. Most states and federal probation and parole require a minimum of a baccalaureate degree to become a probation and parole officer. Many applicants have master's degrees. In addition to criminal justice, common academic degrees include psychology, social work, and sociology. Counseling is a major skill required of

Janine Wiedel Photolibrary/Alamy

probation and parole officers, so criminal justice majors must have the prerequisite counseling skills required for the position.

Measures of Success

The success of probation and parole officers is judged not by the number of clients they return to prison for violating the conditions of release, but by the number of clients who successfully complete probation and parole. To help the offenders succeed, in addition to providing counseling and guidance, the officers help them obtain drug treatment, vocational training, jobs, housing, medical care, rehabilitation services, and other referrals. Probation and parole officers protect the community from any harm that conditionally released offenders may do, and they deter and detect criminal activity on the part of released offenders. The officers also verify compliance with the terms of release, authenticate the clients' residency and employment, and confirm court-ordered payments of fines or restitution and court-ordered attendance at rehabilitation or treatment sessions. Because of their power to initiate revocation proceedings to return clients to prison, probation and parole officers are more influential compared to social workers in motivating clients to be rehabilitated and receive treatment.

▶ Conclusion: You Can Lead a Horse to Water, but …

It is said that you can lead a horse to water, but you can't make it drink. The criminal justice system invests substantially in keeping offenders out of jails and prisons. Many people think that the primary purpose of the criminal justice system is to detect law violators, convict them, and punish them.

Unlike the successful early reforms of Augustus, Maconochie, and Crofton, many of today's conditional release programs appear to be failing in both rehabilitating the offender and protecting the community.

However, through probation and parole, the criminal justice system also tries to rehabilitate offenders and return them to the community.

In the beginning, concerned citizens, alarmed by the awful conditions of jails and prisons and the complete lack of emphasis on rehabilitation, looked for ways to move offenders out of jails and prisons into treatment programs. Those volunteer initiatives became an integral part of the criminal justice system. Unfortunately, many offenders do not take advantage of the "act of grace" offered them. Unlike the successful early reforms of Augustus, Maconochie, and Crofton, many of today's conditional release programs appear to be failing in both rehabilitating the offender and protecting the community. John Augustus's work was not formally evaluated, but he concluded that "most of his probationers eventually led law abiding lives."[43] Less than 3% of the 1,450 inmates discharged from Maconochie's penal colony under the mark system were convicted of new crimes.[44] Between 1856 and 1861, 1,227 tickets of leave were issued by Crofton's Irish system and only 5.6% were revoked.[45] Those results are enviable in light of today's programs, wherein success rates of people on probation and parole are only 30% to 65% and have been as low as 14%.[46]

Although many are critical of probation and parole, and the federal and state criminal justice systems have been abandoning the use of parole, too many offenders are under correctional supervision to be able to house all of them in prison. Furthermore, despite the discouraging statistics, other data suggest that prison is not the most appropriate punishment for many offenders. As you will see in the next chapter, with regard to corrections, the criminal justice system is undergoing major changes to attempt to provide rehabilitation services to offenders, to provide corrections in the community, and to prevent crime.

New Territory for Arkansas

The prison population of Arkansas has doubled in the past 20 years. A 2010 study by the Pew Center on States projected that the prison population would continue to rise and cost Arkansas citizens $1.1 billion over the next decade. To avoid this financial catastrophe, Arkansas adopted new sentencing reform laws and changes in probation in August 2011.

The study found that more than 44% of Arkansas prison inmates released in 2004 went back to prison within three years, giving the state one of the highest recidivism rates in the nation.[47] The new sentencing reform laws and changes in probation are designed to reduce the recidivism rate and at the same time reduce the number of inmates sentenced to prison and the length of the sentence.

The new sentencing guidelines provide for lesser sentences for some nonviolent offenses, especially drug-related crimes.

The law also makes some nonviolent offenders eligible for parole earlier.[48] It reduces the penalty for technical violations of parole. Technical violators could be sentenced to serve up to seven consecutive days in jail rather than be sent back to prison to serve the remainder of their full sentence.[49] Also, the new law allows probationers and parolees to earn credits toward early release from supervision.

The new program is expected to cost about $9 million to implement. Still, the new approach is expected to save Arkansas $875 million over the next decade.

Initially, state prosecutors and law enforcement opposed the new law, fearing it would put violent criminals on the street.[50] As a result, it was necessary to revise the law to gain their endorsement. Governor Mike Beebe said of the new law, "This is new territory" for corrections in Arkansas.

This case raises several interesting questions. Among them are the following:

1. What precautions must be taken to balance the cost of imprisonment with the risk to public safety?

2. What could Arkansas do to reduce its 44% recidivism rate?

3. Like Arkansas, will other states be forced to adopt reforms in sentencing, probation, and parole? Explain.

ZUMA Wire Service/Alamy

LEARNING OUTCOMES 1 Explain why the criminal justice system provides for early release of inmates and the differences between diversion, probation, and parole and between mandatory release, good-time release, and pardon or commutation of sentence.

Academic studies have suggested that long-term incarceration may not be the best use of public resources for offenders. Hence, there has been a movement toward better use of probation and parole as a means to reduce correctional costs. In probation, the offender is diverted from prison time and given a suspended sentence. In parole, the offender is released before the maximum term of the sentence is completed. Another method for reducing a prisoner's sentence is through the application of good-time credit. Here, a prisoner's sentence is reduced for obeying institutional rules and participating in rehabilitation programs.

1. How does probation differ from parole?

2. Name different types of diversions a defendant could be given.

3. What is an executive pardon?

diversion An alternative to criminal trial and a prison sentence, such as drug court, boot camp, or a treatment program, offered to a defendant.

suspended sentence Another term for *probation*, a sentence based on the fact that convicted offenders must serve their full sentence if they violate their terms of release.

parole The release of an inmate before his or her maximum sentence has been served.

mandatory release The release of prisoners required by law after they have served the entire length of their maximum sentence.

good-time credit A strategy of crediting inmates with extra days served toward early release in an effort to encourage them to obey rules and participate in programs.

executive pardon An act by a governor or the president that forgives a prisoner and rescinds his or her sentence.

commutation of sentence A reduction in the severity or length of an inmate's sentence issued by a state governor or the president of the United States.

LEARNING OUTCOMES 2 Identify the origins of, reasons for, processes of, and pros and cons of probation.

Probation can be traced back to the efforts of John Augustus (1785–1859), a Boston shoemaker who used his personal finances to guarantee bail for defendants selected for diversion from jail. Today, probation is a common sentencing option for judges. A shortcoming with probation is the fear of future criminal activity by the offender and the lack of perceived punishment for the crime committed. However, by remaining in the community, the probationer avoids the negative effects of prison and maintains family relationships and employment—at a cost much lower than that of imprisonment.

1. What is another term for *probation*?

2. Describe how probationers are supervised by a probation officer.

3. Why is probation less of a burden on the taxpayer?

probation The conditional release of a convicted offender prior to his or her serving any prison time.

probation officer A state or federal professional employee who reports to the courts and supervises defendants released on probation.

technical violation Grounds for imprisonment of a probationer or parolee based on his or her violation of a condition of release.

LEARNING OUTCOMES 3 Identify the origins of, reasons for, processes of, and the pros and cons of parole.

The historical roots of parole can be traced to practices of the French, the English, and the Irish of releasing prisoners for good behavior and their word of honor to obey the law. In 1854, Sir Walter Crofton pioneered the conditional release of Irish inmates before they completed their sentences. Crofton's Irish system became the model for the American parole system. Parole serves to reduce prison overcrowding. In today's society, the public is strongly opposed to the use of parole. The public fears the release of parolees into the community because of the significant number of crimes they commit.

1. What was the mark system? Who developed it?

2. How does the general public typically view parole?

3. What is a parole board?

4. Describe the conditions of release that a federal parolee must follow.

parole d'honneur The practice of releasing a prisoner for good behavior based on his word of honor that he would obey the law upon release.

mark system An early form of parole invented by Alexander Maconochie in which prisoners demonstrated their rehabilitation by earning points for good behavior.

ticket of leave In the mark system, the unconditional release from prison purchased with marks earned for good behavior.

Irish system An early form of parole invented by Sir Walter Crofton based on the mark system in which prisoners were released conditionally on good behavior and were supervised in the community.

indeterminate sentence A sentence in which the defendant is sentenced to a prison term with a minimum and maximum number of years to serve.

parole board Individuals appointed to a body that meets in prisons to make decisions about granting parole release to inmates.

independent model The system in which decision making about parole is under the authority of an autonomous parole board.

consolidated model The system in which decision making about parole is a function of a state department of corrections.

U.S. Parole Commission (USPC) The agency responsible for parole decisions of federal and Washington, DC, inmates.

parole hearing A meeting with an inmate, his or her attorney, and others in which the parole board decides whether to grant, deny, or revoke parole.

standard conditions of release Federal and state guidelines with which parolees (and probationers) must comply to meet their conditions of release.

Morrissey v. Brewer The case that secured the right to notice and a revocation hearing for parolees.

LEARNING OUTCOMES 4

Summarize how people on probation and parole are supervised.

Probation and parole officers enforce compliance with the terms of release and oversee a client's lifestyle for potential signs of danger to the community. In addition to their role as law enforcement officers, probation and parole officers also perform as social workers and community resource brokers. The success rates of people on probation and parole have been very low. Many people are critical of probation and parole, but there are far too many offenders under correctional supervision for them all to be housed in prison.

1. Describe the role of a parole officer.

2. What type of assistance might a parole officer provide his or her client?

probation and parole officer A state or federal professional employee who reports to the courts and supervises defendants released from prison on parole.

compliance with the terms of release The enforcement role of probation and parole officers to verify that probationers and parolees fulfill the mandatory terms of their release.

community resource broker The role of a probation and parole officer in helping his or her clients secure the services and necessities that are required for successful reentry.

MyCJLab

Go to Chapter 11 in *MyCJLab* to test your mastery of chapter concepts, access your Study Plan, engage in interactive exercises, complete critical-thinking and research assignments, and view related online videos.

☑ **Review:** Complete the pretest in the Study Plan to confirm what you know and what you need to study further. Then complete the post-test to confirm your mastery of the concepts. Use the key term flash cards to review key terminology.

⚙ **Apply:** Complete the interactive simulation activity.

🔍 **Analyze:** Complete assignments as directed by your instructor.

📁 **Current Events:** Explore CJSearch for current topical videos, articles, and news pieces.

Additional Links

Go to the Federal Bureau of Investigation's national sex offender public website at **http://www.fbi.gov/scams-safety/registry/registry** to view the registry for the state in which you live.

Go to **http://www.appa-net.org** to view the website of the American Probation and Parole Association. The APPA is the voice for thousands of probation and parole practitioners, including line staff, supervisors, and administrators.

Go to **http://bjs.ojp.usdoj.gov/index.cfm?ty=tp&tid=151** to read statistics about probation as compiled by the Bureau of Justice Statistics.

Go to **http://vimeo.com/25191368** to listen to a Massachusetts parole board member discuss what she considers when making a parole decision.

Go to **http://www.uscourts.gov/federalcourts/ProbationPretrialServices.aspx** and learn about the U.S. Probation and Pretrial Services System and pretrial services functions in the U.S. district courts. Through its officers and other employees, the system works to make the criminal justice process effective and the public safe.

Go to **http://www.probation.saccounty.net/home/Content.aspx?TID=164** and learn more about the historic origins of probation and the County of Sacramento (California) Probation Department.

Go to **http://www.tdcj.state.tx.us/bpp/index.htm** to learn about state policies and guidelines for the Texas Board of Pardons and Paroles.

Corrections in the Community

"For a punishment to be just it should consist of only such gradations of intensity as suffice to deter men from committing crimes."

—Cesare Beccaria

1 Summarize the role of community corrections sanctions in corrections.

2 List the various community corrections sanctions and explain how they differ from traditional early-release programs.

3 Explain how community corrections programs promote successful reentry into the community.

4 Summarize the role of reentry programs for drug offenders.

12

INTRO REENTRY INTO SOCIETY

The criminal justice system consists mostly of government agencies and personnel. However, nonprofit community organizations play a significant role in helping offenders successfully reenter society after prison. While probation and parole services offer some assistance to offenders reentering society, it is nonprofit community organizations that provide essential services to ex-offenders, such as counseling, housing, and employment.

One of the earliest organizations that provided reintegration assistance to released prisoners was the John Howard Association (JHA), named after the English prison reformer John Howard (1726–1790). The JHA was created in 1867 by a church group focused on providing spiritual care to prisoners in a Toronto, Canada, prison.

Today, one of the necessities of successful reintegration is employment. Prisoners often have a poor or no employment record, lack basic skills, and do not know how to interview for jobs; in addition, employers may be reluctant to hire ex-cons. Prisons do little, if anything, to prepare inmates to readjust to living within the law after they have been released. Prisoners reentering society require basic necessities such as counseling, housing, and employment, and they are often disadvantaged in obtaining these due to the stigma of being an ex-offender. This is where nonprofit organizations step in to provide these services.

One nonprofit organization that helps ex-offenders reintegrate into the community is Safer. Safer has operated in the Chicago area for nearly 40 years and has helped thousands of ex-offenders obtain employment.[1]

Safer provides job-preparedness classes and supportive services such as housing and drug treatment. Safer also provides a vetting process so that its clients are more acceptable to employers. The overall recidivism rate in Illinois is 51%. The rate for those who come to Safer is 22%. For those who keep a job for a year, it is as low as 8%.[2]

> **DISCUSS** Rather than depending on community organizations, should the government put more emphasis and money on reentry services for offenders? Explain.

▶ *Early Release and Financial Crisis*

This chapter examines the alternatives to traditional early-release programs. These alternative programs attempt to balance the need for cost containment with public safety to achieve the successful reentry of prisoners back into society.

Often early release is motivated by the financial crisis that states are experiencing. States find that they cannot support the nearly 40-year record-high incarceration rate and seek alternatives. The growth in the prison population is illustrated by Michelle Alexander, author of *The New Jim Crow: Mass Incarceration in an Age of Colorblindness*. Alexander points out that to return to incarceration rates of the 1970s, four out of five inmates would have to be released from prison.

To deal with the crisis, states turned to traditional early-release programs such as probation and parole, but these early-release programs were often seen as posing a serious risk to public safety. For example, in 2010, Illinois suspended an early-release program when the public became concerned that those released were a threat to public safety. Of the 1,754 inmates who were released early, 65% were returned to prison within three months. The program was suspended, and Illinois had to find $175 million per year to house the inmates who would have been released under the program.

Why Intermediate Sentences?

The criminal justice system may spend millions to convict a defendant and $25,000 or more per year to incarcerate a prisoner, but it spends little to provide for reentry despite the fact that 95% of inmates will be released back into the community. Reentry programs are often the first to be cut in a budget crisis. For example, in 2007, Texas began focusing on developing alternatives to prison and reentry services. As a result, in 2011, there were 7,000 fewer inmates in Texas prisons than the number that had been projected in 2007. In 2010, the number of inmates actually decreased by 1,250 from 2009.

However, when the state suffered an estimated $15 to $27 billion budget shortfall, its legislators proposed cutting $162 million from rehabilitation and treatment programs. Supporters of reentry programs urged legislators to find other cuts because those proposed would have undone the progress made in reducing recidivism. If that happened, Texas could have found itself back where it was in 2007, looking at the need to build new prisons rather than funding reentry and treatment programs.

Why do prisoners return to prison at such a high rate? One reason is that many prisoners were not successful citizens in society to begin with. Once incarcerated, prison did little to improve their lot, and many argue that prison only makes it more difficult for these people to live successful lives within

Michelle Alexander says that to return to incarceration rates of the 1970s, four out of five inmates would have to be released from prison.

2/3

The number of adults (two out of three) that are released from prisons and jails that will be rearrested within three years.

the law. For example, three out of four people released from prison and jail have a substance abuse problem, but only 10% in state prisons and 3% in local jails receive formal treatment prior to release. About 41% of inmates in the nation's state and federal prisons and local jails have not completed high school or its equivalent, compared to 18% of the general population.[3] Nearly half of those in jail earned less than $600 per month just prior to incarceration. More than one out of three jail inmates have some physical or mental disability. Ten thousand parolees will be homeless when they are released.[4] It comes as little surprise that two out of three adults released from prisons and jails will be rearrested within three years. Incarceration, probation, and parole are expensive and fail to stop a large number of ex-prisoners from returning to prison because the criminal justice system traditionally has not prepared inmates to return to society.

Traditional incarceration, probation, and parole are failing to stem the tide of prisoners returning to prison after their release. Many people are calling for new strategies and programs in offender rehabilitation. Despite long prison terms, prison time alone does not change behavior. Experts are recognizing that community-based organizations, not prisons, have the best chance of rehabilitating prisoners.[5] The "get tough on crime" philosophy of the 1980s has proven both costly and ineffective in achieving long-term rehabilitation. Furthermore, given that nearly all of the people sentenced to prison return to the community, incarceration without rehabilitation does not guarantee community safety.

As a result, the criminal justice system is turning to new sanctions for offenders. These sanctions are known as intermediate sanctions—sanctions somewhere between prison and traditional probation and parole. These sanctions are carried out in the community rather than in prison. These new sanctions create a challenge: to rehabilitate the offender while ensuring community safety.

Huge Expense and Number of Prisoners

The United States is transforming itself into a nation of ex-convicts. In 2010, more than 7 million people were on probation, in jail or prison, or on parole—3.2% of all U.S. adult residents, or 1 in every 32 adults.[6] The United States imprisons people at 14 times the rate of Japan, 8 times the rate of France, and 6 times the rate of Canada. Thirteen million people, or about 7% of the U.S. adult population, have been convicted of a felony and spent

Prisons and jails have become a mammoth industry with powerful constituencies that favor the status quo.

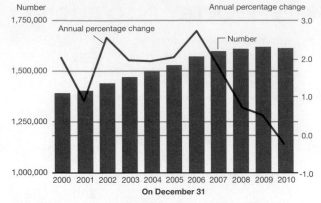

FIGURE 12-1 Adult Correctional Populations, 2000–2010
For many states, corrections is the fastest-growing budget item. In 2009, for the first time in nearly 40 years, the growth of the correctional population declined as indicated by the bars and scale on the left side of the graph. The red line indicates the annual percentage change of prisoners. There was virtually no change in the prison population from 2009 to 2010. It is not known if this is the start of a downward trend or just a brief pause before the prison population begins to rise again.
Source: Paul Guerino, Paige M. Harrison, and William J. Sabol, *Prisoners in 2010* (Washington, DC: Bureau of Justice Statistics, 2011), p. 1

some time in prison. That number is more than the population of Sweden, Bolivia, Senegal, Greece, or Somalia.[7]

The United States has the largest, most expensive, and fastest-growing prison system in the world. (See Figure 12–1.) The United States spends more than $60 billion per year for corrections, compared to just $9 billion a year two decades ago. Corrections is the second fastest–growing expense in state budgets after Medicaid.[8] To keep up with the demand for new bed space, the federal government and states have had to build a record number of prisons in the last decade. As a result, prisons and jails have become a mammoth industry with powerful constituencies that favor the status quo. Many rural communities and politicians who represent these communities depend on prisons for their economic viability.[9] As a result, changes in sentencing and prison policy are not a simple matter. However, states cannot keep pumping more and more money into prisons.

Record Numbers of Released Prisoners

Despite the record number of people sentenced to prison, a record number are being released. (See Figure 12–2.) This creates a double crisis: prisons that are overcrowded and prisoners who are returning to the community with unmet needs. Nationwide at least 95% of all state prisoners will be released from prison. This financial burden has caused 25 states to ease mandatory and long-term sentencing policies and to reinstate early-release and treatment programs for drug offenders; this is about 25% of the nation's prisoners.[10] At the same time, while

1/32

The number of adults (1 out of 32) that are on probation, on parole, or in jail or prison.

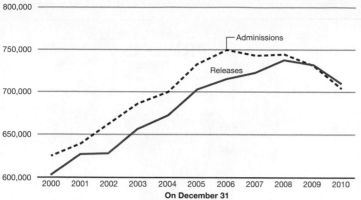

FIGURE 12–2 **Admissions and Releases**
The total prison population is determined by the number of new prisoners admitted and the number of incarcerated prisoners released. Up until 2009, the number of new admissions exceeded the number released; so the prison population grew. Since 2009, the number of new admissions has declined, but the number of releases also has declined. Releases have declined due to longer sentences and mandatory sentencing laws. The decline in prisoner releases keeps the total prison population higher than if the number of releases had continued to increase.
Source: Paul Guerino, Paige M. Harrison, and William J. Sabol, *Prisoners in 2010* (Washington, DC: Bureau of Justice Statistics, 2011), p. 5.

concerned about increased costs of corrections, some people are concerned about the economic impact of declining prison populations. Those communities that have come to depend on the revenues generated by the prison industry will suffer economic distress.

In effect, the attempt to make communities safe and allow them to prosper from the prison industry is having the opposite effect. Most offenders sentenced to prison return to the community within two years. In California in any given year, about 40% of its prisoners are released back into the community. Tougher and longer sentencing strategies only result in more offenders being released back into the community because those policies increase the total prison population, of which 95% are eventually released.[11] Nationwide nearly 640,000 inmates arrive yearly on the doorsteps of the community,[12] compared to fewer than 170,000 released offenders in 1980.[13]

Incarceration Fails to Prepare Offenders for Reentry

Unsuccessful Reentry into Communities

Unfortunately, most released offenders do not make a successful reentry back into the community. Nationwide only 48% of parolees and 35% of probationers successfully complete the conditions of their release.[14] In California, the failure rate of

Because the vast majority of offenders come from economically disadvantaged, culturally isolated inner-city neighborhoods, they return there upon release.

58% The percentage of California paroled felons who reoffend within 36 months.

paroled inmates is so high that "40% of all admissions to state prisons are parole violators."[15] In 1978, parole violators accounted for only 8% of the total felons admitted to prison in California.[16] Two major longitudinal studies of recidivism indicate that in the United States, about 43% to 45% of offenders are reincarcerated within three years.[17]

Most states require offenders to be returned to the counties in which they lived before entering prison. According to Joan Petersilia, a leading researcher in corrections, "Since the vast majority of offenders come from economically disadvantaged, culturally isolated, inner-city neighborhoods, they return there upon release."[18] Once returned to their old neighborhoods, most offenders quickly fall into the lifestyle that led to their arrest. Most will last only six months on the street before they are rearrested. Two-thirds of all parolees are rearrested within three years.[18]

Lack of Support Services

Furthermore, there is an inverse relationship between time in prison and successful reentry. For example, offenders who served five years or more in federal prison were more likely to return to federal prison (25%) than those who served terms of less than five years (15%).[20] Upon their release from prison, most inmates are not prepared to successfully reenter the community. Among state prisoners expected to be released, 84% report being involved in drugs or alcohol at the time of the offense that led to their incarceration. Nearly 25% were alcohol-dependent. Twenty-one percent reported that they had committed the offense to obtain money for drugs. Fourteen percent were classified as having mental illness upon their release. Most will have nowhere to go because they have no family or friends to support them, and 12% reported being homeless at the time of their arrest. Those communities to which offenders are returned are not prepared to provide the services these people need. For example, in Connecticut, almost half of the prison and jail population is from just a handful of neighborhoods in five cities that have the most concentrated levels of poverty and nonwhite populations in the state.[21] In Chicago, only 24% of identified organizations that provide services to reentering individuals were located in any of the six communities to which the highest numbers of people returned from prison in 2001. No services were located in two of those six neighborhoods.[22] California had 200 shelter beds for more than 10,000 homeless parolees. A 2009 study released by the Pew Center on the States documented that 1 in 25 adults in Detroit is under correctional control. Whereas Detroit is home to 44% of the county's adults, it accounts for over 75% of the county's correctional population.[23]

Ineffectiveness of Parole

Offenders released under traditional parole find that the shortage of probation and parole officers means that they infrequently see their supervising officer. Many parolees see their parole officer for less than two 15-minute face-to-face

GLOSSARY

community-based corrections Prevention and treatment programs designed to promote the successful transition of offenders from prison to the community.

NIMBY "Not in my backyard"—opposition to community corrections programs in one's neighborhood.

contacts per month.[24] They quickly discover that "parole is more a legal status than a systematic process of reintegrating returning prisoners."[25] There is little oversight of their activities and little assistance to help them successfully reenter the community. An important fact is that "the majority of inmates leave prison with no savings, no immediate entitlement to unemployment benefits, and few job prospects. One year after release as many as 60 percent of former inmates are not employed in the legitimate labor market."[26]

Problems for the Community

The failure of offenders to be reintegrated into the community poses a serious problem for the criminal justice system. As these unprecedented numbers of offenders go home, their failure results in other social problems, such as increases in child abuse, family violence, the spread of infectious diseases, homelessness, and community disorganization.[27]

Also, incarceration of adults results in problems for children. Among those born in 1990, 1 in 4 African-American children, compared to 1 in 25 white children, had a father in prison by the time they were 14.[28] Adult imprisonment has economic, sociological, and psychological impacts on children that often result in behavioral and psychological problems. Without alternatives to incarceration that separates parents from children, the criminal justice system fosters a new generation of potential offenders. The criminal justice system and society in general do not appear to have prepared for this problem. As Petersilia states, "Virtually no systematic, comprehensive attention has been paid by policymakers to dealing with people after release."[29] The rate of failure suggests that the criminal justice system lacks the organizational capacity to manage the integration of released offenders.[30]

Offenders who routinely enter, leave, and reenter prison are said to be "serving a life sentence on the installment plan." This pattern of repeated incarceration and release is costly in terms of dollars to the taxpayers and harm to the community.

Thus, as measured by recidivism, traditional incarceration, probation, and parole programs have not been successful. In light of serious threats to community safety, new community-based correctional programs and innovative sanctions are being developed and implemented to promote effective crime prevention, treatment, and offender reentry into the community.

1/4
The number of African-American children (one out of four) that had a father in jail by the time they were 14.

Based on past trends, criminal justice experts predict that two out of every five inmates released this year will be reincarcerated within three years. Offenders who routinely enter, leave, and reenter prison are said to be "serving a life sentence on the installment plan." This pattern of repeated incarceration and release is costly in terms of dollars to the taxpayers and harm to the community.

Concern for Community Safety

Community-based corrections are sanctions that are alternatives to incarceration in jail or prison, such as boot camp, house arrest, community service, electronic monitoring, and supervision in the community after a sentence of incarceration has been served (for example, furloughs, work releases, and halfway houses). Citizen opposition to locating community-based programs in their neighborhoods is one of the primary obstacles to community-based corrections. Few politicians are willing to risk the wrath of their constituents who are opposed to locating community-based treatment and prevention programs near their homes. Community opposition to locating prisons and correctional facilities in their neighborhood is so strong and common that there is a name for it—**NIMBY**, or "not in my back yard."

Sometimes public fear is such that a single incident of harm to the community can close down an entire program. The dilemma is that public demand for imprisonment is strong, but those who are imprisoned are returned in a condition not much improved from the one that led to their imprisonment.[31]

Not only are communities opposed to community-based facilities being located in their neighborhoods, but crime victims and the police also are opposed to reentry of individual offenders back into the community. Crime victims fear contact with the offender and can be resentful of memories triggered by the offender's presence in the community. Police fear that offenders released back into the community will contribute to the crime problem.

► Intermediate Sanctions and Community Corrections

Community-based **intermediate sanctions** are correctional punishments other than imprisonment that are designed to reduce the prison population, promote the successful reentry of the offender into the community, and protect the community.

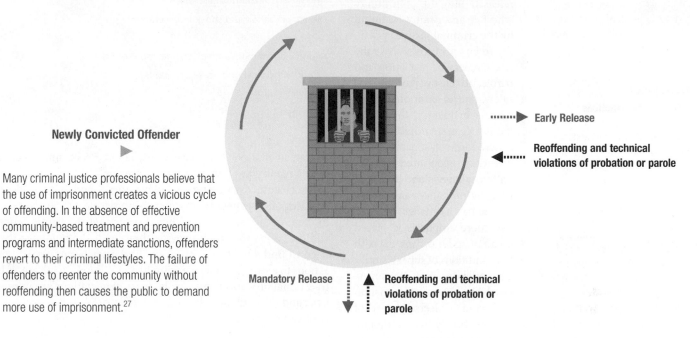

Cycle of Offending

Newly Convicted Offender ▶

Many criminal justice professionals believe that the use of imprisonment creates a vicious cycle of offending. In the absence of effective community-based treatment and prevention programs and intermediate sanctions, offenders revert to their criminal lifestyles. The failure of offenders to reenter the community without reoffending then causes the public to demand more use of imprisonment.[27]

Early Release

Reoffending and technical violations of probation or parole

Mandatory Release

Reoffending and technical violations of probation or parole

Community-based treatment and prevention programs were virtually unknown before the late 1960s. One of the pioneers of community-based programs was the Vera Institute of Justice in New York,[32] which, in the 1980s, spearheaded the use of community-based programs to promote the successful transition of offenders from prison to society. These programs were described as intermediate punishments and later as intermediate sanctions.[33]

Many early programs addressed pressing concerns of prison overcrowding and skyrocketing costs and were not built on research and experimentation related to criminological or correctional theory. Instead, early programs grew out of the search for practical and expedient solutions to pressing problems.[34] Thus, many of the programs have not lived up to expectations. Some have even resulted in substantial harm to the community. According to subsequent research, rehabilitation programs and new forms of supervision in the community have been faulted for not reducing recidivism or providing adequate safeguards for community protection.[35]

Returning prisoners who cannot rejoin the community as law-abiding citizens can have a detrimental impact on the community's quality of life. The impact of this influence is made greater by the fact that prisoners tend to return to certain neighborhoods in a city or state rather than being distributed throughout the state. For example, 11% of the city blocks in Brooklyn, New York, are home to 50% of the people in that borough who are on parole.[36] Also, approximately 1,800 out of 7,400 adult prisoners released each year in Kansas return to a handful of neighborhoods in Wichita.[37] The failures of the returning prisoners influence what are known as the "tipping points," beyond which communities can no longer favorably influence residents' behavior.[38] Sociologist Elijah Anderson argues that as more street-smart young offenders are released back into the community, they exert a strong influence on community disorganization, general

demoralization, and higher unemployment. They can weaken the influence of family values and legitimate role models.[39] As the number of offenders in the community increases, their negative influence can reach the point where the community is powerless to influence them in stable, positive ways. The structure of the community changes, disorder and incivilities increase, out-migration follows as desirable residents leave, and crime and violence increase.[40] This flood of returning offenders also increases the influence of gang activity in the community.[41]

The intermediate sanctions most often used are intensive probation supervision, split sentencing, shock probation, boot camps, and home confinement with electronic monitoring.

Intensive Probation Supervision (IPS)

The three roles of the probation and parole officer, discussed in Chapter 11, include law enforcement officer, caseworker, and community resource broker. However, a factor contributing to the offender's failure is a lack of clarity or agreement about the purpose of probation and parole.[42] There also is a certain amount of conflict among the three roles. The probation and parole officer is faced with conflicting goals and objectives as he or she tries to enforce obedience to the conditions of supervised release and at the same time act as counselor and encourager. Often the role mix favors caseworker and community resource broker; as a result, critics have charged that probation and parole officers have not been very good at ensuring that their clients fulfill the conditions of treatment.[43] Sometimes probationers or parolees simply abscond, and probation and parole officers are unable to locate them. For example, in 2009, parole agents in California lost track of about one-fifth of the parolees they were assigned.[44] Nationwide in 2010, 1% of probationers and 9% of parolees absconded.[45] This amounts

Crime victims and the police are opposed to individual offenders reentering the community.

LEARNING OUTCOMES 2 List the various community corrections sanctions and explain how they differ from traditional early-release programs.

GLOSSARY

intermediate sanctions Punishments that restrict offenders' freedom without imprisoning them and/or that consist of community-based prevention and treatment programs to promote the successful transition of offenders from prison to the community.

intensive probation supervision (IPS) Probation supervised by probation and parole officers with smaller caseloads, placing a greater emphasis on compliance with the conditions of supervision.

split sentencing An intermediate sanction where, after a brief period of imprisonment, the judge brings the offender back to court and offers the option of probation.

shock probation A sentence for a first-time nonviolent offender who was not expecting a sentence, intended to impress on the offender the possible consequences of his or her behavior by being exposed to a brief period of imprisonment before probation.

shock incarceration Programs (boot camps) that adapt military-style physical fitness and discipline training to the correctional environment.

boot camps Programs modeled after military-style entry-level training programs for youthful nonviolent offenders.

home confinement A court-imposed sentence requiring offenders to remain confined in their own residence.

electronic monitoring An approach in home confinement programs that ensures compliance through electronic means.

to 40,555 probationers and 75,660 parolees, respectively, released into the community who flee and cannot be found by the criminal justice system.

In an effort to improve the effectiveness of probation and parole, to ensure community safety, and to promote greater success in reentry, the criminal justice system has adopted a new form of supervision of offenders called **intensive probation supervision (IPS)**. In IPS, the probation and parole officer has a smaller caseload and more emphasis is placed on an offender complying with the conditions of supervision.[46] The offender may be supervised by a team of probation and parole officers. Instead of meeting briefly twice a month, the offender may be required to report daily and to submit to on-site visits by the probation and parole officer. IPS can be used with either probationers or parolees. Its use dates back to the early 1950s when California's probation and parole programs began experimenting with different-size probation caseloads.[47] Today, IPS programs have been implemented in every state as well as in the federal system.

Upon reflection, some probation and parole administrators admit that traditional programs may have been too lenient in enforcing the conditions of release.[48] Probation and parole officers often believed, incorrectly, that released offenders would assume responsibility for compliance with the conditions of release. Leniency also stemmed from impossible caseloads and insufficient funding. Despite increases in spending for corrections, few dollars have gone to rehabilitation or probation and parole. Most of the new dollars have gone primarily to building new prisons, maintaining facilities, and paying for the correctional staff to

The most commonly used community corrections programs:
Intensive probation supervision programs
Shock probation and shock incarceration
Boot camps
Home confinement with electronic monitoring
Work and education release programs
Halfway houses
Day reporting centers

operate institutions.[49] However, only about 5% of inmates complete a reentry program prior to release.[50]

Accustomed to being told what to do and how to do it, parolees often expect their supervising parole officers to relate to them in the same way.[51] They assume that the parole officer will find a job for them; provide them with the guidance they need to find a treatment program; and, in general, direct their actions to ensure compliance with their conditions of release.[52] In traditional probation and parole, these expectations are unrealistic, and released offenders often need more direct supervision than can be given.

Strict Supervision

IPS was designed to provide that direct supervision. As a result, it is more punitive and controlling than regular probation and is more intrusive in the offenders' lives. Probation and parole officers may awaken them with phone calls during the night to verify that they are at home. Supervisors may visit offenders at work sites and at home and routinely conduct searches for evidence that they are not in compliance with the conditions of release. Officers search for drugs, child pornography, excessive alcohol, firearms, or expensive possessions that would not be consistent with the offenders' legitimate income.

In 1982, Georgia implemented one of the earliest IPS programs. In that program, probation and parole officers acted more like law enforcement officers than caseworkers.[53] Offenders were held to strict accountability for compliance with the conditions of probation and parole.

New Jersey has one of the most successful and prominent IPS programs, which is designed to handle about 1,200 offenders at a time. The program provides strict supervision and requires such strict compliance with the terms of release that more than 25% of participants have been expelled from the program for violations.[54] However, of offenders who successfully completed the program and have been in the community for nine years, fewer than 17% have committed new, indictable offenses, compared to a nationwide average of about 52%.[55]

Many other communities have adopted similar programs that have achieved goals of accountability, public safety, and cost savings.[56] Still, some probation and parole officers complain that IPS programs substantially change the relationship they have with their clients. Probation and parole officers

Despite increases in spending for corrections, few dollars have gone to rehabilitation or probation and parole.

who view their primary role as counselor and facilitator find that the role of law enforcement officer often runs counter to many of the characteristics that promote effective counseling. In addition, the effective implementation of IPS requires new working conditions and hours, including nights and weekends. As a result, not all probation and parole officers are comfortable with the call for more IPS programs.

Split Sentencing and Shock Probation

When first-time nonviolent offenders, especially youthful offenders, are convicted of a crime, they assume that they will receive a suspended sentence. Most of the time, they are correct in this assumption. As a result, these offenders often view their first conviction as a minor inconvenience, and their encounter

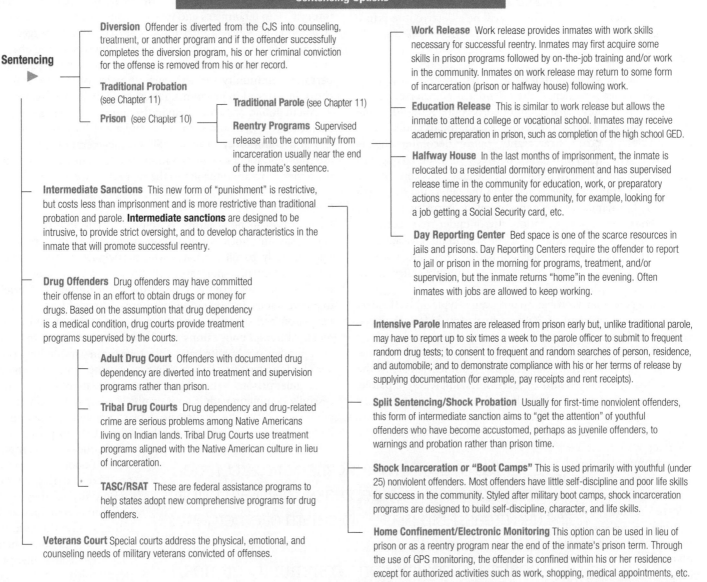

Sentencing Options

Sentencing ▶

Diversion Offender is diverted from the CJS into counseling, treatment, or another program and if the offender successfully completes the diversion program, his or her criminal conviction for the offense is removed from his or her record.

Traditional Probation (see Chapter 11)

Prison (see Chapter 10)

Traditional Parole (see Chapter 11)

Reentry Programs Supervised release into the community from incarceration usually near the end of the inmate's sentence.

Intermediate Sanctions This new form of "punishment" is restrictive, but costs less than imprisonment and is more restrictive than traditional probation and parole. **Intermediate sanctions** are designed to be intrusive, to provide strict oversight, and to develop characteristics in the inmate that will promote successful reentry.

Drug Offenders Drug offenders may have committed their offense in an effort to obtain drugs or money for drugs. Based on the assumption that drug dependency is a medical condition, drug courts provide treatment programs supervised by the courts.

Adult Drug Court Offenders with documented drug dependency are diverted into treatment and supervision programs rather than prison.

Tribal Drug Courts Drug dependency and drug-related crime are serious problems among Native Americans living on Indian lands. Tribal Drug Courts use treatment programs aligned with the Native American culture in lieu of incarceration.

TASC/RSAT These are federal assistance programs to help states adopt new comprehensive programs for drug offenders.

Veterans Court Special courts address the physical, emotional, and counseling needs of military veterans convicted of offenses.

Work Release Work release provides inmates with work skills necessary for successful reentry. Inmates may first acquire some skills in prison programs followed by on-the-job training and/or work in the community. Inmates on work release may return to some form of incarceration (prison or halfway house) following work.

Education Release This is similar to work release but allows the inmate to attend a college or vocational school. Inmates may receive academic preparation in prison, such as completion of the high school GED.

Halfway House In the last months of imprisonment, the inmate is relocated to a residential dormitory environment and has supervised release time in the community for education, work, or preparatory actions necessary to enter the community, for example, looking for a job getting a Social Security card, etc.

Day Reporting Center Bed space is one of the scarce resources in jails and prisons. Day Reporting Centers require the offender to report to jail or prison in the morning for programs, treatment, and/or supervision, but the inmate returns "home" in the evening. Often inmates with jobs are allowed to keep working.

Intensive Parole Inmates are released from prison early but, unlike traditional parole, may have to report up to six times a week to the parole officer to submit to frequent random drug tests; to consent to frequent and random searches of person, residence, and automobile; and to demonstrate compliance with his or her terms of release by supplying documentation (for example, pay receipts and rent receipts).

Split Sentencing/Shock Probation Usually for first-time nonviolent offenders, this form of intermediate sanction aims to "get the attention" of youthful offenders who have become accustomed, perhaps as juvenile offenders, to warnings and probation rather than prison time.

Shock Incarceration or "Boot Camps" This is used primarily with youthful (under 25) nonviolent offenders. Most offenders have little self-discipline and poor life skills for success in the community. Styled after military boot camps, shock incarceration programs are designed to build self-discipline, character, and life skills.

Home Confinement/Electronic Monitoring This option can be used in lieu of prison or as a reentry program near the end of the inmate's prison term. Through the use of GPS monitoring, the offender is confined within his or her residence except for authorized activities such as work, shopping, medical appointments, etc.

with the criminal justice system does little to deter them from further criminal activities.

What can a judge do when faced with a first-time offender who is wise to the ways of the system and is anticipating a suspended sentence? To deal with such an offender, judges have adopted the use of split sentencing and shock probation. Both sentences are similar in their goal of impressing on offenders the possible consequences of their behavior by exposing them to a brief period of imprisonment before probation.

Split Sentencing

In **split sentencing**, after sentencing and a brief period of imprisonment (usually in a jail for as few as 30 days rather than in a long-term confinement facility), the offender is brought back to court. At that time, the judge offers the option of probation. In split sentencing, the offender does not have to apply for parole, have a parole hearing, or present a parole plan to obtain his or her release from prison. Split sentencing is effective in two ways. First, the offender was not expecting any prison sentence. Thus, even a brief period of imprisonment comes as a shock. Second, the sentence exposes the offender to the realities of institutional confinement, but the offender is removed before he or she has time to adjust to institutionalization. The belief is that this "shock" will be a deterrent to future criminal behavior.

Shock Probation

The sentence of **shock probation** is similar to split sentencing, except that after sentencing, the offender is transferred to the custody of the state's department of corrections rather than the local jail and must apply for parole. Again, the offender serves only a brief period of incarceration before becoming eligible for parole. The major difference between split sentencing and shock probation is that in the former, the judge has control over the release of the offender, whereas in the latter, the offender's fate is in the hands of the department of corrections or the parole board. In shock probation, the offender must convince the paroling authorities that he or she should be released from prison. Technically, this is a form of parole because of the very brief period of incarceration, but it is commonly called shock probation rather than shock parole.

New Jersey's shock probation program is typical.[57] Offenders must serve a minimum of 30 days in prison before they can apply for release. They must submit a personal plan describing what they will do upon release. This plan has many of the same requirements as a parole plan. It must detail the problems the inmate has that may jeopardize successful completion of parole, such as alcohol or drug abuse, lack of anger management, or lack of legitimate employment. The plan must detail the community resources the offender can use to help with these problems. The offender also must have a community sponsor and is required to reside with the sponsor upon release. If the paroling authority is satisfied with the offender's personal plan, the offender will be granted a 90-day trial

release period. If the offender is successful in complying with the conditions of the release plan during this period, he or she will be granted conditional early release (or shock probation).[58]

Shock Incarceration: Boot Camps

Another form of **shock incarceration** programs is commonly called "boot camps" because they are modeled after military-style entry-level training programs. **Boot camps** are designed to provide alternative sentencing for young nonviolent offenders. Offenders who participate in boot camps are offered a reduced sentence (usually by about one-third) followed by parole if they successfully complete the program.[59] If they do not complete the program, they are returned to the regular prison population. Although Ohio passed the first shock incarceration law in 1965, the practice did not become common until after 1980.[60] The first shock incarceration programs of nationwide significance began operating in 1983 in Oklahoma and Georgia.[61]

Shock incarceration programs adapt military-style physical fitness and discipline training to the correctional environment, as in basic training in military boot camps. Inmates participate in drill and ceremony, physical training, work (usually hard manual labor), and education. Inmates are organized into platoons of 50 to 60 inmates and may be required to wear military-style clothing. Correctional leaders are called drill sergeants, and inmates are expected to demonstrate unquestioning obedience to drill sergeants' orders. Inmates in boot camps frequently perform community service work. Inmates of the New York shock incarceration programs, for example, help cut firebreaks, maintain public-use areas, help in the aftermath of emergencies such as forest fires and tornadoes, and assist local municipalities and community groups.[62] Shock incarceration programs are rigorous, and a substantial number of inmates do not complete them and are returned to the regular prison population.[63]

Effectiveness of Boot Camps

Participation in boot camps is voluntary. The inducement to participate in shock incarceration programs is the opportunity for early parole. Inmates who participate in boot camps serve substantially shorter prison time. A typical boot camp may last only six months. One of the main purposes of brief, intensive shock incarceration programs is to reduce the need for prison bed space by permitting shorter terms of imprisonment. Although boot camps may be more expensive to operate on a per day, per inmate basis, they save money in the long run because inmates serve less time in a boot camp than they would in a regular prison.[64] The return-to-prison rate for offenders successfully completing adult boot camps is comparable to that of parolees who did not participate in or complete the program.[65] Supporters of the program argue that if the return-to-prison rate for offenders is comparable, if boot camps pose no increased risk to the community, if they cost less than prison does, and if they reduce the need to build more prisons, then they are effective alternatives to prison.[66]

Inmates of the New York shock incarceration programs help cut firebreaks, maintain public-use areas, help in the aftermath of emergencies such as forest fires and tornadoes, and assist local municipalities and community groups.

In shock incarceration, the inmate is released to the community well before the normal parole date. The underlying premise is that boot camps promote public safety by building character, instilling responsibility, and promoting a positive self-image so that nonviolent offenders can return to society as law-abiding citizens.[67] There is little direct evidence to support this claim, but boot camps remain popular with the public because they are perceived as being tough on crime.[68] Many state departments of corrections recognize the lack of research underlying the use of boot camps and describe their programs as "experiments."[69]

Home Confinement and Electronic Monitoring

Home Confinement

Home confinement is a sentence imposed by the court in which offenders are legally ordered to remain in their own residence.[70] Similar to parents telling their teenager that he or she is grounded as punishment for some misdeed, home confinement severely restricts the offender's mobility. Schedules are worked out that allow the offender to leave home for work, medical appointments and services, court-ordered treatment or community service, grocery shopping, and other necessary responsibilities. Offenders cannot leave home for entertainment, for visits to friends or family, for vacations, or for any other purpose not explicitly authorized by the court. Rehabilitation was not one of the goals of early home confinement programs. Early home confinement programs were an intermediate sanction or punishment adopted primarily to reduce prison populations, reduce costs, and increase control of offenders in the community.[71]

The sentence of home confinement is a kind of probation or suspended sentence that more greatly restricts the freedom of the offender in the community. Offenders must live in their own home or in that of a sponsor (usually a relative) and must pay all of their housing costs. Thus, a prerequisite for home confinement is to have a place to live and a job or other financial resources for self-support.

> The breakthrough in home confinement programs came with the use of electronic monitoring to ensure the offender's compliance.

A difficulty of early home confinement programs was ensuring that the offender abided by the restrictions of his or her release and did not leave the home. Probation officers used a combination of phone calls and random home visits or stakeouts to verify that the offender was at home. These practices were labor-intensive, however, and ineffective due to the shortage of probation officers to conduct a sufficient number of random home visits to ensure compliance.

Electronic Monitoring

The breakthrough in home confinement programs came with the use of electronic monitoring to ensure the offender's compliance. **Electronic monitoring** uses signaling technology to achieve a greater degree of certainty in compliance and at a fraction of the cost of using probation officers for this purpose. The first formal electronic monitoring program was implemented in 1983 in Albuquerque, New Mexico, when a district court judge, Jack Love, reputedly inspired by a Spiderman comic strip, placed a probation violator on electronic monitoring.[72]

Since 1983, the use of electronic monitoring has expanded rapidly. It has been adopted in all 50 states by local, state, and federal correctional agencies.[73] The Florida Community Control Program has one of the most ambitious home confinement and electronic monitoring programs in the United States.[74] Spurred in part by an explosive rise in the need for prison bed space, Florida's Correctional Reform Act of 1983 authorized the use of electronically monitored house arrest as a means to reduce the prison population.

Technological Advances in Electronic Monitoring

The past two decades have seen significant changes in the technology for monitoring offenders sentenced to home confinement.[75] Early systems were passive-programmed contact systems that used a computer program to make random calls to the offender at times when he or she was supposed to be home.

The next generation of electronic monitoring systems used continuous signaling systems. The advantage of this system is that it monitors the offender's movements all of the time. The older passive-programmed contact systems had loopholes in that offenders willing to take the risk could slip out of the house as long as they did not miss one of the programmed contacts.

With both the passive-programmed and continuous signaling reporting devices, the probation officer needs to confirm that an actual violation has occurred. When the offender fails to answer the telephone or when there is a break in the continuous signal when the offender is supposed to be home, a probation officer must contact the offender to confirm the violation.

The third generation of electronic monitoring devices began to emerge in 1997. These devices incorporated the advantages of global positioning system (GPS) technology, involving the use of satellites, not only to monitor the offender at home, but also to track every movement of the offender in real time.[76] This technology allows the system to confirm that the offender is at home when he or she is supposed to be and that he or she is not violating restraining orders, visiting places where drugs are known to be sold or used, and frequenting off-limits places such as schools and playgrounds. Another advancement in electronic monitoring is the ability to monitor all communications by the offender via the Internet.[77] This ability is especially useful for monitoring sex offenders to ensure that they do not use the Internet to contact and entice potential victims.

Evaluation and Critique of Electronic Monitoring

Counting the number of people on electronic monitoring as potential prison inmates, compared to the costs of incarceration, home confinement and electronic monitoring have saved the states money. Significant start-up costs are required for the equipment purchases needed to use home confinement and electronic monitoring, but even after factoring in these costs, most jurisdictions report that the program saves money over prison confinement.[79] Critics claim that this is a false savings because offenders selected for release subject to home confinement and electronic monitoring probably would have been given a suspended sentence.[80] Another criticism is that the system discriminates against the homeless and the unemployed. These offenders usually are excluded from home confinement programs because they have no place to live, no telephone, and no means of support.

A potentially serious criticism of electronic monitoring is that it may interfere with First and Fourth Amendment rights of offenders and of others with whom offenders come in contact.[81] New GPS tracking technologies combined with other emerging technologies could identify people the offender contacts or could listen in on conversations. At what point will technological advances overintrude on people's privacy and other constitutional rights?

▶ Reentry Programs: Preparing Offenders to Take Responsibility

The *Washington Post* reported that in February 2010, Louis Sawyer, an African-American, was released from the Federal Correctional Institution at Allenwood, Pennsylvania. He returned to the Washington, DC, area and checked into a halfway house. He had four months to find permanent housing. In May, he had not found new housing or a job, but was invited to testify before a House subcommittee concerning the Revitalization Act, which addressed court services and offender supervision in Washington, DC. Sawyer said that someone returning from prison needs five things: transportation, clothing, physical and mental health care, employment, and housing. Sawyer found housing, but it took him six months to find a job. Many returning prisoners find neither.

In addition to the intermediate sanctions of IPS, shock probation, shock incarceration, home confinement, and electronic monitoring, there is a need for programs that focus on preparing inmates for reentry rather than punishing them.[82] Many states and the federal correctional system have implemented programs for preparing returning inmates through treatment and therapeutic programs, work-release programs, education-release programs, halfway houses, day reporting centers, and drug-treatment programs. For example, Ohio has taken the initiative to move corrections "toward a new vision of the offender reentry dialogue,"[83] and Michigan has created the Office of Community Corrections with the specific purpose of improving rehabilitative services and strengthening offender accountability.[84]

The federal system has recognized the importance of reentry programs. U.S. Code Title 18, Section 3624 requires that authorities should "to the extent practicable, assure that a prisoner serving a term of imprisonment spends a reasonable part" of the last six months or 10% of his or her sentence "under conditions that will afford the prisoner a reasonable opportunity to adjust to and prepare for the prisoner's reentry into the community."[85] The Reentry Partnership Initiative is a federal effort to help jurisdictions meet the challenges of offenders returning to the community. The goal is "to improve the risk management of released offenders by enhancing surveillance and monitoring, strengthening individual and community support systems, and repairing the harm done to victims."[86] Other federal legislation recognizes the need for effective community-based reentry programs for adults and juveniles that focus on treatment as well as punishment. Programs organized with the assistance of the Serious and Violent Offender Reentry Initiative divide reentry programs into three phases:

1. Protect and Prepare
2. Control and Restore
3. Sustain and Support[87]

In 2004, the Department of Justice announced that it was committing $6.7 million to the Serious and Violent Offender Reentry Initiative in an effort to improve public safety by

GLOSSARY

faith-based programs Programs provided by religious-based and church-affiliated groups; their role in rehabilitation is controversial because they receive federal money and may combine religious instruction with rehabilitation.

work release A program that allows facilities to release inmates for paid work in the community.

education release A program in which inmates are released to attend college or vocational programs.

halfway house A transition program that allows inmates to move from prison to the community in steps.

day reporting center An intermediate sanction to provide a gradual adjustment to reentry under closely supervised conditions.

addressing the successful reintegration of high-risk, serious offenders returning to their communities from imprisonment. Since 2004, the initiative estimates that more than $300 million has been committed to designing and carrying out adult and juvenile reentry strategies. Other government-sponsored reentry initiatives include the Council of State Governments Reentry Project, the Federal Bureau of Prisons National Institute of Corrections, and the National Reentry Resource Center.

Faith-Based Programs

A new strategy to promote successful reentry has been the use of **faith-based programs**. In his 2004 State of the Union address, President Bush proposed a $300 million initiative for reentry programs to be conducted by religious-based groups. The faith-based rehabilitation movement extends beyond community services and reaches into the prisons. Many prisons are allowing faith-based groups to provide programs such as vocational classes combined with religious instruction inside the prisons in an effort to prepare the offender for release.

The American Civil Liberties Union opposes faith-based groups receiving government money for their programs, claiming it is a violation of the separation of church and state. Others criticize faith-based programs because the programs often require inmates to participate in Bible studies and attend church services. To avoid these criticisms, some faith-based programs operate without receiving government funding.

It is too soon to evaluate the effect of faith-based programs on successful reentry. One study of the faith-based rehabilitation group InnerChange suggested that offenders who participated in the program were 50% less likely to be arrested and 60% less likely to be reincarcerated than those who did not participate.[88]

A significant appeal of reentry programs is that they cost much less than imprisonment. Whereas prison costs can average about $25,000 or more a year, reentry programs cost about $3,000 annually per inmate. Also, in addition to being less expensive, reentry programs allow states and the federal

1913 The year the Huber Law initiated the first work-release program in Wisconsin.

government to focus on removing the obstacles that keep recidivism rates high. With two out of three adult offenders returning to prison within three years, there is room for improvement. Some legislators have championed reentry programs as significant breakthroughs that would break the cycle of offending. In 2004, Senator Sam Brownback (R–Ks.) expressed his belief that reentry programs could reduce recidivism to 20%.[89]

The most often used reentry programs are work release programs, education release programs, halfway houses, day reporting centers, and drug-treatment programs.

Work Release

How can state and federal programs help to sustain and support inmates in the community? Former inmates have more difficulty than other people in finding and keeping a job.[90] **Work-release** programs were first initiated under Wisconsin's Huber Law in 1913, but they did not become commonplace until the latter half of the twentieth century.[91] Wisconsin's Huber Law permitted county correctional facilities to release misdemeanants for paid work in the community. In 1965, the Prisoner Rehabilitation Act of 1965 authorized work release for inmates in federal institutions. By 1975, all 50 states and the federal system had some form of work release operating.[92]

Obstacles to Employment

The most serious obstacles facing offenders looking for jobs are as follows:

1. Public prejudice against hiring ex-offenders
2. Lack of knowledge of how to find jobs
3. Lack of basic job skills, motivation, and attitude
4. Lack of the kinds of documentation required by employers

Public Prejudice

Public prejudice against hiring ex-offenders is strong. In one survey, 65% of all employers said that they would not knowingly hire an ex-offender, regardless of the offense, and 30% to 40% said that they check criminal records when hiring.[93] Furthermore, ex-offenders are barred from many occupations that require occupational licenses, including law, real estate, medicine, nursing, physical therapy, dentistry, engineering, pharmacy, security, and education.[94] Often employers refuse to hire offenders for fear of potential lawsuits because they are liable for negligent hiring should an offender commit a crime or harm the employers' customers.[95] Employers' fears are not groundless. For example, a family film company that hired inmates as telemarketers was sued by a woman who claimed that a prisoner misused company information by sending her 14-year-old daughter a personal letter.[96] A company that hired a woman who, unknown to them, had been convicted of embezzlement found that after six years with the company, she allegedly had embezzled more than $5 million from the organization.[97]

Lack of Knowledge and Job Skills

Ex-offenders often lack the basic knowledge to conduct a successful job search. Many do not know how to fill out employment applications, how to conduct themselves during

65% The percentage of employers that said that they would not knowingly hire an ex-offender.

interviews, how to dress for job interviews, or how to present the attitude of self-confidence that employers want in their employees. Frequently, offenders have had little experience or success in employment prior to prison. Thus, they do not have basic life skills related to job hunting that the general population often takes for granted.

Furthermore, offenders need to unlearn passive behavior patterns that work well in prison but are a liability in searching for and retaining a job.[98] In prison, offenders become accustomed to being told what to do, when to do it, and how to do it. Obedience to the rules is one of the most important values in prison. When asked to show initiative, demonstrate decision-making skills, and be innovative, inmates often cannot because they do not have these abilities.[99]

Lack of Documents

A unique problem that offenders have in getting employment is lack of proper identification (ID). Most people leave prison without a driver's license, a passport, a Social Security card, a birth certificate, or some other photo ID. The only ID they may have is their prison ID card, and when applying for a job, that does not impress employers. Many of them are clueless as to how to obtain the identification they need.[100] Offenders find that even if they are successful in obtaining employment, they may lose their jobs because they cannot supply their employers with proof of identification and citizenship, as required by law.[101]

Work-Release Strategies

Removing the obstacles to employment requires both community-based and in-prison programs. For example, Texas's Project RIO (Re-Integration of Offenders) provides in-prison vocational training programs to prepare inmates for the workforce and helps them obtain the IDs and documentation needed in the outside world, such as their birth certificate, Social Security identification, and state photo ID. Authorities hold the documentation for the prisoner and then forward it to the employer or agency as needed after the inmate is released.[102] New York provides inmates with a work-release furlough for six weeks to three months to allow them to find employment.

Limited Protection against Discrimination

Recognizing the difficulty that ex-offenders face in finding employment, several states have laws that limit when and to what extent an employer may consider an applicant's criminal record. These laws make it illegal for an employer to discriminate against an ex-offender unless his or her conviction record is related to

the duties of the job. Some states allow ex-offenders to seal or expunge their criminal records. Some states offer certificates of rehabilitation to ex-offenders who have minimal criminal histories or have remained out of the criminal justice system for specified periods.[103] Title VII of the Federal Civil Rights Act of 1964 offers some protection against job discrimination against ex-offenders. The Equal Employment Opportunity Commission has determined that policies that exclude individuals from employment on the basis of their arrest and conviction records may violate Title VII because these policies disproportionately exclude minorities.[104]

Many employers complain, however, that laws banning them from considering a job applicant's criminal record are not "business-friendly." They claim that such laws "ignore the liability employers face regarding the actions of their workers. Employers get squeezed in the middle. If you don't hire, you get sued, but if you do hire and something happens to customers or other workers, you get sued."[105] To induce employers to hire ex-offenders, the federal government has made tax credits available to employers who do so and has established insurance programs to reduce the employer's exposure to liability for possible misdeeds by inmates.[106]

Job Fairs

Some state correctional agencies are becoming more proactive in helping inmates find jobs after their release by sponsoring job fairs. Some job fairs are held within the correctional institutions. Prison officials help the inmates prepare résumés and train them in job interview skills. The Ohio Department of Rehabilitation and Correction has sponsored more than 140 job fairs and even holds teleconferences for companies that cannot send representatives.[107]

Partnerships with Businesses

Other correctional agencies have entered into joint ventures with private businesses to offer inmates the chance to work for private companies while in prison and then to transition to civilian employment with the company when they are released from prison.[108] Such partnerships are made possible by changes in federal and state laws that formerly prevented inmates from working in private-sector prison jobs. In 1979, Congress enacted Pub. L. 96–157 [18 U.S.C. 176(c) and 41 U.S.C. 35], which created the Prison Industry Enhancement Certification Program. This program authorizes correctional agencies to engage in the interstate shipment of prison-made goods for private businesses, providing certain conditions are met.[109] The law allows private companies to operate businesses from within the prison and to use inmate labor. The law requires that inmates must be paid at a rate not less than the rate paid for work of a similar nature in the locality in which the work takes place. Prison officials allow the inmates to send some of the money to support their families and to keep a small portion for themselves; the

> Policies that exclude individuals from employment on the basis of their arrest and conviction records may violate Title VII because these policies disproportionately exclude minorities.

rest is retained for them until their release. These partnerships help reduce the burden on the state of supporting the inmates' families, provide a source of labor for the businesses, and help the inmates make successful transitions from prison to work after release.

Education Release

About 68% of state prison inmates lack a high school diploma. About half of those reported that they had learning disabilities. Without a minimum education, prisoners reentering the community have little chance of finding employment that will provide a sustainable income. Studies indicate that those inmates who obtain a general education development (GED) or college degree while in prison are more likely to find employment when released.

Thus, education is recognized as a factor that can make an important difference in the successful transition of offenders from correctional systems back to their communities.[110] It costs an estimated minimum of $22,000 to $60,000 per year to incarcerate an offender, which is much more than the average cost for one year of college or vocational training.[111] Correctional officials have recognized the importance of education, and while in prison, it is usually mandatory that inmates without a high school education be given the opportunity to earn a high school equivalency or GED degree.

Some correctional institutions bring educational programs into the institution so that inmates can further their education there. Others provide education-release opportunities for inmates while they are in prison and as part of their parole plan. In prison, education programs are expensive because degree programs must be offered by accredited institutions and must use certified instructors. Often educational institutions offer in-prison programs because inmates may be eligible for GI bill educational benefits or state and federal educational loans/grants that cover tuition costs.

While online education is commonplace outside the prison environment, within prisons, it is virtually nonexistent. Experts in correctional education are skeptical that online education will work in prisons. They point to the high number of inmates who report having learning disabilities and the near absolute opposition of prison security officials to allow inmates to have access to the Internet.

The typical **education-release** program for prisoners in community corrections facilities gives them the opportunity to attend vocational, college, or university classes but requires them to return to the community corrections facility each day. When educational release is a part of an inmate's parole plan, the inmate is required to attend a vocational training program, community college, or university rather than go to a full-time job. However, inmates must have the means to support themselves and pay for their schooling.

Effectiveness

Research has shown that offenders who participate in education programs are less likely to commit new crimes compared to inmates who do not participate in such programs.[112] One study tracked 2,305 inmates over three years at the Bedford Hills Correctional Facility for Women, a maximum-security prison

7.7% The percentage of inmates who had taken college courses while in prison and had returned to jail after their release, compared to 29.9% of those who did not take courses.

in New York that has an educational program sponsored by a consortium of private colleges. The study found that only 7.7% of the inmates who had taken college courses while incarcerated committed new crimes and were returned to prison after their release, whereas 29.9% of the inmates who did not take courses were jailed again.[113]

College Discrimination

However, despite the demonstrated benefits of education, similar to employers who are prejudiced against hiring released prisoners, colleges can be prejudiced against admitting ex-offenders—even those who have served their time. For example, in 2005, the University of Alaska refused to admit Michael Purcell to its social work program. Purcell had served 20 years for killing a convenience store clerk when he was 16 years old. He was released on parole in September 2004. Upon his release, he entered a halfway house and took classes at the University of Alaska. However, when he applied for admission to the social work program, he was denied admission. In rejecting Purcell's application, the social work department cited its policy that they considered people with criminal records unfit for social work practice.[114] The University of Alaska is not the only university that has such policies discriminating against ex-felons.

Halfway Houses

Halfway houses are transition programs that allow inmates to move from prison to the community in steps. The first halfway houses in the United States were opened in the mid-1800s, but their use did not become commonplace until the 1950s.[115] The use of halfway houses was encouraged because such a program provided what was considered an essential transition—an inmate could gradually adjust to freedom through a short stay, usually about six months, in a halfway house at the end of his or her sentence.[116]

Gradual Transition

Today, most halfway houses are nonprofit foundations.[117] The state departments of corrections contract with these nonprofit organizations to provide a gradual transition for the offender from an environment that maintains total control to one that permits partial control before the offender is released into the community. The typical halfway house provides services for 6 to 30 inmates in a minimum-security facility, often a residential home that has been converted into a halfway house. Inmates who do not follow the rules or who "walk away" from the halfway house are returned to prison or charged with the felony offense of escape. The combination of nearing the end of their sentence and risking return to prison with possible added time is an effective deterrent for most participants.

Halfway houses have full-time staff members who provide for the custody and treatment of the offenders. Offenders observe strict curfews, participate in treatment programs conducted by the house staff or community-based agencies, and seek employment or enroll in vocational training or college classes. The program allows a transition period from prison to freedom in that the offender is closely supervised but is given limited freedom within the community and is required to take responsibility for preparing for his or her successful reentry into the community.

During the offender's stay in the halfway house, he or she does not have to report to a probation officer because the house staff performs this function. After his or her stay, the offender is released from the halfway house into the community under the supervision of a parole officer. His or her stay at the halfway house gives the person the opportunity to obtain employment and housing upon leaving. Halfway houses are excellent resources for inmates seeking parole who have no family or sponsors in the community to help them when they leave prison. Without halfway houses, many of these inmates would not be able to prepare an acceptable parole plan because they would be homeless and without employment.

Community Opposition

The most significant obstacle to halfway houses is the strong community opposition to having such a facility located in one's neighborhood. As mentioned previously, even those who support the concept of halfway houses suffer from NIMBY—"not in my back yard." Who wants to live next to a halfway house? Who wants to raise a family and have their children play in the yard and in parks that are near a halfway house? Locating communities that are close to employment opportunities and public transportation, essential characteristics for a successful halfway house program, and that are willing to allow halfway houses to operate in the community is a challenge.

Day Reporting Centers

Day reporting centers are relatively new reentry programs dating to the early 1970s.[118] **Day reporting centers** provide

for release from prison that is closely supervised by the state's department of corrections. Inmates live at home rather than being imprisoned or housed in a privately managed halfway house. As the name suggests, inmates report to supervisory centers on a daily basis. Inmates may be sentenced to day reporting centers rather than prison or may be released from prison to day reporting centers during the last months of their sentence. Also, day reporting centers are used by jails.

Inmates report to and leave the center during the day to work, to participate in treatment programs, to attend classes or training programs, or to find employment. Day reporting centers maintain daily schedules that must accurately account for inmates' time while in the community. Participants must submit to certain conditions similar to those in a parole plan, such as random drug tests.

The purpose of the day reporting center is to act as an intermediate sanction for some inmates and to permit a gradual adjustment to reentry for others. Day reporting centers allow departments of corrections to reduce the need for prison bed space by placing low security–risk inmates in day reporting centers.[119] These inmates do not sleep in the institution at night and, thus, do not need a cell or bed. For inmates transitioning from prison, day reporting centers allow them the opportunity to reenter the community under closely monitored conditions.

Because day reporting centers are not widely used, extensive data are not available to judge their effectiveness. However, data from the Metropolitan Day Reporting Center in Boston indicate that inmates who enter the community from the day reporting center rather than directly from jail are less likely to commit new crimes and are more likely to be employed. Furthermore, another source reported that only about 1% of inmates committed a crime while they were in the program.[120]

▶ Reentry Programs for Drug Offenders

Drug use forecasting (DUF) data collected on defendants in 23 cities indicated that 51% to 83% of arrested adult men and 41% to 84% of arrested adult women were under the influence of at least one illicit drug at the time of arrest.[121] In addition, drug use is a significant factor in property offenses—16% of adult prisoners indicated that they committed their offenses to get money for drugs.[122] Although drug offenders may be thought of as nonviolent, about one in ten convicted federal

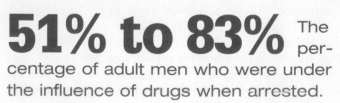

51% to 83% The percentage of adult men who were under the influence of drugs when arrested.

drug defendants received a sentence enhancement for the use or possession of a firearm or another weapon.[123]

Drug offenders consume considerable resources of the criminal justice system. Starting in the mid-1980s with "get tough" and mandatory sentencing laws, the number of defendants charged with a drug offense in the federal courts increased from 11,854 in 1984 to 29,306 in 1999.[124] In 2010, prisoners incarcerated for drug offenses comprised 51% of federal prisons and 17.8% of state prisons[125]. In addition to people sentenced for drug offenses, the Bureau of Justice Statistics estimates that two-thirds of federal and state prisoners and probationers could be characterized as drug involved.[126] In response to the increased frequency of drug crimes, the criminal justice system has enhanced drug law enforcement efforts and has adopted a "get tough" sentencing policy for drug offenders. This federal stance has resulted in 62% of convicted federal drug defendants receiving statutory minimum sentences of five years or more.

However, enhanced enforcement and tough sentencing policies have failed to stem the number of drug offenders. Over 73% of state inmates reentering prison have admitted to drug or alcohol involvement while released.[127] Even when sentenced to prison, inmates continue to find ways to obtain drugs. Thus, incarceration in itself does little to break the cycle of illegal drug use and crime. Furthermore, the traditional case disposition process appears to lack the capacity to bring about any significant reduction in drug use by individuals convicted of drug offenses.[128] A new strategy to break the cycle of drug use and crime that has led to the revolving door syndrome for drug offenders has been the drug court. The **drug court** approach was started in 1989 as an experiment by the Dade County (Florida) Circuit Court. Today, nearly every state uses some form of drug court program to handle drug offenders. Drug courts have proven to be effective with adult and juvenile offenders and for use in tribal courts.

LEARNING OUTCOMES 4

Summarize the role of reentry programs for drug offenders.

Adult Drug Courts

In states that have adult drug courts, adult offenders arrested for drug offenses are diverted from traditional case disposition processing as soon as possible. These offenders are offered the opportunity to participate in the drug court program rather than traditional case disposition that results in incarceration. Drug court programs use intermediate sanctions, community-based treatment, and IPS to achieve two purposes:

1. To get offenders clean and sober

2. To compel offenders to participate in a comprehensive treatment program while being monitored under strict conditions for drug use

Almost all drug courts require participants to obtain a GED if they have not finished high school, to maintain or obtain employment, to be current in all financial obligations (including drug court fees and any court-ordered support payments), and to have a sponsor in the community. Some drug programs require offenders to perform community service hours.[129] Figure 12–3 illustrates how offenders are selected for inclusion in the Superior Court Drug Intervention Program in Washington, DC. This process is typical of the admission process used in most drug courts.

If offenders accept the offer to enter into the drug court program and are accepted by the program, "they are referred immediately to a multi-phased out-patient treatment program entailing multiple weekly (often daily) contacts with the treatment provider for counseling, therapy, and education; frequent urinalysis (usually at least weekly); frequent status hearings before the drug court judge (biweekly or more often at first); and a rehabilitation program entailing vocational, education, family, medical, and other support services."[130] Figure 12–4 shows the variety of treatment programs and support services that are available to participants in drug court programs.

Effectiveness

In contrast to the traditional adjudication process in the criminal court, drug court programs are experiencing a significant reduction in recidivism among participants. Whereas about 45% of defendants convicted of drug possession will reoffend with a similar offense within two to three years, only 5% to 28% of drug court participants reoffend and 90% have negative

GLOSSARY

drug court An approach that provides drug offenders the opportunity for intermediate sanctions, community treatment, and intensive probation supervision instead of prison time.

revolving door syndrome The repeated arrest and incarceration of an offender.

Tribal Healing to Wellness Courts Native American drug-treatment programs that adopt traditional cultural beliefs and practices.

Treatment Accountability for Safer Communities (TASC) A federal assistance program that helps states break the addiction-crime cycle.

Residential Substance Abuse Treatment (RSAT) A federal assistance program that helps states provide treatment instead of prison for substance abusers.

The Ten Key Components of Drug Courts

The operations and components of drug courts vary from jurisdiction to jurisdiction, but the following ten key components identify state adult drug court programs as prescribed by the Drug Courts Program Office:

- Drug courts integrate alcohol and other drug treatment services with justice system case processing.

- Using a nonadversarial approach, prosecution and defense counsel promote public safety while protecting participants' due process rights.

- Eligible participants are identified early and promptly placed in the drug court program.

- Drug courts provide access to a continuum of alcohol, drug, and other related treatment and rehabilitation services.

- Abstinence is monitored by frequent alcohol and other drug testing.

- A coordinated strategy governs drug court responses to participants' compliance.

- Ongoing judicial interaction with each drug court participant is essential.

- Monitoring and evaluation measure the achievement of program goals and gauge effectiveness.

- Continuing interdisciplinary education promotes effective drug court planning, implementation, and operations.

- Forging partnerships between drug courts, public agencies, and community-based organizations generates local support and enhances drug court effectiveness.

Source: Defining Drug Courts: The Key Components (Washington, DC: Office of Justice Programs, Drug Courts Program Office, January 1997), pp. 1–3.

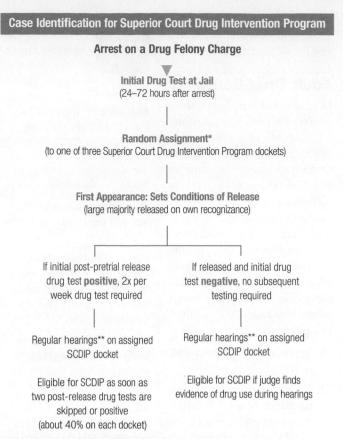

Case Identification for Superior Court Drug Intervention Program

Arrest on a Drug Felony Charge

▼

Initial Drug Test at Jail
(24–72 hours after arrest)

Random Assignment*
(to one of three Superior Court Drug Intervention Program dockets)

First Appearance: Sets Conditions of Release
(large majority released on own recognizance)

If initial post-pretrial release drug test **positive**, 2x per week drug test required

If released and initial drug test **negative**, no subsequent testing required

Regular hearings** on assigned SCDIP docket

Regular hearings** on assigned SCDIP docket

Eligible for SCDIP as soon as two post-release drug tests are skipped or positive (about 40% on each docket)

Eligible for SCDIP if judge finds evidence of drug use during hearings

FIGURE 12–3 **Selection Process for Drug Court**

The selection process for drug court for the Superior Court Drug Intervention Program in Washington, DC, is typical of the process used in most drug courts. Admission to drug court requires confirmation that defendants are drug-dependent. Defendants must meet strict guidelines before they can be diverted from traditional case processing. If admitted to drug court, the focus is on drug treatment, not punishment. Defendants must follow a rigid program of testing and counseling. Failure to conform to the conditions of the drug court program will result in reinstatement of the charges and transfer to the criminal court for prosecution.

*Defendants were not allowed to transfer to another SCDIP docket.

**Plea offers were made at regular docket hearings and could occur before, after, or at the same time as defendant became eligible for SCDIP, and the program offer was not contingent upon acceptance of the plea. However, if the plea was rejected, the defendant transferred out of the SCDIP dockets to a trial docket.

Source: Adele Harrell, Shannon Cavanaugh, and John Roman, *Evaluation of the D.C. Superior Court Drug Intervention Programs* (Washington, DC: U.S. Department of Justice, April 2000), p. 3.

urinalysis drug reports.[131] Drug court programs also have been shown to save money. By avoiding the high cost of incarceration, some cities have been able to save up to $2.5 million per year in criminal justice costs.[132] By eliminating the **revolving door syndrome**, drug court programs not only save on the cost of incarcerating repeat offenders, but also save police, prosecutors, and courts the additional costs of processing the offenders through the system. Drug court programs also help save welfare benefits because offenders who are employed when arrested often maintain their employment and continue to support themselves and their families. By not having drug offenders repeatedly entering and exiting the criminal justice system, criminal justice agencies can more efficiently allocate

their resources to address more pressing needs and crimes.[133] A testament to the effectiveness of drug court programs is that in a poll of 318 police chiefs, almost 60% advocated court-supervised treatment programs over other justice system options for drug users.

Tribal Drug Courts

Unique problems of crime on Native American reservations include a disproportionately high rate compared to general crime statistics. Alcohol and other substance abuse contributes substantially to the crime problem on Native American lands because more than 90% of the criminal cases in most tribal courts involve alcohol or substance abuse.[134] In addition to alcohol abuse, many Native American communities have substantial problems with use of toxic inhalants.

Drug courts were first adopted by Native American and Alaska Native tribal courts in 1997. Interest is growing, however, because drug court programs are more closely aligned with tribal justice concepts and methods than are traditional criminal justice processes.[135] Nevertheless, unique problems are associated with adapting the drug court concept to meet the specific needs of Native Americans:[136]

- Tribal courts must address the specific cultural needs of their individual communities, including the challenge of incorporating tribal custom and tradition into the tribal drug court.

- The nature and high volume of alcohol abuse cases in most tribal courts present unique adaptation issues.

- Tribal courts face jurisdictional barriers that complicate their ability to implement an effective drug court process.

- Tribes seeking to establish drug court systems often face a broad range of other issues and challenges, including isolated rural locations, small-community issues, lack of resources and services, and lack of funding.

Tribal drug courts generally are called **Tribal Healing to Wellness Courts**. Some programs have developed individual names, using words from the tribe's native language.[137] Healing to Wellness Courts may use traditional treatment processes involving tribal elders, traditional healing ceremonies, talking circles, peacemaking, sweats and sweat lodge visits with a medicine man or woman, the sun dance, and a vision quest.[138]

Jurisdictional barriers to tribal drug courts include the lack of criminal jurisdiction over non-Native Americans, concurrent state jurisdiction, legal limits in sentencing (to one year or a fine of $5,000, or both), and a historically strained relationship with state courts and state agencies.[139] Also, more than 50% of the reservation population is under the age of 18,[140] requiring greater demand for juvenile drug court programs than is the case in the

$2.5 million
The amount saved by sending offenders to drug court programs rather than prison.

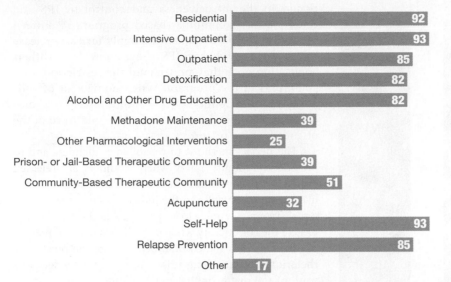

Types of Dedicated and External Treatment Programs

Program	Percentage
Residential	92
Intensive Outpatient	93
Outpatient	85
Detoxification	82
Alcohol and Other Drug Education	82
Methadone Maintenance	39
Other Pharmacological Interventions	25
Prison- or Jail-Based Therapeutic Community	39
Community-Based Therapeutic Community	51
Acupuncture	32
Self-Help	93
Relapse Prevention	85
Other	17

Percentage of Courts Reporting (n=212 courts)

Support Services Available to Program Participants

Service	Percentage
Mental Health Treatment	91
Mental Health Referral	96
Vocational Training	86
Job Placement	77
Housing Assistance	59
Housing Referral	72
Parenting Education	84
Educational Remediation/GED	92
Domestic Violence Intervention Services	73
Transportation Assistance	59
Anger Management	87
Life Skills Management	79
Stress Management	72
Relapse Prevention	93
Child care	32

Percentage of Courts Reporting (n=212 courts)

FIGURE 12–4 Unlike prison, offenders directed into drug-treatment programs participate in a number of rehabilitation programs as indicated above. Often referred to as the "medical model," drug courts focus on treating and rehabilitating, not punishing, offenders. The programs include not only breaking an offender's dependence on drugs, but also equipping him or her with what is needed to become a fully functional member of society.

traditional criminal justice system. Data for traditional drug court programs are promising, however, and it is hoped that the drug court concept will prove flexible enough to work with traditional Native American justice concepts and methods.[141]

TASC and RSAT

Federal assistance programs such as **Treatment Accountability for Safer Communities (TASC)** and **Residential Substance Abuse Treatment (RSAT)** for the State Prisoners Formula Grant Program have helped states adopt new comprehensive programs for drug offenders. Federal legislation designed to help states break the addiction-crime cycle of nonviolent, drug-involved offenders includes the 1972 Drug Abuse and Treatment Act and the Violent Crime Control and Law Enforcement Act of 1994. Both laws provide federal funds to states to allow them to link the legal sanctions of the criminal justice system with the federally funded therapeutic interventions of drug-treatment programs.[142] The major premise of programs funded by the grants is that criminal sanctions can be combined with the reintegration of offenders into the community and that this can be done through a broad base of support from both the criminal justice system and the treatment community.[143] Combining intermediate sanctions and drug offender treatment programs is both effective and cost-efficient. To prevent an offender's return to drug use, these programs provide treatment in prison and after release through postincarceration supervision. The combination of treatment strategies can reduce recidivism by about 50%. In addition to reducing recidivism, drug-treatment costs are about $6,500 per year per inmate, whereas imprisonment costs are four to ten times higher.[144]

▶ Conclusion: Try, Try Again

The criminal justice system involves a dynamic process that is undergoing constant change, including the corrections component. Many correctional programs, philosophies, and challenges are new and evolving. Jails and prisons used for more than 100 years are being replaced by new structures that are radically different. Probation and parole, which emerged in the early twentieth century, are already being transformed by IPS and electronic monitoring. In the past 20 to 30 years, new intermediate sanctions have appeared that focus on control and treatment in the community. In the past decade, new programs for addressing the crisis of drug-addicted inmates are winning greater acceptance by the criminal justice system and the public.

When inmates leave prison and return to the community, it is much better if they are rehabilitated individuals rather than recidivists.

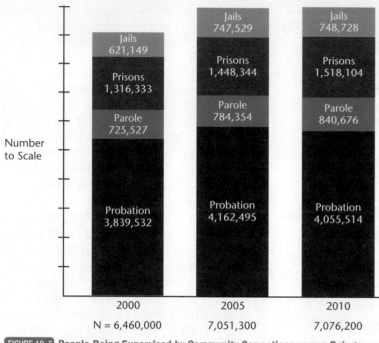

Community Corrections Versus Jails and Prisons 2000–2010

2000

Jails
621,149

Prisons
1,316,333

Parole
725,527

Probation
3,839,532

N = 6,460,000

2005

Jails
747,529

Prisons
1,448,344

Parole
784,354

Probation
4,162,495

7,051,300

2010

Jails
748,728

Prisons
1,518,104

Parole
840,676

Probation
4,055,514

7,076,200

Number to Scale

FIGURE 12–5 **People Being Supervised by Community Corrections versus Being Incarcerated in Jails and Prisons**

In 2010, nearly 5 million people were under community corrections supervision compared to just over 2.2 million in jails and prisons.

Source: Lauren E. Glaze, *Correctional Populations in the United States, 2010* (Washington, DC: Bureau of Justice Statistics, 2011), p. 3.

Ways of looking at corrections are changing as new experiments in control and treatment are being tried. New research indicates that prisoners may prefer prison to many of the new intermediate and community-based sanctions. When polled as to their opinion of the harshness of punishments, many offenders say that they prefer prison to the intrusiveness and control of IPS and other various community-based programs.[145] Fifteen percent of the participants who apply for early release under the New Jersey IPS program withdraw their application once they understand the restrictions and conditions of the program. When nonviolent offenders in Marion County, Oregon, were offered a choice between prison and release under IPS, one-third of the offenders chose prison.[146]

The perfect methods to rehabilitate offenders and to provide community safety when offenders are released back into the community have not been found. However, like law enforcement and the judicial system, the correctional system continues to look for new and better ways to protect the community while providing successful reentry of offenders into the community. Despite the boisterous rhetoric promoting long prison terms for offenders, the truth of the matter is that most offenders remain under supervision in the community rather than in prison. Figure 12–5 illustrates that more than twice the number of people are under community supervisions as are in jails and prisons.

Why should you be concerned about the success of reentry programs? When Oklahoma prisons started a six-part course on maintaining a healthy marriage, many questioned the expense and resources of inaugurating marriage programs in the prison. The response by prison officials to this challenge was simple and direct. "There are 600,000 Americans leaving prison in the next few years. And those guys are all coming to an apartment complex near you."[147] When inmates leave prison and return to the community, it is much better if they are rehabilitated individuals rather than recidivists.

Cops versus Cons

Leroy Delphie, 42, was released on parole from Shawnee Correctional Center (Illinois) on February 27, 2012. He had been convicted and sentenced to prison in 2009 and in 1999. Also, he had served time for drug and attempted murder charges in 1991. Five days after his release on parole in 2012, he was arrested for bank robbery.[148]

Delphie is fairly typical of ex-offenders in the community. Nearly 30% of inmates released from prison are rearrested within six months of their release and nearly 68% are rearrested within three years of their release. Thus, it is no wonder that law enforcement sees ex-offenders in the community as a threat to public safety. Law enforcement officers may be a significant challenge to the ex-offender's successful reentry into the community.

The criminal justice system is not a single unified system of agencies having a shared mission and centralized oversight. The conflict between law enforcement and offenders in the community is an example of how agencies can have different perspectives and objectives. The goal of community corrections is to successfully reintegrate the offender into the community. Law enforcement often sees reentering offenders as a challenge to their mission of public safety.

Officers may target ex-offenders in field stops, as crime suspects, and as a danger to public safety. In unhealthy cases, this attitude toward ex-offenders may reflect the "dirty Harry" syndrome—in which law enforcement officers believe that the early release of offenders or community correction sanctions in lieu of imprisonment reflect a failure of the criminal justice system. To protect the public, these officers may resort to violent and illegal activities.

Numerous scandals have documented law enforcement officials engaging in illegal activities to obtain convictions. The Los Angeles Police Department Rampart Division scandal was one of the most egregious cases. These officers were convicted of planting evidence, obtaining confessions by torture, and violating the civil rights of those arrested. Other scandals have been documented in dozens of other cities.

This case raises several interesting questions. Among them are the following:

1. Do law enforcement officers unfairly target ex-offenders in the community for extra scrutiny? Explain.

2. Are the risks posed by early release and community correction sanctions in lieu of imprisonment justified? Explain.

3. What, if anything, could be done to promote a more positive view of community corrections by law enforcement?

Ernest Prim/Fotolia

Summarize the role of community corrections sanctions in corrections.

Many state governments are facing financial hardship as the nation's incarceration rates reached 40-year highs. In response, states typically used early-release programs such as probation and parole, but these early-release programs often pose serious risks to public safety given high recidivism rates. As a consequence, the criminal justice system is turning to new sanctions for offenders: intermediate sanctions and community-based corrections. Community-based corrections are alternatives to incarceration in jail or prison, such as boot camps, house arrest, community service, and electronic monitoring. However, many communities are opposed to community-based facilities being located in their neighborhoods.

1. What are the advantages of using community-based corrections?

2. Why do so many offenders fail to reintegrate into the community?

3. What does NIMBY mean?

community-based corrections Prevention and treatment programs designed to promote the successful transition of offenders from prison to the community.

NIMBY "Not in my backyard"—opposition to community corrections programs in one's neighborhood.

List the various community corrections sanctions and explain how they differ from traditional early-release programs.

Community-based intermediate sanctions are correctional programs other than imprisonment designed to reduce the prison population and promote successful reentry of the offender into the community. Some forms of supervision in the community have been criticized for not reducing recidivism or not providing adequate safeguards for community protection. The intermediate sanctions most often used include intensive probation supervision (IPS), split sentencing, shock probation, boot camps, and home confinement with electronic monitoring.

1. How is IPS performed?

2. After what is shock incarceration modeled?

3. Describe a criticism of electronic monitoring.

intermediate sanctions Punishments that restrict offenders' freedom without imprisoning them and/or that consist of community-based prevention and treatment programs to promote the successful transition of offenders from prison to the community.

intensive probation supervision (IPS) Probation supervised by probation and parole officers with smaller caseloads, placing a greater emphasis on compliance with the conditions of supervision.

split sentencing An intermediate sanction where, after a brief period of imprisonment, the judge brings the offender back to court and offers the option of probation.

shock probation A sentence for a first-time nonviolent offender who was not expecting a sentence, intended to impress on the offender the possible consequences of his or her behavior by being exposed to a brief period of imprisonment before probation.

shock incarceration Programs (boot camps) that adapt military-style physical fitness and discipline training to the correctional environment.

boot camps Programs modeled after military-style entry-level training programs for youthful nonviolent offenders.

home confinement A court-imposed sentence requiring offenders to remain confined in their own residence.

electronic monitoring An approach in home confinement programs that ensures compliance through electronic means.

LEARNING OUTCOMES 3

Explain how community corrections programs promote successful reentry into the community.

There is a need for rehabilitation programs that emphasize preparing inmates for reentry rather than punishing them. Several states and the federal correctional system have implemented various programs for preparing inmates for release. These programs may utilize treatment and therapeutic programs, work-release programs, education-release programs, halfway houses, day reporting centers, and drug-treatment programs. A goal of reentry programs is to improve the supervision of released offenders by enhancing surveillance and monitoring, strengthening individual and community support systems, and mending the harm done to victims.

1. What are the obstacles for an offender who is looking for work upon being released from prison?

2. How do correctional agencies partner with private businesses?

3. Describe how an educational release program works.

faith-based programs Programs provided by religious-based and church-affiliated groups; their role in rehabilitation is controversial because they receive federal money and may combine religious instruction with rehabilitation.

work release A program that allows facilities to release inmates for paid work in the community.

education release A program in which inmates are released to attend college or vocational programs.

halfway house A transition program that allows inmates to move from prison to the community in steps.

day reporting center An intermediate sanction to provide a gradual adjustment to reentry under closely supervised conditions.

LEARNING OUTCOMES 4

Summarize the role of reentry programs for drug offenders.

For the criminal justice system, drug offenders account for a considerable amount of time and money. The vast majority of state inmates reentering prison have acknowledged drug or alcohol involvement prior to being arrested again. A new approach to assist offenders in breaking this cycle of drug usage has led to the creation of drug court. Here, strict guidelines are established for the defendant to comply with while in rehabilitation. If the defendant is admitted to drug court, the focus is on drug treatment, not punishment.

1. What is meant by the revolving door process?

2. What drove the creation of drug courts?

3. How many people are currently under correctional supervision in the United States?

drug court An approach that provides drug offenders the opportunity for intermediate sanctions, community treatment, and intensive probation supervision instead of prison time.

revolving door syndrome The repeated arrest and incarceration of an offender.

Tribal Healing to Wellness Courts Native American drug-treatment programs that adopt traditional cultural beliefs and practices.

Treatment Accountability for Safer Communities (TASC) A federal assistance program that helps states break the addiction-crime cycle.

Residential Substance Abuse Treatment (RSAT) A federal assistance program that helps states provide treatment instead of prison for substance abusers.

MyCJLab

Go to Chapter 12 in *MyCJLab* to test your mastery of chapter concepts, access your Study Plan, engage in interactive exercises, complete critical-thinking and research assignments, and view related online videos.

 Review: Complete the pretest in the Study Plan to confirm what you know and what you need to study further. Then complete the post-test to confirm your mastery of the concepts. Use the key term flash cards to review key terminology.

 Apply: Complete the interactive simulation activity.

 Analyze: Complete assignments as directed by your instructor.

Current Events: Explore CJSearch for current topical videos, articles, and news pieces.

Additional Links

Go to **http://www.erie.gov/veterans/veterans_court.asp** to view information on the Buffalo Veterans Treatment Court in New York.

Go to **http://www.nationalreentryresourcecenter.org** and learn how the National Reentry Resource Center provides education, training, and technical assistance to states, tribes, territories, local governments, service providers, nonprofit organizations, and corrections institutions working on prisoner reentry.

Go to **http://www.judiciary.state.nj.us/probsup/isp_intro.htm** and learn about the New Jersey Intensive Supervision Program.

Go to **http://www.youtube.com/watch?v=iG5EgPBgpe8** and watch a video that explains what community corrections is all about, with a focus on drug and alcohol counseling.

Go to **http://www.dcor.state.ga.us/Divisions/Corrections/BootCamps.html** to learn about Georgia's boot camp program.

The Juvenile Justice System

> "We may not be able to prepare the future for our children, but we can at least prepare our children for the future."
>
> —*Franklin D. Roosevelt*

1 Identify the foundations of the juvenile justice system.

2 Summarize the jurisdiction of the juvenile justice system and the classification of juvenile offenders.

3 Explain how landmark court cases have influenced the due process rights of juveniles.

4 Summarize why and in what ways states are changing the age of accountability.

5 Describe the juvenile justice system, including post-adjudications options for treatment and punishment of juveniles.

6 Summarize the contributions of research and theory to understanding the causes of juvenile delinquency and offending, including youth gangs and substance abuse.

7 Identify the challenges of preventing school violence and bullying and strategies that have been used to respond to this problem.

8 Describe the role of the juvenile justice system in protecting juveniles from abuse and victimization.

.shock/Fotolia

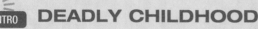
Childhood is often portrayed as a time of innocence, growth, and evolving self-awareness. However, for some, it is a time of murder. For example, on April 20, 1999, in the deadliest high school shooting in the United States, Eric Harris, 18, and Dylan Klebold, 17, killed 12 and wounded 23 at Columbine High School (Colorado). In 2005, there were two high school shootings: Jeffrey Weise, 16, a high school sophomore at Red Lake Senior High School (Minnesota) killed nine and himself on March 21, 2005, and Kenneth Bartley, Jr., 14, killed the principal and wounded two assistant principals at Campbell County Comprehensive High School (Tennessee) on November 8, 2005. On February 27, 2012, T. J. Lane, 17, killed three students and wounded two at Chardon High School (Ohio).

For some, their murderous rage is expressed when they are young men rather than juveniles. For example, on March 16, 2007, Seung-Hui Cho, 24, killed 32 and wounded 17 on the Virginia Tech campus. In another attack on January 8, 2011, Jared Loughner, 23, opened fire on a political gathering held by U.S. Representative Gabrielle Giffords, killing 6 and wounding 12 in a Tucson, Arizona, shopping center. In the most deadly public massacre in the United States, James Eagan Holmes, 24, allegedly killed 12 and wounded 58 when he opened fire on the audience of a Century 16 theater in Aurora, Colorado.

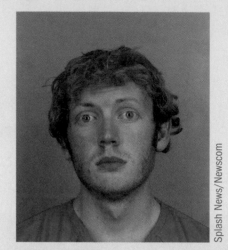

James Holmes

Splash News/Newscom

The goal of the juvenile justice system is radically different from that of the adult criminal justice system. The juvenile justice system seeks to understand the root causes of criminality and to intervene in order to achieve desistance of criminal behavior. If the goal of the juvenile justice system to reduce or eliminate offending were achieved, it could be argued that a significant reduction of adult criminality would ensue.

DISCUSS **Are young people who are capable of such violence different from "ordinary" people?**

▶ *A Changing View of Young Offenders*

The juvenile justice system is based on the premise that young offenders can be rehabilitated and that society would be better served by rehabilitating children rather than punishing them. Juveniles have not always enjoyed the benefits of the juvenile justice system. The separation of juveniles and adults in the criminal justice system is a relatively new practice, dating back only to 1899. However, children may not be as secure in relying on the protection of the juvenile justice system because recent events have caused some to give considerable thought to its function.

School shootings, gang violence, depraved killings, rape, and even accusations of juvenile suicide bombers have caused some to call for the examination of the very principles on which the juvenile justice system is founded, the criminological theories that focus on young offenders, and the ability of the juvenile justice system to rehabilitate offenders and protect society from juvenile violence and mayhem.

Despite statistics that show otherwise, the public perceives a widespread violent juvenile crime wave that has had substantial influence on the juvenile justice system. Juvenile offenders are

---

TIMELINE **Timeline of Key Events**

1825	**1899**	**1925**	**1966**	**1966**
New York House of Refuge juvenile reformatory opens.	***Cook County, Illinois*** (Chicago) establishes juvenile court with original jurisdiction.	All but two states have established juvenile courts with original jurisdiction.	***Charles Whitman*** kills 14 and wounds 31 on University of Texas (Austin) campus.	***Kent v. United States*** Courts must provide the "essentials of due process" in transferring juveniles to the adult system.

GLOSSARY

social safety net Government programs that provide for people in need.

New York House of Refuge An early juvenile reformatory established by New York State in 1824 that was to become the model for most juvenile reformatories.

indenture agreements Agreements whereby employers would supervise youths in exchange for their labor.

Despite statistics that show otherwise, the public perceives a widespread violent juvenile crime wave that has had substantial influence on the juvenile justice system.

seen as a threat to be punished and incarcerated rather than rehabilitated. Those who believe juvenile crime is "out of control" also believe that the juvenile justice system is perceived as an "easy out that gives a meaningless slap on the wrist to violent youth."[1] After just over 100 years from the time the juvenile justice system first emerged, forces are at work that continue to transform it.

This chapter examines the development of the juvenile justice system, including its goals, agencies, processes, and results. It explores the two-sided problem of juveniles as victims and juveniles as offenders. The examination of juvenile offenders focuses on substance abuse, violent crimes, gangs, and school violence. The examination of juveniles as victims focuses on violence against children, sexual exploitation and child pornography, and missing children.

▶ Development of the Juvenile Justice System

Before There Was a Juvenile Justice System

In his classical theory of crime causation, Cesare Beccaria (1738–1794) made no distinction between adult and juvenile offenders and suggested no special considerations for the punishment of juvenile offenders. Neoclassical criminological theorists such as Jeremy Bentham (1748–1832) carved out an exemption for very young offenders, allowing that young offenders cannot appreciate the criminality of their actions. The legal system of the American colonies allowed this defense based on youth. (See Table 13–1.)

Juvenile cases were fairly rare in the founding years of the United States. State courts preferred to let parents or local officials handle juvenile offenders. However, as industrialism and immigration gave rise to swelling populations in cities such as New York and Philadelphia, the public began to see a problem with the "disorderly conduct" of children that was not being contained by parents. As a result, young offenders found themselves being processed by a criminal justice system that often failed to distinguish whether the young offender's behavior was motivated by criminal intent or poverty and need. Many believed that if imprisonment could help the adult criminal, it would surely assist a youth less practiced in crime; so the courts became more disposed to using the criminal justice system to deal with the problem of juvenile disorderly conduct.[2]

Political, social, and economic practices of the eighteenth and nineteenth centuries tended to provide little distinction between the poor, the mentally ill, and the criminal element of society. In a society that had no **social safety net** to provide for people in need, institutions of confinement often housed all "offenders" together without regard for offense, age, or gender. Thus, the orphan, runaway child, debtor, or widow without means of support could end up in the same conditions of confinement as the criminal. Needless to say, such penal institutions were appalling places in terms of sanitation, safety, and rehabilitation. They were characterized by disease as well as violence and victimization of the young, women, and the helpless by fellow inmates and their guards.

Reform Movements

The modern juvenile justice system has its roots in reform movements to "save" children from such conditions. The foundation of the various movements was society's acceptance of the premise that there are significant and fundamental differences between adults and juveniles. As early as the sixteenth century, various reform movements argued against the traditional wisdom that children were "miniature adults." These reform movements advocated that children had less-developed moral and cognitive capacities.[3]

In the 1800s, several reform movements focused on the general well-being of children, which included not only children charged with crimes, but also children who had come into the

1967	1970	1971	1974
In re Gault In hearings that could result in commitment to an institution, juveniles have four basic constitutional rights.	**In re Winship** In delinquency matters, the State must prove its case beyond a reasonable doubt.	**McKeiver v. Pennsylvania** Jury trials are not constitutionally required in juvenile court hearings.	Juvenile Justice and Delinquency Prevention Act establishes standards for juveniles in custody.

1975	1977	1979	1980s	1982
Breed v. Jones Waiver of a juvenile to criminal court following adjudication in juvenile court constitutes double jeopardy.	**Oklahoma Publishing Co. v. District Court**	**Smith v. Daily Mail Publishing Co.** The press may report juvenile court proceedings under certain circumstances.	**Hybrid youth gangs emerge.**	**Eddings v. Oklahoma** Defendant's youthful age should be considered a mitigating factor in deciding whether to apply the death penalty.

custody of the state due to poverty, abandonment, and vagrancy. Many private reform movements focused on providing care for children and removing them from the criminal justice system. During the 1800s, the criminal court did not distinguish between juveniles in the custody of the state for criminal offenses and orphaned, runaway, or abandoned children. In the nineteenth century, children were incarcerated or placed under state control for a variety of "offenses," including petty crime, vagrancy, and begging. Juveniles could be sent to juvenile reformatories because they were "incorrigible minors" or "disorderly children." In 1865, in New York, any child could be sent to the House of Refuge upon the complaint of a guardian, a magistrate, or a justice of the peace that the child was "disorderly." For this reason, early reform movements offered services that tried to encompass the entire spectrum of children's needs, not just the juvenile who committed a criminal offense.

Foundations of the Juvenile Justice System

The New York House of Refuge

In the early 1800s, various private reform groups provided services to divert young offenders and remove juveniles in need from the criminal justice system. The primary focus of these groups was to place youths in group houses, institutions, and other facilities that were designed to provide for their care, education, and rehabilitation. The focus was on rehabilitating and providing for the needs and welfare of the child rather than punishing and imprisoning them. The **New York House of Refuge** was the first of such juvenile reformatories in the nation. It was initiated by the private efforts of a philanthropic association originally called the Society for the Prevention of Pauperism.

The New York House of Refuge juvenile reformatory was established in 1824 and on January 1, 1825, admitted nine children (six boys and three girls) committed for vagrancy and petty crimes.[4] The House of Refuge was privately managed and funded but was endorsed and financially supported by the state of New York. The state passed legislation authorizing courts statewide to commit juveniles convicted of crimes or adjudicated as vagrants to the New York House of Refuge rather than the state's criminal justice system.[5] Like most of the juvenile reformatories of the era that were to follow, supervised labor, education, and discipline were considered the essential elements of rehabilitation for children.[6] In addition, the New York House of Refuge and other early reform movements separated children by gender and took into account the reason they were committed.

The New York House of Refuge had the authority to place those under its charge in private industry through **indenture agreements** by which employers agreed to supervise the youths in exchange for their labor. Those placed in private industry were sent primarily to work on farms and as

TABLE 13–1 COLONIAL AMERICAN COURT TREATMENT OF YOUTHFUL OFFENDERS

Age	Ability to Form *Mens Rea*	Response of the Justice System
Below age 7	Child does not have the ability to form *mens rea* (guilty intent) and cannot be held accountable for any crime.	Parents of offending children were expected to assume responsibility for the child. The juvenile could not be prosecuted in criminal court.
Between ages 7 and 14	The capacity for *mens rea* was a rebuttable defense. Prosecution would have to prove the capacity for *mens rea*, and defense could present evidence against the capacity to form *mens rea*.	If the defense was successful, the offender would be treated the same as children under age 7. If not, the offender would be tried in adult criminal court and sentenced to adult institutions. Some colonies provided a reduction in sentence for children.
Over age 14	The capacity for *mens rea* was presumed, but incapacity for criminal intent could be offered as a defense. Most often this applied to those with mental retardation.	Without benefit of a defense of youth, the offender older than 14 would be tried in adult criminal court and sentenced like adult offenders, including execution by hanging.

1983	1984	1988	1994	1999
Los Angeles Police Department initiates **Drug Abuse Resistance Education (DARE)** program, one of the most popular in-school drug education programs.	**Schall v. Martin** Preventive "pretrial" detention of juveniles is allowable under certain circumstances.	**Thompson v. Oklahoma** The U.S. Supreme Court banned the execution of minors under 16 years old as cruel and unusual punishment.	Rate of juvenile offending peaks and starts to decline.	Columbine High School shooting in Littleton, Colorado, results in nationwide change of law enforcement policy in responding to school shootings.

January 1, 1825

The New York House of Refuge juvenile reformatory admitted nine children (six boys and three girls).

HOUSE OF REFUGE, RANDALL'S ISLAND, NEW YORK.

CORBIS

January 1, 1825: The New York House of Refuge juvenile reformatory admitted nine children (six boys and three girls).

By the mid-1800s, private institutions had proliferated in all of the large cities but still did not have sufficient services to provide alternative incarceration for children.

Other Reformatories Followed

Other states quickly imitated New York's model and adopted similar alternative institutions for juveniles. Like the New York House of Refuge (some of these institutions were also named "House of Refuge"), they could be characterized as "work houses," "training schools," "reform schools," "schools of industry," or other such names whose primary purpose was to develop employable skills for youths.

domestic laborers, and a few of the boys were indentured to merchant sailing ships.[7] The popularity—and the number of wards—of the House of Refuge quickly grew. The New York House of Refuge was visited by and received praise from people all over the world, including Alexis de Tocqueville (a French historian), Frances Trollope (an English novelist), and Charles Dickens (an English writer). In 1857, it was the largest juvenile reformatory in the United States (with over 1,000 youths) and was praised as "the greatest reform school in the world."[8]

The juvenile court was established not as a criminal court, but as a government agency to provide youthful offenders and children who were victimized or in need with a comprehensive and balanced approach to justice.

TIMELINE

Timeline of Key Events

2003	2005	2010	2012	2012
Office of Juvenile Justice and Delinquency Prevention publishes two-year longitudinal study on causes of delinquency.	**Oklahoma Publishing Co. v. District Court**	**Graham v. Florida** Life without parole for juveniles can violate the Eighth Amendment.	**President Obama** issues an executive order titled "White House Initiative on Educational Excellence" to encourage schools to reduce punishments for violation of school rules/violence that disproportionately impact minorities.	In **Miller v. Alabama**, the U.S. Supreme Court extends to homicide offenses the ban on sentences of life without parole for juveniles.

21% The percentage of Maryland penitentiary prisoners in 1897 who were between the ages of 10 and 20.

These quasi-public juvenile reformatories, despite their emphasis on job training and the subsequent income produced by that endeavor, did not prove to be financially sustainable. Further, because each reformatory was independently established, governed, staffed, and financed, there was little or no oversight over the conditions of confinement, the rights of the children, or the qualifications of the staff. There was no standard of care. Many institutions were criticized as being ineffective in their mission, providing substandard care and abusing the rights of children.[9] Many of the reformatories operated on limited funding and could not provide the level of services needed for proper care and reform. As a result, these reform programs failed to rehabilitate the youths or provide them with employable skills; as a result, the children returned to crime, the streets, or the reformatory.

Crisis in the System

By the mid-1800s, private institutions had proliferated in all of the large cities but still did not have enough services to provide alternative incarceration for children. After the Civil War, the growing population and the increase in immigration in America's large cities added to the juvenile problem. By the end of the nineteenth century, there was a crisis in the criminal justice system as to how to handle children in the system. For example, in 1849, approximately 8% of Maryland penitentiary prisoners were between the ages of 13 and 18. In 1897, 15% of the prisoners in the penitentiary were between 12 and 20 years of age and 21% were between 10 and 20 years old. Many states found it necessary to assume control over the various private juvenile reformatories or to provide greater financial support and oversight. States began to see the necessity of providing dedicated court agencies to deal with the problem of young offenders.

▶ The Jurisdiction of the Juvenile Justice System

Toward the end of the nineteenth century, the concept of *parens patriae*, or "state as parent and guardian," began to become the predominant theme in structuring state agencies responsible for juveniles. For example, the adoption of legal reforms that granted the state the inherent right to assume custody of children and a codified assemblage of children's laws culminated in the creation of a separate children's court system in 1892.[10] Cook County (Chicago), Illinois, is recognized as the site of the first juvenile court. Established in 1899, the distinguishing characteristic of the Illinois juvenile court was the concept of **original jurisdiction**. Unlike other states that had separate courts for young offenders who were part of the criminal justice system, the Chicago juvenile court had exclusive jurisdiction over juveniles. Juveniles could not be tried, for any offense, by the criminal court unless the juvenile court granted permission for an accused juvenile to be moved from the authority of the juvenile court. This process was referred to as "**waiving**" the juvenile to the criminal court.

Furthermore, only the juvenile judge—not the prosecutor, the police, or the criminal court judge—had the authority to waive the juvenile to criminal court. The juvenile court was self-contained in that it had its own intake process; it did not depend on the prosecutor to bring cases before the court. Also, it had its own probation and parole system and its own correctional system. The juvenile court did share the services of the police in that the court did not have its own law enforcement agents responsible for the detection and apprehension of juvenile offenders.

The beginning of the twentieth century, known as the Progressive Era, was a time of extensive social reform. Social reform movements had been active in campaigning against "social evil" in the latter part of the nineteenth century. Thus, it is not surprising that with the emergence of a juvenile court with original jurisdiction in Cook County, Illinois, other states quickly adopted this model. By 1910, 32 states had established juvenile courts and/or probation services. By 1925, all but two states had established juvenile courts with exclusive original jurisdiction.[11]

LEARNING OUTCOMES 2 Summarize the jurisdiction of the juvenile justice system and the classification of juvenile offenders.

GLOSSARY

parens patriae The legal assumption that the state has primary responsibility for the safety and custody of children.

original jurisdiction The concept that because juvenile court is the only court that has authority over juveniles, they cannot be tried, for any offense, by a criminal court unless the juvenile court grants permission for an accused juvenile to be waived to criminal court.

waiving Granting permission for an accused juvenile to be moved from juvenile court to criminal court.

juvenile court A court that handles juvenile welfare cases and cases involving status offenders and delinquents; some juvenile courts handle additional matters related to the family.

status offender A child who has committed an act or failed to fulfill a responsibility for which, if he or she were an adult, the court would not have any authority over him or her.

delinquent A juvenile accused of committing an act that is criminal for both adults and juveniles.

juvenile superpredator A term used by the Office of Juvenile Justice and Delinquency Prevention to describe a juvenile who commits violent felony crimes.

1899 The year Cook County, Illinois, established the first juvenile court.

1925 The year in which all but two states had established juvenile courts.

In addition to processing youthful offenders for criminal offenses, the Cook County juvenile court assumed total—and in a sense "absolute"—control over the juvenile. In exercising the right of *parens patriae*, the juvenile court assumed superior authority over the authority of the "natural" parent(s) or guardian. The juvenile court was established not as a criminal court, but as a government agency to provide youthful offenders and children who were victimized or in need with a comprehensive and balanced approach to justice.[12] The court operated on the principle of "the best interests of the child."[13] As a result, the court had original exclusive jurisdiction not only of children who had committed crimes, but also of any child whose welfare and well-being was in question. In a sense, the court had the same interest in the overall welfare and well-being as did the child's parent(s) or guardian. The philosophy underlying this authority was that "the delinquent child or the child in need was seen as in need of the court's benevolent intervention."[14]

The **juvenile court** removed the child from the authority of the criminal court, but it also assumed greater authority over the child than the criminal court had over accused adults. Besides being "benevolent," the juvenile court was more intrusive and had the power to intervene in noncriminal matters. The juvenile court assumed authority over children in three situations:

1. When the welfare of the child was threatened
2. When the child was a status offender
3. When the child was a delinquent

In court review of welfare cases, the child did not commit a crime, but the court's focus was on what was best for the child. Juveniles who committed offenses were classified as status offenders or delinquents.

Classification of Juvenile Offenders

Status Offenders

Juveniles are classified as **status offenders** or delinquents. Status offenders are children who have committed an act or failed to fulfill a responsibility for which, if they were adults, the court would not have any authority over them. Common status offenses are failing to attend school; running away from parents or guardians; and engaging in behaviors that while legal for adults, are considered harmful for children, such as smoking and drinking alcoholic beverages.

Delinquents

On the other hand, **delinquents** are accused of committing an act that is criminal for both adults and juveniles. The criminal justice system divides crimes into felonies and misdemeanors,

Juvenile delinquents include offenders who have committed petty crimes such as theft, vandalism, and simple assault (or fighting) as well as robbery, rape, and murder.

but there is no similar division in the juvenile court. Because the focus of the court is on the welfare of the child, there is less concern about serious versus minor offenses as such concern focuses on the punishment for the offense and not on the welfare of the offender.

Further, the authority of the juvenile court is time-limited. Felonies have sentences of 5, 10, or 20 years or even life without parole. The juvenile court has custodial authority of the offender only during his or her youth. This limit has been defined differently by the various states. In some states, the custodial authority of the juvenile court extends until the offender is 18 years old; in other states, the juvenile court may retain custodial authority until the offender is 23. With such limited custodial authority, it is not possible for the court to impose lengthy sentences for "serious" offenses. Thus, the distinction between misdemeanor crimes and felony crimes is not as pivotal in juvenile court as it is in the criminal justice system.

Hence, a juvenile delinquent is a person under the authority of the juvenile court who has committed an offense for which, if he or she were an adult, would be considered criminal. Therefore, the term *juvenile delinquent* fails to clearly identify the nature of the offender's crime. Juvenile delinquents include offenders who have committed petty crimes such as theft, vandalism, and simple assault (or fighting) as well as robbery, rape, and murder. However, in 2000, the Office of Juvenile Justice and Delinquency Prevention sought to identify juveniles who had committed serious crimes. They used the term **juvenile superpredators** to identify juvenile delinquents who engage in serious violent crime such as murder, rape, and assault. The term *juvenile superpredator* is not a legal term recognized by the juvenile court, but is used in literature describing juveniles who commit more serious offenses.

▶ Due Process for Juveniles

In the beginning, unlike the criminal justice system, neither state supreme courts nor the U.S. Supreme Court provided significant review and oversight of juvenile justice courts. The Supreme Court essentially adopted a hands-off policy similar to its view of prisoner rights for adults prior to the Warren Court. Juvenile jurisdiction extended well beyond the jurisdiction the criminal courts exercised over adults. As such, juveniles were effectively denied the rights afforded by the equal protection clause of the Fourteenth Amendment. The justification for this exclusion was that the juvenile received less due process but that the court demonstrated a greater concern for the interests of the juvenile. Essentially, the view underlying the position of the Court was that operating under the doctrine of *parens patriae*, the purpose of the court was not to punish the juvenile, but to provide "solicitous care and regenerative treatment."[15]

From the beginning, some were critical of the lack of due process based on the assumption of the benevolent nature of the juvenile court. For example, the Maryland Children's Code Commission of 1922 published a report critical of the lack of due process for juveniles. It cited the case of a two-year-old child committed to reform school as an incorrigible minor until the age of 21. However, these complaints were ignored because juvenile courts appeared to offer compensating benefits to the juvenile that offset the lack of due process rights.

LEARNING
OUTCOMES
3

Explain how
landmark court
cases have
influenced the due
process rights of juveniles.

GLOSSARY

Kent* v. *United States A Supreme
Court case that marked the departure of the Supreme Court from its
acceptance of the denial of due
process rights to juveniles.

In re Gault A case in which the
Supreme Court provided due process rights to juveniles, including
notice of charges, counsel, right
to examine witnesses, and right to
remain silent.

In re Winship A case in which
the Supreme Court ruled that the
reasonable doubt standard, the
same used in criminal trials,
should be required in all delinquency adjudications.

burden of proof The standard
required for adjudication.

McKeiver* v. *Pennsylvania
A case in which the Supreme
Court denied juveniles the right to
a trial by jury.

Breed* v. *Jones A case in which
the Supreme Court ruled that once
a juvenile has been adjudicated
by a juvenile court, he or she cannot be waived to criminal court to
be tried for the same charges.

Schall* v. *Martin A case in which
the Supreme Court upheld the
right of juvenile courts to deny
bail to adjudicated juveniles.

**Juvenile Justice and
Delinquency Prevention Act
of 1974** An act that provides the
major source of federal funding
to states for the improvement
of their juvenile justice systems,
services, and facilities.

Although there were
some abuses of due process,
many of the juvenile courts
did operate with the intent
to promote the best interests of the child. Oregon, for
example, adopted legislation
in the 1930s declaring that
juveniles were not responsible
for the underlying causes of
their delinquency because
they had no control over their
environment or heredity,
which were identified as the
underlying causes of juvenile
delinquency.[16] Thus, based
on the juvenile court's balance between prevention and
treatment goals versus punishment, the Supreme Court
did not require juvenile courts
to provide due process protection to juveniles.

During the 1960s, the
U.S. Supreme Court aban-
doned its hands-off doctrine
and began to examine the
need for due process rights
for juveniles. In a series of
decisions, the Court radically
redefined the due process
rights of juveniles. (Supreme
Court decisions regarding
the juvenile death penalty
will be discussed in a later
section.) These decisions
examined whether juveniles
should receive due process
rights similar to those of adult
defendants in criminal court.

Kent v. *United States*—Waiver Hearing Rights

The first due process case the
Supreme Court considered
was ***Kent* v. *United States***
(1966),[17] which marked the
departure of the Supreme Court from its acceptance of the
denial of due process rights to juveniles based on the assumption that juveniles received compensating benefits. In 1961,
while on probation from an earlier case, Morris Kent, aged
16, was charged with rape and robbery. Kent confessed to the
offenses and to several similar incidents.[18] Because of Kent's age
and the fact that he was considered a repeat violent offender,
his attorney, believing that the case may be waived to criminal court, filed a motion requesting a hearing on the issue of

jurisdiction. The judge denied the hearing and ruled that the
case would be transferred to criminal court. The judge stated
that the court had made a "full investigation" of the case but
refused to disclose the details of the investigation or to provide
Kent's attorney with the opportunity to refute the waiver.

At the time, the decision of juvenile judges could not be
appealed based on the concept of original jurisdiction; so
Morris Kent was tried in criminal court. He was found guilty
and sentenced to 30 to 90 years in prison. His attorney appealed
the conviction to the Supreme Court, arguing that Kent's due
process rights were violated when he was waived to criminal
court without the opportunity of a hearing. The Supreme Court
ruled that Kent was deprived of the "compensating benefit of
the solicitous care and regeneration treatment postulated for
children" and thus received the "worst of both worlds"—neither
the protection accorded to adults nor the benefits promised
for juveniles.[19] The Court ruled that Kent was entitled to
due process rights under the equal protection clause of the
Fourteenth Amendment.

In re Gault—Due Process Rights

In 1967, one year after the Kent case, the Supreme Court
expanded the due process rights of juveniles. In reviewing ***In re
Gault*** (1967),[20] the Court abandoned the arguments justifying lack of equal protection for juveniles under the Fourteenth
Amendment. Gerald Gault, aged 15, was on probation in
Arizona for a minor property offense when, in 1964, he and
a friend made a crank telephone call to an adult neighbor. At
the court proceedings, Gault did not have an attorney. The
victim did not testify, and it was not established that Gault
was the one who made the "obscene" remarks during the call.
However, he was committed to a training school until he was
21 years old—a sentence of six years. The maximum sentence
for the same offense had Gault been an adult in criminal court

Kent* v. *United States
Established that juveniles were
entitled to the following due process rights:

1. The right to a waiver hearing
2. The right to counsel at waiver hearings
3. The right to access any reports and records
   used by the court in deciding waiver
4. The right to a statement issued by the juvenile
   judge justifying waiver to the criminal court

would have been a $50 fine or two months in jail. Under state juvenile proceedings, Gault was not entitled to an appeal of the adjudication.

After being committed to training school, Gault obtained an attorney who appealed the case to the Supreme Court. The issue presented was that Gault's constitutional rights to notice of charges, counsel, questioning of witnesses, protection against self-incrimination, a transcript of the proceedings, and appellate review were denied.[21] The Supreme Court agreed with the challenge and ruled that in hearings that could result in commitment to an institution, juveniles have the right to due process.

The Supreme Court criticized the "welfare of the child" doctrine of the juvenile court, concluding the following: "Juvenile court history has again demonstrated that unbridled discretion, however benevolently motivated, is frequently a poor substitute for principle and procedure."[22] The Supreme Court made significant changes to the very nature of the juvenile justice court proceedings giving juveniles due process rights similar to those of adults in criminal court with regard to notice of charges, counsel, confrontation of witnesses, and self-incrimination.

In re Winship—Burden of Proof

Juvenile court proceedings are not criminal trials; so one of the differences between juvenile court proceedings and criminal trials prior to **In re Winship** was the standard of proof required for a judge to adjudicate, which is to hear and judge, an offender. In civil cases, the **burden of proof** is "a preponderance of the evidence"; that is, is it more likely that the matter is true or not true? In criminal cases, the burden of proof is a much stricter "proof beyond a reasonable doubt." Again, because of the mission of the juvenile court, the Supreme Court was silent on which standard should apply to juvenile court proceedings. State supreme courts were also silent on the issue or operated under the "preponderance of evidence," or the 50 percent rule. Judges based their rulings on whether they believed it was more likely than not that the accused juvenile committed the act. *In re Winship* concerned Samuel Winship,

aged 12, who was charged with stealing $112 from a woman's purse in a store.[23] No eyewitnesses saw Winship steal the money, but a witness did claim to have seen Winship running from the scene just before the woman noticed that the money was missing. The New York juvenile court, where Winship's case was heard, used the preponderance of evidence rule. The court agreed with Winship's attorney that there was "reasonable doubt" of Winship's guilt but that it was more likely that he committed the act than not.[24]

Again, the state argued before the U.S. Supreme Court that because juvenile courts were designed to rehabilitate children rather than to punish them, it was not necessary for the state to use the higher standard of proof. As in the *Kent* and *Gault* cases, the Court rejected the juvenile court's claim to waiver of due process protections based on benefits afforded the juvenile. It ruled that the reasonable doubt standard, the same used in criminal trials, should be required in all delinquency adjudications.

McKeiver v. Pennsylvania—Right to Jury Trial

In 1966, 1967, and 1970 rulings, the Supreme Court significantly expanded the due process rights of juveniles when accused of acts for which they could be confined, even if that confinement was in a state facility with the stated purpose of "helping" the juvenile. With these expanded due process rights, juvenile hearings adhered to many of the standards used in criminal trials. One of the due process rights denied juveniles was trial by a jury of their peers. A judge presided over the juvenile hearing and rendered the final judgment and disposition. Joseph McKeiver, 16, was charged with robbery and larceny as well as receiving stolen goods. He was accused of being with a gang of other youths who chased three children and took 25 cents from them.

At McKeiver's adjudication hearing, his attorney requested a jury trial. The request was denied, and McKeiver was adjudicated and placed on probation. The case was appealed to the Supreme Court. Unlike previous cases that favored the expansion of due process rights, the Court ruled that the due process clause of the Fourteenth Amendment did not require jury trials in juvenile courts. The decision also noted that judges presided in bench trials in criminal court and that there was no evidence to suggest that juries are more accurate than judges in the adjudication stage. In **McKeiver v. Pennsylvania**, the Supreme Court agreed with the state's argument that a jury trial would most likely "destroy the traditional character of juvenile proceedings."

In the case of *In re Gault*, the U.S. Supreme Court extended the due process rights of juveniles to include the following:

1. Right to reasonable notice of the charges
2. Right to counsel as well as appointed counsel if indigent
3. Right to confront and cross-examine witnesses
4. Right against self-incrimination, including the right to remain silent

In *McKeiver* v. *Pennsylvania*, the Supreme Court agreed with the state's argument that a jury trial would most likely "destroy the traditional character of juvenile proceedings."

Breed v. Jones—Double Jeopardy

In 1970, Gary Jones, aged 17, was charged with armed robbery. Jones appeared in Los Angeles juvenile court and was adjudicated delinquent on the original charge and two other robberies.[25] The prosecutor sought to try Jones in criminal court for the same actions after his adjudication in juvenile court. Jones's attorney asserted that trial in criminal court on the same charges violated the double jeopardy clause of the Fifth Amendment. The state argued that juvenile adjudication was not a trial and that, therefore, trial in a criminal court constituted the "first trial" for the offense and did not constitute double jeopardy. The California Court upheld the ruling, and the case was appealed to the U.S. Supreme Court. In *Breed v. Jones* (1975), the Supreme Court ruled that juvenile adjudication is equivalent to a trial in criminal court and once a juvenile has been adjudicated by a juvenile court, he or she cannot be waived to criminal court to be tried for the same charges.

Schall v. Martin—The Right to Bail

Gregory Martin, 14, was arrested in 1977 and charged with robbery, assault, and possession of a weapon. He and two other youths allegedly hit a boy on the head with a loaded gun and stole his jacket and sneakers.[26] Arguing that there was a serious risk that Martin would commit another crime, rather than release him to a parent or guardian, the state held Martin in a juvenile facility pending adjudication.[27] Martin's attorney filed a *habeas corpus* action, arguing that because in most cases an adjudicated child was released back to the custody of his or her parent(s) or guardian, preventive detention was punishment. Martin's attorney argued that his client was being denied the right to bail. The lower appellate courts agreed with Martin's attorney and reversed the juvenile court's detention order.

The case was appealed to the U.S. Supreme Court, where the state argued that preventive detention serves a legitimate state objective in protecting both the juvenile and society from pretrial crime and is not intended to punish the juvenile. In **Schall v. Martin** (1984), the Supreme Court upheld the constitutionality of the preventive detention of juveniles. It agreed that the doctrine of *parens patriae* applied to preventive detention of juveniles and accepted that the state was acting in the best interest of the child.[28] The ruling allowed the juvenile court to deny the right to bail to juveniles prior to adjudication.

▶ Characteristics of Juvenile Court Proceedings

One of the characteristics distinguishing juvenile court proceedings from criminal trials is that juvenile court proceedings are not open to the public. Not only are the court proceedings private, but many courts prohibit news media from publishing the names of juveniles involved.

However, in a 1977 case and a 1979 case, the Supreme Court granted the news media the right to publish the names of juveniles involved in court proceedings under certain circumstances. In *Oklahoma Publishing Company v. District Court in and for Oklahoma City* (1977)[29] and *Smith v. Daily Mail Publishing Company* (1979),[30] the Court refused to uphold

> One of the characteristics distinguishing juvenile court proceedings from criminal trials is that juvenile court proceedings are not open to the public.

the traditional ban on publishing juveniles' names. In the *Oklahoma Publishing Company* case, a court order prohibited the press from reporting the name and printing a photograph of a youth involved in a juvenile court proceeding, which the Oklahoma Publishing Company had obtained legally from a source outside the court. Likewise, in the *Daily Mail* case, the juvenile court sought to prohibit the publishing of a juvenile's name that had been obtained by the media independently of the court. In both cases, the Supreme Court ruled that the First Amendment interests in a free press take precedence over the interests in preserving the anonymity of juvenile defendants. The Court ruled that in cases where the media obtains the name or photograph of a juvenile legally and independently of the court record, they have the right to publish or broadcast the information. The Court's ruling was narrow in what it permitted, and it did not open juvenile court proceedings or juvenile court records to the public or the media.

Separation of Juveniles and Adults

Due process rights for juveniles are extensively influenced by the federal **Juvenile Justice and Delinquency Prevention Act of 1974** (JJDPA), amended in 2001. The act provides the major source of federal funding to states for the improvement of their juvenile justice systems, services, and facilities. The JJDPA influences state juvenile justice systems by requiring states to maintain the standards set forth in the JJDPA if they receive federal funds. The primary intent of the JJDPA is to ensure that children do not have contact with adults in jails and other institutional settings and that status offenders are not placed in secure detention.

The provisions of the JJDPA provide that juveniles may not be detained in adult jails and lockups except for limited times before or after a court hearing. Recognizing the difference in the level of resources between urban and rural juvenile courts, juveniles may be detained up to 6 hours before or after a court hearing in urban areas but up to 24 hours plus weekends and holidays in rural juvenile courts. Also, the JJDPA regulates the travel conditions for juveniles. The JJDPA regulations do not apply to children who are tried or convicted in adult criminal court of a felony-level offense.

When children are placed in an adult jail or lockup, except as provided by the exceptions in the JJDPA, "sight and sound" separation is required between adults and juveniles to keep children safe from verbal or psychological abuse that could occur from being within sight or sound of adult inmates. Children also cannot be housed next to adult cells; share dining halls, recreation areas, or any other common spaces with adults; or be placed in any circumstances that could expose them to threats or abuse from adult offenders.

The provisions of the JJDPA do not have the same force as the U.S. Constitution or U.S. Supreme Court decisions, but compliance is influenced by the "purse strings." Under the JJDPA, federal moneys are channeled to state agencies. Moneys can be withheld from those agencies that do not comply with the standards set forth in the JJDPA. Thus, the JJDPA does not guarantee due process rights with the same authority as the Constitution or U.S. Supreme Court, but it plays a pivotal role in setting standards for the holding of juveniles in institutions.

Community-Based Facilities

The JJDPA provides that juvenile status offenders should not be housed in secure facilities while waiting for their juvenile court hearing or waiting for the juvenile intake officer to review their case. Juvenile status offenders are to be housed in community-based facilities, day treatment, or residential home treatment facilities, foster homes, or other age-appropriate nonsecure facilities. The JJDPA does allow juvenile status offenders to be held up to 24 hours in secure detention or confinement under some circumstances. Also, the JJDPA stipulates that juvenile status offenders should receive appropriate treatment, counseling, mentoring, alternative education, and job development support while in state custody.

Treatment of Minority Juveniles

Finally, a broad mission of the JJDPA is to address the problem of disproportionate confinement of minorities. Minority children make up approximately one-third of the youth population but two-thirds of children in confinement. Further, studies indicate that minority youths receive tougher sentences and are more likely to be incarcerated than are nonminority youths for the same offenses. The JJDPA requires states to assess their treatment of minority juveniles to ensure that they are being treated fairly and equitably by the juvenile justice system.

▶ Judicial Waiver: Abandoning the Great Experiment

In the twenty-first century, the juvenile court remains distinct from the criminal court, but the state juvenile courts provide juvenile offenders with most of the same rights as adult offenders. The U.S. Supreme Court has declared that the rights in the Fifth, Sixth, and Seventh Amendments are not restricted by age or the professed intent of the court to "help" the child. However, public perception that the juvenile crime rate is dangerously high has resulted in public pressure to remove some of the protections of the juvenile justice system for juvenile offenders.

Juvenile offending peaked in the mid-1990s with about 2.9 million arrests of teenagers younger than 18. The incidences of juvenile offending decreased substantially from the mid-1990s to the present, dropping to under 2 million arrests. The rate of arrests rose from 2004 to 2006, but since 2006, the juvenile crime rate has continued to decline. The juvenile crime rate has dropped more than the adult crime rate. The FBI Uniform Crime Report recorded an 8.9% drop in juvenile arrests for all offenses in 2009 compared to 2008; the adult rate declined only 1.2%.

However, public perception of the threat from juvenile crime has continued to exert pressure on the juvenile justice system to change its focus from rehabilitation to punishment. Contrary to statistical data, public perception is that juvenile offenders pose a serious and increasing threat to community safety.[31]

Comparison of National Crime Victimization Survey data and self-reported data complicates the analysis. Changes in record keeping—in reporting requirements for crimes on school property—suggest that a discrepancy may exist between reported changes in the rate of juvenile crime and actual increase or decrease in juvenile crime. For example, prior to the adoption of federally mandated reporting requirements, many schools did not report crimes such as theft, assault, and robbery that occurred on school property. If a child took money by force from another child on school property, the incident was handled by school authorities and the offender was punished by school authorities without the intervention of the police and the juvenile court system. However, as a result of new reporting requirements, schools must now report these incidents as crimes, which results in a rise in the juvenile crime rate but, in reality, no change in the actual number of incidences.

Despite the inclusive conclusions derived from crime statistics as to whether there is a greater rate of violent juvenile crime in the twenty-first century, the public perception is that violent juvenile crime is a serious problem. Thus, the past two decades have seen significant changes in the processing of juveniles by the juvenile and criminal justice systems. Spurred by public concern over violent juvenile crimes, states have abandoned the "great experiment" that juveniles were not responsible for the crimes they commit. Many states have adopted a philosophy of accountability for violent crimes and have changed the provisions for transferring juveniles to the criminal court.

Mens Rea and Youthful Violent Offenders

One of the problems with juveniles who commit violent offenses, even murder, is the debate as to whether the youthful offender has sufficient *mens rea* to appreciate the criminality of his or her act. The causes of youth violence have been attributed to neighborhood decay and poverty in U.S. urban centers; unemployment (especially due to lack of minimal education, training, and skills); weak social networks such as those found in impoverished and ethnically diverse neighborhoods; and family and individual risk factors.[32]

LEARNING OUTCOMES 4 Summarize why and in what ways states are changing the age of accountability.

GLOSSARY

waiver The process of moving a juvenile from the authority of juvenile court to the adult criminal justice system.

statutory exclusion The provision that allows juveniles to be transferred to criminal court without review by and approval of the juvenile court.

blended sentencing option An option that allows the juvenile or criminal court to impose a sentence that can include confinement in a juvenile facility and/or in an adult prison after the offender is beyond the age of the juvenile court's jurisdiction.

Many researchers argue that youthful offenders:

1. Are not fully responsible for their criminal actions

2. Because of their immaturity, do not have the same *mens rea*, or criminal intent, as do adults

Often this belief is reflected in state law and was the basis for the decision in *Roper* v. *Simmons* (2005), which prohibited the death penalty for offenses committed by juveniles when they were younger than 18. However, public perception does not necessarily conform to statistical data, and the public has exerted pressure on state legislatures to remove violent juvenile offenders from the protection of the juvenile court.

Waiver to Criminal Court—Age of Accountability

The age at which a juvenile has the necessary maturity to form criminal intent and be fully accountable for his or her crime has not been resolved by researchers or state law. The minimum age for criminal liability varies by state.

In 1899, when the Cook County (Chicago), Illinois, court system implemented the first separation of juvenile offenders from adult offenders, it was necessary to set an age that divided the two systems. Cook County set the legal end of childhood at age 18, which was quite old compared to the life experiences of the time. The average life expectancy at birth for white men in 1900 was 46.3 (most delinquents were men). For African-American men, the average life expectancy was only 32.5 years. At age 18, the average African-American male could be considered "middle aged" in that he had a life expectancy of less than 15 years. In 1899, it was not uncommon for 17-year-olds to marry, have gainful employment, and live separately from their parents. There is no evidence that Cook County used any scientific evidence or any criminological theories or studies to set the dividing line between adult and juvenile at 18 years.

There is no agreement among states as to what constitutes the age of accountability. Thirty-seven states, the District of Columba, and the federal government have set the age of adult criminal responsibility at 18. Eleven states have set the age at 17; New York and North Carolina, at 16. Also, each state has established a lower age at which the juvenile offender can be transferred to the adult court for violent offenses such as murder. Some states have set this age at 14; others, even lower. Some states (Pennsylvania, for example) have no minimum age limit. In these states, even a four- or five-year-old child can be tried and sentenced as an adult in criminal court for certain crimes of murder. On any given day, about 3,000 youth aged 18 and under are in custody of an adult prison system.[33] Approximately 250,000 youth end up in the adult system each year.[34]

In recent years, many have questioned at what age an offender should be treated differently by the criminal justice system. Some members of the public believe 17 years of age is too old to avoid criminal responsibility based on a defense of youth. They argue that children are more mature today; have access to and use guns in the crimes they commit; belong to violent gangs; and use the protection of the criminal justice system to avoid punishment for serious crimes such as murder, rape, drug trafficking, robbery, gang-related violence, and burglary. To a degree, this argument is based on the fact that from 1985 to the early 1990s, the number of teenagers arrested for murder nearly tripled before declining sharply in the mid- and late 1990s. Despite this drop in juvenile offending, juveniles were still involved in about one in ten arrests for murder.[35] The public appears to welcome the fact that the juvenile crime rate has dropped. Other factors causing public fear are media reports of violent attacks by youth gangs. For many people, juvenile violence is perceived as "out of control" and more violent than ever before.[36]

Beginning in the 1970s, state legislatures began moving more juvenile offenders into criminal court based on age and/or offense seriousness, without the case-specific consideration offered by the discretionary juvenile court judicial waiver process.[37] In 2009, about 9% of cases of offenders under the age of 18 were disposed of in adult criminal court.[38] This movement reduced the exclusive original jurisdiction of juvenile courts over youthful offenders. Each state has its own name for the process of moving the juvenile from the authority of the juvenile court to the adult criminal justice system. Common terms for the process include judicial **waiver**, *certification*, *remand*, *bind over for criminal prosecution*, *transfer*, and *decline* (when waiver is denied). New provisions have provided a variety of methods by which a juvenile can be waived to criminal court without the approval of or, in some cases, without any intervention by the juvenile court.

Seriousness of the Offense

Some states have established waiver criteria based on the offense independent of the age of the accused offender. Often the criteria involve commission of crimes with firearms or other weapons or capital offenses. About 15 states have revoked the exclusive original jurisdiction granted to juvenile courts and replaced it with concurrent jurisdiction. In concurrent jurisdiction, the prosecutor has discretion to file certain cases, generally involving juveniles charged with serious offenses, in either criminal or juvenile court. In states with concurrent jurisdiction, when a case meets certain criteria, such as minimum

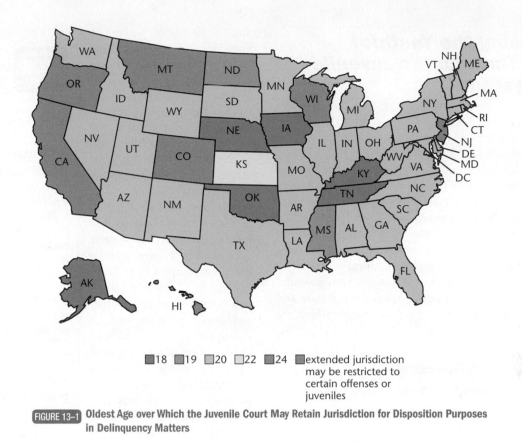

18 ■ 19 □ 20 □ 22 ■ 24 ■ extended jurisdiction may be restricted to certain offenses or juveniles

FIGURE 13–1 Oldest Age over Which the Juvenile Court May Retain Jurisdiction for Disposition Purposes in Delinquency Matters

age, crime committed with a weapon, prior criminal record, certain felonies (murder), or special circumstances, the prosecutor, not the juvenile court, has the discretion of filing the case in criminal court. This **statutory exclusion** provision allows juveniles to be transferred to criminal court without review by and approval of the juvenile court.

A majority of states have adopted statutory exclusion and have excluded certain serious offenses from juvenile court jurisdiction. The offenses most often excluded are capital crimes, murder, and other serious offenses against persons.[39] Also, a majority of the states stipulate that if the juvenile has ever been tried and convicted as an adult, he or she must be prosecuted in criminal court for any subsequent offenses regardless of the offense or the juvenile's age. Thus, if a juvenile is waived to criminal court for an offense at age 14, is released, and is then rearrested before age 18, regardless of the second offense, the defendant will be under the jurisdiction of the criminal court.

In addition, about half the states have **blended sentencing options** to create a middle ground between traditional juvenile sanctions and adult sanctions. Blended models differ by state but generally allow the juvenile court to retain jurisdiction of delinquents past the age of 18. The juvenile court retains custody of the delinquent until he or she is 18 years old. After 18, the youth may be transferred to an adult institution for a further period of time. The oldest age over which the juvenile court may retain jurisdiction for disposition purposes in delinquency matters varies by state. (See Figure 13–1.) In this model, after adjudication/conviction, the offender enters a juvenile facility until he or she is 18. At that point, the court evaluates the offender and has the authority to decide without a new trial whether the offender is to be transferred to an adult facility to serve additional time or if the offender is to be released. This decision is based on an assessment as to whether the youthful offender is rehabilitated and needs no additional incarceration.

22 The number of states that have no minimum age for some juveniles to be waived to criminal court for violent offenses.

(Think About It . . .

Juvenile crime is very focused as to time and place of occurrence. Nationwide, juvenile violence peaks in the after-school hours on school days and in the evenings on nonschool days. Most (63%) violent crimes committed by juveniles occur on school days. Nearly one-fifth of juvenile violent crimes occur in the four hours between 3 P.M. and 7 P.M. on school days. Studies indicate that juvenile crime is concentrated in public and commercial areas where youth gather. Why is juvenile crime so focused as to time and place? How can police use this information?

▶ Processing the Youthful Offender Through the Juvenile Justice System

The adult criminal justice system has been shaped and influenced by extensive Supreme Court rulings, legislation, and oversight by the public and media. As a result, a general overview of the adult criminal justice system fairly accurately reflects the processing of adult offenders in the various states. However, the juvenile justice system is more diverse. Although U.S. Supreme Court decisions have provided more commonality in the due process rights of juveniles, the actual processing, the agencies, and the personnel involved in moving a juvenile from intake to rehabilitation differs from state to state. In a sense, there is no single juvenile justice system, but a collection of juvenile justice systems. How juveniles are processed through the system depends on the state and sometimes the geographical region of the state in which the juvenile court is located.

Classification of Processing

States can be divided into three general models of juvenile justice processing:

1. Centralized states
2. Decentralized states
3. Combination states[40]

The classification is based on how states organize their juvenile system, how services are delivered to juveniles, and who has authority over the juvenile system. The 12 centralized states[41] are characterized by a state executive agency having across-the-board state control of delinquency services, including state-run juvenile probation services, institutional commitments, and aftercare. The 18 states with decentralized juvenile systems are characterized by local control of the various juvenile services, such as juvenile courts, child welfare agencies, and aftercare services (for example, probation services).[42] Twenty-one states are classified as having a combination juvenile system. Each of these states has a different juvenile system that is often an evolutionary outcome reflecting the unique problems, geography, and resources of the state. In combination states, the organization of the juvenile system is a mixture of state-controlled and locally operated juvenile services.[43] In these states, the juvenile court may be state-controlled and aftercare facilities may be locally controlled. Another option is that the juvenile court may be a combination of state-controlled courts for rural areas and locally controlled juvenile courts for major metropolitan areas. The authority responsible for the various juvenile services may be split between the executive and judicial branches. A common example of such a split is juvenile courts controlled by the judicial branch of the state government and juvenile lockup facilities controlled by the executive branch of the state government (governor).

The unique nature of the juvenile system of each state provides some difficulty in generalizing the case flow through the juvenile justice system. The case flow for each state differs, and the names of the various agencies, courts, detention facilities, and aftercare services are not consistent from state to state. For example, in this chapter, the term *juvenile court* has described the place and agency where juvenile court proceedings occur, but most states do not use this term. Such courts may be called *family court*; *probate court*; or terms similar to those used to identify the adult court system, such as *district court*, *superior court*, or *circuit court*. These courts may have jurisdiction over a number of issues concerning children, such as delinquency, status offense, child welfare due to abuse or neglect, adoption, termination of parental rights, and emancipation. Some courts may even have jurisdiction over adult criminal acts involving the family, such as spouse abuse. For these reasons, the following flowchart, which shows a general diagram of the processing of a case through the juvenile justice system, may not be a good representation of each state. However, it does provide a general overview of the processing of juveniles from intake to disposition.

Intake

There is significant difference in terminology in describing the juvenile justice system and the adult justice system, starting with the term to describe how the juvenile is processed into the system. In the adult system, the suspected offender is "arrested." Juveniles are not "arrested." The process whereby a juvenile enters the juvenile justice system is called **juvenile intake**. About 85% of juvenile intakes are initiated by the police. Larger police departments have special units staffed by police officers who are trained and specialize in handling juvenile offenders.

Describe the juvenile justice system, including postadjudications options for treatment and punishment of juveniles.

GLOSSARY

juvenile intake officer A person who is responsible for processing a juvenile into the juvenile justice system and seeing to aftercare if the juvenile is adjudicated; this person has duties similar to those of a police officer and a probation and parole officer.

juvenile intake The process whereby a juvenile enters the juvenile justice system.

life history An assessment by the juvenile intake/probation officer of the juvenile and his or her past behavior, living conditions, parents/guardians, and school behavior.

consent decree A written summary of the specific conditions and requirements to be placed on the child and/or parent(s) or guardian by the juvenile intake officer.

juvenile adjudication hearing The formal hearing held by a juvenile judge to conduct an inquiry of the facts concerning a case and to decide the disposition of the case and any rehabilitation, supervision, or punishment for the juvenile.

delinquency petition A request to a judge to hear and judge a juvenile case in a formal hearing to determine whether the juvenile is to be declared delinquent.

teen courts Courts for younger juveniles (aged 10 to 15) with no prior arrest record who are charged with less serious law violations wherein juvenile peers rather than adults determine the disposition.

juvenile drug courts Alternatives to the traditional adjudication process for juveniles with substance abuse problems that focus on rehabilitating the juveniles and eliminating drug abuse.

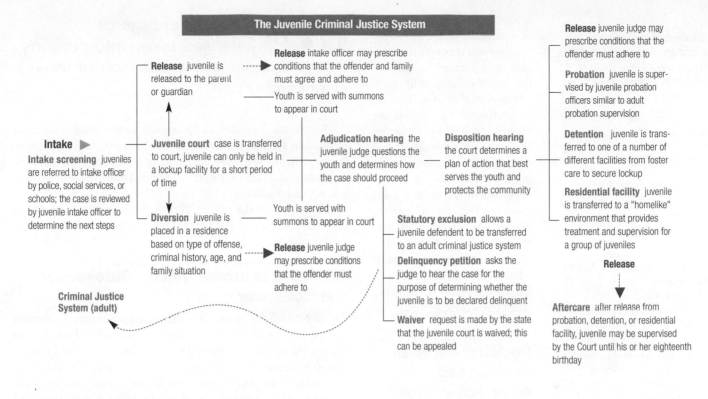

The Juvenile Criminal Justice System

Intake ▶

Intake screening juveniles are referred to intake officer by police, social services, or schools; the case is reviewed by juvenile intake officer to determine the next steps

Criminal Justice System (adult)

Release juvenile is released to the parent or guardian

Juvenile court case is transferred to court, juvenile can only be held in a lockup facility for a short period of time

Diversion juvenile is placed in a residence based on type of offense, criminal history, age, and family situation

Release intake officer may prescribe conditions that the offender and family must agree and adhere to

Youth is served with summons to appear in court

Youth is served with summons to appear in court

Release juvenile judge may prescribe conditions that the offender must adhere to

Adjudication hearing the juvenile judge questions the youth and determines how the case should proceed

Statutory exclusion allows a juvenile defendent to be transferred to an adult criminal justice system

Delinquency petition asks the judge to hear the case for the purpose of determining whether the juvenile is to be declared delinquent

Waiver request is made by the state that the juvenile court is waived; this can be appealed

Disposition hearing the court determines a plan of action that best serves the youth and protects the community

Release juvenile judge may prescribe conditions that the offender must adhere to

Probation juvenile is supervised by juvenile probation officers similar to adult probation supervision

Detention juvenile is transferred to one of a number of different facilities from foster care to secure lockup

Residential facility juvenile is transferred to a "homelike" environment that provides treatment and supervision for a group of juveniles

Release

Aftercare after release from probation, detention, or residential facility, juvenile may be supervised by the Court until his or her eighteenth birthday

---

This special training is necessary because legislation and federal programs encourage and provide for the separation of adults from juveniles in all stages of processing through the system. The other 15% of juveniles can enter the system through *referral* by a parent or guardian, school official, social worker, juvenile probation officer, or juvenile court officer.

Unlike adults who are apprehended by the police for criminal activity, juveniles are not booked and generally are not placed in a lockup facility. Also, unlike adults who enter the criminal justice system because they are charged with

criminal activity, juveniles may enter as status offenders or delinquents or for protective custody. In cases where the juvenile is a status offender or is being held for protective custody, federal regulations generally permit the police to detain the juvenile in a lockup facility for only a short period of time (six hours) to contact the parent(s), guardian, or juvenile court. However, such juvenile lockup facilities cannot be within sight or sound of adult inmates.

If the juvenile is not a danger to self or society, the police may simply gather information concerning the alleged incident,

---

Comparison of State Juvenile Courts and Criminal Courts

Juvenile Justice System		Criminal Justice System
Rehabilitation Rehabilitation of the juvenile is the primary goal	versus	**Sanctions** Sanctions are used against the offender
Prevention Focus on all risk factors, including the family and the environment	versus	**Prevention** Prevention activities are generalized and aimed at deterrence
Law Enforcement Specialized juvenile units are used, and the confidentiality of juvenile identity is ensured	versus	**Law Enforcement** Open public access to all information is required
Intake Intake based on social service model; the court is seen as the guardian of the defendant	versus	**Prosecution** Advisorial system
Detention Separate detention facilities for juveniles	versus	**Jail/lockup**
Adjudication Different rights afforded and no jury trial for juveniles	versus	**Conviction** At criminal trial with right to appeal to higher court
Disposition Rehabilitation of the juvenile is the primary goal	versus	**Sentencing**
Juvenile Justice System Offenses classified as status offense or delinquent	versus	**Criminal Justice System** Misdemeanors or Felonies

adjudicated Determined the disposition of the charges against the juvenile and the treatment or punishment options, done by the juvenile judge.

ward of the state A person for whom the state assumes responsibility for his or her health and well-being.

juvenile boot camp A military-style group-oriented rehabilitation program designed to alter the character and values of the juvenile offender.

Roper, Superintendent, Potosi Correctional Center* v. *Simmons A case in which the Supreme Court held that the Eighth and Fourteenth Amendments forbid imposition of the death penalty on offenders who were under the age of 18 when their crimes were committed.

Graham* v. *Florida A case in which the U.S. Supreme Court held that juveniles tried as adults cannot be sentenced to life in prison without parole for nonhomicide offenses.

Miller* v. *Alabama A case in which the U.S. Supreme Court extends the ban on sentences of life without parole for juveniles guilty of homicide offenses.

return the child to the custody of a parent or guardian, notify the juvenile court of the contact, and forward a copy of the report to the juvenile court. The parent(s) or guardian may be instructed to contact the juvenile court to make an appointment with an intake officer, or the juvenile court may contact the parent(s) or guardian when the court receives the police report. About 22% of juveniles who are apprehended by the police for criminal activity or status offenses are released to a parent or guardian after being taken into custody.[44]

Deciding between Juvenile and Adult Jurisdiction

As previously mentioned, there are a number of offenses and circumstances for which the prosecutor for the criminal justice system may have concurrent jurisdiction or, in some cases, original jurisdiction over the juvenile offender. If state law provides for statutory exclusion, the juvenile is transferred to the adult (criminal justice) system when the criteria for exclusion are satisfied. In cases of concurrent jurisdiction, the prosecuting attorney or district attorney and the juvenile court judge may confer as to whether to transfer the juvenile to the adult system.

In some states, the prosecuting attorney has the authority to request transfer without the consent of the juvenile court. In cases of certain violent crimes, in all states, the prosecuting attorney may request waiver of the juvenile to the adult system. In states with a minimum age for waiver, however, the juvenile may not be waived to the adult system if he or she was younger than the stipulated age when he or she was alleged to have committed the crime. However, some states have no minimum age for waiver for certain violent crimes, usually premeditated murder. In about 9% of serious cases (murder or violent crime, for example), the juvenile offender may be placed under the jurisdiction of the criminal court.[45]

67% The percentage of juveniles taken into custody that are under the jurisdiction of the juvenile court.

Before the juvenile can be waived to the adult system for other than statutory waivers, he or she is entitled to a waiver hearing in the juvenile court and is guaranteed due process rights discussed previously. If it is decided that the juvenile court will retain jurisdiction over the child, he or she is referred to a juvenile court intake officer. If the juvenile is waived to adult criminal court, the prosecuting attorney assumes responsibility for the case.

The Juvenile Intake Officer: Gatekeeper and Counselor

About 67% of the time a juvenile is apprehended for serious crimes or is thought to be a danger to himself or herself or to society, the juvenile is referred to the juvenile court and may be placed in a juvenile institution.[46] The juvenile and/or his or her parent(s) or guardian first meets with the juvenile intake officer. In some states, juvenile court intake officers may be called "juvenile probation officers," but unlike the adult system, where probation officers become involved after conviction, **juvenile intake officers** or juvenile probation officers are involved when the child enters the system and when aftercare is required. Juvenile court intake officers "screen" cases with the purpose of diverting as many as possible from formal processing by the juvenile court judge.

Juvenile intake officers have significant latitude in making decisions about how a juvenile case is to be processed. Their mission is to consider what is best for the child and, if possible, provide minimum contact with the formal juvenile justice system. Juvenile intake officers, unlike police in the adult system, are not bound by rigid prohibitions regarding "interrogation" and Miranda rights. The Supreme Court has provided juveniles with due process protection at certain points in the juvenile justice system, but in general, the juvenile intake officer can extensively question the youth and/or the parent(s) or guardian not only about the specific incident in question, but also about the child's home life, behavior at school, past problems, social development, and general health.

In a typical intake interview, the juvenile intake officer interviews the child and the parent(s) or guardian and takes a **life history** of the child. For example, the juvenile intake officer may ask a child referred by the police for shoplifting to complete psychological and social assessments. Rather than focus on the immediate "crime" in question, as is required in the adult system, the juvenile intake officer may attempt to determine whether other emotional, cognitive, or affective

22% The percentage of juvenile intakes that are processed by law enforcement and released.

9% The percentage of juveniles taken into custody that are under the jurisdiction of the criminal court.

Think About It . . .

About 63% of police departments have a centralized juvenile unit or some form of youth services division.[47] Most juvenile units (63%) are staffed with sworn officers. Other departments staff their juvenile unit with civilians or volunteers or a combination of the three. A survey of police departments indicated that the top three needs for their juvenile unit are more staff, increased and better quality training opportunities for personnel, and more funding. Overall, law enforcement departments reported that they need to improve juvenile operations. How can police improve juvenile programs?

behaviors or environmental issues should be examined. The juvenile intake officer, in a sense, tries to find the cause of the behavior and assess the overall well-being of the child. He or she wants to know why the child shoplifted. Was it due to poor parental supervision? Gang involvement? Peer pressure? Need? Do other behaviors, such as depression or suicidal thoughts, need to be addressed? Is the child in an abusive environment? Frequently, the juvenile intake officer who handles children accused of crimes also handles other referrals, such as child abuse, school delinquency, and status offenders. Regardless of the reason for which the child is referred to the juvenile court, the intake process strives for a thorough review of the total conditions in the child's life.

One purpose of this review during the intake process is to determine whether the child can be diverted from further processing by the formal juvenile justice system. If possible, in lieu of further processing, the juvenile intake officer will refer the juvenile and/or parent(s) or guardian to mental health care, a welfare agency, a diversion program, a counseling program, a school program, or a similar alternative. The juvenile intake officers may simply "counsel" the juvenile and/or parent(s) or guardian and close the case. About half the cases referred to juvenile court are handled informally. About 44% of cases are disposed of in such a manner.[48]

Likewise, the juvenile intake officer might believe that the case merits further review. Even a referral for a minor offense can result in extensive mandatory psychological examinations and investigations into the well-being and living environment of the child. If it is decided that the living environment of the child is a major contributor to the delinquent behavior and/or is a threat to the welfare of the child, the juvenile intake officer may initiate proceedings to remove the child from the parent(s) or guardian and place him or her in foster or residential care. In such cases, the child is not being punished. The juvenile intake officer makes such recommendations because he or she is concerned about the welfare and best interests of the child.

If a case is handled "informally" by the juvenile intake officer, he or she often prescribes behaviors and conditions to which the juvenile and/or parent(s) or guardian must agree. These conditions may include regular school attendance, attendance in drug or alcohol programs, attendance in special diversion programs designed to change the child's behavior, curfew, restitution if there was property damage, counseling, and no gang involvement. The juvenile intake officer will commit these conditions to writing, specify the time frame, and obtain the agreement of the child and/or parent(s) or guardian. These conditions are generally called a **consent decree**.

Juvenile intake officers have authority similar to that of prosecuting attorneys in that they act as gatekeepers as to which cases are forwarded to the court and which are handled by diversion.

The discretion and power of juvenile intake officers is extensive, and there is no equivalent position in the adult criminal justice system. Juvenile intake officers have authority similar to that of "beat" police officers in that they can decide to handle a referral informally or to process the youth formally. They also have authority similar to that of prosecuting attorneys in that they act as gatekeepers as to which cases are forwarded to the court and which are handled by diversion.

Formal Processing

If the juvenile intake officer determines that it is appropriate to refer the child to the juvenile court for formal processing, he or she must decide whether the child is to remain with the parent(s) or guardian or be placed in the care of the state while awaiting processing. Most children remain in the custody of their parent(s) or guardian while waiting for their court appearance before the juvenile judge. Thus, no arraignment, grand jury, or preliminary hearing is necessary, or even possible, as there is in bringing an adult offender before a criminal court for trial.

Once the case is referred to the juvenile court for formal processing, known as a **juvenile adjudication hearing**, the juvenile judge becomes the central figure in determining how the case is to be processed. He or she is more involved in the formal hearing than the judge in a criminal trial and may question the youth and witnesses and inquire about facts concerning the case. Again, there is a difference in the terminology describing the juvenile justice system and the criminal justice system. Juveniles have hearings or formal court proceedings but not trials. If the juvenile intake officer deems a formal hearing appropriate, a **delinquency petition** or waiver petition is forwarded to the juvenile court judge. A delinquency petition asks a judge to adjudicate, or hear and judge, the case in a formal hearing to determine whether the juvenile is to be declared delinquent. A waiver petition requests that the judge transfer the youth to criminal court.

Unlike adult criminal trials that are rigorously scripted as to form and procedure, there is more leeway in juvenile adjudication hearings. This apparent informality in court procedure is not surprising given that until *In re Gault* (1967), attorneys representing the defense were conspicuously absent from the juvenile adjudication hearing. However, as previously mentioned, recent Supreme Court rulings have established that the juvenile be afforded certain due process rights at these court proceedings; as a result, the juvenile hearing now has more characteristics of a "trial." The Court granted the juvenile three rights: (1) to cross-examine witnesses, (2) to challenge the evidence against him or her, and (3) to call witnesses on his or her behalf. However, juvenile hearings are distinct from criminal trials. One of the most obvious differences is that neither juvenile hearings nor transcripts of the trials are available to the public. If the case is referred to the juvenile court for formal processing, one of the options of the court is to deem it appropriate and legally permissible to transfer the juvenile to the adult system. An alternative to formal processing by the juvenile court is to refer the juvenile to an alternative court, such as teen court or drug court. These courts handle specialized cases.

Teen Courts

Teen courts are usually used for younger juveniles (aged 10 to 15) with no prior arrest record who are charged with less serious law violations such as shoplifting, vandalism, and disorderly conduct.[49] The Office of Juvenile Justice and Delinquency Prevention (OJJDP) describes teen courts as being different from other juvenile justice programs because young people rather than adults determine the disposition, given a broad array of sentencing options made available by adults overseeing the program.[50] The premise underlying teen courts is that peer pressure is a powerful deterrent to delinquent behavior.

Juvenile Drug Courts

Drug use among teenagers is a significant problem, and **juvenile drug courts** are being used instead of traditional adjudication processes to work toward long-term success and rehabilitation of these offenders. According to the OJJDP, "Juvenile drug courts provide (1) intensive and continuous judicial supervision over delinquency and status offense cases that involve substance-abusing juveniles and (2) coordinated and supervised delivery of an array of support services necessary to address the problems that contribute to juvenile involvement in the justice system."[51] Juvenile drug courts, like adult drug courts, have emerged only since the 1980s but are quickly being adopted nationwide. Today, nearly all large cities have juvenile drug courts.

> Juvenile drug courts are designed to respond as quickly as possible to delinquent activity so that offenders are held accountable and intrusive intervention can occur to provide treatment and sanction options.

½ to ¾ The number of youths who enter juvenile drug court programs that complete the program.

Juvenile drug courts are designed to respond as quickly as possible to delinquent activity so that offenders are held accountable and intrusive intervention can occur to provide treatment and sanction options.[52] Programs provide for court-supervised substance abuse treatment and core services addressing the needs of the juveniles and their families, including educational needs, behavioral problems, and family therapy. The hallmark of juvenile drug courts is the intensive, continuous judicial monitoring and supervision of participants.[53]

Juvenile drug court programs recognize the challenge of addressing family issues. The operating premise is that if family issues are not addressed, the child will likely continue his or her involvement with drugs and delinquent activity. As a result, a number of programs require supervision by the parent(s) or guardian and utilize the Multisystemic Therapy (MST) approach to provide family-based treatment and to teach parenting skills.[54]

Extensive data are not available to evaluate the effectiveness of juvenile drug courts, but "judges anecdotally report that these programs are able to achieve greater accountability and provide a broad array of treatment and other services to youth and their families than traditional juvenile courts."[55] One-half to three-fourths of youths who enter juvenile drug court programs complete the program.[56] Initial analysis of indicators such as recidivism, drug use, and educational achievement seems to indicate that juvenile drug courts are providing better rehabilitation of youths than are traditional juvenile courts.[57]

Adjudication

The juvenile judge has great latitude in conducting juvenile hearings than do judges conducting criminal trials. There is no constitutional right to a jury trial (although a few states do have this option), so the judge makes the final decision as to the outcome of the case. If the judge concludes beyond a reasonable doubt that the juvenile committed the offense, the judge does not find the juvenile "guilty," but "delinquent."

If the youth is declared delinquent, similar to the sentencing hearing in the adult criminal justice system, a procedure known as aftercare determines the appropriate course of action. This procedure is called a *disposition hearing* in some states. However, unlike the adult criminal justice system, delinquency does not mean that the juvenile is to be punished. Delinquency means that the court will develop a plan of action that best benefits the youth and provides for the safety of the community. The juvenile judge has the option of referring the delinquent to a secure lockup facility similar to a prison, mandating counseling, or imposing an informal plan of action. Judges can be quite creative in their action plans. For example, when a 14-year-old Roanoke, Virginia, youth was adjudicated of sending threatening e-mails to federal officials, including a threat to kill President Bush, bomb the White House, and bomb the library, Juvenile and Domestic Relations District Court Judge Joseph Bounds ordered the youth to complete a stay at a group home for boys, complete 48 hours of community service, and write a research paper on homeland security without using the Internet.

Similar to the presentence investigation prior to the dispositional hearing, a juvenile probation officer or court officer may be asked to make a dispositional recommendation. The recommendation is based on data about the juvenile's past criminal and/or gang involvement; background investigations, especially the performance and behavior of the youth in school; interviews and/or psychological evaluations and diagnostic tests; and information gathered from the delinquent's parent(s) or guardian. At the dispositional hearing, the court officer prosecuting the case and the juvenile or his or her attorney have the opportunity to make their own recommendations and to comment on the recommendations of the juvenile probation officer or court official.

Detention and Probation (Aftercare)

Unlike the adult criminal justice system, juveniles are not sentenced to jail or prison. When a juvenile is **adjudicated** and his or her petition is sustained, the judge then decides whether the delinquent youth should become a **ward of the state** and be placed in a residential facility or enter a course of rehabilitation such as drug or alcohol counseling, restitution, or community service. If the juvenile is declared a ward of the state, it means that the state exercises its right of *parens patriae* and assumes primary responsibility for the health and well-being of the child. This action may mean that the child is removed from the custody of his or her parent(s) or guardian and placed in a juvenile facility or foster care, or it may mean a consent decree stipulating intrusive intervention to determine that the parent(s) or guardian is fulfilling the conditions required by the court.

The action of the juvenile judge is not a "sentence" and is not prescribed by legislation or sentencing guidelines. Thus, juvenile judges have great latitude in setting a course of action for the delinquent. The judge may place a specific time for the termination of the court's authority over the adjudicated delinquent. The jurisdiction of the juvenile court is limited by legislation when the juvenile reaches a certain age, usually 21, but notwithstanding this limit, the orders of the court may specify that the delinquent remain under the court's jurisdiction until specific requirements are met or until the delinquent is "cured."

Data from the California Legislative Analyst's Office indicate that few juveniles are processed through the entire juvenile justice system and arrive at this end point. For every 1,000 juveniles in the California system cited by the police, only 25 will be referred for formal hearings, and of that 25, only 12 will have a formal hearing. Of the 12 formal hearings, six juveniles will be referred to formal probation. Only 1 in 1,000 youths will be moved to residential placement. Nationwide data indicate a higher figure. Nationwide, 95 out of 1,000 juveniles are adjudicated and placed in a residential facility.[58]

Residential Placement

As in the case of adult prisons, juvenile residential placement has levels of security. Residential placement must accommodate not only juveniles who have committed serious violent crimes, but also status offenders and juveniles who have been removed from parents or guardians for their own welfare due to neglect or physical or sexual abuse.[59] Thus, residential placement facilities can range from foster care in individual homes to group homes to long-term placement residential facilities to secure lockup facilities that resemble adult medium-security prisons. The type of placement depends on the characteristics of the youth, such as age and mental health, and the crime. Violent offenders who have committed crimes against persons, especially gang-related crimes and crimes involving firearms, are generally be placed in secure lockup facilities, whereas nonviolent and status offenders are more likely to be placed in homelike settings with minimum security. Often the latter will be placed in a residential facility but will attend a local school. On the other hand, violent juvenile offenders are not allowed to leave the secure lockup facility in which they are placed, and the state must provide continued opportunities for education within the facility.

Mental Health Concerns

One of the major concerns of the juvenile court when a child is placed in a residential facility is the mental health of the child. Surveys indicate that a high percentage of children under the authority of the juvenile system have psychiatric disorders. One survey by the Office of Justice Programs reported that approximately 67% of youths in the juvenile justice system have mental health problems that may have contributed to their criminal behavior and that are likely to interfere with rehabilitation. Also, these children have emotional impairments due to an untreated mental disorder that may contribute to an adverse reaction to confinement.[60] Mental disorders can be divided into two primary groups: (1) those related to alcohol and drug use and (2) those described as nonsubstance use disorders, such as anxiety disorders, conduct disorders, depression, obsessive-compulsive disorders, posttraumatic stress, and social phobias. Most disorders of youths in the juvenile setting (49.3%) are related to substance use. Another concern for the mental health of youths is juvenile suicides. According to the Centers for Disease Control and Prevention (CDC), juvenile suicides are the third leading cause of death for young people aged 12 to 18. In fact, the number of youth aged 13 to 14 who commit suicide equals the number who are murdered.[61] The CDC reports that in a typical 12-month period, 14% of American high school students seriously consider suicide; nearly 11% make plans about how they would end their lives; and 6.3% actually attempt suicide.

9.5% The percentage of juveniles who are adjudicated and placed in a residential facility.

67% The percentage of youths in the juvenile system that have mental health problems.

> Mental disorders can be divided into two primary groups: (1) those related to alcohol and drug use and (2) those described as nonsubstance use disorders.

Juvenile Probation (Aftercare)

Juvenile probation or aftercare is similar to the concept of adult probation. In fact, John Augustus, a founder of the probation movement, started the movement by diverting boys between 7 and 15 years of age away from sentencing. Juvenile probation is also called *aftercare*. The goal of probation or aftercare is to provide treatment services that will eliminate the delinquent behavior and prevent the juvenile from reentering the juvenile justice system or the adult criminal justice system. Probation service agencies and their personnel are divided into those agencies that provide juvenile probation services and those that provide adult probation services. Similar to the criminal justice system, the juvenile justice system has experimented with various forms of probation services, including intensive probation. However, an evaluation of model juvenile intensive aftercare programs does not suggest any difference between "regular" juvenile aftercare services and intensive aftercare services, as measured by participants' subsequent delinquent/criminal involvement and areas of youth functioning (for example, substance abuse and family functioning) that are theoretically and empirically linked to recidivism.[62] One suggestion of the study that explained the lack of difference in aftercare services was that unlike "typical" adults on probation, juveniles already receive a relatively high level of probation services and that the intensity of supervision provided by the intensive aftercare programs may not have been significantly different from that of the control group.[63]

Juvenile Boot Camps

A hybrid model of treatment for juveniles that involves elements from both residential placement and probation is **juvenile boot camp**. Juvenile boot camps are popular treatment programs for juvenile delinquents.[64] The goal of treatment is to alter the character and values of the offender, as juveniles are seen as more likely to change than are older offenders.[65] Some authorities are critical of this type of treatment for juvenile offenders, however. They argue that the military-style strict discipline and group-oriented environment "is a direct opposition to the type of positive interpersonal relationships and supportive atmosphere that are needed for youths' positive development."[66]

Another major criticism of juvenile boot camps is the lack of follow-up after release. Adults released from boot camp usually are released to the supervision of probation and parole. In fact, many adult shock incarceration programs release offenders into intensive probation programs rather than regular probation and parole supervision. Critics of juvenile boot camps express the concern that if juveniles are released back into the community after these brief periods in boot camps, without community-based supervision and follow-up support, they will "revert to their old ways of surviving in and relating to the community in which they live."[67] Research indicates that youths who participate in boot camps have more positive perceptions of their institutional environment than do juveniles in traditional facilities, but the lack of follow-up data makes it difficult to judge the impact of boot camps on recidivism rates.[68]

Private Boot Camp Programs

An interesting development in shock incarceration or boot camp programs is the proliferation of private programs for troubled youths. These private programs occur in a variety of settings, including wilderness camps, at-sea camps, and military-style camps. These private camps mimic state-operated camps, but charge parents for treatment programs that promise to help them with their delinquent or out-of-control children. Some states allow juveniles to be diverted from the formal juvenile justice system to these private camps. Although they may appear similar to state-operated programs, many are unregulated businesses that have been criticized for their lack of standards and the safety of the environment in which the juveniles are placed. One Arizona state senator, critical of the lack of regulation, said of private boot camps in his state, "You have to provide more documents to get a fishing license than to run a camp for young boys. We require nothing to demonstrate you have the qualifications to engage in this type of activity."[69]

Nationwide, there are approximately 400 private boot camps for juveniles.[70] Many are not regulated by the state in which they operate, and there have been numerous complaints of child abuse and questionable therapeutic programs and practices. Often parents who place their children in these facilities have high hopes but little knowledge of the practices and competency of the staff.[71] As a result of the reports of abuse and questionable practices, there is a movement toward bringing proper oversight to private boot camps and strengthening state laws to regulate them to protect the children and youths they are intended to serve.[72]

Juvenile Death Penalty

The death penalty is not a sanction permitted by the juvenile court. However, juveniles who have been waived to the criminal justice system or who have committed murder in a state where the criminal court has concurrent or original jurisdiction over juveniles have been sentenced to the death penalty. The practice of allowing people under the age of 18 at the time of their crime to be in jeopardy of capital punishment, even though they have been declared an adult by the court system or state legislation, is highly controversial in the United States.

Thompson v. Oklahoma

Nationwide concern over the evolving standards of decency has resulted in scrutiny of the issue by the U.S. Supreme Court. The courts have been actively involved in monitoring the juvenile death penalty as illustrated by the fact that 50% of under-age-18 death sentences have been reversed.[73] In early cases, the Supreme Court considered the merits of each case in deciding whether to reverse the death sentence but did not make a general ruling on the constitutionality of the juvenile death penalty. However, in *Thompson v. Oklahoma* (1988), the Supreme Court ruled that national standards of decency did not permit the execution of any offender under age 16 at the time of the crime.[74] The plurality of the Court concluded that "it would offend civilized standards of decency to execute a person who was less than 16 years old at the time of his or her offense." The Court cited the U.S. Anglo-American heritage, the practices of the state, the standards of Western Europe, and the practices of other nations as the criteria for arriving at a standard of decency that prohibited the death penalty for those younger than 16 at the time they committed their crime. Also, the opinion of the Court was based on its belief that there was less culpability for offenders under age 16 and that offenders under 16 did not engage in "the kind of cost-benefit analysis that attaches any weight to the possibility of execution," thereby making the death penalty an ineffective deterrent. A year later, the Supreme Court ruled in *Stanford v. Kentucky* that although standards of decency prohibited the execution of juveniles under 16 years old at the time of their crime, the Eighth and Fourteenth Amendments did not prohibit the execution of juvenile offenders over 15 years old but under 18 years old.[75]

Juvenile Death Penalty Revisited

In 2005, the Supreme Court again visited the question of the juvenile death penalty. In 1993, at the age of 17, when he was still a junior in high school, Christopher Simmons conspired with two friends, aged 15 and 16, to commit burglary and murder. Simmons, the ringleader, assured his coconspirators that they could "get away with it" because they were minors. The 16-year-old renounced his intention to conspire with the other two to follow through with the crimes on the night of the murder, but the other two carried out their plan, which resulted in the death of the victim, Shirley Crook. Simmons was quickly connected to the crime because of his public statements about killing Crook. He was arrested by the police, advised of his Miranda rights, and after two hours of interrogation confessed to the crime. Citing aggravating factors, the state of Missouri was successful in obtaining the death penalty for Simmons in adult court. The prosecutor argued to the jury that the murder "involved depravity of mind and was outrageously and wantonly vile, horrible, and inhuman." Simmons's attorney appealed the death sentence to the Missouri Supreme Court and to the U.S. Supreme Court, but both upheld the death sentence.[76]

Roper, Superintendent, Potosi Correctional Center v. Simmons

After Simmons lost his appeal, the Supreme Court held in *Atkins v. Virginia* (2002) that the Eighth and Fourteenth Amendments prohibit the execution of adult persons with mental retardation,[77] which was held to be subject to the excessive sanctions clause of the Eighth Amendment due to the reduced culpability of offenders with mental retardation. When the Court recognized diminished culpability as a mitigating factor in the death penalty and previous Court cases had already established that juveniles have diminished culpability, Simmons's attorney asked the Court to reconsider the case. In **Roper, Superintendent, Potosi Correctional Center v. Simmons** (2005), the Supreme Court held that the Eighth and Fourteenth Amendments forbid imposition of the death penalty on offenders who were under the age of 18 when their crimes were committed. The ruling closes the debate on the juvenile death penalty for now. The ruling also voided the death sentence of approximately 70 juveniles on death row. (The ruling does not void their conviction, but their sentence will be changed from death to life in prison.)

Life Imprisonment without Parole for Nonhomicide Offenses

The United States was virtually alone in allowing juveniles who did not commit homicide to be sentenced to life without parole. In **Graham v. Florida** (2010), the Court reconsidered the application of the Eighth Amendment to life sentences for juveniles for nonhomicide offenses. States such as Texas had already banned such sentences, but 37 states and the federal government allowed life sentences without parole for juveniles.

When the Court heard arguments in the case that such sentences were so harsh as to be unconstitutional, 129 juveniles in 11 states had not committed homicides but were serving sentences of life without parole.

The Court found that "denying juveniles a chance to ever rejoin society is counter to national and global consensus" and violates the Constitution's ban on cruel and unusual punishment.

Think About It ...

The U.S. Supreme Court struck down sentences of life in prison without parole for juvenile offenders. Any juvenile with this sentence must be resentenced. In July 2012, Iowa governor Terry Branstad commuted to a minimum of 60 years the life sentences of 38 inmates covered by the Court's ruling. No current inmate would be eligible for release before the age of 74. Branstad called the inmates, "very, very dangerous ... violent ... murderous individuals." Is a 60-year minimum sentence appropriate? Why or why not?

Life Imprisonment without Parole for Homicide Offenses

In March 2012, the U.S. Supreme Court heard arguments in the case of **Miller v. Alabama** concerning the constitutionality of sentences of mandatory life without parole for juvenile offenders in cases including murder. The Court issued its ruling on June 25, 2012, striking down the mandatory sentences as cruel and unusual punishments in violation of the Eighth Amendment to the Constitution. Justice Elena Kagan wrote for the majority of the court "that mandatory life without parole for those under age of 18 at the time of their crime violates the Eighth Amendment's prohibition on cruel and unusual punishments.... Mandatory life without parole for a juvenile precludes consideration of his chronological age and its hallmark features—among them, immaturity, impetuosity, and failure to appreciate risks and consequences.... It prevents taking into account the family and home environment that surrounds him—and from which he cannot usually extricate himself—no matter how brutal or dysfunctional."

The ruling did not require defendants sentenced to life with parole to be retried, only to be resentenced. The Court did not specify what conditions would satisfy its ruling and left it to each state to assess what sentence short of life without parole would be constitutional. The Court justified the prohibition, arguing that as previous decisions had prevented states from executing juvenile offenders, the states were not allowed to sentence juveniles to die in prison.

▶ The Juvenile as Offender

Sociological Explanations

The various theories explaining criminal offending and victimization were discussed in Chapter 2, "Crime: The Search for Understanding." Of these theories, sociological explanations of criminal behavior are most popular. Various sociological theories have been the foundation of prevention programs and treatment models for juveniles.

In general, sociological research and theories focusing on juveniles attempts to identify when children first start offending, what influences their decision, what reinforces delinquent behavior, and what is the impact of influences such as social norms, school, culture, self-image, and parenting on juvenile behavior. Especially in the mid-twentieth century, the predominant sociological theories explaining criminal behavior identified environmental and social factors as strong determinants of criminal behavior. Theorists hypothesized that adult criminals did not suddenly undergo a transformation in adult life from being a law-abiding citizen to a criminal. The underlying assumption of these sociological theories was the proposition that criminal behavior was learned behavior or was behavior that resulted from social, environmental, and economic influences acting over time to shape and determine behavior. Thus, criminologists reasoned that if one could isolate and identify the variables that promoted criminal behavior and that suppressed criminal behavior, it would be possible to understand the processes that caused a person to become an adult criminal. Sociologists studied populations of children to identify the onset of delinquency and the earliest determinants that influenced children's behavior and development.

Over time, some of the hypotheses as to the causes of juvenile delinquency (and later adult criminality) were discarded or minimized. However, research and criminal justice practitioners have reinforced the hypothesis of other theories. Many of the researchers whose theories have been helpful in the clarification of juvenile delinquency tended to focus their research on delinquency in school-aged children. Recent research has suggested that the origins of serious and violent juvenile criminality (and later adult criminality) may be found in risk factors that begin early in life.

LEARNING OUTCOMES 6 Summarize the contributions of research and theory to understanding the causes of juvenile delinquency and offending, including youth gangs and substance abuse.

GLOSSARY

youth gangs Difficult-to-define juvenile groups distinct from adult gangs that mimic adult gangs.

hybrid gangs A new type of youth gang with distinctive characteristics that differentiate them from traditional gangs; they are frequently school-based, less organized, less involved in criminal activity, and less involved in violence than are traditional gangs.

Drug Abuse Resistance Education (DARE) A popular in-school antidrug program initiated by the Los Angeles Police Department in 1983 but abandoned when data failed to support its effectiveness.

OJJDP's Study Group on Very Young Offenders

The study of very young children may yield knowledge that can suggest strategies to reduce juvenile delinquency and diminish the number of delinquents that continue their criminality into adulthood. In 1998, the OJJDP formed a Study Group on Serious and Violent Juvenile Offenders. The group undertook a two-year analysis of existing data that focused on the preschool and elementary years. The OJJDP described the group as consisting of 16 primary study group members and 23 coauthors who were experts on criminology, child delinquency, psychopathology, and the law. The group reviewed hundreds of studies, undertook many special analyses, and gathered data from a survey of more than 100 practitioners in the field, concentrating on the delinquent behavior of children aged 7 to 12 and on children's persistently disruptive and precociously deviant behavior from the toddler years up to adolescence.[78]

Early Delinquency Leads to Later Delinquency

The Study Group on Very Young Offenders reported that child delinquents (juveniles between the ages of 7 and 12) are two to three times more likely to become serious, violent, and chronic offenders than adolescents whose delinquent behavior begins in their teens.[79] "In more than 20 studies they reviewed, the Study Group found a significant relationship between an early onset of delinquency and later crime and delinquency (See Figure 13-3). Child delinquents, compared to a later onset of delinquency, are at greater risk of becoming serious, violent, and chronic offenders and have longer delinquency careers."[80] The Study Group reported that there is a significant relationship between delinquency and persistent disruptive behavior as a young

2 The age at which child delinquency can be identified.

child (that is, preschool age).[81] Further, the data showed that children with persistent disruptive behavior are likely to become child delinquents and, in turn, child delinquents are likely to become serious, violent, or chronic juvenile offenders. The research data showed that the antisocial careers of male juvenile offenders start, on average, at age 7. The conclusion of the Study Group was that the preschool period is critical in setting a foundation for preventing the development of disruptive behavior and, eventually, child delinquency.[82] The group concluded that the majority of child delinquents have a history of disruptive behavior, such as aggressive, inattentive, or sensational-seeking behavior, in the preschool period, but the majority of preschoolers with such behavior problems do not go on to become young offenders.[83] Figure 13–1 shows the relationship between child delinquency and serious, violent, or chronic offending as a teen or an adult.

At-Risk Factors

The Study Group reported that behavior and influences that place a child at risk for an early career of disruptive behavior and child delinquency can be identified as early as two years of age and include many factors that have been identified by the more popular criminological theories of crime causation.[84] The Study Group concluded that no single risk factor explains child delinquency, but the greater the number of risk factors, the greater the number of risk-factor domains (for example, family and school), and the greater the exposure to these risks, the greater the likelihood of early-onset offending.[85]

During the preschool years, the most important risk factors stem from the individual and family. This finding is consistent with theories that state that genetic factors, personality, and family environment and parenting skills influence behavior. As the child matures, later influences include peers, school, and community. The data are especially supportive of Sutherland's differential association theory, Reckless's containment theory, and Hirschi's social bond theory regarding the prediction of delinquent behavior. The data showed a correlation between factors such as delinquent behavior and deviant peers; commitment to school and community; and the presence or lack of supervision or outside forces to prevent or intervene in the event of aggressive, antisocial, or disruptive behaviors. Also, the data supported social disorganization and zone theories of crime causation. The study showed a high correlation between a high level of poverty in a neighborhood and early onset of aggressive, inattentive, or sensation-seeking behavior in the preschool years. The data did not demonstrate a relationship between very young offending and race and gender.[86] Figure 13–2 summarizes the risk factors associated with disruptive and delinquent behavior identified by the Study Group.

The Study Group concluded that there should be a shift of focus from adolescent delinquents to child delinquents to prevent high-risk children from

The study did not demonstrate a relationship between very young offending and race and gender.

becoming tomorrow's incarcerated offenders.[87] The group also concluded that current juvenile justice, mental health, and child welfare programs were ineffective in dealing with child delinquents.[88] According to the study, effective preventive intervention required the coordinated delivery of services from numerous agencies but that these agencies were severely fragmented, resulting in ineffective preventive intervention. As a result, the juvenile court has come to serve as a "dumping ground for a wide variety of problem behaviors of children that other institutions (e.g., social, mental health, and child protective services) fail to serve adequately."[89] Finally, the Study Group concluded that policymakers were misguided in focusing on programs for older adolescent delinquents. Early preventive interventions were said to be more effective in terms of reducing delinquency and minimizing costs. For example, the Study Group asserted that for every dollar spent on preventive interventions for very young at-risk children, taxpayers and crime victims were saved more than $7.[90]

The Study Group concluded that policymakers were misguided in focusing on programs for older adolescent delinquents. Early prevention interventions were said to be more effective in terms of reducing delinquency and minimizing costs.

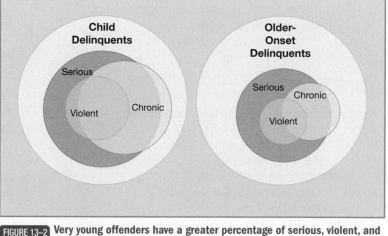

FIGURE 13–2 Very young offenders have a greater percentage of serious, violent, and chronic careers than do older onset delinquents.

Source: R. Loeber, D. Farrington, and D. Petechuk, *Child Delinquency: Early Intervention and Prevention* (Washington, DC: U.S. Department of Justice Office of Juvenile Justice and Delinquency Prevention), May 2003.

Desistance Study

In 2011, the OJJPD released a seven-year study of 1,354 serious juvenile offenders aged 14 to 18. The study had collected the most comprehensive data set currently available about serious adolescent offenders and their lives in late adolescence and early adulthood.[91] The primary findings of the study are counter to the beliefs of those who advocate a "get tough" policy for juveniles. The surprising finding of the study was that most (91.5%) youth who commit felonies greatly reduce their offending over time, regardless of the intervention.[92] Other findings were that longer stays in juvenile institutions did not reduce recidivism.[93] The study found that community-based supervision and substance abuse treatment were effective in reducing offending.[94] The study suggests that substance abuse is connected to offending. The study supported previous findings that stability in family environment and work and school attendance were effective in reducing recidivism.[95]

The major finding of the study was that "incarceration may not be the most appropriate or effective option, even for many of the most serious adolescent offenders."[96] In fact, no treatment may be better than incarceration, as over 90% of offenders reduced reoffending. The study highlights that there are substantial differences in adult offending versus juvenile offending. It reinforces the mission of the juvenile justice system to provide rehabilitation and treatment rather than punishment.

Youth Gangs

According to the *Highlights of the 2010 Youth Gang Survey*, there are 29,400 gangs with 756,000 gang members in the United States.[97] There are various types of gangs—motorcycle gangs, hate or ideology groups, prison gangs, and others. Many researchers are especially interested in **youth gangs**. The term *youth gangs* is difficult to define. Even the OJJDP depends on local definitions when it conducts its national survey on youth gangs. In the survey, a youth gang is defined as "a group of youths or young adults in your jurisdiction that you or other responsible persons in your agency or community are willing to identify or classify as a 'gang.' "[98] The imprecise definition reflects the lack of knowledge about youth gangs. However, the proliferation of youth gangs starting in the 1980s has resulted in researchers and the criminal justice system examining the causes, characteristics, and mitigation of youth gang membership.

One of the reasons for the intense concern over the problem of youth gangs is that although gangs have differing characteristics from city to city and gang to gang, many youth gangs

Approximate Development Ordering of Risk Factors Associated with Disruptive and Delinquent Behavior		
Risk Factors Emerging during Pregnancy and from Infancy Onward		**Risk Factors Emerging from Mid-childhood Onward**
Child	Pregnancy and delivery complications	*Child* Stealing and general delinquency
	Neurological insult	Early onset of other disruptive behaviors
	Exposure to neurotoxins after birth	Early onset of substance use and sexual activity
	Difficult temperament	Depressed mood
	Hyperactivity/impulsivity/attention problems	Withdrawn behavior
	Low intelligence	Positive attitude toward problem behavior
	Male gender	Victimization and exposure to violence
Family	Maternal smoking/alcohol consumption/drug use during pregnancy	*Family* Poor parental supervision
	Teenage mother	*School* Poor academic achievement
	High turnover of caretakers	Repeated grade(s)
	Poorly educated parent	Truancy
	Maternal depression	Negative attitude toward school
	Parental substance abuse/antisocial or criminal behavior	Poorly organized and functioning schools
	Poor parent-child communication	*Peer* Peer rejection
	Poverty/low socioeconomic status	Association with deviant peers/siblings
	Serious marital discord	*Community* Residence in a disadvantaged neighborhood
	Large family size	Residence in a disorganized neighborhood
		Availability of weapons
Risk Factors Emerging from Toddler Years Onward		**Risk Factors Emerging From Mid-adolescence Onward**
Child	Aggressive/disruptive behavior	*Child* Weapon carrying
	Persistent lying	Drug dealing
	Risk taking and sensation seeking	Unemployment
	Lack of guilt, lack of empathy	*School* School dropout
Family	Harsh and/or erratic discipline practices	*Peer* Gang membership
	Maltreatment or neglect	
Community	Television violence	

FIGURE 13–3 A two-year study by the OJJDP suggests that identifiable factors show that young children may exhibit serious delinquent behaviors later in life.
Source: R. Loeber, D. Farrington, and D. Petechuk, *Child Delinquency: Early Intervention and Prevention* (Washington, DC: U.S. Department of Justice Office of Juvenile Justice and Delinquency Prevention), May 2003, p. 9.

are significant sources of criminal activity and violence. Often youth gangs are the gateway into adult criminal gangs, an even greater criminal problem. In an effort to prevent the recruiting of children into criminal gangs, the federal government and the states have adopted legislation making it an offense to attempt to entice a juvenile to join a criminal gang or to prevent a juvenile from leaving a criminal gang.

According to a review of the research data by the OJJDP, historically, gang members have been primarily young adult males from homogeneous lower-class, inner-city ghetto or barrio neighborhoods. Traditionally, gangs have been racially/ethnically segregated and actively involved in a variety of criminal activities.[99] The typical age for gang members is 15 to 24, and the peak age for joining a gang is 15.[100] About 50% of gang members are aged 18 to 24.[101]

Hybrid Youth Gangs

One of the interesting discoveries to emerge from research on youth gangs is the evolving nature of these groups. Contemporary youth gangs appear to have characteristics that are different from those of gangs before the 1980s. The differences are sufficiently different that post-1990 youth gangs have been given a new name—**hybrid gangs**. A majority of members in gangs that emerged prior to 1981 were Hispanic (58%), whereas the majority of gang membership is white (37% to 40%) for gangs emerging after 1991.[102] New hybrid gangs have younger members, have more female members, and are less involved in drug trafficking and violent crimes than are traditional youth gangs.[103] Hybrid gangs are less territorial, are more likely to migrate, frequently begin as school-based gangs, and are more likely to appear outside large cities.[104]

Hybrid gangs have significantly different patterns of membership and organizational structure than do traditional gangs. Hybrid gangs may use the names and gang symbols of traditional gangs, but they are different in how they operate. Traditional gangs tend to have an age-graded structure of subgroups or cliques, organizational charts,

explicit rules of conduct and regulations, concepts of "territory," and coalitions with other gangs often for the purpose of defining "turf."[105] Hybrid youth gangs are less territory-based, are racially mixed, lack formal organizational structure and rules, and are more transient in membership. In some ways, hybrid gangs are quite unremarkable in their ability to imitate more traditional gangs. Starbuck and colleagues describe hybrid youth gangs as "cut and paste bits of Hollywood's media images and big-city gang lore into new local versions of nationally known gangs with which they may claim affiliation."[106] Fleisher described one such gang as "a haphazardly assembled social unit composed of deviant adolescents who shared social and economic needs and the propensity for resolving those needs in a similar way."[107] Gang expert David Kennedy called such gangs "hyperactive street groups of high-rate offenders."[108]

Although hybrid gangs appear less of a concern because they engage in less violent criminal activity and do not have the high degree of organization and strict membership code of more traditional gangs, they actually pose a significant problem for society. Hybrid youth gangs frequently are school-based gangs.[109] According to a report of the National Center of Education Statistics, *Indicators of School Crime*

Characteristics of hybrid youth gangs

- Local gangs may adopt the symbols of large gangs in more than one city.

- Gang members may change their affiliation from one gang to another.

- When gang members move, they may leave their old gang and align themselves with a new local gang that has no ties to their original gang.

- Members of rival gangs may cooperate in criminal activity.

- Existing gangs may change their name or merge with other gangs to form new ones.

- Gangs are not organized along strict racial/ethnic lines.

- Gang members may have multiple affiliations, including membership in rival gangs.

- Hybrid gangs may borrow symbols, graffiti, and gang colors from different gangs and mix them. For example, gang graffiti may illustrate symbols from the Blood gang in blue, which is the color of the rival Crip gang.

Source: David Starbuck, James C. Howell, and Donna J. Lindquist, *Hybrid and Other Modern Gangs* (Washington DC: Office of Juvenile Justice and Delinquency Prevention, December 2001).

Think About It . . .

When Congress refused to pass the DREAM Act to provide adolescent children of illegal immigrants a path to U.S. citizenship, President Obama issued an executive order providing temporary deferred action for childhood arrivals, exempting certain people from deportation, and extending employment authorization. Obama's executive order does not provide a path to citizenship or amnesty and does not provide the opportunity for permanent residence. People applying for deferred action must have come to the United States before they were 16 and meet other requirements. Should adolescent children of illegal immigrants receive special consideration? Why or why not?

Jim West/Alamy

and Safety: 2011, 16% of public schools reported that gang activities had occurred during the 2009–2010 school year. About 20% of students aged 12 to 18 reported that gangs were present at their schools. Any activity that promotes school violence is considered a serious problem.

Unlike traditional gangs, hybrid gangs tend to migrate. Because of the younger age of the gang members, migration can be due to reasons such as the child's family moving to another city. In fact, the most common reason for gang migration "is family relocation to improve the quality of life or to be near relatives and friends."[110] Hybrid youth gangs can be invisible to the community and law enforcement because they often do not behave in such a way as to quickly identify themselves as a "gang" and their membership is small. Some rural youth gangs depend on only one or two people to maintain "the gang."[111] Thus, unlike traditional gangs that are associated with a specific geographical area, hybrid gangs can spread rapidly into new areas.[112] A school that had no gang activity one year can find that a new school year brings hybrid gang problems as new students move into the school district.

As a result of these characteristics, the most significant problem in addressing hybrid gangs is that programs that successfully reduced gang membership and activity in large cities have little or no effect on hybrid gangs.[113] Further, because of the unique characteristics of each local gang and the absence of centralized and organized leadership, what succeeds in reducing gang membership and activity in one city may have little effect in another.[114] Community and law enforcement efforts to reduce gang membership and activity must be based on local conditions, culture and knowledge of the community, and the juveniles involved. In fact, some stereotypes about traditional gangs are just the opposite for hybrid gangs. For example, research has found that traditional gangs flourish in large inner-city environments characterized by declining prosperity and social conditions, but hybrid gangs prosper in cities with populations of less than 50,000 during times of economic prosperity. Also, because members may leave a gang, often with little or no consequences, law enforcement efforts to break up a gang may result in gang members migrating and forming other gangs or joining other gangs. Some experts argue that when the community and law enforcement agencies attempt to respond to hybrid youth "gang problems" using knowledge and experience gained from "traditional" gangs, often the result is that the agencies are "extremely ineffective at both seeing what's right in front of … [them], and doing something about it."[115]

Female Gangs

Gathering data about youth gangs is difficult. Gangs are secret societies; outsiders are easily identified; and the gang seldom wants to reveal its inner workings to scholars, researchers, or the media. However, as difficult as the problem of researching youth gangs is, those problems pale in comparison to the problems of obtaining data to describe female gangs. Significant scholarly gang research has emerged only since the 1980s, and most of that research has focused exclusively on male gangs. Some researchers have argued

> As difficult as the problem of researching youth gangs is, those problems pale in comparison to the problems of obtaining data to describe female gangs.

that female gangs are not "real gangs" or are only "imitations of male gangs" or "extensions" of male gangs.[116] The lack of research data on female gangs results in conflicting descriptions of gang members, activities, and values. Chesney-Lind and colleagues assert that public knowledge of female gangs is based primarily on media-produced stereotypes, which are largely inaccurate.[117]

Despite the reported increase of female membership in hybrid gangs, estimates of the number of female gang members remain low. Nationwide surveys of law enforcement agencies result in various estimates of female gang members, ranging from 3.7% to 11%.[118] Data from self-reported studies indicate a higher number of members, ranging from 8% to 38%.[119] A review of the research concerning female gangs by the OJJDP indicates that, similar to hybrid gangs, female gangs are more likely to be found in small cities and rural areas than in large cities. Most female gangs are either African-American or Latina, with a smaller number of Asians and whites.[120] Latina gangs (Mexican Americans in the Southwest and Puerto Ricans in New York) have been studied more than African-American female gangs.[121]

A review of the literature of female gangs by an OJJDP study indicates that female gangs have significantly different and unique characteristics when compared to male gangs.[122] One difference reported in the study is that females tend to leave the gang by the time they have reached their late twenties. Another characteristic the data suggest is that in general, female gang members commit fewer violent crimes than do male gang members. Drug offenses are among the most common offenses committed by female gang members. The data tend to suggest that females join gangs because of victimization at home, especially sexual abuse. For example, in Los Angeles, 29% of Mexican American female gang members reported being sexually abused at home, and a study of female gang members in Hawaii found that almost two-thirds reported sexual abuse at home.[123]

Juvenile Substance Abuse

Drug use and addiction are a serious problem in the United States. Juvenile drug use is a serious problem as well and is becoming more serious. There appears to be a link between

29% The percentage of Mexican American female gang members that reported being sexually abused at home.

The Office of Juvenile Justice and Delinquency Prevention (OJJDP) reports that more needs to be known about female gangs before they can be understood. The OJJDP issued a report citing a need for the following information about female gangs:

1. What factors cause the formation of female gangs?

2. Why do females join gangs?

3. What is the role of ethnicity in female gangs?

4. What is the role of gender in female gangs and between male and female gangs?

5. What are the patterns of delinquency and criminality in female gangs?

6. What are the later-life consequences of female gang membership?

Source: John Moore and John Hagedorn, *Female Gangs: A Focus on Research* (Washington, DC: Office of Juvenile Justice and Delinquency Prevention, March 2001), pp. 1–2.

substance abuse and delinquency, as data indicate that 80% to 90% of youths detained for delinquency offenses reported use of an illicit substance in the past six months and virtually all of them had used drugs during their lifetime.[124]

Education Programs

The U.S. government and criminal justice system have chosen to take a different approach to juvenile drug use from its "war on drugs" approach for adult offenders. The cornerstone of the White House Office of National Drug Control Policy is education rather than law enforcement.

The history of drug education has not been a stellar example of an effective antidrug strategy. One of the first attempts at drug education was the 1936 pseudodocumentary *Reefer Madness*, which is now viewed as a farce and comedy. (See http://www.youtube.com/watch?v=Azf320JDdqU.) Early drug education programs used fear and exaggeration in an attempt to convince the viewer not to use drugs. For example, one popular media campaign in the 1980s showed an egg sizzling in a frying pan as the narrator announced, "This is your brain on drugs." Rather than dissuade youths not to use drugs, most of these educational programs by the media seem to convince youth not to believe the government's message about drugs.

DARE

Other than media advertising, the **Drug Abuse Resistance Education (DARE)** program initiated by the Los Angeles Police Department in 1983 was a very popular antidrug education program. Given that 35% of youths who reported using drugs said that they first used them at or before age 11, the DARE program targeted children in kindergarten through ninth grade. The DARE program was unique in that it was an in-school program and its instructors were local law enforcement officers. Despite its nationwide use by schools (80% of U.S. public schools used the DARE program), the program's effectiveness has come under criticism. Data have been inconclusive as to its effectiveness. Studies have not demonstrated that DARE is an effective research-based antidrug program.[125] The federal government no longer provides funding to schools and law enforcement for DARE programs. As a result, many law enforcement agencies and schools have dropped it. DARE dismisses this criticism. Furthermore, the DARE program claims to have "re-invented" itself and "evolved to be more than just about resisting drug abuse."[126] DARE now claims to include programming on "Internet safety, prescription and over-the-counter drug abuse, cyber-bullying, and safety and health."

Drug Use by Juveniles

There are indicators that juvenile drug use is increasing in some niches. Methamphetamine use by students in smaller cities, especially in the West and Midwest appears to be a growing problem.[127] Also, abuse of prescription drugs is becoming a serious problem among juveniles. Teens said that the number one factor for using prescription medications was "ease of access." Most of them reported that they obtained the drugs from the medicine cabinet at home or at a friend's home.[128] The Monitoring the Future (MTF) survey by the National Institute on Drug Abuse has measured drug and alcohol use among adolescent students nationwide since 1975.

Think About It . . .

A number of schools have adopted or have considered adopting drug-testing programs for students who are engaged in extracurricular activities or who have on-campus parking privileges. Typically, the programs require random testing of a sample of students. Students who fail the drug test usually are suspended from their activities or parking privileges and may be suspended from school. They usually are not subject to criminal prosecution. Supporters of the policy claim that random testing deters drug use. Opponents claim that it violates the rights of the students and does not work. What do you think?

Radius Images/Alamy

TABLE 13–2	PERCENTAGE OF STUDENTS REPORTING USE OF ANY ILLICIT DRUGS, 2008–2010					
	8th Grade		10th Grade		12th Grade	
	2008	2010	2008	2010	2008	2010
Lifetime	19.6	21.4	34.1	37.0	47.4	48.2
Past Year	14.1	16.4	26.9	30.2	36.6	38.3
Past Month	7.6	9.5	15.8	18.5	22.3	23.8

Source: National Institute on Drug Abuse, DrugFacts: High School and Youth Trends.

The 2011 survey indicated that daily marijuana use was at its highest point among twelfth graders since the early 1980s. In 2010 and 2011, marijuana use was ahead of cigarette smoking by high school seniors—36.4% reported using marijuana compared to 10.3% of seniors reporting daily use of cigarettes. (See Table 13–2.) In the 2011 survey, for the first time, high school seniors reported the use of synthetic marijuana, also known as K2 or Spice. Almost one in nine high school seniors (11.4%) reported using Spice in the past year. The increase in marijuana use is attributed to the fact that students' attitudes toward substance abuse show a decline in the perceived risk of harm associated with its use. After marijuana, prescription and over-the-counter medications account for most of the top drugs abused by twelfth graders.[129]

1 in a million The chances of a child being killed at school.

Most Frequent Prescription and Over-the-Counter Medications Abused by High School Seniors

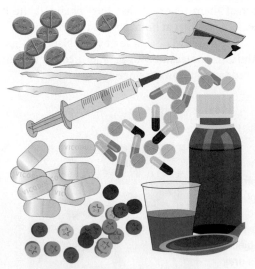

Vicodin, Adderall, Salvia, Tranquilizers, Cough Medicine, MDMA (Ecstasy) Hallucinogens, OxyContin, Sedatives, Inhalants, Cocaine (any form), Ritalin

▶ Schools and Juvenile Violence

In August 1966, Charles Whitman, a college student, dragged a foot locker filled with hunting rifles onto the observation deck of the clock tower at the University of Texas at Austin and opened fire, killing 14 and wounding 31 others. Prior to the Whitman attack, schools and colleges were considered among the safest places in the United States.

Today, school violence is a major concern of society. In the 2009–2010 school year, 25 homicides involving students and staff occurred at schools.[130] This rate of victimization is far lower than the rate of victimization in general. For example, in school year 2008–2009, there were 1,579 homicides among school age youths aged 5 to 18, of which 17 occurred at school. During the 2008 calendar year, there were 1,344 suicides of youths aged 5 to 18, of which 7 occurred at school.[131] While violent acts do occur at school, a student is less likely to be a homicide victim there.

The Justice Policy Institute, the research arm of the Center on Juvenile and Criminal Justice, has determined that the chances of a child being killed at school are nearly 1 in a million.[132] Again, despite these statistics, parents, students, school officials, public officials, and the general public express genuine concern over the problem of school violence. The fear and reaction to school violence may be due in part to the media coverage of such incidents and to the historical expectation of relative safety that has characterized schools.

Further, it is not just large, crowded inner-city schools that have suffered these attacks. In fact, the most serious attacks have occurred at schools in suburban or rural environments, such as Moses Lake, Washington; Pearl, Mississippi; West Paducah, Kentucky; Jonesboro, Arkansas; Springfield, Oregon; Littleton, Colorado; Conyers, Georgia; Edinboro, Pennsylvania; Santee, California; Red Lake, Minnesota; Nickel Mines, Pennsylvania; Dekalb, Illinois; and Blacksburg, Virginia.

Strategies for Safe Schools

The sudden rise of school violence appears to be a mystery. Why does a child with an unremarkable history become a

LEARNING OUTCOMES 7 Identify the challenges of preventing school violence and bullying and strategies that have been used to respond to this problem.

GLOSSARY

contain-and-wait A law enforcement strategy for responding to shootings at schools and colleges in which perimeter security is established and law enforcement officers negotiate with the shooter.

active-shooter A law enforcement strategy for responding to shootings at schools and colleges in which the first officers on the scene seek and find the shooter and neutralize him or her.

bullying Making physical and/or psychological threats or abusing or tormenting another person.

zero-tolerance policies School disciplinary policies that provide for mandatory disciplinary actions for any and all violations of school rules regardless of the student or circumstance.

school-to-prison pipeline School disciplinary policies that increase the likelihood of suspended and expelled students dropping out of high school and having contact with the juvenile justice system.

The fear and reaction to school violence may be due in part to the media coverage of these incidents and to the historical expectation of relative safety that has characterized schools.

mass murderer who randomly kills teachers and classmates? The reasons given by juvenile murderers are diverse and do not seem adequate to explain the crime. For example, consider the following explanations offered by students who murdered or threatened to murder fellow students and teachers. Victor Cordova, Jr., aged 13, said that he shot a 13-year-old classmate in the head because "other kids were bothering me."[133] A seventh grader shot and killed his teacher because he had been sent home for throwing water balloons in class.[134] A 12-year-old student pulled a gun in class and threatened to shoot the teacher and classmates because he wanted to join his mother, who was in jail.[135] Two teens accused of killing two Dartmouth College professors did so because they were committed to "an evil-game dare."[136] John Romano, aged 16, walked into Columbia High School (New York) on February 9, 2004, and opened fire with a shotgun, hitting a teacher in the leg. In his police statement, Romano's explanation was, "I have had fantasies for about the last year of going into Columbia and shooting up the place."[137] Finally, two second-grade boys and an 11-year-old schoolmate buried a loaded handgun in a playground sandbox and plotted to shoot and stab a third-grade student during recess. The students told authorities that they intended to kill the third-grade girl "because she had teased two of them."[138]

Numerous studies of violent offenders have attempted to understand what causes them to kill. Sociological theories point to diverse reasons, such as environmental influence, bullying, peer pressure, lack of opportunity for legitimate advancement, and learned behavior. None of these theories alone can explain the increase in homicides and violent crimes at schools. A study by the Secret Service National Threat Assessment Center of 40 cases of school violence or shootings over a 20-year period concluded that there is no single profile of a school shooter. However, schools have engaged in a number of strategies in an attempt to prevent school violence. Besides simply expelling or arresting disruptive students, among the more frequently used strategies are programs to reduce weapons on school property, programs to address the problem of bullying, and increased presence of police officers on school property.

Responding to Violence on School Property

School shootings, nonfatal violence, and crime have resulted in a number of significant changes in security and response to violence and crime by law enforcement and school administration. In 2010, students aged 12 to 18 were victims of about 828,000 nonfatal victimizations at schools, including 470,000 thefts and 359,000 violent victimizations.[139] Students actually experience a greater number of nonfatal victimizations at school than away

from school.[140] According to a report of the National Center of Education Statistics, *Indicators of School Crime and Safety: 2011*, about 4% of students aged 12 to 18 reported being victimized at school, 8% reported being threatened or injured with a weapon, about 10% of teachers reported being threatened with injury, and 6% of elementary school teachers reported being physically attacked.[141] During the 2009–2010 school year, schools reported to the police 689,000 crimes that occurred at school.[142] In addition, students attending public schools reported being victimized at twice the rate of students attending private schools.[143] This level of violence has forced schools to take active steps to respond to and prevent violence.

One of the landmark cases of school violence was the 1999 Columbine High School schooling in Littleton, Colorado. As a result of the Columbine High School shooting by Eric Harris and Dylan Klebold, Colorado law enforcement and school administrators throughout the nation changed their strategy for responding to school shootings.

Prior to the Columbine High School shooting, law enforcement officers were trained to respond to school shootings in a strategy known as **contain-and-wait**, which had its origins in the 1966 sniper attack at the University of Texas at Austin in which Charles Whitman killed 14 people. The contain-and-wait strategy emphasized the deployment of SWAT teams, negotiations, and perimeter containment. When applied to the Columbine High School shooting, the result was a disaster. Initially, the shooters were unchallenged as police waited for SWAT teams to respond, resulting in continued shooting as Harris and Klebold were not interested in negotiating, only killing. One victim bled to death because the police failed to aggressively enter the high school.

When shooters have no desire to negotiate and their only goal is to kill as many people as possible, rapid response is absolutely necessary. The new police strategy adopted since Columbine is called the **active-shooter** response. Instead of waiting for SWAT or special response teams, this strategy trains police officers to form on-the-spot response teams, called "contact teams," and to enter the building and make their way toward the shooter while ignoring all other demands such as wounded victims and people who need to be evacuated. The purpose of the contact team is to locate and neutralize the shooter. Studies suggest that in a mass shooting, a gunman kills someone every 15 seconds. The police cannot delay or wait for the SWAT team. This strategy has become standard training for law enforcement responding to school shootings. Also, states have passed legislation requiring schools, colleges, and universities to engage in active planning and preparation for school shootings and other emergencies.

Firearms and School Shootings

Many claim that the availability of firearms, especially handguns, is a major contributing factor in the occurrence of violent crime at schools. Proponents of this theory believe that school shootings are possible only because weapons are so easily available to children. They argue that gun control legislation mandating safer guns and penalties against adults who allow children to obtain guns would help promote a safer school environment. Firearms have been brought to school by kindergartners to high school seniors to college students; thus, any strategy that would promote a gun-free environment at schools appears to have merit.

Unfortunately, such strategies are unlikely to have much impact on school violence, as schools and state legislatures have already recognized that weapons, especially guns, on school property are an inherent risk and have taken measures to make schools a weapon-free environment. In every case in schools where students have used guns in violent crimes, it was illegal to bring guns to school. Rather than focus on new laws or stiffer penalties, school administrators have focused on screening for weapons and adopting strategies to respond to shooters.

Schools, even elementary schools, have adopted the use of metal detector screening and zero-tolerance policies prohibiting any weapon, including sharp scissors, pocket knives, and any other object that could be used as a weapon. States have passed laws mandating schools as "gun-free" zones. Often these laws have mandatory sentences or lengthy prison sentences for anyone violating the policy. Even in states that permit private citizens to carry concealed firearms, the law often does not permit them to carry the weapon on school property.

Despite laws and punishments, students continue to bring weapons and guns onto school property. The 2011 report of the National Center of Education Statistics, *Indicators of School Crime and Safety: 2011* data indicated that 17% of students reported carrying a weapon anywhere during the past 30 days and 6% of students reported carrying a weapon at least one day on school property.[144]

Reducing Bullying

Bullying has been identified as a common factor among school shooters. The Secret Service National Threat Assessment Center's analysis of school shooters found that two-thirds of school shooters saw themselves as being bullied. In 2009, about 28% of 12- to 18-year-old students reported having

A Secret Service study of 40 cases of school violence concluded that there is no single profile of a school shooter.

been bullied at school during the school year and 6% reported having been cyber-bullied.[145] In 2009, more students reported that they were afraid of being attacked or harmed at school than away from school.[146] About 1 out of every 20 high school students said that they skipped at least one day of school because of fear for their safety. A 2005 study conducted by Adrienne Nishina of the University of California Los Angeles reported that about half of the students in sixth grade reported being bullied on at least one out of five school days. A larger percentage of students reported witnessing someone else getting bullied. Many of these students stated that teachers appeared to take no action against the bullies.[147] The study reported that children who were bullied, including verbal abuse, or who witnessed others being bullied frequently suffered emotional anxiety and physical symptoms such as feeling sick. The study stated that "the more bullying they [the students] experience, the more they dislike school and want to avoid school." Whereas those bullied suffer emotionally and physically, other studies report that "bullies are often popular and viewed by classmates as the 'coolest' in their classes; they don't show signs of depression or social anxiety, and do not suffer from low self-esteem."[148]

Estimates of the extent of bullying in schools vary and are difficult to validate. One report is that there are an estimated 3.7 million bullies—children who regularly verbally taunt or physically torment others—in sixth to tenth grades. Jim Snyder, a psychologist at Wichita State University, reported that his study of bullying in kindergartners showed that they bully each other once every six minutes.[149] The Suicide Prevention Resource Center reports that nearly 9% of students reported being physically injured as a result of bullying and that bullying is associated with an increased risk of suicide in young people.[150] Furthermore, the Suicide Prevention Resource Center warns that the rate of bullying for lesbian, gay, bisexual, and transgender (LGBT) youth is at a rate two to four times higher than that of their heterosexual peers.[151] In a 2005 survey of LGBT students aged 13 to 18, 90% reported being verbally or physically harassed or physically assaulted over the past year because of their perceived or actual appearance, gender, sexual orientation, or gender expression.[152]

These findings have stimulated many school administrators to reexamine their reaction to bullies and bullying. Studies have reported that bullies often are popular and are protected not only by students, but also by teachers and administrators eager to promote "superstars." These studies suggest that cultural values condone and support "rudeness as a means to get ahead not just on the playground, but into adulthood."[153] While the criminal justice system and law enforcement play a role in preventing and responding to bullying, most antibullying strategies are educational programs. Most of the programs are school-related or school policy programs. The goal of these programs is to teach students mediation and negotiation skills, train teachers and staff in intervention techniques, and stress the importance

There is debate as to what level of force police should use on school children in response to violent behavior or aggression.

of intervening. Some states have adopted criminal laws to reduce bullying, but these laws have proven difficult to enforce and there is no data to suggest that criminal laws are effective in preventing bullying.

Police Presence on School Campuses

One strategy for responding to violence and bullying at schools and colleges is the use of unarmed and armed law enforcement officers and/or school safety agents to patrol school property. Uniformed, armed law enforcement officers have been commonplace on state college campuses, but K–12 schools are now inviting law enforcement officers onto their school property. For example, in 2004, New York City schools targeted "problem schools" and assigned extra police officers and safety agents to patrol them. The targeted schools adopted the successful zero-tolerance policies from the broken windows crime prevention model that has been credited for reducing crime in New York City. The schools adopted **zero-tolerance policies** on violation of school rules and emphasized paying attention to details such as a clean environment and no graffiti. The schools use police officers and school safety agents to enforce these rules. These officers issue citations for criminal and noncriminal incidents, screen students with metal detectors, patrol hallways, and strictly enforce security rules. For example, one school saw 115 arrests, summonses, and juvenile reports for the period from January 5 to March 22, 2004.[154]

New York schools using the police strategy to reduce school violence reported a 48% decrease in major crime, but one of the problems of the programs that use on-campus law enforcement officers is the conflict between school administrators and teachers and the law enforcement officers. Often school administrators and teachers are opposed to the presence of armed law enforcement officers on school property and believe that such a strategy is only treating the symptoms and not the cause of the problems of violence. School administrators, teachers, and staff may be critical of police policies, such as arresting and handcuffing students for apparently minor violations. In some cases, law enforcement officers have been criticized for arresting and handcuffing students as young as five years old.

The presence of police officers in schools has raised serious questions, such as "What is the relationship between law enforcement and students, teachers, and staff." School administrators have criticized school law enforcement officers for using excessive force on students. Officers have used Tasers, pepper stray, physical force, and deadly force to subdue allegedly violent students. School principals who often see themselves as the people in charge often find themselves in an adversarial relationship with school law enforcement officers. Sometimes this relationship is worsened by the attitude of school law enforcement officers who view their relationship with students differently than that of teachers and staff. For example, the Twin Rivers Police Department (California) police union sold T-shirts with a picture of a child behind bars and the slogan: "U raise 'em, we cage 'em' as a fund-raiser. The public reaction to the T-shirt was less than enthusiastic.

Also, there is debate as to what level of force police should use on school children in response to violent behavior or aggression. In some cases, police have used pepper spray to subdue second graders. There are cases where police used Tasers to subdue juveniles in school and the child suffered cardiac arrest and died. While the threat of students using deadly force on school property does exist, often the public is uncomfortable with police requests for more firepower. For example, in 2012, the Plainfield Police Department (Illinois) asked the school board to allow them to store AR-15 assault rifles on school property for use in case of a heavily armed "live shooter" in a school building.[155] Nationally, the number of school resource officers armed with high-powered rifles is growing, and requests for these types of weapons are becoming more common.

Some states have passed legislation requiring schools and law enforcement to conduct training and exercises to develop effective practices for responding to school violence and active shooters. While schools may be reluctant to engage in these exercises because of the potential violence and threat of death they suggest, they are becoming commonplace and necessary.[156]

As a result of the changing role of law enforcement on school campuses, principals of some school districts are meeting regularly with police officials to break down the "silos between police and school administrators."[157] For example, high school principals in violent neighborhoods in Chicago hold regular talks with local police commanders to get rid of the perception that police are responsible for the streets and principals are responsible for the school campus.

Some School Safety Programs Create New Problems

In an attempt to reduce school violence, schools and communities have adopted a plethora of programs. However, the effectiveness of the various preventive programs is not clear. Although the data suggest that specific categories of interventions or arrangements in schools can reduce or prevent delinquent behavior, drug use, and school disorder, the data do not suggest that schools have adopted the more effective programs or have implemented good programs.[158] "A national study completed in 2000 found that despite the increase in knowledge about 'what works' in school delinquency prevention, most of the [n]ation's schools use prevention practices that are either unproven or known to be ineffective."[159] Poor implementation, even of good programs, results in poor quality and ineffective programs. Only 10% of the nation's schools that adopt "best practices" programs report using the minimally adequate activities and instructional and behavioral programs to plausibly expect the program to have a measurable effect on reducing problem behavior or increasing safety.[160]

In 2010, prosecutors brought felony charges against six students at South Hadley High School (Massachusetts), charging them with bullying 15-year-old Phoebe Prince to the point that she hanged herself. In 2011, the students admitted responsibility for their actions and accepted a plea bargain that resulted in sentences of probation for misdemeanor charges. About one-third of students aged 12 to 18 report being bullied. Studies show that bullying is associated with increases in suicide risk and depression. What is the role of the criminal justice system in reducing bullying?

micromonkey/Fotolia

Bans on Cell Phones

Some school strategies have met with conflict from parents. For example, while cell phones are not linked directly with school violence and bullying, many schools claim that serious problems are associated with cell phones. Cell phones can be used to coordinate acts of violence and can be instrumental in promoting bullying. Because of these problems as well as the in-class disruptions caused by cell phone use, some schools have banned them. However, parents have protested such bans. Parents ignore the problems that can result from the abuse of cell phones in the classroom and focus on them as an essential means of communicating with their children, especially in the event of an emergency, such as a school shooting. Whereas school administrators see the problems associated with abuse of cell phones, parents see cell phones as "security." These conflicts only make it more difficult for schools and communities to promote safe schools.

Transfer to Juvenile Court

Some programs used to enhance school safety seem to create as many problems as they solve. For example, two popular strategies to promote safe schools are (1) to transfer "troublemakers" to juvenile court and (2) to expel disruptive or violent students. Many states have passed legislation that allows schools to refer students who commit school-based offenses to juvenile court.

In these schools, misdemeanor charges can be filed against a student for anything from disrupting a class to assaulting a teacher. Rather than school administrators handling problems as disciplinary issues, police take violators into custody and charges are filed in juvenile court. As school administrators encounter more disruptions, they rely more on arrests and referrals to the juvenile court. In some school districts, referrals to the juvenile court for school-based offenses have increased 300% in the last ten years. Schools are referring offenders to juvenile court for turning off the lights in the girls' bathroom, not listening in class, not going to class, violating school dress codes, and disrupting the learning process.[161] The problem with this strategy is that juvenile court intake officers

74% The percentage of Hispanic male students that had at least one discretionary violation.

become overwhelmed with school-related cases. Ohio, Virginia, Kentucky, and Florida juvenile court judges have complained that their courtrooms are at risk of being overwhelmed by student misconduct cases that should be handled in the schools.[162]

Suspensions and Expulsion: Pipeline from School to Prison

Another frequently used strategy to promote school safety that produces serious unintended side effects is the expulsion of disruptive or violent students. Many schools have adopted a "get tough" approach with disruptive students, especially those cases involving firearms or violence. Students who are found to have violated the school's prohibition against firearms or who are violent are not being allowed to attend their regular school. However, most states require young children below a certain age to remain in school. Thus, while they are expelled from attending "regular school," the state must provide an alternative educational experience. Some school districts have created "alternative" schools or "second opportunity schools" for these disruptive students. The schools are a student's last chance before being placed in a secure facility. This solution places all of the most disruptive students in a single environment. Often these schools lack the resources to provide students with the counseling and individual attention necessary to rehabilitate them and end their disruptive behavior. Teachers are unable to provide quality educational experiences because an entire class of disruptive students proves impossible to teach. Principals of these schools have problems with high truancy rates, violent-prone students who assault each other and teachers, and overwhelmed teachers.[163]

The operation of these alternative schools is expensive. They have high failure rates, and few of the students complete their high school education or GED. Nearly all of the students perform below grade level or lack basic skills necessary for

83% The percentage of African-American male students that had at least one discretionary violation.

59% The percentage of white male students that had at least one discretionary violation.

academic success. Frequently, students are court-supervised due to their delinquency; therefore, multiple agencies, such as the Department of Education, the Juvenile Court, and state child welfare agencies, are involved in monitoring the students. Also, juvenile delinquents who have been in the custody of the state for violent offenses or delinquency but are released from a secure facility while they are still required to attend school are frequently placed in these alternative schools. The integration of these new court-involved students, often at various times during the school year, creates significant challenges for the school. The students have a high risk for failure in school.[164] While the initial policy of the school may have been well intended in its effort to promote safety, there have been serious unintended consequences of strategies that have relied on zero tolerance, transfer to juvenile court, and suspensions.

Suspensions and expulsions have become relatively common policies in the pursuit of safe schools.[165] A study of the Texas public school system indicated that in nearly all cases (97%), disciplinary actions were for conduct for which state law does not mandate suspension. The suspensions were primarily at the discretion of school officials.[166] About 54% of students experienced suspensions, but minorities were suspended at a much greater rate than whites were. The great majority of African-American male students had at least one discretionary violation (83%), compared to 74% for Hispanic male students and 59% for white male students.[167] Overall, African-American students had a 31% higher likelihood of facing a school discretionary action compared to otherwise identical white and Hispanic students.[168] Studies of the Los Angeles Unified school district, the Clark County school district (Nevada), the Fairfax County public schools (Virginia), and the Illinois public schools revealed similar data in the wide gap in suspension rates between African-American and white students.[169]

The study of Texas students showed that suspensions had an adverse impact on student academic success and delinquency.[170] A student who was suspended or expelled was twice as likely to repeat his or her grade compared to a student who had the same characteristics and had not been suspended or expelled. Of all students who were suspended or expelled, 31% repeated their grade at least once compared to only 5% of students without a suspension.[171] About 10% of students suspended or expelled between seventh and twelfth grade dropped out.[172] Finally, the Texas data revealed that "a student who was suspended or expelled for a discretionary violation was nearly three times as likely to be in contact with the juvenile justice system the following year."[173]

The association between school discipline and delinquency has become a concern for federal authorities. In 2011, Attorney General Eric Holder and Secretary of Education Arne Duncan announced the launch of the Supportive School Discipline Initiative, a collaborative project between the Departments of Justice and Education that will address the **school-to-prison pipeline** and the disciplinary policies and practices that can push students out of school and into the juvenile system.[174] Attorney General Holder said that the purpose of the initiate is "ensuring that our educational system is a doorway to opportunity—and not a point of entry to our criminal justice system."[175] In 2012, President Obama issued an executive order titled "White House Initiative on Educational Excellence" to encourage schools to reduce punishments for violation of school rules/violence that disproportionately impact minorities. This executive order emphasizes the importance of implementing strategies that promote safe schools but do not have adverse unintended consequences on minority and special needs students.

▶ *The Juvenile as Victim*

The juvenile justice system is concerned not only about juvenile offenders, but also about children who are victims of crime and the health and welfare of children. Under the doctrine "the state as parent and guardian," the state takes an active role in promoting the health and welfare of juveniles through direct intervention and programs for juvenile victims, as well as through legislation, social workers, and police, who work to reduce offenses committed by adults against juveniles.

While law enforcement and the criminal justice system play an important role in protecting children from victimization and promoting the health and welfare of children, other agencies often are central to protecting children from victimization and harm. One of the agencies that focuses primarily on the welfare of the child is **child protective services (CPS)**. CPS is a social service agency of the state that provides services to children who are abused, neglected, or victimized or are in need of care. CPS has the legal responsibility to conduct assessments or investigations of reports of child abuse and neglect and to offer rehabilitative services to families where maltreatment has occurred or is likely to occur.[176] It also has the authority to remove a child from his or her parent(s) or guardian or living environment and place

3x The greater likelihood that a student who was suspended or expelled will be in contact with the juvenile justice system the following year.

Unique to the juvenile justice system is the fact that children are vulnerable victims. Each state has an agency devoted to child protection. These agencies are not law enforcement agencies, but they have broad powers to protect children from all kinds of abuse. For example, an Ohio third grader who weighed more than 200 pounds was taken from his family and placed in foster care after county social workers said that his mother was not doing enough to control his weight. When should children be removed from their parents or guardians?

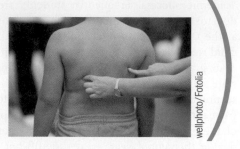

wellphoto/Fotolia

the child under the care of the state if it deems there is a serious threat to the health or welfare of the child.

CPS officers, who are not sworn law enforcement officers, do not have the powers of arrest or search and seizure or the authority to carry concealed weapons. CPS officers are social welfare workers, but they must work closely with law enforcement as many incidents that threaten the welfare of the child are violations of the law. The juvenile justice system also is involved in children's well-being and safety because data show an increased risk of delinquency for children who are abused and victimized.[177]

While children may be offenders, they also are victims of crime. Thus, the criminal justice system must respond to the victimization of children. Three major concerns of the criminal justice system and the public are violence against children, sexual exploitation of children and child pornography, and missing children. Usually, these criminal offenses are committed by adults; thus, law enforcement and the criminal courts are primarily the agencies focused on these offenses and offenders.

Often the public is motivated by sensational crimes against children to push for new laws aimed at punishing perpetrators of crimes against children. For example, the 1932 kidnapping of the 18-month-old son of Charles Lindbergh resulted in the federal government passing the **Federal Kidnapping Act (Lindbergh Law)** that made it a federal crime to transport a kidnap victim across state lines. The 1994 death and sexual assault of Megan Kanda, aged 7, resulted in the **1996 federal sex offender registry**. In another example, the 1996 abduction and death of Amber Hagerman, aged 9, resulted in the development and nationwide use of the **Amber Alert system**. This system enables law enforcement to broadcast timely alerts of missing or abducted children by use of media, Twitter, and smartphones. The 2003 death and kidnapping of Polly Klass, aged 12, resulted in legislation requiring enhanced sentencing for repeat offenders. This sentencing model was applied to other offenses and became known as the three-strikes law. Finally, the death of Caylee Anthony, aged 2, and the subsequent trial of Casey Anthony for her daughter's murder, have resulted in states passing laws, often known as **Caylee's Law**, that make it a crime to fail to report a missing child in a timely manner.

In the effort to protect children from victimization, in some cases, the criminal justice system has provided special protection to children by mandating the reporting of suspected abuse or making certain crimes strict liability crimes. For example, school officials, social workers, doctors, and certain caregivers are required to report suspected abuse of children to law enforcement. Unlike law enforcement officers who must have reasonable suspicion or probable cause that a person committed a crime before intervening, these officials are required by law to report signs of abuse that may not rise to the threshold necessary for law enforcement officers to act. Also, certain crimes such as sexual intercourse by adults with underage juveniles may be designed as a **strict liability crime**. A strict liability crime does not require the prosecutor to prove *mens rea*, or criminal intent, by the perpetrator. Thus, even if the minor child consents to the sexual intercourse, the act is illegal.

▶ Conclusion: Innocence Lost?

It has been just a little over 100 years since the first juvenile court assumed jurisdiction over children. However, in the century that has passed, the juvenile justice system has undergone significant changes. Today, juvenile courts must yield some of the exclusive jurisdiction they exercised over young offenders back to the criminal justice system. As a result, some young violent offenders find themselves right back where they were in the 1800s when they are charged and sentenced as adults. The U.S. Supreme Court has banned the use of the death penalty for juveniles tried as adults, but these offenders can find themselves being sentenced to long prison terms for their crime.

The public has been more willing to accept that juvenile delinquents, especially violent offenders, are fully culpable for their actions. The public has lost faith that, with treatment, a change of environment, discipline, education, and training, juvenile delinquents can be "saved." At the same time, the public continues to recognize that the state has an important role in overseeing the health and welfare of juveniles. Thus, even as more juveniles are being diverted from the juvenile justice system to the criminal justice system, the state is pumping more resources into prevention programs and child welfare programs.

One of the challenges of the juvenile justice system is to provide the proper balance between the competing goals of public safety and age-appropriate response. This challenge must

Some young violent offenders find themselves right back where they were in the 1800s when they are charged and sentenced as adults.

be fulfilled in a changing environment of social norms and values. Today's society is far removed from the society that existed at the turn of the twentieth century. New influences such as mobility, media, availability of firearms, and changing social norms provide a different environment in which children grow up. Even the attitude of parents concerning their role in child rearing has changed.

The public seems less willing to recognize the "innocence" and "immaturity" of juveniles and more willing to accept that due to changes in environment and values, children are more adultlike at a younger age. Thus, the "get tough" policy characteristic of dealing with adult offenders appears to be migrating to juvenile offenders and is resulting in changes to the juvenile justice system.

However, the juvenile justice system is a complex legal and social institution and is not well served by simplistic views of its functions. The proper functioning of the juvenile justice system is extremely important. Historically, the juvenile court has often been a place where theories of delinquency can be tested, with the hope that if they are valid, they will enable the juvenile court to respond so as to prevent the juvenile offender from becoming an adult offender. However, example after example has often proven that the response of the juvenile court has not been correct in eliminating criminal behavior in juveniles. Some segments of the public appear willing to return to pre-1899 treatment of juvenile offenders by transferring them to the criminal justice system.

The financial crisis experienced by many states has resulted in a review of the services the state can offer to juvenile offenders. In response to record budget deficits, many states had to cut juvenile counseling, vocational training, treatment programs, and diversion programs. Often these programs cost little and appear promising in keeping juveniles out of the criminal justice system. However, as states had to make deep cuts in their budgets, even the most promising and inexpensive programs are being cut.

Parents no longer believe that childhood is a time of innocence. They fear their children will be abducted and molested by child sex offenders. They fear the influence of gangs on their children and the danger gangs pose. They fear their children will abuse drugs. They fear their children will be murdered at school. In the midst of all this fear, it is important for the public to realize that despite the well-publicized failures of the juvenile justice system and the dangers parents fear will befall their children, the juvenile justice system has been successful; thus, the public should not be so quick to abandon or radically change it. Children are still safer at school than they are at home, and an overburdened and underfunded juvenile justice system has been providing for the welfare of children and diverting the majority of children from a career of crime.

Duty to Protect Children

Social institutions have a duty to protect children from abuse. However, in some cases, they have failed to do so. Three cases include the Los Angeles Unified School District, the Catholic Archdiocese of Philadelphia, and the Pennsylvania State scandal. The common thread in these cases is that the administrators were aware of the abuse of children but failed to act.

The Los Angeles Unified School District is the second-largest district in the nation. In 2012, a series of arrests of teachers and staff exposed widespread sexual and physical abuse of children. The abuse went unchecked for years because the district administration did not appear to keep any records of accusations of abuse and was reluctant to report suspected child abuse to law enforcement officials even though state law required it.

The Catholic Church has battled allegations of priests sexually abusing children for more than four decades. In July 2012, a landmark trial in Philadelphia resulted in Monsignor William Lynn being sentenced to three to six years in state prison for child endangerment. The case marked the first time an official of the church was held criminally responsible for failure to report abuse by priests. The court found that Lynn helped shuffle and protect priests who had been accused of or admitted to abusing children. In sentencing Lynn, Judge Teresa Sarmina told him you "turned a blind eye while 'monsters in clerical garb' sexually abused children. You knew full well what was right, but you chose wrong."

The Jerry Sandusky sex scandal at Penn State shocked the nation. The report of an independent investigation concluded that as early as 1998, high-ranking university administrators and football coach Joe Paterno knew about allegations of Sandusky sexually abusing children. The report concluded that the most senior leaders at Penn State showed a "total disregard for the safety and welfare of Sandusky's child victims" for 14 years and "empowered" Sandusky to continue his abuse. The National Collegiate Athletic Association imposed severe sanctions against Penn State, but criminal charges were not filed against anyone except Sandusky, who was convicted of 45 counts of sexual abuse.

STAN HONDA/AFP/Getty Images/Newscom

Monsignor William Lynn

This case raises several interesting questions. Among them are the following:

1. Why do administrators fail to report child sexual abuse?

2. Should criminal sanctions be more strictly pursued against administrators who fail to report child abuse? Explain.

3. How do child abuse scandals harm the community and criminal justice system?

LEARNING OUTCOMES 1

Identify the foundations of the juvenile justice system.

In the early 1800s, private reform groups attempted to divert young offenders from the criminal justice system. In 1824, the New York House of Refuge opened as the nation's first juvenile reformatory. This facility had the authority to place children in private industry through indenture agreements by which employers agreed to supervise the youths in exchange for their labor. By the mid-1800s, private institutions had increased in major cities but could not provide adequate services. Eventually, many states found it necessary to assume control over the various private juvenile reformatories to provide greater financial support and oversight.

1. Who was responsible for establishing the first juvenile reformatories?

2. What fueled the crisis in juvenile reformatories during the late nineteenth century?

3. What was the purpose of early reform schools?

social safety net Government programs that provide for people in need.

New York House of Refuge An early juvenile reformatory established by New York State in 1824 that was to become the model for most juvenile reformatories.

indenture agreements Agreements whereby employers would supervise youths in exchange for their labor.

LEARNING OUTCOMES 2

Summarize the jurisdiction of the juvenile justice system and the classification of juvenile offenders.

The first juvenile court was established in Cook County, Illinois, in 1899. This court exercised the right of *parens patriae* by assuming power over the authority of a child's natural parent or guardian. The juvenile court was established not as a criminal court, but as a government agency to provide youthful offenders with a comprehensive and balanced approach to rehabilitation. More focus is placed on the best interests of the child.

1. How do juvenile courts differ from adult courts?

2. What year was the first juvenile court established?

3. Give examples of status offenses.

parens patriae The legal assumption that the state has primary responsibility for the safety and custody of children.

original jurisdiction The concept that because juvenile court is the only court that has authority over juveniles, they cannot be tried, for any offense, by a criminal court unless the juvenile court grants permission for an accused juvenile to be waived to criminal court.

waiving Granting permission for an accused juvenile to be moved from juvenile court to criminal court.

juvenile court A court that handles juvenile welfare cases and cases involving status offenders and delinquents; some juvenile courts handle additional matters related to the family.

status offender A child who has committed an act or failed to fulfill a responsibility for which, if he or she were an adult, the court would not have any authority over him or her.

delinquent A juvenile accused of committing an act that is criminal for both adults and juveniles.

juvenile superpredator A term used by the Office of Juvenile Justice Delinquency and Prevention to describe a juvenile who commits violent felony crimes.

LEARNING OUTCOMES 3

Explain how landmark court cases have influenced the due process rights of juveniles.

Not until the 1960s did the Supreme Court abandon its hands-off approach to juvenile cases and become more concerned with examining the need for due process rights for juveniles. Decisions during the Warren Court era redefined the due process rights of juveniles. The Supreme Court made significant changes to the very nature of the juvenile justice system, declaring that juveniles do have due process rights. One unique aspect of juvenile court proceedings is that they are not open to the public.

1. What was the Supreme Court's earliest position regarding juvenile proceedings?

2. What rights has the Supreme Court prescribed for juveniles?

3. What due process rights were set forth in the *In re Gault* case?

Kent v. United States A 1961 Supreme Court case that marked the departure of the Supreme Court from its acceptance of the denial of due process rights to juveniles.

In re Gault A case in which the Supreme Court provided due process rights to juveniles, including notice of charges, counsel, right to examine witnesses, and right to remain silent.

In re Winship A case in which the Supreme Court ruled that the reasonable doubt standard, the same used in criminal trials, should be required in all delinquency adjudications.

burden of proof The standard required for adjudication.

McKeiver v. Pennsylvania A case in which the Supreme Court denied juveniles the right to a trial by jury.

Breed v. Jones A case in which the Supreme Court ruled that once a juvenile has been adjudicated by a juvenile court, he or she cannot be waived to criminal court to be tried for the same charges.

Schall v. Martin A case in which the Supreme Court upheld the right of juvenile courts to deny bail to adjudicated juveniles.

Juvenile Justice and Delinquency Prevention Act of 1974 An act that provides the major source of federal funding to states for the improvement of their juvenile justice systems, services, and facilities.

LEARNING OUTCOMES 4

Summarize why and in what ways states are changing the age of accountability.

The age at which a juvenile can be fully accountable for a crime varies by state. A common term for the process of moving a juvenile into adult court is called a *judicial waiver*. Some states have a statutory exclusion provision that allows transferring juveniles to criminal court without review by and approval of the juvenile court. A majority of states have adopted statutory exclusion and exclude certain serious offenses from juvenile court jurisdiction, such as homicide and other serious crimes against persons.

1. What does it mean to have concurrent jurisdiction of a youthful offender?

2. Why might a youthful offender be tried as an adult?

3. How does a blended sentencing option work?

waiver The process of moving a juvenile from the authority of juvenile court to the adult criminal justice system.

statutory exclusion The provision that allows juveniles to be transferred to criminal court without review by and approval of a juvenile court.

blended sentencing option An option that allows the juvenile or criminal court to impose a sentence that can include confinement in a juvenile facility and/or in an adult prison after the offender is beyond the age of the juvenile court's jurisdiction.

LEARNING OUTCOMES 5

Describe the juvenile justice system, including postadjudications options for treatment, and punishment of juveniles.

The juvenile justice system is far more diverse than the adult criminal justice system. Before a juvenile can be waived into adult court, he or she is entitled to a waiver hearing in the juvenile court. A juvenile intake officer interviews the child and the parent(s) or guardian and gathers a life history of the child. If a case is referred to the juvenile court for formal processing, it is called a juvenile adjudication hearing. A delinquency petition asks a judge to hear the case in a formal hearing and determine whether the juvenile is delinquent. The judge also decides whether a delinquent youth should become a ward of the state and be placed in a residential facility or in a course of rehabilitation.

1. What is the name of the process by which a juvenile enters the juvenile justice system?

2. What is a consent decree?

3. Who makes a dispositional recommendation?

4. How does a boot camp treatment program work?

juvenile intake officer A person who is responsible for processing a juvenile into the juvenile justice system and seeing to aftercare if the juvenile is adjudicated; this person has duties similar to those of a police officer and a probation and parole officer.

juvenile intake The process whereby a juvenile enters the juvenile justice system.

life history An assessment by the juvenile intake/probation officer of the juvenile and his or her past behavior, living conditions, behavior of parents/guardians, and school behavior.

consent decree A written summary of the specific conditions and requirements to be placed on the child and/or parent(s) or guardian by the juvenile intake officer.

juvenile adjudication hearing The formal hearing held by a juvenile judge to conduct an inquiry of the facts concerning a case and to decide the disposition of the case and any rehabilitation, supervision, or punishment for the juvenile.

delinquency petition A request to a judge to hear and judge a juvenile case in a formal hearing to determine whether the juvenile is to be declared delinquent.

teen courts Courts for younger juveniles (aged 10 to 15) with no prior arrest record who are charged with less serious law violations wherein juvenile peers rather than adults determine the disposition.

juvenile drug courts Alternatives to the traditional adjudication process for juveniles with substance abuse problems that focus on rehabilitating the juveniles and eliminating drug abuse.

adjudicated Determined the disposition of the charges against the juvenile and the treatment or punishment options, done by the juvenile judge.

ward of the state A person for whom the state assumes responsibility for his or her health and well-being.

juvenile boot camp A military-style group-oriented rehabilitation program designed to alter the character and values of the juvenile offender.

Roper, Superintendent, Potosi Correctional Center* v. *Simmons A case in which the Supreme Court held that the Eighth and Fourteenth Amendments forbid imposition of the death penalty on offenders who were under the age of 18 when their crimes were committed.

Graham* v. *Florida A case in which the U.S. Supreme Court held that juveniles tried as adults cannot be sentenced to life in prison without parole for nonhomicide offenses.

Miller* v. *Alabama A case in which the U.S. Supreme Court extends the ban on sentences of life without parole for juveniles guilty of homicide offenses.

LEARNING OUTCOMES 6

Summarize the contributions of research and theory to understanding the causes of juvenile delinquency and offending, including youth gangs and substance abuse.

Sociological research and theories focus on what influences a juvenile's decision to choose delinquent behavior. Many researchers are especially interested in youth gangs. An interesting emergence has been hybrid youth gangs. Another area of interest involves female gangs. Juvenile drug use also is a serious problem, as there appears to be a strong link between substance abuse and delinquent behavior.

1. Why is research of young offenders important for rehabilitation efforts?

2. How do hybrid hangs differ from traditional gangs?

3. Describe the characteristics of a hybrid gang.

4. What percentage of youths detained for delinquency report having used an illicit substance?

youth gangs Difficult-to-define juvenile groups distinct from adult gangs that mimic adult gangs.

hybrid gangs A new type of youth gang with distinctive characteristics that differentiate them from traditional gangs; they are frequently school-based, less organized, less involved in criminal activity, and less involved in violence than are traditional gangs.

Drug Abuse Resistance Education (DARE) A popular in-school antidrug program initiated by the Los Angeles Police Department in 1983 but abandoned when data failed to support its effectiveness.

LEARNING OUTCOMES 7

Identify the challenges of preventing school violence and bullying and strategies that have been used to respond to this problem.

School violence is a major concern of society. The fear and reaction to school violence may be due in part to the media coverage of school shootings. School shootings, nonfatal violence, and crime have resulted in significant changes in security. Schools have adopted the use of metal detector screening and zero-tolerance policies prohibiting weapons. Reducing school bullying is another challenge for school administrators in seeking to reduce violence.

1. What is an active-shooter response strategy?

2. How does a zero-tolerance school policy work?

3. How commonplace is bullying in U.S. schools?

contain-and-wait A law enforcement strategy for responding to shootings at schools and colleges in which perimeter security is established and law enforcement officers negotiate with the shooter.

active-shooter A law enforcement strategy for responding to shootings at schools and colleges in which the first officers on the scene seek and find the shooter and neutralize him or her.

bullying Making physical and/or psychological threats or abusing or tormenting another person.

zero-tolerance policies School disciplinary policies that provide for mandatory disciplinary actions for any and all violations of school rules regardless of the student or circumstance.

school-to-prison pipeline School disciplinary policies that increase the likelihood of suspended and expelled students dropping out of high school and having contact with the juvenile justice system.

LEARNING OUTCOMES 8

Describe the role of the juvenile justice system in protecting juveniles from abuse and victimization.

The juvenile justice system is concerned about children who are victims of crime and about the health and welfare of children. A social service agency that focuses primarily on the welfare of the child is child protective services (CPS). Three major concerns of the criminal justice system in protecting youth are violence against children, sexual exploitation of children, and missing children. In the effort to safeguard children from victimization, the criminal justice system has mandated the reporting of suspected abuse and has made certain acts against youth a strict liability crime.

1. What is the purpose of CPS?

2. What is the Amber Alert system?

3. Identify three occupations that must report suspected child abuse.

child protective services (CPS) A government agency responsible for the health and welfare of children.

Federal Kidnapping Act (Lindbergh Law) An act that made it a federal offense to transport a kidnapping victim across state lines.

1996 federal sex offender registry A database of convicted sex offenders who are required to register with law enforcement; the registration data are available to the public.

Amber Alert system A system that provides law enforcement with the ability to notify the public of a missing or abducted child through media, technology, and social networks.

Caylee's Law A law that requires parents and/or guardians to reporting missing children in a timely manner.

strict liability crime A criminal act that does not require the prosecutor to prove *mens rea*, or criminal intent, by the perpetrator in order to prosecute.

MyCJLab

Go to Chapter 13 in *MyCJLab* to test your mastery of chapter concepts, access your Study Plan, engage in interactive exercises, complete critical-thinking and research assignments, and view related online videos.

Review: Complete the pretest in the Study Plan to confirm what you know and what you need to study further. Then complete the post-test to confirm your mastery of the concepts. Use the key term flash cards to review key terminology.

Apply: Complete the interactive simulation activity.

Analyze: Complete assignments as directed by your instructor.

Current Events: Explore CJSearch for current topical videos, articles, and news pieces.

Additional Links

Go to **www.findlaw.com/casecode/supreme.html** to locate the complete text of the U.S. Supreme Court decisions covered in this chapter.

Go to **http://www.ojjdp.gov/compliance/index.html** to find numerous resources regarding the monitoring of juvenile justice issues.

Go to **http://www.reclaimingfutures.org/blog/posts/%252Fwww.reclaimingfutures.org/www.ncchild.org/action/images/ opportunityboard?page=81&v=v9XRp69hkn6RV** and watch a video on teen drug courts.

Go to **http://www.ojjdp.gov/about/ojjdpact2002.html** to view the complete text of the Juvenile Justice and Delinquency Prevention Act.

Go to **http://doc.state.wy.us/institutions/whcc/boot_camp_whcc.html** and learn about the Wyoming Department of Corrections boot camp for youthful offenders.

Go to **http://articles.cnn.com/keyword/youth-crime** and read numerous articles related to youth crime.

Homeland Security

"Those who surrender freedom for security will not have, nor do they deserve, either one."

— *Benjamin Franklin*

1 Define terrorism and explain the difference between domestic and International terrorism.

2 Summarize the role of the primary agencies responsible for preventing and responding to terrorism.

3 Summarize the importance of intelligence in preventing and responding to terrorism.

4 Explain the changing role and challenges of federal agencies and first responders in preventing and responding to terrorism.

5 Describe the role of border security in the war on terrorism.

6 Describe the challenge of balancing civil rights and homeland security.

14

WHEN TERRORISM STRIKES HOME

On August 5, 2012, Army veteran, rock band leader, and white supremacist Wade M. Page, 40, approached a Sikh temple in Oak Creek, Wisconsin, as members were preparing langar, a Sikh communal meal, for services later in the day. He opened fire with a semiautomatic handgun, killing six people and wounding four. When police responded to the shooting and wounded Page in an exchange of gunfire, Page shot himself in the head. He had been on the radar of those who track the movements of white supremacist groups but had not committed any violent attacks.

Law enforcement officials said that the attack will be treated as an act of domestic terrorism. Preliminary investigations determined that no one else was involved in the attack; for that reason, it has been classified as a lone wolf attack, the most difficult to detect in advance. It is assumed that the attack was motivated by anti-Muslim hatred. Past incidences have occurred in which attacks on Sikhs were carried out under the mistaken belief that the victims were Muslim.

Hatred, discrimination, and attacks against Muslims became a concern immediately after the September 11, 2001, attacks by Muslim extremists. Muslims were randomly victimized under the pretense of revenge for the 9/11 attacks. The Federal Bureau of Investigation (FBI) targeted Muslims in a serious of undercover stings and infiltration of mosques to discover home-grown terrorist groups. The New York Police Department (NYPD) showed training videos claiming that Muslims were planning to infiltrate and dominate America.

HARISH TYAGI/EPA/Newscom

DISCUSS **Has the effort to defend the United States against domestic and international terrorism been too aggressive, just right, or too lax? Explain.**

Also, the NYPD engaged in extensive and widespread surveillance of Muslims and mosques. The secret surveillance extended well beyond the borders of New York City into neighboring states and academic institutions. The surveillance resulted in hundreds of American citizens being entered into secret intelligence databases without probable cause or suspicion that they were in any way connected to terrorism or criminal activity.

Following the 9/11 attacks, billions of dollars have been spent in an attempt to promote homeland security. Some have suggested that these efforts have been misdirected and wasteful and have infringed on people's civil liberties. These efforts have impacted law enforcement, society, and, some claim, the democratic foundations of the United States.

► *Terrorism, Homeland Security, and the Criminal Justice System*

This chapter discusses U.S. efforts to ensure homeland security. It discusses the difficult problem of defining terrorism, explains the development of the Department of Homeland Security, and explains how American policing and the criminal justice system have changed as a result of the war on terrorism. It closes with a discussion of issues raised by concerns over border security, cyberterrorism, and threats of civil liberties.

What Is Terrorism?

Although the United States has long endured horrific assaults on individuals and society (for example, the Sikh Temple shooting in Oak Creek, Wisconsin; the movie theater shooting in Aurora, Colorado;

Some have suggested that efforts to promote homeland security have been misdirected and wasteful and have infringed on people's civil liberties.

and the Fort Hood shooting), these attacks have not impacted the criminal justice system the same way the threat of international terrorism has since September 11, 2001. For the most part, the criminal justice system has effectively responded to the attacks of individuals and groups, and these attacks do not cause widespread public fear and loss of confidence in the government. However, effective counterterrorism actions against international groups using terrorism require resources that far exceed local police budgets and require international intelligence-gathering powers that only federal and military agencies possess. Although local and state police have a vital role as first responders in homeland security, their traditional relationship with federal and military agencies has been significantly changed by international terrorism.

To a large degree, U.S. criminal justice agencies abstain from the political and ethical debates regarding the justification for use of violence. Whether one is robbing a bank for self-gain or for the purpose of distributing the money to the poor does not matter to law enforcement or the criminal justice system. Robbing a bank is a crime, and law enforcement responds to the crime without regard to the motive of the offender. The criminal justice system focuses on the criminal nature of acts of terrorism regardless of the motivation or political ideology, and pursues the goals of protecting the public, apprehending perpetrators of such violence, and determining the guilt and punishment of the accused.

Acts of terrorism are a violation of criminal law. Federal and state laws define certain acts that intend to influence public opinion by the use of force or that use fear and intimidation as separate offenses beyond assault, homicide, bombing, or any other criminal offense. Crimes that are motivated by hate of an ethnic group, race, religion, gender, or sexual orientation may also be **hate crimes**. Hate crimes can have enhanced sentencing options but are not usually considered acts of terrorism. Also, legislation that provides enhanced powers of search and seizure to federal law enforcement in the investigation of terrorism does not apply to hate crimes. Thus, one of the critical elements of crimes of terrorism is the motive of the perpetrators. Generally, acts of terrorism are defined as "the premeditated use of violence against noncombatants agents intended to influence an audience." Noncombatants usually mean the general civilian population as opposed to military troops. What this means is that random acts of violence, no matter how deadly, are not acts of terrorism. Some assaults may be more difficult to categorize. For example, acts of violence against an ethnic group may be a crime, a hate crime, an act of terrorism, or some combination of them.

Terrorism is usually associated with political desires to change or overthrow a government or to influence policy or law. One of the strategies for achieving this goal is for groups to use acts of terrorism to convince the citizens of a legitimate government that their government has rendered them powerless, that there are great injustices in society, and that they are oppressed. Terrorists want citizens to believe that they are victims of social injustice and oppression and that their only recourse is violence against the government.

The use of terrorism is widespread throughout the world. In many Middle Eastern countries, terrorism is a daily concern as opposition groups regularly employ violence and suicide bombings. Compared to other countries, the United States has a relatively low occurrence of terrorist acts. One of the factors that has suppressed widespread terrorism in the United States is that the government and the criminal justice system reflect changing social values. During the course of U.S. history, laws and the criminal justice system have at times discriminated against classes of people, have been unjust in their protection of civil and constitutional rights for all people, and have turned a blind eye toward justice for some. However, these offenses are often corrected without resorting to terrorism or

> To a large degree, the impact of a terroristic attack depends on the ability of the mass media to magnify terrorist actions and to broadcast these images internationally.

overthrowing the government. These corrections can be seen in U.S. laws and Supreme Court rulings that have promoted social justice and equality and offered greater protections to citizens. An example of legislation is the Civil Rights Act of 1964 and various amendments that followed that promoted equality among citizens. One of the most significant examples of U.S. Supreme Court decisions was *Brown* v. *Topeka Board of Education* (1954); it overturned *Plessy* v. *Ferguson* (1896), which established the "separate but equal" doctrine of racial discrimination. Other examples of changing standards of justice established by U.S. Supreme Court cases include requiring states to provide indigent defendants with free legal counsel and enacting rulings that restrict the power of the police in interrogating suspects.

Terrorist Tactics

Generally, groups that engage in terrorism use tactics such as random attacks on noncombatants (civilians), on symbolic buildings and landmarks, and on the infrastructure of a society (bridges, dams, and transportation, for instance) to achieve their goal of causing general disruption and widespread fear. They typically do not expect this destructiveness to topple the legitimate government. On the contrary, groups that use terrorism hope to achieve their goals through the response of the government to their acts. They count on the government and the media to overreact. The ability to create widespread fear does not depend on military strength, the size of the attack, or even the number of causalities. To a large degree, the impact of a terroristic attack depends on the ability of the mass media to magnify terrorist actions and to broadcast these images internationally. Furthermore, terrorists can count on the media to make their actions widely known. As early as 1976, the *Report of the Task Force on Disorder and Terrorism* by the National Advisory Commission on Criminal Justice Standards and Goals concluded that "[t]he spectacular nature of terrorist activities assures comprehensive news coverage; modern communications make each incident an international event."[1]

LEARNING OUTCOMES 1 Define terrorism and explain the difference between domestic and international terrorism.

GLOSSARY

hate crimes Crimes that are motivated by hate of an ethnic group, race, religion, gender, or sexual orientation.

domestic terrorism Acts of terrorism committed in the United States by individuals or groups that do not have ties with or sponsorship from foreign states or organizations.

homegrown terrorism Another name for domestic terrorism that emphasizes that there is no foreign involvement in the violence even though homegrown terrorism may act in support of foreign causes.

lone wolf terrorism terrorist Acts committed by a single individual or a single individual assisted by a small number of other people.

Transportation Security Administration (TSA) The federal agency responsible for airport security and the screening of airline passengers.

Terrorist or Freedom Fighter?

Are the terrorists the "good guys" or the "bad guys"? It depends. It is said that "one man's terrorist is another man's freedom fighter." Whether someone is viewed as a terrorist or a freedom fighter depends to a great degree on whether one agrees or disagrees with the political ideology and goals of those engaged in violence. The American Revolution against England, the Russian Revolution against the Czar, the Hungarian revolt against the Soviet Union, Castro's overthrow of the government of Cuba, the Iranian revolution against the Shah, the Solidarity union movement of Poland, the Irish Republican Army's rejection of British rule, and the Palestinian struggle for a homeland are examples of situations in which political leaders used violence to achieve the political and social change they desired. Depending on which side one favors determines whether the actors are seen as terrorists or freedom fighters.

For example, depending on one's viewpoint, the violence of the Arab Spring represents the overthrow of despotic governments or the violent overthrow of legitimate governments. The overthrow of the governments of Egypt and Libya were celebrated in the United States as democratic movements. In the battle for Syria, the United States finds itself in opposition to China and Russia as it supports the "rebel movement" and China and Russia support the existing government of Syria. The United States would see the "rebels" as "freedom fighters" whereas Syria, China, and Russia would see them as "terrorists."

Domestic and International Terrorism

If a violent act is classified as an act of terrorism, law enforcement agencies (LEAs) distinguish between terrorist acts committed by domestic perpetrators and by foreign perpetrators.

The primary purpose of this distinction is related to investigative strategies rather than seriousness of the attack. Different investigative strategies and different agencies are involved in investigating domestic terrorism as opposed to international terrorism. For example, the Central Intelligence Agency (CIA), the State Department, and military agencies frequently are involved in the investigation and prevention of international terrorism but not domestic terrorism.

According to the FBI's Office of Domestic Terrorism and Counterterrorism Planning, perpetrators of **domestic terrorism** receive no assistance or funding from groups or countries outside the United States. The perpetrators of domestic terrorism are U.S. residents but not necessarily U.S. citizens. Domestic terrorism is frequently referred to as **homegrown terrorism**. Domestic terrorism includes acts by both groups and single individuals. Terrorist acts commited by a single individual or a single individual assisted by a small number of other people are called **lone wolf terrorism**. Acts of violence by lone wolf terrorists are the most difficult to detect and prevent. Lone wolf terrorists may be part of an extremist group, or they may have no association with such groups. Their acts of violence are not coordinated with, planned by, or financed by any group. Lone offenders often are seeking revenge for individual grievances, carrying out vendettas against other citizens, or protesting against government policies or laws that may have had an adverse impact on them (for example, seizure of their property). Lone wolf offenders may be mentally unstable, but they usually are not "crazy" or "insane." However, they may have extreme beliefs that cannot be rationally justified. Lone wolf terrorists may belong to countercultures that believe in the violent overthrow of government or support racial violence, but their actions are independent of the group to which they belong.

Some common acts of domestic terrorism are:

• Declared separation from the authority of the U.S. government and its agencies. These actions may include the refusal to pay income tax or the establishment of a "headquarters" that is declared to be sovereign and not subject to U.S. jurisdiction. Declarations of sovereignty may end in violent and deadly exchanges between the group and U.S. law enforcement agents.

• Violent acts to support terrorists' beliefs. For example, antiabortion extremist groups may protest abortion clinics by blocking clients from entering the building. More violent acts may include bombing abortion clinics or assassinating doctors and staff who perform abortions. Bombings are a commonly used attack by domestic terrorist groups and individuals. Lynchings and cross burnings are common acts of racially motivated hate groups.

• Property damage, vandalism, and arson are common strategies used by single-issue extremists and ecoterrorist groups. For example, ecoterrorists burn down construction sites in forest areas they object to being developed. Animal rights groups vandalize research facilities that conduct animal testing.

The distinction as to whether a violent assault is an act of domestic terrorism, a hate crime, or just a crime can be difficult to determine. For example, the Fort Hood shooting by Nidal Malik Hasan, a military officer of Palestinian descent, was determined not to be an act of international or domestic terrorism. The Century movie theater shooting by James Holmes was a crime committed by a mentally ill person. The Sikh Temple shooting by Wade Page was declared an act of domestic terrorism and a hate crime. Do you agree with these conclusions? Explain.

Acts of domestic terrorism range from murder and bombings to less serious violence. Single-issue extremists and eco-terrorist groups may focus on damaging property or using strategies to gain media attention for their cause. For example, animal rights groups may vandalize research facilities that use animals in testing products or medicines, throw red liquids representing blood on people wearing fur clothing, or protest naked. Other actions used by all domestic terrorist groups include making false bomb threats and mailing threatening letters that contain substances that the person claims to be or that appears to be a biological agent but is not.

International terrorism is terrorism planned, funded, and executed in part or whole by foreign states, subnational groups, or an extremist group outside the United States. While domestic terrorist groups have committed more actions of terrorism in the United States, the focus of the U.S. government since the September 11, 2001,

attacks has been on international terrorism. To a large extent, this focus has concentrated on Muslim extremist groups.

Since 2001, a number of international terrorist acts have been detected or prevented. For example, in 2009, Umar Farouk Abdulmutallab, a Nigerian Islamist, attempted to detonate plastic explosives onboard Northwest Airlines Flight 253 from Amsterdam to Detroit, Michigan. The CIA claims the plot was financed and planned by al-Qaeda in the Arabian Peninsula. Furthermore, they claim Anwar al-Awlaki was involved in the planning and recruiting of Abdulmutallab. (al-Awlaki was later successfully targeted for assassination by the U.S. military using a drone attack.)

The Department of Homeland Security, the FBI, and even local LEAs have focused most of their antiterrorism efforts at detecting and preventing violence by international terrorists groups and individuals. For example, the NYPD has undertaken extensive

What Is Terrorism?

What is terrorism?
Terrorism is a strategy, not a person, group, or nation. Terrorism can be used both by governments and people and groups opposed to government.

What is the origin of the term?
Although the use of terrorism as a tactic and strategy can be traced back to ancient times, the terms *terror, terrorism,* and *terrorist* originated in the Reign of Terror of the French Revolution (1793–1794). Maximilien Robespierre, one of the leaders of the revolution, used violence as the primary strategy to overthrow the existing monarchy and install a new democratic government for France.

What is terrorism?
Title 22 of the United States Code Section 264f(d)— **terrorism** is the premeditated, politically motivated violence perpetrated against noncombatant targets by subnational groups or clandestine agents, usually intended to influence an audience. The term **international terrorism** means terrorism involving citizens or the territory of more than one country. The term **terrorist group** means any group that practices, or has significant subgroups that practice, international terrorism. For the purposes of this definition, the term *noncombatant,* in addition to civilians, includes military personnel who at the time of the incident are unarmed and/or not on duty. It also includes acts of terrorism on military installations or on armed military personnel when a state of military hostilities does not exist at the site.

What are some actions used by terrorists?
Attacks on civilians; indiscriminate bombings, assasinations, destruction of buildings, symbolic targets, or infrastructure targets such as bridges, airports, transportation facilities, energy and communication networks; and attacks using weapons of mass destruction. Terrorists attack their target in stealth and then blend back into the civilian population.

What is the international definition of terrorism?
None. Terrorism is a value-laden term and what one nation considers terrorism another nation or people consider freedom fighting, liberation movement, or overthrowing of an oppressive government or occupying army.

What is the appeal of terrorist groups?
Groups using terrorism for political influence emphasize the social injustice of the existing government or military occupation.

What are the goals of groups/nations that use terrorism?
Nations use terrorism to keep populations under state control. Groups opposed to existing governments use terrorism to generate widespread fear, to get government to overreact, and to gain media attention. Terrorists do not engage in "military battle" for geopolitical territory. Rather than military superiority, they use hit-and-run tactics to win by gradual surrender due to a lack of will to continue the "fight."

intelligence surveillance of potential terrorists. The FBI has made defending the United States against terrorist attacks its primary mission. As such, the FBI has pulled resources from other investigations, such as white-collar crime and civil rights violations, to focus on terrorism. The Department of Homeland Security is more focused on international terrorism than domestic terrorism.

Much of the anti-international terrorism efforts are directed at preventing another hijacking of a commercial airliner. The **Transportation Security Administration (TSA)** is responsible for airport security and the screening of airline passengers. As such, it is one of the prominent agencies involved in preventing international terrorism.

Domestic Terrorism			
Planned, funded, and executed by person or persons living within the United States without any assistance from a foreign group or state.			
	Ideology	**Examples**	**Actions**
Militias and Extremist Groups	Includes right-wing and left-wing extremist groups. Right-wing terrorist groups often are race-based, antigovernment. Left-wing groups profess a revolutionary socialist doctrine, which is anti-capitalism and anti-imperialism	Ku Klux Klan, World Church of the Creator, Aryan Nations, Southeastern States Alliance, Armed Forces for Puerto Rican National Liberation (FALN), Workers' World Party, Reclaim the Streets, and Carnival Against Capitalism	FALN carried out bombings in NYC, race-based hate crimes, assaults on judicial personnel. Many groups engage in public rhetoric and protests, which encourage race-based or anti-government violence but may be protected by the First Amendment
Single-Issue Extremist	Focus on special interests that are considered foundational to the values of the group. Groups have different special interests and seldom do these groups work with other special interest groups. Includes lone wolf individuals not associated with a group.	Army of God, Black Liberation Army, Symbionese Liberation Army, Weathermen, and other antigay rights groups, pro-life groups, anti-immigration groups, antiwar groups, and antinuclear groups	Ted Kaczynski Unabomber attacks, 1978–1995; Timothy McVeigh and Terry Nichols Oklahoma City Federal Building bombing, 1996; Centennial Olympic Park bombing by Eric Robert Rudolph, 2001; anthrax attacks on Congress and media; 2009 Holocaust Memorial Museum shooting
Ecoterrorist Groups	Similar to single-issue groups but their focus is on environmental issues or animal rights	Animal Liberation Front (ALF), Earth Liberation Front (ELF)	Arson fires in Vail, Colorado, 1998; destruction of laboratory research facilities and the "liberation" of animals used in testing; attacks on car dealers selling SUVs
International Terrorism			
Planned, funded, and executed in part or whole by a foreign state, a subnational group, or an extremist group. The violent acts of the group are intended to intimidate or coerce a civilian population, influence the policies of a government, or affect the conduct of a government.			
	Ideology	**Examples**	**Actions**
Loosely Affiliated Extremists	Motivated by political or religious beliefs. Often the goal of the group is to achieve power to force adoption of radicalized religious ideologies	al-Qaeda, Sunni Islamic extremists, various religious-based jihad movements	August 1998 bombings of U.S. embassies in East Africa, the planning and carrying out of large-scale, high-profile, high-casualty terrorist attacks against U.S. interests and citizens
Formal Terrorist Organizations	Transnational organizations have their own infrastructures, personnel, financial arrangements, and training facilities	Hizballah, Palestinian Hamas, Irish Republican Army, the Egyptian al-Gama'a al-Islamiyya, and the Lebanese Hizballah	Hizballah is responsible for the 1983 truck bombings of the U.S. Embassy and the U.S. Marine Corps barracks in Lebanon, the 1984 bombing of the U.S. Embassy Annex in Beirut, and the 1985 hijacking of TWA Flight 847
State-Sponsored Terrorism	Countries that view terrorism as a tool of foreign policy	Iran, Sudan, Libya, Syria, Cuba, and North Korea	Targets dissidents living outside the country, supports anti-Western acts of terrorism by others, engages in cyberattacks against the United States. North Korea is of particular concern due to its pursuit of nuclear weapons and long-range rockets

Source: Adapted from L. J. Freeh, *Threat of Terrorism to the United States: Congressional Testimony Before the United States Senate, Committees on Appropriations, Armed Services, and Select Committee on Intelligence* (May 10, 2001).

September 11, 2001: The Tipping Point

The founding fathers of the United States drafted a constitution that reflected a distrust of a strong centralized government. The Constitution defined a government consisting of three independent branches of government (executive, legislative, and judicial) with checks and balances to prevent any one branch from becoming too powerful. Law enforcement was primarily a local or state responsibility. There were only two federal LEAs (the U.S. Marshal's Office and the Office of Postal Inspector) and few federal crimes defined by law. However, the result of the new focus on homeland security is an increase in federal law enforcement powers and a shift from local to federal law enforcement. The model established by the founding fathers has undergone significant change as the federal government acquires greater responsibilities and powers.

As a result of the greater focus on antiterrorism, new federal law enforcement powers, new federal agencies, new federal legislation, and a changing national political ideology have had a great impact on the criminal justice system. In defending the homeland, there has been a shift from local law enforcement to federal law enforcement. Federal agencies and federal legislation have assumed greater importance than have local agencies and state laws in the war on terrorism.

Capacity of State and Local Criminal Justice Systems Questioned

As early as 1998, some authorities questioned whether the United States was facing a new upsurge of terrorism[2] and whether the U.S. law enforcement system, with its thousands of semiautonomous local LEAs, would prove effective in fighting international terrorism.[3] The escalation of terrorist attacks resulted in greater reliance on the federal government and use of the military.

Shift to Reliance on the Federal Government

The tipping point as to significant reliance on the federal government was the September 11, 2001, attacks on the World Trade Center and the Pentagon. On September 12, 2001, in response to those attacks, President Bush declared war on terrorism and began pursuing a two-prong strategy of:

1. Aggressive use of military force overseas
2. Greater reliance on federal agencies in responding to terrorism on U.S. soil

Following the September 11, 2001, attacks, the FBI made counterterrorism its highest priority, but the Bush administration claimed that this was not sufficient in fighting terrorism. The criminal justice system as it existed was considered inadequate in its ability to prevent terrorism by foreign perpetrators. Thus, the Bush administration requested new powers for federal agencies; the formation of new federal agencies; and the suspension of certain civil rights of accused terrorists, known as enemy combatants.

> Following the September 11, 2001, attacks, the FBI made counterterrorism its highest priority, but the Bush administration claimed that this was not sufficient in fighting terrorism.

Others concurred with the assessment that the criminal justice system as structured prior to 2001 had inherent organizational and legal obstacles that precluded it from preventing future attacks by international terrorists.[4] The report of the *Strategies for Local Law Enforcement Series* concluded that one of the critical obstacles in responding to terrorism in the United States was that law enforcement did not have the necessary infrastructure and powers to respond to international terrorism. The report declared that September 11, 2001, was a turning point for U.S. law enforcement because immediately following the attacks, local, state, and federal LEAs faced service demands, problems, and issues they had never encountered. The report concluded that in examining the collective response and capacity of the various government agencies prior to the September 11 attacks, U.S. law enforcement was not prepared for major attacks by international terrorists. Furthermore, the report concluded that there was no simple fix, no quick solution to equipping LEAs with the ability to prevent and respond to terrorism. The report called for significant and long term changes, asserting the following: "... American law enforcement has been organized around the principles of independence and decentralization. Some 18,000 local, state and federal agencies operate as autonomous entities, often unconnected to those in neighboring jurisdictions or at different levels of government. The threat of terrorism in America's cities and towns, however, has revealed the critical need to develop a formidable strategy to counter future acts of terrorism."[5]

Thus, the September 11, 2001, terrorism attacks were considered the tipping point for changes in U.S. law enforcement and the criminal justice system.[6]

The New Federalism for Counterterrorism

The criminal justice system in the United States lacks the resources, training, intelligence-gathering capacity, and coordinated programs necessary to counter international terrorism. Prior to the September 11, 2001, terrorist attacks, the federal government's role in responding to major disasters was defined by the Stafford Act,[7] which makes most federal assistance contingent on a finding that the disaster is so severe as to be beyond the capacity of state and local governments to respond effectively.[8] Prior to the 9/11 terrorist attacks, few police departments trained and prepared to respond to a major terrorist attack. State and local LEAs are best prepared to respond to crime, to provide crime prevention services, and to provide and maintain order. Despite the call for counterterrorism strategies and capacities, local LEAs are grossly unprepared to respond to terrorism or to mount an effective counterterrorism campaign. As a result, federal agencies have been tasked with the primary responsibility of fighting terrorism and the powers of these agencies have been greatly enhanced by the USA PATRIOT Act, which gives federal LEAs expanded powers to detect, detain, and prosecute terrorists. Other federal legislation and presidential executive orders also have expanded the powers of federal law enforcement.

22 The number of federal agencies that were combined to create the DHS.

75,000 The number of new passenger and baggage screeners the TSA hired in 2002.

Department of Homeland Security (DHS): Building a Better Defense

The overlapping system of federal, state, and local governance in the United States results in more than 87,000 different jurisdictions. Prior to the September 11, 2001, terrorist attacks, lack of coordination of the mission, resources, and programs of these thousands of agencies to create a unified defense against and response to terrorism was a key weakness in the war on terrorism. In an effort to increase homeland security following the September 11 terrorist attacks on the United States, President Bush sought to organize for a secure homeland by issuing the National Strategy for Homeland Security in July 2002 and signed legislation creating the **Department of Homeland Security (DHS)** in November 2002; the cabinet-level DHS was implemented in March 2003.[9] Homeland security is defined as "a concerted national effort to prevent terrorist attacks within the United States, reduce America's vulnerability to terrorism, and minimize the damage and recover from attacks that do occur."[10] Many other federal, state, and local agencies are involved in homeland security, but the DHS has the dominant role because it is the lead federal agency in most homeland security initiatives and has the dominant share of homeland security funding.[11]

Creating the Department of Homeland Security

The DHS is described as "a historic moment of almost unprecedented action by the federal government to fundamentally transform how the nation protects itself from terrorism."[12] The creation of the DHS is the most significant reorganization of the U.S. government since 1947. The DHS consolidates 22 federal agencies and 180,000 employees to create a single agency whose primary mission is to protect the homeland of the United States. In all, the DHS has homeland security responsibilities that are dispersed among more than 100 government organizations.[13] The changes brought about the creation of the DHS, enabling legislation and changing political ideology, have had a significant impact on the criminal justice system.

One of the important new missions of the DHS is to increase the domestic intelligence capacity of federal and local agencies. The DHS works with the CIA, the FBI, the Defense Intelligence Agency (DIA), and the National Security Agency (NSA) to analyze intelligence and information and to disseminate that intelligence to agencies that need it to counter terrorism. Despite the many responsibilities of the DHS for homeland security, the FBI is the primary federal law enforcement agency responsible for the investigation of crimes of terrorism and the apprehension of suspected terrorists.

Transportation Security Administration

With the exception of the TSA, most of the 180,000 staff of the DHS consisted of existing personnel from existing federal agencies. The DHS reorganized federal agencies to move those agencies with homeland security responsibilities under the DHS, as opposed to creating completely new federal agencies and hiring new personnel. The TSA is the exception in that prior to its formation, airport security and passenger screening were the shared responsibility of the government and the private airlines. After the September 11, 2001, attacks, this responsibility was transferred exclusively to the federal government. The Aviation and Transportation Security Act of November 2001 (Pub. L. 107–71) created the TSA to oversee security in all modes of travel.

The DHS assumed responsibility for the TSA on March 1, 2002, with the passage of the Homeland Security Act of 2002. The primary goals of the newly formed TSA were to increase the effectiveness and efficiency of (1) identifying passengers who were potential threats and (2) screening passengers and luggage for potential weapons and explosives. Shortly after assuming responsibility for aviation security, the TSA hired and deployed over 55,000 federal passenger screeners, hired and deployed more than 20,000 baggage screeners, implemented all screening of all checked baggage, and implemented screening of all cargo carried aboard commercial passenger aircraft. The creation of the TSA was the largest increase in federal employees in recent history.

Status Report of the DHS

The goal of the DHS is to prevent the most nightmarish attacks and the most consequential threats. The DHS has been challenged to meet this difficult goal. It appears that the DHS has not achieved the results promised in the rhetoric justifying the creation of this new federal agency. An April 2005 report by the Government Accountability Office (GAO) reported that in an earlier review of the DHS in 2003, the GAO designated the DHS's transformation as a high risk due to the enormous challenges in implementing an effective transformation process, developing partnerships, and building management capacity.

Think About It . . .

Justified by the war on terrorism, significant changes have been made to the U.S. criminal justice system. The powers of federal LEAs have been significantly expanded, detainees have been denied access to legal counsel and the courts, accused terrorists have been tortured and held in prison without charges for over a decade, and American citizens are killed solely on the authorization of the president. Does the threat posed by international terrorists justify these fundamental changes to the American criminal justice system? Why or why not?

Mike Rieger/FEMA News Photo

The 2005 report credited the DHS with making "some progress in its management integration efforts" but cited the need for continued improvements. In July 2005, then-DHS Secretary Michael Chertoff announced his plans to reorganize the DHS and promised to address many of the deficiencies pointed out by the GAO. Chertoff said that the DHS did not have the resources to protect against every threat and that the DHS must reorganize and "identify the most catastrophic possible terrorist attacks and do what it can to prevent them."

Assessing the New TSA

Responsibility for airport security and passenger screening was transferred to the DHS because the previous partnership between the Federal Aviation Agency (FAA) and the airlines was thought to have failed to provide adequate security for the traveling public. Prior to 2001, the FAA issued several reports critical of the ability of airline employee screeners to prevent passengers from boarding with potential weapons and explosives.[14] Unfortunately, transferring responsibility to a federal agency did not seem to achieve the anticipated increase in effectiveness and efficiency of identifying passengers who were potential threats and screening passengers and luggage for potential weapons and explosives. Evaluations by the GAO in September 2002 and February 2004 of the performance of TSA personnel concluded that the new federal agency performed no better than the system it replaced and that the TSA continued to face the same challenges in hiring, deploying, and training its screener workforce as before.[15]

▶ Multiple Agency Coordination

One of the premises underlying the prevention of and response to terrorist attacks, especially attacks involving weapons of mass destruction, is that no single agency has the capacity to prevent and respond to a terrorist attack. Prevention of catastrophic terrorism is dependent on a united effort not only by federal agencies, but also between federal and local agencies and among the various local and state agencies at both the operational and tactical levels.[16] Although the DHS provides overall guidance and coordination for the 22 agencies under its control, there is still a need to provide guidance and coordination for numerous other federal, state, and local agencies.

United States Government Interagency Domestic Terrorism Concept of Operations Plan (CONPLAN)

To promote a coordinated response by federal agencies, the federal government developed the **United States Government Interagency Domestic Terrorism Concept of Operations Plan (CONPLAN)**. The CONPLAN was developed through the efforts of the primary departments and agencies with responsibilities for preventing and responding to terrorist attacks.[17] The purpose of the CONPLAN is to outline an organized and unified capability for a timely, coordinated response by federal agencies to a terrorist threat or act. It establishes conceptual guidance for assessing and monitoring a developing threat; notifying appropriate federal, state, and local agencies of the nature of the threat; and deploying the requisite advisory and technical resources to assist the lead federal agency (LFA) in facilitating interdepartmental coordination of crisis and consequence management activities.[18]

The CONPLAN establishes a **lead federal agency (LFA)**. The LFA is responsible for providing leadership, crisis management, and consequence management actions in the event of a catastrophic terrorist attack. The CONPLAN identifies the LFA that has been established by policy and legislation for various aspects related to a terrorist attack. The purpose of the CONPLAN is to ensure the implementation of a coordinated response by federal agencies.

First Responders

Historical Lack of Coordination of First Responders

In responding to terrorist attacks, it is essential that there be cooperation between the federal government and local or state agencies known as **first responder agencies** and among the various first responder agencies themselves.[19] The most important first responders at the operational/tactical level are police departments, fire departments, and local and state health providers. However, historically, the semiautonomous status of the thousands of first responder agencies has not promoted cooperation between federal agencies and first responders or interagency cooperation among first responders. Instead of cooperation, the various agencies have sought to control each other and "to be in charge" at the scene of the crisis.

In responding to terrorist attacks, it is essential that there be cooperation between the federal government and local or state agencies known as first responder agencies.

LEARNING OUTCOMES 2 Summarize the role of the primary agencies responsible for preventing and responding to terrorism.

GLOSSARY

Department of Homeland Security (DHS) A newly created federal agency responsible for a wide range of security measures to protect against terrorist attacks.

United States Government Interagency Domestic Terrorism Concept of Operations Plan (CONPLAN) A plan that establishes the role and responsibilities of federal agencies for preventing and responding to terrorist attacks.

lead federal agency (LFA) The agency that is designated as being primarily in charge of an incident and has the power to direct the actions of other agencies and to call for the use of their resources even though the lead agency may not have direct authority over the other agencies.

first responder agencies Law enforcement, firefighters, and medical personnel who are the first to respond to a crisis or an incident.

mutual aid agreements Agreements that ensure that neighboring jurisdictions can assist in providing personnel and resources to their impacted counterparts.

History: What Became Part of the Department of Homeland Security?

The following agencies became part of the Department of Homeland Security in 2003.

Original Agency (Department)	Current Agency/Office
The U.S. Customs Service (Treasury)	U.S. Customs and Border Protection—inspection, border and ports of entry responsibilities U.S. Immigration and Customs Enforcement—customs law enforcement responsibilities
The Immigration and Naturalization Service (Justice)	U.S. Customs and Border Protection—inspection functions and the U.S. Border Patrol U.S. Immigration and Customs Enforcement—immigration law enforcement: detention and removal, intelligence, and investigations U.S. Citizenship and Immigration Services—adjudication and benefits programs
The Federal Protective Service	U.S. Immigration and Customs Enforcement
The Transportation Security Administration (Transportation)	Transportation Security Administration
Federal Law Enforcement Training Center (Treasury)	Federal Law Enforcement Training Center
Animal and Plant Health Inspection Service (part) (Agriculture)	U.S. Customs and Border Protection—agricultural imports and entry inspections
Office for Domestic Preparedness (Justice)	Responsibilities distributed within FEMA
The Federal Emergency Management Agency (FEMA)	Federal Emergency Management Agency
Strategic National Stockpile and the National Disaster Medical System (HHS)	Returned to Health and Human Services, July 2004
Nuclear Incident Response Team (Energy)	Responsibilities distributed within FEMA
Domestic Emergency Support Teams (Justice)	Responsibilities distributed within FEMA
National Domestic Preparedness Office (FBI)	Responsibilities distributed within FEMA
CBRN Countermeasures Programs (Energy)	Science & Technology Directorate
Environmental Measurements Laboratory (Energy)	Science & Technology Directorate
National BW Defense Analysis Center (Defense)	Science & Technology Directorate
Plum Island Animal Disease Center (Agriculture)	Science & Technology Directorate
Federal Computer Incident Response Center (GSA)	US-CERT, Office of Cybersecurity and Communications in the National Programs and Preparedness Directorate
National Communications System (Defense)	Office of Cybersecurity and Communications in the National Programs and Preparedness Directorate
National Infrastructure Protection Center (FBI)	Dispersed throughout the department, including Office of Operations Coordination and Office of Infrastructure Protection
Energy Security and Assurance Program (Energy)	Integrated into the Office of Infrastructure Protection
U.S. Coast Guard	U.S. Coast Guard
U.S. Secret Service	U.S. Secret Service

The following three directorates, created by the Homeland Security Act of 2002, were abolished by a July 2005 reorganization and their responsibilities transferred to other departmental components:

- Border and Transportation Security
- Emergency Preparedness and Response
- Information Analysis and Infrastructure Protection

Source: Department of Homeland Security, http://www.dhs.gov/xabout/history/editorial_0133.shtm.

The negative impact of this lack of interagency cooperation was clearly demonstrated during the response to the attacks on the World Trade Center. Lacking a culture of cooperation among the first responder agencies, police, fire, and health agencies "neglected to perform the critical task of information sharing."[20] Even if the police and the fire departments had wanted to share critical information during the crisis, it would not have been possible because the two departments did not have compatible emergency communications equipment. Further, the lack of compatible emergency communications capabilities and interoperable systems is not unique to New York City's police and fire departments. It is

The CONPLAN defines the following lead federal agencies and their responsibilities:

• The **attorney general**, the head of the U.S. Justice Department, is responsible for ensuring the development and implementation of policies directed at preventing terrorist attacks domestically, and will undertake the criminal prosecution of acts of terrorism that violate U.S. law. The Department of Justice has charged the FBI with execution of its lead federal agencies (LFA) responsibilities for the management of a federal response to terrorist incidents. As the lead agency for crisis management, the FBI will implement a federal crisis management response. As an LFA, the FBI is responsible for designating a federal on-scene commander to ensure appropriate coordination of the overall U.S. government response with federal, state, and local authorities until such time as the attorney general transfers the lead federal agency role to the Federal Emergency Management Agency.

• The **Federal Emergency Management Agency** (FEMA) is the LFA responsible for implementing the Federal Response Plan to manage and coordinate the federal consequence management response in support of state and local authorities.

• The **Department of Defense** is responsible for providing military assistance to the LFA and/or the CONPLAN primary agencies during all aspects of a terrorist incident upon request by the appropriate authority and approval by the secretary of defense.

• The **Department of Energy** is responsible for providing scientific-technical personnel and equipment in support of the LFA during all aspects of a terrorist attack involving a nuclear or radiological weapon of mass destruction.

• The **Environmental Protection Agency** (EPA) is responsible for providing technical personnel and supporting equipment to the LFA during all aspects of a terrorist incident involving a weapon of mass destruction. The EPA assistance and advice includes threat assessment; consultation; agent identification; hazard detection and reduction; environmental monitoring; sample and forensic evidence collection/analysis; identification of contaminants; feasibility assessment and cleanup; and on-site safety, protection, prevention, decontamination, and restorative activities.

• The **Department of Health and Human Services** (HHS) serves as a support agency to the FBI for technical operations and a support agency to FEMA for consequence management. The HHS provides technical personnel and supporting equipment to the LFA during all aspects of a terrorist incident. Technical assistance to the FBI may include identification of agents and medical management planning. Operational support to FEMA may include mass immunization, mass prophylaxis, mass fatality management, pharmaceutical support operations, contingency medical records, patient tracking, and patient evaluation and definitive medical care provided through the National Disaster Medical System.

more common than not that state and local government first responders lack these systems.[21]

Improving Coordination

Since 2001, the federal government and first responders have taken action to improve response capacity, communication, cooperation, and interoperable communication systems.

One important change to improve coordination has been the development of mutual aid agreements among first responders. **Mutual aid agreements** ensure that neighboring jurisdictions can assist in providing personnel and resources to their impacted counterparts. There are three types of mutual aid agreements:

1. Mutual aid agreements with adjacent jurisdictions

2. Mutual aid agreements between states or between agencies of different states

3. Mutual aid agreements that allow states and local governments to leverage existing and new assets to the maximum extent possible. Typically, they address such things as the mutual sharing of personnel resources and equipment, communications interoperability, and training.

Think About It ...

The National Counterterrorism Center (NCTC) was created in 2004 to collect information from about 30 databases, including credit card and travel records. The NCTC failed to "connect the dots" on Umar Farouk Abdulmutallab, the 2009 Christmas "underwear" bomber, even though it had information that could have identified the plot. To improve the effectiveness of the NCTC's intelligence ability, the Obama administration has extended the time the NCTC can retain information on someone—from 180 days to 5 years—even if that person is not connected to terrorism. The NCTC calls the time limit reasonable, but the American Civil Liberties Union (ACLU) is concerned about potential abuse and loss of privacy. What do you think?

Radio Codes

One of the changes made to improve interagency communication has been inexpensive, but has received universal notice among the public and police. This change is that first responder agencies no longer use "radio ten codes" in radio communication. These codes, such as "10-4" meaning "acknowledge," have been ubiquitous in radio and personal communication, especially for police. However, there is no uniformity among departments as to the meanings of the various radio codes. The federal government and other studies of crisis response found that these codes have the potential to cause confusion and can result in inappropriate or dangerous responses if codes are misunderstood by the various departments responding to a common crisis. Therefore, based on its power to regulate by controlling the purse strings, the federal government mandated that first responder departments that receive federal grants and funding (all police and fire departments) will use plain English rather than radio ten codes.

Conflict between Police and Fire Departments

Police and fire departments are considered the most important first responders in responding to a terrorist attack, but the autonomous relationship between the two departments has created serious debates regarding crisis management command and control. When responding to an incident, fire and police departments often clash over who is in charge. In some extreme incidents, police officers have arrested firefighters on obstruction charges as police and fire personnel disagree over who has the final authority to give orders and make decisions at the scene.

Most cities have favored placing the fire department in charge of hazardous materials incidents. Some cities have devised compromise plans to ensure public safety and coordinate the efforts of the fire department and police department. However, for some cities, the question has generated significant debate. The conflict between New York's police and fire departments serves as a powerful example. In New York City, the fire department is in command at hazardous materials incidents until it determines whether a crime or a terrorist act has taken place.

Training and Joint Exercises

The federal government has developed an extensive training program for first responders. The program provides a common vocabulary for strategic and operation terms that are used in a multijurisdictional response to an incident. It also ensures a common strategy for multijurisdictional responses to incidents. The federal government provides grants and resources to cover most of the costs of training agency personnel. Under federal guidelines, first responders who would assume positions of command and control at a multijurisdictional incident must have completed the training at the appropriate level of command.

The importance of joint exercises to practice multijurisdictional response to major incidents has been recognized, and again, federal guidelines have mandated joint exercise of first responders. As in the mandatory training, the federal government provides grants and resources to assist in covering the costs of the training and joint exercises.

▶ Intelligence and Homeland Security

A large city has an infinite number of targets that terrorists could choose to attack: buildings, bridges, tunnels, the electrical grid, the water supply, shopping malls, subways, buses, and more. No LEA has the resources to provide security for every potential target. Thus, it is necessary to pick and choose which targets to protect. Accurate and timely intelligence that provides advance warning of possible terrorist attacks is critical if local and state LEAs are to engage in preventive actions to minimize these threats.

LEARNING OUTCOMES 3 Summarize the importance of intelligence in preventing and responding to terrorism.

Historic Separation of FBI and CIA

The FBI is responsible for domestic intelligence, and the CIA is responsible for foreign intelligence. Prior to September 11, 2001, the FBI and CIA did not share intelligence. Intelligence gathered by the CIA was fed primarily to the president, to various federal government agencies, and to the Pentagon and various military units. Local and state LEAs were critical of their dependency on the FBI for intelligence, and they complained that the information flow between federal and local agencies was one-way: Local agencies give more to the federal agencies than they get in return.[22]

The 9/11 Commission criticized the lack of intelligence sharing among agencies as one of the reasons the United States failed to "connect the dots" and piece together the intelligence information that would have enabled action to prevent the September 11 terrorist attacks. For example, there are claims that a secret military intelligence unit called "Able Danger" identified Mohamed Atta and three of the other 9/11 hijackers as likely members of a cell of al-Qaeda operating in the United States but did not share this information with the FBI.[23] Other criticisms include charges the FBI's failure to integrate intelligence gathered from its own field offices that could have alerted them to the fact that international terror suspects were taking flight training lessons.

GLOSSARY

the wall Separation of the Central Intelligence Agency and the Federal Bureau of Investigation in the production and dissemination of intelligence data.

Information Analysis and Infrastructure Protection (IAIP) directorate The intelligence unit of the Department of Homeland Security.

Terrorist Threat Integration Center (TTIC) The agency charged with comprehensive intelligence gathering and dissemination.

joint local–federal counter-terrorism task force (JTTF) A working group of FBI and state and/or local law enforcement officers that focuses on preventing terrorism through their joint cooperation and intelligence sharing.

Fusion Centers Intelligence agencies set up by states or major urban areas and run by state or local authorities that are designed to collect, analyze, and disseminate information critical to state and local law enforcement operations related to both homeland security and crime fighting.

Post–September 11, 2001, Intelligence Reforms

Following the September 11, 2001, attacks, intelligence gathering and sharing has been reengineered and a greater emphasis has been placed on intelligence sharing between federal and local law enforcement. New legislation, including the PATRIOT Act, allows the FBI and CIA to share terror-related intelligence. The FBI and the DHS have been charged with gathering and disseminating intelligence to local and state LEAs. New counter-intelligence strategies call for coordination among the different agencies responsible for terror-related intelligence and the ability to take preemptive action before a terrorist attack occurs.

One of the reforms was to remove **the wall,** which the FBI and CIA claimed was established by the Foreign Intelligence Surveillance Act that prevented criminal investigators from using intelligence gathered in national security cases in criminal cases such as terrorist attacks. Prior to the PATRIOT Act, the Justice Department did not use intelligence gathered in national security cases to obtain search warrants when subjects were suspected of criminal activity. Under the provisions of the Foreign Intelligence Surveillance Act, search warrants and wiretaps could be obtained by showing that "there was probable cause that the subject was the agent of a foreign power." However, under the Fourth Amendment, search warrants require that the LEA establish probable cause that a crime has occurred.

Several reorganizations of the intelligence community have occurred in an attempt to promote coordination and cooperation between the CIA, the FBI, and the DHS.[24] The DHS has its own intelligence directive agency, the **Information Analysis and Infrastructure Protection (IAIP) directorate.** The responsibilities of the IAIP are to coordinate the gathering of intelligence from all possible sources, both public and covert; to assess the scope of terrorist threats to the homeland from the intelligence gathered; and to respond appropriately by disseminating this information to those agencies that are responsible for providing security against terrorist attacks. In addition to the IAIP, another newly created agency whose goal is to promote sharing of intelligence is the **Terrorist Threat Integration Center (TTIC).** The mission of the TTIC is to "merge and analyze terrorist-related information collected domestically and abroad in order to form the most comprehensive possible threat picture."[25] The TTIC will have "unfettered access to all terrorist threat intelligence information, from raw reports to finished analytic assessment, available to the U.S. government."[26]

> Local LEAs "often get little back from their investment" in the joint local–federal counterterrorism task force.

Joint Local–Federal Counterterrorism Task Forces

Some large police departments have turned to joint local–federal counterterrorism task forces to counter the threat of terrorist attacks. **Joint local–federal counterterrorism task forces (JTTFs)** are used to provide additional personnel to focus on counterterrorism activities and to funnel intelligence from federal agencies to local agencies. However, many local departments are critical of JTTFs and do not believe they are a viable long-term solution.[27] The primary argument is that federal agencies often "do not draw on the full capabilities" of local law enforcement and that local LEAs "often get little back from their investment" in the JTTF.[28]

Informal Intelligence Networks

Frustrated by the "slow and sometimes grudging way that federal officials share information about terrorist incidents," police chiefs are creating their own informal networks for exchanging intelligence.[30] Local law enforcement officials say that they still are not getting all of the information they need from the federal government and that what they are getting does not come in a timely fashion.[31] For example, William J. Bratton, former Los Angeles police chief, said that joint terrorism task forces and the DHS are not geared "to providing real-time intelligence to local police," and as a result, he often has to rely on cable news networks, not the DHS or other federal agencies, for information.[32] Charles H. Ramsey, former chief of the Washington Metropolitan Police, said, "Terrorism always starts as a local event. We're the first responders."[33] He emphasized that local police need real-time raw intelligence immediately, as opposed to the threat advisories and terror analysis issued by the DHS and the FBI. Local police executives emphasize that they often must make decisions immediately as to how to respond to a possible terrorist attack and that even waiting a day for information passed through federal intelligence networks may be too late.[34]

Think About It ...

The cornerstone of the U.S. system to detect a biological attack is BioWatch. It was launched in 2003 and is now deployed in about 30 cities at a cost exceeding $1 billion. When BioWatch was implemented, the DHS knew that it was prone to false alarms. Studies continue to show that BioWatch triggers false alarms. Scientists at the Centers for Disease Control and Prevention called the system ill-conceived and unworkable. The DHS continues to assert that the system has performed flawlessly.[29] The DHS plans to continue to invest in improvements to BioWatch and has advised local officials that they should take additional steps to determine the credibility of a threat reported by BioWatch. What, if any, are the negative effects of false alarms involving biological attacks?

TFoxFoto/Shutterstock

TABLE 14–1 | DIFFERENCE BETWEEN FUSION CENTERS AND JOINT TERRORIST TASK FORCES (JTTFS)

Fusion Centers	Joint Terrorism Task Forces
Run by state and local authorities	Sponsored by the FBI
State/local-centric	Regionally and nationally focused
Deal with terrorism, criminal, and public safety matters	Deal exclusively with terrorism matters
Produce actionable intelligence for dissemination to appropriate LEAs but do not generally conduct investigations	Conduct investigations
	Local and state law enforcement personnel are "loaned" to JTTFs to promote federal-local cooperation
Financed and staffed by state and local funds but also may be supported by the FBI	

Source: Adapted from Federal Bureau of Investigation, "Fusion Centers," March 12, 2009.

Fusion Centers

To overcome the deficiencies of JTTFs and the delay in obtaining intelligence from federal sources, local and state LEAs have established **Fusion Centers**. Fusion Centers, usually set up by states or major urban areas and run by state or local authorities, are intelligence networks designed to collect, analyze, and disseminate information critical to state and local law enforcement operations related to both homeland security and crime fighting. Fusion Centers are more than depositories for information already gathered. Fusion Center personnel integrate, evaluate, and analyze data to generate data that will assist police departments in responding to homeland security threats and crime.[35]

Local Law Enforcement Intelligence Units

Few local or state LEAs have an intelligence unit dedicated to gathering terrorism-related intelligence. Most states limit local and state LEAs from gathering data on citizens unless it is justified by probable cause or at least reasonable suspicion that they are connected to criminal activity. State legislation prohibits gathering data on citizens because of their race, ethnic background, or religious beliefs. Thus, state and local intelligence units focus on surveillance and investigation of people linked to specific crimes.

The NYPD is one of the few local LEAs that have an intelligence unit dedicated to gathering terrorism-related data. The NYPD's Demographic Unit uses covert surveillance and data mining to compile databases on people who are not suspected of criminal activity or terrorism but may be potential perpetrators of terrorist activities. The intelligence unit conducts covert surveillance primarily on Muslims. The unit has compiled a database of mosques, meeting places, and places where Muslims shop and live. Undercover agents attend mosques and observe speakers, leaders, and people who may be connected with religious extremism. The New York City unit conducts surveillance and data-gathering operations in other states and on college and university campuses in New York and surrounding states. The NYPD's intelligence unit is unique, and few other departments aspire to having such comprehensive and expensive capabilities.

▶ Expanding Federal Power to Fight Terrorism

One of the most significant changes in the criminal justice system has been the shifting balance of power between federal and state and local LEAs. The federal government has sought and received new powers to fight terrorism. In fact, during times of national security crises, the federal government often is given new powers as a means to defend the country.

Thus, it is not surprising that in the focus on homeland security, the federal government has asked for new powers to promote national security and fight terrorism. Many of these early efforts to promote national security were through classified presidential **national security decision directives (NSDDs)**. Prior to 2001, the most significant antiterrorism legislation was the Anti-Terrorism and Effective Death Penalty Act of 1996. After 2001, the cornerstone legislation in the war on terrorism became President Bush's **enemy combatant executive order** and the USA PATRIOT Act.

Enemy Combatant Executive Order

President Bush authorized a military invasion of Afghanistan, claiming that Afghanistan was the base for al-Qaeda and state-sponsored terrorist attacks on the United States, particularly the September 11, 2001, terrorist attacks. On November 13, 2001, President Bush issued an executive order concerning how certain prisoners who were captured in Afghanistan would be detained and treated. The executive order declared these people unlawful combatants as opposed to prisoners of war. As unlawful combatants, their status is similar to that of enemy spies or saboteurs who are captured behind enemy lines without uniform. The executive order also provided that those captured would be detained in a military prison without charges, without access to an attorney, without access to the civilian courts, and without protection of constitutional rights.

The Bush administration declared that these combatants were not entitled to the rights accorded to prisoners of war under the Geneva Convention. The Geneva Convention's provisions for prisoners of war (Section 1, Article 17) says that

680

The approximate number of enemy combatants captured in Afghanistan.

when questioned, prisoners do not have to reveal information other than their name, rank, and serial number. Furthermore Section 1, Article 17 says, "No physical or mental torture, nor any other form of coercion, may be inflicted on prisoners of war to secure from them information of any kind whatever. Prisoners of war who refuse to answer may not be threatened, insulted, or exposed to any unpleasant or disadvantageous treatment of any kind." Articles 14 and 26 provide for humane treatment with regard to housing and food. Articles 9 and 13 guarantee fair treatment of prisoners and protection against criminal charges or the soldier's battlefield participation except in certain circumstances where the captured soldier is charged with war crimes. The pact also provides that in the event of criminal charges against a prisoner, the prisoner has the right to legal representation and has the right to a trial in a civilian or military court. The provisions of the Geneva Convention (Article 71) provide for the right of prisoners to communicate and to receive communication. Also, Article 9 provides the right of international humanitarian organizations such as the Red Cross to inspect the imprisonment of prisoners.

The approximately 680 enemy combatants captured in Afghanistan, including several juveniles, were deemed to be terrorists and were not given the rights accorded by the Geneva Convention or U.S. civilian law. They were transported to a military prison camp at Guantanamo Bay, Cuba. There, they were interrogated using tactics that some, including the International Red Cross and Amnesty International, have characterized as torture. The Bush administration claimed to have the right to hold these prisoners indefinitely without charging them or giving them access to the civilian courts.

As stated, enemy combatants are held in a military prison at Guantanamo Bay, Cuba. Initially, the nearly 700 enemy combatants were held in outdoor makeshift facilities. The enemy combatants were reduced in number to fewer than 200 through various reviews, pleas, and transfers to other countries. Those remaining are held in permanent facilities built to replace the temporary ones.

The U.S. military base at Guantanamo Bay may be the only site at which prisoners can be held under the conditions of President Bush's enemy combatant executive order denying them basic constitutional rights. If the prisoners were held in a military prison in another country, they would have the right to appeal their detention to the civil courts of the host country.

If the prisoners were held in a facility on U.S. soil, they could appeal their incarceration to the U.S. Supreme Court. However, the United States has no diplomatic ties with Cuba. The United States does not recognize the government of Cuba. Thus, those held at Guantanamo Bay cannot appeal to the Cuban courts, and the U.S. Supreme Court does not have jurisdiction.

When campaigning for president in 2008, candidate Obama promised to close the prison facilities at Guantanamo Bay and move the captives to prison facilities on U.S. soil within the first year of his presidency. Once in office, President Obama found that Congress opposed the move of enemy combatants to U.S. prisons and refused to allot the money for their transfer. Furthermore, Attorney General Eric Holder suggested abandoning the use of military tribunals established under the Bush administration for the trial of the prisoners, proposing to try them in the criminal courts of New York instead. A public outcry ensued.

Military Tribunals

The Bush administration provided that these accused terrorists would be tried by special military tribunals.[36] These tribunals are unlike civilian courts or traditional military court martial courts. Unlike a military court martial governed by the Uniform Code of Military Justice, these military tribunals consist of three to seven judges, all of whom must be commissioned military officers. The accused does not have the right to confront witnesses or to challenge evidence that in the opinion of the tribunal would reveal national security information. The prisoner does not have the right of *habeas corpus*—that is, the right to challenge the lawfulness of his imprisonment. (This original restriction was amended by the U.S. Supreme Court in 2012.) Attorneys who represent accused terrorists in military tribunals must agree to certain conditions regarding disclosure of information and are prohibited from consulting civilian lawyers.[37] (Also, some of the original restrictions on defendants' attorneys were modified by the U.S. Supreme Court in 2012.)[38] The military tribunal can sentence the prisoner to incarceration or impose the death penalty.[39]

(## Think About It ...

Attorney General Eric Holder wanted to try accused terrorists held at Guantanamo Bay in criminal court in New York City. New York City and state officials protested the change of venue, claiming that such trials would last years, costs millions of dollars, and create a security nightmare. Are military tribunals a fair venue for determining whether detainees are guilty of terrorism? Should detainees at Guantanamo be transferred to the United States and given the same rights as accused criminals? Why or why not?

Rapport Press/Newscom

U.S. Citizens as Enemy Combatants

Initially, President Bush's enemy combatant executive order extended only to people captured on the battlefields of Afghanistan. However, the Bush administration extended the authority of the executive order to include U.S. citizens whom the president declared enemy combatants. The Bush administration claimed jurisdiction over U.S. citizens even on U.S. soil. The exercise of this power was highlighted by the Jose Padilla case. Jose Padilla, an American citizen, was taken into military custody at Chicago O'Hare Airport in May 2002. Padilla was a former Chicago gang member with a long criminal record who converted to Islam. The government arrested him after he returned from a trip to Pakistan. Government officials claimed that he was associated with al-Qaeda, met officials of the group in Afghanistan, and received training in explosives in Pakistan. In June 2003, President Bush declared Padilla an enemy combatant and he was moved from a federal jail in Lower Manhattan to a Navy brig in Charleston, South Carolina.[40] As an enemy combatant, Padilla was held without charges, denied an attorney, and did not have access to the courts. The legality of denying U.S. citizens access to the courts and to constitutional rights has been an ongoing dispute in the courts. The circumvention of the criminal court system to prosecute and punish people accused of terrorism has alarmed many constitutional scholars.

Criminal Justice System Ill-Equipped to Try Terrorists

Public opinion regarding whether "terrorists" should be tried in civilian criminal courts or military tribunals is sharply divided. When Attorney General Eric Holder proposed trying accused terrorists Khalid Sheikh Mohammed and others for the 2001 terrorist attacks in civilian criminal courts in New York City, Senators John McCain (R–Ariz.) and Joseph Lieberman (I–Conn.) proposed legislation to ban the use of civilian courts in prosecuting terrorists. Supporters of military tribunals argue that evidentiary rules should reflect battlefield conditions, but critics argue that constitutional rights are the foundation of a democratic government.

Those opposed to civil trials argue that if accused terrorists were granted traditional constitutional rights, it would jeopardize national security, create unnecessary risk, create a significant financial burden for the city, and give the accused a forum for propaganda.

For example, in a civilian criminal trial, defendants would have the right of discovery (the right to examine all the evidence of the prosecutor) and the right to confront witnesses. These rights would mean that evidence gathered by intelligence agencies and operatives would have to be revealed to the defendant. It is argued that the defendant could pass this information along to terrorist networks.

Also, it is feared that civilian criminal trials would expose civilian jurors, prosecutors, and judges to potential violence and retaliation. The necessary actions to ensure courtroom and public safety would impose an extreme financial burden on the city and state. New York officials estimated that it would have cost $200 million for additional security to try Khalid Sheikh Mohammed there.

Finally, those opposed to granting civilian criminal trials to accused international terrorists claim that the defendant would use the public forum of the trial as a means to promote radical ideologies and propaganda and defame the image of the United States.

Civil Rights Concerns

Advocates of civil criminal trials for accused terrorists acknowledge the problems such trials propose, but they argue that denying civil rights to accused terrorists is dangerous. Attorney General Holder argued that denying accused terrorists, including international terrorists, constitutional rights traditionally granted to the accused in criminal trials would harm—not promote—U.S. national security. He said to deprive the accused of important constitutional rights would change the principle of the rule of law upon which the American criminal justice system is based.[41] The rule of law guarantees that all people accused of wrongdoing before the courts will be judged by a single standard of justice that does not depend on who they are, but whether they violated the legal codes of the land. Supporters of civilian criminal trials argue that public trials are the best way to show the world that the United States respects the rights of everyone.

Furthermore, it is feared that if certain civil rights can be denied to accused terrorists based on arguments of national security, public safety, and costs, these same arguments can be used to strip other accused people of their civil rights. However, in the end, political and public opinion forced Attorney General Holder to abandon his intent to try the accused terrorists in criminal court and return to the use of military tribunals.

The USA PATRIOT Act

Following the September 11, 2001, terrorist attacks, Congress quickly enacted legislation to enhance national security. In October 2001, the **USA PATRIOT Act** (commonly called the PATRIOT Act) was quickly passed by Congress by an overwhelming majority and signed into law by the president. In the words of then-Attorney General John Ashcroft, the PATRIOT Act provided new powers to federal LEAs "to close gaping holes in our ability to investigate terrorists."[42]

Think About It . . .

A program called Secure Communities allows local LEAs to determine the immigration status of people booked for an offense. A congressional study by the nonpartisan Congressional Research Service examined 46,734 illegal immigrants who were booked into jail but released before immigration officials took them into custody. Of this number, about 16% were rearrested within three years. Nineteen were arrested for murder, 3 for attempted murder, 142 for sex crimes, and the remainder for lesser offenses. Do you think illegal immigrants released without deportation are a significant threat to public safety? Why or why not?

Photo courtesy of ICE

The USA PATRIOT Act gave broad new powers to federal LEAs such as the FBI. The enhanced powers were so controversial that many of them had sunset provisions. A sunset provision provides a period of time for which the law is effective. At the end of this period of time, if Congress does not renew the law, the law automatically expires and the power is revoked.

Despite the new powers granted to federal law enforcement by the PATRIOT Act, there was little consideration and debate by the public or Congress as to the impact of these new powers pertaining to basic principles of due process on which the criminal justice system is based. In the post–September 11 environment, while the Justice Department continues to uphold the necessity and effectiveness of the PATRIOT Act, there is extensive criticism that it infringes on constitutional rights and has given federal law enforcement too much unchecked power. The extent of this opposition is evident by the fact that over 150 local governments and several states have passed resolutions objecting to the legislation.[43]

The PATRIOT Act provides federal law enforcement greater surveillance powers, it expands federal jurisdiction of terror-related crimes, and it removes some civil liberties protections for those accused or detained under its provisions. The act provides less judicial review of federal LEAs with regard to wire taps, intelligence gathering, and search and seizure.

Expanded Search Powers

One of the most significant effects on the criminal justice system is that the authority of federal law enforcement agents to execute searches has been greatly expanded under the PATRIOT Act. Prior to the act, LEAs could conduct searches without a search

Section 213 of the PATRIOT Act authorizes expanded search powers of federal LEAs.

warrant issued by the court only under a number of limited circumstances, such as incidents to arrest, plain view searches, and emergency situations. Otherwise, law enforcement agents had to present evidence to the court that there was probable cause to conduct the search. Further, the court search warrant limited the scope of the search.

The PATRIOT Act authorized expanded search power; required less judicial oversight of these search powers; and, in some cases, allowed secrecy concerning the search. A controversial provision of the PATRIOT Act is Section 213, the so-called sneak-and-peek provision. This provision gives federal law enforcement agents the authority to conduct a search with limited judicial review and authorization and provides for delayed notification of the search. Thus, federal agents can enter a house or business and execute a search in secret. If authorities do not find any incriminating evidence, they do not have to inform anyone of the search at that time. If the authorities do find incriminating evidence, they can use it to obtain a search warrant from the court.

The PATRIOT Act does not limit the use of this authority only to terrorist-related cases. In addition to the increased power to search under the PATRIOT Act, federal authorities can use the Foreign Intelligence Surveillance Act to perform similar searches as authorized by Section 213 of the PATRIOT Act. However, unlike the PATRIOT Act that provides for delayed notification, the Foreign Intelligence Surveillance Act stipulates that the subject may never be told about the search. The FBI first publicly acknowledged the use of this expanded authority granted by the PATRIOT Act and the Foreign Intelligence Surveillance Act in the search of the home of Brandon Mayfield,

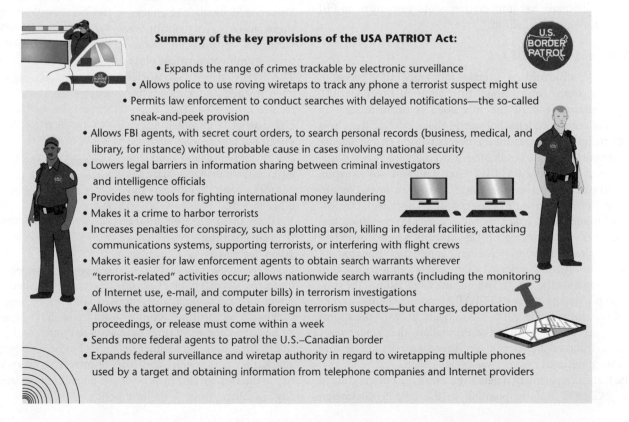

Summary of the key provisions of the USA PATRIOT Act:

- Expands the range of crimes trackable by electronic surveillance
- Allows police to use roving wiretaps to track any phone a terrorist suspect might use
- Permits law enforcement to conduct searches with delayed notifications—the so-called sneak-and-peek provision
- Allows FBI agents, with secret court orders, to search personal records (business, medical, and library, for instance) without probable cause in cases involving national security
- Lowers legal barriers in information sharing between criminal investigators and intelligence officials
- Provides new tools for fighting international money laundering
- Makes it a crime to harbor terrorists
- Increases penalties for conspiracy, such as plotting arson, killing in federal facilities, attacking communications systems, supporting terrorists, or interfering with flight crews
- Makes it easier for law enforcement agents to obtain search warrants wherever "terrorist-related" activities occur; allows nationwide search warrants (including the monitoring of Internet use, e-mail, and computer bills) in terrorism investigations
- Allows the attorney general to detain foreign terrorism suspects—but charges, deportation proceedings, or release must come within a week
- Sends more federal agents to patrol the U.S.–Canadian border
- Expands federal surveillance and wiretap authority in regard to wiretapping multiple phones used by a target and obtaining information from telephone companies and Internet providers

a Portland, Oregon, lawyer who was wrongly arrested and jailed in 2004 in connection with the March 2004 train bombings in Madrid, Spain.[44]

Another controversial section of the PATRIOT Act is Section 215. Under this authority, the FBI can demand access to certain records without obtaining a warrant or demonstrating probable cause to the court. Under this provision, any third party—such as a doctor, a library, a bookstore, a university, a bank, or an Internet service provider (ISP)—must turn over records requested by the FBI. Furthermore, they are forbidden by law to reveal the subject of this information or to inform the public about its release.[45]

One of the most controversial debates related to Section 215 is the right of the FBI to use a national security provision to demand records of the reading habits of library patrons. Under this provision, the FBI can demand that library personnel provide any information they have about a patron and the FBI can request information about documents a patron has borrowed from the library. The request does not have to identify the patron. It can be broad, such as a request for the names and information related to anyone who has checked out books on explosives. Unlike a search warrant, which names a specific person to be searched, the FBI can amass information on any and all patrons. Obviously, such a search results in many people being entered into FBI investigation files who have no connection to terrorist activities. Further, library personnel cannot tell the patron they have released this information to the FBI and cannot make any public comment about the release of the information. The Justice Department argues that if it was revealed that the FBI was seeking information from a certain library or about an individual, that information could jeopardize an FBI counterterrorism investigation.

Criticisms of the PATRIOT Act

Calls by the public and congressional members for repeal of some of the more controversial provisions of the PATRIOT Act were mounting until the July 2005 terrorist attacks on the London transit system. Following these attacks, there was renewed belief by Congress of the necessity for a strong defense against terrorism. As a result, the movement to repeal some of the provisions of the PATRIOT Act that were set to expire at the end of 2005 lost momentum.[46] However, revelations in December 2005, just prior to the expiration of some of the provisions of the PATRIOT Act, that the Bush administration had engaged in extensive spying on U.S. citizens, secretly searched mosques for radioactive material, and conducted thousands of searches without court authorization resulted in a backlash of opposition against the act. In last-minute negotiations, the controversial provisions of the PATRIOT Act were extended and its renewal was approved in early 2006. Again, in 2009, the apprehension over Umar Farouk Abdulmutallab, the "underwear" bomber, reinforced belief that enhanced search and seizure powers were necessary in the war on terrorism.

The Justice Department defends the use of the powers granted by the PATRIOT Act by pointing to the over 5,000 foreign nationals who have been detained since the September 11, 2001, attacks. However, of these thousands of detainees, very few have been charged with a crime.[47] Also, there have been over 1,000 complaints of PATRIOT Act–related abuse of civil rights or civil liberties.[48]

In some cases, local police have not been in complete agreement regarding the constitutionality of the powers given to federal law enforcement by post–September 11 legislation. As a result, at times, conflicts have occurred between local and federal agencies as to the "legality" of certain law enforcement actions. One of the most prominent was when the Portland (Oregon) Police Department refused to interview foreign students as requested by the FBI. The police department refused to conduct the interviews because it claimed that the FBI did not offer specific information about any crimes in which the individuals might be involved. Furthermore, the police department believed that the FBI's questions were not appropriate because they pertained to noncriminal matters such as religious beliefs and other issues not specifically related to criminal activity or knowledge.[49]

Fortress Urbanism: Terror-Focused Policing

Federal, state, and local LEAs have been diligent since the September 11, 2001, terrorist attacks in trying to detect perpetrators planning another attack on the United States. Since the September 11 attacks, there have been continuous warnings of possible, sometimes imminent, terrorist plots. The DHS threat advisories have warned of terrorist plots to attack the New York financial district, commuter trains, symbolic landmarks such as the Brooklyn Bridge and the Golden Gate Bridge, Christmas parades, bank buildings, and other targets.

Fear of a terrorist attack is transforming cities into **urban fortresses** as authorities have reshaped the cityscape; increased security; blocked off streets; established security screening checkpoints; and imposed searches of baggage and backpacks of airline, subway, train, and ferry passengers. Although federal authorities have assumed much of the responsibility for preventing another major 9/11 aviation-type terrorist attack, the responsibility and costs of providing everyday security to the average citizen as he or she goes about business in the city has fallen primarily on local police.

habeas corpus A writ or request to the court to review whether a person is imprisoned lawfully; it alleges that a person is detained or imprisoned illegally.

USA PATRIOT Act Legislation that gives federal law enforcement agencies expanded powers to detect, detain, and prosecute suspected terrorists.

urban fortresses Cities that have adopted extensive and visible physical security measures and barriers in response to the threat of terrorist attacks.

Homeland Security Advisory System (HSAS) A color-coded threat advisory to government agencies, police, and the public that recommended appropriate actions in response to the forecasted risk of terrorist attacks.

Few departments have the budget to purchase equipment or to provide officers with the necessary training to properly respond to a biological, chemical, or nuclear terrorist attack.

$800,000 Additional amount spent on

security per day in New York City following the 2005 London subway bombings.

Homeland Defense: Straining Police Resources

Cities that are considered likely targets by terrorists are being transformed by roadblocks, checkpoints, target hardening, and barriers. Parking lots near buildings thought to be at risk are being closed. Even sidewalks are being closed or transformed with security precautions. Concrete barriers, called Jersey barriers, are popping up as authorities take security measures to protect buildings and people. In cities such as New York and Washington, DC, public officials and citizens are complaining that physical security measures are becoming intrusive, backing up traffic, and making the city look uninviting for tourists and residents.[50] Officials in Washington, DC, complain that the proliferation of concrete barricades and checkpoints is making "this place feel like Fortress Washington."[51] One of the primary reasons for this increased security is fear of terrorists exploding a car or truck bomb, as in the bombings of the 1993 World Trade Center and the Murrah Federal Building in Oklahoma City, or a terrorist suicide bomber.

Such threats are difficult to prevent. It is costing police departments millions of dollars in overtime, training, and equipment to fulfill this responsibility. During the heightened public transit alert in New York City following the July 2005 London subway bombings, New York police spent nearly $800,000 a day in additional costs to provide subway security.[52]

When the terrorist alert level is raised, it is the local police who are expected to provide increased security. Additional security duties during times of high alert have strained some local resources to the point that they can no longer provide routine services during terrorist alerts. Even large police departments such as New York City reach this point. For example, during the 2004 Republican National Convention, all hearings and trials were suspended in New York City courts because police officers had to devote their time to convention security.

Also, as first responders, police officers need training and equipment to respond effectively and to protect themselves against potential hazards such as toxic substances, chemicals, and radioactivity. Few departments have the budget to purchase

this equipment or to provide officers with the necessary training to properly respond to a biological, chemical, or nuclear terrorist attack.

Terrorist Threat Advisories

Following the 9/11 attacks, the federal government wanted to provide the law enforcement community and the public with timely warnings of potential terrorist attacks. These warnings were to flow from the intelligence gathered by federal agencies such as the CIA, FBI, and DHS. In 2002, the DHS implemented the **Homeland Security Advisory System (HSAS)** as the means to disseminate this information. The HSAS was a color-coded system using green, blue, yellow, orange, and red to indicate the level of threat.

The HSAS was not well received by the public or the law enforcement community. The GAO confirmed the public's skepticism of the effectiveness of the HSAS when its report concluded that warnings were often "vague and inadequate, and had hindered the public's ability to determine whether they were at risk and what protective measures to take in response."[53] The law enforcement community found the HSAS warning expensive to respond to, as a warning of high risk frequently resulted in overtime expenses and additional security-related costs. Furthermore, the heightened diligence of the law enforcement community was never rewarded with the apprehension of a terrorist because the warning did not specify the source or nature of the possible attack. Even worse, sometimes the statements issued by the FBI and the DHS provided conflicting advisory warnings.[54] As a result of strong pressure from the public and the law enforcement community, the DHS eliminated the HSAS and replaced it with a new threat advisory system in April 2011.[55]

The National Terrorism Advisory System (NTAS) is designed to address the shortcomings of the HSAS. It has eliminated the color-coded alerts. The NTAS has only two alert levels: elevated and imminent. "Elevated" means the DHS has no specific information about the timing or location of the threat. "Imminent" means the threat is impending or very soon. NTAS

(Think About It . . .

In August 2012, ten immigration agents filed a federal lawsuit in Texas against Homeland Security Secretary Janet Napolitano, seeking to overturn an Obama administration program that suspends deportations for illegal immigrants who came here as children. The agents claim that the program prevents them from performing their duties to arrest illegal immigrants and infringes on the powers of Congress to make laws. The agents claim that if they arrest the immigrants as required by law, the immigrants will be sanctioned by their employer. Can the president direct law enforcement agents not to enforce the law? Explain.)

National Terrorism Advisory System

Alert

DATE & TIME ISSUED: XXXX

www.dhs.gov/alerts

SUMMARY

The Secretary of Homeland Security informs the public and relevant government and private sector partners about a potential or actual threat with this alert, indicating whether there is an "imminent" or "elevated" threat.

DURATION

An individual threat alert is issued for a specific time period and then automatically expires. It may be extended if new information becomes available or the threat evolves.

DETAILS

- This section provides more detail about the threat and what the public and sectors need to know.
- It may include specific information, if available, about the nature and credibility of the threat, including the critical infrastructure sector(s) or location(s) that may be affected.
- It includes as much information as can be released publicly about actions being taken or planned by authorities to ensure public safety, such as increased protective actions and what the public may expect to see.

AFFECTED AREAS

- This section includes visual depictions (such as maps or other graphics) showing the affected location(s), sector(s), or other illustrative detail about the threat itself.

HOW YOU CAN HELP

- This section provides information on ways the public can help authorities (e.g. camera phone pictures taken at the site of an explosion), and reinforces the importance of reporting suspicious activity.
- It may ask the public or certain sectors to be alert for a particular item, situation, person, activity or developing trend.

STAY PREPARED

- This section emphasizes the importance of the public planning and preparing for emergencies before they happen, including specific steps individuals, families and businesses can take to ready themselves and their communities.
- It provides additional preparedness information that may be relevant based on this threat.

STAY INFORMED

- This section notifies the public about where to get more information.
- It encourages citizens to stay informed about updates from local public safety and community leaders.
- It includes a link to the DHS NTAS website http://www.dhs.gov/alerts and http://twitter.com/NTASAlerts

If You See Something, Say Something™. Report suspicious activity to local law enforcement or call 911.

The National Terrorism Advisory System provides Americans with alert information on homeland security threats. It is distributed by the Department of Homeland Security. More information is available at: www.dhs.gov/alerts. To receive mobile updates: www.twitter.com/NTASAlerts
If You See Something Say Something™ used with permission of the NY Metropolitan Transportation Authority.

New Department of Homeland Security Terrorist Threat Advisory
Source: Department of Homeland Security

alerts are not issued unless there is a specific threat. The NTAS alerts will be disseminated to the press and will be distributed using the DHS's social media channels, including Twitter, Facebook, and RSS feeds. NTAS advisories carry an expiration date. They provide a concise summary of the potential threat, communicate information about actions being taken to ensure public safety, and recommended steps for the public and governments to take in response to the threat.

▶ *Closing the Borders to Terrorists*

Fear that international terrorists could slip into the United States or enter under false pretenses using a student visa or a tourist visa has resulted in a change in public opinion, federal agencies, and legislation concerning border security.

However, border security is a complex issue that raises questions of handling illegal immigrants, providing amnesty for the estimated 12 million illegal immigrants residing in the United States, and designing fair immigrant policies and laws. Border security is a homeland security concern, an economic dilemma, and a humanitarian challenge. Those wanting to cross into the United States illegally include drug and human traffickers, immigrants seeking employment, and terrorists.

However, very little documentation shows that there is a significant problem of terrorists entering the United States illegally from either Canada or Mexico.

The challenge of border security is compounded by demographic shifts in the U.S. population as an increasing number of the nation's residents are nonwhite. Studies find that nonwhites and the younger generation see immigration policy through a different set of values. These groups are more receptive to amnesty programs and open borders.

Sealing the Borders

Border security and immigration control have been long-standing concerns. Prior to September 11, 2001, the primary focus was on the U.S.–Mexican border. The concerns were the economic consequences from people entering the United States without authorization who were seeking employment and cross-border drug and human trafficking. In the post–September 11 environment, the concern is that if "ordinary" people simply seeking employment can so easily enter the United States illegally in such large numbers, then international terrorists intent on committing acts of violence can enter just as easily.

Also of concern is the fear that terrorists could smuggle a nuclear weapon into the United States. Auditors from the GAO and scientists testifying before a House committee warned that "the federal government's efforts to prevent terrorists from smuggling a nuclear weapon into the United States are so poorly managed and reliant on ineffective equipment that the nation remains extremely vulnerable to a catastrophic attack."[56]

Also, the DHS is concerned that terrorists could enter the United States as illegal immigrants and obtain jobs in risk-sensitive facilities that would enable them to carry out a terrorist attack against the United States. The DHS is concerned that illegal immigrants could obtain jobs as airline mechanics or at nuclear facilities or other critical infrastructure facilities.[57] To prevent this possibility, legislation makes employers responsible for verifying that their workers are legally entitled to work in the United States. Despite the DHS's warning that hiring undocumented workers poses a serious threat to homeland security, illegal immigrants do find employment in such industries. The DHS fears that those illegals who cross the border simply to obtain employment can make them vulnerable to potential exploitation by terrorists and other criminals who threaten to expose their illegal status to authorities.

Thus, the DHS **Immigration and Customs Enforcement (ICE)** agency has a two-pronged strategy. The DHS focuses on securing the borders and stopping illegal immigration and on ensuring that employers follow federal laws requiring documentation of the legal status of people seeking employment. In focusing on ensuring that employers hire only documented workers, ICE conducts investigations to determine whether illegal immigrants are employed by companies in critical homeland security industries. Past sweeps by ICE have found illegal immigrants working in facilities considered to be critical infrastructure sites. One raid by ICE in May 2005 resulted in the arrest of 60 illegal immigrants in sensitive jobs in six states, including seven petrochemical refineries, three electric power plants, and a pipeline facility.[58]

Immigration Control and Enforcement

Since 2001, one of the goals of the federal government has been to prevent international terrorists from entering the United States. Terrorists can enter the country several ways. They can use false immigration papers, they can enter under the pretext of being legal tourists and then not leave when their tourist visa expires, they can enter using student visas, and they can enter illegally and undetected at some point along the 8,000 miles of the Canadian and Mexican borders in addition to the Atlantic and Pacific coastlines.

The power to regulate immigration is an exclusive power given to the federal government by the U.S. Constitution. The federal agency primarily responsible for immigration control and border security is the DHS. Prior to 2001, the Immigration and Naturalization Service (INS) was responsible for the regulation and control of immigration. However, due to critical reports of the performance of the INS, especially in its role of granting visa documents to people who were involved in the 9/11 attacks, the INS was abolished. The DHS assumed the charge of border security and immigration control.

Under the DHS, two agencies have primary responsibility for border security and immigration: U.S. Customs and Border Protection (CPB) and ICE. The TSA shares in this responsibility by protecting the transportation systems of the United States. The office of CBP is responsible for border security. According to the mission statement of CBP, this agency is "one of the Department of Homeland Security's largest and most complex components, with a priority mission of keeping terrorists and their weapons out of the United States. It also has a responsibility for securing the border and facilitating lawful international trade and travel while enforcing hundreds of U.S. laws and regulations, including immigration and drug laws."[59] ICE is the principal investigative arm of the DHS and the second-largest investigative agency in the federal government with 20,000 employees.[60] ICE was created in 2003 through a merger of the investigative and interior enforcement elements of the U.S. Customs Service and the INS.

Under ICE, the Enforcement and Removal Operations (ERO) agency enforces the nation's immigration laws. ERO identifies and apprehends removable aliens, detains these individuals when necessary, and removes illegal aliens from the United States.[61]

In an attempt to seal the borders against terrorists, the DHS has initiated a number of changes, including better tracking of foreign visitors, airline passenger screening, smart passports, stricter accountability for foreign students and scholars, and border security.

United States Visitor and Immigrant Status Indicator Technology

The cornerstone of the DHS's efforts to track foreign nationals entering and exiting the United States is the **United States Visitor and Immigrant Status Indicator Technology (US-VISIT)** program. It requires most foreign visitors to be fingerprinted and

> The DHS fears that even those illegals who cross the border simply to obtain employment can make them vulnerable to exploitation by terrorists.

photographed when they enter the United States. At first, the program applied only to those visitors arriving at airports from countries for which entry visas were required. Today, the program has expanded to include most foreign travelers and continues to expand to include anyone arriving at seaports and land border crossings.

Smart Passports

In addition to passenger screening and enhanced airport security, the federal government has initiated the adoption of **smart passports**. Smart passports contain microchips and a radio frequency identification system. The microchips contain about 64 kilobytes of data such as name; birth date; issuing office; and biometric identifier such as a photograph, iris scans, and a digital fingerprint of the traveler. The wireless technology allows travelers to pass through a checkpoint with their passport and have their data confirmed electronically. In August 2005, the first use of radio frequency identification system passports was tested at a Canadian border crossing. Similar to radio frequency identification systems used to collect highway tolls, the radio-tagged passports can be read by electronic equipment from 30 feet away as a person passes through the border checkpoint. A DHS spokesperson said that the new electronic passports could "help relieve congestion at border crossings, while also helping authorities weed out potential terrorists, drug dealers and other criminals."[62]

Despite attempts to improve passport security, a 2009 study by the GAO reported that fraudulent passports continue to be a concern. One point noted in the report was that DHS offices are evaluated on the number of passports they issue, not on the quality of the screening to prevent people from obtaining passports using fraudulent documents. The GAO report recommended that the DHS focus on ensuring that the documents used to obtain passports are valid.

Student and Exchange Visitor Information System (SEVIS)

Several of the hijackers involved in the September 11, 2001, terrorist attacks entered the United States on student visas. Under the system in place prior to September 11, 2001, the INS had limited ability to verify whether students actually enrolled in and attended the college or program stated on their student visa application.

LEARNING OUTCOMES 5 — Describe the role of border security in the war on terrorism.

GLOSSARY

Immigration and Customs Enforcement (ICE) A new federal agency under the Department of Homeland Security that is responsible for the enforcement of immigration laws.

United States Visitor and Immigrant Status Indicator Technology (US-VISIT) A new system of registering the entry of foreign visitors to the United States and tracking when and where they exit the United States.

smart passports New passports that contain machine-readable data about travelers.

To end this vulnerability, a new tracking system for international students and scholars was implemented. The new system converted what was a manual procedure into an automated process and provided stricter monitoring of the attendance of international students. The new system, called the **Student and Exchange Visitor Information System (SEVIS)**, is a Web-based system for maintaining information on international students and exchange visitors in the United States. It is administered by ICE and CBP. The cost of the SEVIS program is paid for by fees collected from those applying for student, exchange visitor, or scholar visas.

Student and Exchange Visitor Information System (SEVIS) A Web-based database containing information on international students studying in the United States.

No-Fly List A secret list maintained by the Department of Homeland Security that includes the names of people who are prohibited from flying on a commercial airplane under any circumstances; it also contains the names of people who should receive additional screening prior to being allowed to board an aircraft.

racial profiling Allegations that police search and seizures, traffic stops, field interrogations, and arrests are made on nonbehavioral factors related to race and/or ethnicity rather than suspicious behavior or probable cause.

REAL ID Act Legislation that requires all state driver's licenses to conform to uniform standards set by the Department of Homeland Security.

The Fence

The United States shares a vast land border with Canada to the north and Mexico to the south. As a strategy of the Secure Border Initiative begun in 2003, the United States planned to construct a physical or virtual fence along the entire U.S.–Mexican border and to significantly enhance security of the U.S.–Canadian border. Hundreds of miles of the physical and virtual border fence between the United States and Mexico have been constructed. The physical fence aims to prevent illegal crossings into the United States. The virtual fence is a network of towers equipped with cameras, sensors, and communications equipment. However, both strategies have been plagued with problems and shortcomings. In 2011, the DHS canceled the billion-dollar virtual fence project, citing technical problems, cost overruns, and delays. The DHS says that it plans to use other technologies, such as aerial surveillance (including drones) and border patrol to perform border surveillance.

The fence has been praised and condemned. Those who praise the fence cite its ability to stem the flow of illegal immigrants, drug traffickers, human smugglers, and terrorists into the United States. Those who oppose the fence cite its marginal effectiveness, detrimental impact on the environment, and negative impact on good-neighbor relations with Mexico and Canada.

Frustrated with the stop-and-start progress of federal efforts to build a fence, Arizona enacted legislation in 2010 authorizing the state to build a border fence funded in part by private donors.[63] However, by 2012, only a fraction of the money necessary to build the fence had been raised from private donors. Still, authorities responsible for the project said they were hopeful that construction could start by the end of 2012.[64] The Arizona legislature authorized $2.8 million to build 200 miles of border fencing. No other state has undertaken such an ambitious border fencing project.

Passenger Screening and No-Fly List

The TSA is responsible for airport security and passenger screening. In this capacity, the TSA is one of the last lines of defense for preventing terrorists from entering the United States. The primary strategies used by the TSA to stop terrorists from using U.S. transportations systems, especially commercial airlines, are passenger screening and the No-Fly List. The TSA has focused on screening every passenger on commercial airlines for threats. This approach is labor- and time-intensive and requires every passenger to be subject to search. The TSA has tried to adopt innovative technology to identify passengers who are threats. Some of these technologies, such as "puffers" or "sniffers," which attempted to detect the chemical signature of explosives, were expensive and did not work. In 2012, the TSA is using full-body scanners in addition to metal detectors and searches to detect threats. Full body scanners and intrusive body searches have been criticized by some as an invasion of privacy.

The **No-Fly List** is created and maintained by the U.S. government's Terrorist Screening Center (TSC), not the TSA. The list is compiled by intelligence data gathered from different sources, and people on the list are not permitted to board a commercial aircraft for travel in or out of the United States. The number of names on the list is unknown but is estimated at about 10,000.

The No-Fly List is different from the Terrorist Watch List, a larger list of about 400,000 people the government considers connected to terrorism or supporters of terrorists groups.

The No-Fly List works two ways: (1) Information is gathered about people purchasing commercial airline tickets, and people on the list cannot purchase tickets. (2) The airlines are required to forward the passenger manifest of a flight to the government, and if a person's name on the No-Fly List appears on the manifest, the flight is diverted and the passenger removed.

The list has been criticized on civil liberties and due process grounds. A significant concern is that the public does not know how names are added to the list. The list is secret, and once someone is on the list, there is no procedure for appeal for removal or correction. Past errors have indicated that the list is prone to false positives as infants and even U.S. senators have been placed on it.

Criticisms of Border Security

Many of the efforts of the DHS to seal the borders have been controversial. The program to identify "special interest" immigrants was criticized as **racial profiling**. The US-VISIT program has been criticized as ineffective. Air travelers have claimed that their names have been included on the No-Fly List for reasons unknown to them and that they have been unable to appeal the inclusion of their names due to the secrecy that surrounds how the list is created.

In an effort to detect and deport illegal immigrants who have managed to enter the United States, the DHS has adopted an aggressive policy of immigration enforcement. This policy includes checking the names of people sentenced to jail and prison to determine whether any of the inmates are immigrants who can be deported due to their arrest. It also includes enforcement of immigration laws requiring employers to obtain documentation confirming that the employees they hire are legal immigrants.

Some policies of the DHS have been criticized as being "overly aggressive" and creating public safety concerns because the DHS has used various deceptions to identify illegal workers. One example was the DHS's stepped-up efforts to crack down on illegal immigrants working at chemical plants, nuclear plants, and other sensitive facilities.[65] To discover whether illegal immigrants were working at these facilities, the DHS conducted a sting operation. The DHS posted notices announcing that to keep their job, employees were required to attend mandatory safety training by the Occupational Safety and Health Administration (OSHA). When the workers showed up for the "training session," immigration officials identified illegal immigrants and arrested them. Many OSHA officials protested the subterfuge, claiming that the use of OSHA's name in the ruse could have serious consequences in getting workers to attend legitimate safety training.[66]

The 9/11 Commission concluded that immigration policies initiated by DHS have been "ineffective, producing little, if any, information leading to the identification or apprehension of terrorists."[67] The Commission criticized the immigration policies as neither preventing potential terrorists from entering the country nor clearly distinguishing potential terrorists who should be removed from the country. For example, after assuming control over visas, the new DHS-supervised departments issued visas to 105 foreign men who should have been prevented from entering the United States because their names appeared on government lists of suspected terrorists.[68]

In 2012, the DHS adopted new guidelines regarding enforcement of immigration laws. The DHS changed its focus to detecting and deporting illegal aliens who engaged in criminal activity. (See Figure 14–1.)

Those illegal aliens who were deemed not to be a threat to U.S. security became a low priority for ICE and CBP. In 2012, President Obama issued an executive order suspending deportation actions against illegal aliens who entered as children and met certain conditions for two years. Obama's executive order contained provisions of the DREAM Act, which had failed to pass Congress.

State and Local Actions to Curtail Illegal Immigration

Although immigration is the responsibility of the federal government, many state and city governments are greatly concerned and impacted by illegal immigration. State and local governments have expressed concern over public safety issues caused by illegal immigration.

The actions of state and local governments are not aimed specifically at detecting and apprehending terrorists, but

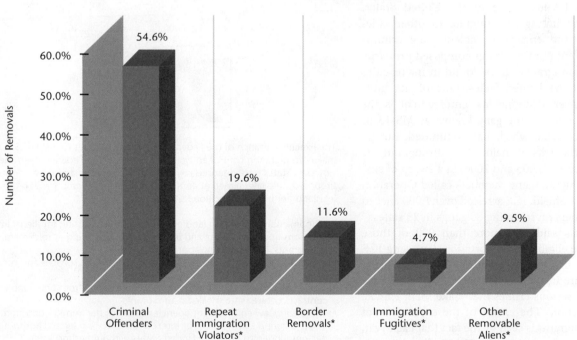

Immigration and Customs
Enforcement Fiscal Year 2011
Removal Statistics

FY2011 as of IIDS v1.10 10/7/2011. Departure data through 9/30/2011.
*These categories may include convicted criminals because of shortcomings in certain data related to criminal conviction.

FIGURE 14–1 ICE Removals by Priority
Source: http://www.ice.gov/removal-statistics.

1,000 The number of alleged gang members arrested by ICE in 2005 and 2006.

900 The number of those alleged gang members who were eligible for deportation.

focusing more on the public safety and economic concerns related to illegal immigrants. States claim that illegal immigrants commit acts of violence, including murder, drug trafficking, human smuggling, and property damage. For example, illegal immigration posed such a threat that in August 2005, the governors of Arizona and New Mexico issued a state of emergency declaration in response to what they described as a public safety concern caused by illegal immigration.[69] Former New Mexico governor Bill Richardson declared that as a result of the illegal border crossings, citizens of New Mexico were "devastated by the ravages and terror of human smuggling, drug smuggling, kidnapping, murder, destruction of property, and death of livestock."[70] The extent of the problem is illustrated by the fact that at one point on the New Mexico border, the Border Patrol estimated that an average of 175 people per day were caught trying to enter the United States illegally.[71]

The concern for public safety extends beyond border towns because once in the United States, some illegal immigrants migrate to other cities and states and engage in violent gang criminality.[72] Violent criminal gangs composed primarily of illegal immigrants can be found in major cities throughout the United States. One of the most serious concerns among law enforcement is the criminal activity of the gang known as MS-13 or Mara Salvatrucha, which has committed numerous violent attacks in major cities throughout the United States. In 2005 and 2006, in a sweep of suspected immigrant gang members called Operation Community Shield, ICE arrested over 1,000 alleged gang members representing 80 gangs in 25 states.[73] ICE officials said that more than 900 of those arrested are eligible for deportation. Antigang ICE officials claim that thousands of suspected gang members are in the United States illegally or have committed serious crimes that make them eligible for deportation. The extent of the criminality of illegal immigrants is seen by the fact that each year, ICE deports approximately 80,000 illegal immigrants for criminal activity.[74]

Furthermore, the states claim that illegal immigration places great strains on public safety, health, and educational budgets. States cite the educational costs associated with unauthorized immigrant school children, the costs of welfare medical care, and the costs of public safety and health services responding to unauthorized immigration populations. These actual costs and the adverse impact of unauthorized immigration on state budgets are disputed.[75]

While primarily focused on the issues of public safety and economic costs, states' efforts to stem the flow of illegal immigrants embrace antiterrorism goals. They claim that their efforts contribute to stopping terrorists from entering the United States.

In the forefront of state immigration legislation are Alabama, Georgia, Indiana, South Carolina, and Utah.[76] State immigration legislation bills are being considered by other states as they await the outcome of court decisions on existing legislation.[77] Prior to the adoption of state immigration laws, state and local LEAs have never had the authority to arrest immigrants simply for lacking valid immigration status unless agreements existed with federal agencies for LEAs to enforce civil violations of immigration law.[78] State immigration laws have granted state and local LEAs broad powers to detain and investigate suspected unauthorized immigrants and have legalized a number of actions by unauthorized immigrants. (See Figure 14–2.) State and local LEAs have been divided as to their endorsement of state immigration laws.[79]

Also, state and local immigration laws have been beset by a number of lawsuits challenging the constitutionality of the legislation and powers granted to LEAs. The courts' rulings regarding immigration laws have been split between upholding the legislation and declaring it unconstitutional. A September 2012 decision by Judge Susan Bolton of the U.S. District Court in Phoenix upheld the contested "show me your papers"

The Executive Branch of the Federal government argues that the U.S. Constitution makes immigration control an exclusive power of the Federal government. However, states have disagreed with this interpretation and have adopted or proposed state laws aimed at controlling illegal immigration within the state. State legislation or bills have included the following:

- Economic sanctions upon landlords who provide housing for illegal immigrants
- Sanctions upon employers and individuals for providing employment to illegal immigrants, including day laborers
- Prohibiting illegal immigrants access to public health services and public education, including colleges and universities
- Restricting civil rights by preventing the state courts from enforcing any contracts entered into by illegal immigrants
- Authorizing law enforcement agencies to check the immigration status of persons during a lawful stop or arrest and requesting federal authorities to arrest persons judged to be in the United States without authorization
- Making it a crime of trespass for illegal immigrants to be in the state
- Giving state law enforcement agencies the power to enforce state laws that duplicate federal immigration laws, such as state laws making it a state crime to fail to carry immigration registration documents

FIGURE 14–2 **State Provisions of Immigration Bills**

provision of Arizona's SB 1070. Court rulings in Alabama and Georgia have likewise upheld the right of LEAs to question suspected unauthorized immigrants and to ask to see proof of their immigration status. Other provisions of the states' immigration laws have been declared unconstitutional. Lawsuits seeking to overturn state immigration legislation claim that states lack the constitutional authority to enact such legislation and/or such legislation would result in racial profiling and discrimination by LEAs.

Enforcement of federal immigration laws and the adoption of state immigration laws have become a political and constitutional "hot button" issue. The controversy arises in some interesting circumstances. For example, in *Padilla* v. *Kentucky* (2010), the U.S. Supreme Court ruled that lawyers must advise their immigrant clients facing criminal charges that pleading guilty could lead to deportation. In another example, in May 2010, during a televised visit to an elementary school, a second grader confessed to First Lady Michelle Obama that she was concerned about U.S. immigration policy because her mother "did not have papers."

National Identification Card

To enhance national security, the DHS has advocated a national identification card. There is controversy over the merits of a national identification card and the potential threat to civil liberties if such a program were adopted. Although not embracing the idea of a national identification card, Congress has been favorable toward adopting uniform standards for state driver's licenses as indicated by the passage of the REAL ID Act.

REAL ID Act

The adoption of a standardized state driver's license as required by the **REAL ID Act** will create a national database because it requires states to share driver's license information. Critics of the REAL ID Act argue that it will create a *de facto* national identification card and database.

Estimates suggest that the REAL ID Act would require approximately $100 to $700 million for states to conform to its requirements.[81] States would have to pick up most of these costs. Governors have argued that if the provisions of the REAL ID Act are implemented, "this is going to drive the cost of driver's licenses for ordinary folks through the roof."[82]

$100 to $700 million

The cost for states to conform to the requirements of the REAL ID Act

Proponents of the legislation believe that the REAL ID Act will eliminate the ability of illegal immigrants to obtain driver's licenses. Presently, many states issue driver's licenses to illegal immigrants because the state does not require a person to prove that he or she is a legal resident. It is estimated that the REAL ID Act would prevent tens of thousands of undocumented people from obtaining a driver's license.[83] Critics of the act argue that it would create a public safety danger because undocumented immigrants would continue to drive without the benefit of being tested to determine whether they have the knowledge and ability to operate a motor vehicle. Those who support the act argue that denying illegal immigrants the right to drive is not "punishment" because they are not entitled to be in the United States in the first place.[84]

Securing U.S. Cyberborders

On January 24, 2000, nearly half of the computing power in the world went dead. The top-secret NSA's massive array of supercomputers—which crunch information from America's spy satellites and global eavesdropping network—mysteriously shut down for three days. Government officials feared that hackers might have caused the shutdown. In the end, the shutdown was attributed to human and computer error, but the fear that it was deliberate is justified. Previously, hackers had been successful in shutting down 9-1-1 emergency service, severing NASA uplinks to the Atlantis shuttle, shutting down state governments' web pages, infiltrating and defacing the Senate's main website, defacing the U.S. Army's main website, and penetrating Defense Department national defense databases and stealing sensitive information.

Responding to cyberterrorism is difficult because cyberattacks can be executed from anywhere in the world and it is difficult to establish the source of attacks. Cyberattacks

In *Padilla* v. *Kentucky*, the Court ruled that lawyers must advise their immigrant clients facing criminal charges that pleading guilty could lead to deportation.

(Think About It . . .

At a time when all states face financial challenges and are making deep cuts to public safety and LEAs, state immigration laws will cost states millions to implement and defend in court. Some estimates are that Arizona's immigration laws could cost the state nearly $100 million in law enforcement, detention, and legal fees.[80] Tennessee, Kentucky, and Louisiana withdrew state immigration legislation when financial analysis showed that it would cost millions of dollars per year to enforce the legislation. Studies suggest that business and agricultural industries of states with immigration laws could lose millions of dollars. Are state immigration laws worth the costs? Why or why not?

Capital City Images/Alamy

can emanate from remotely controlled computers whose owners are not even aware that control of their computers has been hijacked and they are being used for attacks. This strategy was used in the summer of 2009 when U.S. and South Korean computers were attacked. In the United States, the computers of the DHS, the FAA, and the Federal Trade Commission were attacked. News released by the United States and South Korea suggested that the cyberattacks were connected to the North Korean government.[85] Shortly after these attacks, former Defense Secretary Robert M. Gates issued an order establishing a command that will defend military networks against computer attacks and develop offensive cyberweapons. The new cybercommand will be under the NSA, not the DHS, and will provide assistance to civilian systems.

In addition to using the Internet to launch cyberattacks, extremist groups use the Internet to recruit new members, to provide online training for jihadists plotting violent attacks, and to disseminate their message worldwide. In an unusual finding, the federal government has discovered that the relatively low expense and high quality of U.S. servers seems to attract jihadists and that many of the Taliban websites use ISPs located in the United States but run from the Middle East. Usually, the ISP does not know the content or purpose of these websites. Shutting them down can be complicated by the fact that doing so may come close to the line regarding constitutional rights of free speech and privacy.

Terrorists have launched cyberattacks against the United States, which has responded in kind. For example, concerned that Iran would use its nuclear program to produce nuclear weapons rather than electricity, as claimed by Iran, the United States engaged in a number of diplomatic and economic strategies to deter Iran from achieving this objective. When these measures did not stop Iran's nuclear program, a malicious cyberattack was launched on the computers that controlled the speed of the centrifuges spinning to enrich uranium. The worm, called Stuxnet, caused the centrifuge motors to spin faster and faster until it destroyed the centrifuges. Just before destroying the centrifuge, the program returned all operating systems to normal, thus concealing the reason for the failure. The United States has not admitted to the attack, but based on its complexity, most authorities conclude that it must have been a state-sponsored cyberattack. The United States and Israel are both high on the list of possible suspect nations.[86] Many think that cyberattacks, including those originated by terrorists groups, will be the new wave of terrorism and may accomplish as much or more damage as physical attacks.[87] In January 2012, FBI director Robert Mueller told the Senate Select Committee on Intelligence that "cyber-threats would surpass terrorism as the country's top concern."

Defending against cyberattacks and developing cyberweapons is the responsibility of the newly created Department of Defense cyberwarfare unit Cyber Command. Cyber Command is assisted in its mission by the NSA, the Secret Service, and the FBI.

> Extremist groups use the Internet to recruit new members, to provide online training for jihadists plotting violent attacks, and to disseminate their message worldwide.

One of the major challenges of cybersecurity is privacy concerns.[88] One of the best strategies in the fight to detect and stop terrorist cyberattacks in the United States is extensive and intrusive monitoring of Internet communication and websites. However, such monitoring may be in conflict with citizens' rights of privacy.

▶ Civil Rights and Homeland Security

The U.S. criminal justice system is based on the principle that people are entitled to certain inalienable rights provided by the U.S. Constitution and its amendments. People are guaranteed the right of freedom from unreasonable search, the right to confront witnesses, the right to a public trial, the right to know the charges against them, the right to an attorney, and the right of free speech and association. These rights have served as the cornerstone of the U.S. criminal justice system. However, public opinion polls indicate that most Americans believe that some civil rights must be sacrificed in the war on terrorism. The challenge is to balance the loss of civil rights with appropriate national security concerns.

Fewer Liberties, Greater Security?

In the post–September 11, 2001, environment, some acts and behaviors have been prohibited in an effort to promote national security. In the pursuit to discover terrorists who may be in the United States, Congress has provided law enforcement officials with new powers that diminish Fourth Amendment (search and seizure) rights. Often, these powers provide federal law enforcement with the authority to perform acts that prior to September 11, 2001, would not have been approved by the public or would have been considered unconstitutional. The justification for curtailing these rights is that the new powers and laws promote national security and enhance the ability of law enforcement to detect terrorist cells within the United States and secret plots by terrorists before they can launch an attack. **Terrorist cells** in the United States are organized into small groups of terrorists (usually four to six individuals) who have entered the country and have "blended in" as they plot or await orders to launch a terrorist attack.

Related efforts to promote national security by discovering these terrorist cells have impacted many citizens. For example, in an effort to make it harder for terrorists to avoid detection, policies and practices have been adopted to prevent terrorists from obtaining employment. The purpose of these policies and laws is to make it more difficult for terrorists to remain in the United States or to obtain jobs in critical businesses where they could use their employment to carry out a terrorist attack. However, as a result of such practices, thousands of airline workers who are not terrorists lost their jobs when U.S. citizenship became a job requirement. Also, fearing that terrorists may recruit converts from the criminal population, legislation was passed that prohibited people with felony convictions from obtaining certain employment (for example, truck drivers who could transport hazardous materials) or from obtaining jobs on military bases. Because there is no time limit on when a person was convicted, some workers with long-past felony convictions have found that they are denied employment or have lost their job because of this provision.

In the name of national security, citizens have fewer expectations of privacy rights. Increased domestic intelligence action by the Justice Department has resulted in government access to bank accounts, credit histories, medical records, academic records, travel plans, Internet communications, and cell phone communications. In an effort to ensure national security, the FBI and other LEAs have engaged in extensive spying on Americans, secret searches of mosques, and scrutiny of hundreds of social action groups such as the ACLU.

Calls for independent bipartisan panels to monitor the possible abuse of civil rights have not overcome the majority's belief that loss of a certain number of civil rights may be necessary to prevent future terrorist attacks.

Free Speech and Protest versus Terrorism

As federal LEAs have gained new powers to conduct domestic intelligence, critics are concerned about possible abuses of these powers. These concerns were heightened when a 2008 Justice Department report concluded that the FBI had abused its intelligence-gathering powers made possible by noncourt-approved search warrants called "national security letters."[89]

Some antiterrorism laws are vague and may prohibit legitimate activities. For example, federal law prohibits providing material support to groups that the State Department has deemed terrorist organizations. Any form of aid to a "terrorist organization," including health, social welfare, or legal assistance, is illegal. Solicitor General Elena Kagan defended the law, saying, "It was impossible to separate support of any terrorist group's peaceful activities from its violent goals." Critics argue that such vague material support laws hinder international efforts to promote human rights and peace through nonviolent means.[90]

Denial of Due Process

Critics accuse the Justice Department of denying due process to many people accused or suspected of terrorism. For example, a report by Human Rights Watch accuses the federal government of indiscriminate and arbitrary arrests of men from

A 2008 Justice Department report concluded that the FBI had abused its intelligence-gathering powers.

predominately Muslim countries without sufficient probable cause or even reasonable suspicion.[91]

Also, Human Rights Watch and the ACLU accuse the Justice Department of abusing the **material witness law** to detain terror suspects. This law, enacted in 1984, allows federal authorities to hold a person indefinitely without charging him or her with a crime if the authorities suspect that the person has information about a crime and might flee or be unwilling to cooperate with law enforcement officials.[92] Human Rights Watch and the ACLU charge that the Justice Department has used the material witness law to detain 70 people, about one-third of them U.S. citizens, on suspicion of terrorism where questionable evidence existed for such detentions. The Justice Department has apologized to at least 13 people for wrongly detaining them under the material witness law.[93] One of the more publicized abuses of the law was the detention of Portland, Oregon, lawyer Brandon Mayfield, whom the FBI wrongly accused of being connected to the Madrid train bombings in 2004.

Of great concern to those who fear that the loss of due process is eroding due process rights is the Justice Department's denial of access to the civilian courts for those accused or suspected of terrorism. The use of the enemy combatant executive order to detain alleged terrorists and al-Qaeda members has seriously alarmed proponents of constitutional rights. The use of this executive order, combined with the use of military tribunals instead of civilian court trials, denies accused enemy combatants access to the civilian courts. This process of determining guilt denies them the due process rights to have an attorney, to confront the witnesses against them, to know the evidence the government has against them, and to be tried by their peers.

The federal courts have responded to this concern. In 2008, the U.S. Supreme Court ruled that terrorist suspects held at the Guantanamo Bay naval base in Cuba have constitutional rights to challenge their detention in U.S. courts. In a 2009 ruling, the Supreme Court ruled that enemy combatants held in military prisons on U.S. soil have the right to sue in civil courts regarding their imprisonment and interrogation. The decision resulted in the federal government removing Jose Padilla, an accused enemy combatant, from solitary confinement in the

Think About It . . .

In 2011, U.S. Representative Peter King (R–NY), chair of the House Homeland Security Committee, held a hearing on the threat of Islamic radicalization in the United States. King claims that more than 40 Americans have been recruited by Islamic radical groups to join al-Shabaab in Somalia and 15 have been killed in fighting. King claims that radicalized Islamic groups are recruiting American youths to travel overseas for "programming"; then they return to carry out attacks against the United States. One such person is Carlos Bledsoe, who attacked a military recruiting center in Little Rock, Arkansas. Furthermore, King asserts that mosques discourage members from cooperating with law enforcement. Critics accuse King of inflaming Islamophobia and McCarthyism. What do you think?

Charleston, South Carolina, military brig where he was being held without charges and filing charges against him in federal criminal court. (Padilla was convicted and sentenced to 17 years in prison.)

In September 2012, the federal court granted detainees held at Guantanamo Bay further due process rights. The court ruled that certain restrictions imposed by the government on attorneys defending enemy combatants held at Guantanamo violated the detainees' right to challenge their confinement in the courts.[94] Chief U.S. District Judge Royce C. Lamberth ruled, "Access to the courts means nothing without access to counsel.... The Government's attempt to supersede the Court's authority is an illegitimate exercise in Executive power." David Remes, who represents 17 of the Guantanamo prisoners said, "The government has never accepted the right of the detainees to effective legal representation."[95] The government sought to restrict lawyers' access to six detainees as well as information about their cases. The ruling, along with U.S. Supreme Court rulings that detainees have the right of *habeas corpus*—to challenge their confinement—could significantly impact the remaining 160 detainees at Guantanamo Bay as they seek their release.

Racial Profiling

Over the years, law enforcement has made much progress in addressing the problem of racial profiling. Public opinion polls have indicated that most people disapprove of racial profiling by law enforcement. Prior to 9/11, racial profiling was seen as a problem directed primarily against African-Americans and Latinos. However, since September 11, 2001, racial profiling has become a particular concern for Middle Eastern–looking men, as public opinion and legislators seem less opposed to racial profiling of these people, especially at airports and on public transportation. Since September 11, 2001, some have been so bold as to publicly voice that they favor profiling young Middle Eastern or Islamic men at airports and other high-risk security venues.[96]

The DHS and the Justice Department have denied that any of their policies related to immigration enforcement, screening, or investigation are based on racial profiling. In 2003, the Justice Department issued a policy statement regarding guidelines on racial profiling. The guidelines govern the conduct of 70 federal LEAs. However, the guidelines do not ban racial profiling. They do bar federal agents from using race or ethnicity in routine investigations, but the guidelines allow for clear exemptions for investigations involving terrorism and national security matters.

Muslims in the United States point out that hate crimes against them have increased since 9/11 and rose again after the 2005 London transit bombings. They also point out that in some cities with large Muslim populations, the number of Middle Easterners cited for offenses by law enforcement has been significantly higher than all other people charged with offenses.[97] Many Muslims report that they fear that "the motives behind some of the post-9/11 security efforts seem aimed at Muslims."[98] As a result, they report that they "keep as low a profile as they can" because they believe that Americans "feel the next terrorist attack will be from a Muslim."[99]

LEARNING OUTCOMES 6 Describe the challenge of balancing civil rights and homeland security.

GLOSSARY

terrorist cells Small groups of individuals with a common goal of carrying out terrorism.

material witness law A law that allows for the detention of a person who has not committed a crime but is alleged to have information about a crime that has been committed.

rendition The illegal transportation of a person to a foreign country for the purpose of having officials of that country interrogate the person using torture or practices not permitted in the United States.

Rendition and Torture

One of the most serious concerns of denial of due process is allegations of torture and the practice of rendition. As a result of the International Committee of the Red Cross's revelation of the torture of the prisoners of Abu Ghraib prison in Iraq and the report of alleged torture of prisoners at Guantanamo Bay, Cuba, some have alleged that evidence suggests that the United States has chosen to systematically engage in or permit the torture of terror suspects. They argue that the fear of another 9/11–type terrorist incident has caused the U.S. government to be willing "to consider doing almost anything—including actions previously thought morally suspect—to prevent another such catastrophe."[100]

The emergence of "torture memos" exchanged between the Justice Department and President Bush seem to suggest that the Bush administration operated on the premise that in a time of necessity, the president and the military could disregard torture conventions, international treaties, and the law of the land.[101] In legal memorandums by the Justice Department and the Defense Department, President Bush was advised that the Geneva Convention and other antitorture covenants do not apply to suspected terrorist detainees.[102]

Think About It . . .

In 2012, Muhammad Salah of Bridgeview, Illinois, filed a federal law suit claiming "internal banishment." In 1995, Shalah was imprisoned in Israel for providing support to Hamas. When he returned to the United States, federal prosecutors in Chicago charged him with supporting Hamas extremists, but he was acquitted. In 2007, he was found guilty of lying in a civil lawsuit and sentenced to 21 months in prison. Upon his release, the U.S. Treasury Department classified him as a "specially designated terrorist." The government can monitor or bar all of his economic transactions. He cannot open a bank account, buy property, transfer money, donate to charities, or make purchases without governmental approval. His lawsuit challenges the constitutionality of the restrictions. What do you think?

meryl/Fotolia

Another serious charge by critics regarding the denial of due process related to torture is that the federal government has engaged in a practice called **rendition**. Rendition is when the U.S. government arranges for the transfer of a suspected terrorist from the United States or another country to a country such as Pakistan or Egypt where local authorities there can interrogate the suspect using torture. Rendition often involves the clandestine kidnapping of the "terror suspect" and the clandestine transportation of the suspect to such a country. The Bush administration is accused of using this extreme denial of due process rights to those suspected of terrorism both in the United States and in other countries such as Germany and Italy.

Charges of torture or rendition were never directed at federal, state, or local LEAs, but at the executive office (President Bush) and the CIA. (FBI agents were present during some of the interrogations in which "enhanced interrogation methods" were used, but the FBI was not the lead agency in conducting the interrogations.) The CIA maintains that only three prisoners were waterboarded: Khalid Sheikh Mohammed, Abu Zubaida, and Abd al-Rahim al-Nashiri.[103] All three are still imprisoned at Guantanamo Bay. However, a 2012 report by Human Rights Watch alleges that the CIA carried out renditions and waterboarding more extensively than it admits to and for much longer than it admits. The report, "Delivered Into Enemy Hands: U.S.-Led Abuse and Rendition of Opponents to Gaddafi's Libya," alleges that at least 14 detainees were tortured by the CIA in Afghanistan, transferred to Libya in 2004, and held in that country's prison system until August 2011.[104]

The Obama administration has renounced the use of rendition and torture or enhanced interrogation. There is sharp debate between the Obama administration and supporters of "harsh treatment or enhanced interrogation" as to whether valuable information was obtained from the detainees and terrorist plots were foiled. Some who support the Bush administration's use of enhanced interrogation, such as Liz Cheney, attorney, political activist, and daughter of former vice president Dick Cheney, claim that valuable information obtained from these interrogations led directly to finding and killing Osama bin Laden.

Although the Obama administration has declared that it will not use executive orders to imprison enemy combatants without *habeas corpus* rights, it also has said that terrorist suspects could be held in "prolonged detention" without trial. This practice has been referred to as "preventive detention." Many legal scholars argue that there is no constitutional foundation for "preventive detention" and any person detained on U.S. soil is entitled to due process rights and access to the civil courts to appeal his or her detention.[105]

Killing U.S. Citizens

A serious concern regarding due process rights of accused terrorists is the recent use of drone attacks to kill U.S. citizens living abroad. The U.S. has been carrying out drone missile attacks against alleged terrorist since the Bush administration. These attacks target alleged terrorists and, on the sole authority of the U.S. president as commander in chief of the U.S. military, authorize the killing of the person. Under the Bush administration, all drone attacks were carried out against non-U.S. citizens on foreign soil. The Obama administration carried out the first attack against an American-born alleged terrorist, Anwar al-Awlaki.

American-born citizen Anwar al-Awlaki was designated an enemy combatant by the Obama administration and targeted for death by a military drone attack while living in Yemen. The authority of the president to authorize the death of a U.S. citizen without due process or court order stirred considerable controversy. Al-Awlaki's father had sued to try to stop the government from killing his son, arguing that he had to be afforded the constitutional right to due process. However, the U.S. courts refused to intervene, claiming that they had no jurisdiction to review the president's military decisions.[106]

U.S. Attorney General Eric Holder rejected the argument that the president had to get permission from a federal court before killing al-Awlaki. Holder argued al-Awlaki was guaranteed "due process" not "judicial process."[107] Holder claimed that the United States was engaged in a war with a stateless enemy and had the power to take preventive actions "to protect the nation from any imminent threat of violent attack."[108] Holder said that the president is justified in using deadly force without authorization of the court when (1) the citizen poses an imminent threat of violent attack against the United States, (2) capture is not feasible, and (3) the killing would be consistent with laws of war.[109]

Again, this controversy does not concern the actions of federal, state, or local law enforcement, but it does call into question the foundations of due process rights in the U.S. criminal justice system. Can the president authorize the death of a U.S. citizen without charges, trial, right to an attorney, or defense? Can the president declare that a state of war exists against a stateless enemy without a declaration of war authorized by Congress?

▶ Conclusion: Turning the Criminal Justice System Upside Down

Homeland security concerns have had a significant impact on law enforcement and the criminal justice system. Doubtful that the criminal justice system is up to the challenge of responding to terrorism, the federal government has assumed considerable new powers; at the same time, it has curtailed civil rights that have been considered the foundation of the U.S. criminal justice system, such as the right to an attorney, the right of a defendant to know the charges against him or her, the right to remain silent, and the right to a public trial.

The DHS and the FBI have assumed major responsibilities in homeland security. In their new roles, the traditional relationships between federal and local law enforcement have changed and federal agencies have assumed the lead role in investigating terrorist incidents. The role of police as first responders and the need for coordinated multiagency response to terrorist attacks have exposed critical shortcomings in infrastructure, training, and equipment. The powers of federal agencies have been bolstered by new legislation. However, many of these new powers have been challenged as serious and needless infringements on civil rights.

In summary, the criminal justice system has been turned upside down. Whereas the focus of the criminal justice system was traditionally the local government, the new focus today is on the federal government. The war on terrorism has resulted in a reexamination of some of the most basic practices underlying the criminal justice system.

Finally, the focus on homeland security poses a unique challenge for criminal justice scholars and programs. Criminal justice scholars have spent considerable effort and research during the past half century describing and understanding the U.S. criminal justice system. The focus on homeland security is fundamentally changing the criminal justice system, and scholars will need to examine and explain to what extent the focus on homeland security is altering the criminal justice system. Although hundreds of years of criminology research have produced extensive knowledge of criminals and victims, now research is now needed to increase our understanding of terrorism. We need to know the answer to questions such as these: Why do some people choose terrorism? Why do some people choose to be suicide bombers? What is the impact of terrorism on victims? What are the best practices for responding to terrorism? The more information scholars can bring to focus on understanding terrorism and terrorists, the more likely the government and the criminal justice system can respond with effective actions that diminish terrorism and preserve civil liberties.

Negotiating with Terrorists

September 4, 2012, was the fortieth anniversary of the 1972 Munich massacre in which Palestinian militants killed 11 members of the Israeli Olympic team. This event marked the emergence of an era of terrorism and shaped the U.S. response to terrorism for the next four decades.

President Reagan started the policy that was to doom the victims to death—do not negotiate with terrorism. In 1986, President Reagan issued National Security Decision Directive 207 declaring that U.S. policy was not to negotiate with terrorists regarding their demands. This policy continued as the guiding principle in dealing with terrorists. The underlying assumption was that terrorists were not legitimate actors and negotiations were futile and immoral. Terrorists were "bloodthirsty fanatics bent on spreading destruction and anarchy."

The policy of not negotiating with terrorists is still the official U.S. policy. However, the nature of "terrorism" and "terrorist" has changed significantly in the past 40 years. For example, since June 2007, Hamas has governed the Gaza portion of the Palestinian territories, after it won a majority of seats in the Palestinian Parliament in the January 2006 Palestinian parliamentary elections and then defeated the Fatah political organization in a series of violent clashes. The European Union, the United States, Canada, Israel, and Japan classify Hamas as a terrorist organization, while the Arab nations and countries such as Russia and Turkey do not. Are the rebels involved in overthrowing Middle Eastern totalitarian governments of the Arab Spring terrorists or freedom fighters? Should the United States negotiate with them—even provide them with assistance?

Terrorist and *terrorism* are political value terms that predispose someone to form negative images and expectations of those labeled as such. However, in a complex, multivalued society, the difference between "right" and "wrong" may be subjective. A no-negotiation policy assumes that those seeking negotiations, even though it is through violence, have no legitimate claims. A no-negotiations policy may make resolution and peace impossible.

The problem is complicated by the fact that it is difficult to distinguish between someone threatening violence in the hope of achieving political objects and someone conducting a violent criminal assault in which he or she has no interest in negotiating—only murdering. With the former, it is possible to negotiate a successful resolution to a potentially violent situation; with the latter, however, negotiations only give the perpetrator more time for violence.

This case raises several interesting questions. Among them are the following:

1. Should the no-negotiation policy of the United States be modified? Why or why not?

2. If a person is to negotiate with "terrorists," what guidelines should he or she follow? What demands can be granted?

3. How does a person distinguish between "legitimate" groups that use violence to achieve political means and individuals who are criminals or fanatics or are bent on destruction?

4. Are there causes that are so deeply held that the use of violence is a legitimate strategy to achieving the goals when other means are blocked? Explain.

James Steidl/Fotolia

369

Define terrorism and explain the difference between domestic and international terrorism.

The criminal justice system focuses on the criminal nature of terrorism, notwithstanding the motivation or political beliefs of such a group, and seeks to protect the public by apprehending perpetrators of terrorism. Law enforcement agencies (LEAs) differentiate between terrorist acts committed by domestic perpetrators of terrorism and foreign perpetrators of terrorism. Perpetrators of domestic terrorism include lone offenders and extremist elements of groups, whereas international terrorism is planned, funded, and executed in part or whole by foreign states.

1. What motivates a domestic terrorist to carry out violence against other citizens?

2. Which agency is responsible for airport security and screening?

3. Define what constitutes a hate crime.

hate crimes Crimes that are motivated by hate of an ethnic group, race, religion, gender, or sexual orientation.

domestic terrorism Acts of terrorism committed in the United States by individuals or groups that do not have ties with or sponsorship from foreign states or organizations.

homegrown terrorism Another name for domestic terrorism that emphasizes that there is no foreign involvement in the violence even though homegrown terrorism may act in support of foreign causes.

lone wolf terrorism Terrorist acts committed by a single individual or a single individual assisted by a small number of other people.

Transportation Security Administration (TSA) The federal agency responsible for airport security and the screening of airline passengers.

Summarize the role of the primary agencies responsible for preventing and responding to terrorism.

The new attention on homeland security has resulted in an increase in both federal agencies and federal law enforcement powers. This has had a great impact on the criminal justice system as a result of a greater shift of power from local to federal law enforcement. Local law enforcement agencies (LEAs) are underprepared to respond to terrorism; as a result, federal agencies have been given the responsibility of fighting terrorism. The powers of these federal agencies have been greatly enhanced by the USA PATRIOT Act. The federal government has taken steps to improve response capacity, communication, and cooperation of first responders at the local level.

1. What is the purpose of CONPLAN?

2. Name some of the federal agencies that have become part of the DHS.

3. Describe a type of mutual aid agreement.

Department of Homeland Security (DHS) A newly created federal agency responsible for a wide range of security measures to protect against terrorist attacks.

United States Government Interagency Domestic Terrorism Concept of Operations Plan (CONPLAN) A plan that establishes the role and responsibilities of federal agencies for preventing and responding to terrorist attacks.

lead federal agency (LFA) The agency that is designated as being primarily in charge of an incident and has the power to direct the actions of other agencies and to call for the use of their resources even though the lead agency may not have direct authority over the other agencies.

first responders Law enforcement, firefighters, and medical personnel who are the first to respond to a crisis or an incident.

mutual aid agreements Agreements that ensure that neighboring jurisdictions can assist in providing personnel and resources to their impacted counterparts.

Summarize the importance of intelligence in preventing and responding to terrorism.

Police departments lack the resources to provide security for every potential terrorist target—hence, gathering accurate and timely intelligence is important so that local and state police can prevent terrorist attacks. Joint local and federal counterterrorism task forces (JTFFs) are used to funnel intelligence from federal agencies to local agencies. Local and state law enforcement agencies (LEAs) have also established Fusion Centers, which are intelligence networks designed to collect, analyze, and disseminate information critical to state and local law enforcement operations.

1. What did the 9/11 Commission say about intelligence sharing among agencies?

2. How many new passenger screeners did the TSA hire in 2002?

3. Who usually creates a fusion center?

the wall Separation of the Central Intelligence Agency and the Federal Bureau of Investigation in the production and dissemination of intelligence data.

Information Analysis and Infrastructure Protection (IAIP) directorate The intelligence unit of the Department of Homeland Security.

Terrorist Threat Integration Center (TTIC) The agency charged with comprehensive intelligence gathering and dissemination.

joint local–federal counterterrorism task force (JTTF) A working group of FBI and state and/or local law enforcement officers that focuses on preventing terrorism through their joint cooperation and intelligence sharing.

Fusion Centers Intelligence agencies set up by states or major urban areas and run by state or local authorities that are designed to collect, analyze, and disseminate information critical to state and local law enforcement operations related to both homeland security and crime fighting.

LEARNING OUTCOMES 4

Explain the changing role and challenges of federal agencies and first responders in preventing and responding to terrorism.

A major change for the criminal justice system has been the shifting of power between federal and local law enforcement agencies (LEAs) as a result of the war on terrorism. President Bush's enemy combatant executive order and the USA PATRIOT Act have served to broaden the scope of authority of federal officials in handling suspected terrorists. A key controversy has centered on whether to grant civilian criminal trials to accused international terrorists. In certain situations, local police have not been in complete agreement about the constitutionality of the powers given to federal law enforcement by post–September 11 legislation.

1. How does the enemy combatant law erode constitutional rights?

2. How does the PATRIOT Act broaden federal law enforcement powers?

3. What do Sections 213 and 215 of the PATRIOT Act allow the FBI to do?

national security decision directives (NSDDs) Directives issued by the president that are binding on federal agencies under executive command; NSDDs may forbid an agency from taking certain actions or may direct the agency to take certain actions.

enemy combatant executive order An order issued by President Bush providing for the detention of terrorists without access to due process rights.

habeas corpus A writ or request to the court to review whether a person is imprisoned lawfully; it alleges that a person is detained or imprisoned illegally.

USA PATRIOT Act Legislation that gives federal law enforcement agencies expanded powers to detect, detain, and prosecute suspected terrorists.

urban fortresses Cities that have adopted extensive and visible physical security measures and barriers in response to the threat of terrorist attacks.

Homeland Security Advisory System (HSAS) A color-coded threat advisory to government agencies, police, and the public that recommended appropriate actions in response to the forecasted risk of terrorist attacks.

LEARNING OUTCOMES 5

Describe the role of border security in the war on terrorism.

U.S. border security is a multifaceted issue and raises great concern about how to deal with the estimated 12 million illegal immigrants in the United States. Since 2001, one of the goals of the federal government has been to prevent international terrorists from entering the country. Two agencies are primarily responsible for border security and immigration: the U.S. Customs and Border Protection (CPB) and Immigration and Customs Enforcement (ICE). The Department of Homeland Security (DHS) initiated a number of changes to seal the border from terrorists, including better tracking of foreign visitors, airline passenger screening, and the use of smart passports. In addition, a No-Flight List has been established by the Terrorist Screening Center (TSC).

1. What is the two-part strategy of ICE in combating illegal immigration?

2. What information is contained in a smart passport?

3. How does the TSC work?

Immigration and Customs Enforcement (ICE) A new federal agency under the Department of Homeland Security that is responsible for the enforcement of immigration laws.

United States Visitor and Immigrant Status Indicator Technology (US-VISIT) A new system of registering the entry of foreign visitors to the United States and tracking when and where they exit the United States.

smart passports New passports that contain machine-readable data about travelers.

Student and Exchange Visitor Information System (SEVIS) A Web-based database containing information on international students studying in the United States.

No-Fly List A secret list maintained by the Department of Homeland Security that includes the names of people who are prohibited from flying on a commercial airplane under any circumstances; it also contains the names of people who should receive additional screening prior to being allowed to board an aircraft.

racial profiling Allegations that police search and seizures, traffic stops, field interrogations, and arrests are made on nonbehavioral factors related to race and/or ethnicity rather than suspicious behavior or probable cause.

REAL ID Act Legislation that requires all state driver's licenses to conform to uniform standards set by the Department of Homeland Security.

LEARNING OUTCOMES 6

Describe the challenge of balancing civil rights and homeland security.

In the post–September 11, 2001 environment, the effort to promote national security has arguably diminished Fourth Amendment (search and seizure) rights. Another concern has been the racial profiling of Muslims in the United States. In addition, using torture and rendition, as well as killing Americans living abroad by drone missile strikes, raises grave concern about due process rights. The focus on homeland security poses challenges for both the government and the criminal justice system to respond with effective actions that combat terrorism and preserve civil liberties.

1. What does the material witness law allow federal authorities to do?

2. Describe a government practice that demonstrates a denial of due process in dealing with suspected terrorists.

3. How does the U.S. government use the practice of rendition to bypass due process?

terrorist cells Small groups of individuals with a common goal of carrying out terrorism.

material witness law A law that allows for the detention of a person who has not committed a crime but is alleged to have information about a crime that has been committed.

rendition The illegal transportation of a person to a foreign country for the purpose of having officials of that country interrogate the person using torture or practices not permitted in the United States.

MyCJLab

Go to Chapter 14 in *MyCJLab* to test your mastery of chapter concepts, access your Study Plan, engage in interactive exercises, complete critical-thinking and research assignments, and view related online videos.

 Review: Complete the pretest in the Study Plan to confirm what you know and what you need to study further. Then complete the post-test to confirm your mastery of the concepts. Use the key term flash cards to review key terminology.

 Apply: Complete the interactive simulation activity.

Analyze: Complete assignments as directed by your instructor.

Current Events: Explore CJSearch for current topical videos, articles, and news pieces.

Additional Links

Go to **http://www.dhs.gov** to view the home page of the Department of Homeland Security, where you can learn more about its efforts to protect the American people from terrorist threats.

Go to **http://www.tsa.gov** and learn more about the nearly 50,000 security officers, inspectors, directors, air marshals, and managers who protect our nation's transportation systems.

Go to **http://www.ice.gov** and learn about the mission of ICE and its responsibilities for investigating a wide range of domestic and international activities arising from the illegal movement of people and goods into, within, and out of the United States.

Go to **http://www.fema.gov** to view the home page for the Federal Emergency Management Agency and read about its mission, its leadership, and its policies as well as employment opportunities with the agency.

Go to **http://www.cbp.gov** to read about recent criminal incidents, seizures, and the way the agency works to prevent the illegal entry of people and goods into the United States.

Go to **http://www.c-spanvideo.org/program/307297-2** and watch homeland security and law enforcement officials talking about recent cases and responses by intelligence agencies and law enforcement.

References

Chapter 1, Introduction to Criminal Justice

1 Stephanie Simon, "In Contraceptive Debate, Bishops Vie for Flock's Ear," *Chicago Tribune*, February 19, 2012, Sec. 1, p. 30.

2 Dawn Rhodes, "George: Government Impinging on Religious Freedoms Regarding Contraception," *Chicago Tribune*, February 18, 2012.

3 Rex W. Huppke, "Contraception Debate Neglects Catholics at Odds with Doctrine," *Chicago Tribune*, February 19, 2012, Sec. 1, p. 2.

4 Rhodes, "George: Government Impinging on Religious Freedoms Regarding Contraception."

5 Megan Barr and Ryan J. Foley, "Occupy Protests Cost Nation's Cities at Least $13M," *Chicago Tribune*, November 23, 2011.

6 Tracey Kyckelhahan, "Justice Expenditures and Employment, FY 1982–2007—Statistical Tables," U.S. Department of Justice, Bureau of Justice Statistics: GPO, December 2011, p, 2.

7 President's Commission on Law Enforcement and the Administration of Justice, *The Challenge of Crime in a Free Society* (Washington, DC: GPO, 1967).

8 Symposium on the 30th Anniversary of the President's Commission, *The Challenge of Crime in a Free Society: Looking Back Looking Forward* (Washington, DC: U.S. Department of Justice).

9 Thomas Cohen and Tracey Kyckelhahn, *Felony Defendants in Large Urban Counties, 2006* (Washington, DC: Bureau of Justice Statistics, May 2010), p. 1.

10 Bureau of Justice Statistics website, http://www.bjs.gov/index.cfm?ty=pbdetail&iid=2193 (accessed March 3, 2012).

11 Cohen and Kyckelhahn, *Felony Defendants in Large Urban Counties, 2006.*

12 Samuel Walker, *The Police in America: An Introduction* (New York: McGraw-Hill, 1999).

13 *Brown v. Board of Education of Topeka*, 347 U.S. 483 (1954).

14 Michelle Alexander, *The New Jim Crow: Mass Incarceration in the Age of Colorblindness* (New York: The New Press, 2010).

15 James Q. Wilson, *Thinking about Crime* (New York: Basic Books, 1975), p. 65.

16 Robert Fogelson, "Reform at a Standstill," in Carl Klockars and Stephen Mastrofski, eds., *Thinking about Police* (New York: McGraw-Hill, 1991), p. 117.

17 Edwin H. Sutherland and Donald R. Cressey, *Criminology*, 10th ed. (Philadelphia: Lippincott, 1978).

18 Ibid.

19 Jason Meisner and Ryan Haggerty, "Jury Quickly Acquits Woman Accused of Recording Cops," *Chicago Tribune*, August 25, 2011.

20 Andy Grimm, "Woman Acquitted in Eavesdropping Case Files Lawsuit against Chicago Police," *Chicago Tribune*, January 14, 2012.

21 Edith Brady-Lunny, "Eavesdropping Charges Dropped: SA Thinks Law Unconstitutional," *Pantagraph*, February 29, 2012.

22 Ryan Haggerty, "Bill Would Let People Record Audio of Cops," *Chicago Tribune*, January 12, 2012.

23 Ibid.

Chapter 2, Crime—*The Search for Understanding*

1 Amima Khan, "Dutch Scientist Accused of Fraud: Pressures of Academia Blamed," *Chicago Tribune*, November 9, 2011, Sec. 1, p. 25.

2 Ibid.

3 Erica Goode, "Many in U.S. Are Arrested by Age 23, Study Finds," New York Times Online, December 19, 2011. Web posted at http://www.nytimes.com.

4 "Son, Is Your Name Trouble?" *Chicago Tribune*, January 30, 2009, Sec. 1, p. 3.

5 "Is Crime Drop Out of the Blue?" *Chicago Tribune*, December 19, 2008, Sec. 1, p. 5.

6 Norimitsu Onishi, "Sinatra Song Often Strikes Deadly Chord," New York Times Online, February 7, 2010. Web posted at http://www.nytimes.com.

7 Steve Chapman, "Rick Santorum's Moral Delusions," *Chicago Tribune*, January 8, 2012, Sec. 1, p. 23.

8 Ibid.

9 Cesare Bonesana and Marchese Beccaria, *Of Crimes and Punishments* (Philadelphia: Philip Nicklin, 1819).

10 Jeremy Bentham, "An Introduction to the Principles of Morales and Legislation," In J. E. Jacoby, ed., *Classics of Criminology* (Oak Park, IL: Moore, 1979).

11 Richard Louis Dugdale, *The Jukes: A Study in Crime, Pauperism, Disease and Heredity*, 3rd ed. (New York: G.P. Putnam's Sons, 1985).

12 Henry Herbert Goddard, *The Kallikak Family: A Study in the Heredity of Feeblemindedness* (New York: Macmillian, 1912).

13 Cesare Lombroso, *Crime: Its Causes and Remedies*, trans. Henry P. Horton (Boston: Little, Brown, 1918); and Cesare Lombroso, *Criminal Man*, Mary Gibson and Nicole Hahn Rafter, eds. (Durham, NC: Duke University Press, 2005).

14 Cesare Lombroso and Gina Lombroso-Ferrero, *Criminal Man* (Montclair, NJ: Patterson Smith (1911), 1972.

15 Ibid.

16 Karl Christiansen, "A Preliminary Study of Criminality among Twins," in Sarnoff Mednick and Karol O. Christiansen, eds., *Biosocial Bases of Criminal Behavior* (New York: Simon & Schuster, 1985).

17 William H. Price, John A. Strong, Peter Whatmore, and William F. McClemont, "Criminal Patients with XYY Sex Chromosome Complement" *Lancet*, Vol. 287 (March 12, 1966), pp. 565–566.

18 Jonathan R. Beckwith, "The Myth of the Criminal Chromosome," in *Making Genes, Making Waves: A Social Activist in Science* (Cambridge, MA: Harvard University Press, 2002), pp. 116–134.

19 Sigmund Freud, *A General Introduction to Psychoanalysis* (New York: Norton Press, 1963).

20 Adrian Raine, "The Psychopathology of Crime: Criminal Behavior as a Clinical Disorder" (Orlando, FL: Academic Press, 1993).

21 Robert E. Park and Ernest Burgess, *Introduction to the Science of Sociology*, 2nd ed. (Chicago: University of Chicago Press, 1942).

22 Robert E. Park, Ernest Burgess, and Roderick McKenzie, *The City* (Chicago: University of Chicago Press, 1925).

23 Clifford R. Shaw, *Juvenile Delinquency in Urban Areas* (Chicago: University of Chicago Press, 1942).

24 Park, Burgess, and McKenzie, *The City*.

25 Clifford R. Shaw and Henry D. McKay, "Social Factors in Juvenile Delinquency," in *Volume II of the Report on the Causes of Crime, National Commission on Law Observance and Enforcement, Report no. 13* (Washington, DC: U.S. Government Printing Office, 1931).

26 Mark H. Moore, Robert C. Trojanowicz, and George L. Kelling, *Crime and Policing* (Washington, DC: U.S. Department of Justice, June 1988).

27 Edwin H. Sutherland, *Principles of Criminology*, 6th ed. (Philadelphia: Lippincott, 1966).

28 Albert K. Cohen, *Delinquent Boys: The Culture of the Gang* (Glencoe, IL: Free Press, 1958).

29 Thorsten Sellin, *Culture and Conflict in Crime* (New York: Social Science Research Council, 1938).

30 Associated Press, "Group Urges More Polygamy Prosecutions," New York Times Online, June 16, 2005. Web posted at http://www.nytimes.com.

31 Francis T. Cullen, *Rethinking Crime and Deviance Theory* (Totowa, NJ: Rowman & Allanheld, 1969).

32 Ibid.

33 Gresham Sykes and David Matza, "Techniques of Neutralization: A Theory of Delinquency," *American Sociological Review*, Vol. 22 (1957), pp. 664–670.

34 Robert Merton, "Social Structure and Anomie," *American Sociological Review*, Vol. 3 (1938), pp. 672–682.

35 Ibid.

36 Michael J. Lynch and W. Byron Graves, *A Primer in Radical Criminology*, 2nd ed. (Albany, NY: Harrow and Heston, 1989).

37 Richard Quinney, *The Social Reality of Crime* (Boston: Little, Brown, 1970).

38 Ivan Taylor, Paul Walton, and Jock Young, *The New Criminology* (New York: Harper & Row, 1973).

39 Richard Quinney, *The Crime Problem* (New York: Dodd, Mead, 1970).

40 Austin Turk, *Criminality and the Legal Order* (Chicago: Rand McNally, 1969).

41 Freda Adler, *Sisters in Crime: The Rise of the New Female Criminal* (New York: McGraw-Hill, 1975).

42 Chesney-Lind, M., *The Female Offender: Girls, Women and Crime* (Thousand Oaks, CA: Sage Publications, 1997).

43 Kathleen Daly and Lisa Maher, eds., *Criminology at the Crossroads: Feminist Readings in Crime and Justice* (London: Oxford University Press, 1998).

44 Sally S. Simpson, "Feminist Theory, Crime and Justice," *Criminology*, Vol. 27 (1989).

45 Gwynn Nettler, *Explaining Crime*, 2nd ed. (New York: McGraw-Hill, 1978).

46 William J. Chambliss, "Toward a Radical Criminology," in D. Kairys, ed., *The Politics of Law: A Progressive Critique* (New York: Pantheon Books, 1982).

47 Sabrina Tavernise, "Teenager Is Charged in Killing of 3 at a School," New York Times Online, March 1, 2012. Web posted at http://www.nytimes.com.

48 Campbell Robertson, "New Orleans Struggles to Stem Homicides," New York Times Online, December 7, 2011. Web posted at http://www.nytimes.com.

49 Ibid.

50 Ibid.

Chapter 3, Measuring Crime and Victimization

1 Josiah Stamp, *Some Economic Factors in Modern Life* (London: P. S. King & Son, 1929), p. 258.

2 Thomas Reppetto, *The Blue Parade* (New York: Free Press, 1978), p. viii.

3 The Cleveland Foundation Survey of the Administration of Justice in Cleveland, Ohio, Criminal Justice in Cleveland (Cleveland, OH: Cleveland Foundation, 1922); and Illinois Association for Criminal Justice, The Illinois Crime Survey (Chicago: Illinois Association for Criminal Justice, 1929).

4 Robert Tannehill, "The History of American Law Enforcement," in Dae Change and James Fagin, eds., *Introduction to Criminal Justice: Theory and Application*, 2nd ed. (Lake Geneva, WI: Paladin House of the Farley Court of Publishers, 1985), p. 159.

5 Federal Bureau of Investigation, *Crime in the United States, 2010* (Washington, DC; U.S. Department of Justice), September 2011.

6 Ibid.

7 C. Kindermann, J. Lynch, and D. Cantor, *Effects of the Redesign on Victimization Estimates* (Washington, DC: Bureau of Justice Statistics, 1997), p. 1.

8 U.S. Department of Justice, Office of Justice Programs, Bureau of Justice Statistics, NCVS Resource Guide, October 2004.

9 Department of Justice, "The Nation's Two Crime Measures," (Washington, DC: U.S. Department of Justice, October 2004), p. 2.

10 Bureau of Justice Statistics, "National Incident-Based Reporting System (NIBRS) Implementation Program," March 18, 2012. Web posted at http://www.bjs.gov/index.cfm?ty=dcdetail&iid=301.

11 Federal Bureau of Investigation, "What Is the National Incident-Based Reporting System (NIBRS)?", March 18, 2012. Web posted at http://www2.fbi.gov/ucr/faqs.htm.

12 Ibid.

13 Office of Justice Programs website, http://www.ojp.usdoj.gov/index.cfm?ty=abu.

14 National Criminal Justice Reference Service, "About NCJRS," March 20, 2012. Web posted at https://www.ncjrs.gov/whatsncjrs.html.

15 Ibid.

16 Sourcebook of Criminal Justice Statistics, "About Sourcebook," http://albany.edu/sourcebook/about.html.

17 Bureau of Justice Statistics, "About the Bureau of Justice Statistics," March 19, 2012. Web posted at http://bjs.ojp.usdoj.gov/index.cfm?ty=abu.

18 R. B. Felson and S. F. Messner, "Disentangling the Effects of Gender and Intimacy on Victim Precipitation in Homicide," *Criminology*, Vol. 36, No. 2 (1998), p. 414.

19 Ross Macmillan and Candace Kruttschnitt, *Patterns of Violence Against Women: Risk Factors and Consequences* (National Institute of Justice, January 2005).

20 L. E. Cohen and M. Felson, "Social Change and Crime Rate Trends: A Routine Activity Approach," *American Sociological Review*, Vol. 44, No. 4 (1979), pp. 588–608.

21 Ibid.

Chapter 4, Criminal Law—*Crimes and the Limits of Law*

1 A. G. Sulzberger, "Kansas Law on Sodomy Stays on Books Despite a Cull," New York Times Online, January 20, 2012. Web posted at http://www.nytimes.com.

2 Ibid.

3 Joel Samaha, *Criminal Law* (Belmont, CA: West/Wadswoth, 1999), p. 3.

4 American Law Institute, *Model Penal Code and Commentaries*, Vol. 1 (Philadelphia: American Law Institute, 1985), pp. 1–30.

5 Steve Schmadeke and Dennis Sullivan, "Bans on Saggy Pants Are All the Rage," *Chicago Tribune*, August 23, 2011, Sec. 1, p. 1.

6 Matthew Walberg, "Drive Is on for Uniformity," *Chicago Tribune*, March 4, 2012, Sec. 1, p. 14.

7 U.S. Constitution, Article X, Section 10. Based on the seventeenth-century philosophy expressed by Lord Edward Coke, "No Crime without Law. No Punishment without Law," and Jerome Hall, *General Principle of Criminal Law*, 2nd ed. (Indianapolis: Bobbs-Merril, 1960).

8 *Lonzetta* v. *New Jersey*, 306 U.S. 451, 453 (1939).

9 *Weems* v. *United States*, 217 U.S. 349, 30 S.Ct. 544, 54 L.Ed 793 (1910).

10 *Harmelin* v. *Michigan*, 501 U.S. 957, 111 S.Ct. 2680, 115 L.Ed.2d 836 (1991); and *Robinson* v. *California*, 370 U.S. 660 82 S.Ct. 1417, 8 L.Ed.2d 758 (1962).

11 *People* v. *Lauria*, 251 Cal.App.2d 471, 59 Cal.Rptr. 628 (1967).

12 *Young* v. *State*, 32 Wis.2d 294, 145 N.W.2d 79 (1966).

13 *Le Barron* v. *State*, 32 Wis.2d 294, 145 N.W.2d 79 (1966).

14 "The Rough Sex Defense," *Time*, May 23, 1988, p. 55.

15 *People* v. *Alderson and Others*, 144 Misc.2d 133, 540 N.Y.S.2d 948 (N.Y. 1989).

16 *People* v. *Goetz*, 68 N.Y.2d 96, 506 N.Y.S.2d 18, 497 N.E.2d 41 (1986).

17 Alan Dershowitz, *The Abuse Excuse and Other Cop-Outs, Sob Stories, and Evasions of Responsibility* (Boston: Little, Brown, 1994).

18 *State* v. *Mitcheson*, 560 P.2d 1120 (Wash. 1977).

19 *State* v. *Valentine*, 935 P.2d 1294 (Wash. 1977).

20 Thomas A. Johnson, *Introduction to the Juvenile Justice System* (St. Paul, MN: West, 1975), pp. 1, 3.

21 Samaha, *Criminal Law*, p. 317.

22 M'Naghten's Case, 8 Eng. Rep. 718 (1843).

23 American Law Institute, *Model Penal Code and Commentaries*, Section 221.1.

24 Samaha, *Criminal Law*, p. 358.

Chapter 5, An Overview of Law Enforcement—*History, Agencies, Personnel, and Strategies*

1 Barbara Ortutary, "Facebook Warns Employers: Asking for Passwords on Job Seekers Called an Invasion of Privacy," *Pantagraph*, March 24, 2012, p. 7.

2 Erica Goode, "Police Lesson: Social Network Tools Have Two Edges," New York Times Online, April 7, 2011. Web posted at http://www.nytimes.com.

3 Brian A. Reeves, "Census of State and Local Law Enforcement Agencies, 2008" (Washington, DC: Bureau of Justice Statistics, 2011), p. 1.

4 U.S. Department of the Interior, Indian Affairs website, http://www.bia.gov/WhoWeAre/BIA/index.htm (accessed May 8, 2012).

5 Carrie Johnson, "Justice Dept. Focusing on Indian Country Crime," *Washington Post*, June 15, 2009.

6 Ibid.

7 Thomas A. Reppetto, *The Blue Parade* (New York: Free Press, 1978), p. 17.

8 Samuel Walker, *Popular Justice: A History of American Criminal Justice* (New York: Oxford University Press, 1980), p. 191.

9 Don Van Natta, Jr. and David Johnson, "Wary of Risk, Slow to Adapt, F.B.I. Stumbles in Terror War," New York Times Online, June 2, 2002. Web posted at http://www.nytimes.com.

10 DEA website, http://www.justice.gov/dea/about/mission.shtml (accessed May 20, 2012).

11 Reaves, "Census of State and Local Law Enforcement Agencies," p. 1.

12 Ibid., p. 2.

13 Ibid.

14 Brian A. Reaves, "Local Police Departments, 2007" (Washington, DC: Bureau of Justice Statistics, December 2010).

15 Ibid.

16 Ibid.

17 Reaves, "Census of State and Local Law Enforcement Agencies, 2008," p. 3.

18 James Fagin, "Authority," in Jay M. Shafritz (ed.), *International Encyclopedia of Public Policy and Administration* (Boulder, CO: Westview Press, 1998), p. 163.

19 Charles R. Swanson, Leonard Territo, and Robert W. Taylor, *Police Administration: Structures, Processes, and Behavior* (Upper Saddle River, NJ: Prentice Hall, 1998), pp. 160–161.

20 Title VII of the Civil Rights Act of 1964 as amended in 1972 by the Equal Employment Act requires that employment screening be based on bona fide occupational requirements (BFOQ). This requirement was further defined in *Griggs* v. *Duke Power Company* (1971), 401 U.S. 424; *Albemark Paper Company* v. *Moody* (1975), 422 U.S. 405, and *Washington* v. *Davis* (1979), 426 U.S. 299.

21 Brian A. Reaves and Andrew L. Goldberg, *Law Enforcement Management and Administrative Statistics, 1997. Data for Individual State and Local Agencies with 100 or More Officers* (Washington, DC: U.S. Department of Justice, April 1999), pp. 31–40.

22 Herman Goldstein, *Policing a Free Society* (Cambridge, MA: Ballinger, 1977), pp. 283–284.

23 Robert E. Worden, "A Badge and a Baccalaureate: Policies, Hypotheses, and Further Evidence," *Justice Quarterly*, Vol. 7 (September 1990), pp. 565–592; and Reaves and Goldberg, *Law Enforcement Management and Administrative Statistics, 1997. Data for Individual State and Local Agencies with 100 or More Officers*, pp. 31–40.

24 National Advisory Commission on Criminal Justice Standards and Goals, *Police* (Washington, DC: Government Printing Office, 1973), p. 369.

25 Kenneth J. Peak, *Policing in America* (Upper Saddle River, NJ: Prentice Hall, 1997), p. 86.

26 Bureau of Justice Statistics, Local Police website, http://www.bjs.gov/index.cfm?ty=tp&tid=71 (accessed May 20, 2012).

27 Ibid.

28 Peak, *Policing in America*, pp. 160–161.

29 Peak, *Policing in America*.

30 Bureau of Justice Statistics, Local Police.

31 Charles R. Swanson, Leonard Territo, and Robert W. Taylor, *Police Administration: Structures, Processes, and Behavior* (Upper Saddle River, NJ: Prentice Hall, 1998).

32 Dan Hinkel, "Prosecutors: Shooters Thought Police Were Rivals," *Chicago Tribune*, March 12, 2011.

33 Associated Press, "Calif. Man Convicted in Booby Trap Police Attacks," November 7, 2011. Web posted at http://news.yahoo.com/calif-man-convicted-booby-trap-police-attacks-0221588745.html (accessed September 14, 2012).

34 Allison Klein, Matt Zapotosky, and Josh White, "Killings in Line of Duty Haunt Police Officers," *Washington Post*, February 10, 2012.

35 Ibid.

36 Matthew Walberg, "College of DuPage Gives Emergency Training a Dose of Reality." Web posted at http://www.chicagotribune.com (accessed August 18, 2011).

37 "Suspect Threatens to Eat Police, Dogs," *Pantagraph*, January 13, 2012, p. A7.

38 Reaves, "Census of State and Local Law Enforcement Agencies, 2008," p. 8.

39 Peak, *Policing in America*, pp. 64–65.

40 ASIS International website, http://www.asisonline.org.

41 Egon Bittner, "Popular Conceptions about the Character of Police Work," In Carl B. Klockars and Stephen D. Mastrofski, eds., *Thinking about Police: Contemporary Readings* (New York: McGraw-Hill, 1991), pp. 35–51.

42 James Q. Wilson, *Police Behavior: The Management of Law and Order in Eight Communities* (Cambridge, MA: Harvard University Press, 1968, 1978).

43 Robert M. Fogelson, "Reform at a Standstill," in Carl B. Klockars and Stephen D. Mastrofski, eds., *Thinking about Police: Contemporary Readings* (New York: McGraw-Hill, 1992), pp. 117–119.

44 Samuel Walker, "Does Anyone Remember Team Policing? Lessons of the Team Policing Experience for Community Policing." *American Journal of Police*, Vol. XII, No. 1 (1993), p. 33.

45 Ibid.

46 Mark H. Moore and Robert C. Trojanowicz, "Corporate Strategies for Policing," *Perspectives on Policing*, No. 6 (Washington, DC: National Institute of Justice, November 1988).

47 George Kelling, "Police and Communities: The Quiet Revolution," *Perspectives on Policing*, No. 1 (Washington, DC: National Institute of Justice and Harvard University, June 1988).

48 Herman Goldstein, *The New Policing: Confronting Complexity* (Washington, DC: National Institute of Justice, December 1993), p. 1.

49 George Kelling and Mark H. Moore, "The Evolving Strategy of Policing," *Perspectives on Policing*, No. 4 (Washington, DC: National Institute of Justice and Harvard University, November 1988), p. 1.

50 George Kelling and William J. Bratton, "Implementing Community Policing: The Administrative Problem," *Perspective on Policing*, No. 17 (Washington, DC: National Institute of Justice and Harvard University, July 1993), p. 2.

51 Goldstein, *The New Policing: Confronting Complexity*, p. 4.

52 Lee P. Brown, "Community Policing: A Practical Guide for Police Officials," in *Perspectives on Policing*, No. 12 (Washington, DC: National Institute of Justice and Harvard University, September 1989).

53 Kelling and Bratton, "Implementing Community Policing: The Administrative Problem," p. 2.

54 "Jaywalking Ban," *Honolulu Advertiser*, August 8, 1998, p. E1.

55 Edwin Meese III, "Community Policing and the Police Officer," *Perspectives on Policing*, No. 15 (Washington, DC: National Institute of Justice and Harvard University, January 1993).

56 Ibid.

57 William Spelman and John E. Eck, *Problem-Oriented Policing* (Washington, DC: National Institute of Justice, January 1987), p. 2.

58 Ibid., p. 3.

59 Ibid., p. 4.

60 James Hernandez, *The Custer Syndrome* (Salem, WI: Sheffield, 1989), p. 184.

61 Meese III, "Community Policing and the Police Officer," p. 5.

62 Hernandez, *The Custer Syndrome*.

63 Hubert William and Patrick V. Murphy, "The Evolving Strategy of Police: A Minority View," *Perspectives on Policing*, No. 13 (Washington, DC: National Institute of Justice and Harvard University, January 1990), pp. 2, 12.

64 George L. Kelling, *What Works—Research and the Public* (Washington, DC: National Institute of Justice, 1988), p. 2.

65 Erica Goode, "With Green Beret Tactics, Combating Gang Warfare," New York Times Online, May 1, 2012. Web posted at http://www.nytimes.com.

66 Ibid.

67 Ibid.

68 Ibid.

Chapter 6, Oversight and Professionalism of Law Enforcement

1 Lycia Carter and Mark Wilson, "Measuring Professionalism of Police Officers," *Police Chief: The Professional Voice of Law Enforcement*, February 2012.

2 Ashley Halsey III and Tim Craig, "No More Jail Time for Expired License Plates, D.C. Council Says," *Washington Post*, October 18, 2011.

3 *Weeks* v. *United States*, 232 U.S. 383 (1914).

4 *Mapp* v. *Ohio*, 367 U.S. 643 (1961).

5 *Silverthorne Lumber Co.* v. *United States*, 251 U.S. 385 (1920).

6 *Wolf* v. *Colorado*, 338 U.S. 25 (1949).

7 *Mapp* v. *Ohio* (1961).

8 Edith Brady-Lunny, "Ruling May Alter City Police Search Policy," *Pantagraph*, December 14, 2011, p. A1.

9 Edith Brady-Lunny, "Judge Stands by Ruling that BPD Did Not Have Right to Search Car," *Pantagraph*, February 23, 2012.

10 Eric Lichtblau, "Police Are Using Phone Tracking as a Routine Tool," New York Times Online, March 31, 2012. Web posted at www.nytimes.com.

11 Ibid.

12 *Chimel* v. *California*, 395 U.S. 752 (1969).

13 *Harris* v. *United States*, 390 U.S. 234 (1968).

14 *Horton* v. *California*, 110 S.Ct. 2301 47 CrL. 2135 (1990).

15 *Arizona* v. *Hicks*, 107 S.Ct. 1149 (1987).

16 *Horton* v. *California*, (1990).

17 *Florida* v. *Jimeno*, 111 S.Ct. 1801 (1991).

18 *Carroll* v. *United States*, 267 U.S. 132 (1925).

19 *Ormelas* v. *United States*, 116 S.Ct. 1657, L.Ed. 2d 911 (1996).

20 *Colorado* v. *Bertive*, 479 U.S. 367, 107 S.Ct. 741 (1987).

21 *Terry* v. *Ohio*, 3129 U.S. 1 (1968).

22 *Minnesota* v. *Dickerson*, 113 S.Ct. 2130, 124 L.Ed. 2d 334 (1993).

23 *Hibel* v. *Sixth Judicial District Court of Nevada*, No. 03-5554 (2004).

24 Although a search warrant is required to conduct such an intrusive search, this does not rule out other approaches. The court has ruled that a suspect may be X-rayed and detained until the subject passes the swallowed objects. See *United States* v. *Montoya de Hernandez*, 473 U.S. 531, 105 S.Ct. 3304 (1985).

25 *New York* v. *Quarles*, 104 S.Ct. 2626, 81 L.Ed. 2d 550 (1984).

26 *Florida* v. *Bostick*, 111 S.Ct. 2382 (1991).

27 *United States* v. *Martinez-Fuerte*, 428 U.S. 543 (1976).

28 *Safford Unified School District* v. *Redding*, No. 08-479 2009.

29 *Illinois* v. *Gates*, 416 U.S. 318 (1982).

30 *United States* v. *Leon*, 468 U.S. 897, 104 S.Ct. 3405, 82 L.Ed. 2d 677, 52 U.S.L.W. 5515 (1984); and *Massachusetts* v. *Sheppard* 104 S.Ct. 3424 (1984).

31 *Olmstead* v. *United States*, 277 U.S. 438 (1928).

32 *Katz* v. *United States*, 389 U.S. 347 (1967).

33 Shankar Vedantam, "Confessions Not Always Clad in Iron," *Washington Post*, October 1, 2007, p. A3.

34 Annie Sweeney, "Burge Given 4½ Years in Prison," *Chicago Tribune*, January 21, 2011.

35 Dan Hinkel, "Ex-Waukegan Cop at Center of Rivera Case," *Chicago Tribune*, April 6, 2012.

36 Ibid.

37 *Gideon* v. *Wainwright*, 372 U.S. 335 (1963).

38 *In re Gault*, 387 U.S. 1 (1967).

39 *Escobedo* v. *Illinois*, 378 U.S. 478 (1964).

40 Kevin Johnson and Gary Fields, "Jewell Investigation Unmasks FBI 'Tricks,'" *USA Today*, April 9, 1997, p. 13A.

41 *Leyra* v. *Denno*, 347 U.S. 556 (1954).

42 *Miranda* v. *Arizona*, 384 U.S. 436 (1966).

43 *United States* v. *Karo*, 468 U.S. 705 (1984).

44 *United States* v. *Dionisio*, 410 U.S. 1 (1973).

45 *United States* v. *Wade*, 388 U.S. 218 (1967); *Kirby* v. *Illinois*, 406 U.S. 682 (1972); and *Foster* v. *California*, 394, U.S. 1 (1973).

46 *Tennessee* v. *Garner*, 471 U.S. 1 (1985).

47 Terry R. Sparher and David J. Goacopassi, "Memphis Revisited: A Reexamination of Police Shootings after the *Garner* Decision," *Justice Quarterly*, Vol. 9 (1992).

48 *Graham* v. *Conner*, 490 U.S. 386, 396–397 (1989).

49 Ian Lovett, "Pasadena Police Arrest 911 Caller After Unarmed Suspect Is Killed," New York Times Online, March 29, 2012. Web posted at http://www.nytimes.com.

50 Christine Eith and Matthew R. Durose, "Contacts between Police and the Public, 2008" (Washington, DC: Bureau of Justice Statistics, October 2011), p. 1.

51 Federal Bureau of Investigation, *Uniform Crime Reports: Crime in the United States, 2010*, "Persons Arrested." Web posted at http://www.fbi.gov.

52 Eith and Durose, "Contacts between Police and the Public, 2008," p. 1.

53 Eric H. Holder, Jr., Laurie O. Robinson, and John H. Laub, *NIJ Research in Brief: Police Use of Force, Tasers and Other Less-Lethal Weapons* (Washington, DC: National Institute of Justice, May 2011), p. ii.

54 Ibid., p. 5.

55 Ibid.

56 Ibid., p. 1.

57 Ibid., p. 2.

58 Ibid.

59 Ibid., p. 1.

60 Ibid., p. 4.

61 Ibid., p. 5.

62 Ibid., p. 6.

63 Ibid., p. 10.

64 Ibid., p. 16.

65 Don Van Natta, "Accused of Defying Orders, Miami Police Chief Is Fired," New York Times Online, September 12, 2011. Web posted at http://www.nytimes.com.

66 "Civil Rights and Resisting Arrest," New York Times Online, October 18, 2011. Web posted at http://www.nytimes.com.

67 Peter Applebome, "Police Gang Tyrannized Latinos, Indictment Says," New York Times Online, January 24, 2012. Web posted at http://www.nytimes.com.

68 Ibid.

69 Peter Applebome, "After Charges of Latino Abuse, Anger Shifts to a Mayor for His 'Taco' Remark," New York Times Online, January 25, 2012. Web posted at http://www.nytimes.com.

70 John Eligon, "Taking on Police Tactic, Critics Hit Racial Divide," New York Times Online, March 22, 2012. Web posted at http://www.nytimes.com.

71 Ibid.

72 *Jacobsen* v. *United States*, 112 S.Ct. 1535 (1992).

73 Holder, Robinson, and Laub, *NIJ Research in Brief: Police Use of Force, Tasers and Other Less-Lethal Weapons*, p. 11.

74 Matthew J. Hickman, "Citizens Complaints about Police Use of Force" (Washington, DC: Bureau of Justice Statistics, June 2006), p. 1.

75 Ibid., p. 3.

76 *Gray* v. *Bell*, 712 F. 2d 490, 507 (D.C. Cir. 1983); and *Hans* v. *Louisiana*.

77 *Northern Insurance Company of New York* v. *Chatham County*; and *Jinks* v. *Richland County*.

78 *Messerschmidt* v. *Millender*, No. 10-704; and *Malley* v. *Briggs* (1986).

79 Michael Kinsley, "When Is Racial Profiling Okay?" *Law Enforcement News*, October 15, 2001, p. 9.

80 Human Rights Watch, *Presumption of Guilt: Human Rights Abuses of Post-September 11 Detainee* (New York: Human Rights Watch, 2002), pp. 3, 6, 46, 55.

81 Eric Lichtblau, "Two Groups Charge Abuse of Witness Law," New York Times Online, June 27, 2005. Web posted at http://www.nytimes.com.

82 Human Rights Watch, *Presumption of Guilt: Human Rights Abuses of Post-September 11 Detainee*, p. 5.

83 Associated Press, "Bloomberg: NYPD's Monitoring of Muslims Was Legal," New York Times Online, February 24, 2012. Web posted at http://www.nytimes.com.

84 Matt Apuzzo and Adam Goldman, "NYPD Monitored Where Muslims Shopped, Prayed," *Pantagraph*, August 31, 2011.

85 Joseph Goldstein, "Kelly Defends Surveillance of Muslims," New York Times Online, February 27, 2012. Web posted at http://www.nytimes.com.

86 Associated Press, "NYPD Document: Gather Intel Info at Shiite Mosques," New York Times Online, February 2, 2012. Web posted at http://www.nytimes.com.

Chapter 7, The Court System

1 Administrative Office of the United States Courts, *Understanding the Federal Courts* (Washington, DC: Office of Judges Programs, Administrative Office of the United States Courts, 2003), p. 4.

2 Statistics Division Office of Judges Program, *Judicial Business of the United States Courts: 2011 Annual Report of the Director* (Washington, DC: Administrative Office of the United States Courts, 2011).

3 "Trust and the Supreme Court," New York Times Online, February 10, 2012. Web posted at www.nytimes.com.

4 Amy Gardner and Matt DeLong, "Newt Gingrich's Assault on 'Activist Judges' Draws Criticism, Even from Right," *Washington Post*, December 18, 2011.

5 "Trust and the Supreme Court," New York Times Online, February 10, 2012. Web posted at www.nytimes.com.

6 Supreme Court of the United States website, http://www.supremecourt.gov/about/traditions.aspx.

7 Ibid.

8 Administrative Office of the United States Courts, *Understanding the Federal Courts*.

9 Ibid.

10 CNN website, http://articles.cnn.com/1996-09-16/us/9609_16_simpson.case_1_murder-trial-sharon-rufo-ronald-goldman?_s=PM:US.

11 Supreme Court of the United States website, http://www.supremecourt.gov/about/institution.aspx.

12 Administrative Office of the United States Courts, *Understanding the Federal Courts*.

13 http://www.supremecourt.gov/about/constitutional.aspx.

14 Administrative Office of the United States Courts, Understanding the Federal Courts, p. 11.

15 United States Courts website, http://www.uscourts.gov/FederalCourts/UnderstandingtheFederalCourts/Jurisdiction.aspx.

16 Statistics Division Office of Judges Program, *Judicial Business of the United States Courts: 2011 Annual Report of the Director*.

17 Ibid.

18 Ibid.

19 Administrative Office of the United States Courts, *Understanding the Federal Courts*, p. 11.

20 http://www.uscourts.gov/FederalCourts/UnderstandingtheFederalCourts/Jurisdiction.aspx.

21 Associated Press, "Obama Moves at Historic Pace to Diversify Federal Bench: White Males under Half His Choices," *Washington Post*, September 13, 2011.

22 Ibid.

23 Jodi Kantor, "Justices Sit on Highest Court, but Still Live Without Top Security," New York Times Online, February 18, 2012. Web posted at www.nytimes.com.

24 Ibid.

25 Sourcebook of Criminal Justice Statistics website, http://www.albany.edu/sourcebook/pdf/t5702010.pdf.

26 State of Illinois website, http://www.state.il.us/court/supremecourt/annreport.asp#2010.

27 The United States Judicial System of Pennsylvania website, http://www.pacourts.us/links/public/aboutthecourts.htm.

28 Ibid.

29 State of Illinois website, http://www.state.il.us/court/supremecourt/historical/home.asp.

30 William Glaberson, "Broken Bench: In Tiny Courts of N.Y., Abuses of Law and Power," New York Times Online, September 25, 2006. Web posted at www.nytimes.com.

31 Ibid.

32 State of Illinois website, http://www.state.il.us/court/general/proceed.asp.

33 State of Oklahoma website, http://www.ok.gov/section.php?sec_id=67#skipcontent.

34 Texas Courts website, http://www.courts.state.tx.us.

35 New York State Unified Court System website, https://www.nycourts.gov/courts/townandvillage.

36 Glaberson, "Broken Bench: In Tiny Courts of N.Y., Abuses of Law and Power."

37 Ibid.

38 Ibid.

39 Ibid.

40 Ibid.

41 Glaberson, "Broken Bench: In Tiny Courts of N.Y., Abuses of Law and Power."

Chapter 8, Courtroom Participants and the Trial

1 Robert Barnes, "Supreme Court to Take Another Look at Prosecutorial Misconduct," *Washington Post*, October 30, 2011.

2 Bail is not required in a civil trial because the court has no jurisdiction to incarcerate either party of a civil suit prior to trial.

3 *Hudson* v. *Parker*, 156 U.S. 277 (1895).

4 *McKane* v. *Durston*, 153 U.S. 684 (1894).

5 *Stack* v. *Boyle*, 342 U.S. 1 (1951).

6 *Carlson* v. *Landon*, 342 U.S. 524 (1952); and *United States* v. *Salerno*, 55 U.S.L.W. 4663 (1987).

7 Bail Reform Act of 1984, 18 U.S.C. 4142(e).

8 *U.S.* v. *Hazzard*, 35 CrL. 2217 (1984); and *United States* v. *Motamedi*, 37 CrL. 2394, CA 9 (1985).

9 Erica Goode, "Stronger Hand for Judges in the 'Bazaar' of Plea Deals," New York Times Online," March 22, 2012. Web posted at http://www.nytimes.com.

10 Adam Liptak, "Justices' Ruling Expands Rights of Accused in Plea Bargains," New York Times Online, March 21, 2012. Web posted at http://www.nytimes.com.

11 Wayne R. LaFave and Jerald H. Israel, *Criminal Procedure* (St. Paul, MN: West, 1984), p. 626.

12 *United States* v. *Werker*, 5335 F.2d 198 (2d Cir. 1976), *certiorari* denied 429 U.S. 926.

13 Erica Goode, "Stronger Hand for Judges in the 'Bazaar' of Pleas Deals."

14 Richard Oppel, Jr., "Sentencing Shift Gives New Leverage to Prosecutors," New York Times Online, September 25, 2011. Web posted at http://www.nytimes.com.

15 Ibid.

16 Ibid.

17 *Klopfer* v. *North Carolina*, 386 U.S. 213 (1967).

18 *Beavers* v. *Haubert*, 1998 U.S. 77 (1905).

19 *Klopfer* v. *North Carolina*, 386 U.S. 213 (1967).

20 *Barker* v. *Wingo*, 407 U.S. 514 (1972).

21 Benjamin Weiser, "In New Jersey, Rules Are Changed on Witness IDs," New York Times Online, August 24, 2011. Web posted at http://www.nytimes.com.

22 Adam Liptak, "Eyewitness Evidence Needs No Special Cautions, Court Says," New York Times Online, January 11, 2012. Web posted at http://www.nytimes.com.

23 A 30-day extension is granted for indictment if the grand jury is not in session, and a 110-day extension can be granted between indictment and trials in cases in which the delay is due to problems associated with calling witnesses.

24 One of the strategies used against organized crime figures is to grant them immunity so that they cannot take the Fifth Amendment and then ask them questions regarding their organized crime activities and partners. If they refuse to answer, they can be incarcerated for contempt of court.

25 "A New Lawyer's Duty," The New York Times Online, May 1, 2012. Web posted at http://www.nytimes.com.

26 Bureau of Justice Statistics, *Indigent Defendants* (Washington, DC: Bureau of Justice Statistics, February, 1996).

27 Bureau of Justice Statistics, *Indigent Defense Services in Large Counties, 1999* (Washington, DC: Bureau of Justice Statistics, November 2000), p. 1.

28 Ann Fagan Ginger, *Minimizing Racism in Jury Trials* (Berkeley, CA: National Lawyers Guild, 1969).

29 *Taylor* v. *Louisiana*, 419 U.S. 522 (1975).

30 Bureau of Justice Statistics, *Report to the Nation on Crime and Justice* (Washington, DC: U.S. Department of Justice, 1988), p. 86.

Chapter 9, Sentencing

1 Robbie Brown, "Criminal Charges for 13 in Florida A&M Hazing Death," New York Times Online, May 2, 2012. Web posted at http://www.nytimes.com.

2 Associated Press, "Teen Who Threw Up on Teacher Sentenced," New York Times Online, July 27, 2005. Web posted at http://www.nytimes.com.

3 Associated Press, "Man Jailed for Not Licensing Cat in N.D.," New York Times Online, November 5, 2005. Web posted at http://www.nytimes.com.

4 Joyce Punick, "Can Bench Set Rules for Bedroom?" New York Times Online, May 13, 2004. Web posted at http://www.nytimes.com.

5 Associated Press, "Convicted Rapist Tells Judge He's Rude," New York Times Online, November 11, 2005. Web posted at http://www.nytimes.com.

6 Catrin Einhorn, "4 Decades after Shooting, Effort to Make Punishment Fit the Crime," New York Times Online, February 23, 2008. Web posted at http://www.nytimes.com.

7 Ibid.

8 Associated Press, "Conn. Police Fine Students for Cursing," New York Times Online, December 1, 2005. Web posted at http://www.nytimes.com.

9 "Britain Toughens Punishment Laws," *Honolulu Advertiser*, January 19, 2000, p. A3.

10 Associated Press, "Woman Sentenced to 100 Lashes for Extramarital Sex," *Pocono Record*, August 13, 2001, p. A5.

11 Associated Press, "Fourteen Men Lashed in Public in Iran for Drinking," *Pocono Record*, August 15, 2001, p. A5.

12 Associated Press, "Mayor: Sever Thumbs of Graffiti Artists, New York Times Online, November 5, 2005. Web posted at http://www.nytimes.com.

13 *Los Angeles Times*, "Sweden Pays 200 Who Were Forcibly Sterilized," *Honolulu Advertiser*, November 14, 1999, p. A17.

14 Associated Press, "Japanese Sterilized in Eugenics Program Demand Apology, Money," *Honolulu Advertiser*, December 21, 1997, p. G12.

15 Ira J. Silverman and Manuel Vega, *Corrections: A Comprehensive View* (Minneapolis: West, 1996), p. 63.

16 Associated Press, "That Man Needs to Be Dragged Himself," *Honolulu Advertiser*, February 24, 2000, p. A6.

17 Brown, "Criminal Charges for 13 in Florida A&M Hazing Death."

18 Associated Press, "Woman Gets House Arrest in Fla. Hit-and-Run," New York Times Online, November 5, 2005. Web posted at http://www.nytimes.com.

19 Paul J. Weber, "Police: Mother Says Devil Made Her Decapitate Infant Son," *Pantagraph*, July 28, 2009.

20 Joel Samaha, *Criminal Law* (Belmont, CA: West/Wadsworth, 1999), p. 317.

21 18 U.S.C. Section 17.

22 *United States* v. *Cameron*, 907 F.2d 1051, 1065 (11th Cir. 1990).

23 Michael Luo, "Some with Histories of Mental Illness Petition to Get Their Gun Rights Back," New York Times Online, July 2, 2011. Web posted at http://www.nytimes.com.

24 Ira Mickenberg, "A Pleasant Surprise: The Guilty but Mentally Ill Verdict Has Both Succeeded in Its Own Right and Successfully Preserved the Traditional Role of the Insanity Defense," *University of Cincinnati Law Review*, Vol. 55 (1987), pp. 987–991.

25 Samaha, *Criminal Law*, p. 315.

26 Ibid.

27 Carrie Johnson, "Parity in Cocaine Sentences Gains Momentum," *Washington Post*, July 25, 2009.

28 Adam Liptak, "Rendering Justice with One Eye on Re-election," New York Times Online, May 25, 2008. Web posted at http://www.nytimes.com.

29 Associated Press, "Louisiana: New Orleans Backtracks on Labeling Suspected Drug Houses," New York Times Online, February 15, 2012. Web posted at http://www.nytimes.com.

30 Ashley Surdin, "Radio Hosts Gleefully Try to Taint Jurors," *Washington Post*, May 17, 2008, p. A2.

31 Matthew R. Durose and Patrick A. Langan, *Felony Sentences in State Courts, 2002* (Washington, DC: Bureau of Justice Statistics, 2004), p. 9.

32 Even the Supreme Court has argued both sides of the argument on the constitutionality of victim impact statements. In *Booth* v. *Maryland*, 197 S.Ct. 2529 (1987), the U.S. Supreme Court ruled that victim impact statements in capital murder cases could lead to the risk that the death penalty would be imposed in an arbitrary and capricious manner. In *Payne* v. *Tennessee*, 501 U.S. 808 (1991), the U.S. Supreme Court reversed itself and ruled that in imposing sentence, victim impact statements were a legitimate method of presenting the harm done by the defendant.

33 G. Kleck, "Racial Discrimination in Criminal Sentencing: A Critical Evaluation of the Evidence with Additional Evidence on the Death Penalty," *American Sociological Review*, Vol. 46, 1981, pp. 783–805.

34 National Council on Crime and Delinquency, *National Assessment of Structured Sentencing* (Washington, DC: Bureau of Justice Administration, 1996).

35 Associated Press, "Courts Concentrate on Domestic Violence," *Honolulu Advertiser*, November 23, 1997, p. A16.

36 Alexandra Marks, "Prisons Review Results from Get Tough Era," *Christian Science Monitor*, May 12, 2004, p. 2.

37 Dean E. Murphy, "California Rethinking '3-Strikes' Sentencing," *New York Times Online*, October 24, 2004. Web posted at http://www.nytimes.com.

38 Associated Press, "ABA: End Mandatory Minimum Prison Terms," *New York Times Online*, June 23, 2004. Web posted at http://www.nytimes.com.

39 Ibid.

40 Ibid.

41 U.S. Sentencing Commission, *Federal Sentencing Guidelines Manual* (Washington, DC: Government Printing Office, 1987).

42 *Mistretta* v. *United States*, 488 U.S. 361 (1989).

43 *Melendez* v. *United States*, 117 S.Ct. 383, 136 L.Ed.2d 301 (1996).

44 Charles Lane, "Justices Order Review of 400-Plus Sentences," *Washington Post*, January 25, 2005, p. 7.

45 Linda Greenhouse, "Supreme Court Transforms Use of Sentence Guidelines," *New York Times Online*, January 13, 2005. Web posted at http://www.nytimes.com.

46 Carl Hulse and Adam Liptak, "New Fight over Controlling Punishments Is Widely Seen," *New York Times Online*, January 13, 2005. Web posted at http://www.nytimes.com.

47 Harry Elmer Barnes, *The Repression of Crime* (New York: George H. Doran, 1926), p. 220.

48 "Pakistan Criminal to Be Strangled," *Honolulu Advertiser*, March 17, 2000, p. A2.

49 Bureau of Justice Statistics, *Capital Punishment 2000* (Washington, DC: U.S. Department of Justice, December 2001).

50 Peter Slevin, "More in U.S. Expressing Doubts about Death Penalty," *Washington Post*, December 2, 2005.

51 Death Penalty Information Center, "Facts about the Death Penalty" (Washington, DC: Death Penalty Information Center, 2012), p. 4.

52 Plato, "Crito," *The Apology, Phaedo and Crito of Plato*, trans. Benjamin Jowett (New York: P.F. Collier & Son, 1937), p. 40.

53 Death Penalty Information Center, "Facts about the Death Penalty," p. 3.

54 Death Penalty Information Center, "Facts about the Death Penalty," p. 4.

55 Death Penalty Information Center, "Facts about the Death Penalty," p. 3.

56 Richard Cohen, "Despite Data, Politicians Continue to Support Death Penalty," *Pocono Record*, October 1, 2000, p. A7.

57 Southern Center for Human Rights website, http://www.schr.org (accessed January 1, 2002).

58 *Witherspoon* v. *Illinois*, 391 U.S. 510 (1968).

59 *Wilkerson* v. *Utah*, 99 U.S. 130 (1878).

60 *In re Kemmler*, 136 U.S. 436 (1890).

61 *Louisiana ex. rel. Francis* v. *Resweber*, 392 U.S. 459 (1947).

62 *Baze et al.* v. *Rees, Commissioner, Kentucky Department of Corrections, et al.* No. 07-539, decided April 16, 2008.

63 *Furman* v. *Georgia*, 408 U.S. 238 (1972).

64 *Woodson* v. *North Carolina*, 428 U.S. 280 (1976)

65 *Coker* v. *Georgia*, 433 U.S. 584 (1977)

66 *Gregg* v. *Georgia*, 428 U.S. 153 (1976).

67 Used in Arizona, Idaho, Montana, and Nebraska.

68 Used in Alabama, Delaware, Florida, and Indiana.

69 Associated Press, "Several States Reconsider Death Penalty Laws," *Honolulu Advertiser*, February 13, 2000, p. A10.

70 Ibid.

71 "Georgia's Electric Chair Found Cruel and Unusual," Southern Center for Human Rights website, http://www.schr.org (accessed December 28, 2001); Associated Press, "Judge Clears Florida to Use Injection for Execution," *Honolulu Advertiser*, February 13, 2000, p. A10; and "Gory Death on Florida Electric Chair Creates Furor," *Honolulu Advertiser*, July 9, 1989, p. A9.

72 "Texas Passes Ban on Executing Mentally Retarded Murderers," *Pocono Record*, May 27, 2001; Charles Lane, "High Court to Review Executing Retarded," *Washington Post*, March 27, 2001, p. 1; and Charles Lane, "Court Hears Death Penalty Case: Justices to Rule If Jury Got Proper Instruction on Retardation," *Washington Post*, March 28, 2001, p. A8.

73 Reuters, "Court Finds Death Penalty Is Misused in Kansas," *New York Times Online*, December 30, 2001. Web posted at http://www.nytimes.com.

74 "An Irrevocable Error," *Washington Post*, August 23, 2005, p. A14.

75 Associated Press, "Executed Woman to Get Pardon in Georgia," *New York Times Online*, August 16, 2005. Web posted at http://www.nytimes.com.

76 Michael L. Radelet and Hugo Adam Bedau, "Fallibility and Finality: Type II Errors and Capital Punishment," in Kenneth C. Hass and James A. Inciardi, eds., *Challenging Capital Punishment: Legal and Social Science Approaches* (Newbury Park, CA: Sage, 1988), pp. 91–112.

77 Adam Liptak, "Study Suspects Thousands of False Convictions," *New York Times Online*, April 19, 2004. Web posted at http://www.nytimes.com.

78 Deborah Hastings, "Police Say Evidence That Led to Execution Doesn't Actually Exist," *Pocono Record*, August 30, 2001, p. A5; and "Reasonable Doubts: Work under the Microscope," *Law Enforcement News*, May 31, 2001.

79 "Condemned Man Exonerated," *Honolulu Advertiser*, May 19, 1999, p. 3.

80 Associated Press, "Prosecutors on Trial in False Charge of Murder," *Honolulu Advertiser*, March 21, 1999, p. A10.

81 Todd S. Purdum, "Los Angeles Police Officer Sets Off Corruption Scandal," *New York Times Online*, September 18, 1999. Web posted at http://www.nytimes.com.

82 Associated Press, "30 Freed from Death Row Support Reform," *Honolulu Advertiser*, November 8, 1998, p. A10.

83 "Center Director Presents Wrongfully Convicted Client to U.S. Senate Judiciary Committee in Calling for Competent Counsel," Southern Center for Human Rights website, http://www.schr.org (accessed January 2, 2002).

84 Associated Press, "Judge Overturns Murder Conviction," *New York Times Online*, December 28, 2001. Web posted at http://www.nytimes.com.

85 Larry McShane, "62,000 Letters and 13 Years Later, Innocent Man Goes Free," *Pocono Record*, September 23, 2001, p. A4.

86 Associated Press, "Charges Dismissed for 17-Year Death Row Inmate," *Honolulu Advertiser*, March 12, 1999, p. A11.

87 Isidore Zimmerman, *Punishment Without Crime* (New York: Manor, 1973).

88 "Justice System Abuses Minorities at All Levels, Study Finds," *Honolulu Advertiser*, May 4, 2000, p. A3.

89 C. Spear, *Essays on the Punishment of Death* (London: John Green, 1844), pp. 227–232.

90 David A. Jones, *The Law of Criminal Procedure* (Boston: Little, Brown, 1981), p. 543.

91 President's Commission on Law Enforcement and Administration of Justice, *The Courts* (Washington, DC: U.S. Government Printing Office, 1967), p. 28.

92 Marvin E. Wolfgang and Marc Riedel, "Race Judicial Discretion and the Death Penalty," *Annals of the American Academy of Political and Social Science*, Vol. 407 (May 1973), p. 129.

93 Thomas J. Kell and Gennaro F. Vito, "Race and the Death Penalty in Kentucky Murder Trials: 1976–1991," *American Journal of Criminal Justice*, Vol. 20 (1995), pp. 17–36.

94 "Judge Overturns Death Sentence for Abu-Jamal," *Pocono Record*, December 19, 2001, p. A8.

95 "Judge Asks Prosecutors to Address Race Question in Death Penalty Case," *Pocono Record*, December 6, 2001, p. A4.

96 *McCleskey* v. *Kemp*, 41 CrL 4107 (1987).

97 Ibid.

98 "Justice System Abuses Minorities at All Levels, Study Finds," *Honolulu Advertiser*, May 4, 2000, p. A3.

99 Ibid.

100 "DNA Tests Clear 3,000 Suspects," *Honolulu Advertiser*, November 30, 1997, p. G2.

101 Associated Press, "Two Inmates Freed after New DNA Tests," *Honolulu Advertiser*, December 7, 1997, p. G10; Associated Press, "DNA Testing Frees Two Inmates Imprisoned 12 Years for Murder," *Honolulu Advertiser*, April 16, 1999, p. A6; Associated Press, "DNA Test Frees 60-Year-Old

Inmate," *Honolulu Advertiser*, September 2, 1999, p. 3A; Helen O'Neil, "False Conviction," *Pocono Record*, October 1, 2000, p. A5; Associated Press, "Convicted Killer Freed on New DNA Evidence," *Pocono Record*, March 16, 2001, p. B6; Associated Press, "Convicted Murderer Finally Acquitted," *Pocono Record*, April 5, 2001, p. A4; and Associated Press, "DNA Clears Man Jailed for 13 Years for Rape," *Pocono Record*, October 19, 2001, p. C10.

102 R. H. Melton, "Gilmore Sets Limit on DNA Evidence; Window Would Close 3 Years after Trial," *Washington Post*, March 28, 2001, p. 1.

103 Brooke A. Masters, "New DNA Testing Urged in Case of Executed Man," *Washington Post*, March 28, 2001, p. B1.

104 F. Carter Smith and Corbis Sygma, "A Life or Death Gamble," *Newsweek*, May 29, 2000, pp. 22–27.

105 Liptak, "Study Suspects Thousands of False Convictions."

106 Smith and Sygma, "A Life or Death Gamble."

107 Ibid.

108 Shaila Dewan, "Prosecutors Block Access to DNA Testing for Inmates," New York Times Online, May 17, 2009. Web posted at http://www.nytimes.com.

109 Death Penalty Information Center, "Facts about the Death Penalty," p. 4.

110 Ibid.

111 Ibid.

112 National Institute of Justice, *Effects of Judges' Sentencing Decisions on Criminal Careers* (Washington, DC: U.S. Department of Justice, November 1999).

113 Ibid.

114 Ibid.

115 Campbell Robertson, "Judge Blocks Death Sentence under Law on Race Disparity," New York Times Online, April 20, 2012. Web posted at http://www.nytimes.com.

116 Ibid.

Chapter 10, Jails and Prisons

1 Bridget O'Shea, "Psychiatric Patients With No Place to Go but Jail," New York Times Online, February 18, 2012. Web posted at http://www.nytimes.com.

2 Pam Belluck, "Life, with Dementia," New York Times Online, February 25, 2012. Web posted at http://www.nytimes.com.

3 Law Enforcement Assistance Administration (LEAA), *Two Hundred Years of American Criminal Justice: An LEAA Bicentennial Study* (Washington, DC: U.S. Department of Justice, 1976), p. 46.

4 Harry B. Weiss and Grace M. Weiss, *An Introduction to Crime and Punishment in Colonial New Jersey* (Trenton, NJ: Past Times Press, 1960), pp. 17–18.

5 Ibid., p. 18.

6 Ibid., p. 64.

7 Ibid., p. 10.

8 Ibid., p. 47.

9 Ibid.

10 Norman Johnston, *The Human Cage: A Brief History of Prison Architecture* (New York: Walker & Company, 1973), pp. 13–14.

11 The society still operates under the name of the Philadelphia Prison Society.

12 Joseph M. Hawes, "Prisons in Early Nineteenth Century America: The Process of Convict Reformation," in Joseph M. Hawes, ed., *Law and Order in American History* (Port Washington, NY: National University Publications, 1979), p. 39.

13 Law Enforcement Assistance Administration (LEAA), *Two Hundred Years of American Criminal Justice: An LEAA Bicentennial Study*, p. 47.

14 Hawes, "Prisons in Early Nineteenth Century America: The Process of Convict Reformation."

15 Ibid., p. 40.

16 Ibid., p. 39.

17 Law Enforcement Assistance Administration (LEAA), *Two Hundred Years of American Criminal Justice: An LEAA Bicentennial Study*, p. 49.

18 Lizette Alvarez "In Florida, Using Military Discipline to Help Veterans in Prison," New York Times Online, December 11, 2011. Web posted at http://www.nytimes.com.

19 O. L. Lewis, *The Development of American Prisons and Prison Customs, 1776–1845* (Montclair, NJ: Patterson Smith, 1996/1922).

20 D. J. Rothman, *The Discovery of the Asylum: Social Order and Disorder in the New Republic* (Boston: Little, Brown, 1971), p. 106.

21 Ira J. Silverman and Manuel Vega, *Corrections: A Comprehensive View* (Minneapolis/St. Paul: West, 1996), p. 78.

22 Ibid.

23 Law Enforcement Assistance Administration (LEAA), *Two Hundred Years of American Criminal Justice: An LEAA Bicentennial Study*, p. 49.

24 Lewis, *The Development of American Prisons and Prison Customs, 1776–1845*.

25 John W. Fountain, "Time Winds Down at a Storied Prison," New York Times Online, December 26, 2001. Web posted at http://www.nytimes.com.

26 E. Ayers, *Vengeance and Justice: Crime and Punishment in the 19th-Century American South* (New York: Oxford University Press, 1984).

27 M. C. Moos, *State Penal Administration in Alabama* (Tuscaloosa, AL: Bureau of Public Administration, University of Alabama, 1942), p. 18.

28 B. McKelvey, *American Prisons: A History of Good Intentions* (Montclair, NJ: Patterson Smith, 1977).

29 Thomas Murton and J. Hyams, *Accomplices to the Crime: The Arkansas Prison Scandal* (New York: Grove Press, 1969).

30 *Holt* v. *Sarver*, 309 F.Supp. 825 (1969); *Holt* v. *Sarver*, 309 F.Supp. 362 (E.D. Ark. 1970); and *Jackson* v. *Bishop*, 404 F.2d 571 (8th Cir., 1968).

31 *Holt* v. *Sarver*, 309 F.Supp. 362 (E.D. Ark. 1970).

32 Albert R. Hunt, "A Country of Inmates," New York Times Online, November 20, 2011. Web posted at http://www.nytimes.com.

33 Adam Liptak, "Inmate Count in U.S. Dwarfs Other Nations," New York Times Online, April 23, 2009. Web posted at http://www.nytimes.com.

34 Ibid.

35 Sandhya Somashekhar, "Webb Sets His Sights on Prison Reform," *Washington Post*, December 29, 2008, p. B-01.

36 Liptak, "Inmate Count in U.S. Dwarfs Other Nations."

37 N. C. Aizenman, "New High in U.S. Prison Numbers: Growth Attributed to More Stringent Sentencing Laws," *Washington Post*, February 29, 2008, p. A-01.

38 Marc Mauer and David Cole, "Five Myths about Americans in Prison," *Washington Post*, June 17, 2011.

39 David Jones, *History of Criminology: A Philosophical Perspective* (New York: Greenwood Press, 1986), p. 123; and Bureau of Justice Statistics, *Census of Jails, 1999* (Washington, DC: U.S. Department of Justice, August 2001), pp. 1–7.

40 American Correctional Association, *The American Prison from the Beginning* (Lanham, MD: American Correctional Association, 1983), p. 220.

41 Ibid.

42 Tim D. Munton, *Jails in Indian Country, 2010* (Washington, DC: Office of Justice Programs, December 2011), p. 5.

43 Bureau of Justice Statistics, *Census of Jails, 1999*, p. 3.

44 Shaila K. Dewan, "Sheriff Accepts Takeover of a Troubled Jail," New York Times Online, July 12, 2004. Web posted at http://www.nytimes.com.

45 Ibid.

46 Bureau of Justice Statistics, *Law Enforcement Management and Administrative Statistics, Sheriffs' Offices, 1999* (Washington, DC: U.S. Department of Justice, May 2001), p. 7.

47 Ibid.

48 Bureau of Justice Statistics, *Census of Jails, 1999*, p. 4.

49 Associated Press, "Arizona: Halt to a Detention Practice," New York Times Online, May 30, 2009. Web posted at http://www.nytimes.com.

50 Paige M. Harrison and Allen J. Beck, *Prisoners in 2004* (Washington, DC: Bureau of Justice Statistics, October 2005), p. 1.

51 Lauren E. Glaze, *Correctional Populations in the United States, 2010* (Washington, DC: Bureau of Justice Statistics, December 2011), p. 7.

52 Samantha Henry, "Prison Consultants Help Inmates Get Good Digs," *Pantagraph*, July 28, 2009.

53 Glaze, *Correctional Populations in the United States, 2010*.

54 American Correctional Association, *The American Prison*, p. 172.

55 Samantha Henry, "Prison Consultants Help Inmates Get Good Digs," *Pantagraph*, July 28, 2009.

56 Kevin Johnson, "Inmate Swap Worked—Until Imposter Fled," *USA Today*, October 25, 2000, p. 2.

57 Ibid.

58 Gary Marx, "Illinois Prisons: Low-Level Inmate Is Killed by Cellmate with Violent Past When Illinois Prison Officials OKd Housing Them Together," *Chicago Tribune*, May 5, 2009.

59 American Correctional Association, *The American Prison*, p. 172.

60 Paul Guerino, Paige M. Harrison, and William J. Sabol, *Prisoners in 2010*, (Washington, DC: Bureau of Justice Statistics, December 2011), p. 29.

61 Allen Beck and Jennifer Karberg, *Prison and Jail Inmates at Midyear 2000* (Washington, DC: U.S. Department of Justice, March 2001), p. 5.

62 John Scalla, *Federal Drug Offenders, 1999, with trends 1984–99* (Washington, DC: U.S. Department of Justice, August 2001), p. 6.

63 Anne L. Stahl, *Drug Offense Cases in Juvenile Courts, 1989–1998* (Washington, DC: U.S. Department of Justice, September 2001), p. 1.

64 Michele Staton-Tindall, "Female Offender Drug Use and Related Issues," http://www.nij.gov/topics/drugs/markets/adam/staton-paper.pdf (accessed September 25, 2012).

65 Ibid.

66 Laura Maruschak, *HIV in Prisons and Jails, 1999* (Washington, DC: U.S. Department of Justice, July 2001), p. 4.

67 Freda Adler, Sisters in Crime: The Rise of the New Female Criminal (New York: McGraw-Hill, 1975).

68 Caroline Wolf Harlow, *Prior Abuse Reported by Inmates and Probationers* (Washington, DC: U.S. Department of Justice, April 1999), p. 2.

69 Lennie Magida, "Doing Hard Time," *Honolulu Weekly*, July 14, 1993, p. 4.

70 Adrienne Lu, "For Transgender Detainees, a Jail Policy Offers Some Security," The New York Times Online, December 22, 2011. Web posted at http://www.nytimes.com.

71 Joan Petersilia, *When Prisoners Return to the Community* (Washington, DC: U.S. Department of Justice, November 2000), p. 4.

72 Marilyn C. Moses, *Keeping Incarcerated Mothers and Their Daughters Together: Girl Scouts beyond Bars* (Washington, DC: U.S. Department of Justice, October 1995), p. 1.

73 Petersilia, *When Prisoners Return to the Community*.

74 Moses, *Keeping Incarcerated Mothers and Their Daughters Together: Girl Scouts beyond Bars.*

75 Ibid.

76 Thomas Bonczar and Allen Beck, *Lifetime Likelihood of Going to State or Federal Prison* (Washington, DC: U.S. Department of Justice, March 1997), p. 1.

77 Ibid.

78 Mauer and Cole, "Five Myths about Americans in Prison."

79 Gannett News Service, "13% of U.S. Black Men Barred from Voting," *Honolulu Advertiser*, October 23, 1998, p. A3.

80 Ibid.

81 Ibid.

82 Nearly all jails, state prisons, and federal prisons have abandoned the use of the term *guard* to describe security personnel. In the federal prisons, these employees are called *correctional officers*. Correctional institutions do not consider the job title "guard" as appropriately describing the duties of the employee, and use of the term is considered rather derogatory and demeaning of the professionalism required for the position.

83 Glaze, *Correctional Populations in the United States, 2010*, p. 7.

84 Lizette Alvarez, "Florida: Senate Votes No on Privatization of Prisons," New York Times Online, February 14, 2012. Web posted at http://www.nytimes.com.

85 Associated Press, "Private Prisons Said to Do Little for Communities," *Pocono Record*, October 22, 2001, p. A5.

86 Ibid.

87 Ibid.

88 Ibid.

89 *Richardson et al. v. McKnight*, No. 96-318.

90 Bureau of Justice Statistics, *Challenging the Conditions of Prisons and Jails: A Report on Section 1983 Litigation* (Washington, DC: U.S. Department of Justice, December 1994).

91 Solomon Moore, "Texas: Inmate's Family Wins $42.5 Million Judgment," New York Times Online, www.nytimes.com, April 10, 2009. Web posted at http://www.nytimes.com.

92 Adam Liptak, "Inmate Was Considered 'Property' of Gang, Witness Tells Jury in Prison Rape Lawsuit," New York Times Online, September 25, 2005. Web posted at http://www.nytimes.com.

93 Ibid.

94 Human Rights Watch, *No Escape: Male Rape in U.S. Prisons*, http://www.hrw.org.

95 Allen J. Beck and Timothy A. Hughes, *Sexual Violence Reported by Correctional Authorities, 2004* (Washington, DC: Bureau of Justice Statistics, 2005), p. 1.

96 Carrie Johnson, "Panel Sets Guidelines for Fighting Prison Rape," *Washington Post*, June 23, 2009.

97 *PREA Data Collection Activities, 2012* (Washington, DC: Bureau of Justice Statistics, June 2012, p. 1.

98 Ibid., pp. 1–2.

99 Petersilia, *When Prisoners Return to the Community*, p. 4.

100 William J. Fraser, "Getting the Drop on Street Gangs and Terrorists," *Law Enforcement News*, November 30, 2001, p. 11.

101 Silverman and Vega, *Corrections*, p. 208.

102 Kevin Dayton, "Release Foreseen for Comatose Halawa Inmate," *Star Bulletin & Advertiser*, December 8, 1991, p. A3.

103 Petersilia, *When Prisoners Return to the Community*, p. 4.

104 Laura M. Maruschak and Allen J. Beck, *Medical Problems of Inmates, 1997* (Washington, DC: Bureau of Justice Statistics, January 2001), p. 1; and Laura M. Maruschak, *Medical Problems of Prisoners* (Washington, DC: Bureau of Justice Statistics, April 2008), Table 1.

105 "Unintended Consequences of Sentencing Policy: The Creation of Long-Term Healthcare Obligations," *Research in Review* (Washington, DC: U.S. Department of Justice, November 2001), p. 1.

106 Bureau of Justice Statistics, *Challenging the Conditions of Prisons and Jails: A Report on Section 1983 Litigation* (Washington, DC: U.S. Department of Justice, December 1994), p. 8.

107 Tammerlin Drummond, "Cellbock Seniors," *Time*, June 21, 1993, p. 60.

108 Ibid.

109 Adam Nossiter, "As His Inmates Grew Thinner, a Sheriff's Wallet Grew Fatter," New York Times Online, January 9, 2009. Web posted at http://www.nytimes.com.

110 Rebecca Widom and Theodore M. Hammett, *HIV/AIDS and STDs in Juvenile Facilities* (Washington, DC: U.S. Department of Justice, April 1996), p. 1.

111 Laura M. Maruschak, *HIV in Prisons and Jails*, p. 1.

112 Ibid.

113 Ibid.

114 Ibid.

115 Ibid.

116 Lawrence K. Altman, "Much More AIDS in Prisons Than in General Populations," New York Times Online, September 2, 1999. Web posted at http://www.nytimes.com.

117 Ibid.

118 Karen Wilcock, Theodore M. Hammett, Rebecca Widom, and Joel Epstein, *Tuberculosis in Correctional Facilities, 1994–1995* (Washington, DC: U.S. Department of Justice, July 1996), p. 1.

119 Ibid.

120 Doris James and Lauren Glaze, *Mental Health Problems of Prison and Jail Inmates* (Washington, DC: Bureau of Justice Statistics, September 2006), p. 1.

121 Fox Butterfield, "Experts Say Study Confirms Prison's New Role as Mental Hospital," New York Times Online, July 12, 1999. Web posted at http://www.nytimes.com.

122 Ibid.

123 Ibid.

124 ACLU Newswire, "Jails No Place for the Mentally Ill, ACLU of Mississippi Says," http://www.aclu.org/news (accessed January 16, 2002).

125 Paula M. Ditton, *Mental Health and Treatment of Inmates and Probationers* (Washington, DC: U.S. Department of Justice, July 1999), p. 1.

126 Petersilia, *When Prisoners Return to the Community*, p. 2.

127 ACLU News Wire, "Jails No Place for the Mentally Ill, ACLU of Mississippi Says."

128 Butterfield, "Experts Say Study Confirms Prison's New Role as Mental Hospital."

129 Erving Goffman, *Asylums: Essays on the Social Situation of Mental Patients and Other Inmates* (Garden City, NY: Anchor Books, 1961).

130 Ditton, *Mental Health and Treatment of Inmates and Probationers*, p. 9.

131 Linda A. Teplin, *Assessing Alcohol, Drug, and Mental Disorders in Juvenile Detainees* (Washington, DC: U.S. Department of Justice, January 2000), p. 1.

132 Kurt Erickson, Report: Prisons Need More Female Guards," *Pantagraph*, January 29, 2012, p. A5.

133 Debbie Cenziper and James Hohmann, "Some Guards at Md. Jail Have Arrest Records," *Washington Post*, July 25, 2008, p. A-01.

134 John Eligon, "Correction Officers Accused of Letting Inmates Run Rikers Island Jail," New York Times Online, January 23, 2009. Web posted at http://www.nytimes.com.

135 David T. Johnson and Meda Chesney-Lind, "Does Hawaii Really Need Another Prison?" *Honolulu Advertiser*, March 29, 1998, p. B1.

136 William D. Nueske, "Four Prisoners Who Killed Themselves Did Us a Favor," *Honolulu Star-Bulletin*, January 13, 1992.

137 Associated Press, "Official Resists Plan of Computers for Jail," *Pocono Record*, January 17, 2002, p. A4.

138 Ibid.

139 Anita Kumar, "Va. Prisons' Use of Solitary Confinement Is Scrutinized," *Washington Post*, January 7, 2012.

Chapter 11, Probation and Parole

1 Ian Urbina, "Virginia Sets Free 3 Sailors Convicted in Rape and Murder," *New York Times*, August 7, 2009.

2 Ibid.

3 Marlin P. Simpson, "Madigan v. Snyder The Illinois Supreme Court Evaluates the Governor's Pardon Power," *The Journal of the DuPage County Bar Association*, Vol. 16 (2003–2004), http://www.dcbabrief.org/vol160404art5.html.

4 Greg Stammar, "72-Year-Old Convicted Murderer Denied Parole," *Pantagraph*, December 16, 2011.

5 Ira Silverman and Manuel Vega, *Corrections: A Comprehensive View* (Minneapolis/Saint Paul, MN: West, 2006), p. 495.

6 Lauren E. Glaze and Thomas P. Bonczar, *Probation and Parole in the United States, 2010* (Washington, DC: Bureau of Justice Statistics, November 2011), p. 2.

7 Glaze and Bonczar, *Probation and Parole in the United States, 2010*, p. 33.

8 Ibid.

9 James M. Byrne, *Probation: A National Institute of Justice Crime File Series Study Guide* (Washington, DC: U.S. Department of Justice, 1988), p. 1.

10 In *Escoe v. Zerbst*, 295 U.S. 490 (135), the Court ruled that probation was an act of grace and thus the probationer was without due process rights. In *Mempa v. Rhay*, 389 U.S. 128 (1967), the Court reversed the ruling of *Escoe v. Zerbst* and ruled that probationers were entitled to due process rights.

11 *Gagnon v. Scarpelli*, 411 U.S. 778 (1973).

12 *Griffin v. Wisconsin*, 483 U.S. 868, 107 S.Ct. 3164 (1987).

13 *Minnesota v. Murphy*, 465 U.S. 420, 104 S.Ct. 1136, 79 L.Ed.2d 409 (1984).

14 *Gagon v. Scarpelli* (1973); and *Mempa v. Rhay* (1967).

15 Glaze and Bonczar, *Probation and Parole in the United States, 2010*, p. 5.

16 Ibid., p. 9.

17 *Kelly v. Robinson*, 479 U.S. 36, 107 S.Ct. 353, 93 L.Ed. 2d 216 (1986).

18 Silverman and Vega, *Corrections: A Comprehensive View*, p. 501.

19 H. Burns, *Corrections Organization and Administration* (St. Paul, MN: West, 1975).

20 G. I. Glardini, *The Parole Process* (Springfield, IL: Charles C. Thomas, 1959), p. 9.

21 David Dresser, *Practice and Theory of Probation and Parole* (New York: National Probation and Parole Association, 1957).

22 Marjorie Bell, ed., *Parole in Principle and Practice* (New York: National Probation and Parole Association, 1957).

23 A. W. Pisciotta, "Scientific Reform: The 'New Penology' at Elmira, 1876–1900," *Crime and Delinquency*, Vol. 29 (1983), pp. 613–630.

24 Chris L. Jenkins, "Ten Years after It Eliminated Parole, VA Considers Costs," *Washington Post*, December 25, 2004, p. B1.

25 Ibid.

26 Glaze and Bonczar, *Probation and Parole in the United States, 2010*, p. 9.

27 Ibid.

28 Glaze and Bonczar, *Probation and Parole in the United States, 2010*, pp. 6, 9.

29 Glaze and Bonczar, *Probation and Parole in the United States, 2010*, pp. 5, 9.

30 Glaze and Bonczar, *Probation and Parole in the United States, 2010*, pp. 10, 33.

31 Jenkins, "Ten Years after It Eliminated Parole, VA Considers Costs," p. B1.

32 Bureau of Justice Statistics, *Likelihood of Going to State or Federal Prison* (Washington, DC: U.S. Department of Justice, March 1997), p. 5.

33 Task Force on Corrections, *Task Force Report: Corrections* (Washington, DC: U.S. Government Printing Office, 1967).

34 William Parker, *Parole: Origins, Development, Current Practices and Statutes* (College Park, MD: American Correctional Association, 1975).

35 *Menechino v. Oswald*, 430 F. 2d 403 (2d Cir., 1970); and *Greenholtz v. Inmates of Nebraska Penal and Correctional Complex*, 422 U.S. 1 (1979).

36 *Johnson, U.S. ex. Rel. v. Chairman, New York State Board of Parole*, 363 F. Supp. 416, *aff'd*, 500 F. 2d 925 (2d Cir. 1971).

37 James Austin, "The Consequences of Escalating the Use of Imprisonment," *Corrections Compendium* (September 1991), pp. 1, 4–8.

38 Ibid.

39 Department of Justice website, http://www.usdoj.gov/uspc/relese.htm (accessed February 4, 2002).

40 Lauren E. Glaze and Seri Palla, *Probation and Parole in the United States, 2004* (Washington, DC: Bureau of Justice Statistics, 2005), p. 1.

41 Glaze and Bonczar, *Probation and Parole in the United States, 2010*, pp. 6, 9.

42 *Morrissey v. Brewer*, 408 U.S. 471 (1972).

43 Silverman and Vega, *Corrections: A Comprehensive View*, p. 495.

44 J. V. Barry, *Alexander Maconochie of Norfolk Island: A Study of Prison Reform* (London: Oxford University Press, 1958).

45 E. E. Dooley, "Sir Walter Crofton and the Irish or Intermediate System of Prison Discipline," *New England Journal on Prison Law*, Vol. 72 (Winter 1981).

46 Bureau of Justice Statistics, *Probation and Parole Violators in State Prison, 1991* (Washington, DC: U.S. Department of Justice, August 1995), p. 1.

47 Bob Moritz, "Changes Coming with New Probation, Sentencing Reform Law, Officials Say," *Arkansas News*, April 18, 2011. Web posted at http://arkansasnews.com/2011/04/18/changes-coming-with-new-probation-sentencing-reform-law-officials-say.

48 Ibid.

49 Ibid.

50 Ibid.

Chapter 12, Corrections in the Community

1 John Keilman, "Where Ex-Cons Get Another Chance," *Chicago Tribune*, October 16, 2011, Sec. 1, p. 20.

2 Ibid.

3 Caroline Wolf Harlow, "Education and Correctional Populations" (Washington, D.C.: Bureau of Justice Statistics, 2003), p. 1.

4 Jeremy Travis, Amy L. Solomon, and Michelle Waul, *From Prison to Home: The Dimensions and Consequences of Prisoner Reentry* (Washington, DC: The Urban Institute, April 2003).

5 Sara B. Miller, "A Shift to Easing Life after Prison," *Christian Science Monitor*, February 23, 2005, p. 1.

6 Lauren E. Glaze, *Correctional Population in the United States, 2010* (Washington, DC: Bureau of Justice Statistics, 2011), p. 3.

7 Jennifer Gonnerman, *Life on the Outside* (New York: Farrar, Straus & Giroux, 2004).

8 "New Strategies for Curbing Recidivism," New York Times Online, January 21, 2005. Web posted at http://www.nytimes.com.

9 Brent Staples, "Why Some Politicians Need Their Prisons to Stay Full," New York Times Online, January 21, 2005. Web posted at http://www.nytimes.com.

10 "Creating the Next Crime Wave," New York Times Online, March 13, 2004. Web posted at http://www.nytimes.com.

11 Joan Petersilia, "Challenges of Prisoner Reentry and Parole in California," California Policy Research Brief Series, June 2000. Web posted at http://www.ucop.educ/cprc/parole.html.

12 Joan Petersilia, *When Prisoners Return to the Community: Political, Economic, and Social Consequences* (Washington, DC: U.S. Department of Justice, November 2000), p. 1.

13 Jeremy Travis, *But They All Come Back: Rethinking Prisoner Reentry* (Washington, DC: U.S. Department of Justice, May 2000), p. 1.

14 Lauren E. Glaze and Thomas P. Bonczar, *Probation and Parole in the United States, 2010* (Washington, DC: Bureau of Justice Statistics, November 2011), pp. 5, 9.

15 Pew Center on the States, *State of Recidivism: The Revolving Door of America's Prisons* (Washington, DC: The Pew Charitable Trusts, April 2011, pp. 10, 14.

16 Ibid.

17 Pew Center on the States, *State of Recidivism: The Revolving Door of America's Prisons*, p. 2.

18 Petersilia, *When Prisoners Return to the Community: Political, Economic, and Social Consequences*, p. 3.

19 Ibid.

20 William J. Sabol, William P. Adams, Barbara Parthasarathy, and Yan Yaun, *Offenders Returning to Federal Prison, 1986–1997* (Washington, DC: Bureau of Justice Statistics, 2000), p. 1.

21 Council of State Governments, "Building Bridges: From Conviction to Employment, A Proposal to Reinvest Corrections Savings in an Employment Initiative," January 2003. Web posted at http://www.csgeast.org/crimpub.asp.

22 Nancy LaVigne, Cynthia A. Mamalian, Jeremy Travis, and Christy Visher, *A Portrait of Prisoner Reentry in Illinois* (Washington, DC: The Urban Institute, 2003).

23 Pew Center on the States, *One in 31: The Long Reach of American Corrections* (Washington, DC: The Pew Charitable Trusts, March 2009), p. 8.

24 Petersilia, *When Prisoners Return to the Community: Political, Economic, and Social Consequences*.

25 Travis, *But They All Come Back: Rethinking Prisoner Reentry*.

26 Sara Rimer, "At Last, the Windows Have No Bars," New York Times Online, April 29, 2004. Web posted at http://www.nytimes.com.

27 Petersilia, When Prisoners Return to the Community: Political, Economic, and Social Consequences.

28 Kirk Eckholm, "In Prisoners' Wake, a Tide of Troubled Kids," New York Times Online, July 5, 2009. Web posted at http://www.nytimes.com.

29 Petersilia, When Prisoners Return to the Community: Political, Economic, and Social Consequences.

30 Travis, But They All Come Back: Rethinking Prisoner Reentry, p. 3.

31 Ibid.

32 Mark S. Umbreit, "Community Service Sentencing: Last Alternative or Added Sanction? Federal Probation, Vol. 45, 1981, pp. 3–14.

33 Ira J. Silverman and Manuel Vega, Corrections: A Comprehensive View (St. Paul, MN: West, 1996), p. 515.

34 Ibid.

35 Travis, But They All Come Back: Rethinking Prisoner Reentry.

36 Analysis by Eric Cadora and Charles Swartz for the Community Justice Project at the Center for Alternative Sentencing and Employment Services (CASE), 1999, cited in Jeremy Travis, Amyu L. Solomon, and Michelle Waul, From Prison to Home: The Dimensions and Consequences of Prisoner Reentry (Washington, DC: The Urban Institute, April 2003).

37 "Report of the Reentry Policy Council: Report Preview: Charting the Safe and Successful Return of Prisoners to the Community." Web posted at http://www.reentrypolicy.org.

38 Petersilia, When Prisoners Return to the Community: Political, Economic, and Social Consequences.

39 Elijah Anderson, Streetwise: Race, Class, and Change in an Urban Community (Chicago: University of Chicago Press, 1990), p. 4.

40 Petersilia, "Challenges of Prisoner Reentry and Parole in California."

41 Joan Moore, "Bearing the Burden: How Incarceration Weakens Inner-City Communities," Paper read at the Unintended Consequences of Incarceration Conference at the Vera Institute of Justice, New York City, 1996.

42 Office of Justice Programs, Rethinking Probation: Community Supervision, Community Safety (Washington, DC: U.S. Department of Justice, December 1998), p. 1.

43 Ibid.

44 Petersilia, When Prisoners Return to the Community: Political, Economic, and Social Consequences.

45 Glaze and Bonczar, Probation and Parole in the United States, 2010.

46 T. Clear and P. Hardyman, "The New Intensive Supervision Movement," Crime and Delinquency, Vol. 35, 1990, pp. 42–60.

47 R. Carter and L. Wilkins, "Caseloads: Some Conceptual Models," in R. Carter and L. Wilkins, eds., Probation, Parole and Community Corrections (New York: John Wiley, 1976).

48 Office of Justice Programs, Rethinking Probation: Community Supervision, Community Safety, p. 2.

49 Petersilia, "Challenges of Prisoner Reentry and Parole in California," p. 2.

50 Ibid.

51 Marta Nelson and Jennifer Trone, Why Planning for Release Matters (New York: Vera Institute of Justice, 2000), p. 2.

52 Ibid.

53 James P. Levine et al. Criminal Justice in America: Law in Action (New York: John Wiley, 1986), p. 549.

54 Administrative Office of the Courts, "New Jersey Intensive Supervision Program, Progress Report 12, No. 1" (Trenton, NJ: State of New Jersey, 1995), p. 3.

55 New Jersey Intensive Probation Supervision Program Statistical Highlights, December 31, 2010. Web posted at http://www.judiciary.state.nj.us/probsup/isp_stat_highlights.pdf.

56 "Going Home: The Serious and Violent Offender Reentry Initiative," February 16, 2002. Web posted at http://www.ojp.usdoj.gov/reentry/communities.htm.

57 Joan Petersilia, Expanding Options for Criminal Sentencing (Santa Monica, CA: The Rand Corporation, 1987).

58 Ibid.

59 Cherie L. Clark, David W. Aziz, and Doris L. MacKenzie, Shock Incarceration in New York: Focus on Treatment (Washington, DC: U.S. Department of Justice, August 1994), p. 2.

60 Silverman and Vega, Corrections: A Comprehensive Review, p. 529.

61 Doris L. MacKenzie and Deanna B. Ballow, "Shock Incarceration Programs in State Correctional Jurisdictions—An Update," NIJ Report, Shock Incarceration (May/June 1989), pp. 9–10; and D. G. Parent, Shock Incarceration: An Overview of Existing Programs (Washington, DC: U.S. Department of Justice, 1989).

62 Clark, Aziz, and MacKenzie, Shock Incarceration in New York: Focus on Treatment, p. 5.

63 Ibid., p. 4.

64 Steve Chapman, "The False Hope of Sex Offender Registries," Chicago Tribune, August 18, 2011.

65 Clark, Aziz, and MacKenzie, Shock Incarceration in New York: Focus on Treatment.

66 Ibid., p. 9.

67 Ibid., p. 10.

68 Ibid., p. 6.

69 Doris MacKenzie and Claire Souryal, Multisite Evaluation of Shock Incarceration (Washington, DC: National Institute of Justice, September 1994), p. 1.

70 Clark, Aziz, and MacKenzie, Shock Incarceration in New York: Focus on Treatment, p. 4.

71 Joan Petersilia, "House Arrest," National Institute of Justice, Crime File Study Guide (Washington, DC: U.S. Department of Justice, 1988), p.1.

72 Silverman and Vega, Corrections: A Comprehensive Review, p. 523.

73 Ibid., p. 524.

74 M. Renzema and D. Skelton, Final Report: The Use of Electronic Monitoring by Criminal Justice Agencies (Washington, DC: U.S. Department of Justice, 1990), pp. 1–3.

75 Petersilia, "House Arrest."

76 David C. Anderson, Sensible Justice: Alternatives to Prison (New York: The New Press, 1998), p. 44.

77 Ibid.

78 John Schwartz, "Internet Leash Can Monitor Sex Offenders," New York Times Online, December 31, 2001. Web posted at http://www.nytimes.com.

79 Christy Gutowski, "Woman Convicted in Notorious Triple Murder: 'I Have Served Enough Time,'" Chicago Tribune, January 22, 2012, Sec. 1, p. 12.

80 Christopher Baird and Dennis Wagner, Evaluation of the Florida Community Control Program (Madison, WI: National Council on Crime and Delinquency, 1990).

81 J. Muncio, "A Prisoner in My Home: The Politics and Practice of Electronic Monitoring," Probation Journal, Vol. 37, 1990, pp. 72–77.

82 Federal Government Information Technology, Electronic Surveillance and Civil Liberties (Washington, DC: Congress of the United States, Office of Technology Assessment, 1985); and R. Ball, R. C. Huff, and J. P. Lilly, House Arrest and Correctional Policy: Doing Time at Home (Newbury Park, CA, Sage, 1988).

83 Reginald A. Wilkinson, "Offender Reentry: A Storm Overdue," January 16, 2002. Web posted at http://www.drc.state.oh.us/Articles/article66.htm.

84 Ibid.

85 "History of the Office of Community Corrections," February 16, 2002. Web posted at http://www.michigan.gov.

86 National Criminal Justice Reference Service, "Prisoner Reentry Resources—Legislation," February 17, 2002. Web posted at http://www.ncjrs.org/reentry/legislation.htm.

87 Ibid.

88 "Going Home: The Serious and Violent Offender Reentry Initiative."

89 Jacqui Goddard, "Florida's New Approach to Inmate Reform: A Faith-Based Prison," Christian Science Monitor, December 24, 2003, p. 1.

90 Fox Butterfield, "Repaving the Long Road Out of Prison," New York Times Online, May 4, 2004. Web posted at http://www.nytimes.com.

91 Nelson and Trone, Why Planning for Release Matters.

92 Elmer H. Johnson and Kenneth E. Kotch, "Two Factors in Development of Work Release: Size and Location of Prisons," Journal of Criminal Justice, Vol. 1 (March 1973), pp. 44–45.

93 Silverman and Vega, Corrections: A Comprehensive Review, p. 520.

94 Harry Holzer, What Employers Want: Job Prospects for Less-Educated Workers (New York: Russell Sage, 1996).

95 Petersilia, When Prisoners Return to the Community: Political, Economic, and Social Consequences, p. 4.

96 U.S. Department of Labor, *From Hard Time to Full Time: Strategies to Move Ex-Offenders from Welfare to Work* (Washington, DC: Department of Labor, June 2001), p. 7.

97 "Woman Files Lawsuit against Company for Using Inmate Telemarketers, *Pocono Record*, November 15, 2001, p. A5.

98 Cheryl Dahle, "What's That Felony on Your Resume," New York Times Online, October 17, 2004. Web posted at http://www.nytimes.com.

99 Nelson and Trone, *Why Planning for Release Maters*, pp. 4–5.

100 Ibid.

101 Ibid., p. 3.

102 Rhonda Cook, "State Prison-to-Work Program Falls Short," *Atlanta Journal-Constitution*, June 1, 2000.

103 Nelson and Trone, *Why Planning for Release Matters*, p. 2.

104 U.S. Department of Labor, *From Hard Time to Full Time: Strategies to Move Ex-Offenders from Welfare to Work*, p. 10.

105 Ibid., p. 11.

106 Susan Kreifels, "New Rules Add Teeth to Convict Hiring Laws," *Honolulu Star-Bulletin*, January 9, 1998, pp. A1, A8.

107 U.S. Department of Labor, *From Hard Time to Full Time: Strategies to Move Ex-Offenders from Welfare to Work*, pp. 9–10.

108 David Koeppel, "Job Fairs Give Ex-Convicts Hope in Down Market," New York Times Online, December 26, 2001. Web posted at http://www.nytimes.com.

109 George E. Sexton, *Work in American Prisons: Joint Ventures with the Private Sector* (Washington, DC: U.S. Department of Justice, November 1995), pp. 2, 10.

110 Ibid.

111 Ronald D. Stephens and June Lane Arnette, *From the Courthouse to the Schoolhouse: Making Successful Transitions* (Washington, DC: U.S. Department of Justice, February 2000), p. 1.

112 Ibid., p. 3.

113 Thomas Barlett, "Prime Numbers," *Chronicle of Higher Education*, January 19, 2002, p. A7.

114 Ibid.

115 Peter Monaghan, "U of Alaska Declines to Admit a Killer to Its Social-Work Program, Raising Questions—and a Lawsuit," *Chronicle of Higher Education*, July 13, 2005.

116 O. I. Keller and B. S. Alper, *Halfway Houses: Community-Centered Corrections and Treatment* (Lexington, MA: Health Lexington Books, 1970).

117 Task Force on Corrections, *Task Force Report: Corrections* (Washington, DC: President's Commission on Law Enforcement and Administration of Justice, U.S. Government Printing Office, 1967); and Task Force on Corrections, *Task Force Report: Corrections* (Washington, DC: National Advisory Commission on Criminal Justice Standards and Goals, 1973).

118 Office of Justice Programs, *Rethinking Probation: Community Supervision, Community Safety*, pp. 19–21.

119 Dale G. Parent, *Day Reporting Centers for Criminal Offenders: A Descriptive Analysis of Existing Programs* (Washington, DC: U.S. Department of Justice, 1990), p. 1.

120 Dale G. Parent, "Day Reporting Centers," in Michael Tonry and Kate Hamilton, eds., *Intermediate Sanctions in Overcrowded Times* (Boston: Northeastern University Press, 1995), p. 15.

121 *Criminal Justice Abstracts* (Monsey, NY: Willow Tree Press, 1998), pp. 105–106.

122 Drug Court Clearinghouse and Technical Assistance Project, "Looking at a Decade of Drug Courts," November 16, 2001. Web posted at http://www.ojp.usdoj.gov.

123 Adele Harrell, Shannon Cavanagh, and John Roman, *Evaluation of the D.C. Superior Court Drug Intervention Programs* (Washington, DC: National Institute of Justice, April 2000), pp. 1–2.

124 John Scalia, *Federal Drug Offenders, 1999 with Trends 1984–1999* (Washington, DC: U.S. Department of Justice, August 2001), p. 10.

125 Ibid.

126 Paul Guerino, Paige M. Harrison, and William J. Sabol, *Prisoners in 2010* (Washington DC: Bureau of Justice Statistics, December 2011), pp. 29, 30.

127 Elizabeth A. Peyton and Robert Gossweiler, *Treatment Services in Adult Drug Courts: Report on the 1999 National Drug Court Treatment Survey Executive Summary* (Washington, DC: U.S. Department of Justice, May 2001), p. 5.

128 Allen J. Beck, "State and Federal Prisoners Returning to the Community: Finding from the Bureau of Justice Statistics," paper presented at the First Reentry Courts Initiative Cluster Meeting, Washington, DC, April 13, 2000.

129 Drug Court Clearinghouse and Technical Assistance Project, "Looking at a Decade of Drug Courts."

130 Ibid.

131 Ibid.

132 Ibid.

133 Harrell, Cavanagh, and Roman, *Evaluation of the D.C. Superior Court Drug Intervention Programs*, p. 2.

134 Ibid.

135 Tribal Law and Policy Institute, *Healing to Wellness Courts: A Preliminary Overview of Tribal Drug Courts* (Washington, DC: U.S. Department of Justice, July 1999), p. 14.

136 Ibid., p. 9.

137 Ibid., p. 2.

138 Ibid., p. 4.

139 Ibid., pp. 9–10.

140 Ibid., p. 12.

141 Ibid., p. 13.

142 Ibid., p. 14.

143 National Institute of Justice, "Reducing Offender Drug Use Through Prison-Based Treatment," *NIJ Journal* (July 2000), p. 21; and Bureau of Justice Assistance, *Treatment Accountability for Safer Communities* (Washington, DC: U.S. Department of Justice, November 1995), pp. 1–2.

144 Bureau of Justice Assistance, *Treatment Accountability for Safer Communities*, p. 1.

145 National Institute of Justice, "Reducing Offender Drug Use Through Prison-Based Treatment."

146 Joan Petersilia and Elizabeth Piper Deschenes, "What Punishes? Inmates Rank the Severity of Prison Versus Intermediate Sanctions," in Joan Petersilia, ed., *Community Corrections: Probation and Parole and Intermediate Sanctions* (New York: Oxford University Press, 1998), pp. 149–159.

147 Joan Petersilia, "When Probation Becomes More Dreaded Than Prison," *Federal Probation*, Vol. 54, 1990, pp. 23–27.

148 Rick Lyman, "Marriage Programs Try to Instill Bliss and Stability Behind Bars," New York Times Online, April 16, 2005. Web posted at http://www.nytimes.com.

149 Liam Ford, "Man Arrested for Bank Robbery, 5 Days after Being Paroled," *Chicago Tribune*, March 5, 2012.

Chapter 13, The Juvenile Justice System

1 *Juvenile Justice: A Century of Change* (Washington, DC: Office of Juvenile Justice and Delinquency Prevention, December 1999), p. 1.

2 "Juvenile Detention in New York—Then and Now," New York City Department of Juvenile Justice, April 28, 2005. Web posted at http://www.correctionhistory.org/html/chronicl/djj/djj20yrs3.htm.

3 *Juvenile Justice: A Century of Change*, p. 2.

4 "A Brief History," New York House of Refuge. Web posted at http://www.archives.nysed.gov/a/research/res_topics_ed_reform_history.shtml.

5 Ibid.

6 Ibid.

7 Ibid.

8 Ibid.

9 "Department of Juvenile Services: Origin," Maryland Department of Juvenile Services. Web posted at http://www.djs.state.md.us/history.html.

10 "Juvenile Delinquency: A Rising Concern: 1861–1916." Web posted at http://www.archives.nysed.gov/a/researchroom/rr_ed_reform_intro.shtml.

11 *Juvenile Justice: A Century of Change*.

12 Ibid., p. 1.

13 Ibid., p. 3.

14 Howard N. Snyder and Melissa Sickmund, *Juvenile Offenders and Victims: 1999 National Report* (Washington, DC: Office of Juvenile Justice and Delinquency Prevention, September 1999), p. 86.

15 *Juvenile Justice: A Century of Change*, p. 6.

16 History of Juvenile Justice in Oregon," Oregon Youth Authority. Web posted at http://www.oregon.gov/OYA/history.shtml.

17 *Kent v. United States*, 383 U.S. 541, 86 S.Ct. 1045 (1966).

18 Snyder and Sickmund, *Juvenile Offenders and Victims: 1999 National Report*, p. 90.

19 Ibid.

20 *In re Gault*, 387 U.S. 1, 87 S.Ct. 1428 (1967).

21 Snyder and Sickmund, *Juvenile Offenders and Victims: 1999 National Report*, p. 90.

22 Ibid., pp. 90–91.

23 *In re Winship*, 397 U.S. 358, 90 S.Ct. 1068 (1970).

24 Snyder and Sickmund, *Juvenile Offenders and Victims: 1999 National Report*, pp. 90–91.

25 Ibid., p. 92.

26 Ibid.

27 Ibid.

28 *Schall* v. *Martin*, 467 U.S. 253, 104 S.Ct. 2403 (1984).

29 *Oklahoma Publishing Company* v. *District Court in and for Oklahoma City*, 480 U.S. 208, 97 S.Ct. 1045 (1977).

30 *Smith* v. *Daily Mail Publishing Company*, 443 U.S. 97, 99 S.Ct. 2667 (1979).

31 Charles Puzzanchera and Benjamin Adams, *Juvenile Arrests 2009* (Washington, DC: Office of Juvenile Justice and Delinquency Prevention, December 2011), pp. 1, 8.

32 Wendy S. McClanahan, *Alive at 25: Reducing Youth Violence through Monitoring and Support* (Philadelphia: Public/Private Ventures, 2004), p. 1.

33 Jason Ziedenberg, *You're An Adult Now: Youth in Adult Criminal Justice Systems* (Washington, DC: National Institute of Corrections, December 2011), p. 15.

34 Ibid., p. 3.

35 Puzzanchera and Adams, *Juvenile Arrests 2009*, p. 7.

36 Ibid., p. 1.

37 Snyder and Sickmund, *Juvenile Offenders and Victims*, p. 103.

38 Puzzanchera and Adams, *Juvenile Arrests 2009*, p.5.

39 Snyder and Sickmund, *Juvenile Offenders and Victims: 1999 National Report*, p. 106.

40 Patrick Griffin and Melanie Bozynski, "National Overviews," *State Juvenile Justice Profiles* (Pittsburgh, PA: National Center for Juvenile Justice, May 1, 2005). Web posted at http://www.ncjj.org/stateprofiles.

41 Ibid.

42 Ibid.

43 Ibid.

44 Snyder and Sickmund, *Juvenile Offenders and Victims: 1999 National Report*.

45 Ibid.

46 Ibid.

47 International Association of Chiefs of Police, *Juvenile Justice Training Needs Assessment: A Survey of Law Enforcement* (Washington, DC: Office of Juvenile Justice and Delinquency Prevention, 2011), pp. 10–11.

48 *OJJDP Statistical Briefing Book*, http://www.ojjdp.gov/ojstatbb/court/JCSCF_Display.asp?ID=qa06601&year=2008&group=1&estimate=1 (accessed May 06, 2011).

49 Jeffrey A. Butts and Janeen Buck, *Teen Courts: A Focus on Research* (Washington, DC: Office of Juvenile Justice and Delinquency Prevention, October 2000).

50 Ibid., p. 1.

51 Caroline S. Cooper, *Juvenile Drug Court Programs* (Washington, DC: U.S. Department of Justice, May 2001), p. 1.

52 Ibid., p. 3.

53 Ibid., p. 6.

54 Ibid., p. 9.

55 Ibid., p. 13.

56 Ibid., p. 11.

57 Ibid., p. 13.

58 *OJJDP Statistical Briefing Book*.

59 Melissa Sickmund, *Juveniles in Correction* (Washington, DC: Office of Juvenile Justice and Delinquency Prevention, June 2004).

60 Gail A. Wasserman, Susan J. Ko, and Larkin S. McReynolds, *Assessing the Mental Health Status of Youth in Juvenile Justice Settings* (Washington, DC: Office of Juvenile Justice and Delinquency Prevention, August 2004), pp. 3–4.

61 Howard N. Snyder and Monica Swahn, *Juvenile Suicides, 1981–1998* (Washington, DC: Office of Juvenile Justice and Delinquency Prevention, March 2004), pp. 1–2.

62 Richard G. Wiebush et al., *Implementation and Outcome Evaluation of the Intensive Aftercare Program: Final Report* (Washington, DC: Office of Juvenile Justice and Delinquency Prevention, March 2005).

63 Ibid., pp. 82–83.

64 Doris MacKenzie, Angela Gover, Gaylene Armstrong, and Ojmarr Mitchell, *A National Study Comparing the Environment of Boot Camps with Traditional Facilities for Juvenile Offenders* (Washington, DC: U.S. Department of Justice, August 2001), p. 1.

65 Ibid., p. 3–4.

66 Ibid., p. 1–2.

67 Ibid., p. 2.

68 Ibid., p. 11.

69 Michael Janofsky, "States Pressed as 3 Boys Die at Boot Camps," New York Times Online, September 7, 2001. Web posted at http://www.nytimes.com.

70 Ibid.

71 Michael Janofsky, "Boot Camp Proponent Becomes Focus of Critics," New York Times Online, August 9, 2001. Web posted at http://www.nytimes.com.

72 James Sterngold, "Head of Camp in Arizona Is Arrested in Boy's Death," New York Times Online, February 16, 2002. Web posted at http://nytimes.com.

73 Snyder and Sickmund, *Juvenile Offenders and Victims*, p. 211.

74 *Thompson* v. *Oklahoma*, 487 U.S. 815, 818–838 (1988).

75 *Stanford* v. *Kentucky*, 492 U.S. 361 (1989).

76 *State* v. *Simmons*, 944 S.W.2d 165 (en banc), *cert. denied*, 522 U.S. 953 (1997); and *Simmons* v. *Bowersox*, 235 F.3d 1124, 1127 (CA8), *cert. denied*, 534 U.S. 924 (2001).

77 *Atkins* v. *Virginia*, 536 U.S. 304 (2002).

78 Rolf Loeber, David P. Farringtron, and David Petechuk, *Child Delinquency: Early Intervention and Prevention* (Washington, DC: Office of Juvenile Justice and Delinquency Prevention, May 2003), p. 3.

79 Ibid., p. 1.

80 Ibid., p. 4.

81 Ibid.

82 Ibid.

83 Ibid., p. 5.

84 Ibid.

85 Ibid., p. 6.

86 Ibid., p. 8.

87 Ibid., p. 14.

88 Ibid., p. 10.

89 Ibid., p, 11.

90 Ibid., p. 13.

91 Edward P. Mulvey, "Highlights From Pathways to Desistance: A Longitudinal Study of Serious Adolescent Offenders," (Washington, DC, Delinquency Prevention, March 2011), p. 1.

92 Ibid.

93 Ibid.

94 Ibid.

95 Ibid., p. 3.

96 Ibid.

97 Arlen Egley, Jr. and James C. Howell, *Highlights of the 2010 Nation Youth Gang Survey* (Washington, DC: Office of Juvenile Justice and Delinquency Prevention, April 2012), p. 1.

98 Arlen Egley, Jr., and Aline K. Major, *Highlights of the 2002 National Youth Gang Survey* (Washington, DC: Office of Juvenile Justice and Delinquency Prevention, April 2004), p. 1.

99 James C. Howell, Arlen Egley, Jr., and Debra K. Gleason, *Modern-Day Youth Gangs* (Washington, DC: Office of Juvenile Justice and Delinquency Prevention, June 2002), p. 1.

100 Karl G. Hill, Christina Lui, and J. David Hawkins, *Early Precursors of Gang Membership: A Study of Seattle Youth* (Washington, DC: Office of Juvenile Justice and Delinquency Prevention, December 2001), p. 4.

101 Arlen Egley, Jr., *Highlights of the 1999 National Youth Gang Survey* (Washington, DC: Office of Juvenile Justice and Delinquency Prevention, November 2000), p. 1.

102 Howell, Egley, Jr., and Gleason, *Modern-Day Youth Gangs*, p. 3.

103 David Starbuck, James C. Howell, and Donna J. Lindquist, *Hybrid and Other Modern Gangs* (Washington, DC: Office of Juvenile Justice and Delinquency Prevention, December 2001); and Howell, Egley, Jr., and Gleason, *Modern-Day Youth Gangs*.

104 Starbuck, Howell, and Lindquist, *Hybrid and Other Modern Gangs*.

105 Ibid.

106 Ibid., p. 5.

107 M. S. Fleisher, *Dead End Kids: Gang Girls and the Boys They Know* (Madison, WI: University of Wisconsin Press, 1998), p. 264; and Starbuck, Howell, and Lindquist, *Hybrid and Other Modern Gangs.*

108 "Sending Gangs the Message: Change, or Else," *Law Enforcement News*, Vol. xxxi, No. 620, March 2005, p. 4.

109 Simone Roberts et al., *Indicators of School Crime and Safety: 2011* (Washington, DC: U.S. Department of Education, February 2012), p. v.

110 Starbuck, Howell, and Lindquist, *Hybrid and Other Modern Gangs*, p. 4.

111 Ralph A. Weisheit and L. Edward Wells, "Youth Gangs in Rural America," *National Institute of Justice Journal*, Vol. 251, July 2004, p. 4.

112 Egley, Jr. and Howell, *Highlights of the 2010 National Youth Gang Survey*, p. 3.

113 Starbuck, Howell, and Lindquist, *Hybrid and Other Modern Gangs*, p. 6.

114 Howell, Egley, Jr., and Gleason, *Modern-Day Youth Gangs*, p. 8.

115 "Sending Gangs the Message: Change, or Else."

116 John Moore and John Hagedorn, *Female Gangs: A Focus on Research* (Washington, DC: Office of Juvenile Justice and Delinquency Prevention, March 2001), pp. 1–2.

117 M. Chesney-Lind, R. Sheldon, and K. Joe, Girls, Delinquency, and Gang Membership, in C. R. Huff, ed., *Gangs in America*, 2nd ed. (Newbury Park, CA: Sage Publications, 1996).

118 Moore and Hagedorn, *Female Gangs: A Focus on Research*, p. 2.

119 Ibid.

120 Ibid., p. 6.

121 Ibid.

122 Ibid.

123 Ibid., p. 3.

124 Gary M. McClelland, Linda A. Teplin, and Karen M. Abram, *Detection and Prevalence of Substance Use among Juvenile Detainees* (Washington, DC: Office of Juvenile Justice and Delinquency Prevention, June 2004).

125 "Has the DARE Curriculum Gone to Pot?" *Law Enforcement News*, December 15/31, 2001, p. 6.

126 Elizabeth Armstrong, "Leave Them Alone," *Christian Science Monitor*, September 23, 2003, p. 12.

127 Associated Press, "States Grapple with Growing Teen Meth Use," New York Times Online, April 10, 2005. Web posted at http://www.nytimes.com.

128 Associated Press, "AP: 1 in 5 Teens Abused Prescription Drugs," New York Times Online, April 21, 2005. Web posted at http://www.nytimes.com.

129 "NIDA InfoFacts: High School and Youth Trends" (Washington, DC: National Institute on Drug Abuse, March 2011), p. 2.

130 Roberts, *Indicators of School Crime and Safety: 2011*, p. iii.

131 Ibid., p. iv.

132 Jill F. DeVoe, Katharin Peter, Amanda Miller, Thomas D. Snyder, and Katrina Baum, *Indicators of School Crime and Safety: 2004* (Washington, DC: National Center for Education Statistics, November 2004), p. 1.

133 Associated Press, "Schoolmate Held in Shooting Death of Girl, 13," *Honolulu Advertiser*, November 21, 1999, p. A22.

134 Jon Nordheimer, "Seventh-Grade Boy Held in Killing of Teacher," New York Times Online, May 26, 2000. Web posted at http://www.nytimes.com.

135 Associated Press, "12-Year-Old Pulls Gun on Classmates," *Honolulu Advertiser*, March 24, 2000, p. A5.

136 Associated Press, "Expert: Suspects Spurred by Dares," New York Times Online, February 24, 2002. Web posted at http://www.nytimes.com.

137 Associated Press, "Student Guilty in Albany School Shooting," New York Times Online, November 23, 2004. Web posted at http://www.nytimes.com.

138 Associated Press, "Neb. Teen Charged in School Murder Plot," New York Times Online, March 19, 2004. Web posted at http://www.nytimes.com.

139 Ibid.

140 Ibid.

141 Ibid.

142 Ibid.

143 Ibid.

144 Ibid., p. vi.

145 Ibid., p. v.

146 Ibid., p. vi.

147 "Bullying among Sixth Graders a Daily Occurrence, UCLA Study Finds," *UCLA News*, March 28, 2005. Web posted at http://newsroom.ucla.edu/page. asp?RelNum 6006 (accessed April 5, 2005).

148 Ibid.

149 Patrik Jonsson, "Schoolyard Bullies and Their Victims: The Picture Fills Out," *Christian Science Monitor*, May 12, 2004, p. 1.

150 Suicide Prevention Resource Center, "Suicide and Bullying: Issue Brief" (Newton, MA: Suicide Prevention Resource Center, March 2011), p. 2.

151 Ibid., p. 4.

152 Ibid., p. 3.

153 Jonsson, "Schoolyard Bullies and Their Victims: The Picture Fills Out."

154 Elissa Gootman, "Crime Falls as Citations Surge in Schools with Extra Officers," New York Times Online, March 25, 2004. Web posted at http://www.nytimes.com.

155 Andy Grimm and Alicia Fabbre, "Cops Ask for More Firepower in Schools," *Chicago Tribune*, August 23, 2012, Sec. 1, p. 10.

156 Joe Taschler, "Schools, Firms Hold Drills for Shootings," *Chicago Tribune*, August 24, 2012, Sec. 1, p. 14.

157 John Byrne, "Principals to Meet Regularly with Police," *Chicago Tribune*, December 1, 2011, Sec. 1, p. 11.

158 Gary D. Gottfredson, Denise C. Gottfredson, Ellen R. Czeh, David Cantor, Scott B. Crosse, and Irene Hantman, *Toward Safe and Orderly Schools—The National Study of Delinquency Prevention in Schools* (Washington, DC: National Institute of Justice, November 2004), p. 2.

159 Ibid., p. 1.

160 Ibid., p. 4.

161 Sara Rimer, "Unruly Students Facing Arrest, Not Detention," New York Times Online, January 4, 2004. Web posted at http://www.nytimes.com.

162 Ibid.

163 Sara Rimer, "Last Chance High," New York Times Online, July 25, 2004. Web posted at http://www.nytimes.com.

164 Cora Roy-Stevens, *Overcoming Barriers to School Reentry* (Washington, DC: Office of Justice Programs, October 2004).

165 Tony Fabelo and Dottie Carmichael, *Breaking Schools' Rules: A Statewide Study of How School Discipline Relates to Students' Success and Juvenile Justice Involvement* (Texas A&M University: Public Policy Research Institute Justice Center, July 2011).

166 Ibid., p. x.

167 Ibid.

168 Ibid.

169 Joel Hood, "Illinois Tops in Black Student Suspensions," *Chicago Tribune*, August 8, 2012, Sec. 1, p. 4.

170 Fabelo and Carmichael, *Breaking Schools' Rules: A Statewide Study of How School Discipline Relates to Students' Success and Juvenile Justice Involvement*, p. xi.

171 Ibid.

172 Ibid.

173 Ibid., p. xii.

174 "Attorney General Holder, Secretary Duncan Announce Effort to Respond to School-to-Prison Pipeline by Supporting Good Discipline Practices" (Washington, DC: U.S. Department of Justice, July 21, 2011).

175 Ibid.

176 Howard N. Snyder and Melissa Sickmund, *Juvenile Offenders and Victims: 2006 National Report* (Washington, DC: U.S. Department of Justice, Office of Justice Programs, Office of Juvenile Justice and Delinquency Prevention, 2006), p. 47.

177 Ibid.

Chapter 14, Homeland Security

1 National Advisory Commission on Criminal Justice Standards and Goals, *Report of the Task Force on Disorder and Terrorism* (Washington, DC: U.S. Government Printing Office, 1976).

2 Jonathan S. Landay, "As Radicalism Declines, Terrorism Surges," *Christian Science Monitor*, August 20, 1998, pp. 1, 10.

3 Peter Grier and James N. Thurman, "Age of Anonymous Terrorism," *Christian Science Monitor*, August 20, 1998, p. 10; and Evan Thomas et al., "The Road to September 11," *Newsweek*, October 1, 2001, p. 40.

4 Gerald R. Murphy and Martha R. Plotkin, *Protecting Your Community from Terrorism: Strategies for Local Law Enforcement, Volume I: Local-Federal Partnerships* (Washington, DC: U.S. Department of Justice, 2003), p. 61.

5 Ibid., p. 1.

6 Ibid., p. 11.

7 Robert T. Stafford Disaster Relief and Emergency Assistance Act (42 U.S.C. § 121 et seq.).

8 Patricia A. Dalton, *Effective Intergovernmental Coordination Is Key to Success* (Washington, DC: General Accounting Office, August 2002), p. 3.

9 Homeland Security Act of 2002, Pub. L. 107–296 (November 25, 2002); Normal J. Rabkin, *Homeland Security* (Washington, DC: Government Accountability Office, April 2005), p. 3.

10 *National Strategy for Homeland Security* (Washington, DC: Office of Homeland Security, July 2002), p. 2.

11 Rabkin, *Homeland Security: Overview of Department of Homeland Security Management Challenges*, p. 3.

12 Ibid., p. 5.

13 *National Strategy for Homeland Security*, p. 13.

14 Gerald L. Dillingham, *Transportation Security: Post-September 11th Initiatives and Long-Term Challenges* (Washington, DC: United States General Accounting Office GAO-03-616T, April 1, 2003), p. 3.

15 *Aviation Security: Screener Training and Performance Measurement Strengthened, But More Work Remains* (Washington DC: Government Accountability Office GAO-05-457, May 2005).

16 *National Strategy for Combating Terrorism: February 2003* (Washington, DC: Department of State, Publication 11038, April 2003), p. 27.

17 *CONPLAN: United States Government Interagency Domestic Terrorism Concept of Operations Plan* (Washington, DC: Government Printing Office, 2001).

18 Ibid., p. iii.

19 Dalton, *"Effective Intergovernmental Coordination Is Key to Success,"* p. 10.

20 Mike McIntire and Michelle O'Donnell, "Fire Chief Challenges New York Emergency Plan." New York Times Online, May 10, 2005. Web posted at http://www.nytimes.com.

21 Dalton, *Effective Intergovernmental Coordination Is Key to Success*, p. 14.

22 Murphy and Plotkin, *Protecting Your Community from Terrorism: Strategies for Local Law Enforcement, Volume I: Local-Federal Partnerships*, p. 53.

23 Douglas Jehl, "Four in 9/11 Plot Are Called Tied to Qaeda in '00." New York Times Online, August 9, 2005. Web posted at http://www.nytimes.com; Douglas Jehl and Philip Shenon, "9/11 Commission's Staff Rejected Report on Early Identification of Chief Hijacker," New York Times Online, August 11, 2005. Web posted at http://www.nytimes.com; and Dan Eggen, "Sept. 11 Panel Explores Allegations about Atta," *Washington Post*, August 12, 2005, p. A9.

24 Dan Eggen and Walter Pincus, "Bush Approves Spy Agency Changes," *Washington Post*, June 30, 2005, p. A1.

25 George W. Bush, "Fact Sheet: Strengthening Intelligence to Better Protect America," http://www.whitehouse.gov/news/release/2003/01/print/2003012812.html (accessed January 28, 2003).

26 Associated Press, "Details of Counterterror Center Unveiled," New York Times Online, February 14, 2003. Web posted at http://www.nytimes.com.

27 Murphy and Plotkin, *Protecting Your Community from Terrorism: Strategies for Local Law Enforcement, Volume I: Local-Federal Partnerships*, p. 31.

28 Ibid., p. 32.

29 David Willman, "Records: Scientists Knew of U.S. BioWatch System Flaws," *Chicago Tribune*, August 23, 2012, Sec. 1, p. 15.

30 John M. Broder, "Police Chiefs Moving to Share Terror Data," New York Times Online, July 19, 2005. Web posted at http://www.nytimes.com.

31 Eric Lichtblau and William K. Rashbaum, "U.S. Steps Down Threat Level for Mass Transit Systems by a Notch," New York Times Online, August 12, 2005. Web posted at http://www.nytimes.com.

32 Broder, "Police Chiefs Moving to Share Terror Data."

33 Ibid.

34 Ibid.

35 Federal Bureau of Investigation, "Headline Archives—Fusion Centers: Unifying Intelligence to Protect Americans," March 12, 2009.

36 Associated Press, "Feds Outline Plan on Enemy Combatants," New York Times Online, December 17, 2003. Web posted at http://www.nytimes.com.

37 Associated Press, "ABA Panel Wants Tribunal Rules Changed," New York Times Online, August 12, 2003. Web posted at http://www.nytimes.com.

38 Ibid.

39 Neil A. Lewis, "Rules on Tribunal Require Unanimity on Death Penalty," New York Times Online, December 28, 2001. Web posted at http://www.nytimes.com.

40 William Glaberson, "Judges Question Detention of American," New York Times Online, November 18, 2003. Web posted at http://www.nytimes.com.

41 Spencer S. Hus, "Holder Prefers Keeping Option of Civilian Courts for Terrorism Suspects," *Washington Post*, April 16, 2010, p. A11.

42 Dante Chinni, "Ashcroft on Tour and Unplugged," *Christian Science Monitor*, http://www.csmonitor.com (accessed August 26, 2003).

43 Brian Knowlton, "Ashcroft Pushes Defense of Terror Law," New York Times Online, August 19, 2003. Web posted at http://www.nytimes.com.

44 Dan Eggen, "Flawed FBI Probe of Bombing Used a Secret Warrant," *Washington Post*, April 7, 2005, p. A3.

45 Jeffrey R. Young, "FBI Seeks Library Data from Connecticut Institution Under Patriot Act, Court Records Show," *Chronicle of Higher Education*, August 29, 2005.

46 Dan Eggen, "Renewed Patriot Act Gets Boost in House, Senate Panel," *Washington Post*, July 22, 2005, p. A12.

47 Warren Richey and Linda Feldmann, "Has Post-9/11 Dragnet Gone Too Far?" *Christian Science Monitor*, http://www.csmonitor.com (accessed September 12, 2003).

48 Philip Shenon, "Report on USA Patriot Act Alleges Civil Rights Violations," New York Times Online, July 21, 2003. Web posted at http://www.nytimes.com; and Paul von Zielbauer, "Detainees' Abuse Is Detailed," New York Times Online, December 19, 2003. Web posted at http://www.nytimes.com.

49 Jennifer Nislow, "Portland Just Says 'No' to FBI," *Law Enforcement News*, November 30, 2001, pp. 1, 9.

50 David W. Dunlap, "Financial District Security Getting New Look," New York Times Online, November 27, 2003. Web posted at http://www.nytimes.com.

51 Rachel L. Swarns, "Is Anti-Terrorist Anti-Tourist? New York Times Online," October 31, 2004. Web posted at http://www.nytimes.com.

52 Thomas J. Lueck, "Convention to Delay Some Cases in City Courts," New York Times Online, July 210..0.2, 2004. Web posted at http://www.nytimes.com.

53 Eric Lichtblau, "Report Questions the Value of Color-Coded Warnings," New York Times Online, July 13, 2004. Web posted at http://www.nytimes.com.

54 Eric Lichtblau, "F.B.I. Issues and Retracts Urgent Terrorism Bulletin," New York Times Online, May 29, 2004. Web posted at http://www.nytimes.com.

55 Stephen E. Flynn, "Color Me Scared," New York Times Online, May 25, 2005. Web posted at http://www.nytimes.com; and John Mintz, "DHS Considers Alternatives to Color-Coded Warnings," *Washington Post*, May 10, 2005, p. A6.

56 Eric Lipton, "U.S. Borders Vulnerable, Witnesses Say," New York Times Online, June 22, 2005. Web posted at http://www.nytimes.com.

57 Associated Press, "Illegal Workers Raise Security Concerns," New York Times Online, April 13, 2005. Web posted at http://www.nytimes.com.

58 John Mintz, "DHS Arrests 60 Illegals in Sensitive Jobs," *Washington Post*, May 21, 2006, p. A3.

59 U.S. Customs and Border Protection website, http://www.cbp.gov/xp/cgov/about.

60 U.S. Immigration and Customs Enforcement website, http://www.ice.gov/about/overview.

61 U.S. Immigration and Customs Enforcement website, http://www.ice.gov/about/offices/enforcement-removal-operations.

62 Associated Press, "Officials Test Radio Tags at Canada Border," New York Times Online, August 9, 2005. Web posted at http://www.nytimes.com.

63 Associated Press, "New Border Fence: Arizona Plans Its Own 200-mile Fence, *Christian Science Monitor*, http://www.csmonitor.com (accessed August 27, 2012).

64 Ibid.

65 Steven Greenhouse, "Immigration Sting Puts 2 U.S. Agencies at Odds," New York Times Online, July 16, 2005. Web posted at http://www.nytimes.com.

66 Ibid.

67 Michael Janoesky, "9/11 Panel Calls Policies on Immigration Ineffective," New York Times Online, April 17, 2004. Web posted at http://www.nytimes.com.

68 Associated Press, "United States Issued Visas to 105 Men on Anti-Terror List," *Pocono Record*, November 27, 2002, p. A5.

69 Ralph Blumenthal, "Citing Violence, 2 Border States Declare a Crisis," New York Times Online, August 17, 2005. Web posted at http://www.nytimes.com.

70 Ralph Blumenthal, "For One Family, Front Row Seats to Border Crisis," New York Times Online, August 23, 2005. Web posted at http://www.nytimes.com.

71 Ibid.

72 Timothy Egan, "A Battle against Illegal Workers, With an Unlikely Driving Force." New York Times Online, May 30, 2005. Web posted at http://www.nytimes.com.

73 Dan Eggen, "Customs Jails 1,000 Suspected Gang Members," *Washington Post*, August 2, 2005, p. A2.

74 Ibid.

75 Immigration Policy Center, *A Q&A Guide to State Immigration Laws: What You Need to Know if Your State is Considering Anti-Immigrant Legislation* (Washington, D.C.: Immigration Policy Center, 2012), p. 8.

76 Ibid., p. 3.

77 Ibid.

78 Ibid., p. 7.

79 Brooks Barnes, "California Sheriffs Oppose Bill on illegal Immigrants," New York Times Online, August 28, 2012. Web posted at http://www.nytimes.com.

80 Immigration Policy Center, "A Q&A Guide to State Immigration Laws: What You Need to Know if Your State is Considering Anti-Immigrant, p.11.

81 Dibya Sarkar, "Fight Over Driver's License Standards," *Federal Computer Week*, http://fcw.com (accessed June 23, 2005).

82 Associated Press, "Governors: Drivers License Costs to Soar," New York Times Online, July 18, 2005. Web posted at http://www.nytimes.com.

83 T. R. Reid and Darryl Fears, "Driver's License Curtailed as Identification," *Washington Post*, April 17, 2005, p. A3.

84 Daniel B. Wood, "Driver IDs for Illegals Raise Security Concerns," *Christian Science Monitor*, July 12, 2004, p. 3.

85 Ellen Nakashima, Brian Krebs, and Blaine Harden, "U.S., South Korea targeted in Swarm of Internet Attacks," *Washington Post*, July 9, 2009.

86 Ellen Nakashima, "U.S. Accelerating Cyberweapon Research," *Washington Post*, March 18, 2012.

87 Ellen Nakashima, "Several Nations Trying to Penetrate U.S. Cyber-Networks, Says Ex-FBI Official," *Washington Post*, April 17, 2012.

88 Ellen Nakashima, "White House, NSA Weigh Cybersecuirty, Personal Privacy," *Washington Post*, February 28, 2012.

89 Office of the Inspector General, A Review of the FBI's Use of National Security Letters: Assessment of Corrective Actions and Examination of NSL Usage in 2006 (Washington, DC: U.S. Department of Justice, 2008).

90 Robert Barnes, "Supreme Court Weighs Free Speech Against Aid to Terrorists," *Washington Post*, February 24, 2010, p. A3.

91 Human Rights Watch, *Presumption of Guilt: Human Rights Abuses of Post-September 11 Detainee* (New York: Human Rights Watch, 2002), pp. 3, 6, 46, 55.

92 Eric Lichtblau, "Two Groups Charge Abuse of Witness Law," New York Times Online, June 27, 2005. Web posted at http://www.nytimes.com.

93 Human Rights Watch, *Presumption of Guilt: Human Rights Abuses of Post-September 11 Detainee*, p. 5.

94 *IN RE: Guantanamo Bay Detainee Continued Access to Counsel* No. 12-398 (2012).

95 Del Quentin Wilber, "Federal Judge Blocks Restriction of Lawyer Access to Guantanamo Detainees," *Washington Post*, September 7, 2012.

96 Tracey Maclin, " 'Voluntary' Interviews and Airport Searches of Middle Eastern Men: The Fourth Amendment in a Time of Terror," *Mississippi Law Journal* (January 21, 2005), p. 521.

97 Associated Press, "Dearborn, Mich., Arabs Cited More Often," New York Times Online, November 20, 2003. Web posted at http://www.nytimes.com.

98 Laurie Nadel, "For Island's Muslims, a Time to Be Wary," New York Times Online, September 4, 2005. Web posted at http://www.nytimes.com.

99 Ibid.

100 Peter Grier, "Bush Team and the Limits on Torture," *Christian Science Monitor*, June 10, 2004, p. 1.

101 Ibid.

102 Ibid.

103 Greg Miller, "From Former Libyan Prisoners, New Claims about CIA Renditions, Abuses," *Washington Post*, September 5, 2012.

104 Ibid.

105 William Glaberson, "President's Detention Plan Tests American Legal Tradition," *New York Times*, May 23, 2009.

106 Nedra Pickler, "Holder Offers First Legal Justification for Killing U.S.-Born al-Qaida Operative Overseas," *Chicago Tribune*, March 5, 2012.

107 Ibid.

108 Richard A. Serrano and Andy Grimm, "President May Order Killing of American Terrorists, Holder Says," *Los Angeles Times*, March 5, 2012.

109 Ibid.

Glossary

1972 Equal Employment Opportunity Act The act that ended discrimination in law enforcement and corrections based on race, gender, and other protected categories.

1996 federal sex offender registry A database of convicted sex offenders who are required to register with law enforcement; the registration data are available to the public.

abolitionists People opposed to the death penalty.

active-shooter A law enforcement strategy for responding to shootings at schools and colleges in which the first officers on the scene seek and find the shooter and neutralize him or her.

actual damages Losses or harm that can be documented and on which a monetary value can be placed.

actus reus An element of crime in which people are punished for their actions; thus, the law does not prosecute people for actions that are not voluntary or that are accidental and do not involve recklessness or negligence.

Ada Jukes A woman labeled by Richard Dugdale as the "mother of criminals."

adjudicated Determined the disposition of the charges against the juvenile and the treatment or punishment options, done by the juvenile judge.

administrative-maximum prison The highest security level of prison operated by the U.S. Bureau of Prisons. Supermax prisons are considered escape-proof regardless of the resources of the inmate.

affirm the case A finding by the Supreme Court that there was no substantial judicial or constitutional error and that the original opinion of the lower court stands.

affirmative defense A defense in which the defendant admits that he or she committed the *actus reas* of the crime but claims that he or she should not be found guilty of the crime because his or her actions were justified or he or she had an excuse.

aggravating factors Actions that may increase the seriousness of a crime.

Amber Alert system A system that provides law enforcement with the ability to notify the public of a missing or abducted child through media, technology and social networks.

American Society for Industrial Security (ASIS) One of the largest professional societies for promoting the ethics and professionalism of private protection services.

anomie A feeling of "normlessness" and lack of belonging that people feel when they become socially isolated.

appellate courts State courts that have the authority to review the proceedings and verdicts of general trial courts for judicial errors and other significant issues.

arraignment A criminal proceeding where the defendant is formally charged with a crime and is asked to enter a plea.

arraignment hearing A hearing where charges are read and the defendant is asked to enter a plea.

arrest To restrict the freedom of a person by taking him or her into police custody.

arson The willful and malicious burning of a structure.

Article 3, Section 2 The part of the U.S. Constitution that defines the jurisdiction of the federal courts.

assault The act of inflicting injury on another, whereas battery is the act of unlawfully striking another.

atavism The failure of humans to fully develop into modern men and women.

atavistic stigmata The study of the physical traits of criminals.

attempt An incomplete criminal act; the closest act to the completion of a crime.

bail Temporary release of the defendant prior to trial.

bail bonds agent An agent of a private commercial business that has contracted with the court to act as a guarantor of a defendant's return to court.

bailiffs The people who provide courtroom security. Deputy sheriffs provide security for state courts, and Deputy U.S. Marshals provide security for federal courts.

banishment The removal of an offender from the community.

Barker v. Wingo The case in which the court ruled that the defendant's failure to request a speedy trial does not negate the defendant's right to a speedy trial.

bench trial A trial in which the judge rather than a jury makes the determination of guilty.

beyond a reasonable doubt A unanimous verdict—the standard required for a verdict in a criminal case.

bifurcated trial A two-part trial structure in which the jury first determines guilt or innocence and then considers new evidence relating to the appropriate punishment.

biocriminology Research into the roles played by genetic and neurophysiological variables in criminal behavior.

biological determinism The school of thought that says that crime is caused by a biological or biochemical influence over which the offender has no control.

blended sentencing option An option that allows the juvenile or criminal court to impose a sentence that can include confinement in a juvenile facility and/or in an adult prison after the offender is beyond the age of the juvenile court's jurisdiction.

booking Police activity that establishes the identification of an arrested person and formally charges that person with a crime.

boot camps Programs modeled after military-style entry-level training programs for youthful nonviolent offenders.

Breed v. Jones A case in which the Supreme Court ruled that once a juvenile has been adjudicated by a juvenile court, he or she cannot be waived to criminal court to be tried for the same charges.

brief A written statement submitted by an appellant's attorneys that states the substantial constitutional or federal issue they believe the court should address.

broken window theory The belief that ignoring public-order violations and disruptive behavior leads to community neglect, which fosters further disorder and crime.

Brown v. Board of Education Topeka (1954) The U.S. Supreme Court decision that resulted in the movement to integrate schools, public transportation, business, and society.

bullying Making physical and/or psychological threats or abusing or tormenting another person.

burden of proof The standard required for adjudication.

Bureau of Alcohol, Tobacco, Firearms and Explosives (ATF) The federal agency responsible for regulating alcohol, tobacco, firearms, explosives, and arson.

Bureau of Justice Statistics (BJS) A primary source for criminal justice statistics that compiles reports on many aspects of the criminal justice system, including data about federal, state, and local criminal justice.

burglary A combination of trespass and the intent to commit a crime.

capital punishment The sentence of death.

Carroll doctrine Terms allowing admissibility of evidence obtained by police in a warrantless search of an automobile when the police have probable cause that a crime has occurred and delaying a search could result in the loss of evidence.

causal variables Variables that directly influence the outcome of relationships.

Caylee's Law A law that requires parents and/or guardians to reporting missing children in a timely manner.

certiorari power The authority of the Supreme Court, based on agreement by four of its members that a case might raise significant constitutional or federal issues, to select a case for review.

Cesare Beccaria The founder of Classical School theories.

Cesare Lombroso An Italian doctor who collected data to support his Darwinist-based theory that criminal behavior is a characteristic of humans who have failed to develop normally from their primitive origins.

chain gang In the southern penal system, a group of convicts chained together during outside labor.

checks and balances The authority of the legislative branch, the executive branch, and the judicial branch to provide a constitutional check on the actions of each other.

chief law enforcement officer The highest-ranking law enforcement official within a system; the sheriff is the chief law enforcement officer of a county, the attorney general is the chief law enforcement officer of a state, and the U.S. attorney general is the chief law enforcement officer of the United States.

chief of police The chief administrative officer of the police department.

child protective services (CPS) A government agency responsible for the health and welfare of children.

circuits Geographic divisions of the federal court system.

citizen complaint board A citizen review board that hears alleged complaints of police misconduct.

civil commitment examination A determination of whether the defendant should be released or confined to an institution for people with mental illness.

civil death The legal philosophy that barred a prison inmate from bringing a lawsuit in a civil court related to his or her treatment while incarcerated or related to conditions of incarceration.

civil disobedience A nonviolent approach of protest in the civil rights movement.

civil law Also called private law, the body of law concerned with the definition, regulation, and enforcement of rights in noncriminal cases in which both the person who has the right and the person who has the obligation are private individuals.

Civil Rights Act of 1964 The act declaring that it is illegal for businesses, hotels, restaurants, and public transportation to deny citizens service based on their race.

civil service status Protection of an employee in that his or her employment can only be terminated for cause and the employer must follow certain due process procedures in terminating the employee.

Classical School The school of thought that individuals have free will to choose whether to commit crimes.

clear and present danger A condition related to public safety that may justify police use of deadly force against a fleeing suspect.

clearance rate The percentage of crimes that are solved versus crimes that are unsolved.

clearing cases In reference to the status of a criminal offense, knowing the perpetrator of the crime, as asserted by the police or prosecutor.

command-and-control structure A hierarchical administrative structure organized by ranks with a single person responsible for all personnel in the organization.

common law Unwritten, simply stated laws based on traditions and common understandings in a time when most people were illiterate.

community policing Decentralized policing programs that focus on crime prevention, quality of life in a community, public order, and alternatives to arrest.

community resource broker The role of a probation and parole officer in helping his or her clients secure the services and necessities that are required for successful reentry.

community-based corrections Prevention and treatment programs designed to promote the successful transition of offenders from prison to the community.

commutation of sentence A reduction in the severity or length of an inmate's sentence issued by a state governor or the president of the United States.

competent to stand trial The defendant's ability to comprehend the charges against him or her and to assist counsel in his or her defense.

compliance with the terms of release The enforcement role of probation and parole officers to verify that probationers and parolees fulfill the mandatory terms of their release.

concentric zone model (Burgess model) A theory developed by Park and Burgess that social environments based on status disadvantages such as poverty; illiteracy; and lack of schooling, unemployment, and illegitimacy are powerful forces that influence human interactions.

conditional release A bail alternative in which the defendant is released from custody if he or she agrees to court-ordered terms and restrictions.

conducted energy devices Devices that deliver powerful electric shocks, causing incapacitation.

conflict theories Theories that the most politically and socially powerful individuals and organizations use the legal system to exploit less powerful individuals and to retain their power and privileges.

congregate work system The practice of moving inmates from sleeping cells to other areas of the prison for work, meals, and recreation.

consent decree (law enforcement agency) A court order that establishes a monitoring team over a law enforcement agency.

consent decree (juvenile court order) A written summary of the specific conditions and requirements to be placed on the child and/or parent(s) or guardian by the juvenile intake officer.

consolidated model The system in which decision making about parole is a function of a state department of corrections.

conspiracy The planning by two or more people to commit a crime.

contain-and-wait A law enforcement strategy for responding to shootings at schools and colleges in which perimeter security is established and law enforcement officers negotiate with the shooter.

contempt of court A charge against any violator of the judge's courtroom rules, authorizing the judge to impose a fine or term of imprisonment.

contingency A situation in a civil case when an attorney agrees to forgo payment in return for a percentage of the potential settlement.

contraband Smuggled goods, such as drugs, cigarettes, money, and pornography.

contract services Security personnel who work for a third-party company and are hired by another company to provide specific services at the direction of the client.

convict lease system The practice of some southern penal systems leasing prisoners to private contractors as laborers.

corporal punishment The administration of bodily pain as punishment for a crime.

correctional officers Uniformed jail or prison employees whose primary job is the security and movement of inmates.

correlation The state of two variables being associated with each other in that when one increases, the other increases or decreases in a predictable pattern.

county department of corrections An independent county department that supervises a county jail when the sheriff does not.

court docket The schedule of cases and hearings.

court of last resort A state court of final appeals that reviews lower court decisions and whose decisions can be appealed to the U.S. Supreme Court.

courts of general jurisdiction Courts that handle felony crimes.

courts of limited jurisdiction State courts of original jurisdiction that handle traffic violations and criminal violations, small claims, misdemeanors, and violations of local ordinances and laws within the geographic jurisdiction of the town or village.

courts of record Courts in which trial proceedings are transcribed.

Crime Awareness and Campus Security Act of 1992 A law requiring college campuses to make a public disclosure of crimes occurring on their campuses.

crime clock A method used by the Federal Bureau of Investigation to report how often crimes occur.

crime statistics The gathering, analysis, and interpretation of crime data.

Crime Victims' Rights Act A law enacted in 2004 that guarantees crime victims a number of rights, including the right to protection and restitution.

crime-control (public-order) model A model of the criminal justice system in which emphasis is placed on fighting crime and protecting potential victims.

criminal justice system The enforcement, by the police, the courts, and correctional institutions, of obedience to laws.

criminal man Lombroso's belief that criminals were born inferior and prehuman.

criminology The body of knowledge regarding crime as a social phenomenon.

cruel and unusual punishment An Eighth Amendment right based on the premise of classical criminology that punishment should be appropriate to the crime.

cultural deviance theories The idea that, for the most part, the values of subcultural groups within the society are more influential upon individual behavior and interactions than laws are.

dark figure of crime statistics Crimes that are not reported and thus are unknown to police.

day reporting center An intermediate sanction to provide a gradual adjustment to reentry under closely supervised conditions.

deadly force The power of police to incapacitate or kill in the line of duty.

defendant The party whom a lawsuit is brought against.

defense of duress A legal claim by a defendant that he or she acted involuntarily under the threat of immediate and serious harm by another.

defenses Justifications or excuses defined by law by which a defendant may be released from prosecution or punishment for a crime.

deinstitutionalization The movement of mentally ill offenders from long-term hospitalization to community-based care.

delinquency petition A request to a judge to hear and judge a juvenile case in a formal hearing to determine whether the juvenile is to be declared delinquent.

delinquent A juvenile accused of committing an act that is criminal for both adults and juveniles.

Department of Homeland Security (DHS) A newly created federal agency responsible for a wide range of security measures to protect against terrorist attacks.

deputy chief The second in command below the chief of police. In a large police department, there may be several deputy chiefs, each commanding a large unit within the police department.

deputy sheriff officers Law enforcement officers who assist the sheriff.

determinate sentencing A model of sentencing in which the offender is sentenced to a fixed term of incarceration.

determinist Scholars and scientists who believe that causes of criminal behavior are not controlled by free-will choice; rather, they are influenced by factors that are beyond the control of the individual.

deterrence The philosophy and practices that emphasize making criminal behavior less appealing.

deviant subculture group One subcultural group in which its values do not conform to social values of the larger part of society.

differential association theory The concept that criminal and delinquent behaviors are learned entirely through group interactions, with peers reinforcing and rewarding those behaviors.

diplomatic immunity The granting of immunity, or protection from any kind of criminal prosecution, to foreign diplomats.

direct oversight Laws and judicial decisions that prohibit specific law enforcement behavior.

dislocation Crackdowns on crime by police in larger cities that cause offenders to relocate to the suburbs or rural areas that have less law enforcement resources.

disproportionate confinement The nonrandom distribution of people by race in correctional institutions. If the prison population reflected the same demographics as the general population, confinement would not reflect racial bias.

diversion An alternative to criminal trial and a prison sentence, such as drug court, boot camp, or a treatment program, offered to a defendant.

domestic terrorism Acts of terrorism committed in the United States by individuals or groups that do not have ties with or sponsorship from foreign states or organizations.

domino theory A claim that the continued fall of governments to communist rule would threaten democracy.

double jeopardy The act of trying a person twice for the same offense.

Drug Abuse Resistance Education (DARE) A popular in-school antidrug program initiated by the Los Angeles Police Department in 1983 but abandoned when data failed to support its effectiveness.

drug court An approach that provides drug offenders the opportunity for intermediate sanctions, community treatment, and intensive probation supervision instead of prison time.

Drug Enforcement Administration (DEA) The federal agency that enforces U.S. laws and regulations regarding controlled substances and that supports nonenforcement programs intended to reduce the availability of illicit controlled substances domestically and internationally.

dual court system The political division of jurisdiction into two separate systems of courts: federal and state; in this system, federal courts have limited jurisdiction over state courts.

due process Court rules that define the standards for a "fair" trial.

due process amendment The Fourteenth Amendment of the U.S. Constitution prohibiting local governments from depriving persons of life, liberty, or property without due process.

due process model A model that ensures that individuals are protected from arbitrary and excessive abuse of power by the government.

due process rights Rights guaranteed to persons by the Constitution and its amendments.

education release A program in which inmates are released to attend college or vocational programs.

ego The rational mind.

electronic monitoring An approach in home confinement programs that ensures compliance through electronic means.

elements of a crime The illegal actions (*actus reus*) and criminal intentions (*mens rea*) of the actor along with the circumstances that link the two, especially causation.

Eleventh Amendment A provision that prohibits a citizen from one state from suing the government of another state in federal court.

enemy combatant executive order An order issued by President Bush providing for the detention of terrorists without access to due process rights.

enemy combatants The suspension of due process rights for accused terrorists under the enemy combatant executive order.

enhanced interrogations Interrogation methods that allow for the use of pain, threats, and waterboarding to extract information from a subject.

entrapment The illegal arrest of a person based on criminal behavior for which the police provided both the motivation and the means, tested in *Jacobsen* v. *United States* (1992).

ethical standards of behavior Legal sanctions that prohibit experimentation that may harm subjects and regulate the degree of deception of subjects that researchers may use in an experiment.

ex post facto laws Laws providing that citizens cannot be punished for actions committed before laws against the actions were passed and that the government cannot increase the penalty for a specific crime after the crime was committed.

excessive bail Bail that is prohibited by the Eighth Amendment, but there is no uniform standard as to what "excessive" is.

exclusionary rule A rule that prohibits the use of evidence or testimony obtained in violation of the Fourth and Fifth Amendments of the U.S. Constitution, established in *Weeks* v. *United States* (1914) and extended to all state courts in *Mapp* v. *Ohio* (1961).

executive orders Presidential directives regarding the execution of legislative acts that oversee the behavior of officers and agencies of the executive branch.

executive pardon An act by a governor or the president that forgives a prisoner and rescinds his or her sentence.

factual impossibility Circumstances under which it is not possible for a person to commit the crime intended.

faith-based programs Programs provided by religious-based and church-affiliated groups; their role in rehabilitation is controversial because they receive federal money and may combine religious instruction with rehabilitation.

father of scientific criminology The title bestowed on Cesare Lombroso because he was the first to use the scientific method in the search to explain criminal behavior.

Federal Bureau of Investigation (FBI) The federal agency responsible for protecting the United States from terrorist attacks, foreign intelligence and espionage, cyber-based attacks, and high-tech crimes and for combating public corruption at all levels.

Federal Bureau of Prisons (BOP) The agency responsible for the administrative oversight of federal prisons and jails.

Federal Judiciary Act The congressional act of 1789 that created the lower federal courts.

Federal Kidnapping Act (Lindbergh Law) An act that made it a federal offense to transport a kidnapping victim across state lines.

federal law enforcement agencies Agencies that enforce only federal laws and are under the control of the executive branch of the federal government.

felicitic calculus The balancing of pain and pleasure as a means to discourage criminal behavior.

felony Serious criminal conduct punishable by incarceration for more than one year.

feminist criminology The proposal that female criminal behavior is caused by the political, economic, and social inequality between men and women.

field-training program A probationary period during which police academy graduates train in the community under the direct supervision of experienced officers.

first responder agencies Law enforcement, firefighters, and medical personnel who are the first to respond to a crisis or an incident.

first responders Law enforcement, firefighters, and medical personnel who are the first to respond to a crisis or an incident.

fleeing-felon doctrine The police practice of using deadly force against a fleeing suspect, made illegal in *Tennessee* v. *Garner* (1985), except when there is clear and present danger to the public.

formal sanctions Social norms enforced through the laws of the criminal justice system.

fruit of the poisoned tree doctrine A rule of evidence that extends the exclusionary rule to secondary evidence obtained indirectly in an unconstitutional search, established in *Silverthorne Lumber Co.* v. *United States* (1918) and in *Wolf* v. *Colorado* (1949).

Fusion Centers Intelligence agencies set up by states or major urban areas and run by state or local authorities that are designed to collect, analyze, and disseminate information critical to state and local law enforcement operations related to both homeland security and crime fighting.

gag order A judge's order to participants and observers at a trial that the evidence and proceedings of the court may not be published, broadcast, or discussed publicly.

general deterrence The concept based on the logic that people who witness the pain suffered by those who commit crimes will want to avoid that pain and will refrain from criminal activity.

general prison population The nonrestricted population of prison inmates who have access to prison services, inmate interactions, programs, and recreation.

general trial courts State courts of original jurisdiction that hear all kinds of criminal cases.

good faith exception An exception to the requirement that police must have a valid search warrant or probable cause when they act in good faith on the belief that the search was legal.

good-time credit A strategy of crediting inmates with extra days served toward early release in an effort to encourage them to obey rules and participate in programs.

Graham v. Florida A case in which the U.S. Supreme Court held that juveniles tried as adults cannot be sentenced to life in prison without parole for nonhomicide offenses.

grand jury An alternative method, which is confidential, to determine whether there is sufficient evidence to charge the defendant with a crime.

grass eaters Police officers who engage in minor illegitimate activities that are considered "acceptable behavior" by fellow officers.

guilty but mentally ill A new type of verdict in which the jury finds a defendant mentally ill but sufficiently aware to be morally responsible for his or her criminal acts.

habeas corpus A writ or request to the court to review whether a person is imprisoned lawfully; it alleges that a person is detained or imprisoned illegally.

habitual offender laws Tough sentencing laws that punish repeat offenders more harshly.

halfway house A transition program that allows inmates to move from prison to the community in steps.

hate crimes Crimes that are motivated by hate of an ethnic group, race, religion, gender, or sexual orientation.

Henry Goodard A sociologist who studied Martin Kallikak's family tree attempting to link heredity to criminality.

hierarchy rule An old police method of counting only the most serious crime in a single incident involving multiple crimes.

highway patrol State law enforcement agencies that focus on traffic enforcement.

HIV/AIDS A disease that damages the body's immune system. Acquired immunodeficiency syndrome (AIDS) is caused by the human immunodeficiency virus (HIV). A person can be HIV-positive and not have AIDS.

home confinement A court-imposed sentence requiring offenders to remain confined in their own residence.

homegrown terrorism Another name for domestic terrorism that emphasizes that there is no foreign involvement in the violence even though homegrown terrorism may act in support of foreign causes.

Homeland Security Advisory System (HSAS) A color-coded threat advisory to government agencies, police, and the public that recommends appropriate actions in response to the forecasted risk of terrorist attacks.

homicide The killing of one human being by another.

honor killings Killings for dishonoring or disrespecting cultural or religious values.

hybrid gangs A new type of youth gang with distinctive characteristics that differentiate them from traditional gangs; they are frequently school-based, less organized, less involved in criminal activity, and less involved in violence than are traditional gangs.

id Unconscious desires and drives.

Immigration and Customs Enforcement (ICE) A new federal agency under the Department of Homeland Security that is responsible for the enforcement of immigration laws.

impeachment A process for removing judges or elected officials from office.

imperfect defense The defense that results in the defendant's liability or punishment for a crime being reduced.

In re Gault A case in which the Supreme Court provided due process rights to juveniles, including notice of charges, counsel, right to examine witnesses, and right to remain silent.

In re Winship A case in which the Supreme Court ruled that the reasonable doubt standard, the same used in criminal trials, should be required in all delinquency adjudications.

incapacitation Deterrence based on the premise that the only way to prevent criminals from reoffending is to remove them from society.

incarceration The bodily confinement of a person in a jail or prison.

inchoate offense An action that goes beyond mere thought but does not result in a completed crime.

incorporate To grant rights defined by the U.S. Constitution to the citizens of a state.

indenture agreements Agreements whereby employers would supervise youths in exchange for their labor.

independent model The system in which decision making about parole is under the authority of an autonomous parole board.

indeterminate sentence A sentence in which the defendant is sentenced to a prison term with a minimum and maximum number of years to serve.

indeterminate sentencing A model of sentencing in which judges have nearly complete discretion in sentencing an offender.

indictment The formal verdict of the grand jury that there is sufficient evidence to bring a person to trial.

indigent defense The right to have an attorney provided free of charge by the state if a defendant cannot afford one, established in *Gideon* v. *Wainwright* (1963).

indirect oversight A remedy, usually at a criminal trial, if the standards of the court are not observed by agencies or officers.

informal sanctions Social norms that are enforced through the social forces of the family, school, government, and religion.

Information Analysis and Infrastructure Protection (IAIP) directorate The intelligence unit of the Department of Homeland Security.

initial placement The assignment by the classification process as to the first institution placement and security level of a convicted defendant.

input-output model A model of how people are processed through the criminal justice system until they exit the system.

insanity A legal claim by a defendant that he or she was suffering from a disease or mental defect and that the defect caused the defendant not to understand the difference between right and wrong.

inside cell block Prison construction in which individual cells are stacked back-to-back in tiers in the center of a secure building.

intensive probation supervision (IPS) Probation supervised by probation and parole officers with smaller caseloads, placing a greater emphasis on compliance with the conditions of supervision.

intermediate sanctions Punishments that restrict offenders' freedom without imprisoning them and/or that consist of community-based prevention and treatment programs to promote the successful transition of offenders from prison to the community.

internal affairs investigation unit A special unit whose mission it is to investigate the actions of officers for the purpose of recommending disciplinary actions or criminal prosecution.

Internal Affairs Unit or Office of Internal Affairs An office that conducts investigations of criminal, abusive, or unprofessional behavior by law enforcement officers within the department.

International Association of Police The world's oldest and largest nonprofit membership organization of police executives.

Irish system An early form of parole invented by Sir Walter Crofton based on the mark system in which prisoners were released conditionally on good behavior and were supervised in the community.

jails Short-term multipurpose holding facilities that serve as the gateway into the criminal justice system.

Jim Crow laws (Black Codes) Laws passed after the Civil War to overstep the basic human rights and civil liberties of African-Americans.

joint local–federal counterterrorism task force (JTTF) A working group of FBI and state and/or local law enforcement officers that focuses on preventing terrorism through their joint cooperation and intelligence sharing.

judgment A ruling by the court regarding the liability for injury or the claim alleged by the plaintiff.

judicial review The power of the courts to declare congressional and presidential acts unconstitutional.

jumped bond Failed to appear for a court appearance.

jurisdiction (court) The authority of the court to try a case. Usually, jurisdiction is established when some part of the crime was committed within the geographic jurisdiction of the district court.

jurisdiction (law enforcement agencies) The geographic limits, such as the municipality, county, or state, in which officers of the agency are empowered to perform their duties.

jurisprudence A philosophy or body of written law used to settle disputes.

juvenile adjudication hearing The formal hearing held by a juvenile judge to conduct an inquiry of the facts concerning a case and to decide the disposition of the case and any rehabilitation, supervision, or punishment for the juvenile.

juvenile boot camp A military-style group-oriented rehabilitation program designed to alter the character and values of the juvenile offender.

juvenile court A court that handles juvenile welfare cases and cases involving status offenders and delinquents; some juvenile courts handle additional matters related to the family.

juvenile drug courts Alternatives to the traditional adjudication process for juveniles with substance abuse problems that focus on rehabilitating the juveniles and eliminating drug abuse.

juvenile intake The process whereby a juvenile enters the juvenile justice system.

juvenile intake officer A person who is responsible for processing a juvenile into the juvenile justice system and seeing to aftercare if the juvenile is adjudicated; this person has duties similar to those of a police officer and a probation and parole officer.

Juvenile Justice and Delinquency Prevention Act of 1974 An act that provides the major source of federal funding to states for the improvement of their juvenile justice systems, services, and facilities.

juvenile superpredator A term used by the Office of Juvenile Justice and Delinquency Prevention to describe a juvenile who commits violent felony crimes.

Kent v. United States A Supreme Court case that marked the departure of the Supreme Court from its acceptance of the denial of due process rights to juveniles.

kidnapping The taking away of a person by force against his or her will and holding that person in false imprisonment.

Klopfer v. North Carolina The case that requires states to grant defendants a speedy trial.

labeling theory The theory that explains deviant behavior, especially juvenile delinquency, by examining society's reactions to behaviors that are labeled as deviant.

landmark case A U.S. Supreme Court case that marks a significant change in the interpretation of the Constitution.

larceny The wrongful taking of another's property with the intent to permanently deprive its owner of its possession.

lateral transfers Transfers that involve changes in the duties the officer performs and the unit to which he or she is attached, but no changes in his or her rank or pay grade.

Law Enforcement Assistance Administration (LEAA) A conduit for the transfer of federal funds to state and local law enforcement agencies.

Law Enforcement Assistance Administration (LEAA) program A federal grant/loan program to promote educational advancement of law enforcement officers.

Law Enforcement Code of Ethics Professional standards of behavior to which law enforcement officers should aspire.

Law Enforcement Educational Program (LEEP) A program created to promote education among criminal justice personnel by offering loans and grants to pursue higher education.

lazy cop syndrome A term used to refer to officers who eschew the use of conflict resolution skills in favor of Tasers to control subjects.

lead federal agency (LFA) The agency that is designated as being primarily in charge of an incident and has the power to direct the actions of other agencies and to call for the use of their resources even though the lead agency may not have direct authority over the other agencies.

legalistic style A style of policing that focuses on law enforcement and professionalism and is associated with reform-minded cities with mixed socioeconomic communities.

legally sane An assumption that a defendant knows right from wrong and that his or her behavior was willful.

legislative immunity The protection of senators and representatives of Congress from arrest only while the legislature is in session, except for felonies and treason.

life history An assessment by the juvenile intake/probation officer of the juvenile and his or her past behavior, living conditions, parents/guardians, and school behavior.

lifestyle theories of victimization A concept that personal victimization is an outgrowth of a victim's high-risk behavior patterns and associations.

Lombroso-based correctional philosophies Philosophies that divided people into two distinct types: criminal and noncriminal. Noncriminals were biologically determined and therefore not amenable to rehabilitation or reform.

lone wolf terrorism Terrorist acts committed by a single individual or a single individual assisted by a small number of other people.

longitudinal comparisons Examinations of crime data recorded at one time period with crime data from another time period, such as year-to-year comparisons and comparisons over a number of years.

mala in se Acts that are crimes because they are inherently evil or harmful to society.

mala prohibita Acts that are prohibited because they are defined as crimes by law.

mandatory release The release of prisoners required by law after they have served the entire length of their maximum sentence.

mandatory sentencing The strict application of full sentences in the determinate sentencing model.

manslaughter The killing of another without the specific intent to kill.

Marbury* v. *Madison The 1803 case that established the court's power of judicial review.

mark system An early form of parole invented by Alexander Maconochie in which prisoners demonstrated their rehabilitation by earning points for good behavior.

material witness law A law that allows for the detention of a person who has not committed a crime but is suspected of having information about a crime and might flee or refuse to cooperate with law enforcement officials.

McKeiver* v. *Pennsylvania A case in which the Supreme Court denied juveniles the right to a trial by jury.

meat eaters Officers who engage in serious criminal conduct, corruption, and illicit money-making opportunities.

medical model The rehabilitation model that views criminality as a disease to be cured.

mens rea An element of crime in which a person must have criminal intent, or a "guilty mind," for his or her actions to be criminal.

meta-influence A phenomenon that results in encompassing transformative changes.

military police Police who are members of the military and provide law enforcement services on military bases, on certain federal lands, and in cases involving military personnel.

Miller* v. *Alabama A case in which the U.S. Supreme Court extends the ban on sentences of life without parole for juveniles guilty of homicide offenses.

Miranda rights Rights that provide protection from self-incrimination and confer the right to an attorney, of which citizens must be informed before police arrest and interrogation, established in *Miranda* v. *Arizona* (1966).

misdemeanor Less serious criminal conduct punishable by incarceration for less than a year.

Missouri* v. *Frye* and *Lafler* v. *Cooper The two cases that extended the constitutional rights of criminal defendants to effective counsel during plea negotiations.

mistake or ignorance of fact An affirmative legal defense in which the defendant made a mistake that does not meet the requirement for *mens rea*.

mitigating factors Actions that show the offender's remorse or responsibility.

Model Penal Code Guidelines for U.S. criminal codes published in 1962 by the American Law Institute that classify and define crimes into categories.

Montgomery bus boycott A boycott of public transportation initiated by the arrest of Rosa Parks.

Morrissey* v. *Brewer The case that secured the right to notice and a revocation hearing for parolees.

move and shoot High-tech simulations that mimic real-world scenarios where officers must respond to the simulated environment to detect and respond to threats.

municipal jails City incarceration facilities separate from the county jail for holding detainees and inmates sentenced for violation of city codes.

murder All intentional killings and deaths that occur in the course of aggravated felonies.

mutual aid agreements Agreements that ensure that neighboring jurisdictions can assist in providing personnel and resources to their impacted counterparts.

narcoterrorism Terrorism in which drug lords in some countries operate virtually unchecked by law enforcement.

National Crime Information Center (NCIC) The nation's largest database of computerized criminal information on wanted felons; people on parole; criminal history; and stolen items such as automobiles, boats, guns, and securities.

National Crime Victimization Survey (NCVS) A survey of a representative sample of U.S. households that gathers detailed information about crimes from victims.

National Criminal Justice Reference Service (NCJRS) A federally funded resource offering justice and drug-related information to support research, policy, and other programs.

National Incident-Based Reporting System (NIBRS) An incident-based reporting system in which more comprehensive crime information is gathered.

National Organization for Victim Assistance (NOVA) An organization that helped pass the 1984 Victims of Crime Act and the 1982 Victim and Witness Protection Act, both of which provide counseling, information, and assistance to crime victims.

national security decision directives (NSDDs) Directives issued by the president that are binding on federal agencies under executive command; NSDDs may forbid an agency from taking certain actions or may direct the agency to take certain actions.

Native American country jails Short-term incarceration facilities on Native American land under the sovereign control of the Native American tribe.

necessity An affirmative legal defense claiming that the defendant committed an act out of need, not *mens rea*.

Neoclassical School of criminology A school of thought that is similar to Classical School theories except for the belief that there are mitigating circumstances for criminal acts, such as the age or mental capacity of the offender, and that punishment should fit the crime.

neoclassical theories A contemporary view of Classical School theory that believes that there are mitigating circumstances for criminal acts, such as the age or mental capacity of the offender, and that punishment should fit the crime.

neutralization theory The concept that most people commit some type of criminal act in their lives and that many people are prevented from doing so again because of a sense of guilt, but criminals neutralize feelings of guilt through rationalization, denial, or an appeal to higher loyalties.

New York House of Refuge An early juvenile reformatory established by New York State in 1824 that was to become the model for most juvenile reformatories.

NIMBY "Not in my backyard"—opposition to community corrections programs in one's neighborhood.

No-Fly List A secret list maintained by the Department of Homeland Security that includes the names of people who are prohibited from flying on a commercial airplane under any circumstances; it also contains the names of people who should receive additional screening prior to being allowed to board an aircraft.

nonscientific theories Theories that emphasize moral weakness and evil spirits as the cause of criminality.

nonsworn personnel Employees such as secretaries, office workers, and technicians who do not have "police" powers and are not authorized to carry firearms.

not guilty by reason of insanity A verdict by which the jury finds that a defendant committed the crime but was insane.

Office of Tribal Justice An office established in 1995 to coordinate tribal issues for the Department of Justice (DOJ) and to increase the responsiveness of the DOJ to Native American tribes and citizens.

officers of the court Law enforcement officers who serve the court by serving papers, providing courtroom security, and transporting incarcerated defendants.

Omnibus Crime Control and Safe Streets Act of 1968 An act that provided resources to local and state government to assist in the adoption of reforms, including the Law Enforcement Assistance Administration.

order maintenance Activities of law enforcement that resolve conflicts and assist in the regulation of day-to-day interactions of citizens.

original jurisdiction The first court to hear and render a verdict regarding charges against a defendant.

pain–pleasure principle A philosophical axiom that people are rational and seek to do that which brings them pleasure and to avoid that which causes them pain.

parens patriae The legal assumption that the state has primary responsibility for the safety and custody of children.

parole The release of an inmate before his or her maximum sentence has been served.

parole board Individuals appointed to a body that meets in prisons to make decisions about granting parole release to inmates.

parole d'honneur The practice of releasing a prisoner for good behavior based on his word of honor that he would obey the law upon release.

parole hearing A meeting with an inmate, his or her attorney, and others in which the parole board decides whether to grant, deny, or revoke parole.

Part I offenses A Uniform Crime Report category group used to report murder, forcible rape, robbery, aggravated assault, burglary, larceny-theft, motor vehicle theft, and arson.

Part II offenses A Uniform Crime Report category group used to report less serious offenses involving an arrest.

pat-down doctrine The right of the police to search a person for a concealed weapon on the basis of reasonable suspicion, established in *Terry* v. *Ohio* (1968).

penitentiary A correctional institution based on the concept that inmates could change their criminality through reflection and penitence.

per curiam **opinion** A case that is disposed of by the U.S. Supreme Court without a full written opinion.

perfect defense The defense that results in the person being excused from all criminal liability and punishment.

picket fence model The model of the criminal justice system in which the local, state, and federal criminal justice systems are depicted as horizontal levels connected vertically by the roles, functions, and activities of the agencies that comprise them.

plain-view search The right of the police to gather without a warrant evidence that is clearly visible.

plaintiff The party who files a civil lawsuit against the party who is alleged to have done harm.

plea bargaining A pretrial activity that involves the negotiation between defendant and prosecutor for a plea of guilty for which in return the defendant will receive some benefit, such as reduction of charges or dismissal of some charges.

police academy A facility or program for the education and training of police officers.

police holding cells Also called booking cells and lock-up facilities, secure detention facilities for the purpose of temporarily housing arrestees until they can be booked, can be moved to another facility, can pay their bail, or are released.

police lineup An opportunity for victims to identify a criminal from among a number of suspects.

Positive School Modern theories of crime, primarily based on sociology and psychology, that people commit crimes because of uncontrollable internal or external factors that can be observed and measured.

Posse Comitatus Act of 1878 An act that limits the powers of local governments and law enforcement agencies in using federal military personnel to enforce the laws of the land.

predatory crime Acts involving direct physical contact between at least one offender and at least one person or object which that offender attempts to take or damage.

preliminary hearing A hearing before a magistrate judge in which the prosecution presents evidence to convince the judge that there is probable cause to bring the defendant to trial.

preponderance of the evidence A majority vote of the jury—the standard required for a judgment in a civil case.

presentence investigation An in-depth interview and investigation into the background of a convicted defendant and the impact of his or her crime on victims and the community.

presentence investigation report A report that contains a recommendation for specific criminal sanctions, including a recommendation for prison time, probation, fines, community service, or other sanctions.

presentence investigator A person who works for the court and has the responsibility of investigating the background of the convicted offender and the circumstances surrounding the offense.

President's Task Force on Victims of Crime A task force that makes recommendations for new legislation to be enacted to protect the rights and interests of crime victims in the criminal justice system.

presumption of innocence The most important principle of the due process model requiring all accused persons to be treated as innocent until proven guilty in a court of law.

presumptive sentencing A structured sentencing model that attempts to balance sentencing guidelines with mandatory sentencing and at the same time provide discretion to the judge.

principle of legality The principle that citizens cannot be punished for conduct for which no law against it exists.

prison code The informal rules and expected behavior established by inmates. Often the prison code is contrary to the official rules and policies of the prison. Violation of the prison code can be punished by use of violence or even death.

prison consultants Private people who give convicted defendants advice and counsel on how best to present themselves during classification and how to behave in prison.

prison economy The exchange of goods, services, and contraband by prisoners in place of money.

prison farm system In the southern penal systems, the use of inmate labor to maintain large, profit-making prison farms or plantations.

prison industry The sale of convict-made products and services.

Prison Rape Elimination Act of 2003 An act that required the Bureau of Justice Statistics to survey jails and prisons to determine the prevalence of sexual violence within correctional facilities.

prisoner classification The reception and diagnosis of an inmate to decide the appropriate security level in which to place him or her and the services of placement.

prisonization Socialization into a distinct prison subculture with its own values, mores, norms, and sanctions.

private investigators Investigators who are licensed by the state and are authorized to conduct investigations.

private prisons Prisons that house local, state, or federal inmates for a fee.

privatization The trend to house inmates in privately administered prisons.

privilege A type of defense in which the defendant claims immunity from punishment for an admitted violation of the law because it was related to his or her official duties.

probable cause The likelihood that there is a direct link between a suspect and a crime.

probable cause hearing A hearing to determine whether there is a direct link between a suspect and a crime.

probation The conditional release of a convicted offender prior to his or her serving any prison time.

probation and parole officer A state or federal professional employee who reports to the courts and supervises defendants released from prison on parole.

probation officer A state or federal professional employee who reports to the courts and supervises defendants released on probation.

problem-oriented policing A community policing strategy that emphasizes attacking the root problem that causes crime instead of responding to the symptoms of the problem.

procedural due process The process and procedure the government can use to prosecute an individual.

procedural law The body of laws governing how things should be done at each stage of the criminal justice process.

Prohibition Amendment The Eighteenth Amendment passed in 1919 that prohibited the manufacture, sale, and possession of alcoholic beverages.

proprietary services Private protection security forces that are owned and managed by a company.

prosecutorial discretion The power of a prosecutor to decide whether to charge a defendant and what the charge(s) will be, as well as to gather the evidence necessary to prosecute the defendant in a court of law.

psychoanalytic theory The concept that behavior is not a matter of free will, but is controlled by subconscious desires, which includes the idea that criminal behavior is a result of unresolved internal conflict and guilt.

psychological profiling Profiles based on the personality traits according to psychoanalytic theories.

psychological theory The idea that criminal behavior is a result of emotions, drives, and mental defects.

public safety exception The right of the police to search without probable cause when not doing so could pose a threat of harm to the public.

punitive damages Claims for a monetary award to punish the defendant for his or her misconduct.

racial profiling Allegations that police search and seizures, traffic stops, field interrogations, and arrests are made on nonbehavioral factors related to race and/or ethnicity rather than suspicious behavior or probable cause.

radical criminologists Those who advocate conflict theories and class and power inequality as the causes of crime.

rape Sexual assault; nonconsensual sexual acts.

reaction formation A term that describes how lower-class youths reject middle-class values.

REAL ID Act Legislation that requires all state driver's licenses to conform to uniform standards set by the Department of Homeland Security.

rehabilitation Deterrence based on the premise that criminals can be "cured" of their problems and criminality and can be returned to society.

release on recognizance (ROR) To secure the pretrial release of the accused based merely on the defendant's unsecured promise to appear at trial.

remanded After the U.S. Supreme Court's reversal of a decision of a lower court, the return of the case to the court of original jurisdiction with instructions to correct the judicial error.

rendition The illegal transportation of a person to a foreign country for the purpose of having officials of that country interrogate the person using torture or practices not permitted in the United States.

Residential Substance Abuse Treatment (RSAT) A federal assistance program that helps states provide treatment instead of prison for substance abusers.

restorative justice A model of deterrence that uses restitution programs, community work programs, victim-offender mediation, and other strategies not only to rehabilitate the offender, but also to address the damage done to the community and the victim.

retribution Deterrence based on the premise that criminals should be punished because they deserve it.

reverse stings Tactics involving law enforcement officers who pose as providers of illegal substances, goods, or services.

reversing the case A finding by the Supreme Court that a judicial error or an unconstitutional issue was central to the lower court's decision and voided the lower court's ruling.

revolving door syndrome The repeated arrest and incarceration of an offender.

Richard Dugdale A psychologist who conducted an early study attempting to link heredity to criminal behavior in his study of the Jukes family.

right to privacy The principle that laws that violate personal privacy cannot be upheld.

robbery The taking away of property from a person by force or the immediate threat of force.

Roper, Superintendent, Potosi Correctional Center v. Simmons A case in which the Supreme Court held that the Eighth and Fourteenth Amendments forbid imposition of the death penalty on offenders who were under the age of 18 when their crimes were committed.

routine activities theory A theory that assumes that all humans are motivated by the desire to have things that give them pleasure or benefit them and to avoid those things and situations that inflict pain.

rules of evidence Administrative court rules governing the admissibility of evidence in a trial.

Safe and Drug-Free Schools and Communities Act of 1996 A law requiring the collection of data, frequency, seriousness, and incidences of violence in elementary and secondary schools.

SARA A community policing strategy based on a highly modified version of the scientific method that attempts to identify the root cause of crime in a community.

Schall v. Martin A case in which the Supreme Court upheld the right of juvenile courts to deny bail to adjudicated juveniles.

school-to-prison pipeline School disciplinary policies that increase the likelihood of suspended and expelled students dropping out of high school and having contact with the juvenile justice system.

scientific method The assumption that repeated testing of a hypothesis should result in similar results.

search incident to lawful arrest The right of police to search a person who has been arrested without a warrant.

search warrant Legal permission, signed by a judge, for police to conduct a search.

secondary victimization The victimization caused not by the criminal act, but through the inappropriate response of institutions and individuals.

Section 1983 lawsuits Civil lawsuits filed in federal court alleging that the government has violated a constitutional right of the inmate.

security-risk groups Groups in prisons that raise special threats, such as prison gangs.

self-defense An affirmative legal defense in which a defendant claims that he or she acted to protect himself or herself or another person against a deadly attack or invasion of his or her home.

self-incrimination Statements made by a person that might lead to criminal prosecution.

sentence bargaining Negotiating with the prosecutor for a reduction in length of sentence, reduction from capital murder to imprisonment, probation rather than incarceration, or institution where the sentence is to be served in return for a guilty plea.

sentencing guidelines A sentencing model in which crimes are classified according to their seriousness and a range of time to be served is mandatory for crimes within each category.

sentencing hearing A hearing at which the prosecution and the defense have the opportunity to challenge the recommended criminal sanctions.

service style A style of policing that focuses on protecting a homogenous suburban, middle-class community against outsiders and providing service to community residents.

shock incarceration Programs (boot camps) that adapt military-style physical fitness and discipline training to the correctional environment.

shock probation A sentence for a first-time nonviolent offender who was not expecting a sentence, intended to impress on the offender the possible consequences of his or her behavior by being exposed to a brief period of imprisonment before probation.

signature bond Bond that releases the defendant based on his or her signature on a promise to appear in court, usually for minor offenses such as traffic violations.

silent system The correctional practice of prohibiting inmates from talking to other inmates.

slave patrols White militia who were responsible for controlling, returning, and punishing runaway slaves.

smart passports New passports that contain machine-readable data about travelers.

social control theory A theory that focuses on the social and cultural values that exert control over and reinforce the behavior of individuals.

social determinism The idea that social forces and social groups are the cause of criminal behavior.

social disorganization theory Park and Burgess's research that criminal behavior is dependent on disruptive social forces, not on individual characteristics.

social norms The expected normative behavior in a society.

social safety net Government programs that provide for people in need.

Sociological School of criminology The school of thought that says that crime is caused by socioeconomic conditions and social interactions and values.

sociology The study of human social behavior.

solicitation The requesting or commanding of another to commit a crime.

solitary confinement The practice of confining an inmate such that there is no contact with other people.

Sourcebook of Criminal Justice Statistics A publication funded by the U.S. Department of Justice, a research body that brings together data from more than 200 sources about many aspects of criminal justice in the United States.

sovereign immunity Immunity from civil lawsuits granted to federal and state governments.

special police Police who have limited jurisdiction in geography and in police powers.

special prison populations Inmates with characteristics that may result in significant risks to themselves, other inmates, or staff.

specific deterrence A concept based on the premise that a person is best deterred from committing future crimes by the specific nature of the punishment.

Speedy Trial Act of 1974 The act that requires a specific deadline between arrest and trial in federal courts.

split sentencing An intermediate sanction where, after a brief period of imprisonment, the judge brings the offender back to court and offers the option of probation.

standard conditions of release Federal and state guidelines with which parolees (and probationers) must comply to meet their conditions of release.

standard operating procedures (SOP) manual A manual that describes the policies that regulate behavior and the performance standards for police officers.

stare decisis The U.S. system of developing and applying case law on the basis of precedents established in previous cases.

state liability A state's liability for violations of an inmate's constitutional rights.

state prisons Correctional facilities for prisoners convicted of state crimes.

status offender A child who has committed an act or failed to fulfill a responsibility for which, if he or she were an adult, the court would not have any authority over him or her.

statute of limitations The length of time between the discovery of the crime and the arrest of the defendant.

statutory exclusion The provision that allows juveniles to be transferred to criminal court without review by and approval of the juvenile court.

stings Tactics in which law enforcement officers pose as buyers of illegal substances or goods.

strain theory The assumption that individuals resort to crime out of frustration from being unable to attain economic comfort or success.

strict liability crime A criminal act that does not require the prosecutor to prove *mens rea*, or criminal intent, by the perpetrator in order to prosecute.

strict liability crimes Actions that are considered criminal without the need for criminal intent.

structured sentencing A sentencing model (including determinate sentencing, sentencing guidelines, and presumptive sentencing) that defines punishments rather than allowing indeterminate sentencing.

Student and Exchange Visitor Information System (SEVIS) A Web-based database containing information on international students studying in the United States.

substantive due process Due process that refers to the constitutionality of laws.

suicide by police Situations created by citizens in which law enforcement officers are forced to fire on them.

superego The moral values system.

suspended sentence Another term for *probation*, a sentence based on the fact that convicted offenders must serve their full sentence if they violate their terms of release.

sworn personnel Officers who have police powers of arrest and search and seizure and the authority to carry a firearm.

system of social control A social system designed to maintain order and regulate interactions.

Taylor v. *Louisiana* The case that ruled that the exclusion of women from jury duty created an imbalance in the jury pool.

team policing Teams of officers assigned to a specific geographic area with the charge to ensure public safety, maintain order, and deliver community services to the residents of that community.

technical violation Grounds for imprisonment of a probationer or parolee based on his or her violation of a condition of release.

teen courts Courts for younger juveniles (aged 10 to 15) with no prior arrest record who are charged with less serious law violations wherein juvenile peers rather than adults determine the disposition.

ten-code radio communications A system of communicating events, actions, and services by use of numbered code, each beginning with the number 10 followed by another number.

Tenth Amendment A provision that states that powers not specifically delegated to the federal government are reserved for the states.

terrorist cells Small groups of individuals with a common goal of carrying out terrorism.

Terrorist Threat Integration Center (TTIC) The agency charged with comprehensive intelligence gathering and dissemination.

the wall Separation of the Central Intelligence Agency and the Federal Bureau of Investigation in the production and dissemination of intelligence data.

theory A statement regarding the relationship between two or more variables.

three-strikes law The law that applies mandatory sentencing to give repeat offenders longer prison terms.

ticket of leave In the mark system, the unconditional release from prison purchased with marks earned for good behavior.

tort A private wrong that causes physical harm to another.

total institutions Prisons that meet all of the inmate's basic needs, discourage individuality, punish dissent, and segregate those who do not follow the rules.

transportation The eighteenth-century practice by Great Britain of sending offenders to the American colonies and later to Australia.

Transportation Security Administration (TSA) The federal agency responsible for airport security and the screening of airline passengers.

Treatment Accountability for Safer Communities (TASC) A federal assistance program that helps states break the addiction-crime cycle.

trial *de novo* A new trial granted by an appellate court.

trial penalty The fact that the sentences for people who go to trial have grown harsher relative to sentences for those who agree to a plea.

Tribal Healing to Wellness Courts Native American drug-treatment programs that adopt traditional cultural beliefs and practices.

tribal police Police that provide law enforcement services on Native American reservations, where local and state police have no jurisdiction and federal police have only limited jurisdiction.

true bill A jury's decision that authorizes the prosecutor to arraign the defendant.

truth in sentencing Legislation that requires the court to disclose the actual prison time the offender is likely to serve.

tuberculosis (TB) A contagious infectious disease caused by a bacterial infection that primarily affects the lungs.

U.S. courts of appeal The third tier of the federal court system where decisions of lower courts can be appealed for review of significant judicial error that may have affected the verdict.

U.S. district courts The federal system's trial courts of original jurisdiction.

U.S. magistrate courts Federal lower courts whose powers are limited to trying lesser misdemeanors, setting bail, and assisting district courts with various legal matters.

U.S. Marshals Service The federal agency that provides security for federal courts; is responsible for the movement, custody, and capture of federal prisoners; and provides protection of witnesses in federal cases.

U.S. Parole Commission (USPC) The agency responsible for parole decisions of federal and Washington, D.C., inmates.

U.S. Postal Inspection Service The federal agency responsible for the security of U.S. mail and mail carriers and for investigation of mail fraud.

U.S. Secret Service The federal agency that protects the president, the vice president, members of their families, major candidates for president and vice president, and visiting heads of foreign governments.

U.S. Supreme Court The highest court in the U.S. judiciary system whose rulings on the constitutionality of laws, due process rights, and rules of evidence are binding on all federal and state courts.

undersheriff The second in command of the sheriff's office.

Uniform Code of Military Justice (UCMJ) Legal statutes that govern the behavior of military personnel and prescribe the due process to be followed to determine guilt and punishment.

Uniform Crime Report (UCR) A database of information about reported crimes collected by the Federal Bureau of Investigation over time.

United States Government Interagency Domestic Terrorism Concept of Operations Plan (CONPLAN) A plan that establishes the role and responsibilities of federal agencies for preventing and responding to terrorist attacks.

United States Visitor and Immigrant Status Indicator Technology (US-VISIT) A new system of registering the entry of foreign visitors to the United States and tracking when and where they exit the United States.

unsecured bond Bond that releases the defendant based on his or her signing a promissory note agreeing to pay the court an amount similar to a cash bail bond if he or she fails to fulfill the promise to appear at trial.

urban fortresses Cities that have adopted extensive and visible physical security measures and barriers in response to the threat of terrorist attacks.

USA PATRIOT Act Legislation that gives federal law enforcement agencies expanded powers to detect, detain, and prosecute suspected terrorists.

use of force continuum A policy that requires officers to use appropriate force depending on the circumstances they confront.

utilitarianism A philosophy stating that a rational system of jurisprudence provides for the greatest happiness for the greatest number of people.

victim impact statements Testimony by victims at a convicted offender's sentencing hearing.

victim-precipitation theories Theories based on the concept that victims themselves precipitate, contribute to, provoke, or actually cause the outcome of their victimization.

victimization The process of being victimized or becoming a victim of crime.

victimology The study of victims and the patterns of how they are victimized.

victims' right movement The dissatisfaction of victims with the neglect and minimization of harm they suffered, leading to a victims' movement for the criminal justice system to provide them with specific rights.

Vietnam War A war from 1955 to 1975 Vietnam, Laos, and Cambodia.

Violent Crime Index The rate of crimes reported in the Part I offenses.

void for overbreadth The principle that laws go too far in that they criminalize legally protected behavior in an attempt to make some other behavior illegal that cannot be upheld.

void for vagueness The principle that laws not using clear and specific language to define prohibited behaviors cannot be upheld.

voir dire process The questioning of potential jurors to determine whether they have biases that would disqualify them from jury service.

Volstead Act Another name for the Prohibition Amendment.

waiver The process of moving a juvenile from the authority of juvenile court to the adult criminal justice system.

waiving Granting permission for an accused juvenile to be moved from juvenile court to criminal court.

War on Crime A declaration by President Lyndon Johnson in 1965 to counter crime and social disorder.

war on terrorism President George W. Bush's declaration regarding the response of the United States to the events of September 11, 2001.

ward of the state A person for whom the state assumes responsibility for his or her health and well-being.

Warren Court The U.S. Supreme Court years (1953–1969) during which Chief Justice Earl Warren issued many landmark decisions greatly expanding the constitutional rights of inmates and defendants.

watchman style A style of policing that focuses on maintaining order and is associated with declining industrial, blue-collar communities.

waterboarding An interrogation technique in which a large volume of water is poured over a bound person to simulate the sensation of drowning.

wiretapping A form of search and seizure of evidence involving communication by telephone.

witness immunity A situation in which a defendant admits to committing a crime but is granted immunity from prosecution in exchange for cooperating with a government investigation.

work release A program that allows facilities to release inmates for paid work in the community.

writ of *certiorari* An order to a lower court to forward the record of a case to the U.S. Supreme Court for review.

XYY chromosome theory of violent behavior The idea that violent behavior in males can in part be attributed to the presence of an extra Y chromosome in male offenders.

youth gangs Difficult-to-define juvenile groups distinct from adult gangs that mimic adult gangs.

zero-tolerance policies School disciplinary policies that provide for mandatory disciplinary actions for any and all violations of school rules regardless of the student or circumstance.

zero-tolerance strategy Strict enforcement of the laws, even for minor violations.

Name Index

Subject Index

Note: Page ranges in **bold** indicate chapter-level discussions.

Internet
　　jury access to, 201
　　victimization through, 51
Interrogations and confessions,
　　134–137, 144
IPS (intensive probation supervision),
　　281–283, 294
Irish system of parole, 262, 263

J

Jacobsen v. *United States,* 141
Jails and prisons, **219–253**. *See also*
　　Prisons
　　classification and assignment to, 232
　　community corrections compared
　　　　to, 294
　　contemporary correctional system,
　　　　224–227
　　described, 247–248
　　development of, 220–224
　　generally, 227–230
　　mentally ill persons in, 220
　　population in, 237, 278
　　privatization of, 239–241
　　sheriff's departments and, 104
Jim Crow laws, 13
John Howard Association, 277
Joint local-federal counterterrorism
　　task force, 350, 351, 352
Judges
　　diversity of, 157–158
　　granting of probation by, 259–260
　　impeachment of, 199, 200
　　power of, 182–183
　　sentencing models for, 201–206
Judgment, defined, 154
Judicial error, 156–157, 160–161
Judicial review, 155, 157
Judicial system. *See* Court system
Judicial waiver, 309
Jumping bond, 176
Jurisdiction
　　defined, 93
　　juvenile justice system, 314
　　original, 156, 160, 161, 162, 304
　　in policing, 94, 105
　　trials and, 170–171
Jurisprudence, 150, 151

Jury, 183–184, 200, 201, 208
Jury trials for juveniles, 3–7
Just-desserts principle, 194–195
Justice courts in New York, 164
Justice Systems Improvement
　　Act (1979), 60
Justinian code, 150–151
Juvenile courts, 304, 305, 308–309, 330
Juvenile intake, 312–314
Juvenile intake officers, 312, 314–315
Juvenile Justice and Delinquency
　　Prevention Act (1974), 306, 308
Juvenile justice system, **299–338**
　　court proceedings in, 308–309
　　development of, 301–304
　　due process in, 305–308
　　goals of, 332–333
　　judicial waiver, 309–311
　　jurisdiction of, 304–305
　　processing through, 312–320
　　theories and explanations in, 320–326
　　views of young offenders, 300–301
Juveniles. *See also* Children
　　interrogation of, 137
　　as superpredators, 304, 305
　　as victims, 331–332

K

Katz v. *United States,* 125, 133
Kent v. *United States,* 300, 306
Kidnapping, 85, 86, 331, 332
Klopfer v. *North Carolina,* 179–180
Knapp Commission, 139–140

L

Labeling theory, 40–41
Lafler v. *Cooper,* 177, 178, 185
Landmark cases, 160–161
Larceny, defined, 85, 87
Last resort, courts of, 162
Lateral transfers, 109
Law enforcement, **92–121**. *See also*
　　Law enforcement officers
　　antiterrorist activities of, 347
　　city, 104–106
　　county, 102–104
　　development of policing, 93–94

federal, 94–101
　　operational strategies, 113–116
　　private protection services,
　　　　112–113
　　shift work, 110
　　special police, 111–112
　　state, 101–102
　　stress and danger, 110–111
Law Enforcement Assistance
　　Administration, 14, 15, 66, 107, 109
Law Enforcement Code of Ethics, 124
Law Enforcement Education Program, 5,
　　14, 15, 107
Law enforcement officers
　　career path for, 109
　　conflict between ex-offenders and, 295
　　external oversight of, 126–127
　　hiring of, 93, 107, 108
　　misconduct by, 137–143
　　professionalism of, 124–128
　　recording of, 18
　　relationship with prosecutors, 173
　　on school campuses, 329
　　views of, 123–124
Lawrence v. *Texas,* 73
Laws. *See also* Criminal law; *specific laws*
　　abortion, 88, 129
　　Blue, 73
　　civil, 151–154
　　common, 74, 75, 151
　　ex post facto, 76–77
　　fair sentences and, 198–199
　　international, 213
　　Jim Crow, 13
　　making of, 73–74
　　mandatory sentencing and habitual
　　　　offender, 201, 202, 203–204
　　material witness, 143–144, 365, 366
　　procedural, 126
　　public, 182
　　sodomy, 73
　　sources of, 73
　　"stand your ground," 68, 84
　　state and local immigration, 362–363
　　three-strikes, 201, 203–204
　　unenforceable, 73
Lazy cop syndrome, 139, 142
Lead federal agency, 347
Learning theories, 37
Legalistic style of policing, 113, 114

Legally sane, 196

Legislative immunity, 81, 82

Lethal injection, 206, 208

Leyra v. *Denno*, 135–136

Life history, 312, 314

Life imprisonment for juvenile offenders, 319–320

Lifestyle victimization theories, 51, 63–64, 68

Limited jurisdiction, courts of, 161–162, 170

Lindbergh Law, 331, 332

Local courts and probation, 259

Local criminal law, 75–76

Local governments and illegal immigration, 361–363

Lombroso-based correctional philosophies, 224, 226

Lone wolf terrorism, 340, 341, 342

Longitudinal comparisons, 61

Long-term health care of prisoners, 243–244

Los Angeles Police Department Rampart Division scandal, 295

Los Angeles Unified School District Case, 334

M

Magistrate courts, 155, 156, 157

Mala in se, 74

Mala prohibita, 74

Mandatory release, 255–256

Mandatory sentencing, 201, 202, 203–204, 269

Manslaughter, defined, 85–86

Mapp v. *Ohio*, 125, 127–128, 160

Marbury v. *Madison*, 153, 154–155, 157

Marital rape exception, 86

Mark system, 262

Marriage, 16, 35, 38–39

Maryland v. *Shatzer*, 135

Material witness law, 143–144, 365, 366

McCleskey v. *Kemp*, 213, 215

McDonald v. *City of Chicago, et al.*, 15

McKeiver v. *Pennsylvania*, 301, 307

McNabb-Mallory rule, 135

Measurement of crime and victimization, **50–71**. *See also* Victimization

Bureau of Justice Statistics, 59, 60

limitations of, 61

National Crime Victimization Survey, 26, 52, 57–59

National Criminal Justice Reference Service, 59, 60

National Incident-Based Reporting System, 52, 57, 59

public demand for, 51–52

school crime data, 60

Sourcebook of Criminal Justice Statistics, 60

state surveys and self-reports, 60–61

Uniform Crime Report, 52, 53–57, 58–59, 98

Meat eaters, 140, 142

Medical model, 33, 194, 195

Medical records and right to privacy, 129

Megan's Law, 74, 284

Mempa v. *Rhay*, 261

Mens rea, 78, 79, 80, 141–142, 196, 309–310

Mental health

of juveniles, 317

in prisons, 246–247

Mental illness, offenders with, 196–198, 220, 234, 246–247, 249

Meta-influences on criminal justice system, 12–15

Michigan v. *Jackson*, 135

Military police, 95–96

Military prisons, federal, 239

Military tribunals, 353

Miller v. *Alabama*, 303, 314, 320

Minorities. *See also* Muslims; Native Americans

disproportionate confinement rate for, 236

racial profiling of, 140–141, 145, 360, 366

Miranda rights, 135, 136

Miranda v. *Arizona*, 5, 125, 136

Misconduct by law enforcement

entrapment, 81–82, 141–142

racial profiling, 140–141, 145, 360, 366

remedies for, 142–143

types of, 139–140

use of force, 137–139

Misconduct in death penalty cases, 211–212

Misdemeanor, 74, 75

Missouri v. *Frye*, 177, 178, 185

Mistake or ignorance of fact, 82–83

Mitigating factors, 204

M'Naughten standard, 84

Model Penal Code, 85, 197

Montgomery bus boycott, 13

Morrissey v. *Brewer*, 263, 269

Motive. *See Mens rea*

Move and shoot strategy, 110, 111

Munich Olympics terrorism, 369

Municipal jails, 228, 230

Murder

defined, 85

in New Orleans, 46

wrongful convictions for, 211–212

Muslims, 141, 145, 340, 352, 366

Mutual aid agreements, 347, 349

N

Napoleonic Code, 151

Narcoterrorism, 99, 101

National Center for Education Statistics, 52

National Counterterrorism Center, 349

National Crime Information Center, 98, 99

National Crime Victimization Survey (NCVS), 26, 52, 57–59

National Criminal Justice Reference Service, 59, 60

National identification cards, 363

National Incident-Based Reporting System (NIBRS), 52, 57, 59

National Organization for Victim Assistance, 66, 67

National Security Agency, 101

National security decision directives, 352, 353, 369

Native Americans, 96, 228, 292–293

NCVS (National Crime Victimization Survey), 26, 52, 57–59

Necessity, 83

Negotiation with terrorists, 369

Neoclassical theories of crime, 27–30, 301

Neutralization theory, 38, 39

New Orleans, murder in, 46

New York House of Refuge, 301, 302–303